Death by Night

Death by Night

No. 630 Squadron – An Operational History

Peter Sharpe

First published 2024 by Aviation Books Ltd., Merthyr Tydfil, CF47 8RY, United Kingdom

Publisher's email address for correspondence: aviationbooksuk@gmail.com

Copyright 2024 © Peter Sharpe

The right of Peter Sharpe to be identified as Author of this work is asserted by him in accordance with the Copyright, Designs and Patents Act 1988.

All rights reserved. No part of this publication may be reproduced, stored in a retrieval system, transmitted in any form or by any means, electronic, mechanical, or photocopied, recorded or otherwise, without the written permission of the copyright owners.

Any queries or objections to the use of any images or other material should be referred to the publisher.

A CIP catalogue reference for this book is available from the British Library.

Cover artwork: Piotr Forkasiewicz

Cover design: Topics – The Creative Partnership www.topicsdesign.co.uk

ISBN 9781915335500

Author's royalties all donated to Lincolnshire Aviation Heritage Centre.

Table of Contents

East Kirkby – A Poem by Walter Scott	6
Introduction	7
Sources	8
Acknowledgements	9
Formation	10
November 1943	14
November 1943 - Operations Commence for No. 630 Squadron	20
December 1943	26
January 1944	43
February 1944	63
March 1944	76
April 1944	100
May 1944	121
June 1944	144
July 1944	171
August 1944	203
September 1944	234
October 1944	252
November 1944	265
December 1944	283
January 1945	298
February 1945	310
March 1945	323
April 1945	338
May 1945	366
June 1945	371
July 1945	373
Awards	375
Aircraft of 630 Squadron	378
East Kirkby	381
Footnotes	385
The Faces of Aircrew Representing 630 Squadron	394

East Kirkby – A Poem by Walter Scott

Now these aged limbs of mine,
Take me back through mists of time,
Down this quiet village street,
Which once I trod with youthful feet.
And in this darkening village street,
Do blue-clad spirits walk, and meet,
As wayward breezes sigh, and mourn,
Through the wayside grass, and tall hawthorn.
The friendly people, friendly still,
The village inn, the distant hill,
The welcome lights of our home base,
Set within this tranquil place.
The airfield acres, vanished now,
Surrendered to the rending plough,
With growing crops, where once it knew,
That gleaming flarepath, straight and true.
That sense of freedom, wild and strong,
The thrusting wings, the merlin's song,
The mighty cloudbanks drifting by,
White mountains in that fateful sky.
Gaunt, bearded spectre, with the scythe,
Last enemy of those alive,
That spectre of our youthful fears,
Pursues us through the dwindling years.
The day is ending, we must part,
We who still, are young at heart,
And you, old friend, as we all know,
Just as you were so long ago.

Walt Scott (630 Squadron poet)

Introduction

No.630 Squadron RAF was a two flight heavy night bomber squadron within No. 5 Group, RAF Bomber Command. The squadron was formed at a vital phase in the wartime service of Bomber Command as the offensive against Berlin was due to begin and the preparations for the liberation of Europe were gaining momentum. 'Six-thirty' was based at East Kirkby in Lincolnshire, thirty miles from the long-established RAF Scampton, in what had mainly been the farmland of Hagnaby Grange. The site was already in use as a dummy airfield to confuse intruding Luftwaffe aircrews seeking a bomber base to attack. RAF East Kirkby could however have been a thousand miles from RAF Scampton in terms of comfort, the pre-war station lacked for very little with its brick accommodation blocks, offices, workshops and briefing rooms whereas the bleak wartime station even lacked sufficient Nissen huts to accommodate the new squadron.

630 Squadron's Lancasters took off on 2,515 sorties to attack enemy targets and the stark figures show that of the 162 crews[1] who flew operationally on its strength, 64 were lost serving with the squadron and 10 were later lost serving with other squadrons. Of the remaining 88 crews, 48 completed their tours with 630 Squadron, 13 completed their tours later with other squadrons, 1 was broken up after their pilot was killed in an accident and 26 were still operational at VE-Day. 46% of these 162 crews (some having transferred to other squadrons) were lost. A total of 1,199 airmen flew operationally on the strength of 630 Squadron, 99 earned awards for bravery and distinguished service during their time with the squadron. A further 15 airmen were killed in flying accidents before commencing operations. Of these operational aircrew, 436 were killed or are missing, 69 became prisoners of war, 29 evaded capture in occupied Europe (2 pilots evaded capture and later returned to ops to complete their tours) and 6 aircrew were interned in neutral Sweden.

The number of aircrew by parent Air Force were:

RAF[2]	985
RAAF	97
RCAF	84
RNZAF	41
SAAF	4
USAAF	2
FFAF	1
TOTAL	1214

Due to the losses sustained by 630 Squadron, none of their assigned Lancasters flew 100 ops; the nearest was ME739 which took off for 90 before it was lost, LM216 flew on 84 and NN702, PB344, ND949 and LM287 flew on 77, 75, 775 and 70 respectively.

The Lincolnshire Aviation Heritage Centre[3] at East Kirkby is a wonderful living memorial to all of those who flew Ops from East Kirkby (No. 57 and No. 630 Squadron) and all of those who toiled in harsh conditions to keep the Lancasters serviceable. We very strongly recommend visiting for a truly historical experience.

Research continues and all additional information, copies of logbook pages/photos are sincerely appreciated. The author can be contacted at 630historian@btinternet.com

---

[1] 8 crews/pilots flew a single op whilst on loan to 630 Squadron, and totals do not include crews of 630 Squadron who flew ops whilst on loan to other squadrons.

[2] RAF includes RAFVR, AuxAF, RAFO, etc

[3] https://www.lincsaviation.co.uk/

Sources

This study is built around contemporary documents using the 630 Squadron Operations Record Book' (National Archives/London Air 27/2152) backed up by the 57 and 630 Squadrons 'Raid Book' (RAF Museum Hendon) and 630 Squadron Ops Record (RAF Museum Hendon) as primary sources.

The above have been supported and supplemented by material from over 120 aircrew flying logbooks, information within recommendations for awards (National Archives Air 2), combat reports (National Archives Air 50/287 and Air 27/2153), reports by Evaders and Escapers (National Archives WO 208) and the records of the Station and Base East Kirkby (National Archives Air 28/244). After cross referring so many contemporary records we have been able to identify and where necessary correct many aircraft serials which had been missing or incorrectly recorded in the ORB, corrected the names of aircrew which had been miss-spelled or even omitted and identified aircraft and entire crews who flew on specific operations but had been completely missed from the ORB by overworked wartime clerks, some several times.

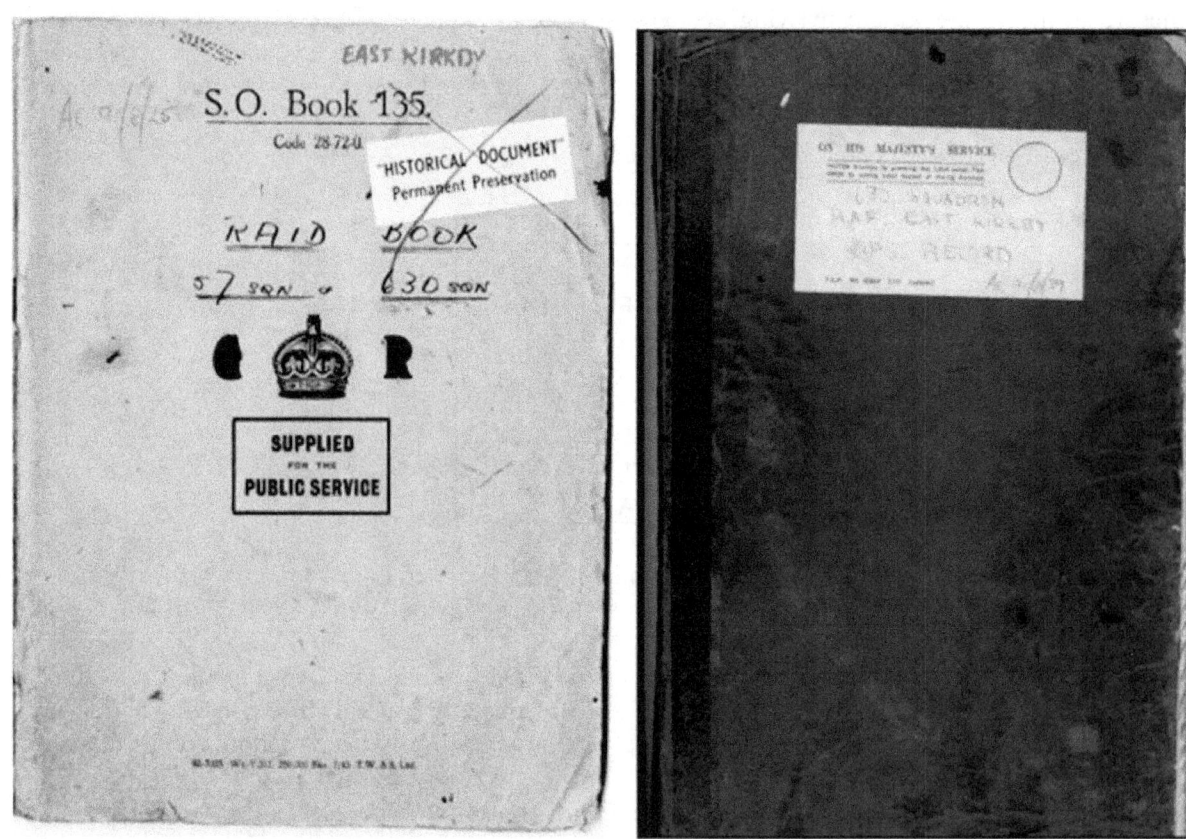

Squadron Ops Record and 57 and 630 Squadron Raid Books (RAF Museum, Hendon)

Acknowledgements

Over forty years a very considerable number of people have assisted in the compilation of information, sadly many of them have passed during this time. Thanks to all of those who assisted, former aircrew of 630 Squadron, the families of former airmen and particularly Group Captain John Grindon CVO DSO AFC, 'Cab' Kellaway DSO and Bar AFC, Len Barnes MBE, 'Blue' Rackley AM DFC AE, Roy Millichap DFC, Roy Calvert DFC and 2 Bars, Steve Nunns DFC AFC, Jerry Monk, Angus Newson and so many others. The staff of the Air Historical Branch and MOD (Miss Mary Locke, Mrs ECM Ford and many others), RAF Museum Hendon (Belinda Day and Iain Duncan), RAAF Museum (Monica Walsh) and the RNZAF Museum and especially Louise Bush at the Lincolnshire Aviation Historical Centre (East Kirkby) all have been particularly generous with advice and assistance as have my friends in the 630 Squadron research group. The staff at the Public Records Office (Chancery Lane) and then National Archives (Kew) were always helpful.

Sincere thanks are due to the late George Griffiths DFM (76/102 Squadrons) for guiding my early research, Geoff Copeman (57 Squadron) for encouragement and advice, to Bomber Command historians Martin Middlebrook, Chris Everett and Bill Chorley, European air warfare historians Emil Nonnenmacher, Jörg Helbig and Theo Boiten, Ron Emeny AFM (207) and Wal Simpson MM (299) of the Air Gunners Association, Rupert Oakley DSO DFC AFC DFM (617), Andrew Panton (East Kirkby), Miss I G Bruce, Pam Rackley, Errol Martyn, Wilf Bickley CGM, Wing Commander Bernard Moorcroft DSO DFC, Neale Wellman in Tasmania, John McCutchion, Robert Hay, Sheila Scott, Walt Scott, Paul Baillie, Roland Hammersley DFM (57), Kay Rowland (Seward), Judith Bentley and Christine Young (family of Bob Adams DFC), Danny Bouchard in Canada, Linda Deakin, Ross McNeill, James Castle, Selina Moore, Shirley Moulsley, Ian Lawton, Karen Shortland, Cassie, Colin, Jackie. Deirdre and Bob (cousins of Bob Smale), Linda (Kellaway family genealogist), Joanna Sassoon, Jane Spencer, Lynne Weller, Kay Thomson, Michael Williamson, Peter Swain, Bob Wilson, Neale McCarthy, Brian Lunn, Richard Millar, Bertrand Letournel of Annecy, Jeff Maynard and the family of G/Capt David Roberts DFC AFC and Bar, Hugh Halliday the RCAF historian. Malcolm Barrass of RAFweb.org has patiently answered numerous queries. Thanks also to Piotr Forkasiewicz for allowing me to use his stunning artwork on the front cover.

The contributor or source of each image is credited in brackets after each caption.

Great support from friends the late Patti Kellaway, Steve Smith (218 Squadron Historian), the late Pete Tresadern (35 Squadron Historian) and Tim and Beryl Raynes (nee Pinches) has been invaluable, quite simply this book would not have happened without them.

The two words '*Thank you*' are insufficient for my always patient wife Eileen.

Invaluable works of reference have been:

Bomber Command War Diaries by Martin Middlebrook and Chris Everett.
Silksheen by Geoff Copeman
Bomber Squadrons at War by Geoff Copeman
Bomber Offensive by Sir Arthur Harris
Nachtjagd Combat Archives by Theo Boiten

Formation

No.630 Squadron RAF was formed within No. 5 Group by order of H.Q. Bomber Command letter (ref. BC/S.21717/13/ORG). dated 26th October 1943. In November 1943 Wing Commander HWH Fisher DFC[i] O.C. 57 Squadron received orders to reduce his squadron's strength to two flights and to hand over his entire 'B' Flight to serve as the nucleus for a new squadron which would also be a two flight squadron.

'B' Flight, its aircraft and crews, complete with flight commander, 26 year old Acting Squadron Leader Malcolm Crocker DFC[ii] were transferred across the station, his orders were to assume command and commence building No. 630 Squadron pending the arrival of its appointed C.O. Wing Commander John Rollinson DFC[iii].

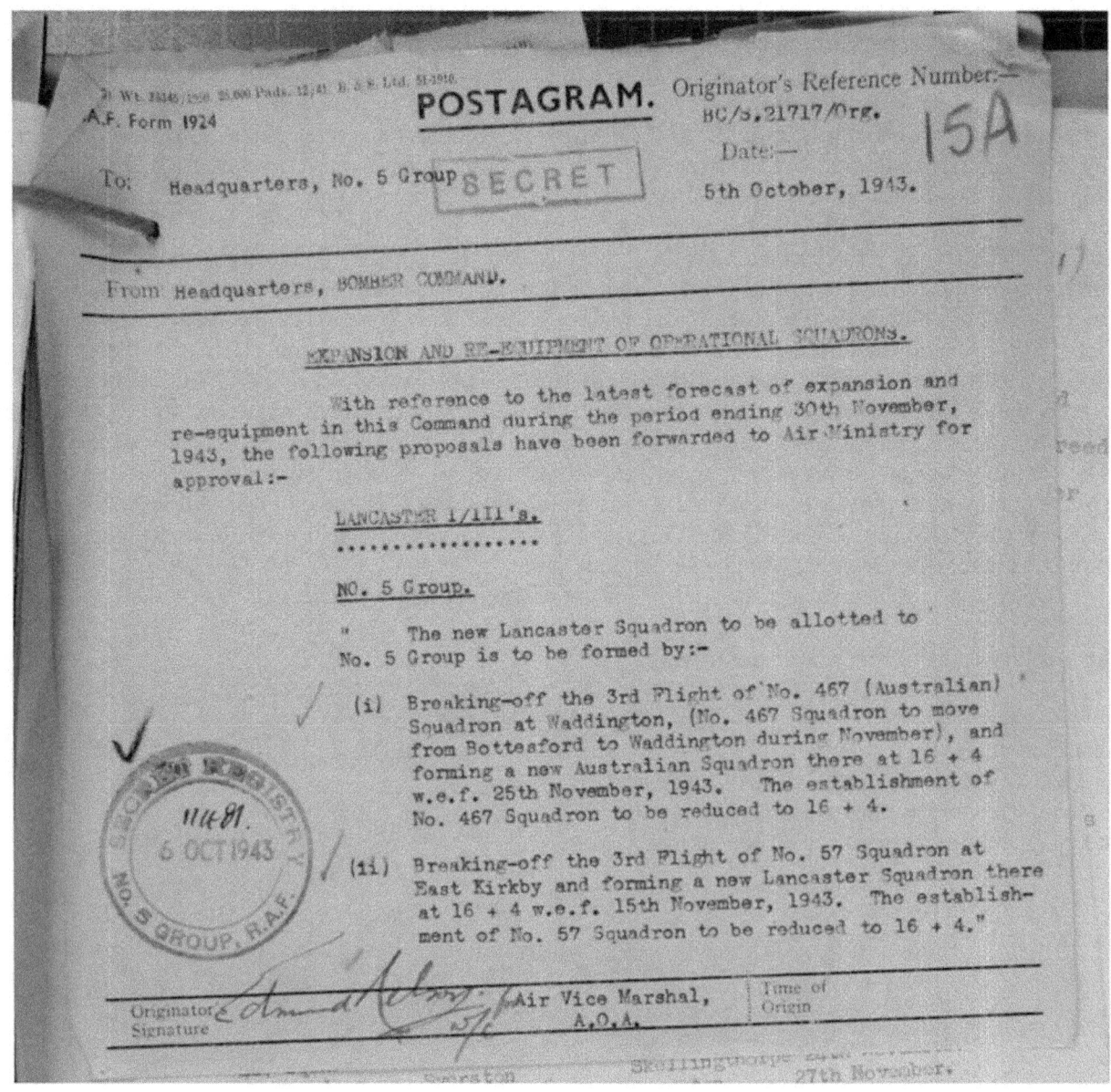

HQ No.5 Group, order for formation of 630 Squadron (The National Archives)

> 15.11.43. Formation of 630 Sqdn. 2 F/L. 16 + 6. WB Squadron. Formed by posting of 'B' Flight, 57 Sqdn., on reduction from 3 F/L to 2 F/L Sqdn. (FL/Com. A/S/L M. Crocker, D.F.C.) S/Commander F.D. Rollinson, D.F.C. Remaining aircrews from various squadrons and ground personnel to be posted by A.O. i/c Records.

57 Squadron records note the formation of 630 Squadron (The National Archives)

Malcolm Crocker was the son of a wealthy American family from Massachusetts. His formative years were spent in a large house at Stockbridge, Berkshire County, Massachusetts with his parents, two brothers, two sisters and several domestic servants. During 1941 while working as an apprentice engineer with Ludlow Manufacturing and already with two years civil flying experience under his belt Crocker followed the events in Europe with interest joining a US based pilot refresher course for prospective RAF aircrew before enlisting in the RAF. He was commissioned Acting Pilot Officer in June 1942 and in the next year as a Flying Officer was quickly advanced to Acting Squadron Leader, only actually becoming a war substantive Flight Lieutenant on 9th November.

It was expected that 'sprog crews' straight from Heavy Conversion Units would be posted-in and that additionally experienced crews would be transferred from other squadrons within 5 Group to supplement the strength of the new 630 Squadron. Heavy Servicing Echelon 9630 was established to provide engineering support manned by the essential ground crews to keep the bombers flying.

Malcolm Crocker pre-war and skiing with friends (Cloe Milek and Crocker family)

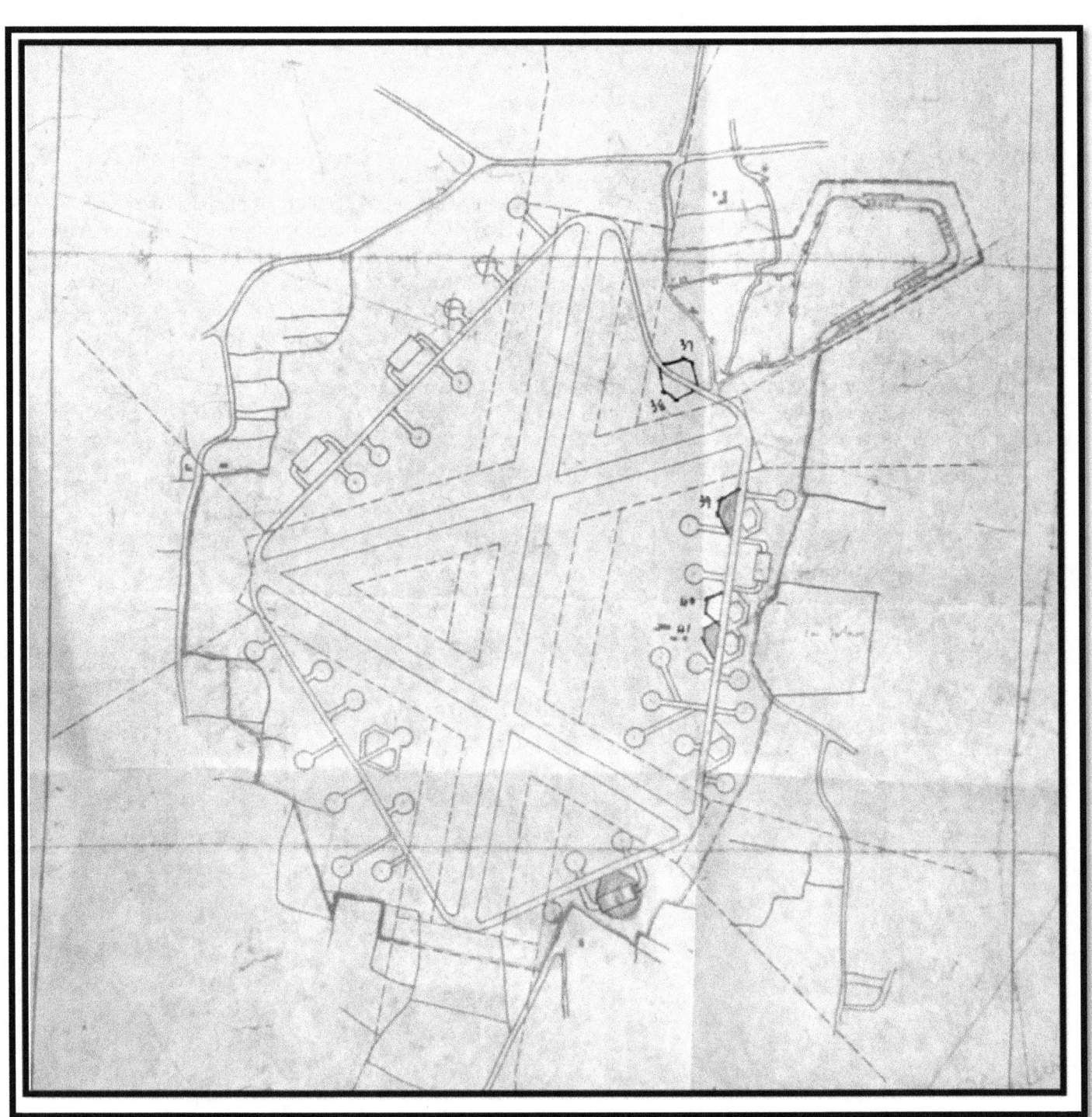

Dispersals at East Kirkby (The National Archives)

'Crocker's crew', (l to r) Jock Glencross (Nav), Jack Arnett (Mid Upper), Harry LeMarchant (Bomb Aimer), Gwyn 'Taff' Llewellyn (Rear gunner) (Natasha Yelland)

Flight Lieutenants JD Henderson RNZAF[iv] and CR Savage DFC RCAF[v] (ex-44 Squadron) were attached from HQ Bomber Command to support Squadron Leader Crocker. On 11th November 1943 the Padre's arrived at East Kirkby, Rev. GR Cooper (C of E)[vi] from RAF Shobden and Rev. CE Heap (Methodist)[vii] from RAF Bottesford.

The following day saw the first issue of 'The Bull', a weekly newspaper for RAF East Kirkby and RAF Spilsby. Dispersal were reassigned, 57 Squadron were allocated numbers 1 – 11, 32, 33 and 34 while 630 Squadron took 12 – 23, number 24 and 25 and visiting aircraft were expected to use 26 and 27. The Appendix to 57 Squadron's Operations Record Book' recorded on 15th November 'All B-Flight including 9 crews and 106 ground staff were transferred to newly formed No. 630 Squadron'.

The following day two new members were attached to Station Staff in recognition of the additional workload.

P/O FH Jones[viii]   (Intelligence) formerly 15 OTU.
F/O HFG Dawson[ix]   Admin (Major Servicing Wing)

November 1943

The records of 630 Squadron commence on Monday 15th November 1943 when, with high winds driving the rain and sleet across East Kirkby airfield, Flight Lieutenant Frank Cheetham[i] arrived from 1668 HCU to take up his post as Squadron Adjutant. Earlier in the war he had been responsible for 'admin' at RAF Swinderby (Wigsley) and would provide administrative and logistical support to Squadron Leader Crocker who had 11 captains and crews as a cadre around which to form the new squadron, reinforced by a further crew which had been captained by 57 Squadron's Pilot Officer F Smith recently hospitalized for an operation, his crew, as the result arriving on strength as 'spare bods' available to fly with other crews as and when required[ii].

S/L Malcolm Crocker DFC (US citizen)
F/L Don Paterson RCAF[iii]
F/L Fred Perrers RNZAF[iv]
F/O John Pratt RCAF[v]
P/O Joseph Howe[vi]
P/O Peter Piggin[vii]
P/O Donald (Tony) Story RAAF[viii]
F/S Sid Edwards[ix]
F/S John Homewood[x]
F/S Jimmy White[xi]
F/S Wilson Yates[xii]

Don Paterson was a 25 year old Canadian born at Fort William, Ontario but resident in Toronto, he joined the RCAF in June 1940 and with 57 Squadron already flown 19 ops since commencing his tour in August. His fellow countryman 23 year old John Pratt from Winnipeg and his crew had been operational with 'Fifty-seven' since June and had flown 18 ops. The crew of recently promoted thirty year old Flight Lieutenant Fred Perrers RNZAF of Remuera, NZ had already survived several close calls and were approaching their 20th op.

Left: Fred Perrers RNZAF (Roy Calvert) Right: Jim White (Frank Elwood)

Unidentified Lancaster (Jerry Monk)

Twenty year olds Peter Piggin from Tanganyika, East Africa and Joe Howe headed less experienced crews as did Flight Sergeants Wil Yates aged 31, Sid Edwards aged 23 and John Homewood aged 21. 'Tony' Story and Jimmy White's crews had only recently arrived with 57 Squadron themselves having operated previously with 61 and 49 Squadrons respectively. Glaswegian Jimmy White was a former soldier who had transferred to the RAF to fly. The official records of Six-thirty[xiii] commenced in handwritten form reportedly scribed by Cheetham himself and would remain as such until clerks were posted in. The squadron offices didn't even have electricity for lighting and there was no provision for black-out curtains. The Adjutant borrowed folding tables, chairs and also some staff who would be trained for clerical duties along with a typewriter which for the meanwhile remained non-operational as nobody could type. Living quarters had no linoleum floor covering and two hundred yards away across the airfield were the barely finished toilet blocks. One 'batman' (valet) rather than the expected ten was available to assist the forty officers but Frank Cheetham reported that 'the spirit was cheerful'.

Eleven Lancasters of 57 Squadron transferred to the new 630 Squadron including ED308, ED413 and ED655 which had each been repaired three times following damage, ED698 which had been twice repaired and ED944 which had not long completed repairs. ED308 was transferred to No. 1654 HCU a week later.

ED308	ED698	ED920	JB135
ED413	ED758	ED944	JB236
ED655	ED777	JA872	

Complete crews arrived promptly at East Kirkby to join 630 Squadron posted from the other 5 Group squadrons. No. 9 Squadron sent 22 year old F/L Bill English[xiv] a former Van Boy for Rivington's Tea in Durham and 26 year old P/O John Syme RAAF[xv] of Adelaide, the 44 Squadron crew of F/S Gordon Burness RNZAF[xvi] of Waimate, Canterbury/NZ, 61 Squadron's crew of Londoner F/O Ken Ames[xvii], 106 Squadron sent 23 year old P/O WA 'Bill' Clark[xxiv] and 23 year old P/O Don Cheney RCAF[xviii] of Ottawa with their crews, 207 Squadron sent P/O Reg Cartwright DFC[xix] and crew, from 619 Squadron the crews of 20 year old F/O Doug MacDonald RCAF[xx] of Regina, Saskatchewan and F/S Bob Hughes[xxi] and a pilotless crew from 49 Squadron (formerly captained by P/O Frank Oglesby who had been hospitalized).

Left: Don Cheney RCAF (Peter Cheney) Right: Gordon Burness RNZAF (Burness family)

Left: Geoff Prober (Mike Barber) Right: David Roberts (Jeff Maynard and the Roberts family)

Six Lancasters (JB546, JB654, JB666, JB597, JB665 and JB672) were delivered from 61 Squadron and a planned bombing attack had to be cancelled due to insufficient change in the miserable weather. Other new crews arriving were those of 29 year old Hanwell man F/O Geoff Probert[xxii] from 1661 HCU on 19th November, 21 year old Londoner F/O David 'Robbie' Roberts[xxiii] (from 1654 HCU), Sergeant Austin Drinkall[xxv] a 28 year old from Lancashire recently married and settled in Southwark and 22 year old Sergeant Allan Johnson[xxvi] all direct from Conversion Units and F/O Cliff Armour[xxvii] a London resident Australian theatrical manager serving in the RAF) on 27th.

John Homewood (Homewood family)

Clifford Armour (Armour family)

Senior figures at this stage were:

Navigator Leader – Flight Lieutenant Leo Ehrman[xxix] born in Russia but who had settled in Hounslow in 1929 with his father Martin Ehrman – Gentleman's Tailor and his brother Rudolph. Leopold became a Member of the Royal Meteorological Society and joined the RAF at the outbreak of war, flying a tour with 44 Squadron in early 1943 for which he was awarded a DFC.

Engineer Leader – Flying Officer Fred Spencer[xxx] a 22 year old second tour man from Shotteswell near Banbury. He completed his first tour with 106 Squadron before instructing at 1654 Conversion Unit. During an exceptionally long tour with 630 Squadron (Nov 1943 to Oct 1944) he flew regularly with Ken Ames' crew and after their tour completed he flew with a variety of other crews.

Bombing Leader – Flying Officer George Farara DFM[xxxi] a 26 year old from Antigua in the West Indies who had returned to the UK with his mother and siblings in 1930. Farara enlisted in 1939 and married before he flew a tour with 61 Squadron over the winter of 1942/43 earning a DFM and being commissioned.

Gunnery Leader – Flight Lieutenant Ernie Stead[xxxii] a 30 year old married Yorkshireman who had completed his first tour as a Sergeant Air Gunner, been Mentioned in Despatches and commenced a second tour with 467 Squadron as a flight gunnery leader. As the former 'B' Flight 57 Squadron lads mixed with

WH "Cab" Kellaway (Patti Kellaway)

Freddie Spencer (Patti Kellaway)

Leo Ehrmann (Ehrman family)

George Farara (Patti Kellaway)

the new crews arriving from elsewhere in 5 Group, there must have been a few eyes on Flight Lieutenant Winston 'Cab' Kellaway[xxviii] who had been identified by 5 Group as 'solid support' for Malcolm Crocker. He wore the ribbon of the Distinguished Service Order (DSO) beneath his pilots' wings, a very rare honour for such a junior ranking officer therefore alluding to an act of great bravery.

Cab was a former Sergeant pilot with No.12 Squadron he had flown with the Advanced Air Striking Force in the Fall of France and the Low Countries in the summer of 1940 when the single engine Fairey Battle equipped squadrons were virtually annihilated. Whilst instructing at 15 OTU Kellaway participated in the first 1000 bomber raids (31st May/1st June 1942 attacking Cologne and then 1st/2nd June against Essen). Converting to heavy bombers 'Cab' Kellaway flew a tour with 149 Squadron in their lumbering great Stirlings before being posted to 617 Squadron in early June 1943 as a replacement for one of the Dambuster crews. On 5th August 1943 while flying over Ashley Walk ranges testing a new type of bomb designed to be released at low level over land to spin into the base of viaduct supports his Lancaster (ED765) was caught in the wake of a leading aircraft and touched the ground. It crashed and caught fire, 6 of the seven man crew had to be hospitalized at RAF Hospital Wroughton due to injuries and on recovery from multiple broken bones 'Cab' Kellaway was posted to 'the new squadron' effective 15th November.

Wednesday 17th November 1943 at 23:06 hours East Kirkby witnessed 57 Squadron's JB315 overshoot the airfield on landing and hit the ground as the pilot attempted to get airborne again. The Lancaster crashed at Southfields Farm, Mavis Enderby near neighbouring Spilsby, sadly two of the crew were killed outright, three were dangerously injured of which one would later die and the other two crewmen sustained less serious injuries.

Don Paterson RCAF and crew with JB135 still in 57 Squadron codes (Andrew Paterson)

November 1943 - Operations Commence for No. 630 Squadron

Thursday 18th November 1943.
Orders were received during the day of Thursday that ops were on that night and 630 Squadron were to participate in a major raid. For the first time in the war Bomber Command was going to make two large scale attacks, a great distance apart, almost simultaneously. 395 bombers would attack Ludwigshafen-am-Rhein as 444 attacked Berlin. At briefing that afternoon when the airmen sat awaiting instructions the curtain covering the huge wall map swept backwards and the crews discovered their target at the end of the long red ribbon between East Kirkby and Germany, it was the Big City, Berlin.

The raid that night was to be the first of a concerted campaign against Berlin the capital of Nazi Germany which would last until the end of January 1944 with return trips in February and even late March 1944. Berlin was a formidable target, one of the most heavily defended in Germany with an incredible concentration of anti-aircraft guns and night fighters. Nine Lancasters of the squadron participated almost all formerly of 57 Squadron, each carrying 9 x 4000lb HC (High Capacity) 'Cookies', 432 x 30lb incendiaries and 7,740 x 4lb incendiaries.

18th/19th November 1943 : Night Bombing Attack on BERLIN
Take Off: from 16:50 hours led by Squadron Leader Crocker in JB236 O Bar'.

JB236-OBar	S/L M Crocker	
JB135-L	P/O J Howe	
ED920-P	F/L W English	
ED944-Z	P/O DW Story RAAF	
ED655-J	F/O DA MacDonald RCAF	RD
ED698-R	P/O PJ Piggin	RD
ED758-H	F/S SA Edwards	
JA872-N	F/S WB Yates	RD[4]
ED413-M	F/S GW Burness RNZAF	

The crews reported dense (10/10ths cloud) over the target area but using green and red target indicators all believed that their bombs had been dropped in the target area and some reported red fires and a large orange explosion. Night fighters were thankfully not encountered and for many the sortie was uneventful although Pilot Officer Peter Piggin flying ED698 was caught by heavy flak and the starboard wing sustained some shrapnel damage. All aircraft returned safely but ED944 'Z-Zebra' flown by Aussie Pilot Officer Don 'Tony' Story had to put down at West Malling in Kent with empty fuel tanks after being nursed across Northern France and the English Channel by pilot and flight engineer Sgt Douglas James[xxxiii]. All aircraft and crews were reported home safely by 01:48 hours, 630 Squadron had been lucky, many must have hoped that the honeymoon period would continue. New Zealander Gordon Burness who had recently arrived from 44 Squadron was no doubt relieved to have had a trouble free op, on one of his trips earlier in the month, a raid on Kassel, his aircraft had been over the target area when the bomb load failed to release due to a mechanical problem. Not a chap to give in easily Burness had a member of his crew ready themselves to release the bombs manually and despite concentrated flak and some night fighter interference he made three bombing runs over the target to ensure a successful result. He was deservedly awarded the Distinguished Flying Medal in the London Gazette of 14 December 1943. (After completion of his tour and having been commissioned he became an instructor and in 1945 was again decorated, receiving the Air Force Cross for his dedicated work with pilots under training).

---

[4] **RD** indicated that the aircraft returned with damage substantial enough to be reported.

A major contributory factor to the lack of opposition over Berlin had been the transfer of several Gruppen of Luftwaffe night fighters which had transferred to Norway on the 18th to counter USAAF raids on the Oslo area and a thick layer of ground fog which kept much of the remaining defending force on the ground. German 'Schlussbericht' – final reports – revealed that bombing was not too well concentrated however four industrial premises were totally destroyed and 28 more damaged, 11 explosives works and 4 chemical plants were counted within these figures. Large numbers of residential properties in the target area were also destroyed or damaged. On Saturday 20th November the AOC 5 Group AVM RA Cochrane CB CBE AFC visited the Station, Flight Lieutenant Cheetham of 630 Squadron recorded the arrival of the first of his ground echelon, two RAF clerks arrived at East Kirkby accompanied by Flight Lieutenant James Harrower[xxxiv] who was to take up the role of Station Education Officer arranging a full range of training courses for all ranks and trades. Two Lancasters were delivered from 61 Squadron, JB532 and JB561.

Monday 22nd November 1943.
Berlin was the destination announced again to a hushed briefing room; ten Lancasters from 630 Squadron were to participate in the latest attack, carrying 10 x 4,000lb 'Cookies', 12,260 x 4lb incendiaries and 700 x 30lb incendiary bombs. It was to be the largest single force of heavy bombers ever to target Berlin with a total of 764 aircraft scheduled to attack between 19:57 and 21:51 hours.

22nd/23rd November 1943 : Night Bombing Attack on BERLIN
Take Off: 16:42 hours led by Flying Officer Doug MacDonald RCAF in ED655.

ED655-J	F/O DA MacDonald RCAF
ED413-M	F/O R Cartwright
ED698-R	P/O PJ Piggin
ED777-Q	F/O JM Pratt RCAF
ED758-H	F/S SA Edwards
JB672-F	F/S WB Yates
JB546-A	F/S GW Burness RNZAF
JB135-L	P/O J Howe
JB236-OBar	F/L FL Perrers
ED920-P	F/L W English

With more aircraft serviceable than crews to fly them 57 Squadron borrowed the 630 Squadron crews of Tony Story to fly JB529 and Jim White to fly JB541 for them. Arriving in the target area Six-thirty's crews again found a heavy blanket of cloud but they could make out a good concentration of target indicators dropped in a timely manner by the Pathfinder Master Bombers. They attacked from 20,500 to 21,500 feet and reported that there were very large deep red/orange explosions in the centre of the target area with black smoke rising through the cloud layer and the glow from the large fires was reflected on the clouds. Flak was reportedly light in the target area but was encountered crossing the Dutch coastline. Fortunately for the RAF the Luftwaffe's 1st Jagdkorps (Fighter Corps) had not detected the incoming bombers over the North Sea and with poor conditions due to icing and dense cloud the night fighters mainly remained on the ground. Unaware of the problems encountered by the enemy, Sergeant John Forrester, Rear Gunner in Doug MacDonald's crew fought lack of oxygen caused by a faulty system but eventually he lost consciousness and the turret had to be left unmanned over enemy held territory. At 00:06 hours Reg Cartwright put ED413's wheels down on the deck just as Doug MacDonald taxied clear and was the last of Six-thirty's crews to return, all crews returned safely to East Kirkby, Lady Luck had held out. Based on German official records and photo reconnaissance this attack was later determined to be the most effective against Berlin during the entire war. A vast area of the city was destroyed across to Spandau and during the following day smoke was still to be found at 19,000 feet. The Germans had to divert the equivalent of three divisions of troops, over 50,000 men, to help with the aftermath and amongst the buildings destroyed or damaged were the Ministry of Weapons and Munitions, the SS Administrative College and barracks, the Imperial Guard barracks at Spandau, five factories conducting war work for Siemens Electrical Group and the Alkett tank factory which had just relocated to avoid the reduction in output caused by bombing attacks in their Ruhr homeland.

A contemporary official document, 630 Squadron, Ops Record[xxxv], held at the RAF Museum at Hendon suggests that Pilot Officer Tony Story flew on the above attack with 630 Squadron and omits the crew of John Pratt, it is certain however that the Pratt crew did fly based on confirmation from his bomb aimer Tony Blois[xxxvi] which is further confirmed by the detailed listing of operations in the recommendation[xxxvii] for John Pratt's DFC dated 24th February 1944 by which time he had completed 27 sorties (between 11th June 1943 and 21st January 1944), possibly there was a late change to the Battle Order.

Tuesday 23rd November 1943.
During the day Lancaster JB556 became the ninth and last aircraft transferred from No. 61 Squadron. Early afternoon as the curtain screening the huge map fell the aircrew gathered for briefing must have wondered at the hand that fate was dealing them, it was Berlin again for a force of 383 bombers. The outward and homeward routes were identical to the previous night. It must have been obvious to all that the German ground defences and the night fighters would be ready and expecting them, 630 Squadron were to provide ten Lancasters bombed up with 10 x 4000lb 'Cookies', 11,700 x 4lb incendiaries and 720 x 30lb incendiary bombs.

23rd/24th November 1943 : Night Bombing Attack on BERLIN
Take Off: at 16:50 hours JB236 (Fred Perrers) was the first airborne.

JB135-L	P/O J Howe
JB236-OBar	F/L FL Perrers
ED920-P	F/L W English
JB597-S	P/O DH Cheney RCAF
JA872-N	P/O DW Story RAAF
ED413-M	P/O R Cartwright
ED698-R	P/O PJ Piggin
JB666-O	F/O JM Pratt RCAF
ED655-J	F/O DA MacDonald RCAF
JB546-A	F/S GW Burness RNZAF

Minutes before 19:00 hours Don Cheney brought JB597 back to East Kirkby, their wireless system had failed and despite an hour work by their Wireless Op it stubbornly refused to work. Shortly after 20:00 hours Peter Piggin returned, heavy icing had prevented him gaining sufficient altitude to proceed and within minutes he was followed by Tony Story suffering with the same problem. Over the North Sea a lot of 'cookies' were jettisoned by Lancasters of the force bound for Berlin as they struggled to gain vital altitude, some taking over 20 minutes to gain 400 feet. Enroute for the target at altitude 19,000 feet at 18:50 hours the mid-upper gunner of Reg Cartwright's 'M-Mother', Sergeant Terry Davidson saw a twin engined night fighter approaching starboard quarter up and instructed a dive to starboard as he opened fire with a 3 second burst. The night fighter took evasive action and was not seen again. No claim was made. On their run up to the target in ED920 'P-Peter' at 20:09 hours Bill English's mid-upper gunner Sgt Derek Carlile observed an aircraft believed to be a JU88 moving across from their port beam to immediately above the Lancaster and dropping a series of fighter flares. Sgt Carlile opened fire with a 4 second burst, the tracer rounds being seen to enter the fuselage of the German fighter which turned to port and was hit in its undersurfaces by a burst from F/Sgt Bill Hewitt RAAF in the rear turret, it dived away on the port quarter and wasn't seen again. Enemy aircraft claimed as damaged. At this point ED920 was still painted as 57 Squadron's 'P' only becoming 'D-Dog' some days later.

Over the cloud covered target area the squadron's Lancasters attacked again from between 20,000 to 21,500 feet reporting explosions quite well concentrated on the green target indicator flares dropped by P.F.F. Some of the crews simply bombed the fires still burning from the night before. Canadian F/O John Pratt noted a *'good hearty glow'* from the fires raging in the city below. Luftwaffe night fighters were active and the anti-aircraft fire was lighter than expected, probably in consideration of the large force of their own fighters seeking out the Lancaster bombers in the night sky. Freed of their payloads of explosives the bombers headed for home avoiding points which were offering the fiercest flak. Determination of the results proved hard as German records apparently simply added 94 wooden barracks, 8 industrial sites and 1 military base with thousands of houses to the losses of the night before. Doug MacDonald's crew landed at 00:23 hours and the vigil continued for P/O Howe's and F/L Perrer's crews. It soon however became obvious that they wouldn't be returning, their fuel loads would have been exhausted and they were marked F.T.R. – Failed to Return.

Lancaster III, JB135 (Code – L)

Pilot	– P/O Joseph Howe. Age 20	Killed
Flight Eng	– Sgt Norman James Yates Goulding. Age 20	Killed
Navigator	– F/O Dennis Edward Caudrey. Age 23	Killed
Bomb Aimer	– P/O Arthur James Matthews . Age 30	Killed
Wireless Op	– Sgt Thomas Walter Blanc. Age 22	Killed
Mid Upper	– Sgt Robert Inglis. Age 23	Killed
Rear Gunner	– Sgt John George Smith. Age 20	Killed

The parents of the crew would soon be receiving the terrible news by telegram, those of Sergeant Norman Goulding a former 'Halton Bratt' RAF Boy Apprentice and regular RAF airman from Kendal, would hear thousands of miles away in Seattle, USA where they were staying. The fate of the Howe crew on their 15th Op was never determined and they are commemorated on the Runnymede Memorial to the Missing. Initially it seemed distinctly possible that in the darkness over the North Sea their Lancaster, weighed down by its payload of explosives and the fuel necessary for flying hundreds of miles into Germany and home again, struggled to gain altitude whilst icing up and that something went catastrophically wrong. Notification received via the International Red Cross in January 1944 reported that the Germans had advised the deaths of five members of the crew of JB135 but made no mention of the pilot or flight engineer. The origin of that information is not as yet known. Since the Germans had the serial number of the Lancaster and names of five of the seven crewmen to be able to confirm their deaths it seems likely that the bomber crashed and exploded on German occupied territory. The graves of these men may have been lost during the 1945 fighting as the Russians fought for Germany.

Lancaster III, JB236 (Code – O Bar)

Pilot	– F/L Frederick Leonard Perrers RNZAF. Age 30	Killed
Flight Eng	– Sgt Charles Harry Pell. Age 21	Killed
Navigator	– F/S John Clapperton . Age 28	Killed
Bomb Aimer	– F/S John Freebairn White. Age 27	Killed
Wireless Op	– F/S Ronald Bertie Mutum. Age 22	Prisoner
Mid Upper	– Sgt Leon Harvey Cooper. Age 19	Killed
Rear Gunner	– F/S Frederick Colin Crowe. Age 19	Prisoner

Shot down by a night fighter, Flight Lieutenant Perrer's Lancaster crashed onto a Luftwaffe bombing range at Fassberg in Germany. German records state that JB236 crashed 1 km south of the Faßberg in the vicinity of Schmarbeck near the airfield of Faßberg- on the way to the target. JB236 was shot down at 19:30 hours by Hauptmann (Flight Lieutenant) Siegfried Hahn of 9 Squadron/ Night Fighter Group 3 (in German

9./NJG 3, which is written in full as 9 Staffel/Nachtjagdgeschwader.3) and claimed as a 4 engine bomber north of Hannover. Investigated on the ground by the Luftwaffe bureaucracy Hahn's claim was fully confirmed when the crashed bomber was located and an entry was made in the records of the regional Luftwaffe command, LG XI, with 19:40 hours as the 'recorded time of crash.' The five dead crewmen are buried at Hanover War Cemetery. Fred Perrers and his crew were flying their 20th op. A tongue in cheek message was later received from Prisoner 263610, 23 year old Ronald Bertie Mutum held at Stalag Luft 6 (Heydekrug) advising that having taken to his parachute over Germany he had landed without even a bruise and asking that his appreciation be conveyed to the manufacturers responsible for his 'chute. Postwar Ron Mutum returned to his job as a Railways Clerk in Norfolk where he married before leaving for Kenya in the 1950's to become a Station Master on the East African railways. Flight Sergeant Fred Crowe the Rear Gunner, an apprentice draughtsman from Hull was held at Stalag IVB allocated the Prisoner number 263575 and survived the war as a Warrant Officer to return home, marry and raise two sons.

The crew had had a very event filled flying career. Fred Perrers had survived a mid-air collision during his training when on 2nd February 1942 with his instructor their Crane Mk.I (7831) was hit by a novice pilot who crashed and was killed. Joining 10 OTU in August 1942 Fred Perrer's crew were amongst a small number of crews who on completion of training were not sent direct to Bomber Command, instead being 'loaned out' to Coastal Command. Attached to 10 OTU equipped with obsolete twin engine Whitley bombers they were to patrol known routes to and from the U-boat bunkers on the Biscay coast of France. Having taken off from St Eval at 10:00 on 10th December 1942 engine failure left no alternative but to force land in the sea off Cape Penas in Northern Spain at 15:20 hours. The waters were unexpectedly shallow and after destroying all secret equipment, documents and maps P/O Perrers, Sgt's White, Crowe, Mutum, Clapperton and an attached 2nd Pilot (Sgt Walpole) waded ashore into Spanish internment. John Clapperton, a pre-war Dunblane police officer reported that he hadn't been interrogated but that the Spanish did attempt to get information from some of the crew who gave ambiguous replies. They were moved to Valladolid, Alhama de Aragon and Madrid before being re-patriated to Gibraltar on 19 February 1943. Arriving back in the UK within a week they were interrogated by M.I.9 before being passed back to the RAF. The crew then had a couple of months at Upper Heyford with 16 OTU before converting to Lancasters at 1661 CU and joining 57 Squadron in time to bomb the V-1 works at Peenemunde in August 1943. After 19 Ops they were transferred to 630 Squadron.

The loss of two crews in a night was a harsh one for the young squadron and the night also marked the final Op' for the crew of Flight Sergeant Gordon Burness RNZAF who had completed their tour. Twenty two year old Burness from Waimate, Otago was awarded a DFM and after a long tour instructing fledgling pilots also later decorated with an AFC, Desmond Hawkins the Navigator would later return to operational flying to do a second tour with 625 Squadron, rear gunner Tom Holmes also flew a second tour as a Warrant Officer with 578 Squadron, both were awarded DFCs. Their bomb aimer Sid Jeapes was not so lucky and on his second tour was shot down and killed serving with 9 Squadron. Flight Engineer Ken Peacock had more ops to fly before completing his tour and remained with the squadron until sadly he also failed to return from an op in late March. On Wednesday 24th November Major Francis Whalley[xxxviii] arrived from RAF Bottesford to take over as Local Defence Adviser because Lt-Colonel Astle had been posted to 5 Group HQ.

Thursday 25th November is marked only in the records to state that a planned night bombing attack was cancelled and that two new typewriters had been delivered. The records are all hand written and convey little of the continued struggle which went on at East Kirkby to find sufficient of anything for the newly formed squadron. Supplies had not arrived, billets had not yet been completed, everything needed to run the squadron was still having to be begged or borrowed from anybody who had it. East Kirkby's MO, Squadron Leader O'Dowd was posted to RAF Cosford on 26th.

Friday 26th November 1943.
A force of 443 Lancasters and 7 Mosquitoes were detailed for an attack on Stuttgart on the night of 26th November. Ten aircraft of 630 Squadron had been scheduled to deliver a payload of 10 x 4000lb 'Cookies',

9,600 x 4lb and 504 x 30lb incendiary bombs onto the German capital city. Three aircraft were on loan from 57 Squadron for the nights Op.

26th/27th November 1943 : Night Bombing Attack on Berlin
Take Off: at 17:09 hours Lancaster ED364 (Tony Story) was the first to take off.

ED364-57	P/O DW Story RAAF
JB546-A	F/L DS Paterson RCAF
ED655-J	F/S RT Hughes
ED920-D	P/O WA Clark
JA872-N	P/O J Syme RAAF
JB526-57	F/S J White
ED698-R	P/O DH Cheney RCAF
JB532-X	F/O R Cartwright
JB666-O	F/S WB Yates
JB597-S	F/S SA Edwards

A common route over northern France by both the main force and that of a diversionary raid on Stuttgart confused the Luftwaffe fighter controllers and left the skies over Berlin relatively clear of night fighters. Bombing between 21:17 and 21:26 hours from 20,000 to 22,000 feet the returning crews reported conditions moderate to quite clear over Berlin, large explosions were seen on the ground with some major concentrations of fire, P/O Cheney's crew could still see the fires behind them 150 miles after leaving the target area, other crews reported dense smoke at 16,000 feet and the fires still visible at 120 miles and 50 miles. The semi-industrial Reinickendorf suburb was badly hit with other clusters of bombs on the electrical factories in the district known as Siemensstadt, the city centre and Tegel districts. Thirty-eight factories supplying the German war effort were destroyed. Large numbers of nearby residential properties were also destroyed or damaged. Due to heavy cloud over East Kirkby with a maximum visibility of 500 yards in the best of spots the returning bombers were instructed to divert to other airfields. At Holme-on-Spalding Moor the runway was still obscure when Flight Sergeant Sid Edwards came into land and he had to crash land JB597 but got his crew home safely. Their Lancaster was classified with Category B Damage and had to be Struck Off Charge as unrepairable. All aircraft were accounted for across bases in Lincolnshire and East Yorkshire. Monday 29th November found Flight Lieutenant Cheetham (Adjutant) in meetings at H.Q. No. 5 Group with his peers amongst the Staff Officers, protesting, pleading and arm twisting to get the men and women, accommodation, supplies and equipment Squadron Leader Crocker needed to be able to run the fledgling squadron.

The following afternoon news was received of the award of an 'Immediate' Distinguished Flying Medal to Flight Sergeant Gordon William Burness, RNZAF (NZ.416191) for his bravery shortly before joining Six-thirty whilst flying over Kassel with 44 Squadron. Immediate awards were made by the RAF in respect of an act of courage or gallantry where Non-Immediate awards recognised sustained bravery and spirit over a period of time. Tour expired, the majority of the Burness crew had departed on leave before proceeding to their next postings. At about the same time the 'all Sergeants' crew of North Wales born 20 year old Herbert 'Cliff' Rogers[xxxix] arrived fresh from Conversion Unit. Tuesday 30th November was also marked as the day that 630 Squadron was allocated the squadron Code LE for the fuselages of its Lancasters which were still painted as they had been on receipt from their former units. At this stage some aircraft had new codes painted, for instance ED920 had been 'P-Pip'' and ED413 had been 'M-Mother' while on the strength of 57 Squadron, they would now become 'D-Dog' and 'T-Tock' with 630 Squadron.

December 1943

During the month a clerk able to operate a typewriter joined the strength of Six-thirty and the eye strain for anybody attempting to decipher the records is reduced however the poor clerk was evidently working from handwritten originals because their struggles to interpret the writing resulted in exactly the same difficulties that readers today encounter with the earlier records.

Thursday 2nd December 1943.
A force of 458 bombers were detailed to attack Berlin. 630 Squadron Lancasters were armed with 1 x 4,000 lb HC, 1,200 x 4lb and 64 x 30lb incendiaries.

2nd/ 3rd December 1943 : Night Bombing Attack on Berlin
Take Off: at 16:12 hours Flight Sergeant Jimmy White and crew were the first away aboard JB651.

JA872-N	F/L W English	
JB546-A	F/L DS Paterson RCAF	
JB665-B	Sgt A Drinkall	
JB561-W	F/S J White	
JB655-J	F/S RT Hughes	RD
ED777-Q	P/O WA Clark	
JB654-C	P/O DH Cheney RCAF	
ED413-M	F/O GH Probert	
JB532-X	F/O DA MacDonald RCAF	
ED944-Z	F/O D Roberts	
ED920-D	P/O J Syme RAAF	
JB666-O	F/S WB Yates	RD
ED698-R	F/S JW Homewood	

Various problems were encountered on the outward leg of the flight resulting in several 'early returns', JB665 with its intercom out of action, a lethal weakness if night fighters were encountered, JB561 suffering from faulty instruments, ED698 wouldn't gain altitude and ED920 turned back when the Flight Engineer (Sgt LT Johnson) noted a rate of fuel consumption by the four engines which would make it impossible to bomb Berlin and then return home. Reluctant to simply jettison his bomb load into the North Sea the crew of Pilot Officer Syme RAAF located the flak batteries at Den Helder on the Dutch coast and dropped their ordnance onto some surprised anti-aircraft gunners below. Inaccurate forecasting of the winds over Germany scattered the bomber stream and the direct route to Berlin permitted the Luftwaffe to identify the likely target as Berlin and to get night fighters into the air with 19 minutes to spare. The Pathfinders struggled to get their markers on position. In hazy cloud between 20:17 and 20:22 hours 'Six thirty's' Lanc's delivered their payloads onto Berlin from 20,000 to 21,000 feet where large fires were noted in the south east of the city and scattered through its West End, some of these were still visible 100 miles away as the bombers flew home. Intense fighter activity was encountered coupled with moderate heavy barrage flak and light 20mm and 40mm cannon fire 'hosed' up to 14,000 feet. The searchlights were rendered relatively ineffective by cloud cover. Flying Officer Probert's crew reported that large fires were burning in built-up areas and that through gaps in the cloud they had seen many streets ablaze, both the MacDonald and Roberts crews noted a huge yellow explosion and column of black smoke. The crews who had bombed Berlin and returned landed safely at East Kirkby before midnight on 2nd December. Both JB655 and JB666 returned with flak damage.

German reports confirmed that two more Siemens electrical factories, a ball bearing plant and several railway installations were badly damaged. Sadly one of the Six-thirty crews Failed To Return.

Lancaster III, ED777 (Codes LE – Q)

Pilot	– P/O William Alfred Clark. Age 23	Killed
Flight Eng	– Sgt George Alfred Crowe. Age 19	Killed
Navigator	– Sgt Richard Hooton Banks. Age 25	Killed
Bomb Aimer	– F/O Leonard Redmond Rinn RCAF. Age 29	Killed
Wireless Op	– Sgt John Ford. Age 23	Killed
Mid Upper	– Sgt Robert Hughes. Age 19	Killed
Rear Gunner	– F/S Clarence Ray McLaren RAAF. Age 22	Killed

Their Lancaster was coned by searchlights of 1./Flakscheinw.Abt 808 at 20.38 hours and downed very quickly by the combined efforts of flak and a night fighter. A Lancaster was claimed shot down at this exact place and time by the 1st and 2nd Batteries of Flakabteilung 211. Unteroffizier Adreas Hartl of 6./JG 302 claimed to have attacked a 4-engined bomber at 20.38 hours in the same area, his claim was never fully confirmed and remained as a 'probable'. ED777 crashed to earth on a ridge near a windmill just 1 mile north-east of Gross Schulzendorf which is itself 16 miles south of Berlin.

The fate of ED777 and crew (National Archives of Australia)

 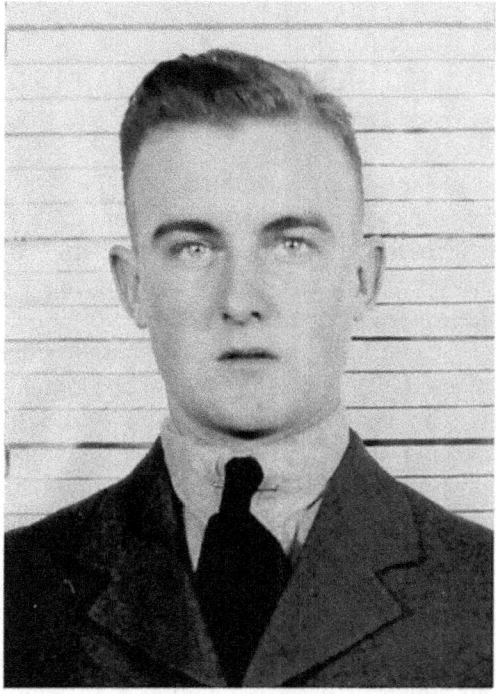

Left: Leonard Rinn RCAF (Rinn family (Canada)) – Right: Doug Macdonald RCAF (RCAF official)

The crew were buried there on the next day in the municipal cemetery where the graves were immediately marked and remained well tended until December 1946 when they were moved to the huge Berlin War Cemetery maintained by the Commonwealth War Graves Commission. Both George Alfred Crowe and Robert Hughes were only 19 years old, Crowe was a former 'Halton bratt' RAF Boy Apprentice and regular RAF airman and Richard Banks had gained a 1st Class Diploma in Agriculture at Wye College, London University. The clerk typing up the returns for the operations in squadron records incorrectly labelled the missing Lancaster as JB546. On Friday 3rd December the Met Officer F/O Charles Lowndes held a gramophone recital of classical music in the Social Club which was well attended by both air and ground crew personnel. During the week the weather in Lincolnshire maintained its usual early mist or fog, drizzle during the day as the clouds grew thicker.

Friday 3rd December 1943.

Ten of the squadrons Lancaster crews were detailed for Ops that afternoon and at briefing the learned that they would be taking off immediately after midnight on the Saturday morning to bomb Leipzig, they were part of a force of 527 bombers taking a direct route to Berlin. Most of the 630 Squadron aircraft carried a 4000lb 'Cookie', 990 x 4lb and 53 x 30lb incendiary bombs.

3rd /4th December 1943 :Night Bombing Attack on Leipzig

Take Off: at 00:11 hours highly experienced Pilot Officer Reg Cartwright DFC and crew previously of 207 Squadron were the first off with a Second Dickie aboard, the recently arrived Cliff Rogers who would be gaining operational experience.

JB666-O	P/O R Cartwright	(Sgt HC Rogers)
JB546-A	P/O DW Story RAAF	
JB654-C	Sgt AGG Johnson	
ED920-D	P/O J Syme RAAF	
JB561-W	F/S J White	RD
JB665-B	Sgt A Drinkall	
JA872-N	F/O CH Armour	
ED698-R	F/S JW Homewood	
JB556-Y	F/O GH Probert	RD
ED944-Z	F/O D Roberts	

JB666 had to jettison its bombload over the North Sea and turned for home after its port outer engine failed and the rear gunners turret malfunctioned, JB654 aborted its mission after instruments failed and then its own rear turret failed. Given the favoured angle of attack by German night fighters was from below and behind a heavy bomber, continuing the mission without rear protection would have been suicidal. The outward route was again direct for Berlin before the Main Force bombers turned sharply for Leipzig leaving a small force of fast Mosquito light bombers to continue and bomb Berlin confusing the German ground and air defences. The night fighters did make contact with the main bomber stream however and Halifaxes and Lancasters began to fall. Glaswegian Flight Sergeant Jim White a 24 year old former Territorial Army soldier was flying JB561/W when it was intercepted between Brandenburg and Leipzig by one of the German night fighters. Raked with heavy cannon and machine gun fire a starboard engine caught fire, the hydraulic system began to fail and the intercom went out of action. At 04:10 hours Jim White had to bomb from only 15,000 feet amongst the worst of the flak due to the damage. The crew didn't know until they landed on two punctured tyres, that their rear gunner, Flight Sergeant Jim Rossiter, RAAF, a 28 year old from Murray Bridge, South Australia had been killed in action. His turret continued to swing from side to side as if he was scanning the dark skies behind the Lancaster. Sergeant Frank Guy, mid upper gunner, fought off an attack by a Messerschmitt 210 twin engined fighter and they continued onwards to bomb Leipzig. James Rossiter was buried alongside many Australian airmen in Cambridge City Cemetery.

The combat report states – Aircraft Lancaster JB561 (W-William) detailed for operations to Leipzig on 3-4.12.43 whilst enroute to the target at position 52° 10' North 12° 25' East height 20,000 feet, magnetic course 182', speed 150mph, AS time 03:50 hours, the mid-upper gunner (Sgt Guy) and the rear gunner (F/S Rossiter) observed an ME210 approaching from astern and slightly above our aircraft, range 300 yards. Instructions were given to corkscrew port and the rear gunner and mid-upper gunner both opened fire. At the same time the enemy opened fire with cannon and machine guns and the return fire from the rear turret of the Lancaster ceased. The rear gunner was heard over the inter-com to exclaim something but almost immediately the inter-com was rendered unserviceable. The fighter broke away to starboard and attacked the Lancaster from dead astern, range 200 yards, again firing cannon and machine guns. Corkscrew manoeuvring was maintained and the mid-upper gunner (Sgt Guy) continued firing until the fighter broke away down and underneath the Lancaster.

Jim Rossiter RAAF died at his guns (Frank Elwood) *Frank Elwood (Frank Elwood)*

Jimmy White's flight engineer Frank Elwood from Poulton-le-Fylde later recalled 'shortly before reaching the target heavy machine gun and cannon fired raked our Lanc, I felt a tug at my sleeve and a hefty smack on my flying helmet and comms died, apparently I'd been almost hit twice but thankfully unhurt. The starboard outer was ablaze issuing bright orange and yellow flames as a beacon to every night fighter for miles and hydraulics were beginning to fail so I had my hands full trying to feather it and extinguish the fire and help our skipper to maintain sufficient height to attack. Another fighter attacked and shot us up from astern'. Bomb aimer Sgt Vince Moor then observed a twin engined aircraft, possibly the same ME210 approaching from the port bow down, firing cannon and machine guns. He fired a two second burst at it from the nose turret as the mid-upper gunner (Sgt Guy) operating his guns and turret manually to fire a short burst as the fighter broke away to port. The ME210 again appeared from dead astern and opened fire. Frank Guy the mid-upper gunner returned fire, still working his guns manually and observed a bright flash of flame appear on the fighter which disappeared from sight not to be seen again. The inter-com being unserviceable Frank Elwood went aft to the rear turret but, thinking the rear gunner was OK as his rear turret apparently swung from left to right, returned to help Jimmy White fighting to maintain control and altitude. 'When we attacked it was from many thousands of feet lower than we'd normally have made a bombing run, medium and heavy flak was exploding all around shaking the Lanc like crazy and other aircraft were dropping their loads from above, bombs were falling all around us'.

Upon landing the rear gunner was found to be dead having sustained multiple injuries from cannon. and machine gun bullets. Extensive damage was caused to our aircraft including two front tyres punctured,

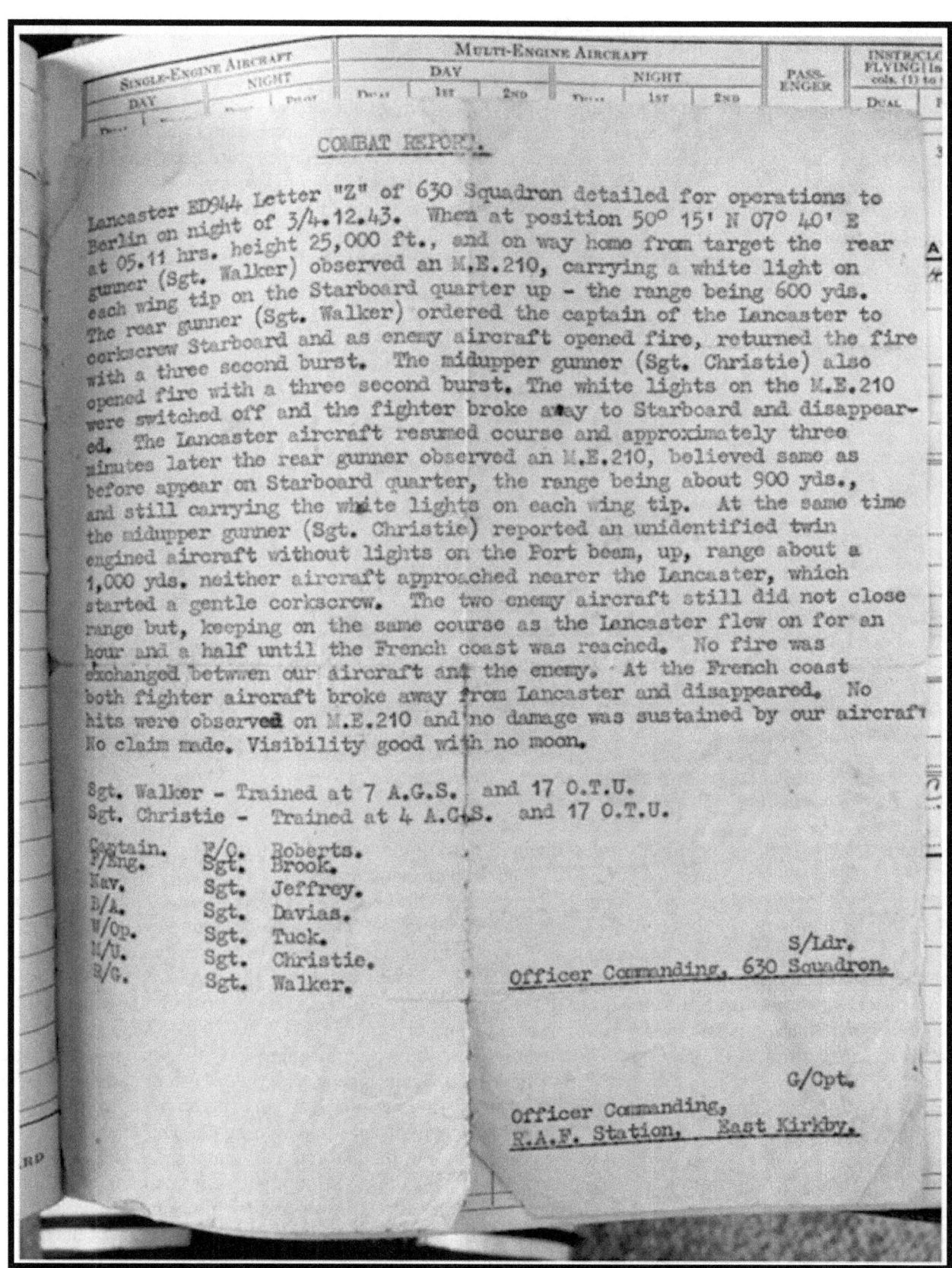

Combat report in David Roberts logbook (Jeff Maynard and the Roberts family)

hydraulics to the rear turret damaged and the whole fuselage cannon shell holed and machine gun bullet holed. Monica indicator received prior to first attack. Weather was clear, visibility was good. Numerous fighter flares in vicinity. Claim : Me210 probably damaged. Assessed to have sustained Category AC Damage, Lancaster JB561 went back to the AV Roe factory for repairs. Shortly after leaving the target area Sergeant Walt Walker in the rear turret of 'Robbie' Roberts' ED944 spotted an ME210 with white wing tip lights in position in the starboard quarter up at 600 yards range. He called for a corkscrew to starboard just as the night fighter opened fire and returned a three second burst of about 200 rounds. The white lights on the fighter were quickly switched off as it broke away. Three minutes later an Me210 was sighted by Walt Walker and simultaneously Sergeant Paul Christie (mid-upper gunner) sighted another twin engined fighter on the port beam at about 1,000 yards. Neither fighter made to attack and Roberts made a gentle corkscrew but the fighters held position and followed the Lancaster to the French coast before they broke away. No hits were claimed.

Flying Officer Cliff Armour's rookie crew reported considerable congestion of aircraft over the target area and the glow of long fires still visible more than 200 miles from the target, Flight Sergeant Homewood's crew added that the fires were dark red and they had also seen the fires from 200 miles distant. Geoff Probert's de-brief report mentioned the glow of the fires reflected on the clouds from 150 miles away, his JB556 was damaged by flak and stray bullets. The appendix to 'Six-thirty's' ORB mentions that heavy flak was bursting in a barrage at about 18,000 feet. Intense fighter activity was noted in the target area and as far south as the Rhine on the return leg. The flak gunners at Koblenz were kept busy that night.

Accurate marking by the Pathfinders resulted in accurate bombing and this raid was regarded as the most successful on Leipzig during the war. The squadron's aircraft attacked between 04:02 and 04:16 hours from 19,500 to 21,500 feet apart from Jim White's crew as mentioned above. The former World Fair buildings which had been occupied by war production factories were devastated, particularly the Junkers bomber aircraft factory. Jim White's battered JB561 was the last of Six-thirty's Lancasters to limp in to land at East Kirkby and it soon became obvious that another of the squadron's crews had Failed To Return.

C Walter Walker saved the Roberts crew that night (Ian Walker)

Lancaster III, ED920 (Codes LE – D)

Pilot	– P/O John Syme RAAF. Age 26	Killed
Flight Eng	– Sgt George Leggott. Age 22	Killed
Navigator	– Sgt Eric Hubbert. Age 21	Killed
Bomb Aimer	– F/O John Christopher Doherty. Age 21	Killed
Wireless Op	– Sgt Dennis Cattley. Age 22	Prisoner
Mid Upper	– Sgt Kenneth Swinchatt. Age 20	Killed
Rear Gunner	– Sgt James Heron. Age 22	Killed

> AIRCRAFT:
>
> At 04.00 hours on the 4th December 1943, a burning, four engined aircraft was observed circling the village of VOLGFELDE (M53/Y64) in an apparent attempt to make a crash landing in one of the nearby fields (?). It suddenly plunged to the ground and crashed about 200 to 300 metres South West of the village (near the main road to Gardelegen). A large explosion was heard and felt in the village which seemed to indicate that the aircraft had crashed with its bomb load. The aircraft burnt fiercely for more than two hours. When the fire, had subsided, it was found that the aircraft pieces had been scattered by the explosion over a wide area and one of the engines had buried itself in the ground nearly fifty metres away.

The fate of ED920 and crew (National Archives of Australia)

John Syme's Lancaster blew up after a night fighter attack enroute to the target over the Altmark and came down south west of Volgfelde, 18 km west of Stendal next to the Volgfelde-Börgitz road. It is impossible to be certain about which night fighter was involved, Hauptman Paul Szameitat of 5./NJG 3 claimed two bombers in the area at 03.36 and 03.41 hours and at 03.36 hours Oberleutnant Günter Köberich

Left: John Syme RAAF (M Syme (Australia)) – Right: Cliff Rogers (Cliff Rogers)

of 11./NJG 3 shot down a Lancaster also in the vicinity. It is known that Syme's Lancaster crashed in the area as did Halifax JD361 flown by P/O FWBG Hingston RCAF of 429 Squadron. Szameitat shot down one aircraft and probably both he and Köberich attacked the other.

The dead airmen were buried at Volgfelde, their remains were moved to Berlin War Cemetery post-war when the names of the pilot, flight engineer and navigator were commemorated on Runnymede Memorial to the Missing as in reality the impact had left nothing identifiable of these men. Pilot Officer John Syme, originally from Adelaide, Australia had travelled halfway across the globe from his job as a plantation manager in New Guinea to fight Nazism, together with five of his crew he paid the supreme sacrifice. George Leggott was a pre-war regular RAF airman. Twenty-two year Dennis Cattley from Wakefield in Yorkshire, the Wireless Operator/Air Gunner was sole survivor of John Syme's crew, he parachuted into captivity where he was issued Prisoner of War number 267151 and sent to Stalag Luft 4b (Mühlberg-Elbe).

On 4th December 28 year old former Queensland trucker Harold 'Mac' Mackintosh[i] and his crew of Australian, Canadian and British lads arrived via an H2S course at 1660 HCU, they had trained at 1661 HCU and 14 OTU. A series of foggy days saw Bomber Command generally undertaking routine work on the ground with limited flying training. For almost two weeks Mosquitoes carried out occasional small raids and tiny numbers of Wellington's flew Radio Counter Measures sorties.

At 630 Squadron Tuesday 7th December saw a party of eleven officers and NCO's drove south to Cambridge for the funeral of Jimmy White's Australian rear gunner Jim Rossiter. In stark contrast the same day saw the founding of the RAF East Kirkby chess club for all ranks, the chairman was Group Captain Taaffe. One WAAF clerk who knew how to use a typewriter was attached to 630 Squadron from No. 5 Group on 8th December, the Adjutant noted that this would ease conditions of work and office machinery including a rotary duplicator arrived. Squadron Leader Crocker carried out an inspection of No.6 living site and found the highly overcrowded NCO's Quarters unsatisfactory as were the Officers ablutions. He reported the shortcomings to Group Captain Taaffe and two aircraftsmen who had just completed a full working day volunteered to work through the night until breakfast time to do what they could to clean-up the squadron offices. Saturday morning saw the arrival of the Air Officer Commanding No.5 Group, Air Vice Marshal Hon. RA Cochrane OBE AFC, who lunched in the mess and then inspected 630 Squadron speaking with the aircrew. He learned in detail from Malcolm Crocker of the battle fought by Jim White's crew a few nights previously. On Friday 10th December the award of a DFC was announced in the London Gazette to Pilot Officer Reg Cartwright for his service with 207 Squadron before joining Six-thirty. On 11th December Squadron Leader WL Dunn[ii] (Accounts) arrived from RAF Grantham as Station Senior Accounts Officer and two days later the Station's Senior Signals Officer F/L Leslie Woolcott exchanged with F/L Joseph Wagstaff[iii] from RAF Coningsby.

Sunday 12th December dawned fine and clear with a sharp frost and after Church Parade Squadron Leader Crocker relinquished his temporary command of the squadron to Wing Commander John Dudley Rollinson DFC but remained temporarily as a Flight Commander. Rollinson was the son of a Workhouse Master in the Poor Law Service and a Workhouse Matron. Thirty-two years old he had grown up in Worcestershire joining in the Royal Auxiliary Air Force pre-war and flown Hawker Hinds and Hawker Hectors with 614 (County of Glamorgan) Squadron. The new CO had completed a tour as a flight commander and finally in command of a Wellington squadron flying from Malta to attack enemy bases in North Africa, Italy and the Balkans. The London Gazette of 2 January 1942 had carried notification of his award of the Distinguished Flying Cross for gallantry and devotion to duty in the execution of aerial operations. His Citation reads: 'Acting Wing Commander J. D. Rollinson, R.A.F.O., No. 38 Squadron.—This officer has carried out 30 operational sorties from Malta first as a flight commander and later as the commanding officer Wing Cdr. Rollinson has performed sterling work. Wing Cdr. Rollinson himself has contributed materially to the outstanding successes achieved by his squadron. Throughout, he has shown cheerfulness and courage and he has been undeterred by difficulties'.

On Thursday 16th December recently returned from service in West Africa 28 year old Flight Lieutenant Howard Derbyshire Elliott MB ChB[iv] was posted to RAF East Kirkby as Senior MO taking the place of Squadron Leader JR O'Dowd. The CO of 2785 Anti-Aircraft Squadron (RAF Regiment) who provided air defence capability for the station, Squadron Leader RN Benjamin MC, was posted away to be shortly

Sam Weller and crew (Lynne Weller)

Left: Weller crew navigator Don Williamson (Michael Weller) Right: Weller crew bomb aimer Andy Kuzma RCAF (Shaun Pattinson)

Derm Hegarty RAAF and crew (back, l to r; Gilly Potter, Laurie Croft, Bob Hay and Hector Scott – front row, Taffy Cross, Dermot Hegarty and Tony Smith (R Hay)

Edward Butler (Patti Kellaway)

replaced by Squadron Leader Robert Clover[v] from RAF Stradishall. 14th December saw the arrival of 22 year old Faversham man JCW 'Sam' Weller[vi] and crew from 1660 HCU and 23 year old Aussie Dermott Hegarty[vii] and his crew direct from 1654 HCU, their 22 year old rear gunner Mike Cross was a veteran who had already completed a tour in Wellington's with 108 Squadron in the Western Desert where he'd shot down a JU88 attacking his aircraft on 5th July 1942.

Also arriving on station at this time were 50 aircrew cadets from RAF Heaton Park who would be visiting for 6 weeks as a part of their training. Squadron Leader Edward Butler DFC and Bar[viii] was posted to No. 630 Squadron on 16th December to command A-Flight, the 33 year old Caversham resident was an outstanding Navigator who had completed a tour of 31 ops with 97 Squadron participating in the historic experimental daylight raids against Augsburg, Le Creusot and Milan in 1942, awarded a DFC (London Gazette 3 November 1942) and an 'Immediate'

Bar to his DFC (London Gazette 20 November 1942). Extremely fortunate to survive the Augsburg MAN engine factory raid in April 1942 when over half of the attacking force was lost and a VC was earned by the leader S/L John Nettleton, Butler was Mentioned in Despatches (London Gazette 1 January 1943) as he commenced a tour training young navigators. Not a man to sit on the sidelines his repeated requests to return to operations had resulted in a posting to Six-thirty.

Thursday 16th December 1943.

Cold, frosty, misty days brought routine work on the ground until 16th December when Six-thirty were warned for a night bombing operation, twelve aircraft and crews were required. 483 Lancasters and 10 Mosquitoes were to attack Berlin again with a force of 5 more Mosquitoes dropping decoy fighter flares south of Berlin to lead night fighters astray. It was another clear, cold, frosty day and Wing Commander Rollinson had put his own name on the Battle Order to fly as 2nd Pilot with Squadron Leader Crocker. Although he had converted from Wellingtons to Lancasters he had as yet not flown night ops and recognised the steep learning curve. Briefing confirmed that the target was Berlin again. Several other crews had '2nd Dickies' assigned for this night and Cliff Rogers was getting a second Op under his belt, 'Mac' Mackintosh and 'Sam' Weller their first.

16th/17th December 1943 : Night Bombing Attack on Berlin

Take Off: at 16:34 hours recently commissioned Pilot Officer Austin Drinkall and crew in JB546 were the first of the eleven Lancasters to lift off.

JB532-X	S/L M Crocker (W/C JD Rollinson)
JB666-O	F/L WH Kellaway
JB556-Y	F/O JH Pratt RCAF
JA872-N	P/O WB Yates (F/S HCL Mackintosh RAAF)
ED944-Z	F/O D Roberts
JB546-A	P/O A Drinkall
JB665-B	F/S J White
JB654-C	P/O DW Story RAAF (F/O JCW Weller)
JB672-F	P/O DH Cheney RCAF
ED655-J	P/O AGG Johnson
ED413-M	P/O R Cartwright (Sgt HC Rogers)

Twelve aircraft had been prepared but Sid Edwards' Lancaster had to abort the operation before taking off due to engine problems. Ninety minutes into the flight, a beeline for Berlin which the German ground defences had very quickly identified, the starboard outer engine of JB532 failed and Squadron Leader Crocker with the new C.O sitting beside him, had to turn for home. Luftwaffe night fighters were vectored into the bomber stream at the Dutch coast where the Luftwaffe ace Oberleutnant Wolfgang Schnaufer shot down a succession of four Lancasters in forty minutes (all confirmed as they matched with crash sites, they were his 37th, 38th, 39th and 40th victories) with other night fighters guided in as the main force droned onward, deeper into Germany, with even more fighters waiting ready in the Target Area. Berlin was again covered by clouds when the 483 Lancasters and 15 Mosquitos arrived between 19:55 and 20:34 hours but the green and yellow Pathfinder sky markers were quite accurate and main force crews could see the glow from fires below. The squadron's aircraft each dropped their 4000lb 'Cookie' and loads of mixed 30lb and 4lb incendiaries from 18,000 to 20,500 feet between 20:01 and 20:09 hours and turned for home on a route across Denmark. German records suggest that bombs fell mainly across Central and Eastern districts doing little damage to local industry but hitting railway tracks, a train standing in Halensee station, the National Theatre and damaging the archive which housed the German military and political records. Six-thirty's Lancasters all returned safely, mostly just after midnight, to find conditions on landing to be fine and cold with a slight haze across the airfield. Sadly twenty-five Lancasters had gone down, 5% of the attacking force, but 630 Squadron had been lucky. Allowing time for his returned airmen to sleep after their de-briefing and meal, Wing Commander Rollinson and his Adjutant (Frank Cheetham) visited the No.6 Living Site to fully understand the cramped situation of the airmen in preparation for the Adjutant representing the squadron's requirements at the Station Commanders conference on the following day. That day a signal arrived advising that HM King George VI had approved a recommendation by the Air Officer Commanding in Chief that 657977 Flight Sergeant James White should be awarded an 'Immediate' D.F.M. which appeared in the London Gazette on 31st December 1943.

Monday 20th December 1943.

The day dawned fine with good visibility although it began to cloud over later. The squadron were called on to contribute 15 Lancasters to a force of 650 bombers attacking Frankfurt, flight commander Malcolm Crocker would fly with Wing Commander Rollinson along as Second Dickie again and F/L Doug MacDonald would have an Army officer along for the ride. Twenty-three year old Major Peter Greenhalgh[ix] originally of The Loyal Regiment and more recently a Searchlight specialist in the Royal Artillery was serving at RAF East Kirkby as Base Defence Officer and Anti-Aircraft Liaison. During his time associated with Bomber Command he flew more often than would be expected and was actually issued with his own log book. Eventually he was one of the few Army officers to be awarded a DFC.

20th/21st December 1943 : Night Bombing Attack on Frankfurt

Take Off: at 16:45 hours Flight Lieutenant Doug Paterson was the first of the fifteen aircraft to take off, each with a 4000lb Cookie and assorted 30lb and 4lb incendiary bombs.

JB546-A	F/L DS Paterson RCAF
ED698-R	F/S JW Homewood
JB556-Y	P/O HC Mackintosh RAAF
JB532-X	F/L DA MacDonald RCAF
ED944-Z	F/O D Roberts
JB665-B	F/O KR Ames
JB654-C	P/O DJ Hegarty RAAF
ED655-J	P/O AGG Johnson
JB672-F	P/O DH Cheney RCAF
ED413-M	P/O R Cartwright
ND335-L	Sgt HC Rogers
ND338-Q	S/L M Crocker
JA872-N	P/O WB Yates
ND337-S	F/S SA Edwards
JB666-O	F/L WH Kellaway

Flying for the first time with 630 Squadron was Ken Ames' crew. Ames is remembered by his navigator Jim Wright (later Wing Cdr, DFC) as an outstanding pilot who only weeks before joining 630 Squadron had earned an Immediate DFC on his 5th Op for getting his Lancaster and crew home after being coned by searchlights and then shot up by three night fighters over Kassel (22nd October 1943). The crew had joined Six-thirty without their navigator, Jim Wright who had been hospitalised with injuries after that night over Kassel. Ken Ames flew that night with Squadron Leader ER Butler DFC and Bar (Flight Commander) as his navigator. Within days Jim Wright rejoined them from hospital and the crew were reunited. The port outer engine of ED413 'M-Mother' played up immediately after take-off but Reg Cartwright's crew pressed on as far as the Dutch coastline before they had to give up having been unable to climb above 16,500 feet and with the engine proving unreliable. 'Cab' Kellaway aborted the mission and jettisoned his 'Cookie' into the North Sea after his rear gunner Sergeant George Cansell reported that the turret, which had only just been repaired, was out of action again. The German control rooms identified the bomber force as it began the outward leg of their flight over the North Sea and a diversionary raid on Mannheim did not confuse the German fighter control teams. There were repeated combats across the night sky and the first

Snow on the airfield. Photo by Walt Scott (supplied courtesy of Ian Walker)

of the 41 bombers to be lost began to fall at 19:10 hours north-east of Liege. The crew of Six-thirty's recently commissioned P/O Harold Mackintosh a 28 year old Aussie, flying his first Op as Captain after a trip as 2nd Dickie some nights earlier had already been in combat before that first bomber fell. Their report tells the story –

Lancaster JB556, Letter 'Y-Yoke', detailed for operations against Frankfurt on the night of 20.12.43. Whilst on the way to the target at position 51° 15' North 04° 50' East, course 180° magnetic, time 18:50 hours, airspeed 150mph, indicated height 20,000 feet, no moon, good visibility, no search lights, no unusual phenomena. Sergeant Charles Bottreill mid-upper gunner reported an ME210 on port parallel on same level and 300 yards range, coming in to attack. Mid upper gunner and rear gunner Flight Sergt Burton Howard RCAF opened fire simultaneously and instructions were given to dive to port. Enemy aircraft followed round in the turn and fired a short burst above the Lancaster, simultaneously both gunners scored hits on the enemy aircraft, the rear gunner in the port engine and the mid-upper in the nose of the enemy aircraft which broke away at 200 yards range in a diving turn to port. The Lancaster then proceeded on to the target after making a short corkscrew, and fighter was not seen again. During combat the rear gunner fired 500 rounds and the mid-upper gunner 300 rounds. Claim : Me210 probably damaged. Their combat report, signed off by F/L Stead (Gunnery Leader), W/C JD Rollinson (Commanding) and G/C R Taafe (Station Commander) combined two fights that night as they were unlucky enough to be attacked again after bombing.

On arrival over Frankfurt most of Six-thirty's crews reported that the Pathfinder marking was inadequate with the red target indicators placed too far east saying however that large fires were growing in the target area which could still be seen from 100 miles away as they flew home. They attacked from 19,000 to 21,000 feet between 19:41 and 19:54 hours. The crews of Doug Paterson, John Homewood, Sid Edwards and the rookie crews of 'Mac' Mackintosh and Cliff Rogers all reported a huge red explosion probably in the north-east suburbs of Frankfurt between 19:46 and 19:48 hours. Squadron Leader Crocker with Wing Commander

Rollinson beside him criticised the PFF marking strongly but did report well concentrated fires around green target indicators. Heading for home 'Mac' Mackintosh's crew had their second encounter of the evening with the Luftwaffe – returning to their report detailed above – the same aircraft after bombing target and at 19:09 hours, position 50° 30' North and 05° 10' East, airspeed 160mph indicated, height 20,000 feet leading 095° magnetic, twenty miles from Liege, no moon, no searchlight, no unusual phenomena. Rear gunner reported one enemy aircraft, identified as a FW200, flying in parallel course on the port quarter, level, range 400 yards. F/Sgt Howard ordered the pilot to dive port and opened fire with a 4 second burst. Enemy aircraft immediately dived down and to port and was not seen again. The Lancaster completed a short corkscrew and resumed course. Rear gunner fired 250 rounds. On the ground the Germans had been lighting wooden pyres in surrounding fields five miles south-east of the city and had burned decoy target indicators in the hope of confusing the bomb aimers above. Various low priority targets were hit, light industry was disrupted and the German forces suffered damage to 4 flak installations, a clothing store, a veterinary department and the Army Music School. All of 630 Squadron's Lancasters landed safely at East Kirkby before midnight. It was Squadron Leader Crocker's last op with 630 Squadron, screened from further Ops he remained at East Kirkby fulfilling the duties of a flight commander while awaiting his replacement before being posted to 1660 Heavy Conversion Unit as a flight commander early in the New Year. On 22nd January he moved to 1661 HCU also as a flight commander. In late spring 1944 Malcolm Crocker was promoted to Acting Wing Commander and posted via 5 Group HQ on 1st May 1944 to 49 Squadron as C.O. where sadly he was killed during the terribly costly attack on the Wesserling Oil Refinery on 22nd June 1944. His service with 630 Squadron was recognised with the award of a Bar to his DFC (London Gazette 18th January 1944).

On the dark wet evening of Tuesday 21st December the first party hosted by the Officers Mess at East Kirky took place with the greater majority of Six-thirty's officers present, the AOC 5 Group AVM 'Cocky' Cochrane, Group Captain WN McKechnie GC DFC[x] and Group Captain Evans-Evans[xi]. On the following day Section Officer Margaret Vickers (6092) WAAF arrived to stand-in for F/L Cheetham who was proceeding on leave for Christmas, she wouldn't be getting home to Twickenham until the New Year.

Thursday 23rd December 1943.

The RCAF liaison officer responsible for the district arrived at East Kirkby with a delivery for Canadian personnel of cigarette filled stockings from Santa Claus, but a call from Group advised that 630 Squadron were to provide 12 aircraft and crews for another attack on Berlin each armed with a 4,000lb Cookie, supplemented by 4lb and 30lb incendiaries.

23rd/24th December 1943 :Night Bombing Attack on Berlin

Take Off: just minutes before midnight ND338 (Wilson Yates) thundered down the runway to become the first of Six-thirty's Lancasters airborne.

JB546-A	F/L DS Paterson RCAF
JB665-B	P/O A Drinkall
JB556-Y	F/O JH Pratt RCAF
ND337-S	F/S SA Edwards
ND338-Q	P/O WB Yates
ND335-L	Sgt HC Rogers
ED655-J	P/O R Cartwright
ED698-R	F/S JW Homewood
JB532-X	P/O DJ Hegarty RAAF
JB654-C	P/O DW Story RAAF
JA872-N	P/O AGG Johnson
JB672-F	P/O PH Cheney RCAF

Cliff Rogers had to return early due to serviceability problems and the crews of David Roberts and 'Mac' Mackintosh were unable to take off due to unserviceability. 379 bombers flew against Berlin however the German controller was briefly deceived by Mosquitos raiding Leipzig and the majority of available night fighters arrived as the raid concluded and were unable to contact the main bomber stream. Covered by cloud Berlin was tough to mark and suffering technical problems with their H2S the resulting Pathfinder markers were scattered. Flak was reportedly light although searchlights were numerous but ineffective due to the heavy cloud cover. The squadron's Lancasters attacked from 19,000 to 22,500 feet between 04:03 and 04:16 hours. Well concentrated fires were reported spreading around the Target Indicators. German records suggest that only the south-eastern suburbs of Köpenick and Treptow were bombed heavily and amongst the usual damage and destruction to housing and property an inland waterways cargo vessel was sunk and three more seriously damaged. All of Six-thirty's crews made it home safely and for most of the crew of Reg Cartwright DFC the tour which they had started on 207 Squadron was completed, their captain became an instructor with 1661 HCU. Sadly John Crawford their navigator was killed on 11th November 1944 flying his second tour by then a Warrant Officer with 97 Squadron. Sergeant Terence Davidson their mid-upper gunner later returned to 630 Squadron to fly operationally in the closing months of the war also as a Warrant Officer.

Christmas Eve dawned with a thick white frost, a signal was received from the Secretary for State for Air conveying congratulations from the Prime Minister (Winston Churchill) to the bomber crews for the attacks on Berlin and Leipzig. Several crews flew on Air Sea Rescue searches but nothing was found. The Sergeants Mess held their Christmas Party that evening and station personnel put on a Concert Party Show in No.2 Dining Hall, it met with such a wave of approval that a second show was immediately booked for New Year's Eve. This was followed by an 'All Ranks' dance in the NAAFI which was swinging into the wee small hours. Christmas Day was foggy, the Station was 'stood down' at 10:00 hours and in keeping with tradition the officers helped with the service of the airmen's festive dinner of soup, fish, turkey and pork, followed by Christmas pudding, mince pies, beer and fruit before playing host to the Sergeant's in the Officers Mess at 19:00 hours. There was a Christmas Dance and Cabaret in No.2 Dining Hall. The highlight of Boxing Day was the showing of 'Road to Morocco' in the Cinema at 19:30 and an 'All Ranks' dance in the NAAFI. The following night saw the most successful dance of the series, the WAAF Christmas Dance in the NAAFI. Several wet days followed and routine work was done on the ground. The 'all NCO' crew of 22 year old Sergeant Ken Rodbourn[xii] of Burton on Trent arrived after training at 1660, 1661 and finally 1668 HCU's ready to start their tour.

After a brief introduction to the role during the previous day, Flying Officer Gordon Brake (Bob Hughes crew navigator) took over temporarily as Squadron Adjutant on 29th to enable Section Officer Margaret Vickers WAAF to get off for New Year leave.

Wednesday 29th December 1943.

Another attack on Berlin was planned for that evening, 712 bombers were scheduled to fly a long outward route passing south of the Ruhr valley, onwards toward Leipzig before changing course for Berlin whilst Mosquitos attacked Leipzig, Düsseldorf and Magdeburg. Each Lancaster of 630 Squadron carried a 4,000lb HC bomb and approximately 1,000 x 4lb and 50-60 x 30lb incendiaries.

29th /30th December 1943 : Night Bombing Attack on Berlin
Take Off: at 16:49 hours JB654 (Don Storey) was the first airborne.

JB546-A	F/L DS Paterson RCAF
JB665-B	F/O KR Ames
JB654-C	P/O DW Storey RAAF
JB672-F	P/O DH Cheney RCAF
ED655-J	F/S RT Hughes
ND335-L	Sgt HC Rogers
ED413-M	P/O DJ Hegarty RAAF

JA872-N*	P/O A Drinkall
JB532-X	F/L DA MacDonald RCAF
JB556-Y	F/O JH Pratt RCAF
ND338-Q	P/O WB Yates RAAF
JB666-O	F/O CH Armour
ND337-S	F/S SA Edwards
ED944-Z	F/S JW Homewood
JA872-N*	W/C JD Rollinson

It is unclear which aircraft were flown by Wing Commander Rollinson and Austin Drinkall, the Operations Record Book' shows both crews aboard JA872, obviously one is wrong. F/S John Homewood aborted the mission bringing ED944 'Z-Zebra' home almost two hours later after his rear turret failed due to a broken oil pipe. Confusion reigned amongst the German fighter controllers given the route and simultaneous diversionary raids, coupled with bad weather the fighter opposition was reduced over Berlin. Between 20:06 and 20:23 hours the squadron's crews attacked from 19,000 to 22,000 feet in 10/10ths cloud over Berlin but Pathfinder Force sky marker flares placing in the Target Area were widely praised with well concentrated flares going down below but heavier flak than usual was noted likely due to reduced chance of hitting their own fighters. Canadian pilot Don Paterson commented that heavy flak burst very close but that his Lancaster wasn't hit. Flying Officer Ken Ames, just recently awarded a DFC as his crew transferred from 61 Squadron to join 630 Squadron for getting his Lancaster home after an epic battle against 3 night fighters left 2 of his crew wounded and his aircraft riddled with cannon shell and machine gun bullet holes, on fire and with ammunition exploding, summed up his latest attack, *'Flak heavy up to 25,000 feet, large numbers of fighters, brilliant glow from beneath clouds 150 miles distant'*. Austin Drinkall noted heavy flak bursting up to 30,000 feet. Three heavy explosions were noted in quick succession at 20:16 by Doug MacDonald's crew and W/C Rollinson added that based on the glow on the clouds there had to be a large area of fire below. Six-thirty delivered 59 tons of bombs to Berlin this night. Bomber Command believed that they had executed a concentrated attack although German records suggested that the bombs fell across the southern and south-eastern districts of the capital with little damage to the war effort. Some of the attacking force this night again made mention of 'scarecrow' flares which were regarded as German countermeasures in the form of a bright orange flash designed to give the appearance that the fuel tanks of a bomber had exploded at altitude, it was followed by clouds of black smoke from which showers of smaller red, white and green flashes fanned out and fell to earth. The sad reality is that the Germans had no 'scarecrow' counter measures to try to put-off the bomber crews and that these instances normally marked a successful attack on a Lancaster or Halifax bomber by a Luftwaffe night fighter pilot.

Twenty-one year old Harold Hill[xiii] and crew were posted from 1654 HCU to Six-thirty very late in December and began the program of cross-country, navigation and high level bombing exercises. On 30th December a signal was received announcing the award of an 'Immediate' DFC to Acting Flight Lieutenant Douglas Allister MacDonald, RCAF for his bravery and skill when an engine failed during a mission. The award for the 20 year old veteran pilot from Rockglenn, Saskatchewan in Canada was published in the London Gazette on 7th January, 1944.

'Flight Lieutenant Macdonald is a highly skilled and most determined pilot who has taken part in very meaty attacks on targets important to the enemy's war effort. He has displayed a high degree of courage and resolution in pressing home his attacks, qualities which have earned him much success. One night in November, 1943, Flight Lieutenant Macdonald piloted an aircraft detailed to attack a target in central Germany. Before reaching the target one engine of his aircraft became Useless. Despite this, and in the face of extremely trying weather, Flight Lieutenant Macdonald completed his task successfully. His achievement was most commendable'.

Squadron Leader Kenneth Vare[xiv] arrived at East Kirkby joining the squadron following command of 'A' Flight of No.5 Lancaster Finishing School based at Syerston apparently to take over from Squadron

Leader Malcolm Crocker who was due to be posted away after completing his tour. Born at Wellington, New Zealand in 1913 and educated at Wellesley Boys' College and Wellington College, Vare gained a civil pilot's 'A' licence in 1936 as a member of the Wellington Aero Club. Earning part of the Bachelor of Commerce degree as an undergraduate of the New Zealand University, he joined the staff of the Department of Agriculture, in whose employ he remained until sailing for the United Kingdom in July 1937 aboard the 'Rotorua' to take up a short service commission with the Royal Air Force. Ken Vare flew Wellingtons on Ops with 40 Squadron from Wyton and Alconbury before being posted to the Middle East with 108 Squadron to fly Wellingtons and later Liberators. After a spell back in the UK during which time he qualified as an instructor in air navigation he joined Ferry Command in Canada then instructing at 111 OTU at Nassau/Bahamas flying Venturas, Mitchells and Liberators. Vare's period in this role earned him the AFC [London Gazette 1st January 1944].

A projected operation was abandoned on Friday 31st December 1943 due to unfavourable weather forecasts, later that day the Sergeant's Mess opened its doors to host the Station New Year's Eve Dance at 20:00 hours. With the WAAF clerk typist still on leave the records are handwritten again at this point. Below - East Kirkby dispersals winter 1943/44

The crew of Don Paterson RCAF (Andrew Paterson)

January 1944

Saturday 1st January 1944.

The weather was good in the morning and at 12:30 hours news of an Op was received from Group, Six-thirty were to provide 14 Lancasters for an attack that evening, the squadron actually despatched 15 in the force of 421 Lancasters attacking. Flight Lieutenant Doug MacDonald had newly arrived Squadron Leader Ken Vare AFC flying as Second Dickie. Part of MacDonald's regular crew were not flying that night, both gunners and the bomb aimer were on loan from other crews. 'Sam' Weller (named for a Dickensian character) and his crew commenced what would be for the regular members of his crew (only the flight engineer changed regularly) a tour to set records.

1st/2nd January 1944 : Night Bombing Attack on Berlin

Take Off: at 23:49 hours Don Cheney at the controls of JB672 was the first of 630 Squadron's fifteen Lancasters airborne most aircraft armed with 1 x 4000lb HC, 900 x 4lb and 48 x 30lb incendiaries.

JB546-A	F/L DS Paterson RCAF (Sgt K Rodbourn)
JB665-B	F/L W English
JB654-C	F/O KR Ames
JB672-F	F/O DH Cheney RCAF
ED655-J	F/S RT Hughes
ND335-L	Sgt HC Rogers
ED413-M	P/O DJ Hegarty RAAF
ED758-H	P/O AGG Johnson
JB532-X	F/L DA MacDonald RCAF (S/L KF Vare)
JB556-Y	F/O JH Pratt RCAF
ND337-S	F/S SA Edwards
ED944-Z	F/S JW Homewood
JB666-O	F/O CH Armour
ND338-Q	F/O GH Probert
JB710-W	F/O JCW Weller

Aussie Dermott Hegarty had to turn for home when an engine cut out and then caught fire, the 22 year old from Pymble, NSW brought ED413 'M-Mother' all the way home to safely 'landing on three' just before 04:00 hours. Six-thirty's bombers arrived over Berlin to find dense cloud cover again and attacked between 03:07 and 03:25 hours from 20,000 to 22,500 feet in the face of intense heavy flak. On their bombing run John Pratt's crew were harried by night fighters. Don Paterson's highly experienced crew nearing the end of their tour aboard 'A-Able' were not caught unawares by a ME110 night fighter which closed to attack. Sgt Pete Vaggs in the rear turret got off an extended burst and as the fighter overshot and dived away Sgt John Leahy RAAF in the mid-upper turret and P/O Harold MacDonald RCAF in the bomb aimers nose gun turret both fired into the twin engined fighter, all three men saw their rounds strike home and the fighter was not seen again (sadly no combat report has been located).

Bill English stated on his return that *'if the markers were placed properly the raid will have been successful because crews were bombing based on the flares'*. The Cheney crew de-brief commented that the green flare route markers had been very effective and noted a large fire in the Target Area, this matched with the report of the Johnson and Rogers crews on a large

W/Cdr. K. F. Vare, A.F.C., of Wellington, missing, believed killed.

glow from fires reflected on clouds. At de-briefing Allan Johnson reported the flashes of exploding 'Cookies' and a terrific reddish flash which lit up the sky. The crew of John Homewood saw two bombers shot down by fighters and placed on record that the route used was too familiar to the enemy. Sgt's RG 'Smudge' Smith and Howell Jones, the mid-upper and rear gunners aboard 'Sam' Weller's JB710 'W-William' observed a FW190 single engined fighter before it was able to attack and they opened fire causing it to break away into a dive when it was lost (sadly no combat report has been located). Sid Edwards landed his usual mount 'S-Sugar' at 08:36 hours and was the last to return. It was soon obvious that one of Six-thirty's crews was missing, the highly reliable crew of Doug MacDonald in JB532 with Squadron Leader Vare aboard.

Lancaster III, JB532 (Codes LE – X)

Pilot	– F/L Douglas Allister MacDonald, DFC RCAF. Age 20	Killed
2nd Pilot	– S/L Kenneth Frederick Vare, AFC. Age 30	Killed
Flight Eng	– Sgt Robert Francis Smale MID. Age 21	Killed
Navigator	– F/O Niels Erik Westergaard, DFC. Age 21	Killed
Bomb Aimer	– F/S John Mowbray Turnbull. Age 22	Killed
Wireless Op	– Sgt William Richard Tyrie, DFM. Age 21	Killed
Mid Upper	– F/S William Jenkins. Age	Killed
Rear Gunner	– F/S William Joseph Roche, RAAF. Age 29	Killed

Aboard the Lancaster were a Canadian, a New Zealander, an Australian, a Dane and 4 British lads. It is believed that the highly experienced crew had completed their attack and were heading home when a flak burst shot one engine clear out of its mount causing the crippled Lancaster to dive steeply and crash 300 yards north-west of Gross Beuthen, 18 miles south-west of Berlin. Surviving Bundesarchiv documentation shows that the Lancaster was shot down by flak gunners of three flak batteries, 1.-4./126, 3.+5./211 (both of Flakgruppe Süd) and 1./418 (Eisenbahn) at 03:05 hours. German records indicate that the crew were buried on 4th January in the Parish Cemetery Gross Beuthen. In 1948 the crew were re-buried at the Commonwealth War Graves Commission Berlin War Cemetery. Niels Westergaard from Denmark had

Left: Bob Smale's grave immediately post-war (Robert Smale) Right: Paddy Parle (Walt Scott/Patti Kellaway)

flown with distinction in the RAF, he and Bill Tyrie had been decorated for their service with 619 Squadron prior to joining Six-thirty. flight engineer Robert Smale had been Mentioned in Despatches a year earlier (London Gazette 01/01/43)

Bill English's comment about the success of the raid being dependant on the accuracy of the P.F.F. markers proved to be spot-on. As the raid developed the sky-marking apparently deteriorated and German reports refer to scattered bombing with a large number of bombs falling in the Grunewald a large, forested area in south-west Berlin. One industrial building and a lock on an important canal were destroyed, shipping was halted for several days. Fighters had been in position to attack the bombers before the reached the target, some were encountered over Berlin and more over France on the way home. Lurching into a different handwriting the squadron records move on to the next night.

Sunday 2nd January 1944.
'Ops tonight' – an attack was announced at 11:30 hours and of course it was Berlin again, in a force of 383 bombers.

2nd/3rd January 1944 : Night Bombing Attack on Berlin
Take Off: at 23:14 hours Canadian John Pratt in JB556 led the squadron into the air with most aircraft carrying 1 x 4000lb HC, 900 x 4lb and 48 x 30lb incendiaries.

JB556-Y	F/O JH Pratt RCAF
ND337-S	F/S SA Edwards
JB710-W	F/O GH Probert
ED944-Z	Sgt K Rodbourn
ND338-Q	F/O KR Ames
JB546-A	F/L DS Paterson RCAF
JB665-B	F/L W English
JB672-F	F/O DH Cheney RCAF
ND335-L	Sgt HC Rogers
JB654-C	P/O DJ Hegarty RAAF
ED758-H	P/O AGG Johnson

Last minute service problems prevented Cliff Armour, Wil Yates, 'Sam' Weller and Bob Hughes from taking off. F/O Geoff Probert and Sgt Ken Rodbourn both returned early, neither of their aircraft being able to climb above 12,000 feet and 13,500 feet respectively, JB710 unable to make full use of super chargers due to a hydraulic leak and ED944 with its starboard inner engine out of service. They landed minutes apart around 02:20 hours. Allan Johnson's crew were awarded the sortie despite an early return (04:41 hours) due to altimeter failure in a huge electrical storm encountered east of the Dutch coast, their Lanc dived almost out of control and they had to jettison their bomb load to enable the pilot to pull out of the steep dive before they hit the sea. Over Berlin the crews bombed between 02:52 and 02:59 hours from 20,000 up to 21,600 feet through 10/10ths cloud as usual. Good PFF route marking with an improved marker flare type was acknowledged. Several crews reported a deep red glow reflected on the clouds which was still visible during their return flight and the explosions of some 4,000 pounders.

In Lancaster 'Q-Queen' (ND338) skipper Ken Ames' gunners found the fighters very active, in the mid-upper turret Irishman Bill Leary and the rear turret Dubliner Richard 'Paddy' Parle a 25 year old who would serve in the Malaya Police and later the Hong Kong Police post-war. The gunners almost exhausted their ammunition in combat with an Me109, a JU88 and an Me110. All three attackers were claimed to have been hit and damaged and the Me110 was possibly destroyed, (sadly no combat report has been located). German fighter control rooms followed the bomber stream directly to Berlin which they correctly assessed as the target forty minutes before the attack commenced. Ten of the Pathfinder Force were shot down, 156 Squadron losing 5 of its 14 deployed aircraft and the raid was not successful with bombing being scattered. A drizzly cold couple of days followed at East Kirkby during which Flight Lieutenant Cheetham returned from leave thanking Flying Officer Brake for sterling work standing-in after Section Officer Vickers had gone on leave despite him flying twice on Ops during his time in office.

Ken Ames (Jim Wright)   *Roy Calvert RNZAF (Roy Calvert)*

Wednesday 5th January 1944.
The day brought a change to the routine of flights across occupied Europe to Berlin,. The target was to be Stettin a major industrial centre and port on the Baltic coast of northern Germany (now in Poland). It would be the first major raid on Stettin since September 1941 and Six-thirty's Lancasters were each bombed up with 3 x 1000lb MC, 1 x 500lb MC, 400 x 4lb incendiaries and 48 x 30lb incendiaries. That same evening a musical quiz was held in Hut 18 at East Kirkby.

5th/6th January 1944 : Night Bombing Attack on Stettin
Take Off: at 23:39 hours 'Cab' Kellaway was the first of the squadron's 13 Lancasters airborne. There would have been fourteen but Sid Edwards aircraft went unserviceable and did not take off.

JB666-O	F/L WH Kellaway
ND338-Q	P/O HCL Mackintosh RAAF
ED698-R	F/O GH Probert
JB710-W	Sgt K Rodbourn
ED944-Z	F/O D Roberts
ED413-M	F/O JCW Weller
JB654-C	P/O DJ Hegarty RAAF
JB672-F	F/O KR Ames
ED655-J	F/S RT Hughes
ED758-H	P/O AGG Johnson
ND335-L	P/O HW Hill
JB665-B	F/S J White
JA872-N	F/O CH Armour

Conditions were sometimes clear in the TA with drifting patches of thin cloud. Attack photos show that bombing was concentrated on well-placed target indicators with huge fires burning in the town as the attack came to an end. That attack was set for 03:45 hours and most of 630 Squadron's crews attacked from between 19,500 and 22,500 feet between 03:50 and 03:55 hours. A spoof attack (diversionary raid) on Berlin apparently led some of the night fighter controllers astray. A great piece of team work by the Mackintosh crew got them to target and attacking on time despite their Navigator being ill on the outward leg, their bomb aimer doubled up as navigator. Ken Rodbourn, 'Cab' Kellaway, Bob Hughes, Ken Ames, Dermott Hegarty and 'Sam' Weller's crews all saw the dockyard area and most noted that it was ablaze. Geoff Probert was amongst those to report good route marking and he added that neutral Sweden was not too friendly after their ground defences opened up. David Roberts and Ken Ames debriefs both mention a major explosion at about 03:49 hours. The port inner engine of JB665 'B-Baker' failed shortly after they attacked and Jim White brought her home on 3 engines landing about an hour later than the other aircraft at 10:25 hours. German assessments of damage show that the early phases of the attack were accurately aimed on the central districts which were very badly fire damaged but later waves of bombers had bombed more to the west. Aside from housing stock 20 industrial buildings were destroyed, 29 were damaged and 8 ships were sunk in the port. Stood down for several days due to the 'moon period' 630 Squadron commenced training sessions. Saturday 8th January brought the welcome news of two missing airmen who had survived as Prisoners of War (doubtless Flight Lieutenant Perrers, Wireless Op and Rear Gunner, Ron Mutum and Fred Crowe) and the donations to the 630 Squadron 'POW comforts box' grew immeasurably. Flight Lieutenant VCS Bach[i] took over from F/L CU Lloyd as MT officer for the station.

Left – Right: Alan Connor RAAF (Jack Martin); Len Barnes (Geoff Copeman); Bill Mooney (Mooney family); Jack Geoghegan RAAF, who gave his life to save another. (June Roberts)

After greeting his newly arrived flight commander on the Sunday, Wing Commander Rollinson went on leave on Monday 10th leaving the Squadron in the hands of Squadron Leader Edward Butler A-flight commander. Squadron Leader Roy Calvert DFC and Bar RNZAF[ii] was posted from 1660 HCU where he'd been instructing for a year, via No.5 Lancaster Finishing School, to take command of 'B' Flight. Roy Calvert was a very experienced operational pilot who had very unusually been decorated with an 'Immediate' DFC and an 'Immediate' Bar to the DFC during his previous 33 op tour with 50 Squadron (DFC London Gazette 20/10/1942, Bar to DFC London Gazette 18/12/1942). He re-commenced flying in late January with a crew comprising several veterans such as Alan Connor DFM RAAF (Wireless Operator) and Bill Mooney DFM (Flight Engineer) formerly of 50 Sqdn

On the next day the Adjutant received official RAF stationary and for the first time was able to equip his clerks with the means to do their jobs without having to scrounge or borrow further. That evening a highly successful dance was held in the WAAF Dining Hall and on the following night Hut 18 hosted a Musical Evening. Two new crews both captained by 23 year old Londoners, Freddy Watts[iii] from Kensington and former printer Len Barnes[iv] from Poplar were posted in from 1654 HCU and commenced the routine of cross countries, night flying and high level bombing exercises.

630 Squadron transferred two of its more 'tired' Lancasters to No. 207 Squadron on 11th and 13th January, ED698 and ED758, these were two of the several times repaired aircraft received from No. 57 Squadron when 630 formed. Another, ED413 would follow to 207 Squadron on the 20th.

Friday 14th January 1944.

A battle order was issued: 630 Squadron were to provide sixteen Lancasters and crews, 100% of their strength, for the night's Op each carried 1 x 4000 HC, 1,400 x 4lb incendiaries, 72 x 30lb incendiaries and 100 x 4lb alternative incendiaries.

14th/15th January 1944 : Night Bombing Attack on Brunswick

Take off: 'Tony' Story in JB654 was the first to take off from East Kirkby at 16:35 hours and fourteen Lancs followed him, Bill English aboard JB665 was detailed to carry a Second Dickie, a recently arrived pilot needing operational experience prior to commencing Ops with his own crew. JB288 developed problems and Allan Johnson had to turn for home over the North Sea.

JB546-A	P/O DJ Hegarty RAAF	
JB665-B	F/L W English	(F/S FHA Watts)
JB654-C	P/O DW Story RAAF	
JB672-F	P/O HW Hill	
JB288-H	P/O AGG Johnson	
ED655-J	P/O RT Hughes	
ND335-L	F/O KR Ames	
JA872-N	F/O JCW Weller	
JB666-O	F/L WH Kellaway	
ND338-Q	P/O HCL Mackintosh RAAF	
JB294-R	F/S JW Homewood	
ND337-S	F/S SA Edwards	
JB710-W	F/O CH Armour	
ED944-Z	F/O D Roberts	
JB556-Y	F/O GH Probert	

With cloud cover in the target area when Six-thirty's Lancasters attacked from 20,000 to 21,000 feet between 19:16 and 19:26 hours very little could be observed however David Roberts, Cliff Armour, Sid Edwards and 'Cab' Kellaway's crews glimpsed what appeared to be fires through breaks in the cloud beneath the Wanganui flares, 'Mac' Mackintosh's crew mentioned a large orange explosion south-east of the city at 19:16 hours. Considerable fighter opposition was in evidence in the TA and the Adjutant noted that on their return that every crew contributed to the 'POW box' such was the effect of the experience. Lancaster ND337 flown by Sid Edwards was the last to land at 23:23 hours. Aboard ED944 'Z-Zebra' David Roberts gunners Sergeants Paul Christie and Walter Walker managed to damage a JU88 night fighter while their pilot corkscrewed away from its attack and 'Sam' Weller's gunners, Sergeants RG 'Smudge' Smith and Howell Jones aboard JA872 'N-Nan' shot up a Messerschmitt Bf109 before it was able to open fire. Both crews were 'awarded' a 'Damaged'. At 21,000 feet Cliff Armour's crew aboard Lancaster JB710 'W-William' had a strange experience at 19:16 hours when red flares suddenly burst all around their aircraft. Inaccurate cannon fire from a night fighter was then seen both above and below them but no damage was sustained and a corkscrew to port lost the fighter. Nineteen minutes later Sgt John Morris and F/S Morris Marks RCAF in the mid-upper and rear turrets of John Homewood's JB294 'R-Robert' were in action after a 'Monica' warning of a night fighter in close proximity. Marks observed tracing in-coming from the port quarter up and called for a corkscrew as he sighted an Me110 approaching. Morris got off a two second burst (200 rounds) but found that his guns wouldn't fire when he hit his trigger and struggled to get off 20 rounds manually before the fighter broke off and disappeared.

On their return flight aboard 'Q-Queen' the crew of 'Mac' Mackintosh realised that their mid-upper gunner 20 year old Charlie Bottriell from East London was not responding to the intercom. Their Aussie wireless op Jack Geoghegan a 27 year old who had briefly served in a medical unit with the Australian 3rd Cavalry before transferring to the RAAF, volunteered to investigate and in the freezing rarified atmosphere of the fuselage found that Bottriell had collapsed and was unconscious. He struggled for fifteen minutes and managed to get the gunner conscious again but by this time he was feeling the effects of the altitude and lack of oxygen himself. On landing at base both men were treated, Charlie Bottriell recovered slowly but was unable to return to ops, sadly Jack Geoghegan's condition deteriorated. The Aussie was admitted to RAF Hospital Rauceby but quickly transferred to RAF Hospital Wilmslow where he was treated for six weeks. Whilst convalescing for two weeks he suffered a relapse and was re-admitted on 2nd April but sadly died two days later. His death as the result of saving his friends life went unrecognised by the authorities. At the time he had been married for less than six months, his English wife Jean gave birth to twins soon after his death, they later settled in Australia. After the war Charlie Bottriell joined the police service in what was then Southern Rhodesia.

The raid on Brunswick, the first major one of the war, was not regarded as a successful attack. A German running commentary was picked up following the progress of the Main Force from only 40 miles out into the North Sea and Luftwaffe night fighters entered the bomber stream soon after it crossed the German coast at Bremen, steadily shooting down bombers as it droned onwards, whilst the bombers attacked and on the homeward leg to the Dutch coast. Thirty eight bombers were lost, eleven of them were Pathfinders. The post-attack report by the civil administration of Brunswick described the 498 bomber attack as a light raid with minimal damage in the south of the city and most of the bombs landing in open countryside or other small neighbouring towns. The Appendix to the ORB states that on the 15th of January information was received via the International Red Cross quoting German information confirming the death of five members of the crew of JB135 (Pilot Officer Howe's crew, missing since 23/24 November 1943) however there was no mention of the pilot or flight engineer. This remains a mystery since the entire crew of JB135 are missing without trace and are commemorated on Runnymede memorial, however it is suspected that the Lanc crashed in woodland near Berlin with its crew buried nearby. During the battles of 1945 grave markers and wreckage likely destroyed. Research continues to ascertain the final fates of Six-thirty's lost crew.

DW Tony Story RAAF (Tony Story)

The first round of the annual inter-station football knock-out competition, the 'Matz Cup' was complete except for one match, Strubby v Scampton. In the preliminary round East Kirkby beat Spilsby 3 – 2. The first of the Stirling trained Conversion Unit crews were posted to squadrons by way of 5 LFS. during the month, the new training policy was in full swing. A total of 35 crews were posted to squadrons of No. 5 Group from 51 Base in January. Another 45 crews progressed from Conversion Units to No.5 LFS. Heavy fog hung over Lincolnshire for the next few days, conditions were frosty and cold resulting in 630 Squadron being grounded. On Monday 17th January news was received that Squadron Leader Malcolm Crocker DFC had been awarded a Bar to his DFC (London Gazette 18 January 1944) which was in respect of his bravery on operations and leadership of the newly formed squadron prior to the arrival of Wing Commander Rollinson.

A signal was also received that an 'Immediate' DFC had been awarded to Flying Officer Niels Erik Westergaard (Danish) who had been missing since the attack of 1st January 1944. (Westergaard's DFC, awarded for his courage flying with 619 Squadron during a raid on Kassel in October 1943 was not actually officially announced until more than 12 months after it was earned (London Gazette 21 November 1944).

Lancaster 'S' East Kirkby 1944

20th/21st January 1944 : Night Bombing Attack on Berlin
Take Off: at 16:10 hours Aussie Tony Story and crew were the first airborne.

JB546-A	F/L DS Paterson RCAF
JB665-B	P/O A Drinkall
JB654-C	P/O DW Story RAAF
JB288-H	P/O AGG Johnson
JB290-D	F/S J White
JB672-F	P/O DH Cheney RCAF
ED655-J	P/O HW Hill
ND335-L	Sgt HC Rogers
JB666-O	F/L WH Kellaway
JA872-N	F/S JW Homewood
ND338-Q	F/O GH Probert
JB294-R	P/O PJ Piggin
ND337-S	F/O D Roberts
JB556-Y	F/O JH Pratt RCAF (P/O L Barnes)

*Billy Davis RCAF, who died in his gun turret.
(Library and Archives Canada)*

After a wide swinging approach to the North the bombers headed for Berlin with night fighters already attacking, the Luftwaffe would attack throughout the raid and again as they made their homeward trip. The target area was shrouded by 10/10ths cloud cover which rendered the search lights ineffective and reduced night fighter activity but did not stop the flak. Between 19:37 and 19:50 hours crews attacked from 19,500 to 21,200 feet based on the Pathfinder 'Wanganui' green and red star marker flares. David Roberts and Jim White's crews commented on the glow of fires over a large area as they left the target area. John Homewood's debrief mentions several fighters sighted, Me109, FW190 and Me110 all closing in on 'spoof' fighter flares. There were a number of positive comments noted about the routing and PFF marking by the Rogers, Hill and Cheney crews, Allan Johnson referred to heavy flak over the Heligoland Bight which was bursting at 25,000 feet and Aussie 'Tony' Story asked that the PFF crews who were returning with surplus marker flares were ordered not to jettison them so close to the enemy coast as they currently did, his crew had noted that the flares were illuminating the returning main force bombers.

Aboard JB294 'R-Robert' flown by Peter Piggin the crew spent much of the homeward trip fighting for the life of 24 year old Warrant Officer Billy Davis RCAF from Fort Francis, Ontario, their mid-upper gunner who had passed out in his turret. Exiting the mid-upper turret where the gunner clambered up onto a saddle with his feet in pedals was always difficult but trying to get an unconscious man out whilst in flight, was a huge struggle. Once free they carried out artificial resuscitation until landing, but sadly Billy Davis did not recover, his death being recorded as caused by oxygen starvation and exposure. Geoff Probert was the last of Six-thirty's pilots to land at 00:24 hours.

Ground trainers were installed at 1660 and 1661 Conversion Units and at 49, 57 and 630 Squadrons, with a view to reducing manipulation failures. Returning from leave Wing Commander Rollinson resumed command of Six-thirty from Squadron Leader Butler and ops were on that night.

Friday 21st January 1944.

Operational orders required 630 Squadron to provide 2 aircraft and crews each armed with 1 x 4000lb HC and 4 x 1000lb HC to participate in a 34 bomber diversionary attack on Berlin and a further 13 armed with 1 x 400lb, and 1.350 x 4lb and 56 x 30lb incendiary bombs for a simultaneous raid on Magdeburg by 648 bombers.

21st /22nd January 1944 : Night Bombing Attack on Berlin

Take Off: at 19:25 hours Pilot Officer Bob Hughes (ED655) was the first to take off.

JB294-R	F/S JW Homewood	– both to attack Berlin	
ND335-L	F/O KR Ames		
JB646-A	F/L DS Paterson RCAF	– all to attack Magdeburg	RD
JB665-B	F/L W English		
JB654-C	P/O DJ Hegarty RAAF		
JB290-D	F/O JCW Weller		
JB672-F	P/O HW Hill	RD	
JB288-H	P/O AGG Johnson		
ED655-J	P/O RT Hughes		
JA872-N	P/O WB Yates		
JB666-O	F/L WH Kellaway		
ND338-Q	F/O GH Probert		
ND337-S	F/O D Roberts		
JB710-W	F/O CH Armour		
JB556-Y	F/O JH Pratt RCAF		

Although the German fighter controllers were slow to identify Magdeburg as the target they did manage to vector their fighters in to the bomber stream early and again they maintained contact and shot bombers down, a total of 57 being lost. Bob Hughes had to abort his mission and bring ED655 home early after the artificial horizon instrumentation failed, landing at 21:16 hours. Several of Six-thirty's crews commented on the heavier than usual coastal flak defences, particularly at Cuxhaven. Crews again bombed on the Pathfinder's Wanganui red and green target indicators although bombing was confused as 27 bombers who arrived before the Pathfinders had bombed independently and may have caused confusion, this issue was commented on specifically by P/O Hill. David Roberts' crew gained a visual pinpoint on the river and commented on a good concentration of bombs on the railway station. Several crews could still see evidence of fires far into their return flight. Barrage flak was encountered at 23,000 feet. Aboard ND338 'Q-Queen' Geoff Probert's rear gunner Sergeant Richard Rogers was in action when a night fighter showed a little too much interest. A timely burst of fire was made without any strikes being observed and the German fighter went on its way. The last to return were Ken Ames and crew who landed 03:14 hours having had continuous trouble with ED335 'L-Love' failing to gain altitude and consequently attacking their secondary target, Berlin. It soon became obvious that having survived their experience with the Me110 on the previous night, John Homewood's crew in JB294 were missing.

Lancaster III, JB294 (Codes LE – R)

Pilot	– F/S John Walter Homewood. Age 20	Killed
Flight Eng	– Sgt William George Yorke. Age 33	Killed
Navigator	– Sgt Alexander William Reedman. Age 20	Killed
Bomb Aimer	– Sgt Peter John Walker. Age 21	Prisoner
Wireless Op	– Sgt Alexander Charles Stopp. Age 21	Killed
Mid Upper	– Sgt John Desmond Morris. Age 21	Killed
Rear Gunner	– F/S Morris Marks. RCAF Age 25	Killed

Morris Marks RCAF and his grave marker (Mike Marks (Canada))

    RAF records apparently suggest that JB294 was shot down by a night fighter but there is no claim made by a night fighter pilot which matches, however at 00:01 hours a Lancaster exploded in mid-air crashing at Wiesenhagen in the southern Flak belt of Berlin. It therefore seems most likely that John Homewood and his crew were shot down by flak. The crew were originally laid to rest in Wiesenhagen Cemetery but are now buried in Berlin War Cemetery having been moved in 1948. Their bomb aimer Peter Walker a machine setter from Dunstable was captured wounded at Berlin just 10 days after his 21st birthday. Briefly held in Stalag IIIA and Stalag Luft 6 (Hydekrug) he spent the last months of the war at Stalag 357 (Thorn and Fallingbostel). Morris Marks was a Canadian Jew who had bravely chosen to fly over Nazi Germany.

    For Canadian John Pratt and his crew their tour which started with 57 Squadron was complete, DFCs were awarded to John Pratt (announced on 22nd May 1944), navigator Tom Smart[v] and bomb aimer Tony Blois[vi] (neither announced till 2nd June 1944). Dermott Hegarty and crew did not fly any further Ops with the squadron and transferred to 83 Squadron Pathfinder Force. Hegarty and Mike Cross his rear gunner were killed before completing their tour with Pathfinders, Hegarty was awarded a DFC. On Saturday 22nd and Sunday 23rd which were very rainy days, records note the strain on the Orderly Room with completion of casualty returns, reports, recommendations for awards and promotions. Squadron Leader The Rev, Thomas Freyne[vii] was posted to RAF East Kirkby on Tuesday 25th January as Roman Catholic Chaplain. A General Mess Meeting was attended by all officers on Wednesday 26th, one of many subjects discussed was the non-arrival of batmen and 50 officers were 'doing' for themselves.

Thursday 27th January 1944.

During the morning preliminary warning was received of Ops requiring 13 of the squadron aircraft each bombed up with 1 x 4000lb HC, 900 x 4lb incendiaries and 48 x 30lb incendiaries were to join a force totalling 515 Lancasters and 15 Mosquitoes to attack Berlin.

27th/28th January 1944 : Night Bombing Attack on Berlin

Take Off: at 17:34 hours JB654 ('Tony' Story) was the first to take off.

JA872-N	P/O WB Yates
JB666-O	S/L RO Calvert RNZAF
ND338-Q	P/O LA Barnes
ND337-S	F/O D Roberts
JB710-W	F/O CH Armour
JB556-Y	F/O GH Probert
JB546-A	P/O A Drinkall
JB665-B	F/L W English
JB654-C	P/O DW Story RAAF
JB290-D	F/O KR Ames
JB672-F	P/O WH Hill
JB288-H	F/O JCW Weller
ND335-L	Sgt HC Rogers

F/O 'Sam' Weller brought JB288 H-How' home early, she had shown dodgy form during the attack on Brunswick and was still not fully serviceable. The Luftwaffe committed its fighters much earlier than usual with a number from the Dutch airfields ranging 75 miles out across the North Sea to attack incoming bombers. Diversionary tactics including a mining operation around Heligoland caused confusion and reduced the number free to attack the main bomber stream. Virtually all crews said that the PFF marking had been good, the main force bombed through the cloud cover based on PFF red/green star markers. The squadron's crews bombed between 20:32 and 20:45 hours from 19,500 to 21,000 feet. Comments from most were regarding heavy fighter activity and the glow from fires seems in the Target Area where searchlights were ineffective as they couldn't penetrate cloud.

Based on their H2S the Hill crew suggested that bombing was concentrated on the city centre. German assessments suggest that the bombs landed right across the city and also on some small neighbouring towns but that 50 industrial premises were hit and several important war industries were bombed out. Cab Kellaway's usual Lancaster JB666 'O-Oboe' on this occasion flown by S/L Roy Calvert on his first op with the squadron was the last to land at 02:42 hours. The Kiwi from Cambridge, Waikato had been a wool grader before joining the RNZAF in December 1940. During 1942 Calvert had flown a tour with 50 Squadron in Manchester's and participated in the same daylight raid on Le Creusot as Squadron Leader Butler who was then with 97 Squadron. Wounded by flak over Hamburg in November 1942 Roy Calvert had completed his tour and been awarded a DFC and Bar (London Gazettes 20th October 1942 and 18th December 1942). A year of instructing had followed before his request to return to operational flying was granted and Roy Calvert was posted to Six-thirty. On 28th January the party of 50 aircrew cadets from RAF Heaton Park return to their training unit and the next group of 50 arrived.

Derm Hegarty's crew, front to back, Taffy Cross, Laurie Croft, Bob Hay, Gilly Potter, Tony Smith and Scotty (Scott Robert Hay).

Friday 28th January 1944, Six-thirty were an aircraft short of their expected commitment when JB655 'J-Jig' was unserviceable at take-off and unable to participate, 677 bombers were despatched to bomb Berlin.

28th/29th January 1944 : Night Bombing Attack on Berlin
Take Off: at 23:45 hours in ND335, Ken Ames led the squadron into the air.

JB546-A	P/O A Drinkall
JB665-B	F/L W English
JB654-C	P/O DW Story RAAF
JB288-H	P/O DH Cheney RCAF
ND335-L	F/O KR Ames
JA872-N	P/O WB Yates RD
JB666-O	W/C JD Rollinson
ND337-S	F/O D Roberts
JB710-W	F/O CH Armour
JB556-Y	F/L WH Kellaway
JB290-D	F/S J White

630's 'D for Dog' repeatedly brought her crew home safely (LAHC Archive)

Lancaster S-Sugar (Walt Walker/Ian Walker)

Lancaster 'S', East Kirkby, 1943

The bomber stream approach over Northern Denmark proved to be a good option and served to split the Luftwaffe fighter forces, however the controller for the region including Berlin retained their fighters over the city and many bombers were shot down. Ground defences were reported to be heavier than recently with bursting heavy flak at 25,000ft and considerable light flak at 16-17000ft. The squadron's crews attacked between 03:15 and 03:39 hours from 19,000 to 21,000 feet. As with most crews Austin Drinkall's crew bombed on the Wanganui red and green star markers and in common with the Ames, Cheney, English and Yates crews, reported a huge explosion, some said yellow, some white, and the glow from well concentrated fires. Arriving 9 minutes after the attack finished and therefore having no markers, Stan Pinches 'Cab' Kellaway's bomb aimer released their bombload on the centre of a huge patch of fire. At 03:29 hours flying at 22,000 feet a JU88 closed on Ken Ames' ND335 'L-Love' on the port quarter down but was spotted at 500 yards by 'Paddy' Parle the rear gunner. Instructing a corkscrew to starboard Parle operated his turret manually as it was partly unserviceable and fired a two second burst. The JU88 broke away to starboard and was not seen again. No claim was made. German post-raid assessments were beginning to deteriorate in quality by this stage, it must have been hard to differentiate between much of the damage night after night. Many industrial firms were however hit and an unusually high proportion of administrative and public buildings such as Hitler's New Reich Chancellery, four theatres, the 'French' Cathedral, six hospitals, five embassies and the State Patent Office.

ND337 'S-Sugar' flown by David Roberts was the last to land at 08:33 hours, soon afterwards two crews had to be declared missing after their fuel must had given out and they had not landed back in England. Six-thirty's O.C. on his 53rd Op and its RAAF Regular airman 'Tony' Story of Hawthorn, Victoria, had Failed To Return.

Lancaster III, JB666 (Codes LE – O)

Pilot	– W/C John Dudley Rollinson DFC. Age 32	Killed
Flight Eng	– Sgt Percy George Kempen. Age 19	Killed
Navigator	– F/L Leopold (Leo) Ehrman DFC	Killed
Bomb Aimer	– Sgt William John Rosser. Age 29	Killed
Wireless Op	– F/S Albert Edward Broomfield. Age 25	Killed
Mid Upper	– Sgt Stanley Robert Loades. Age 29	Killed
Rear Gunner	– W/O Leslie Christie. Age 33	Killed

JB666 was apparently intercepted very shortly after Wing Commander Rollinson's crew released their bomb load and turned eastwards on the planned route away from the target area. Their Lancaster was shot down 20 km east of Berlin crashing into the woods north of Alt-Buchhorst (6 km east of Erkner). Two Luftwaffe night fighter pilots claimed to have shot down Lancasters in the area and it is likely that the loss of JB666 coincides with either the 03:44 hours claim by Oberleutnant (Flying Officer) Hans Leickhardt (of 2/NJG5) or the 03:51 hours claim by Unteroffizier (Junior Sergeant) Ernst Reitmeyer (of 3/NJG5). One of these Lancasters was JB666, the other was LM366 of 207 Squadron. Wing Commander Rollinson and crew, originally buried at Hennickendorf, are now buried together at Berlin War Cemetery.

Lancaster III, JB654 (Codes LE – C)

Pilot	– P/O Donald William (Tony) Story RAAF. Age 24	Killed
Flight Eng	– Sgt Douglas Edward James. Age 23	Killed
Navigator	– P/O Francis James Peacock. Age 21	Killed
Bomb Aimer	– F/O Herbert Laurence Wray Cairns. Age 22	Killed
Wireless Op	– Sgt George Henry Barrington. Age 21	Killed
Mid Upper	– P/O Harold John Barrons RCAF	Killed
Rear Gunner	– F/S George Dove. Age 25	Killed

The fate of 'Tony' Story's crew is unknown and as such they are commemorated on the Runnymede Memorial to the Missing. It is quite likely that JB654 was shot down over the North Sea amongst the three bombers claimed by the Luftwaffe night fighter ace Oberfeldwebel (Warrant Officer) Heinz Vinke of 11 Squadron/ Night Fighter Group 1 (11/NJG1) at 05:10, 05:55 and 06:14 hours. George Dove the crew's rear gunner was a pre-war member of the Royal Auxiliary Air Force's 616 Squadron. Lancaster JA872 flown on Ops by Wil Yates was seriously damaged either that night or on the day following – circumstances as yet unclear – and despatched to the Avro Factory for repairs on 30th and during the day two brand new Lancasters were delivered, ND561 and ND563.

Sunday 30th January 1944.

Six-thirty had to borrow JB526 from 57 Squadron, their elder sister, in order to fulfil the requirement expected by Group and with air gunners also in short supply two were also loaned for the night. The 10 Lancasters were each bombed up with 1 x 4000lb HC, 64 x 30lb and 1,100 x 4lb incendiaries and were part of a force of 534 bombers heading for Berlin.

30th/31st January 1944 : Night Bombing Attack on Berlin
Take Off: at 17:02 hours Bob Hughes (probably in ED655 but serial not recorded in the ORB) was the first of the 10 Lancasters to take off.

JB546-A	F/L DS Paterson RCAF	
JB665-B	F/L W English	
JB290-D	F/S J White	
ED655-J	P/O RT Hughes	
JB288-H	P/O HW Hill	
JB526-57	F/S FHA Watts	
ND530-P	P/O LA Barnes	RD
ND337-S	F/L D Roberts	
JB710-W	F/L CH Armour	
JB556-Y	F/L GH Probert	

Ninety minutes into the outward flight however F/O Gordon Brake (navigator aboard ED655 'J-Jig') realised that their Lancaster was not flying as smoothly as usual and that it was straying off course. Checking on his pilot after failing to get a coherent response on the inter-com he found P/O Bob Hughes barely conscious after his oxygen system had failed. Even after the flight engineer changed his supply Hughes remained unwell and Brake ordered a return to base where they landed at 19:48 hours. Most of Six-thirty's crews attacked between 20:24 and 20:38 hours on Wanganui red, green star markers from 19,500 to 20,500 feet through solid cloud cover although records suggest that Cliff Armour bombed as late as 20:50 hours. Concentrated fires were reported in the TA, and Cliff Armour's crew noted the glow from the fires still visible at 80 miles on their return flight, Len Barnes, who was the last to land at 00:10 hours reported a *'pall of black smoke at 9000 ft'*. Bombers encountered sporadic light flak in loose barrage form bursting at 17,000 -23,000 feet. At 20:47 hours the crew of Len Barnes in ND530 'P – Peter' flying at 21,500 feet above 10/10ths cloud were attacked by a ME210 night fighter. Rear gunner Sergeant Thomas 'Freddy' Fox reported tracer incoming from the starboard quarter up ordering a corkscrew to starboard and immediately sighted the Me210 at 600 yards. He delivered a 2 second burst but saw no hits and made no claim. About 1 minute later another Me210 was sighted by Fox and mid-upper gunner Sgt Jim Overholt RCAF, at 500 yards range and as the pilot began his corkscrew both gunners opened fire with a five second burst, both noting strikes on the nose and engine of the enemy fighter. It broke away and wasn't seen again. Claim: Me210 damaged. Barnes later recalled *'we were attacked over Magdeburg on the way home. 'Jerry' made a couple of passes, my gunners returned fire and he broke away. Smoke was seen from him after that. Later that morning in daylight we assessed the damage he'd done to the aircraft and saw our groundcrew remove an unexploded 20mm cannon shell from a starboard fuel tank. Luck was with us!'*. German reports stress the seriousness of the damage on this particular night, two industrial plants were completely destroyed and fifteen seriously damaged. Amongst the public buildings to be hit were the Nazi Propaganda Ministry of Dr. Josef Goebbels and sections of the German underground railway system, 94 railway carriages being destroyed at the Kreuzberg depot. In summarising the Month-End situation at Six-thirty, the Adjutant, Frank Cheetham, wrote that much progress had been made in knitting together the squadron and that a healthy rivalry existed between 57 and 630. He said that 630 were now well supplied with aircraft but that most other equipment was still slow arriving. Crew rooms were still incomplete but were being used (through necessity) despite having no furniture other than folding chairs and tables. He remained short of office stationery. The living accommodation had improved particularly in last 10 days, morale was high but the loss of the CO was a grievous blow. The water supply at East Kirkby failed completely on Monday 30th January and emergency measures had to be put in place including bringing a supply in and pumping it into tanks. Normal supplies were not resumed until 3rd February.

February 1944

On Tuesday 1st February 1944 a signal was received 'posting in' Acting Wing Commander W. I. Deas DFC and Bar to command the squadron. Several quiet days followed and the new C.O. arrived on Saturday 5th February to assume command. Wing Commander William Inglis 'Bill' Deas[i] was a 29 year old South African from Piet Retief in the Transvaal, South Africa. In 1939 he quickly arranged passage from Durban aboard Union Castle's mail liner 'Winchester Castle' arriving in Southampton on 15th October 1939 and within days joined the RAFVR for pilot training. An experienced bomber pilot by 1944 he'd flown Handley Page Hampden's on his first tour with 61 Squadron in 1941 being awarded a DFC (London Gazette 21 November 1941) returning to 61 Squadron in Lancasters after a spell instructing at 14 OTU to complete a second tour during which he'd been promoted to Squadron Leader, flight commander and awarded a Bar to his DFC (London Gazette 20 April 1943). A natural leader who led from the front, highly popular with his aircrew and ground crews alike, he would make an indelible impression on the young squadron.

Wing Commander Bill Deas (Patti Kellaway)

That evening a concert party from RAF Woodhall Spa gave the first concert at East Kirkby, it was well attended by squadron personnel. Flying Officer Johnny Nall[ii] and crew were posted to the squadron following training at 1661 HCU and via 51 Base. Arriving at about the same time from HCU was the crew of 26 year old Joe Kilgour[iii] from Prescott, Lancashire and from 29 OTU and 1654 HCU the crew of Arthur 'John' Perry[iv] a 24 year old Western Australian. Tuesday 8th February saw a Station Parade to hoist the Colours and a full muster by Six-thirty. From the 5th to the 12th of February the weather was unfavourable for Ops due to the 'moon period' and an extended training program was carried out with all aircrew personnel reporting to their Flight Commanders at 09:30 hours for morning lectures. A visiting officer of the 8th USAAF, Captain Kerr, spoke to aircrew about 'Life in the USA'. Flight Lieutenant Ernie Stead the Squadron Gunnery Leader lectured the gunners and pilots whilst other section leaders addressed their men. Flight Engineers spent the whole of one morning in the hangars, the Electrical Officer lectured aircrew on in-flight failures and the Technical Officer spoke on H2S and Fishpond followed by the Chief Technical Officer who spoke to Flight Engineers and Pilots on 'engine handling'. The Senior Intelligence Officer lectured on 'Raid Assessment'. Finally the squadron were addressed by the Senior Medical Officer and finally the Squadron Commander. The afternoons were used for practice flying.

On the night of Tuesday 8th February an 'Escape and Evasion' exercise was staged with all aircrew being bussed to selected points 6 – 8 miles distant from East Kirkby and left to evade a force of 100 members of the Parachute Regiment tasked to capture the 'escapees'. Seven airmen were captured. Inspections were carried out of the Catering Department, Gas and Fire Sections and Technical Equipment. On Saturday 12th February after the return of Lancaster JA872 from two weeks' worth of repairs at Avro, at 16:00 hours Lancaster W4119 'Y' of 50 Squadron fell through thick cloud and crashed south east of the boundary fence by East Kirkby's No.3 Hangar after port outer engine fail, slightly damaging two of 57 Squadron's Lancasters. Some of those aboard were able to bale out but sadly a number died. Nevertheless a squadron party was held on the night of 12th February with the aircrew hosting the groundcrews. The following day 'Ops were on', twenty-one aircraft and crews were detailed but 45 minutes prior to take off the mission was scrubbed.

On 14th February Don Cheney's crew prepared for their transfer to 617 Squadron on the next day, sadly they failed to return from a sortie in early August 1944. Close behind Joe Kilgour and crew 22 year old Yorkshireman Cliff Allen[v] and crew arrived from training at 14 OTU. and 1660 CU as replacements.

Don Cheney and crew (back, l to r, Reg Pool, Jim Rosher, Noel Wait, Art McRostie RAAF, and front l to r Rob Welch, Don Cheney and A 'Len' Curtis). Four were killed (Peter Cheney)

Clifford Allen (Mike Wraith)   *Joe Kilgour (LAHC Archive)*

Tuesday 15th February 1944.
A battle order was again issued and 21 aircraft were serviceable, two in excess of available crews so two crews were borrowed (one each from 61 and 619 Squadrons). This was a 'maximum plus' as the squadron establishment was 16 + 4 Lancasters, and they were amongst the 891 bombers on course for Berlin that night, each of the squadron's Lancasters bombed up with 1 x 4000lb HC, 48 x 30lb and 900 x 4lb incendiaries.

15th/16th February 1944 : Night Bombing Attack on Berlin
Take Off: at 16:50 hours Bob Hughes and crew were the first off the deck in ND580.

JB546-A	P/O A Drinkall	
JB665-B	F/L W English	
ND554-C	F/L JCW Weller	
JB290-D	W/O J White	
JB672-F	P/O HW Hill	RD
JB288-H	P/O AGG Johnson	
ND580-G	P/O RT Hughes	
ND531-K	P/O HC Rogers	
ND335-L	F/L KR Ames	
ND532-N	P/O WB Yates	
ND527-O	F/L WH Kellaway	
ND530-P	P/O LA Barnes	
ND338-Q	P/O HCL Mackintosh RAAF	

ND561-R	P/O PJ Piggin	
ND337-S	F/L D Roberts	
JB710-W	F/L CH Armour	
ND563-T	W/C WI Deas	
ND583-V	P/O K Rodbourn	
JB556-Y	F/L GH Probert	
ED944-Z	P/O J Golightly	(61 Sqn crew)
ED655-J	P/O K Roberts	(619 Sqn crew – crashed landed)

JB556 'Y-Yoke' (Geoff Probert) aborted and returned to base as the rear gunner's intercom went unserviceable, they landed at 20:52 hours. After a 2 week rest for Berlin 891 bombers had been despatched to resume the attack and a record 2,642 tons of bombs were dropped. The outward flight over Denmark proved to be too distant for many of the Luftwaffe fighters although as they came closer the fighter opposition stiffened and even over the target where the night fighters had been ordered to stay clear leaving the skies open for the flak gunners, the German pilots continued to attack. Flak was found to be moderate in barrage form, Luftwaffe fighters intercepted over Denmark and from that point were active on the track from the Baltic coast to Berlin and Ken Ames crew noted that 'the defences over the target were lively with considerable numbers of fighters'.

Flight Sergeant Reg Findlow the bomb aimer aboard ND532 'N-Nan' (Wil Yates) was preparing for the attack as they approached the target at 21,000 feet at 20:59 hours when he sighted a JU88 night fighter moving from port to starboard bow on a parallel course. The fighter immediately curved around to starboard an approached the Lancaster. At 600 yards the rear gunner (Flight Sergeant Dennis Dawson) ordered a corkscrew to port as the fighter opened fire with cannons and machineguns missing the bomber due to the timely manoeuvre. Dawson's guns refused to fire as his breech block had jammed but the fighter broke away for a moment before attacking again. Yates threw the Lancaster into a starboard corkscrew on Dawson's word as the mid upper gunner (Sergeant Doug Remole) fired a four second burst, 250 rounds. His tracer was visible all around the nose of the night fighter which broke away without opening fire and disappeared into a cloud. No damage was suffered aboard 'N-Nan' and no claim of damage to the night fighter was made.

The attack was timed to begin at 21:15 hours and 630 Squadron crews attacked using the PFF sky markers, Sam Weller commented on 4 Wanganui clusters and the green Target Indicators cascading through the clouds, the Lancasters attacked from 20,000 to 23,500 feet between 21:10 and 21:34 hours. 'Cab' Kellaway's report confirms his crew's H2S fix placed the concentration of bombing in the centre of the city and aside from a very large explosion at 21:19 hours commented on by Wing Commander Bill Deas as it lit up the target area, no results were noted due to 10/10 cloud. After attacking Austin Drinkall and Harold Hill reported accurate flak bursting at 25,000 feet. David Roberts report mentions that the clouds above Berlin were reflecting the glow of the fire from 100 miles distant on their homeward leg. It was a maximum effort raid and Six-thirty had the highest number of aircraft off the ground in No. 5 Group. At 21:23 hours flying at 21,000 feet over the target the Mackintosh crew aboard ND338 'Q-Queen' were suddenly dazzled by fighter flares, the rear gunner Flight Sergeant Burt Howard sighted an ME109 dead astern at 400 yards range and called for a corkscrew to port as he opened fire with a three second burst. No strikes were observed and no claim made.

German assessments show that bombing was heavy on the central and south-western districts with extensive damage in Berlin, 599 large and 572 medium fires being recorded and further destruction to housing stock and 526 temporary wooden housing barracks. Several of the Berlin based major war production factories were hit, particularly Siemensstadt. Berlin had been very badly hit during the campaign and major numbers of its civilian population 'bombed out' having to be evacuated. The experienced crew of Bill English aboard JB665 failed to return.

Lancaster III, JB665 (Codes LE – B)

Pilot	– F/L William English. Age 22	Killed
2nd Pilot	– P/O John Leslie Richards. Age 28	Killed
Flight Eng	– Sgt Norman Harold Mitchell. Age 31	Killed
Navigator	– F/O John Emlyn Evans. Age 24	Killed
Bomb Aimer	– P/O Llewellyn Vivian Fussell. Age 29	Killed
Wireless Op	– F/S Leslie George Lane. Age 21	Killed
Mid Upper	– P/O Derek Reginald Carlile. Age 19	Killed
Rear Gunner	– P/O William Philip Revenall Hewitt RAAF. Age 20	Killed

Bill English and crew were shot down by a night fighter after crossing the Baltic Coast, probably by Oberleutnant Helmuth Schilte of Stab.II/NJG5 about 30km north east of Teterow and crashed about 20:53 hours (German time) at Prebberede near Güstrow, 32 km south of Rostock. The crew were buried there with military honours on 19th February but have since been moved to the Berlin War Cemetery. No trace of their rear gunner could be found and he is commemorated on Runnymede Memorial to the missing. Lancaster III, ED655 (LE – J) P/O K Roberts RAAF (on loan from 619 Squadron) crashed in the funnel on return, clipping the ground 1 mile north of Old Bolingbroke after having to over-shoot and go around again, three of the crew were slightly injured and the rear gunner (Sgt LF Virgo RAAF) suffered a broken leg. On Wednesday 16th, Thursday 17th and Friday 18th February crews were briefed and Lancasters bombed-up and prepared for Ops only to have them cancelled very shortly before take-off.

Saturday 19th February 1944.
In the morning preliminary warning was received for 17 Lancasters to participate in an attack on Leipzig which was mounted by 823 bombers. The 630 Squadron Lancasters each carried 1 x 4000lb HC, 950 x 4lb and 600 x 30lb incendiaries plus 100 x 4X1b incendiaries.

19th/20th February 1944 : Night Bombing Attack on Leipzig
Take off : 23:29 hours Bob Hughes and crew were first airborne again.

JB556-Y	F/L GH Probert
ND530-P	P/O LA Barnes
JB546-A	P/O A Drinkall
ND554-C	F/L JCW Weller
JB672-F	P/O HW Hill
ND580-G	P/O RT Hughes
JB288-H	P/O AGG Johnson
ND531-K	P/O HC Rogers
ND532-N	P/O WB Yates
ND527-O	F/L WH Kellway
ND338-Q	P/O HCL Mackintosh RAAF
ND561-R	P/O PJ Piggin
ND337-S	F/L D Roberts
ND563-T	W/C WI Deas
ND583-V	P/O K Rodbourn
JB710-W	F/L CH Armour
ND335-L	F/L KR Ames

This attack attracted heavy fighter activity after the German fighter controllers turned around a force which they had despatched to deal with RAF minelaying aircraft off the northern port of Kiel to assist the remainder of their aircraft stretched between the Dutch coast and central Germany. Six-thirty's own Ken

Rodbourn made specific comment on the intense activity by the Luftwaffe over the Dutch coast. The result was that the bomber stream was attacked almost continually, Bob Hughes reported that he considered the route too close to well defended Emden an opinion which Wing Commander Bill Deas must have agreed after he was coned there by searchlights. The attack took place early and went from 03:43 to 04:24 hours as many of the bombers arrived early due to strong tail winds which hadn't been predicted, the squadron's Lancasters attacked from 20,000 to 23,500 feet between 03:45 and 04:24 hours. \

Ken Ames's experience concerning heavy cloud cover and bombing based on red and green star markers would have been common. A glow from fires below was seen on the clouds amidst considerable fighter activity. Moments before 'zero' (attack time) Harold Hill and 'Cab' Kellaway saw a major explosion and large blue flash lit up the night sky, it was recorded by Stan Pinches his unflappable bomb aimer. Sam Weller reported a heavy flak barrage bursting about 23,000 feet in the target area. Wing Commander Deas arrived late after struggling to lose the Emden search lights and found well concentrated fires visible. Six-thirty lost two crews that night:

Lancaster III, JB710 (Codes LE – W)

Pilot	– F/L Clifford Harold Armour. Age 32	Killed
Flight Eng	– Sgt John Adams Byars. Age 20	Killed
Navigator	– P/O Harold Kidd. Age 30	Killed
Bomb Aimer	– F/O John Stanley Cross. Age 21	Killed
Wireless Op	– Sgt Ronald Giles. Age 20	Killed
Mid Upper	– Sgt Leslie Alfred Young. Age 20	Killed
Rear Gunner	– Sgt George Henry Griffiths. Age 19	Killed

JB710 was lost without trace and its entire crew are commemorated on the Runnymede Memorial to the missing. It is likely that the Lancaster was one of two shot down over the sea about 15km north-west of Ameland by Oberfeldwebel Heinz Vinke, these two Lancasters were claimed at 00:57 and 01:40 hours. Although shown as a resident of Streatham in South West London, Cliff Armour was actually an Australian born in Sydney who had settled in London where he was in the theatrical business and held a Civil Pilot's Licence. Based on an obituary for Harold Kidd it is possible that he and Cliff Armour crewed up based on their mutual interest in the stage.

Lancaster III, ND532 (Codes LE – N)

Pilot	– P/O Wilson Birwell Yates DFC. Age 31	Killed
Flight Eng	– Sgt William Albert Isaacs. Age 20	Prisoner
Navigator	– Sgt Alan Spence. Age 22	Killed
Bomb Aimer	– F/S Reginald George Findlow RCAF. Age 22	Prisoner
Wireless Op	– Sgt Donald Scott	Prisoner
Mid Upper	– F/L Ernest Stead, MID. Age 30	Killed
Rear Gunner	– F/S Dennis Arthur Dawson	Killed

Ernie Stead Six-thirty's Gunnery Leader was lost aboard ND532, he was a married man from Leeds who had risen through the ranks during his first tour as an Air Gunner and been Mentioned in Despatches (London Gazette 1 January 1943). Captain of the crew, Wilson Yates was posthumously awarded the DFC (London Gazette 21 December 1945 – with effect from 18 February 1944) which had been 'in the system' at the time of his death. Those who died are buried at Berlin War Cemetery. Three members of the crew baled out and became prisoners of war, Isaacs, Scott and Findlow were all held at Stalag 357 Kopernikus with numbers 3523, 2118 and 2111 respectively. During the forced marches of POWs away from the advancing Allied forces, Findlow, Scott and Isaacs escaped from the group heading from Stalag 357 during darkness on 6th April and made their way westwards through the forests on the run until 13th April when

Wil Yates' crew: left to right, Isaacs, Findlow, Yates, Scott, Spence and Rocky Roche (Mike Isaacs)

they were recaptured near Stalsrade and returned to Stalag 357. Bill Isaacs was an engineering fitter from Glossop.

Sunday 20th February 1944.

Ops were on again, the squadron was instructed to take part in an attack on Stuttgart, 598 bombers pounded the city, all of 630 Squadron's aircraft with payloads of 1 x 4000lb HC bomb, 950 x 4lb and 600 x 30lb plus 100 x 4Xlb incendiaries.

20th/21st February 1944 : Night Bombing Attack on Stuttgart

Take Off: at 23:40 hours ND563 flown by the crew of Edgar Murray[vi], who had recently arrived from 1654 CU, was the first to take off but crashed to the ground and exploded clear of the runway. The squadron then took off overflying the crashed 'T-Tare', three of the experienced crews carrying Second Dickies.

JB546-A	P/O A Drinkall	(P/O JB Nall)
ND554-C	F/L JCW Weller	
JB290-D	W/O J White	
JB672-F	P/O HW Hill	
ND580-G	P/O RT Hughes	
ND531-K	P/O HC Rogers	
ND335-L	F/L KR Ames	
ND527-O	F/L WH Kellaway	(P/O CLE Allen)
ND338-Q	P/O HCL Mackintosh RAAF	
ND561-R	P/O PJ Piggin	(F/S AJ Perry RAAF)
ND337-S	F/L D Roberts	
ND563-T	P/O EJ Murray	
ND583-V	P/O K Rodbourn	
JB556-Y	F/L GH Probert	

The port outer engine of ND531 'K-Kitty' (Cliff Rogers) cut out on take-off and at 600 feet burst into flames, the unflappable pilot who would later become Chief Test Pilot to Rolls-Royce aviation, cut the engine and headed calmly out to sea to jettison the incendiaries in his bomb load as he couldn't climb over 1,500 feet. For some unknown reason the 4,000 pounder released with the incendiaries falling with them into the sea, he headed back at East Kirkby at 00:42 hours. A diversionary sweep across the North Sea by 156 aircraft mainly of training units and a diversionary raid on Munich by Mosquitoes confused the German fighter controllers and the bomber stream was not as vigorously attacked as it had been on other nights although spirited Flak was noted over Stuttgart. The main force found cloud in the Target Area and Six-thirty attacked between 03:59 and 04:07 hours from 21,000 to 23,000 feet bombing on green/red star Wanganui Target Indicators which David Roberts, Jim White and 'Sam' Weller all noted were well placed against both banks of the River Neckar near the railway station. Several crews reported the bombing to be well concentrated and Peter Piggin noted large fires in the Target Area while Austin Drinkall and Bob Hughes commented on a large golden/orange explosion. Harold Hill, Ken Rodbourn and David Roberts all reported the long distances over which the fires could still be seen as they flew home. The Rodbourn crew landed at another airfield but Glaswegian Jim White was the last to touch down at 07:55 hours.

Although some of the bombing had been scattered due to the cloud cover, contemporary local reports state that there was considerable damage in the city centre and the north-eastern suburb of Bad Canstatt and north western suburb of Feuerbach. In the latter district the Bosch factory, one of the most important to the German war industry producing dynamos, injection pumps and magnetos, was severely damaged and closer into the centre of the city the Landtag (regional parliament building), state archives and state picture galleries were all badly damaged.

Lancaster III, ND563 (Codes LE – T)

Pilot	– P/O Edgar John Murray. Age 20	Killed
Flight Eng	– Sgt Francis Westhead. Age 19	Killed
Navigator	– Sgt Phillip Gascoyne Mottram. Age 28	Killed
Bomb Aimer	– F/O Harold Knowles Battye. Age 26	Killed
Wireless Op	– Sgt Kenneth James Wallbey. Age 19	Killed
Mid Upper	– Sgt Douglas William Remole RCAF. Age 20	Killed
Rear Gunner	– Sgt William Alfred Cecil Davies. Age 23	Injured

Edgar Murray (LAHC Archive)

On taking off at 23:40 hours after travelling three quarters of the length of the longest runway the Lancaster was reported to have been momentarily airborne before it swung sharply to port, crashed through the airfield boundary fence out of control, lost its undercarriage and the bomb loaded exploded shattering windows for some distance around. Miraculously the Rear Gunner was not killed, he was admitted to Station Sick Quarters, sadly the remaining six lads were all killed instantly.

Having flown his first Op just days before with 'Cab' Kellaway, Sergeant Bill Davies survived the crash on his 2nd Op and on recovery flew during April with Peter Nash's crew until that was disbanded after their pilot's accidental injury and death, then as a spare rear gunner with Wing Commander Stidolph[vii] and in the crew of Bob Hooper in May before finding a home with 'Blue' Rackley's crew, sadly though his luck did run out and he was killed flying with 'Blue' in June 1944 after their aircraft was crippled by a night fighter.

Lancaster III, ND338 (Codes LE – Q)

Pilot	– P/O Harold Charles Leeton Mackintosh RAAF. Age 28	Killed
Flight Eng	– Sgt Elwyn Rees Hughes. Age 20	Killed
Navigator	– F/S Geoffrey Slater. Age 26	Killed
Bomb Aimer	– F/S Owen Preston Smith. RAAF. Age 29	Killed
Wireless Op	– Sgt Angus Newson, Age 22	Prisoner
Mid Upper	– F/S Stephen Tatai RCAF. Age 27	Killed
Rear Gunner	– F/S Burton Dix Howard RCAF. Age 26	Killed

ND338 was shot down by Hauptman Ludwig Meister of 1/NJG 4 at 03:17 hours and crashed to earth at 'Plitterdorf' where her crew were initially buried, they were later moved to Durnbach War Cemetery. His night fighter was equipped with Schraege Musik (Jazz Music) a pair of upward firing cannons which enabled the German pilot to manoeuvre into position in the blind spot beneath a Lancaster and fire vertically upwards. Mackintosh's newlywed South American born Wireless Op, Angus Newson from Exeter, survived as a prisoner of war being held at Stalag 357 Kopernikus having been issued POW number 1750. Navigator Geoff Slater was a former soldier who had transferred to the RAF volunteering for aircrew duty. Of Hungarian heritage Stephen Tatai of Brantford, Ontario was an outdoorsman who worked at Bertram Tool Company in Dundas.

On Wednesday 23rd February a court of enquiry into the recent crash at East Kirkby assembled chaired by Wing Commander Robert Bowes DFC and Bar[viii] of 52 Base. Six-thirty were stood down. In the inquiry the crash was categorized as 'pilot error' in the absence of any contradictory evidence. Getting a fully bombed up Lancaster, loaded with sufficient fuel for many hours flight off the ground was a lethally dangerous business even for a pilot who had done it repeatedly, new crews had to learn very quickly. Funerals were held on the next day for crash victims at Cambridge (P/O Murray and Sgt Wallbey) and at

Angus Newson (Russell Stock)   *Ken Orchiston RNZAF (New Zealand official)*

Harrogate Regional Cemetery (Sgt Remole RCAF). Representatives of 630 Squadron attended both services. The families of the other airmen requested that their boys were returned home for burial and Sergeant's Westhead and Mottram are in buried in Liverpool (Anfield) and Liverpool (Knotty Ash), Flying Officer Battye is buried at Shepley. Arriving that week from No.5 Lancaster Finishing School after training at 1661 HCU was the crew of 23 year old New Zealander Ken Orchiston[ix] ready to commence the pre-operational program of night flying, high level bombing and cross country exercises.

Thursday 24th February 1944, it was confirmed that 'Ops are On' and the AOC No. 5 Group, Air Vice Marshal Hon RA Cochrane CB CBE AFC arrived to attend Six-thirty's aircrew briefing. Germany's main ball bearing production factories had been the target of a raid by the 8th USAAF on the previous day and following up, Bomber Command split its force in a different way this night, with 392 aircraft in an initial attack followed two hour later by 342 more. A Luftwaffe raid was going on over London and some crews experienced the active ground defences. Various bomb loads were carried, 1 x 4000lb HC, 900 x 4lb incendiaries and 60 x 30lb incendiaries, some also having 4lb X incendiaries, other aircraft were bombed up with 4 x 2000lb HC and 1 x 1000lb MC bomb.

24th/25th February 1944 : Night Bombing Attack on Schweinfurt
Take Off: at 20:12 hours Allan Johnson in JB288 led Six-thirty's take off.

JA872-N	F/S AJ Perry RAAF	
ND527-O	S/L RO Calvert RNZAF	
ND530-P	F/O CLE Allen	
ND561-R	P/O PJ Piggin	
ND337-S	F/L D Roberts	
ND583-V	P/O K Rodbourn	
JB556-Y	F/L GH Probert	
JB546-A	F/O JB Nall	
ND554-C	F/L JCW Weller	
JB290-D	W/O J White	
JB672-F	P/O HW Hill	RD
ND335-L	P/O RT Hughes	
JB288-H	P/O AGG Johnson	
ND531-K	P/O HC Rogers	
ND580-G	P/O FHA Watts	RD
ED944-Z	P/O JS Kilgour	

Several of 630 Squadron's Lancasters had serviceability problems, ED944 'Z' (Joe Kilgour) turned for home when the starboard inner engine failed and it couldn't gain sufficient altitude, ND554 'C' (Sam Weller) turned back at Beachy Head when their rear gunner became seriously ill with the symptoms of appendicitis, ND337 'S' (David Roberts) had to abort the mission over the French coast when their starboard inner engine failed and had to be feathered, he was shot at near London on his homeward flight and ND530 'P' (Allen) turned for home over the North Sea as their wireless was not working properly.

Over the North Sea JB672 'F' was involved in a mid-air collision with 9 Squadron's LM432/O but managed to continue and bomb Augsburg. Arriving in the target area both waves of attacking bombers were hampered by poorly placed Path Finder target indicators. The squadron's crews attacked between 01:01 and 01:16 hours from 20,000 to 23,600 feet, Harold Hill's bomb aimer had a good visual of the built up area and river with fires burning but noted concentrated flak up to 25,000 feet, Johnny Nall's report mentions a sea of flames and Cliff Rogers' a major concentration of fire. Having arrived late due to the air attack on London Geoff Probert commented on two large explosions in the TA at 01:48. Jim White's crew in 'D-Dog' also reported heavy flak and search lights. The Watts crew in 'G-George' crew were coned by a dozen search lights over London and fired the correct flare colour but as the lights released them their rear gunner saw a twin engined aircraft which had been hit, fall in pieces. Several German attackers were lost in the area that night. John Nall was the last of the 630 Squadron Lancasters to land at 05:10 that morning. German reports do not make clear what damage had been done in the USAAF attack or the RAF attacks and simply state that 'nominal damage' was done to their war industries. F/O Bill Kirkpatrick[x] transferred to Six-thirty from 463 Squadron to take up the role of Gunnery Leader which had been vacated when Ernie Stead went missing some nights earlier. The 38 year old born in Whitehaven, Cumbria was a very experienced air gunner who had served operationally with 49 and 463 Squadrons. Prevented from enlisting in the RAF until October 1942 he had joined immediately he could and had battled successfully to be accepted for aircrew training.

Friday 25th February 1944.

Preliminary warning for a night attack was received mid-morning. In the first large raid on Augsburg 594 aircraft were despatched with various diversionary raids working to split the Luftwaffe night fighters between Kiel and the Baltic in the far north, Holland in the centre and Augsburg in the far south of Germany. In clear weather outstandingly accurate bombing was achieved and 2,000 tons of bombs dropped by two waves of bombers. Six-thirty's Lancasters were bombed-up with 1 x 4000lb minol, 76 x 30lb, 500 x 4lb and 100 x 4Xlb incendiary bombs for their attack on Augsburg.

25th/26th February 1944 : Night Bombing Attack on Augsburg
Take Off: 17:58 hours David Roberts and crew were the first off the deck.

ND554-C	F/L JCW Weller	
JB672-F	P/O HW Hill	
ND580-G	P/O FHA Watts	RD
JB288-H	P/O AGG Johnson	
ND531-K	P/O HC Rogers	
ND335-L	F/L KR Ames	
JA872-N	F/O JB Nall	
ND527-O	P/O RT Hughes	
ED944-Z	P/O JS Kilgour	
ND530-P	P/O CLE Allen	
ND561-R	P/O PJ Piggin	
ND337-S	F/L D Roberts	
ND583-V	P/O K Rodbourn	
JB556-Y	F/L GH Probert	

JB288 'H' (Allan Johnson) had to abort when the rear turret intercom failed and the turret doors were found to be jammed open. Doubtless cursing in ND554 'C' (Sam Weller) the crew had to turn back for a second night when an oil pipe burst in the rear turret soaking their gunner in oil. David Roberts flying ND337 'S' almost had to abort for a second night when the starboard inner engine started to surge, cut out and produce a heavy vibration. Unwilling to go home early again he feathered the prop and headed for the Kriegsmarine occupied Naval docks at Dieppe which they bombed before heading for base. Approaching the target area to attack at 22:38 hours about 22,000 feet Six-thirty's crews could see the fires in the city centre between the two rivers caused by the earlier attackers. The squadron's crews attacked between 01:01 and 01:16 hours from 20,000 to 23,600 feet, 22:46 and 22:56 hours. After seeing several aircraft shot down Ken Rodbourn and John Nall both noted a huge dark orange explosion at about 23:18 hours, Joe Kilgour commented on heavy flak in barrage form up to 21,000 feet. At 22:48 hours flying near Augsburg at 19,000 feet Sergeant Bob Heggie, the mid-upper gunner of Freddy Watts' ND580 'G-George' sighted a FW190 climbing below their port wing along a searchlight beam which had caught 'George'. The fighter opened fire instantly and cannon and machinegun fire tore holes in the mainplane. Heggie called a warning as he was unable to fire and when the fighter broke to the starboard quarter the rear gunner (Sergeant George

Gordon Brake (Michael Brake) *Geoff Probert (Patti Kellaway)*

Matthews) opened fire at about 200 yards with a long burst (400 rounds), hits were observed on the single engined fighter which dived away, the bomber's tailfin left the mid-upper unsighted and he was unable to join the battle. FW190 claimed as damaged.

All 630 Squadron aircraft returned home safely although ND580 'G-George' (Freddy Watts) had to land at North Killingholme due to the battle damage sustained, 'G-George' was repaired by Avro aircraft factory technicians at the airfield. The crew of Bob Hughes gave a huge sigh of relief, their tour which had started on 619 Squadron was complete.

Distinguished Flying Crosses were awarded to Hughes, his navigator Gordon Brake and a Distinguished Flying Medal to Jimmy Martin their mid-upper gunner (who would sadly be killed in September 1944 flying from East Kirkby on his second tour, with 57 Squadron). Bob Hughes was a former soldier who had transferred to the RAF volunteering for aircrew duties. The old centre of the city of Augsburg was completely destroyed, as was the town hall and several theatres and historic and other civic buildings. Second wave bombers caused serious damage to some of Augsburg's war industries including an aircraft component factory and engineering units of the MAN works. The Social Club in Hut 18 at East Kirkby was by now a great success with social evenings twice weekly, the club room open on other nights and various functions such as a 'mock trial', whist drive and various musical activities. A 'Toc H' Club with a club room and canteen opened just 100 yards from the communal site for use jointly with local villagers. Howard Elliott, the Station MO, recently promoted to Squadron Leader got off on leave just before the weather turned for the worse, two weeks earlier his NCO i/c Station Sick Quarters (Sergeant Jasper) had been posted away but his replacement Flight Sergeant Hair arrived within days reducing disruption. The S.S.Q. had done sterling work attending the Lancaster crashes on 12th, 15th and 20th February and also the crash of a P-38 Lightning of the USAAF which crashed at nearby Eastville killing the pilot. Squadron Leader Elliott or his deputy, F/O AG Hardy[xi], or both, were quickly on the scene at all of these crashes. Flight Lieutenant Cockshott[xii] was the Station Dental Officer. Saturday 26th and Sunday 27th February brought snow to East Kirkby followed by sleet, the squadron was stood down from 11:00 hours and although a mission was on the cards for Monday 28th but Ops were no sooner declared as 'on' than Six-thirty were again stood down. Twenty-two year old pilots Peter Nash[xiii] from Stansted, Kent, Alan 'Happy Jack' Wilson[xiv] from Murrumbeena/Victoria and Ron Bailey[xv] from Northampton arrived with their crews direct from training.

Hot on their tails came the crews of 30 year old John Langlands[xvi] a former Edinburgh policeman and 21 year old Lionel 'Blue' Rackley[xvii] from Brisbane/Queensland. 'Blue' Rackley and crew had joined 3 LFS from RAF Wratting Common on 21st February, promptly completed their 'finishing' on Course No.12 and were posted to No. 51 Base at the end of the first week in March and from there on to join 630 Squadron.

Alan "Happy Jack" Wilson RAAF (Geoff Vigar) *Ron Bailey (Walt Scott/Patti Kellaway)*

LN "Blue" Rackley RAAF (Blue Rackley) *John Langlands. (The Brief History Archive)*

March 1944

Wednesday 1st March 1944.

A battle order was issued and 'Ops were on' for the night and Six-thirty's Lancasters were bombed up with varying loads some had 1 x 4000lb HC, 68 x 30lb and 650 x 4lb incendiaries plus 100 x 4X lb incendiaries or 1 x 5000lb NC, 1 x 4000lb HC and 1 x 1000lb NC or 4 x 2000lb HC, 1 x 1000lb NC and 1 x 500lb NC. 557 bombers were despatched to attack Stuttgart.

1st /2nd March 1944 : Night Bombing Attack on Stuttgart

Take Off: at 22:46 hours Roy Calvert took off in ND527 with a 2nd Dickie beside him.

JB546-A	F/O JB Nall	
ME650-B	F/L JCW Weller	
ND554-C	P/O FHA Watts	
JB290-D	W/O J White	
JB672-F	P/O HW Hill	
JB288-H	P/O JS Kilgour	
ND335-L	F/L KR Ames	
JA872-N	F/S AJ Perry RAAF	
ND527-O	S/L RO Calvert RNZAF	(P/O AW Wilson RAAF)
ND530-P	P/O CLE Allen	
ND561-R	F/O PJ Piggin	
ND337-S	F/O D Roberts	
ME664-T	W/C WI Deas	
JB556-Y	F/L GH Probert	

ND530 'P-Peter' (Clifford Allen) aborted when its air speed indicator froze up, they landed at 02:36 hours. Arriving in the target area virtually unscathed with the 10/10ths cloud cover also screening the bomber screen from Luftwaffe night fighters the 557 bombers attacked. 630 Squadron bombed between 02:58 and 03:16 hours from 20,000-22,000 feet using Pathfinder red/green star markers, through the dense cloud little could be seen however flak was heavy in the target area. Wing Commander Bill Deas believed that attack may have been scattered but some big fires had been seen in built up areas through occasional breaks in the cloud. Roy Calvert also commented on fires his crew had seen through breaks. Ken Ames reported a major explosion in the target area and John Nall, Joe Kilgour, Ken Ames, David Roberts, Harold Hill and 'Sam' Weller's all noted fires being visible for a long time on their return flights, the last three still seeing reflection on the clouds at 150 miles distant. Freddy Watts' crew saw a Me109 in the distance but none of the returning 630 Squadron Lancasters were involved in combats. German reports regarding the attack state that considerable damage was done in the central, western and northern districts of Stuttgart with many civic buildings destroyed or further damaged and serious damage was caused to war industries such as the Bosch works and Daimler Benz factories and the devastated central railway station was further flattened. Joe Kilgour was the last to land at 07:57 hours. The veteran crew of ND561 Failed to Return.

Lancaster III, ND561 (Codes LE – R)

Pilot	– P/O Peter John Piggin. Age 21	Killed
Flight Eng	– F/S Robert Edward Pearson. Age 22	Killed
Navigator	– F/O Rayner Francis Jowett. Age 23	Killed
Bomb Aimer	– P/O Percy Wilfred Green. Age 20	Killed
Wireless Op	– F/O William Egbert Trevor Bladen. Age 22	Killed
Mid Upper	– Sgt Peter Sigston White. Age 24	Killed
Rear Gunner	– F/O William Leopold Carver Kirkpatrick. Age 38	Killed

Born in Tanganyika on the plantation managed by his father, Piggin had spent his entire life in East Africa until enlisting in the RAF and had married just months before 630 Squadron was formed. Percy and Daisy White of Holbeck, Leeds lost their second son when Peter White was killed, his elder brother Jack also an Air Gunner, had been killed on 22nd June 1943 flying over the Netherlands with 35 Squadron. At the age of thirty-eight Flying Officer William Kirkpatrick was double the age of many aircrew and on this night he had taken the seat of Warrant Officer Lorne Todd RCAF who was Peter Piggin's regular rear gunner. The entire crew are buried at Durnbach War Cemetery in Bavaria. Research in German records reveals that on 2nd March 1944 at 03:00 and 03:15 hours two night fighters of 3rd wing/Night Fighter Group 2 (III/NJG2) recorded attacking a Lancaster over Stuttgart so based on the time and crash location it is viewed very likely that ND561 was shot down by either Hauptmann (Captain) Hoffmann or Leutnant (Lieutenant) Heinz Reuter. At East Kirkby several days followed when 'Ops were On' only to then be called off prior to take off.

The crew of 26 year old Australian Ron Clark[i] arriving during March sadly demonstrated the story of many young lads posted to squadrons at that time, they arrived direct from training, their captain completed his op as Second Dickie and on their first op as a crew they Failed To Return. John Perry's crew flew six Ops before they Failed To Return, Ken Orchiston and John Langland's crews only flew two Ops. The odds against survival were terrible. Wing Commander Carter visiting RAF East Kirkby from No 8 Group lectured the aircrew on matters related to the Pathfinder Force. Wing Commander Bill Deas managed to secure the services of a man he knew well and on Wednesday 8th March thirty-two year old Flight Lieutenant Robert Adams DFC[ii], who had flown a tour with 61 Squadron over the winter of 1942/43 arrived and took up duties as Squadron Navigation Officer replacing Leo Ehrman who had been posted missing with Wing Commander Rollinson at the end of January. Born at Jalunda in India Robert Adams was a married man with two young children.

Robert Adams (J Bentley and C Young)   *Ron Clark RAAF (National Archives of Australia)*

Friday 10th March 1944.

A battle order was issued for 16 aircraft and crews. Late in the day the order was amended to remove the 5 least experienced crews and the target was changed to Clermont-Ferrand in a special attack by 3 squadrons to be led by Wing Commander Deas. 630 Squadron aircraft were carrying standardised loads of 1 x 4000lb minol plus 7 x 1000lb MC bombs or multiple incendiaries. No. 5 Group were to carry out a moonlight raid on four factories in France which were being used by the occupying Germans on war-work. Six-thirty were detailed to lead 33 Lancasters against the Michelin works at Clermont-Ferrand.

10th/11th March 1944 : Night Bombing Attack on Clermont Ferrand
Take Off: at 19:32 hours Wing Commander Deas led the squadron from East Kirkby.

ND527-O	F/L WH Kellaway
ND685-Q	S/L RO Calvert RNZAF
ME664-T	W/C WI Deas
ND657-W	F/L D Roberts
JB556-Y	F/L GH Probert
JB546-A	P/O A Drinkall
ME650-B	F/L JCW Weller
ND554-C	P/O FHA Watts
JB290-D	W/O J White
JB672-F	P/O HW Hill
ND335-L	F/L KR Ames

The raid was planned for the early hours of a Saturday morning, attacking from around 10,000 feet in an effort to improve accuracy and avoid civilian casualties. The Lancasters of 630 Squadron bombed from 23:12 to 23:39 hours from 6,000 to 11,000 feet using the Pathfinder markers which were a little to the south of where Bill Deas wanted them. Sam Weller reported that the target area was 'plastered in cookies' and Jim White's crew commented on concentrated fires. All targets were successfully bombed and when Harold Hill landed JB672 safely at 03:03 hours all aircraft and crews were back safely. Austin Drinkall and crew transferred to Pathfinder Force (83 Squadron) after this operation, near the end of their tour they failed to return from an attack in early August 1944. After a wet and misty day on Sunday 12th March when the squadron was stood down a start was made on tidying up and then gardens began to be constructed around the crew rooms and offices on 13th.

Wednesday 15th March 1944.

Flight Lieutenant Tom Neison [iii] a 31 year old former engineer's machinist from Rutherglen in Scotland arrived to take up duties as Squadron Gunnery Leader and Commander Macdonald RN of HMS Vernon (Naval Intelligence) visited the Station Intelligence Officer and gave a lecture to aircrew.

During the day a battle order was issued for 20 aircraft and crews to fly that night. Six-thirty's Lancasters bomb loads were centred around 2 x 1000lb MC, 88 x 30lb, 950 x 4lb and 100 x 4Xlb incendiaries. 863 bombers raided Stuttgart.

15th/16th March 1944 : Night Bombing Attack on Stuttgart
Take Off: at 18:57 hours Ken Rodbourn was the first take off in ND583.

JB546-A	P/O JS Kilgour
ME650-B	F/L JCW Weller
ND554-C	P/O FHA Watts
JB290-D	W/O J White
JB672-F	P/O HW Hill
JB288-H	P/O AGG Johnson

ND655-J	F/O JB Nall
ND531-K	P/O HC Rogers
ND335-L	F/L KR Ames
ND686-M	P/O KW Orchiston RNZAF
ND527-O	F/L WH Kellaway
ND530-P	P/O LA Barnes
ND685-Q	P/O AW Wilson RAAF
ND688-R	S/L RO Calvert RNZAF
ND337-S	F/L D Roberts
ME664-T	F/S AJ Perry RAAF
ND583-V	P/O K Rodbourn
ND657-W	P/O CLE Allen
JB556-Y	F/L GH Probert
ED944-Z	P/O RW Bailey

863 bombers took off to attack Stuttgart flying into adverse winds which delayed the opening of the attack. The German fighter controller split his force of night fighters unsure of Bomber Command intentions as the main force flew directly across France almost to the Swiss frontier before turning north-east towards Stuttgart. The night fighters did meet the main force however just before the target was reached and bombers began to fall. 630 Squadron, bombing between 23:15 and 23:29 hours from 20,000 to 23,000 feet believed that the Pathfinders were late but that their markers had been quite well placed based on their bombing photos which showed the River Neckar and railway lines. Some crews encountered moderate to light defences in the target area whilst others suffered heavier flak and some reported intense fighter activity from Strasbourg and on the line of withdrawal. David Roberts crew had the unnerving experience of seeing a bomber hit the sea on the outward journey and considered the bombing may have been scattered, Cab Kellaway and Cliff Rogers noted large fires burning near the railway station and also east of the River Neckar whilst the crews of Ken Orchiston and Alan Wilson reported scattered fires.

Ron Bailey's de-brief report mentioned fighters near Dieppe on the route homeward, which they avoided. German reports show that the bombing fell in central Stuttgart and did indeed stray out through the south-western suburbs into open countryside. ND554 (Freddy Watts) was the last of the squadron to return safely to East Kirkby, two crews were missing.

Lancaster III, ND530 (Codes LE – P)

Pilot	– P/O Leonard Alfred Barnes. Age 24	Evaded
Flight Eng	– Sgt Kenneth Arthur Walker. Age 20	Evaded
Navigator	– F/O Malcolm Geisler. Age 26	Prisoner
Bomb Aimer	– Sgt Malcolm Elliott Gregg. Age 21	Prisoner
Wireless Op	– Sgt George Edmund Plowman. Age 21	Prisoner
Mid Upper	– Sgt James Henry Overholt RCAF. Age 20	Killed
Rear Gunner	– Sgt Thomas Austin Fox. Age 21	Killed

After attacking the target Len Barnes' Lancaster 'P-Peter' (ND530) was shot up by Oberleutnant Dietrich Schmidt of 8/NJG1 (8th Squadron of Night Fighter Group 1) who recorded his attack as having taken place approx 00.56 hours at 6,300 metres altitude to the West of Reims, he crippled the Lancaster. Surviving crew baled out and ND530 crashed at St.Gilles (Marne) on the west bank of the River Ardre, 24 km west of Reims, 'Freddy' Fox and Jim Overholt the gunners are buried in St-Gilles Churchyard. George Plowman a Leather worker from London was captured wounded, Malcolm Gregg, a Nottingham clerk, was wounded in his hand and captured, Malcolm Geisler a Manchester salesman was captured near Crugny also wounded. Aided by the family of French patriot Leon Coigne and hidden for weeks despite the enormous risks which they faced Len Barnes was eventually moved to Paris where he was one of the very last to escape over the

"Freddy" Fox (Fox family album)   *James Overholt RCAF (Mike Glenn)*

Pyrenees with the Comet Escape line (number 287) on 4th June 1944. They were in neutral Spain on 4th June, routinely arrested by the Spanish Police and on 23rd June he was in Gibraltar ready to fly back to the UK.

Only having recently celebrated his 24th birthday Len Barnes recalled that on their 5th op 'P-Peter' was attacked from below, the hydraulics were shot away and both turrets put out of action. During continued attacks his gunners worked their guns manually but he believed that his rear gunner had been wounded and ordered him to bale out before going into a 360mph dive to 12,000 feet to try to shake the fighter off. Realising that both starboard engines had been badly hit and were ablaze and the rudder controls badly damaged he repeated the order to his crew to bale out before attempting unsuccessfully to clear the nose escape hatch himself. After hitting the bomb sight he regained his senses tumbling through the night sky and pulled the ripcord.

Lancaster III, ND583 (Codes LE – V)

Pilot	– P/O Kenneth Rodbourn . Age 22	Killed
Flight Eng	– Sgt Richard John Harry Easter . Age 21	Killed
Navigator	– Sgt Albert Henry Wilkinson . Age 20	Killed
Bomb Aimer	– F/S Alexander McCowan Freeman RCAF. Age 24	Killed
Wireless Op	– F/S Frank James Hobbs . Age 35	Killed
Mid Upper	– F/S Leslie Hall. Age 23	Killed
Rear Gunner	– F/S Ernest John Philipson RAAF. Age 25	Killed

Hauptmann Ludwig Meister of 1/NJG4 (1st Squadron of Night Fighter Group 4) attacked ND583 at 01:30 hours, altitude 6,300 metres, west of Laon and out of control it crashed and exploded with great force at

Ken Rodbourn and crew (Phillipson family)

Besme near Bourguignon-sous-Courcy, 23 km north-west of Soissons. The entire crew were killed and after a hasty burial in shrouds by the Germans, were almost immediately reburied properly in coffins in the local churchyard by the French people. Meister was a Luftwaffe night fighter ace and this was his second victory of the night.

On 18th March following more than 3 weeks of factory repairs after damage sustained in late February, Lancaster ND580 returned to the squadron.

Saturday 18th March 1944.

A battle order was issued detailing 18 aircraft and crews for Ops that night with standard bomb load of 1 x 4000lb HC, 1,200 x 4lb and 96 x 30lb incendiaries.

18th/19th March 1944 : Night Bombing Attack on Frankfurt
Take Off: at 19:06 hours Jim White took off at the head of 630 Squadron

ND335-L	F/L KR Ames
ND686-M	P/O KW Orchiston RNZAF
ND527-O	F/S AJ Perry RAAF
ND685-Q	P/O AW Wilson RAAF
ND688-R	S/L RO Calvert RNZAF
ND337-S	F/L D Roberts
ME664-T	W/C WI Deas
ND657-W	P/O CLE Allen
JB546-A	P/O JS Kilgour
ME650-B	F/L JCW Weller
ND544-C	P/O FHA Watts
JB290-D	W/O J White
JB672-F	P/O HW Hill
JB288-H	P/O AGG Johnson

ND655-J	F/O JB Nall
ND531-K	P/O HC Rogers
JB556-Y	F/L GH Probert
ED944-Z	P/O RW Bailey

With 98 aircraft making a mine laying diversion to the Heligoland Bight waters frequented by U-boats the main force of 846 bombers sortied into Germany masked by cloud and with the Luftwaffe having already split their available fighter force in response to the diversion. Fighters did make contact shortly before the target was reached but the casualties were not as high as had been feared. Accurate Pathfinder marking led to heavy bombing of the eastern, central and western districts of Frankfurt despite poor visibility. 630 Squadron crews commented that without H2S it would have been hard to find the target in such thick cloud, they attacked between 21:59 and 22:13 hours from 19,000 to 23,000 feet despite intense flak and strong searchlight defences. Wing Commander Deas reported flak bursting as low as 16,000 feet and Cliff Rogers noted flak in box barrage form at 25,000 feet. Enemy aircraft dropping yellow fighter flares did not dissuade Harold Hill's crew as they bombed.

Extensive destruction was done at Frankfurt with the 'Volkischer Beobachter' (Nazi run newspaper) printing a complaining list of 'cultural buildings' destroyed, in short however 56 public buildings, 412 small businesses, 99 factories and thousands of houses were destroyed and a military train was hit. Aboard Alan Wilson's 'Q-Queen' the gunners, Sergeants Jim Hanna and Alastair Henderson, fought an inconclusive combat with a Fw190 night fighter.

Flying at 20,000 feet over the target at 22:03 hours the rear gunner of Ken Ames' ND335 'L-Love' sighted an Me109 approximately 600 yards distant on the starboard quarter, up. Paddy Parle immediately called for a corkscrew to starboard and opened fire with a three second burst. Strikes from his rounds were seen on the enemy fighter. Closing to 400 yards it opened fire but missed. At the same time both gunners returned fire with 3 second bursts and having been hit multiple times the Me109 caught fire and moved to break away. Both gunners continued to engage the enemy aircraft with 2 second bursts and burning fiercely a section of the engine cowling broke off as it went down in flames. The gunners had fired 900 rounds. Claim:

Alan Wilson RAAF and crew (Geoff Vigar)

Me109 destroyed. Sergeant Bud Coffey RCAF of the Langlands crew had been borrowed for the sortie, sadly he died later in the month. Their report was signed off by the new Gunnery Leader F/L Tom Neison before W/Cdr Bill Deas and Group Captain Taaffe endorsed it 'confirmed'. Clifford Allen was the last of the returning Six-thirty Lancasters to touch down at East Kirkby in the small hours of the morning.

One of 630's aircraft had Failed To Return.

Lancaster III, ND686 (Codes LE – M)

Pilot	– P/O Kenneth Watson Orchiston RNZAF. Age 23	Killed
Flight Eng	– Sgt Winston Pescod Clough. Age 19	Killed
Navigator	– F/S Derek Charles Pearse. Age 22	Killed
Bomb Aimer	– F/O Jack Norman Gill. Age 21	Killed
Wireless Op	– Sgt Jack Palmer. Age 22	Killed
Mid Upper	– Sgt Peter Dutchak RCAF. Age 28	Killed
Rear Gunner	– Sgt Alexander Murphie Kiltie. Age 19	Killed

An as-yet unidentified Kriegsmarine Flak Abteilung (Naval anti-aircraft unit) on the Belgian coastline shot ND686 down into the sea at 23:50 hours crashing 2 km west of Adinkerke to the west of Veurne. The bodies of both air gunners were recovered quickly after the crash, the remainder of the crew two days later, they were buried together on 22nd March at Koksidje (Coxyde) Military Cemetery. Jack Gill is also commemorated in St.Andrew's Church, Oxshott.

This crew represent the essence of a Bomber Command crew, Ken Orchiston and Peter Dutchak from New Zealand and Canada, the crew also included two nineteen year olds, one from Scotland, the other from the North East, a regular member of the RAF, a recently commissioned former grammar school boy from the home counties and an irrepressible Yorkshireman. Canadian Peter Dutchak was the eldest of nine children born to a family of Austrian immigrants who had arrived in Canada in 1900. Jack Gill had been a keen member of the 1st Oxshott Scout Group. Ken Orchiston was a married man with a baby son, he left Lincoln Agricultural College (Canterbury, New Zealand) to join the NZ Army Service Corps but transferred to the RNZAF for aircrew training.

Three successive nights saw the squadron advised 'Ops are on' only to later receive the 'stand down' on Sunday 19th, Monday 20th and Tuesday 21st March. On the 21st George Joblin[iv] and crew arrived. A former storeman with the Farmers' Co-Operative at Hawera George Joblin had served in the Queen Alexandra Mounted Rifles, New Zealand Army for 2 years before he volunteered for aircrew duty as a Wireless Operator/ Air Gunner but re-mustered for Pilot training which he completed in Canada under the Empire Air Training Scheme. He gained his pilot's wings and progressed through Wellington equipped 11 OTU. then Stirling equipped 1651 HCU to be 'finished at' No. 5 LFS before joining the squadron. A common progression for crews. The R.A.F.V.R. service record of Joblin's Flight Engineer, W.A 'Ken' Butcher illustrates the crew's progression through training and conversion before arriving at East Kirkby to join No. 630 Squadron.

Wednesday 22nd March 1944.

A battle order was issued on which 16 aircraft and crews were detailed. The Lancasters at East Kirkby were bombed up with various bomb loads again, such as 1 x 2000lb HC and 10 x 1000lb MC or 1 x 4000lb HC, 84 x 30lb and 1200 x 4lb and 100 x 4 x incendiaries. 816 bombers attacked Frankfurt.

Ken Orchiston RNZAF and crew at HCU (Dutchak family album)

22nd/23rd March 1944 : Night Bombing Attack on Frankfurt
Take Off: at 18:40 hours Pilot Officer Freddy Watts (ND554) was the first airborne.   JB546 'A' (Joe Kilgour) returned early with serviceability problems at 21:44 hours.

ND527-O	F/L WH Kellaway	
ND685-Q	P/O AW Wilson RAAF	
ND688-R	S/L RO Calvert RNZAF	
ND337-S	F/L D Roberts	
ME664-T	W/C WI Deas	
ND657-W	P/O CLE Allen	
JB556-Y	P/O RW Bailey	
JB546-A	P/O JS Kilgour	
ND554-C	P/O FHA Watts	
JB290-D	W/O J White	RD
JB288-H	P/O AGG Johnson	
ND655-J	F/O JB Nall	
ND531-K	P/O HC Rogers	
JB672-F	P/O PA Nash	
JA872-N	F/S AJ Perry RAAF	

The outward route took the bomber stream across the Dutch Coast north of the Ijsselmeer (Zuyder Zee) then due south to Frankfurt, a move which confused the German fighter controllers and kept their fighters away from the bombers. Flying at 20,000 feet and just 20 miles from the target at 21:27 hours Jim White's

JB290 'D-Donald' was suddenly hit by cannon and machine gun bullets from somewhere astern and below. Standing up in his rear turret Sergeant Johnny Jukes looked down and sighted a JU88 night fighter at 300 yards on their port quarter passing to starboard. In response to his instruction Jim White threw the Lancaster into a starboard corkscrew but Jukes managed to keep a bearing on the enemy fighter and got in a good four second burst forcing the Germans to break off. Frank Guy's mid-upper turret had been damaged by enemy cannon fire and with the power out he operated his turret manually to turn, engage and fire. Both gunners saw strikes on the JU88 which they reported damaged. Their Lancaster was damaged by the cannon fire and with hydraulics unserviceable were unable to release their bombs leaving Jim White and Frank Elwood to fight to keep their damaged bomber airborne. Their badly shot up Lancaster had to be despatched for repairs which would take a month! Debriefing reports record that Six-thirty's crews had bombed between 21:43 and 22:05 hours from 20,000 to 22,500 feet and they commented on the well concentrate fires centred on green markers. Winston 'Cab' Kellaway's bomb aimer Stan Pinches had a visual of the target as well as a solid H2S reading, he felt that the marking and incendiaries seemed well concentrated.

The crews of Peter Nash and John Perry reported that search lights were very active, Perry's crew saw bombers being coned over the Target Area, one was Freddy Watts' crew, coned by numerous searchlights as they bombed and were blinded by the lights until their bomb load was released and they could corkscrew to evade. Amongst the throng of bombers attacking Wing Commander Deas reported three bombers shot down and a lot of horizontal tracer fire (from night fighters) and Cliff Rogers noted the barrage of heavy flak over the target. The crews of Peter Nash, Ron Bailey, John Nall and Cliff Allen confirmed at be-brief that the glow of major fires could be seen at 100-150 miles distant as they flew home. Cliff Allen added that incendiaries could be seen lining the homeward route from the target and Wing Commander Bill Deas endorsed his point adding that the practice of jettisoning bombloads and flares between the target and the enemy coast must stop immediately. The Wilson crew were the last to land at 01:01 hours. The marking and bombing had been accurate and as the result Frankfurth suffered a heavy blow at the hands of the 816 bombers attacking. Half of the city was left without gas, water and electricity for days, all parts of the city received hits with the western districts hit most heavily. The German TENO administration report details severe damage to the industrial areas along the main road to Mainz. Amongst the list of buildings destroyed ere five important Nazi Party building and 26 less important properties to their administrative system During the day a signal was received that an 'Immediate' DFC had been awarded to Acting. Flight Lieutenant James Charles William WELLER (55014), Royal Air Force. No.630 Squadron.

'One night in March, 1944, this officer piloted an aircraft detailed to attack Stuttgart. Shortly after the take-off several instruments, including the air speed indicator, became unserviceable. Flight Lieutenant Weller continued his mission however and successfully bombed the target. Whilst over the area the oxygen supply failed. Four members of the

Stan Pinches (Beryl Raynes, nee Pinches)

Left: Pete Dutchak RCAF Right: Ken Orchiston RNZAF (Dutchak family album)

Left: George Joblin RNZAF. Right: WA "Ken" Butcher (Shirley Moulsley)

Winston "Cab" Kellaway (Patti Kellaway)   *JCW "Sam" Weller (Lynne Weller)*

INSTRUMENTS USELESS, BUT HE BOMBED TARGET

During a recent attack on Stuttgart, a bomber piloted by Acting Flight-Lieut. James Charles William Weller, R.A.F., No. 630 Squadron, had several instruments, including the air speed indicator, rendered unserviceable.

Flight-Lieut. Weller continued his mission, however, and bombed his target successfully.

While his aircraft was still over the target area, the oxygen supply failed and four of the crew, who were badly affected, had to be assisted by the flight engineer.

Then one of the engines became useless, but Flight-Lieut. Weller brought the bomber back safely.

For this exploit Weller, whose home is at Faversham, Kent, receives the D.F.C. in the latest list of R.A.F. awards.

crew were badly affected but were given assistance by the flight engineer. Later, one of the engines became useless but Flight Lieutenant Weller flew back to an airfield in this country'.

Friday 24th March 1944.

A battle order was issued detailing 15 aircraft and crews for Ops that Friday night, 6 second pilots were to carried to enable pilots newly arrived from training units to gain operational experience. This raid was the last of the series against Berlin and yet again Six-thirty's Lancasters were bombed up with 1 x 4000lb HC bomb, 80 x 30lb, 850 x 4lb, 50 x 4xlb incendiaries. 811 bombers flew against Berlin that night.

24th/25th March 1944 : Night Bombing Attack on Berlin

Take Off: at 18:29 hours Allan Johnson flying JB288 was the first airborne.

JB546-A	P/O JS Kilgour	RD
ND554-C	P/O FHA Watts	
ND531-K	P/O HC Rogers	(F/O CW Rodgers RAAF)
ND335-L	P/O PA Nash	
LL886-I	W/O J White	(Sgt T Southworth)
ED944-Z	F/O JB Nall	
JB288-H	P/O AGG Johnson	
ND527-O	F/L WH Kellaway	(F/O GR Joblin RNZAF)
ND685-Q	P/O AW Wilson RAAF	
ND688-R	S/L RO Calvert RNZAF	(F/O JO Langlands)
ND337-S	F/L D Roberts	(F/S RL Clarke RAAF)
ND788-U	F/S AJ Perry RAAF	
ND657-W	P/O CLE Allen	
JB556-Y	P/O RW Bailey	RD
ME664-T	F/L JCW Weller	(F/S LN Rackley RAAF)

Walt Walker (Ian Walker)

Six-thirty attacked between 22:29 and 22:44 hours from 20,000 to 23,000 feet sighting on red/green ground markers as the sky markers had been badly scattered by winds much stronger than had been forecast. Debriefing of the returning crews saw repeated comments that the broadcast winds had been badly out, searchlights and flak had been intense in the target area, the Nash crew dropped their bomb load to corkscrew and evade the searchlights which had coned them. Most crews heard the Pathfinder Master of Ceremonies despite German jamming. Fighter activity commenced at the Danish coast on the outward flight and continued as far as Osnabruck on the return. At 22:40 hours aboard ND685 'Q-Queen' whilst illuminated by fighter flares and the fires below Aussie Alan Wilson's rear gunner Jim Hanna sighted an Me109 on their starboard quarter down at 700 yards range. Corkscrewing to starboard as the German pilot opened fire caused the attackers cannon shells and machine gun bullets to pass below wide of the Lancaster while Hanna got in a 100 round burst before three of his four .303's jammed. The fighter was lost. No claim was made by the gunners. At 22:48 hours ND337 'S-Sugar' flown by 'Robbie' Roberts was at 21,000 feet when their rear gunner Sergeant CW 'Walter' Walker sighted an Me109 at a range of 700 yards port quarter down. Walker opened fire a three second burst and the enemy fighter turned in towards 'Sugar' leaving its original target. Roberts corkscrewed to port as the rear gunner fired another 3 second burst, this time his rounds were seen to hit the nose of the Me109. It continued to close to 400 yards and opened fire with a single cannon but the shells passed to port. Paul Christie (mid-upper) and 'Walter' Walker returned fire and further hits on the fighter were observed at 300 yards before it went into a spin and dived away off the port beam out of control. Their combat report was signed off by Gunnery Leader Tom Neison, the CO Wing Commander Deas and Station Commander, Group Captain Taaffe their final assessment being - Probably Destroyed.

Sam Weller, reported that the returning bomber stream had straggled or been blown all across the Ruhr Valley attracting very heavy flak, Joe Kilgour was coned by searchlights for 10 minutes north of the Ruhr and received flak damage sufficient that his aircraft Lancaster JB546, one of the squadron's original aircraft, was classified Category AC Damage on their return and required 2 weeks of repairs at the airfield. Yet another close call for the brave young skipper and his crew. Winston 'Cab' Kellaway reported that the established search light belt covering the south-west approaches to Berlin had been extended between Leipzig and Magdeburg and a big searchlight belt had been placed from Munster heading in a north-westerly direction. Allan Johnson was late having struggled with the winds so he bombed the south western district of Leipzig where he encountered very accurate searchlights which twice coned the Lancaster. These radar predicted flak and searchlight batteries scored several successes and it is believed that possibly 50 of the 72 bombers shot down were destroyed by flak. Various buildings in south-western Berlin were hit, 5 military establishments were badly hit including the Berlin-Lichterfelde Depot of the Leibstandarte SS Adolf Hitler, the crack SS bodyguard regiment which had been expanded to divisional strength and was forging a reputation for ruthless hard fighting. All aircraft were diverted to Spilsby on their return due to filthy weather over East Kirkby. ND554 (Freddy Watts) was the last to land at 02:30 hours.

Three 630 Squadron crews had Failed To Return.

Lancaster I, LL886 (Codes LE – I)

Pilot	– W/O James White DFM. Age 24	Killed
2nd Pilot	– Sgt Thomas Southworth. Age 21	Prisoner
Flight Eng	– Sgt Frank Elwood. Age 20	Prisoner
Navigator	– Sgt Robert James Brydon. Age 22	Prisoner
Bomb Aimer	– F/S Vincent Edward Moor. Age 21	Prisoner
Wireless Op	– Sgt Frederick Peter Settle. Age 21	Prisoner
Mid Upper	– Sgt Frank William C Guy. Age 21	Prisoner
Rear Gunner	– Sgt John Lewis A Jukes. Age 19	Prisoner

Jim White's crew Top row: Frank Elwood, Jim Rossiter, Bob Brydon; Bottom row: Frank Guy, Vince Moor, Jim White and Fred Settle (Peter Settle)

Over half way through their already busy tour Jim White's crew aboard 'I-Item' were shot down, he lies in the Reichswald Forest War Cemetery. Frank Elwood believed that his skipper remained at the controls struggling to hold the crippled bomber level to give his crew time to bale out knowing full well that he was unlikely to have time to escape himself. Jim White's crew survived in captivity. LL886 having likely been shot down by a night fighter flown by Oberleutnant Walter Riedlberger of 5/NJG5 near Krefeld at 00:42 hours. Frank Elwood later recalled the feeling that their Lancaster was being *'beaten by giant fists'* and hammered from all directions as cannon and heavy machine gun fire chopped through the fuselage and engines, fires began to engulf the engines followed by Jim White's immediate orders to his crew to bale out as their stricken bomber began to go down.

James Brydon from Newcastle on Tyne, a 22 year old Apprentice Shipbuilding Draughtsman landed by parachute near Munich and went into captivity just 2 weeks after his birthday. At interrogation Brydon was staggered at the depth of information the Germans had concerning 630 Squadron but resisted their demands for details of the Captain's. Initially held at Stalag Luft 6 he was at Stalag 357 by July 1944 remaining at Fallingbostel until 12th April 1945 when he escaped from a marching column and hid out until taken in by a group of French prisoners with plenty of food and limited freedom of movement. British tanks liberated the prisoners very shortly afterwards. Frank Elwood a former Clerk from Poulton-Le-Fylde and John Jukes a Clerk from Nottingham were captured soon after landing going straight 'into the bag' to be held at Stalag Luft 1 (Barth). On landing by parachute Frank Guy was found unconscious by the Germans and later met up with their gunners in Stalag Luft 1. Last to arrive were former GPO Sorting Clerk and Telegraphist Ed Moor from Spalding and Londoner Peter Settle a Solicitors Clerk.

Lancaster III, ND657 (Codes LE – W)

Pilot	– P/O Clifford Leslie Eldridge Allen. Age 22	Killed
Flight Eng	– P/O Kenneth Peacock. Age 21	Killed
Navigator	– F/S Anthony Stanley Leyva. Age 21	Prisoner
Bomb Aimer	– F/S William James McMeekan RCAF. Age 22	Killed
Wireless Op	– Sgt Alexander Ernest McCormick. Age 20	Killed
Mid Upper	– Sgt Leslie Raymond Ingell. RCAF. Age 21	Killed
Rear Gunner	– Sgt Roy Stuart Bourne. Age 19	Killed

Clifford Allen's Lancaster was shot down at 00:24 hours by a night fighter flown by crack ace Oberfeldwebel Rudolf Frank of 3/NJG3 when homeward bound, ND657 crashed at Altharen near Meppen. The crew were buried at Lingen (Ems) New Cemetery but later moved to Reichswald Forest War Cemetery. For the Bourne family it was a second tragedy as their eldest son 22 year old Lance Serjeant Alfred Bourne had been killed on 18th June 1942 in North Africa. Sole survivor Tony Leyva a Bank Clerk from Streatham in south-west London was captured when he landed by parachute near Meppen and saw the wreckage of

Clifford Allen (Allen family collection)   *Les Ingell RCAF (S Ingell (Canada))*

his Lanc at daybreak. He spent three months in Stalag Luft 6 (Heydekrug) and the remainder of the war in Stalag 357 at Thorn and Fallingbostel. Tony Leyva recalled that he was working on his charts when cannon shells tore through the cabin of 'W-William', the aircraft rocked violently and he believed that the bomb aimer or flight engineer opened the nose escape hatch just as their pilot collapsed over the controls sending the Lancaster into a power dive. Leyva had just grabbed his parachute and with it only partially clipped to his chest harness he fell towards the nose hatch of the bomber as it tore earthwards being thrown out into the night. His chute opened and despite being only partly secured it saved his life. Speaking post-war Unteroffizier (Junior Sergeant) Hans-Georg Schierholz remembered this night when he was flying as an aircrew radar operator aboard the Messerschmitt 110 of night fighter ace Oberfeldwebel (Warrant Officer) Robert Frank (I/NJG 3) Ist Wing of Night Fighter Group 3. It was their second sortie of the night as they had missed the bombers on their first mission. Operating with the ground radar stations of Box 'Leghorn' they were vectored onto the returning bomber stream.

'It was a good box-fighting situation. There was good guidance from the ground. They gave us three perfect contacts and we shot all three of them down with 'Schräge Musik'. Not one of them saw us, I think they felt they were already safe on their way home. I recorded the positions in my log book, they were all Lancasters'.

At 6,400 metres Robert Frank and Hans-Georg Schierholz had shot down a Lancaster of 460 Squadron, Six-thirty's own ND657 (the Allen crew) at 00:39 hours and the first Lancaster to be lost by 635 Squadron. Frank had shot down his 39th bomber.

Lancaster III, ND788 (Codes LE – U)

Pilot	– F/S Arthur John Perry RAAF. Age 24	Prisoner
Flight Eng	– Sgt James Dunnet Morrison. Age 28	Evaded
Navigator	– F/S Geoffrey Hather. Age 20	Prisoner
Bomb Aimer	– F/S James Duncomb . Age	Prisoner
Wireless Op	– Sgt John Edmund Naisbitt. Age 23	Prisoner
Mid Upper	– Sgt Montague George Colin Todd. Age 23	Prisoner
Rear Gunner	– Sgt Francis Joseph Giblin. Age 35	Prisoner

Officially recorded as hit by flak from Münster at 23,000 feet whilst heading for home the crew of 'U-Uncle' baled out. John Perry, a former Farmer from Merredin, West Australia, held the Lancaster steady whilst his crew baled out and parachuted to safety himself. In his own words –

'Hit by flak in starboard inner engine which caught fire and later set wing alight. When it became apparent that the fire was gaining hold on the wing and burning near the petrol tanks I gave the order to bail out, these were acknowledged by the whole crew, nobody was injured and all except the navigator left. The Nav

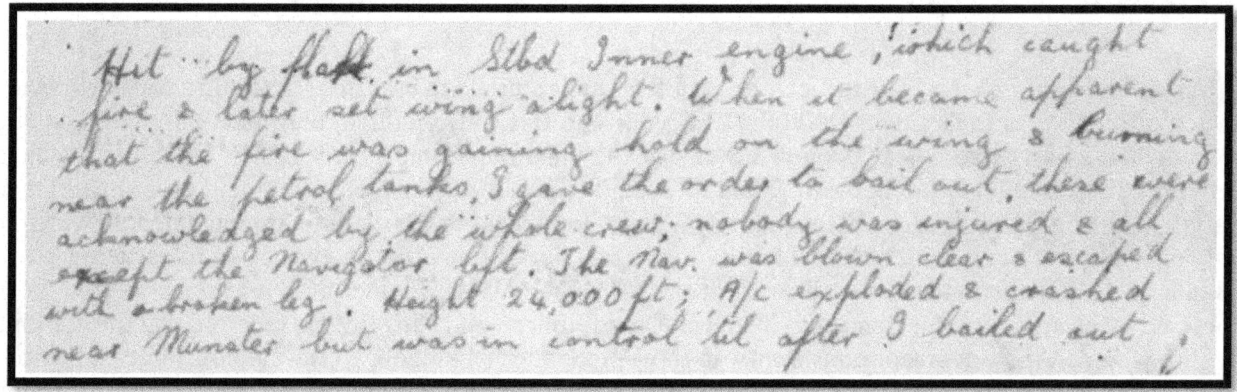

The fate of ND788 and crew (John Perry)

was blown clear and escaped with a broken leg. Height 24,000 feet, aircraft exploded and crashed near Munster'.

Hauptmann Werner Husemann a night fighter pilot made a claim at the same time and in the same area and may have also attacked the Lancaster. Geoff Hather was taken prisoner wounded and treated in the hospital at Ibbenbüren for the next 7 weeks following which he was interrogated and presented with a complete listing of his crew, their trades, full details of the aircraft and its serial numbers. He settled in Canada post-war but returned to the UK in 1949 with his wife and young son. Frank Giblin a farm worker from Hull was quickly captured near Munster and went 'into the bag', after hiding out for 24 hours John Naisbitt a Durham lad was also caught and would spend the remainder of the war at Stalag Lift I (Barth), Colin Todd a timber measurer and estimator from East Grinstead was picked up immediately and ended up at Stalag 357 (Thorn and Fallingbostel).

The crew of twenty-one year old Don Mallinson [v] were posted from 1651 HCU to 3 LFS on 5th March and completed their Lancaster training on No.14 Course being posted on 23rd March to No.51 Base and then onwards to join 630 Squadron arriving about the same time as crews from 5 LFS captained by 22 year old Bridgewater man Bob Hooper[vi] from 1661 HCU, Alfred 'Bob' Jackson[vii] and the Australian skipper Wade Rodgers[viii] from 17 OTU. and 1654 HCU.

Sunday 26th March 1944.
A battle order was issued detailing 14 aircraft and crews for Ops, the 630 Squadron Lancasters were each bombed up with 1 x 4,000lb HC bomb and 1,500 x 4lb and 80 x 30lb incendiaries. Bomber Command despatched 705 aircraft in this attack.

26th/27th March 1944 : Night Bombing Attack on Essen
Take Off: at 19:16 hours Allan Johnson (JB288) was the first of the 14 to take off.

ME650-B	F/L JCW Weller
ND554-C	P/O FHA Watts
JB672-F	P/O PA Nash
JB288-H	P/O AGG Johnson
ND655-J	F/O JB Nall
ND531-K	P/O HC Rogers
JA872-N	P/O JS Kilgour
ND335-L	F/S LN Rackley RAAF
ND527-O	F/L WH Kellaway
ND685-Q	P/O AW Wilson RAAF
ND688-R	S/L RO Calvert RNZAF
ND337-S	F/L D Roberts
ED944-Z	F/O JO Langlands
ME664-T	P/O RW Bailey

Ron Bailey's crew aborted due to technical problems and returned to base at 21:50 hours. The unexpected switch of target area to the industrial Ruhr Valley left the Luftwaffe fighter controllers wrong footed and their night fighters were poorly deployed to attack the incoming bomber stream. The squadron attacked between 22:00 and 22:09 hours from 19,000 to 22,250 feet in 10/10ths cloud, bombing on red and green Target Indicators placed by Oboe Mosquitoes. With no fighters over Essen, light ground defences were the only opposition to begin with but the intensity of the flak opposition grew and was soon in barrage form at 18,000 to 22,000 feet, much of it directed at the Wanganui flares. Fighter activity seems to have been confined to the area between Bonn and Charleroi. David Roberts and Cliff Rogers reported that the marking by PFF was extremely good and consistently in same place and Joe Kilgour's crew noted 2 large explosions in the target area which lasted 2 minutes. Squadron Leader Roy Calvert in ND688 was the last to land at 01:17 hours. In a highly successful raid 48 industrial buildings were seriously damaged and approaching

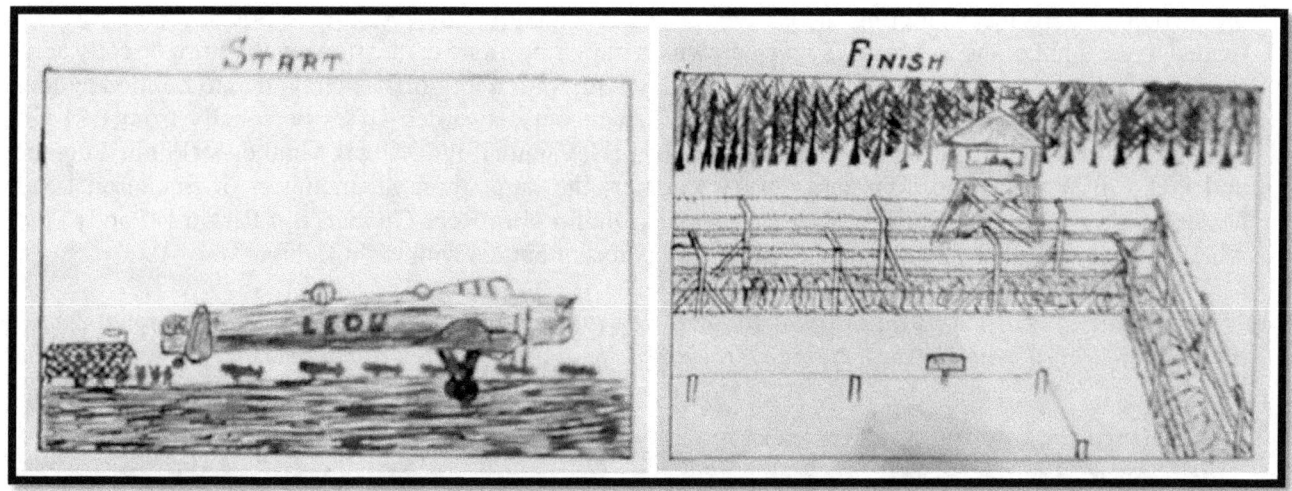

Monty Todd sketched his thoughts later (Dave Finn)

Don Mallinson (Richard and Barry Mallinson)

Bob Hooper (B Jadot)

2,000 homes destroyed. 57 Squadron's CO Wing Commander HWH Fisher DFC[ix] who was preparing to hand over command of the squadron to Wing Commander HY Humphreys[x] decided to remind his crews that despite the normal lack of 'bull' enjoyed by aircrew they were still in the RAF and temporarily instituted a series of morning parades. Delighted by the entertainment offered 'on the other side' (of the station) where the veterans of the 'Senior Squadron' still occasionally teasingly referred to the 'junior squadron' as 'C Flight', the crews of 630 Squadron wasted no time in returning the compliment and re-naming their elder sister '57 ITW' (Initial Training Wing). Marching along the runway on one occasion they were seen as a prime target by a Six-thirty crew carrying out a flight test. The Lancaster roared across the airfield at zero feet scattering the parade. Soon after landing however the 57 Squadron aircrew were treated to the sight of the Lancaster's seven crewmen marching alone up the runway to return directly across the frontage of the applauding 57 crews. On Tuesday 28th March four officers travelled to London to attend an investiture at Buckingham Palace to receive their recently awarded DFCs personally from HM King George VI, they were likely P/O Alexander Gibson (Navigator), P/O Albert Matthews (Flight Engineer) and P/O Jim Worthington (Wireless Op/Air Gunner) the latter three all members of Squadron Leader Malcolm Crocker's crew and possibly Ken Ames' Dublin born Rear Gunner, Sgt Richard 'Paddy' Parle who had been awarded an 'Immediate' DFM for his recent battles with night fighters.

'This airman has participated in very many sorties in the role of rear gunner. He has shot down 2 enemy aircraft, the last of which he destroyed on a recent sortie against Frankfurt. His successes are a fine tribute to

"Bob" Jackson (Jack Porter) Wade Rodgers RAAF (Patti Kellaway)

Thursday 30th March 1944.

A battle order was issued with 16 aircraft and crews detailed. At the briefing Wing Commander Bill Deas named five crews who would be able to go on leave the following day, this was contrary to his normal practice and some of the superstitious amongst the airmen considered it to be a bad move on his part. There was apparently a distinct hush. Of the five crews named, two would abort their mission that night, two would be shot down and only one would complete the sorties without a problem.

Aircraft were bombed up with variations on two main loads, either 1 x 4000lb minol, 900 x 4lb and 68 x 30lb incendiaries or 9 x 1000lb MC and 1 x 500lb MC bombs. The Op would normally have been 'scrubbed' due to the clear moonlight conditions but the Bomber Command Met team had forecast a protective cloud screen on the outward route during the period that the moon would be up. A Met flight Mosquito reported that the cloud was not in place as expected but the Op was still not scrubbed, the night fighters would have excellent vision to hunt the 795 bombers on the outward leg of their flight. 'The Nuremburg Raid' would incur disastrous losses for Bomber Command and forever be identified as an example of a 'hairy do'. Nuremburg was the stage of the enormous highly choreographed pre-war Nazi Party rallies and a city of huge significance to Nazis.

30th/31st March 1944 : Night Bombing Attack on Nuremburg

Take Off: at 21:46 hours both ME650 (Freddy Watts) and ND531 (Cliff Rogers) are as having taken off, three Second Dickies were carried that night.

ND789-I	P/O JS Kilgour	
ME650-B	P/O FHA Watts	
JB672-F	P/O HW Hill	
ND580-G	P/O PA Nash	
JB288-H	P/O AGG Johnson	
ND655-J	F/O JB Nall	
ND531-K	P/O HC Rogers	
ND335-L	F/L KR Ames	(P/O AT Jackson)
ED944-Z	F/S LN Rackley RAAF	
ND527-O	F/L WH Kellaway	(P/O RC Hooper)
ND685-Q	P/O AW Wilson RAAF	
ND688-R	S/L RO Calvert RNZAF	
ND337-S	F/S RL Clark RAAF	
ME664-T	F/O JO Langlands	
ND793-V	F/L GH Probert	(Sgt DR Mallinson)
JB556-Y	P/O RW Bailey	

'Blue' Rackley brought ED944 back at 01:08 hours with oxygen supply problems and at 01:41 hours ND655 (John Nall) landed after their intercom had died. From just before the Belgian border fighters were a menace on the moonlit outward flight and 82 bombers were shot down, a minimum of 574 airmen were aboard them. Combats raged for over an hour. Badly forecast winds blew 120 or more aircraft 50 miles north of Nuremburg where they bombed Schweinfurt in error. Arriving in the target area the aircrew found thick cloud and a fierce crosswind and they turned in to attack still harried by fighters. Six-thirty bombed between 01:05 and 01:22 hours from between 19,000 and 22,000 feet on the centre of Pathfinder flares and 6 Wanganui red/yellow star markers. At debriefing crews commented that PFF had been late marking and said that bombing had possibly been scattered. They were proven to be correct and little of worth had been hit in Nuremburg that night for an overall loss of 95 bombers. Geoff Probert reported that vis had been very clear and they had seen fighters attacking bombers from underneath using the upward firing cannon installed in the centre of Luftwaffe heavy night fighters. At 00:47 hours flying at 21,200 feet Flight Sergeant Derek Todd RCAF the bomb aimer aboard Peter Nash's ND580 'G – George' sighted two ME109's at 900 yards range on the starboard beam, one had its navigation lights on. The fighters instantly swung around onto the Lancasters starboard quarter and the one without lights opened fire just as the 'Monica' early warning system began to earn its keep. The tracer passed by above the bomber as it began to corkscrew to starboard and the rear gunner Flight Sergeant Ed Goehring RCAF opened fire. Sergeant Geoff Jennings in the mid-upper turret found that his turret was out of action, electrical solenoids had failed at the critical moment. The fighters broke off the attack and were not seen again. No claim was made by the gunners.

The Lancasters flown by Ken Ames and Ron Bailey were the last of Six-thirty's to land, both being shown as down safely at 06:17 hours. Many squadrons were badly hit that night, 101 Squadron lost 6 aircraft in combat and 1 crashed. Sadly Six-thirty lost three crews again.

Lancaster III, ND337 (Codes LE – S)

Pilot	– P/O Ronald Leslie Clark RAAF. Age 26	Killed
Flight Eng	– Sgt William Donnan Jones. Age	Killed
Navigator	– F/S Kelvin Carlyle Green RAAF. Age 26	Killed
Bomb Aimer	– Sgt Roy I Smith . Age 33	Prisoner
Wireless Op	– Sgt Norman Worboys . Age 22	Killed
Mid Upper	– Sgt Thomas Hughes. Age	Killed
Rear Gunner	– Sgt David Victor Menell. Age 21	Killed

The 'Clark crew' flying their maiden Op in ND337 'S-Sugar' were aboard the first of 630 Squadron's Lancasters to fall, possibly the 19th aircraft lost that night when a night fighter shot it down at Bickenbach, 4km south-west of Emmelshausen. Their bomb aimer survived to be taken prisoner but the six remaining lads died and are buried at Rheinberg War Cemetery in Germany. Kelvin Green was a pre-war regular airman with the RAAF. Roy Smith landed unhurt by parachute about 30km south west of Coblenz where he evaded capture until 4th April. After initial interrogation at Dulag Luft the former Highway Surveyors Clerk was held at Stalag Luft VI (Heydekrug) and then Stalag 357 at Thorn and Fallingbostel. German records suggest that ND337 was intercepted at about 20,000 feet by either Unteroffizier (Junior Sergeant) Walter Rohlfing or Leutnant (Pilot Officer) Achim Woeste (both flying over Koblenz area with the 3rd Wing of Night Fighter Group 3). Rear Gunner David Menell was a Jewish lad who had chosen to volunteer for aircrew duties and to fly over Nazi Germany.

As the bomber stream closed on the target area a night fighter claimed what was possibly the 62nd bomber to fall, it was ME664 of 630 Squadron flown by John Langlands crew.

Lancaster I, ME664 (Codes LE – T)

Pilot	– F/O John Ogilvie Langlands . Age 30	Prisoner
Flight Eng	– Sgt Norman Goring. Age 19	Prisoner
Navigator	– F/O Robert Martin Guthrie . Age 21	Prisoner
Bomb Aimer	– P/O Harold Bernard Bryans. Age 21	Prisoner
Wireless Op	– Sgt George William Jeffery. Age	Killed
Mid Upper	– F/S Alan George Drake . Age 28	Killed
Rear Gunner	– Sgt Harry Morley 'Bud' Coffey RCAF. Age 21	Killed

Attacked at 20,000 feet the Lancaster exploded over Ruhla (Saettelstadt near Burla in some German records), 14 km west of Gotha at 00:34 hours possibly shot up by Oberfeldwebel Herbert Altner of 8/NJG5. George Jeffery, Alan Drake and 'Bud' Coffey were buried on 4th April by the Germans at Eisenach Cemetery. Occupied in 1945 by the Red Army access to the area was restricted immediately post-war but in October 1950 the three airmen were recovered and on 1st November were re-buried in the Berlin War Cemetery. Flight Sergeant Alan Drake was a pre-war regular airman in the RAF with approaching 10 years' service under his belt. John Langlands was a 30 year old Edinburgh police constable, he survived captivity to return to a long and distinguished police career. Landing heavily near Erfurt Harold Bryans, a former Laboratory Assistant from Leicester who had recently celebrated his 21st birthday, found his left flying boot was missing and hobbled into captivity at the Luftwaffe Wireless School. After 4 days he was transferred to Dulag Luft near Frankfurt where he spent 4 days in solitary confinement refusing to answer questions. The interrogators gave up and on 15th April he was transferred to Stalag Luft I at Barth joining Bob Guthrie from Reading who had landed by parachute 10-15 miles south west of Erfurt, they remained in captivity at Barth until liberated on 1st May 1945. The flight engineer Norman Goring, a Clerk from Hull, was captured near Eisenach when he landed and spent the last 13 months of the war at Stalag Luft 6 and Stalag 357. On 6th April 1945 the Germans marched their prisoners out from Stalag 357 (Fallingbostel)

John Langlands crew (back, left to right) Alan Drake, George 'Jeff' Jeffery, Norman 'Herman' Goring, Harry 'Bud' Coffey and (front left to right) Robert 'Bob' Guthrie, John 'Jock' Langlands, Harold 'Benny' Bryans (The Brief History Archive)

beginning a forced march. Goring and several others escaped on 14th and were liberated by 7th Armoured Division near Soltau. Shortly afterwards and reportedly the 77th bomber to be shot down, JB288 (Allan Johnson and crew on their 16th Op) were caught by another night fighter, German records indicate that this was likely Feldwebel (Flight Sergeant) Ernest Reitmeyer of 1/NJG5 (1st Squadron/ Night Fighter Group 5) at 01:15 hours north-west of Nuremburg.

Lancaster III, JB288 (Codes LE – H)

Pilot	– P/O Allan George Garth Johnson . Age 23	Killed
Flight Eng	– Sgt Geoffrey Ernest Watts. Age 22	Prisoner
Navigator	– F/S Ernest Arthur Farnell. Age 28	Killed
Bomb Aimer	– F/O John Philip Headlam. Age 23	Prisoner
Wireless Op	– Sgt Arthur Henry McGill. Age 23	Killed
Mid Upper	– Sgt William Pearson. Age	Prisoner
Rear Gunner	– Sgt William Edward France . Age 23	Killed

JB288 crashed at Altendorf on the east side of the Donau-Regnitz Canal, 4 km north-west of Eggolsheim. The dead are now buried at Durnbach War Cemetery. Allan Johnson was from Nassau, Bahamas. Bill Pearson was later repatriated aboard the 'Arundel Castle' to Liverpool on 6th February 1945. John Headlam a Middlesbrough Chemical worker was captured on landing by parachute near Hollendorf and taken to Stalag XIIID for a month before being moved to Stalag Luft 3 (Sagan) via Dulag Luft.

Johnny Johnson and crew (Steve Alcock)

Allan Johnson's flight engineer Geoff Watts a 22 year old regular RAF airman from Leamington Spa was taken prisoner slightly wounded after landing by parachute in Germany and placed temporarily in a POW camp housing French and Yugoslav prisoners, which had been hit during the bombing, he later said: *'without exception they saluted me with a formality and dignity they could not have bettered for royalty. It was my first indication of the respect in which they held the RAF. I suppose we were their only allies visibly attacking the common enemy and represented some hope for their final release'.* (Sergeant GE Watts) Geoff Watts was held at Stalag XIIID (Nurnberg) for three weeks before routine interrogation at Dulag Luft and being transferred to Stalag Luft III (Sagan). Ex-policeman Flight Sergeant George Whitby had flown all of the Johnson crew's 19 Ops with them since the start of their tour but on this particular night he'd been unable to fly. They failed to return so he remained at East Kirkby as a spare bod flying a number of Ops filling in when required by crew's who needed a bomb aimer. Eventually completing his tour in January 1945 he was recommended for a Distinguished Flying Cross. Post-war he settled with his wife in Canada and had a long and distinguished career with the Vancouver Police Department.

The A-Flight crew of Harold Hill lost their navigator, 20 year old Spalding lad Maurice Stancer[xi], after the Nuremburg raid, he was posted to 44 Squadron where he would later be awarded the DFM. From this point onwards the Flight Commander, Squadron Leader Edward Butler DFC and Bar flew as their navigator. The crew of young Sergeants captained by an equally young Pilot Officer were staggered to find that their regular Nav was now to be the flight commander, he was remembered as *'very straight and correct, a top notch Nav and enormously keen operational type, but as he was our CO and we were all Sergeants there was always a gulf there'.*

At the end of the Monthly Summary in the Squadron Records Appendix Wing Commander Bill Deas signed off a series of bald statistics:

649.35 hours flown in 109 sorties by 111 aircraft.
80 x 4000lb HC bombs dropped,

42 x 2000lb MC bombs dropped,
149 x 1000lb MC bombs dropped,
15 x 500lb MC bombs dropped,
76,850 x 4lb incendiaries dropped,
7034 x 30lb incendiaries dropped.
10 aircraft lost, 16 officers and 55 men.
German sources advise 3 squadron personnel are POW and 7 have been killed.

Between the last days of January and the end of March, sixteen aircraft and crews had been lost in just 8 weeks or so, the entire official strength of Six-thirty was 16 aircraft plus 4 reserves. Replacements had been posted-in and some of them had now been lost. The Bomber Boys' spirit in the face of such staggering losses was to get up and get back into the fray, they would admit decades later that inside they were shaken by the loss of so many fellow airmen, but every one of them would add that, *'it wouldn't do to show that it bothered you'*, and *'you said that it was shoddy luck and a damn bad show'* and *'then you got on with it'*.

April 1944

Doug Hawker RNZAF (Doug Hawker)

April saw 630 Squadron's long suffering Adjutant, F/L Frank Cheetham posted to HeadquartersNo.5 Group and replaced temporarily by Flying Officer (Acting F/L) Marcus Radcliffe[i] a 38 year old London businessman who had grown up in Dean's Yard, Westminster Abbey where his father was the Solicitor, Chapter Clerk and Receiver to the Dean and Chapter of Westminster Abbey. Flight Lieutenant Percy Alderson the Station Equipment Officer was forced to retire from the RAF on reaching the upper age limit at the end of March and his replacement, Flight Lieutenant Townsend arrived from HQ 93 Group during April. Also replaced was RC Chaplain Freyne by Squadron Leader Rev H Deerin[ii] from RAF Cosford.

Air Vice Marshal Cochrane was readying his No. 5 Group for a transformation at this vital stage leading up to the Invasion of Europe. He wished to dispense with the services of the Pathfinder Force (No. 8 Group) and conduct his own marking for his own squadrons. Several recent experiments had encouraged the No. 5 Group officers given a good degree of success. On April 3rd, 27 year old New Zealander Doug Hawker[iii] and crew arrived, they had completed conversion from Stirlings at 1661 HCU and then 'finished' at No. 5 Lancaster Finishing School at Syerston ready to join 'B' Flight under fellow Kiwi Squadron Leader Roy Calvert.

Freddy Watts and crew had completed 11 operations with Six-thirty before they transferred to 617 Squadron on 5th April. Flying with 617 Squadron they were to take part in all three 'Tirpitz' attacks. With little guidance on transport however they simply flew over to Woodhall Spa in what they regarded as their own Lancaster, ND554 'C for Cleo' which was superbly decorated on the nose as 'Conquering Cleo' and continued to fly with 617 as 'N-Nan Bar' until the aircraft had to be returned to Six-thirty in mid-June (when it was re-coded as 'A-Able').

Wednesday 5th April 1944.
An attack on the aircraft factory at Toulouse being used by the Germans for war work was to be pivotal in the 'marking question'. Six-thirty were mainly bombed up with 1 x 4000lb HC bomb and 10 x 500lb and 36 x 30lb incendiaries. On the same day Freddy Watts and crew transferred to 617 Squadron.

5th/6th April 1944 : Night Bombing Attack on Toulouse
Take Off: at 19:48 hours Ken Ames was first to take off. He had been appointed second deputy leader for the attack and therefore was carrying the normal load but with 36 x 4.5 Recce flares in place of incendiaries, just in case additional marking was required.

ME650-B	F/L KR Ames
JB672-F	P/O HW Hill
ND685-Q	P/O JS Kilgour
ND655-J	F/O JB Nall
ND531-K	P/O HC Rogers

ND688-R   S/L RO Calvert RNZAF
ND527-O   F/L WH Kellaway
ND793-V   F/L GH Probert
ND797-W   F/O GR Joblin

Wing Commander Leonard Cheshire DSO DFC who was OC of No. 5 Group's 617 Squadron made the first low level Mosquito marking flight of the war. In the face of stiff flak Cheshire did not drop his markers until his third pass over the factory building to ensure accuracy. Two Lancasters of 617 Squadron then supplemented the marking by their 'Wing Co' effectively rubber stamping the accuracy for the main force.

The target was well defended but 617 Squadron's Mosquito marker was so fast that it wasn't hit, the marking by the follow up Lancasters was extremely well placed and the bombing by the 144 Lancasters of No. 5 Group was a near perfect concentration despite one Lancaster exploding in mid-air over the target. The Lancasters of 630 Squadron bombed from 00:19 to 00:38 hours from 6,500 to 8,900 feet Geoff Probert's de-briefing makes it clear that the visibility was very clear and there was no doubt that the buildings being attacked were hit repeatedly. John Nall reported concentrated fires burning in the target area and Joe Kilgour's crew commented that the target area was a mass of flames. Many crews noted that German radio interference caused problems on the R/T. All crews landed at Morton-in-Marsh except Ken Ames at Barford St. John and Geoff Probert at Silverstone. ND793 (Geoff Probert) was last of 630 Squadron to land at 04:26 hours.

Freddie Watts and crew with "Conquering Cleo" (Geoff Copeman/FHA Watts)

This attack was enough evidence for the AOC and within hours of the raid Sir Arthur Harris had approved Cochrane's formal request for No. 5 Group to be able to operate independently and doing its own marking. Two of No. 8 Group's Pathfinder Squadrons which had been originally drawn from No. 5 Group (83 and 97 Squadron) and whose crews were still largely drawn from Cochrane's group were returned to him along with a Mosquito squadron (627 Squadron).

De Havilland Mosquito (RAF official)

No.5 Group Order of Battle

617 Squadron   (special duties squadron, Lancasters and Mosquitoes)
627 Squadron   (Mosquito Pathfinder squadron)

Lancaster equipped Pathfinder squadrons.
83 Squadron   97 Squadron

Lancaster heavy bomber squadrons.
9 Squadron   106 Squadron
44 Squadron   207 Squadron
49 Squadron   463 Squadron
50 Squadron   467 Squadron
57 Squadron   619 Squadron
61 Squadron   630 Squadron

On 7th April Lancaster JB546 was returned to the squadron's operational strength after two weeks of repairs.

Sunday 9th April 1944.
Next, in a new type of attack for 630 Squadron, ten aircraft and crews were detailed for mine laying in the Baltic. More than just disrupting normal sea traffic in that part of the Baltic, the aim was to make dangerous a transit area used regularly by U-boats. Mines were carried by the Lancasters, the mission was described as 'Gardening' as were all mine-laying operations and it was in 'Tangerine area' (Danzig Bay).Whilst loading the mines into the bombers one fell from the bomb bay of a Lancaster onto the back of a member of the ground crew knocking him to the ground and injuring his leg and feet. With a dislocated right knee and compound fracture of the right foot he was evacuated to RAF Hospital Rauceby. Ken Ames

was again appointed Deputy leader and Six-thirty's crews used H2S, Fishpond, API and Mandrel to ensure a successful op.

9th/10th April 1944 : Night Minelaying in Danzig Bay
Take Off: at 21:17 hours 'Cab' Kellaway was first to be airborne.

ME650-B	F/L JCW Weller
JB672-F	P/O HW Hill
ND789-I	P/O JS Kilgour
ND655-J	F/O JB Nall
ND335-L	F/L KR Ames
ND580-G	P/O HC Rogers
ND688-R	S/L RO Calvert RNZAF
ND527-O	F/L WH Kellaway
ND793-V	F/L GH Probert
ND797-W	P/O GR Joblin RNZAF

Suffering with engine trouble Geoff Probert brought ND793 'V-Victor' back to East Kirkby at 02:16 hours. In his de-brief Ken Ames confirmed that the datum point had been located and that he'd 'made a steady run over the garden' and then reported heavy flak from 5 coastal guns between Pilau and Palmickan supplemented by several ships. 'Sam' Weller added that his Lancaster had been attacked by a flak ship off Danish coast. George Joblin and others reported the datum point located in clear moonlight and mined successfully fortunately not drawing flak and after mining Cliff Rogers crew saw a fighter over Denmark but were not attacked. At 07:25 hours John Nall set ND655 down at East Kirkby, the last to land.

Winston "Cab" Kellaway (Patti Kellaway)   *Jack Geoghegan RAAF(June Roberts)*

The squadron learned that JT 'Jack' Geoghegan RAAF who had saved the life of crewmate 'Chuck' Bottriell several weeks earlier had died of the effects of his high altitude bravery. Sadly no suitable bravery medal was awarded despite the obvious possibility of a BEM for gallantry. Screened from further Ops 'Cab' Kellaway was posted from 630 Squadron to instruct at No. 5 Lancaster Finishing School. Strongly recommended for a Bar to his DSO by Wing Commander Bill Deas, the award followed in due course (London Gazette 9th May 1944). On 19th May 'Cab' was instructing Flight Sergeant JHG South who was taking off from Syerston in Lancaster DV368 just as the aircraft was about to lift off its port tyre blew-out causing the undercarriage to collapse and the aircraft to crash. Everybody was fortunate to walk away from the crash unhurt. The Station MO and his team rushed to RAF Spilsby during the day on 10th April to assist with casualties after a bomb exploded. Flight Lieutenant Fred Spencer (Engineer Leader) commenced a series of lectures for his Flight Engineers including time spent in both the hangars and briefing room.

Monday 10th April 1944.

Furthering the new operational role of No. 5 Group, 180 of its Lancasters, including 630 Squadron, were to attack railway marshalling yards. The standard bomb load for Six-thirty's Lancasters was 12 x 1000lb long delay (6 hours) bombs and 1 x 1000lb bomb.

10th/11th April 1944 : Night Bombing Attack on Tours

Take Off: at 22:02 hours Wing Commander Bill Deas led the squadron into the air, probably aboard the newly arrived LL972.

ND335-L	F/L KR Ames	
ND688-R	F/L JCW Weller	RD
ND655-J	F/O JB Nall	
ME717-E	F/O CW Rodgers	
JB672-F	P/O HW Hill	
ND789-I	P/O JS Kilgour	
ND580-G	P/O AT Jackson	
ND531-K	P/O HC Rogers	
ND797-W	P/O PA Nash	
ND685-Q	F/S LN Rackley RAAF	
JA872-N	P/O RC Hooper	
ND527-O	F/L WH Kellaway	
ME737-S	F/L D Roberts	
Query-T	W/C WI Deas	
ND793-V	F/L GH Probert	
JB556-Y	P/O RW Bailey	
ED944-Z	Sgt DR Mallinson	

Flying 'T-Tare' Wing Commander Deas marked the target with 6 hooded flares and 4 green TIs accompanied by a 4,000lb minol. David Roberts backed him up with 6 more hooded flares. After attacking between 01:38 and 01:56 hours from 5,250 to 8,000 feet the experiences of the crews were (Sam Weller) 3 large fires burning in the railway and 'one large explosion after we left the target area', John Nall and Joe Kilgour both spoke of encountering light flak over the target. Peter Nash and Don Mallinson reported a concentrated attack with large explosions and Ron Bailey added that his crew had witnessed a number of explosions, one very large which rocked their aircraft and as they left the target a huge explosion which made earth ripples. Winston 'Cab' Kellaway summed it up reporting large fires and a burning petrol dump.

At 01:05 hours flying at 5,000 feet Pat Gillespie the Australian rear gunner of ND531 'K- Kitty' (Cliff Rogers) sighted an Me109 at 700 yards before it had a chance to attack. Calling an instruction to corkscrew to port he fired a burst of 160 rounds at 600 yards and the fighter broke off its attack and disappeared. Sergeant Bob Marshall in the mid-upper turret was not in position to fire. No claim was made by the gunners. The raid was a great success with the railway yards seriously damaged. They would be less able to support German defences and reinforcements when the Liberation of France commenced. Bob Hooper landed JA872 at 04:51 hours being the last of Six-thirty home safely. The crew of Wilf Watt[iv], a former member of staff at the Government Printing Office in Wellington New Zealand, joined 630 Squadron on Tuesday 11th April. They had progressed via the usual route from Wellingtons at OTU. (in this case 11 OTU.) then on to Stirlings at 1661 HCU, Lancasters at 5 LFS and finally to the squadron.

Left – Right: Charles Martin (Becky Martin); Wilf Watt RNZAF (Doug Hawker); Teddy Champness RAAF (Heather Champness)

Flight Lieutenant Charles Martin MM[viii] also arrived at RAF East Kirkby to assume duties as Squadron Adjutant, a former infantryman decorated for bravery whilst a Lance Corporal with 11th Battalion, Rifle Brigade in the Great War (London Gazette 2 November 1917). Heavily involved in motor racing at Brooklands between the wars he had been commissioned into the RAF (General Duties Branch) as an Air Gunner very soon after the outbreak of the Second World War and flew a tour with 214 Squadron as a Wellington rear gunner until injuries received in July 1940 prevented further flying. Transferring to the Admin and Special Duties Branch he served as Adjutant to Guy Gibson at 106 Squadron and RAF Coningsby.

New Zealander Joe Lennon[v] and his crew arrived from 1657 HCU, reuniting their captain with his friend Doug Hawker. At about the same time two Australian captains arrived with their crews Vivian Brown[vi] from 1651 HCU and 'Teddy' Champness[vii] from 1654 HCU. Teddy had worked for St. Mary's Municipal Council, Nepean/NSW from the age of 16 until enlisting in the RAAF aged 17, he trained at RAAF Mallala, then in Canada and the UK where they crewed up. 'Buster' Brown was from Corparoo, Queensland.

Tuesday 11th April 1944.
630 Squadron were detailed to participate in a small attack by a force from several Groups on Aachen. The Lancasters were each armed with 12 x 1000lb bombs and 200 x 4lb incendiaries.

11th/12th April 1944 :Night Bombing Attack on Aachen
Take Off: at 20:29 hours JB556 (Ron Bailey) was the first airborne.

ND797-W	P/O PA Nash	RD
ME717-E	F/S LN Rackley RAAF	
ME737-S	F/L D Roberts	(P/O DE Hawker RNZAF)
JB556-Y	P/O RW Bailey	
ND685-Q	P/O AW Wilson RAAF	
ME789-I	F/O CW Rodgers RAAF	

David Roberts crew witnessed an aircraft shot down over the sea and whilst running in over the target Ron Bailey reported some heavy explosions. The squadron's crews attacked between 22:44 and 22:48 hours from 17,000 to 18,250 feet. In his de-brief report 'Blue' Rackley commented on intense fighter activity on the homeward flight. Flying at 20,000 feet at 23:02 hours soon after bombing Peter Nash's ND797 'W-William' was shot up and badly damaged by cannon fire incoming from port quarter down from an unseen night fighter, he made a violent corkscrew to port as their rear gunner Flight Sergeant Ed Goehring RCAF returned fire (130 rounds) into the blackness where he suspected the enemy aircraft to be, his night vision momentarily destroyed by the cannon flashes. The mid-upper gunner Sergeant Geoff Jennings was unsighted and unable to assist. The Lancaster made it home with serious cannon fire damage to its elevators, flaps, the port inner engine and port radiator which required 17 days repairs. No claim was made of damage to the enemy aircraft. Pete Nash was the last to land in his damaged aircraft at 00:59 hours. The raid was accurate and caused serious damage and widespread fires in the centre and south-western part of Aachen. A communications hub and several of the Ground Defences, Polizei and Air Raid Control posts were hit leaving the Germans unable to coordinate their reaction and the Police HQ was hit. Serious damage was caused to electricity supplied and railway and road communications. Twenty-two year old Salford man Eugene Mitchell[ix] and crew joined Six-thirty having trained at 26 OTU. and 1653 HCU, their wireless operator Walt Scott was delighted to be posted to East Kirkby which was close to his home.

Geoff Burt (mid upper) with Eugene Mitchell (pilot) (Patti Kellaway)

Tuesday 18th April 1944.
The Bomber Command campaign continued against lines of communications and routes which would be useful for re-supply and reinforcement after the invasion. No. 5 Group were detailed to mount a raid by 202 Lancasters, four of the group's own Mosquito markers and three Oboe Mosquitoes from No. 8 Group were assigned marking duties. All of Six-thirty's Lancasters were each bombed-up with 13 x 1000lb MC bombs.

18th/19th April 1944 : Night Bombing Attack on Juvisy
Take Off: at 20:37 hours ND688 (Bob Hooper) was the first airborne.

ND527-O	P/O DE Hawker RNZAF	
ND685-Q	P/O AW Wilson RAAF	
ME737-S	F/L D Roberts	
ND688-R	P/O RC Hooper	
ME729-T	Sgt DR Mallinson	
Unknown	P/O RW Bailey	
ND793-V	F/L GH Probert	(F/S JW Lennon RNZAF)
ME650-B	F/L JCW Weller	
ME739-D	F/O CW Rodgers RAAF	
ME717-E	F/S LN Rackley RAAF	
JB672-F	P/O HW Hill	
ND580-G	P/O PA Nash	
ND789-I	P/O JS Kilgour	
ND655-J	F/O JB Nall	
ND531-K	P/O HC Rogers	
ND335-L	F/L KR Ames	
JA872-N	P/O AT Jackson	

They arrived to find 3/10ths cloud over the target, the marking was good and the squadron's crews attacked between 23:29 and 23:46 hours from 8,050 to 11.500 feet. Most crews reported a good concentration bombs and little opposition although a couple attacked in the face of flak. JA872 'N-Nan' flown by Bob Jackson was late to take off at 21:22 hours but still made a successful attack. In the proximity of three searchlights at 23:57 hours flying at 15,000 feet Sergeant Ron 'Shortie' Adams in the mid-upper turret of Doug Hawker's ND527 'O-Oboe' spotted a single engined fighter, port quarter up, at 600 yards range, it had its wing tip lights lit. He instructed a corkscrew and as the Lancaster began its evasive action 'Shortie' and the rear gunner Sergeant John 'Dusty' Miller opened fire before the enemy pilot had the chance to commence his attack. The enemy was lost and not seen again. No claim was made by the gunners.

No. 5 Group HQ rated the raid as completely successful with the marshalling yards badly damaged. All of the 630 Squadron aircraft returned safely, Don Mallinson and crew the last to land at 02:02 hours.

Thursday 20th April 1944.
The raid on La Chapelle railway yards north of Paris was the first major test of No. 5 Group's new system. AVM Cochrane employed not only 617 Squadron but all three of his transferred former PFF squadrons to mark and make an initial bombing run in an attack by 247 Lancasters of No. 5 Group and 22 Mosquitoes of No's 5 and 8 Group. The bombing force was split into two parts with a one hour interval between. The two attacking forces targeted different sectors of the railway yards. Six-thirty's Lancasters were each armed with 13 x 1000lb MC bombs.

Juvisy Railway yards before and after the attack (Geoff Copeman)

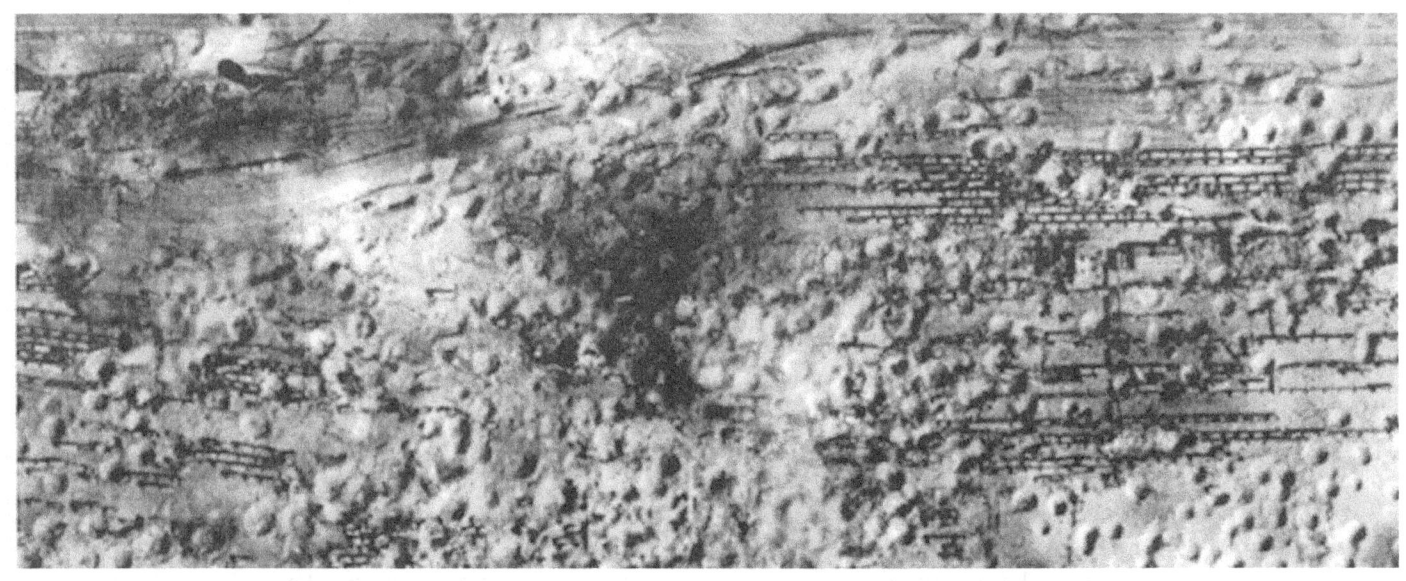

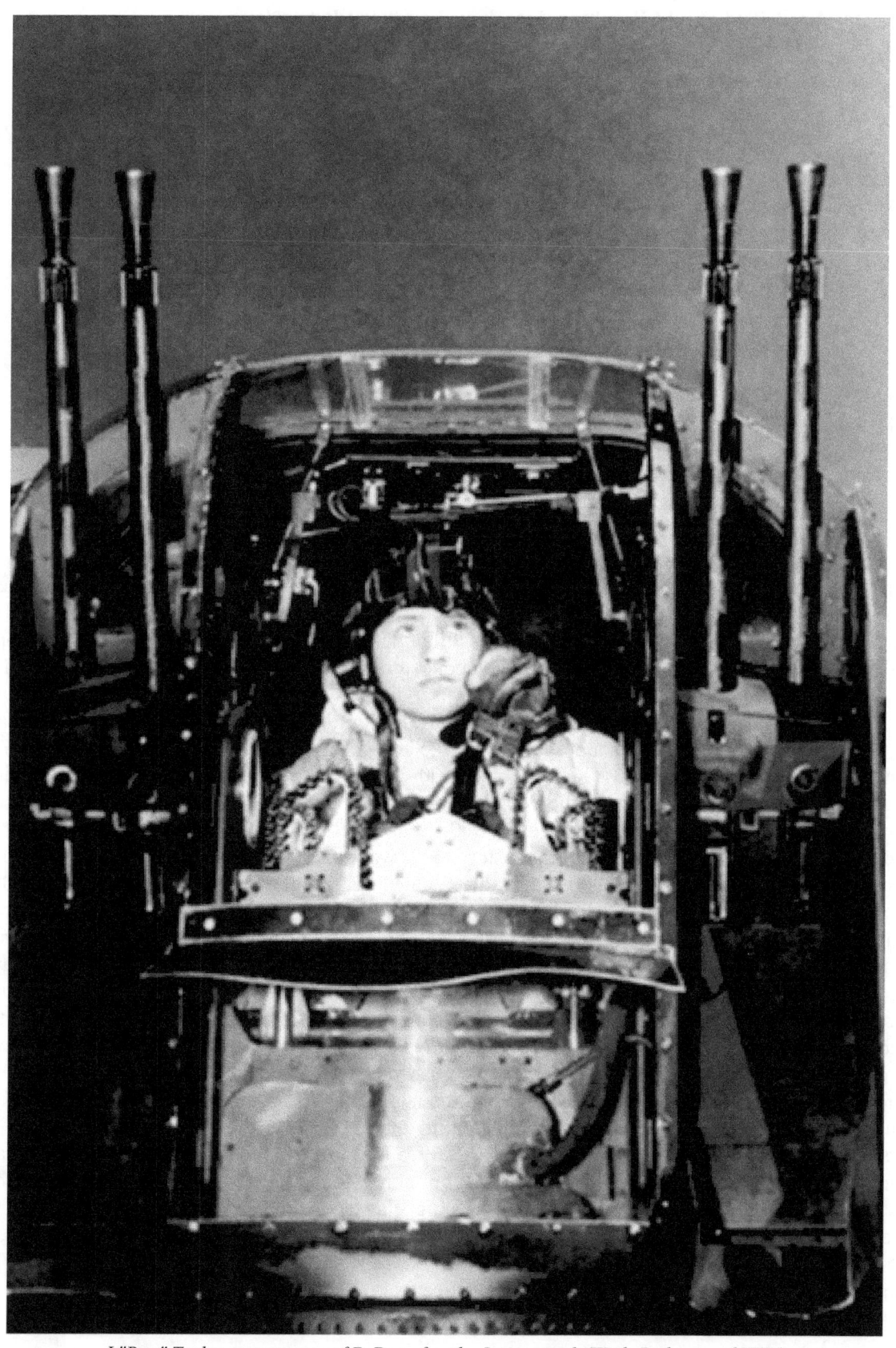
J "Bert" Taylor, rear gunner of D-Dog after the Juvisy attack (Wade Rodgers and IWM)

20th/21st April 1944 : Night Bombing Attack on La Chapelle (Paris)
Take Off: at 21:50 hours ME739 (Bob Jackson) was the first airborne.

ME650-B	F/L JCW Weller
ME739-D	P/O AT Jackson
ME717-E	F/S LN Rackley RAAF
JB672-F	P/O HW Hill
ND580-G	P/O PA Nash
ND789-I	P/O JS Kilgour
ND655-J	F/O JB Nall
ND335-L	F/O GR Joblin RNZAF
ND531-K	F/S JW Lennon RNZAF
JA872-N	P/O RC Hooper
ND527-O	F/O DE Hawker RNZAF
ND685-Q	P/O AW Wilson RAAF
ND688-R	S/L RO Calvert RNZAF
ME737-S	F/L D Roberts
ME729-T	Sgt DR Mallinson
ND793-V	F/L GH Probert
JB556-Y	P/O RW Bailey

Sam Weller had to bring ME650 'B-Baker' home early when its inter-com system failed, he landed back at East Kirkby at 23:24 hours. At de-briefing the reports record that George Joblin arrived early and circled until the marking was in place to ensure a successful attack. The crews of Roy Calvert, Bob Hooper and 'Bob' Jackson believed that there had been a good concentration of bombing on the target and noted a large explosion and Johnny Nall commented that there was a direct hit on an oil or petrol store. This must have been the very large explosion reported by Joe Kilgour during his run-up to bomb and by Peter Nash just after they had left the target. It was a busy night for the crew of David 'Robbie' Roberts flying ME737 'S-Sugar'. On track for the target at 00:36 hours at 10,000 feet Paul Christie in the mid-upper turret sighted a single engined fighter passing from starboard to port directly astern. Calling a warning both gunners opened fire at 600 yards range, Sergeant Walter Walker in the rear turret fired 160 rounds and Sergeant Christie 40 rounds. No results were seen and the course for target was maintained. On their return flight over the Channel at 01:24 hours flying at 14,000 feet Walter Walker sighted an ME109 port quarter, up, at 600 yards range. Just as the Lancaster began a corkscrew to port the German pilot fired a long burst of cannon and machine gun fire which missed and both Lancaster gunners simultaneously opened fire, Walker firing 400 rounds and Christie 320 rounds. A number of strikes were observed on the enemy fighter and a claim was entered for 'damaged'. 'Blue' Rackley's was the last of the Six-thirty crews to land at 03:29 hours. The bombing was assessed as 'extremely accurate and concentrated'. The Operations Record Book for 630 Squadron does not mention the crew of Doug Hawker as participating in this attack however the recommendation for his DFC, his logbook and the Squadron Ops Record held at the RAF Museum, Hendon confirm that they flew that night and according to the latter attacked at 00:29 hours from 10,400 feet on a heading of 045°, successfully returning with a bombing photo.

In accordance with Comber Command letter BC/S.29757/5/Org. dated 22nd April 1944 No. 55 Base was formed with RAF Station East Kirkby as base station taking control of RAF Spilsby (207 Squadron) and RAF Strubby (280 Squadron, Coastal Command, flying Warwicks), effective from 15th April 1944. Group Captain Taaffe OBE assumed temporary command with Wing Commander RN Stidolph DFC formerly CO of 61 Squadron as his Base Operations Officer. In early May Wing Commander JB McGinn MBE[x] would be posted from 1654 HCU as Base Engineering Officer.

Saturday 22nd April 1944.

Next followed an attack on a major German target, it was the first time that the No. 5 Group low level marking technique had been tried on a heavily defended target and although the marking was unquestionably accurate, the raid was not successful as a thick layer of cloud masked the target indicators and communications failures hampered direction of the bombing. All 630 Squadron Lancasters were bombed-up with 1 x 2000lb HC and 12 x 500lb 'J type' 30lb incendiaries.

22nd/23rd April 1944 : Night Bombing Attack on Brunswick

Take Of: at 22:59 hours ND531 (Joe Lennon) was the first airborne. Second Dickies flew aboard two aircraft this night.

ME739-D	P/O AT Jackson	
ME717-E	F/S LN Rackley RAAF	
JB672-F	P/O HW Hill	
ND789-I	P/O JS Kilgour	
ND655-J	F/O JB Nall	(P/O EF Champness RAAF)
ND335-L	F/O GR Joblin RNZAF	
ND531-K	F/S JW Lennon RNZAF	
JA872-N	P/O RC Hooper	
ND527-O	P/O DE Hawker RNZAF	
ND685-Q	P/O AW Wilson RAAF	
ND688-R	S/L RO Calvert RNZAF	(P/O WA Watt RNZAF) RD
ME737-S	F/L D Roberts	
ME729-T	Sgt DR Mallinson	
ND793-V	F/L GH Probert	
JB556-Y	P/O RW Bailey	

The squadron attacked between 01:56 and 02:15 hours from 17,000 to 21,800 feet. On his return 'Robbie' Roberts reported good, concentrated bombing and moderate fires in the TA, stating that the new PIB incendiaries give yellow instead of white light and considerably more smoke. It was noted by many crews that flak over the target stopped during their attack whilst the night fighters hunted.

Roy Calvert's crew in ND688 'R-Robert' were attacked just before they bombed at 01:34 hours. Suddenly at 19,000 feet there was incoming cannon fire from an unseen fighter, Calvert corkscrewed off to starboard as shells tore through his starboard wing. His gunners were unable to spot the fighter which did not press home its attack. The Lancaster required three weeks of repairs at east Kirkby before it was operational again. Sixteen minutes later at 21,500 feet Doug Hawker's crew in ND527 'O' were saved by the outstanding night vision of their rear gunner John 'Dusty' Miller. While experiencing moderate heavy flak he sighted a JU88 on the starboard quarter at 800 yards range, instructed a corkscrew to port and both he and Ron 'Shortie' Adams in the mid-upper turret opened fire before the night-fighter was in position to start its attack. No claim was made by the gunners.

ME729 (Don Mallinson) was the last to land back at East Kirkby at 05:41 hours. As the result of poor visibility and faulty communications between the various Bomber Controllers the raid was not successful and damage to Brunswick was not extensive although the centre of the city was repeatedly hit. The crews of 'Sam' Weller and Peter Nash were on the original Battle Order for this attack but instructions were cancelled and re-issued for them to join a minelaying operation.

Sunday 23rd April 1944.

Bomber Command mounted a 114 aircraft minelaying operation in five areas of the Baltic Sea and Six-thirty were detailed to provide 2 Lancasters to 'plant' in an area code named 'Geranium Bay'.

23rd/24th April 1944 : Night Minelaying off Swinemünde in the Baltic Sea

Take Off: at 21:08 hours Peter Nash was the first of the two bombers to take off and he was also the last to land at 04:17 hours.

ME650-B	F/L JCW Weller
ND789-I	P/O PA Nash

The aircraft made their run down the 'Geranium Bay' and laid mines (Gardening) in the allotted positions, ground defences were reportedly negligible but some fighter activity was seen over Denmark.

Monday 24th April 1944.

In a second attack on a major German target the No. 5 Group technique proved successful, Munich was the birthplace of Nazism and its importance to the Nazis can't be over-rated. 630 Squadron's Lancasters were bombed-up with varying loads, some carried 6 x 500lb Type J incendiaries and 36 x 30 lb incendiaries, others had 18,000 x 4lb incendiaries or 6 x 500lb J type and 136 x 30lb incendiaries, whilst others 1 x 4000lb HC and 132 x 30lb incendiaries.

24th/25th April 1944 : Night Bombing Attack on Munich

Take Off: at 20:40 hours ME739 (Don Mallinson) was the first squadron aircraft in the sky, behind him John Nall had a 2nd Dickie aboard.

JB546-A	P/O EF Champness RAAF	
ME717-E	F/S LN Rackley RAAF	
JB672-F	P/O HW Hill	
ND789-I	P/O JS Kilgour	
ND655-J	F/O JB Nall	(F/S VW Brown RAAF)
JA872-N	P/O RC Hooper	RD
ND527-O	P/O DE Hawker RNZAF	
ME729-T	S/L RO Calvert RNZAF	
ME737-S	F/L D Roberts	
ND793-V	F/L GH Probert	
JB556-Y	P/O RW Bailey	
ND335-L	F/O GR Joblin RNZAF	
ND531-K	F/S JW Lennon RNZAF	
ME739-D	Sgt DR Mallinson	
ME650-B	F/L JCW Weller	
ND685-Q	P/O AW Wilson RAAF	

234 Lancasters and 16 Mosquitoes of No. 5 Group supplemented by 10 Lancasters of No. 1 Group attacked. The low level marking by the Mosquitoes was accurate despite determined ground defences and the main force followed in the face of intense and accurate flak. The squadron's crews attacked between 01:50 and 01:59 hours from 15,500 to 19,250 feet. Alan Wilson and 'Teddy' Champness commented on heavy flak in the target area and Ted's crew saw several bombers coned by searchlights. Veteran Geoff Probert rated the attack the most successful he'd ever seen with the town appearing to be on fire from end to end and 'Sam' Weller supported that stating that the bombing concentration had been excellent, his crew had seen fighters over the target.

Blue Rackley's crashed Lancaster (Blue Rackley and Australians At War Film Archive)

Attacked by two night fighters at 00:15 hours Bob Hooper's JA872 'N' was also hit by flak and badly damaged on its run-up at 17,000 feet. Sergeant Fred Nicholls in the rear turret shouted a warning of a fighter starboard quarter down at 600 yards before he was wounded in the face by splinters from the incoming cannon and machine gun fire. Bob Hooper corkscrewed to starboard as 19 year old Danny Synnot in the mid-upper turret fired a 100 round burst at the second enemy aircraft which broke off its attack and disappeared. Shot up all down the starboard side, the hydraulics powering both Mid Upper and Rear turrets shot away and the rear gunner badly wounded, his turret doors shattered, Hooper managed to evade the remaining fighter and the crew maintained their calm continuing to bomb the target. He managed to get JA872 home and landed on the emergency strip at Thorney where Fred Nicholls was treated and with a damaged eye sent off to hospital. Bob Hooper was awarded an immediate DFC.

At 01:23 hours 'Blue' Rackley's ME717 'E-Edward' was caught by a master searchlight and quickly coned by 25 to 30 more searchlights being continually hit by flak and probably also a night fighter as he manoeuvred violently for 9 minutes to try to evade the blinding lights. Escaping the lights with the intercom dead, port outer engine stopped, engine controls shot up, starboard outer propeller running away and refusing to feather until the engine finally caught fire at 01:50 hours. Rackley's crew had jettisoned their bomb load at 01:35 over the city at 12,000 feet. With only their inner engines working the crew made for Switzerland hoping to avoid going down in Germany but managed to get the engine fire under control. Calculating their fuel load and distances to safety Rackley set course for Corsica. A landing on two engines was bravely attempted at a USAAF airfield with metal landing surface at Borgo in Corsica but ME717 crashed and swung around its rear turret throwing the gunner from his turret. Sadly 21 year old rear gunner Flight Sergeant Maxwell Dunbar RAAF of Dubbo, New South Wales died 30 minutes later just as the US medical team arrived.

Lancaster III, ME717 (Codes LE – E)

Pilot	– F/S Lionel Norman (Blue) Rackley. RAAF	unhurt
Flight Eng	– Sgt Stanley Jones	unhurt
Navigator	– F/O Ian Stuart Gow	unhurt
Bomb Aimer	– F/S Douglas Stewart Morgan. RAAF	unhurt
Wireless Op	– Sgt Joseph (Jock) Watt	unhurt
Mid Upper	– F/S John David (Jack) Jones	unhurt
Rear Gunner	– F/S Maxwell Dunbar RAAF	killed

Stan Jones and Blue Rackley RAAF (Blue Rackley)

Maxwell Dunbar was buried in Biguglia War Cemetery on Corsica on 26th April in the presence of his crew who were fortunate to walk away from the wrecked Lancaster unhurt. Unsurprisingly Blue Rackley's Lancaster ME717 was assessed Category E Damaged and struck off charge. At 01:52 hours, flying at 15,000 feet Johnny Nall's ND655 'J-Jig' was experiencing numerous search lights and both light and heavy calibre flak when their rear gunner Sgt Charles Winter sighted a FW190 on the port quarter at 800 yards range and called for a corkscrew to port as he opened fire. His burst was limited to 200 rounds before stoppages but he still managed to register hits on the enemy fighter. Sergeant Harold Callon RCAF (mid-upper) was unsighted and unable to fire. A claim was not allowed due to lack of witnesses. On their flight home Joe Lennon's crew could still see Munich burning 150 miles away and Roy Calvert's gunners reported the evidence of fires still at 200 miles. ND655 (John Nall) was the last to touch down at 07:34 hours.

Lancaster III, JB556 (Codes LE – Y)

Pilot	– P/O Ronald Walter Bailey. Age 22	unhurt
Flight Eng	– Sgt John Mellor Allwright. Age 23	injured
Navigator	– F/S Charles Henry Richardson, Age 22	unhurt
Bomb Aimer	– Sgt James Mitchell Henderson. Age 35	unhurt
Wireless Op	– Sgt Arthur John Cable. Age 22	unhurt
Mid Upper	– Sgt James Lindsay. Age 22	unhurt
Rear Gunner	– Sgt Martin Ernest Murton. Age 22	unhurt

Less than a minute after taking off in JB556, Ron Bailey's port inner engine caught fire preventing him from gaining height, he attempted a circuit hoping to come in to land but the port outer engine then cut out and he made what was considered to be a very fine crash landing on the edge of the aerodrome. The Lancaster immediately caught fire but an efficient crash party subdued the flames quickly whilst the crew were rescued by Group Captain Taaffe (Station Commander), Squadron Leader H D Elliott (Station Medical Officer) and Flight Lieutenant Tom Neison (630 Squadron Gunnery Leader). The crew were practically unhurt except for the flight engineer who suffered a fracture dislocation of his right ankle, the captain Ron Bailey had his nose skinned, but they survived to fly another day although Sergeant Lindsay was treated for shock and concussion after the rescue crew had had a prolonged battle to free him from his turret. The record states that they took off at 20:55 and crashed at 20:58 hours. Squadron Leader Alan Flowerdew[xi] the new Station Flying Control Officer arrived at East Kirkby on 26th April from RAF Leicester East.

Wednesday 26th April 1944.

Schweinfurt was a major centre of war industry in Nazi Germany and a vital producer of the ball bearings required by every engine and gun mounting in the German forces. No. 5 Group despatched 206 Lancasters and 11 Mosquitoes supported by 9 Lancasters of No. 1 Group. Some 630 Squadron aircraft were armed with 1 x 4,000lb HC and 136 x 30lb incendiaries, others carried a payload of 1,860 x 4lb incendiaries.

26th/27th April 1944 : Night Bombing Attack on Schweinfurt

Take Off: at 21:13 hours ND335 took off at the head of Six-thirty but had to abort its mission shortly afterwards when his crew found their inter-com unserviceable.

JB546-A	P/O EF Champness RAAF	
ME650-B	F/L JCW Weller	
ND580-G	P/O PA Nash	RD
ND789-I	P/O JS Kilgour	
ND655-J	F/O JB Nall	
ND335-L	F/S VW Brown RAAF	
JB672-F	F/O GR Joblin RNZAF	
ND531-K	F/S JW Lennon RNZAF	
ND527-O	P/O DE Hawker RNZAF	
ND685-Q	P/O AW Wilson RAAF	
ME737-S	F/L D Roberts	
ND793-V	F/L GH Probert	
ND949-Z	S/L RO Calvert RNZAF	
ME729-T	Sgt DR Mallinson	
ME739-D	P/O WA Watt RNZAF	

ND531 'K-Kitty' (Joe Lennon) had to return early when the mid-upper turret was found to be unserviceable. Virtually every crew repeated Kiwi Doug Hawker's de-brief comments on the intense fighter activity and incessant attacks from the moment they crossed the French coast on the outward flight, John Nall's crew noted 20 bombers shot down before even reaching the target. David 'Robbie' Roberts and Geoff Probert both reported the unusually heavy fighter activity. Finding the conditions clear over the target apart from a drifting haze and smoke the attack started late due to unexpectedly strong head winds, 630 Squadron attacked between 02:20 and 02:42 hours from 14,000 to 19,600 feet. Young New Zealander Wilf Watt's crew saw aircraft after aircraft caught by search lights as they attacked and then moved away from the target. On track at 02:10 hours flying at 15,000 feet aboard Peter Nash's ND580 'G' Sergeant Roly Locke in the rear turret sighted a twin engined night fighter at 400 yards range below and to starboard. Shouting an instruction for a corkscrew to starboard he opened fire with a 160 round burst. The night fighter broke off his preparation to attack and disappeared as mid upper Lenny Page turned from his search of the port side. The fighter was not seen again. Their Lanc suffered flak damage. The raid on Schweinfurt was a failure as the marking by the 627 Squadron Mosquitoes was not accurate on this occasion and the Lancaster markers were late due to the head winds. Aussie 'Teddy' Champness (JB546) was the last to land at 06:40 hours. It was apparent that the experienced crew of Joe Kilgour were missing.

Inset Bob Middleton. Back row l to r: Davison, Jenkins, Doram, White, Front Dougan, Kilgour (Dougan family)

Lancaster III, ND789 (Codes LE – I)

Pilot	– P/O Joseph Seddon Kilgour. Age 26	Killed
Flight Eng	– Sgt Robert Middleton. Age 20	Killed
Navigator	– F/S Eric Colston Doram. Age 22	Killed
Bomb Aimer	– Sgt John Leslie Davison. Age 31	Killed
Wireless Op	– Sgt Stephen Nelson Dougan. Age 23	Killed
Mid Upper	– Sgt Melvyn White. Age 26	Killed
Rear Gunner	– Sgt Wallace Henry Jenkins. Age 19	Killed

Shot down by a night fighter and crashed at Mühlhausen. ND789 was possibly shot down by Leutnant (Pilot Officer) Otto Keller of 9/NJG 5 (9th Squadron of Night Fighter Group 5), his report stated that at 01:47 hours he attacked a Lancaster flying at 6000 metres altitude east of Pforzheim in night fighter quadrant AS 6. Originally buried by the Germans near the crash site Joe Kilgour and his crew were later moved to Durnbach War Cemetery.

Approaching his second wedding anniversary Joe Kilgour left a young wife in Prescott, Lancashire, Melvyn White from Bedwellty in Monmouthshire had married just before war broke out and left a widow and three year old son.

Saturday 29th April 1944.

The Michelin tyres factory at Clermont-Ferrand was to be the target of a No. 5 Group raid by 54 Lancasters and 5 Mosquito markers. Each of Six-thirty's Lancasters were bombed up with 1 x 4000lb HC and 216 x 30lb incendiaries.

29th/30th April 1944 : Night Bombing Attack on Clermont-Ferrand
Take Off: at 22:09 hours Geoff Probert in ND793 was the first to take off.

JB546-A	P/O EF Champness RAAF
ME739-D	F/L JB Nall
JB672-F	P/O HW Hill
ND580-G	P/O PA Nash
ND335-L	F/S VW Brown RAAF
ME650-B	F/L JCW Weller
ND527-O	P/O WA Watt RNZAF
ME737-S	F/L D Roberts
ND685-Q	P/O AW Wilson RAAF
ND793-V	F/L GH Probert
ND949-Z	S/L RO Calvert RNZAF
LM537-X	F/O GR Joblin RNZAF

The inter-com aboard ND685 failed and Alan Wilson had to turn for home before attacking. All crews attacked successfully between 01:30 and 01:40 hours from 6,300 to 8,800 feet in relatively clear visibility and without opposition. Teddy Champness's crew reported at debrief that the target area was thoroughly saturated with bombs.

On their return flight Sam Weller's ME650 'B' was attacked at 03:28 hours by a FW190 at 9,000 feet above the English Channel. Sighted at 900 yards range as it commenced a diving attack by the mid upper, who that night was the Squadron Gunnery Leader Tom Neison, Sam Weller made a corkscrew to port as the running battle began. Tom Neison fired a three second burst as the fighter closed, Flying Officer Andy Kuzma RCAF the bomb aimer got in an 80 round burst from his nose turret and Sergeant Howell Jones in the rear turret fired 160 rounds. As the fighter made to attack a second time Neison hit it with a second three second burst which resulted in it exploding and falling disintegrating into the Channel followed by a burst from the nose turret. Witnessed by the entire crew the claim 'Destroyed' was accepted. Acting Flight Lieutenant Thomas NEISON (138890), Royal Air Force Volunteer Reserve, No. 630 Squadron was awarded the Distinguished Flying Cross.

'In April 1944, this officer was the mid-upper gunner of an aircraft which attacked an industrial plant at Clermont Ferrand. Soon after crossing the enemy coast, on the return flight, Flight Lieutenant Neison sighted an enemy fighter coming in to the attack. In the ensuing fight, Flight Lieutenant Neison defended his aircraft with much skill and finally struck the enemy aircraft with a well-placed burst of fire causing it to explode in the air. This officer has completed a large number of sorties and has proved himself to be a keen and confident gunner. His determination and fine fighting spirit have set an excellent example'.

JB672 (Harold Hill) was the last of Six-thirty's Lancasters to land at East Kirkby at 05:36 hours. The post-attack photo reconnaissance proved that the factory had been accurately hit. For David 'Robbie' Roberts and his crew the Op was the last of their tour, they had flown 31 and were 'screened'. It was also a defining moment for 630 Squadron because the Roberts crew were the first to join the squadron from training as a 'sprog crew' and actually complete their tour. Many crews had joined from training and been lost, others had transferred to 83, 97 and 617 Squadrons in the intervening months but since its formation none had completed a tour of Ops all flown with 630. Robbie Roberts had been promoted to Flight Lieutenant and was one of the squadron's senior pilots unusually however none of his crew had been commissioned, recommendations for awards were put in by Wing Commander Bill Deas and as expected a well-earned DFC was awarded in June to Roberts but surprisingly it was not until August that DFMs were gazetted for his navigator and bomb aimer, Flight Sergeants Allan Jeffrey and George Davies.

David 'Robbie' Roberts and crew were interviewed by BBC Correspondent Richard North. Imperial War Museum

Andy Kuzma RCAF and JCW "Sam" Weller (Patti Kellaway)

May 1944

Brian Lindsay RAAF (Brian Lindsay)   *Howard Smith RCAF (H W Smith (Canada))*

Replacement crews arrived under 21 year old former farmer Brian Lindsay[i] from King King, Cooran, Queensland and 22 year old Canadian Howard Smith[ii] from Abbotsford, British Columbia. The first crew who were transferred from 1660 CU would complete almost a dozen ops before transferring to No.97 Squadron Pathfinder Force their pilot subsequently earning an Immediate DFC for skill and gallantry in a daylight attack which resulted in ditching at sea, the other would sadly Fail To Return.

Monday 1st May 1944.
The first of the attacks made in May 1944 was a No. 5 Group attack by 46 Lancasters and 4 Mosquitoes on the aircraft repair factory at Tours which was working for the Luftwaffe. All of Six-thirty's Lancasters were bombed up with 2 x 1000lb MC (025) and 11 x 1000lb MC bombs Fused No.37 Mk.V pistol for this attack.

1st/2nd May 1944 : Night Bombing Attack on Tours
Take Off: at 22:02 hours Alan Wilson in ND685 was first airborne.

JB546-A	P/O EF Champness RAAF
ME650-B	F/L JCW Weller
ME739-D	F/O CW Rodgers RAAF
JB672-F	F/O HW Hill
ND580-G	P/O PA Nash
ND531-K	P/O HC Rogers
ND335-L	F/S VW Brown RAAF
ND685-Q	P/O AW Wilson RAAF
ME737-S	P/O WA Watt RNZAF
ME729-U	F/O GR Joblin RNZAF
ND793-V	F/L GH Probert
ND949-Z	F/O RW Bailey

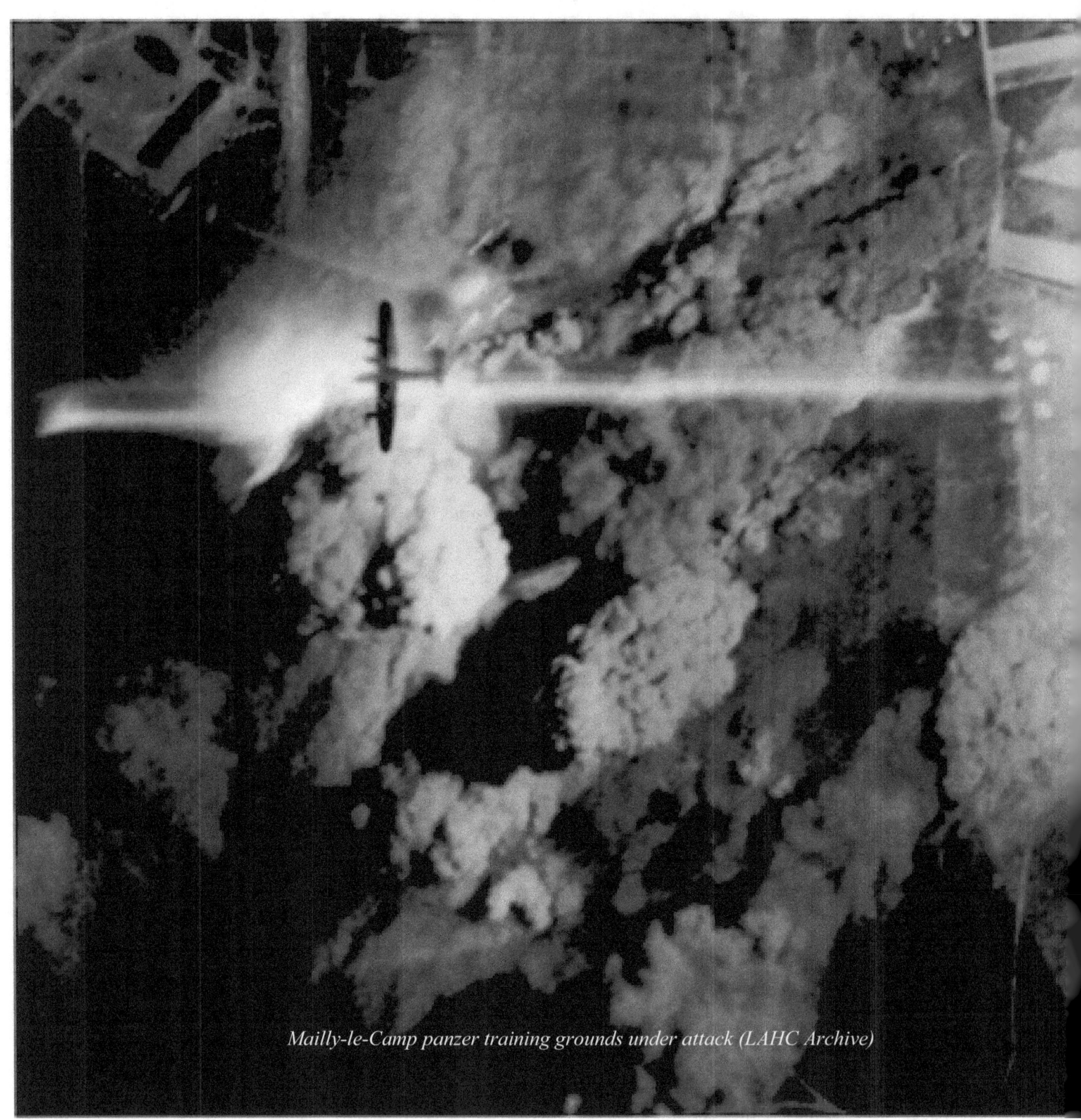
Mailly-le-Camp panzer training grounds under attack (LAHC Archive)

Weather conditions in the target area were good, little cloud, good visibility and only slight ground haze. The target was reportedly promptly and efficiently marked, the squadron attacked between 00:38 hours and 01:08 hours from 6,350 to 9,100 feet. Crews de-briefing stated that the *'bombing appears to have been well concentrated around the red spot flares particularly in the early stages of the attack'*. Bombing instructions should have been backed up by W/T but were not heard, it was noted that fortunately R/T reception was good. Ground defences were light and only one fighter was seen. The target was completely destroyed by bombing. Cliff Rogers was last to land back at base at 03:45 hours.

Wednesday 3rd May 1944.

The enormous Panzer crew training grounds at Mailly-Le-Camp often used by the elite Waffen-SS was a target which Bomber Command couldn't afford to miss and an attack was detailed. A standard bomb load was carried by all of Six-thirty's Lancasters on the night, 1 x 4000lb minol and 15 x 500lb MC (025). Of the attacking force of 346 Lancasters and 14 Mosquitoes of 1 and 5 Groups and two PFF Mosquitoes, 42 Lancasters were lost.

3rd/4th May 1944 : Night Bombing Attack on Mailly-Le-Camp

Take Off: at 21:50 hours the new crew of Eugene Mitchell aboard ND655 were the first off from East Kirkby.

JB546-A	P/O EF Champness RAAF	
ME650-B	F/L JCW Weller	
ME739-D	F/O CW Rodgers RAAF	
JB672-F	F/L HW Hill	
ND580-G	P/O PA Nash	RD
ND655-J	Sgt EP Mitchell	
ND531-K	P/O HC Rogers	
ND335-L	F/S VW Brown RAAF	
ND685-Q	P/O AW Wilson RAAF	
ME737-S	S/L RO Calvert RNZAF	
ME729-U	F/O GR Joblin RNZAF	
LM537-X	P/O WA Watt RNZAF	
ND949-Z	F/L GH Probert	

In the view of 630 Squadron crews, who were fortunate to return unscathed from a raid which developed into a massacre of heavy bombers, the markers were well placed and on time, the bombing seemed to be accurate and concentrated although a good deal of smoke developed which obscured the target area at times. 630 Squadron's Lancasters attacked between 00:11 and 00:30 hours from 5,350 to 8,100 feet. The brightness of the moonlight assisted the ground defences considerably and the flak was heavy and very accurate. Fighter activity was observed to be intense from about 20 miles off the datum point and all along the route home with Bomber Command suffering terrible losses. ND580-G flown by Peter Nash's crew suffered flak damage while Geoff Probert's gunners Sergeants Dennis Bradd and Rick Rogers fought off an attack on ND949-Z and probably destroyed the Me109 fighter. Aussie Wade Rodgers was the last to land at 03:56 hours. On Saturday 6th May 1944 twenty-two year old Peter Nash one of 630 Squadron's pilots was severely injured when he fell from the running board of small car into which his entire crew was crammed roaring along the perimeter track out to dispersal. He landed very badly receiving severe head injuries and despite treatment in the Station Sick Quarters and a prompt transfer to Lincoln Military Hospital sadly he died as the result on 15th May leaving his crew without a captain. They were split up and became 'spare bods'.

Gordon Maxwell RAAF   *HC "Cliff" Rogers (LAHC Archive / Patti Kellaway)*

The crew of RAAF captain Gordon Maxwell[iii] a 27 year old from Sandgate, Queensland who had trained at 29 OTU. and 1654 HCU arrived on the Friday.

Sunday 7th May 1944.
630 Squadron were next detailed to participate in another 5 Group 'bash' attacking the Aerodrome at Tours. Six-thirty's Lancasters were each bombed up with 1 x 4000lb HC and 15 x 500lb MC bombs. Flying with the squadron was a pilot well known to the former 61 Squadron personnel and particularly to the CO, Wing Commander Reg Stidolph DFC a Southern Rhodesian currently serving at No. 55 Base (East Kirkby) as Base Ops Officer.

7th/8th May 1944 : Night Bombing Attack on Tours
Take Off: at 00:15 hours JB672 (Harold Hill) was the first of 630 Squadron to take off.

LL949-E	P/O EF Champness RAAF	
ME650-B	F/L JCW Weller	
ME739-D	F/O CW Rodgers RAAF	
JB672-F	F/L HW Hill	
ND655-J	Sgt EP Mitchell	
ND531-K	P/O HC Rogers	
ND335-L	F/S VW Brown RAAF	
LL950-Y	W/C RN Stidolph	
ME729-T	W/C WI Deas	RD
ND949-Z	S/L RO Calvert RNZAF	
ND793-V	F/L GH Probert	
ND527-O	F/O GR Joblin RNZAF	
ND685-Q	P/O AW Wilson RAAF	
LM537-X	P/O WA Watt RNZAF	

The main buildings, administration and aircraft hangars were all heavily hit and badly damaged. The squadron's crews attacked between 02:55 and 03:13 hours from 6,000 to 8,850 feet. Crews reported that serious fighter opposition was in place but little ground defences were experienced over the target, marking appeared good to them and good visibility made a successful attack possible. Wade Rodgers in ME739 was the last to land at 05:47 hours. The aircraft flown by George Joblin's crew is uncertain but possibly ND527-O. F/S Ted Howard (Wop/AG) one of the 'spare bods' from Frederick Oglesby's crew who flew with many different 630 Squadron crews was loaned to Wing Commander Humphreys (CO, 57 Squadron) who needed a Wireless Operator aboard ME626 for the Op. Wing Commander Deas' recommendation for Cab Kellaway to receive a Bar to the DSO was approved and the award quickly appeared in the London Gazette. Acting Flight Lieutenant Winston Herbert KELLAWAY, D.S.O. (49688), Royal Air Force, No. 630 Squadron.

'This officer has completed a third tour of operations and has continued to display, the highest standard of skill and bravery. Notable amongst his achievements on his last tour are five attacks on Berlin, missions which he completed with great skill and determination. His example has been outstanding and has done much to foster a high standard of morale throughout the squadron. His record is worthy of the greatest praise'.

AVM Sir Ralph Cochrane had signalled his approval of the award on 25th April noting that Kellaway had already flown 70 sorties, 26 since his last award and that he was Deputy Flight Commander.

Tuesday 9th May 1944.
Thirty-nine Lancasters, including 630 Squadron and 4 Mosquitos, all of 5 Group, were allocated an industrial target, the ball bearings factory located beside the railway marshalling yards at Annecy. All Lancasters of the squadron carried a bomb load of 15 x 500lb GP (025) and 2 x 1000lb MC (025) bombs.

9th/10th May 1944 : Night Bombing Attack on Annecy
Take Off: at 21:00 hours 'Sam' Weller in ME650 with a Second Dickie aboard was the first airborne.

ME650-B	F/L JCW Weller	(P/O JHG Smith)
LL949-E	P/O EF Champness RAAF	
JB672-F	F/O CW Rodgers RAAF	
ND531-K	P/O HC Rogers	
ND949-Z	F/L HW Hill	
ND685-Q	P/O AW Wilson RAAF	
ND793-V	P/O RC Hooper	
ND527-O	P/O DE Hawker RNZAF	
ME737-S	P/O DR Mallinson	
LM537-X	P/O JW Lennon RNZAF	
LL950-Y	F/O GR Joblin RNZAF	

On the outward flight foul weather was encountered and 2 Mosquitoes did not reach the target however the other 2 reached Annecy where the weather conditions were fine and they marked accurately. In the third wave of bombers, Six-thirty crews bombed accurately from 6,500 to 6,950 feet between 02:02 and 02:11 hours and the factory was severely damaged. Not only the first airborne, LL950 (George Joblin) was the last to land at 06:35 hours.

Several crews were forced to switch aircraft shortly before take-off due to serviceability problems and the Battle Order was not updated. Aircrew flying logbooks have been used for this record. The Operations Record Book for 630 Squadron does not record the crew of George Joblin participating in the attack on Annecy however the Squadron Ops Record and the 'East Kirkby Raid book'[iv] both held at the RAF Museum shows that they did take part and were one of the two crews (Joblin and Hooper) instructed not to bomb, this is supported by the total number of operations and the detailed list of targets given in his RNZAF

Two views of the Annecy ball bearing factory after the attack (Bertrand Letournel)

official biographical summary and specifically in the list of 'targets attacked' in the recommendation for his DFC.

Thursday 11th May 1944.
In an effort to confuse the German Military about the likely location of the forthcoming landings, No.5 Group were ordered to attack the massive German military depot at Bourg Leopold in Belgium with 190 Lancasters and 8 Mosquitoes supplemented by 3 PFF Mosquitoes of No. 8 Group. Six-thirty's aircraft each carried 1 x 4000lb HC and 16 x 500lb MC bombs.

11th /12th May 1944 : Night Bombing Attack on Bourg Leopold
Take Off: at 22:16 hours Ken Ames in ND335 was the first to take off.

ME650-B	F/L JCW Weller	
JB290-C	F/O HW Smith	
ME739-D	F/L CW Rodgers RAAF	
LL949-E	Sgt EP Mitchell	
JB672-F	F/L HW Hill	
ND580-G	P/O AT Jackson	
ND655-J	F/L JB Nall	
ND531-K	P/O HC Rogers	
ND335-L	F/L KR Ames	
ME782-N	F/O BB Lindsay RAAF	
ND527-O	P/O ED Hawker RNZAF	
LL966-P	F/S GE Maxwell RAAF	
ND685-Q	P/O AW Wilson RAAF	
ME737-S	P/O WA Watt RNZAF	(P/O AG Henriquez)
ND793-V	P/O DR Mallinson	RD
LM537-X	P/O JW Lennon RNZAF	
ND949-Z	P/O RC Hooper	
LL950-Y	P/O RW Bailey	
JB546-A	F/L GR Joblin RNZAF	

In windy, hazy conditions and with civilian housing in close proximity the Master Bomber ordered 'Stop bombing' after 94 Lancasters had attacked. The result was rated disappointing and unsatisfactory although it is believed that civilians were not injured. Records suggest that only the following captains attacked before the order to stop bombing was given, Ames, Bailey, Hooper, Lennon, Lindsay, Maxwell, Mitchell and Rogers and they attacked from 12,350 to 13,850 feet between 00:17 and 00:32 hours. Two aircraft and crews Failed To Return.

Lancaster III, ND580 (Codes LE – G)

Pilot	– P/O Alfred Thomas 'Bob' Jackson. Age	Killed
Flight Eng	– Sgt Harold Edgar Frank Owen . Age 25	Killed
Navigator	– F/S Denis Walter Muddiman. Age 22	Killed
Bomb Aimer	– F/O Joseph Feldman RCAF. Age 23	Killed
Wireless Op	– Sgt Richard Matthew Cartlidge. Age 20	Killed
Mid Upper	– Sgt Arthur William Seago. Age 21	Killed
Rear Gunner	– Sgt Ernest Albert Louis. Age 29	Killed

ND580 was lost without trace and possibly is the Lancaster claimed by Oberleutnant (Flying Officer) Heinz Rökker of 2/NJG 2 (2nd Squadron/ Night Fighter Group 2) at 00:23 hours over the sea near Zeebrugge or otherwise that claimed by Hauptmann (Flight Lieutenant) Ernst-Wilhelm Modrow of 1/NJG 1 at 01:04 hours over the sea west of The Hague. Runnymede Memorial to the missing.

Dennis Muddiman (Muddiman family)

Joe Feldman RCAF (Simon Feldman)

Lancaster I, ME737 (Codes LE – S)

Pilot	– P/O Wilfred Arthur Watt RNZAF. Age 25	Killed
Flight Eng	– Sgt Roy Victor Charles Witham. Age 21	Prisoner
Navigator	– Sgt Leslie St.Clair Thompson. Age 20	Killed
Bomb Aimer	– F/S Keith Angus Michael Stuart RNZAF. Age 21	Prisoner
Wireless Op	– Sgt Philip Amies. Age 22	Killed
Mid Upper	– Sgt Alfred Frederick Grant RCAF. Age 18	Killed
Rear Gunner	– Sgt Peter Robert Rowthorn. Age 19	Killed

Wilf Watt's ME737 is believed to have been shot down by Oberfeldwebel Vincenz Giessuebel of 2/NJG2 north-east of Brussels at 00:42 hours. It apparently crashed at Blauwbroek 3km south east of Herenthout. P/O Watt is buried at Heverlee War Cemetery, his crew are buried at Schoonselhof Cemetery at Antwerp having been moved from Antwerpen-Deurne.

Roy Witham described the attack which is a classic example of the upward firing cannons which night fighters carried (Schrägemusik), *'Without warning a JU88 came up from below and tore us apart from tail through to nose, killing the gunners, wireless operator and navigator. The starboard engines caught fire and I feathered them, we lost height rapidly. The bomb aimer bailed out and I helped the pilot as he tried to maintain height but this was impossible and he told me to get out. I released his harness and baled out at just over 1,200 feet as the starboard main plane broke away. The aircraft exploded just as my chute opened and I landed less than quarter of a mile from the burning wreckage'.*

Wilf Watt RNZAF (Roy Calvert)

Alfred Grant RCAF (Library and Archives Canada)

Ken Ames crew. Back row l to r – Tex Glasby, Ken Ames, Paddy Parle, Fred Spencer with 2 ground crew.
Front row l to r 2 ground crew, Jim Wright, Bill Leary, unknown, Tom Savage (Jim Wright)

Keith Stuart, a sheet metal worker from Greytown, NZ and Roy Witham a motor engineer from South Devon both landed by parachute and went 'straight into the bag' spending the bulk of the remainder of the war at Stalag 357 (Thorn and Fallingbostel). During the April 1945 forced marches of Prisoners Of War by the Germans a group including Roy Witham were left only partly supervised near one of the Elbe bridges which were being prepared for destruction. Witham promptly cut the cables which had been laid by the German Army to blow the bridge up and fortunately the prisoners moved on before his sabotage was detected. Without doubt he would have been summarily shot if he had been caught. Don Mallinson's 'V-Victor' returned from the attack with flak damage. Night fighters had been attacking the force almost continually, Eugene Mitchell's gunners Geoff Burt (mid-upper) and Norman Longbottom (rear gunner) fighting off four attacks to claim a single engine fighter damaged and a Me110 destroyed although it was only recorded by the authorities as confirmed damaged. Canadian Howard Smith landed at 02:40 hours. The highly popular Ken Ames and crew who had started their tour with 61 Squadron before transferring to Six-thirty as founder members were tour expired after this attack. Ames received a Bar to his DFC, rear gunner Richard 'Paddy' Parle had already been awarded an Immediate DFM, navigator Jim Wright received a DFC, Tom Savage (bomb aimer) a DFM and RAAF wireless operator 'Tex' Glasby a DFC. All of the above went on to fly a second tour with 97 Squadron Pathfinder Force where sadly Harvey Glasby was killed operating as a 'spare bod' on an attack with a different crew.

John Nall and his crew transferred to 83 Squadron after the Bourg Leopold raid and survived their tour, navigator Linton Grimshaw and bomb aimer Ken Gouldbourn receiving DFCs at the end of their tours. Tragically at least three members of the crew later died in their forties or early fifties. New crews had been arriving at East Kirkby, one from 16 OTU. and 1660 HCU captained by 28 year old Pilot Officer Alfred Henriquez[v] a black Caribbean pilot from Buff Bay, Jamaica, an extremely brave man as he was Jewish by religion. [Source: NA AIR 2/6876 – Nominal Roll of Coloured Candidates, October 1944]

One was captained by 25 year old Kings Lynn man Doug Gamble[vi] and another by 31 year old Argentine farmer Terence 'Pancho' O'Dwyer[vii] who was born in Colon of Irish/Spanish parents and brought up in the Argentine. Educated in England from 1926-32 he had gained a civil pilot's licence at the age of 18 and sailed back to England aboard the 'Andalucia Star' arriving in September 1941 having left

Alfred Henriquez and his bride (Henriquez family collection)

TG "Pancho" O'Dwyer (Claudio Meunier)

his comfortable lifestyle to join the fight. His crew included a Spanish Basque Navigator Pilot Officer Richard Baudens who was soon to be removed from ops in consideration of his potential fate if shot down and taken prisoner, after the RAF discovered that he'd actually fought alongside the Luftwaffe during the Spanish Civil War. Pending transfer to an instructional role he would rocket up and down the longest runway on a massive motorcycle. The novice O'Dwyer crew were fortunate to be joined by the veteran and unflappable Stan Pinches who had flown previously with 57 and 630 as bomb aimer in the crew of the legendary 'Cab' Kellaway DSO and Bar. Interviewed shortly before his death 'Cab' was delighted to learn that Andy Lucas of his crew had received a DFC which he'd recommended but was horrified to discover that Stan had not received a hard earned DFC, he considered that maybe this and a couple of other notable omissions were the result of the loss of Wing Commander Bill Deas.

Bomber Command HQ reviewed operational statistics in the Spring of 1944 and a policy decision was taken, confirmed in a letter to the Air Ministry BC/C.28437/P/C dated 8th March 1944, to differentiate between 'two entirely different types of operation'. Effectively it had been decided that some targets were 'softer' than others and should be counted only as 'one third' of an Op towards an aircrew's tour. Sir Arthur Harris applied this 'one third of an op' ruling to targets in a region 'West of 70°East and North of 53°North, and West of 6°East between 53°North and 46°North'. Exceptions were mining 'in the inner harbours of Brest, Lorient, St Nazaire and La Pallice'.

630 Squadron records on the night of 11th/12th May 1944 list the 'official' status of operational aircrew with their 'Ops Completed':

F/L Ames	26 ⅔	P/O Hawker	5 ⅔
F/L Rodgers	4 ⅓	P/O Bailey	10 ⅓
Sgt Mitchell	1	P/O Lennon	3 ⅔
F/L Hill	25	P/O Lindsay	⅓
P/O Jackson	4	P/O Hooper	5
F/O Smith	1	P/O Mallinson	6
P/O Rogers	21 ⅔	P/O Wilson	13 ⅔
F/L Weller	21 ⅔	F/S Maxwell	
F/O Nall	18	F/L Joblin	9 ⅓
P/O Watt	4		

A week later, on the night of 19th/20th May 1944 the 'fractions' had been removed and the list updated showing crews operational that night:

F/L Probert	26	P/O Maxwell	2
F/L Weller	24	P/O Wilson	16
F/L Rodgers	6	W/C Deas	56 + 8
Sgt Mitchell	2	P/O Henriquez	1
F/O Smith	2	P/O Lennon	7
P/O Rogers	22	P/O Bailey	11
P/O Mallinson	7	P/O Hooper	8
P/O Lindsay	1	F/L Joblin	13
P/O Hawker	5		
S/L Calvert	33 + 17		

Quite naturally aircrew were deeply upset by this decision which would materially lengthen their tours and obviously further reduce their chances of survival. The ruling was later cancelled.

Lancaster LL966 'P – Peter' regularly flown by Pete Doherty's 'Breeze Boys' (RD Gale)

On Monday 15th May Air Commodore Henry Thornton MBE[viii] assumed command of No.55 Base freeing up Group Captain Taaffe to resume command of RAF East Kirkby. At the time the three 5 Group heavy bomber squadrons were flying from East Kirkby and Spilsby and three Coastal Command squadrons were 'lodging' at Strubby. No. 55 Base staff included a high percentage from RAF East Kirkby (these are marked *).

Wing Commander RGP Jaggard MBE[ix]	(Accounts)
Wing Commander TB McGinn MBE	(Engineering)*
Squadron Officer BB Hayward[x]	WAAF 'G'
Flight Lieutenant KC Brigden[xi]	(Electrical/Engineering)
Squadron Leader WC Hawken MBE	(Armaments)*
Flight Lieutenant AF Norris	(Signals/Radar)*
Squadron Leader EA Dearman	(Intelligence)*
Flight Lieutenant M Carty	(Intelligence)*
Squadron Leader HA Astbury[xii]	(Accounts)
Flight Lieutenant WB Rawling[xiii]	(Admin/Adjutant)*
Section Officer DM deSausmarez	(Admin/Assistant Adjutant)*
Squadron Leader LH Button[xiv]	(Ops/Flying Control)*
Flight Lieutenant Cornwall Walker	(Ops/Flying Control)
Flight Lieutenant CJ Morley	(Catering)*
Section Officer DE Holey[xv]	(Code and Cypher)*
Squadron Leader BV Smith[xvi]	(Signals)

During the day of 19th May a group of staff officers and students at the RAF Staff College visited East Kirkby to see a heavy bomber station in action and witness flight planning and briefing, amongst the party was Wing Commander Guy Gibson VC DSO and Bar DFC and Bar.

Friday 19th May 1944.
One hundred and twelve Lancasters of 5 Group and 9 Mosquito markers of both 5 and 8 Groups were detailed to bomb the railway marshalling yards at Amiens. Wing Commander Bill Deas carried a marking payload of 2 hooded flare clusters, 2 yellow TIs, 2 green TIs, 3 red spots and 5 x 1000lb AN-M65 (025) bombs, the remainder of the squadron each bombed-up with 11 x 1000lb AN-M65 and 4 x 500lb MC (025) bombs.

19th/20th May 1944 : Night Bombing Attack on Amiens
Take Off: at 23:11 hours Cliff Rogers in ME795 was the first to take off.

LL972-T	W/C WI Deas
JB290-C	F/L GH Probert
ME782-N	F/O BB Lindsay RAAF
ND527-O	F/O DE Hawker RNZAF
LL966-P	P/O GE Maxwell RAAF
ND685-Q	P/O AW Wilson RAAF
ND688-R	S/L RO Calvert RNZAF
ND655-J	P/O DR Mallinson
ND797-W	F/L GR Joblin RNZAF
LM537-X	P/O JW Lennon RNZAF
LL950-Y	P/O RW Bailey
ND949-Z	P/O RC Hooper
JB546-A	F/L JCW Weller
ME739-D	F/L CW Rodgers RAAF

LL949-E	Sgt EP Mitchell
JB672-F	F/O HW Smith RCAF
ME795-G	F/O HC Rogers

Six-thirty were to attack in the third wave but at 01:24 hours before any of their bombs had dropped the controller ordered all crews to return to base due to weather conditions making the accuracy of bombing uncertain. Great consideration being again given to avoiding collateral damage and unnecessary civilian casualties. It is possible based on one set of records that the crews of Alan Wilson and Cliff Rogers attacked at 02:22 and 02:23 hours from about 6,800 feet, not having received the instruction. LM537 (Joe Lennon) was the last to land back at East Kirkby at 03:50 hours.

Sunday 21st May 1944. Detailed to participate in 2 separate attacks in a single night 630 Squadron was divided to take part in both Ops. Five Lancasters joined the force of 510 aircraft to attack Duisburg and were allocated to the third wave of bombers, each was armed with 1 x 4000lb Minol, 96 x 30lb and 1,500 x 4lb incendiaries. The other 14 aircraft were detailed for sea mining in the Baltic 'Forget-Me-Not' area and were each armed with 5 x MkVI sea mines.

21st/22nd May 1944 : Night Bombing Attacks on Duisburg
Take Off: at 22:49 hours 'Buster' Brown in ND655 was the first airborne.

ME782-N	P/O BB Lindsay RAAF
ME796-S	P/O AG Henriquez
ND655-J	P/O VW Brown RAAF
ND335-L	P/O GE Maxwell RAAF
JB672-F	F/O HW Smith RCAF

The target was found to be covered by dense cloud but Oboe sky-marking was accurate and bombing based on that caused substantial damage in southern districts of Duisburg. Gordon Maxwell's crew were late to take off due to technical problems so arrived on target late and had to abandon the sortie. Uncertain due to the cloud, P/O Brown's crew in ND655 'J' bombed Cologne at 01:19 hours. Pilot Officer Alfred Henriquez from Jamaica attacked at 01:22 hours and was the last to land back at East Kirkby at 03:49 hours. The crew of Canadian Howard Smith Failed to Return from the raid on Duisburg :

Lancaster III, JB672 (Codes LE – F)

Pilot	– F/O Howard Wallace Smith RCAF. Age 22	Killed
Flight Eng	– Sgt Kenneth Dickinson. Age 21	Killed
Navigator	– F/S Raymond Coates. Age 21	Killed
Bomb Aimer	– WO2 William Baxter RCAF. Age 31	Killed
Wireless Op	– Sgt Ronald Victor Lawrence. Age 21	Killed
Mid Upper	– Sgt Vernon Alfred Goodwin RCAF. Age 19	Killed
Rear Gunner	– Sgt Leonard Spensley RCAF. Age 21	Killed

Attacked by a night fighter flown by Hauptmann Martin Drewes of the Staff Flight of III Gruppe/NJG1 at 00:58 hours near Deventer they were shot down and crashed near Kilder in the Dutch Gelderland, 27 km from Arnhem. Six of the crew are buried at Bergh (Kilder) RC Churchyard but no trace of Sergeant Lawrence was found and he is commemorated on Runnymede Memorial to the missing.

21st/22nd May 1944 : Night Minelaying 'Forget-Me-Not'
Take Off: at 21:49 hours ND685 (Alan Wilson) took off at the head of the Gardeners.

ND527-O	F/O DE Hawker RNZAF	
LL966-P	F/L GH Probert	RD
ND685-Q	P/O AW Wilson RAAF	
ND688-R	S/L RO Calvert RNZAF	
LL972-T	P/O DR Mallinson	
ND797-W	F/L GR Joblin RNZAF	
LM537-X	P/O JW Lennon RNZAF	
LL950-Y	P/O RW Bailey	
ND949-Z	P/O RC Hooper	RD
ME739-D	F/L CW Rodgers RAAF	
LL949-E	Sgt EP Mitchell	
ND531-K	F/O HC Rogers	
ME795-G	F/L JCW Weller	
JB290-C	P/O EF Champness RAAF	

Mines which had been armed and winched aboard the Lancasters under the watchful supervision of Royal Navy Petty Officers were planted in the allocated areas of Kiel Bay and the mission was viewed as very successful. Allan Payne, Geoff Probert's navigator aboard LL966-P recalled that on the last op of their tour their Lancaster was badly shot up by a Junkers JU88 night fighter while in the target area. The gunners of Roy Calvert's 'R-Robert', Sergeant George Cansell and Flight Sergeant Derek Freeman, were in action twice during this op being credited with the destruction of a JU88 night fighter and damaging an unidentified enemy aircraft. Sadly the combat report has not been located. One of Six-thirty's Lancasters was amongst the three which Failed to Return.

Lancaster III, LL950 (Codes LE – Y)

Pilot	– P/O Ronald Walter Bailey. Age 22	Killed
Flight Eng	– P/O Jack Maxwell (Max) Whiting. Age 31	Killed
Navigator	– F/S Charles Henry Richardson. Age 26	Killed
Bomb Aimer	– F/S James Mitchell Henderson. Age 35	Killed
Wireless Op	– F/O Albert Edward (Bertie) Truesdale . Age 22	Killed
Mid Upper	– Sgt James Lindsay. Age 22	Killed
Rear Gunner	– Sgt Martin Ernest Murton. Age 22	Killed

Intercepted at 4,700 metres altitude over the Jylland Peninsula by a night fighter flown by Unteroffizier Heinz Koppe of 10/NJG 3 (10th Squadron/ Night Fighter Group 3) over Denmark at 02:00 hours LL950 crashed at Vesterlund. Ron Bailey and his crew were buried at Esbjerg (Fourfelt) Cemetery. A Danish researcher advises- *'the Lancaster started burning and came down in great circles. It broke up in mid-air and crashed at 02:00 hours just south of the railroad line west of the small village of Vesterlund. The tail fell to the ground some five kilometres away, a little to the east of the village of Dørken. In the wreckage near Vesterlund were found four bodies and in the wreckage east of Dørken were found two bodies. A third body with an unopened parachute was found in a nearby field. The dead airmen were left lying where they were found until the evening of 24th May when the Wehrmacht from Give Barracks collected the bodies and took them to Esbjerg where they were laid to rest in Fovrfelt cemetery on 27th May.'*

Ron Bailey and Max Whiting (LAHC Archive/Patti Kellaway)

Max Whiting's widow Muriel later remarried becoming the second wife of Air Chief Marshal Hugh Dowding, 1st Baron Dowding. The crew of 30 year old Geoff Probert had flown the 34th and last op of their tour and were screened on their return. Like David Roberts' crew they had joined the squadron direct from training and were only the second such crew to survive a full tour. Both pilot and navigator (Alan Payne) later received DFCs in recognition of their sustained bravery and example. Sadly, Geoff Probert died in 1958 aged only 44 leaving a young wife and daughter.

On 22nd May 1944 the crew of Bill Adams USAAF joined No. 630 Squadron, they included Jonny Kiesow another USAAF member also on an exchange posting, two Canadians and three British lads. Both Adams and Kiesow had previously enlisted in the RCAF before being accepted by the USAAF.

Monday 22nd May 1944. During the morning the squadron received preliminary warning for a night attack and the Lancasters were bombed-up with 1 x 2000lb HC and 12 x 500lb J type Cluster Incendiaries and at briefing the crews were warned of the severe risk of icing despite which they were expected to attack from 21,000 feet.

22nd/23rd May 1944 : Night Bombing Attack on Brunswick

Take Off: at 22:25 hours Wing Commander Deas led the take-off. Sam Weller had a Second Dickie, 'Pancho' O'Dwyer, along for the trip.

JB290-C	P/O DR Mallinson	
LL949-E	Sgt EP Mitchell	RD
ME795-G	F/L CW Rodgers RAAF	(P/O Gamble)
ND655-J	P/O VW Brown RAAF	
ND531-K	F/O HC Rogers	
ND335-L	F/L HW Hill	

JB546-A	P/O EF Champness RAAF	
ME650-B	F/L JCW Weller	(F/O TG O'Dwyer)
ME782-N	P/O BB Lindsay RAAF	
ND527-O	F/O DE Hawker RNZAF	
ND685-Q	P/O AW Wilson RAAF	
ND688-R	P/O GE Maxwell RAAF	RD
ME796-S	P/O AG Henriquez	
LL972-T	W/C WI Deas	
ND797-W	F/L GR Joblin RNZAF	
LM537-X	P/O JW Lennon RNZAF	

JB290 (Don Mallinson) returned early due to an unserviceable rear turret, jettisoning their bombload over the sea to reduce to safe landing weight they landed safely. Fighters were active on the outward route, marker flares and supporters were at the target on time but no red spot fires were seen by Six-thirty. Crews made several orbits awaiting markers and at 01:25 hours Wanganui flares and green TIs were visible and orders received by W/T to bomb them. 630 Squadron crews reported that some bombing began at 01:15 hours before markers were visible and R/T discipline was rated as poor. The attack went on between 01:15 to 01:43 hours from 18,000 feet or more and bombing was correctly reported as scattered. Several aircraft received flak damage and 'O-Oboe' possibly received more than most, fortunately no fighters were encountered on the way home. At 02:12 hours the crew of New Zealander Joe Lennon flying Lancaster 'X-X ray' (LM537) got a shock as tracer suddenly appeared on their port bow slightly below aimed at another Lancaster, the night fighter had not seen them as it attacked another bomber. On different courses the two aircraft were soon some distance apart. Eugene Mitchell's and Wade Rodgers' both reported their Lancasters being coned by searchlights and then hit repeatedly by heavy flak.

Gordon Maxwell in ND688 'R-Robert' was the last to land at 05:00 hours, his Lancaster had survived a 'hairy Op'. Already coned by numerous searchlights for several minutes by 02:20 hours he was struggling to evade the blinding lights as flak burst all around them damaging the aircraft when a burst of cannon and machine gun fire came in from their port beam, down, wounding their South Rhodesian rear gunner Sergeant Ron Peake in the legs. Fortunately their violent corkscrews eventually evaded both the fighter and the searchlights at which time the gunner finally admitted having been wounded, the lower section of the fuselage beneath him had been shot away and tail wheel extensively damaged. They landed at Spilsby from where he was rushed to RAF Hospital Rauceby and later down to London, he never flew again. Maxwell's crew were driven home to East Kirkby where a concerned Wing Commander Deas had waited up to welcome them home despite having flown the op himself.

Two Lancasters collided in the funnel over East Kirkby that early morning, F/L Bailey (57 Squadron) was able to crash land on the airfield all of his crew escaping unhurt, sadly the 97 Squadron aircraft of F/O Jardine RCAF crashed at Revesby killing the entire crew. Ambulances from East Kirkby and Woodhall Spa attended the crash site. Two of Six-thirty's crews Failed To Return that night.

Lancaster III, JB546 (Codes LE – A)

Pilot	– P/O Edward Frank Champness RAAF. Age 20	Killed
Flight Eng	– Sgt John Peacock Craig Johnstone. Age 19	Killed
Navigator	– F/S Vernon Stanley John Zucker RAAF. Age 24	Prisoner
Bomb Aimer	– F/S Gerald Melbourne Naugler RCAF. Age 21	Killed
Wireless Op	– Sgt Edmond Adair. Age 21	Prisoner
Mid Upper	– Sgt Leslie Jones. Age 19	Prisoner
Rear Gunner	– Sgt Alan Leslie Pickering. Age 20	Killed

A night fighter attacked JB546 and shot it down near Quackenbrück, this was possibly Oberleutnant (Flying Officer) Heinz Ferger of 3/NJG 3 (3rd Squadron/ Night |Fighter Group 3) who claimed a Lancaster in the vicinity of Holdorf at 00:30 hours. Originally buried locally the bodies of the dead airmen were moved to Rheinberg War Cemetery post-war. Eddie Adair a 21 year old apprentice baker from Belfast baled out and was captured on landing, wounded. After two weeks in hospital he spent the remainder of the war between Stalag Luft 7 (Bankau). Stalag 344 (Lamsdorf) and Stalag IIIA (Luckenwalde). His crewmate Les Jones an assistant Storekeeper from Liverpool recorded his date of capture as 29th May 1944 at Osnabrück, he was also held at Stalag Luft 7 and Stalag IIIA Australian Vernon Zucker was captured slightly wounded on 27th by rural policemen near Lingen and after interrogation and some months at Stalag Luft 7 Zucker joined his fellow survivors at Stalag IIIA. Back home at Upper La Have, Nova Scotia, Gerald Naugler's mother Etta May had lost a second son, Gerald's brother Reginald had died serving at sea with the Canadian Merchant Navy aboard the S.S. 'Bic Island' torpedoed in October 1942.

Lancaster III, ND655 (Codes LE – J)

Pilot	– P/O Vivian William Brown RAAF. Age 23	Killed
Flight Eng	– Sgt David Beattie Haig. Age	Killed
Navigator	– W/O Kenneth Arthur Sinclair RAAF . Age 22	Killed
Bomb Aimer	– Sgt Thomas William Connor. Age 22	Killed
Wireless Op	– Sgt William John Saxby . Age 22	Killed
Mid Upper	– Sgt James Binnie. Age 21	Killed
Rear Gunner	– F/S William Irving Taylor RAAF . Age 27	Killed

ND655 was almost certainly the Lancaster shot down by Oberleutnant (Flying Officer) Dietrich Schmidt of 8/NJG 1 (8th Squadron/ Night Fighter Group 1) from 5,400 metres over the sea 70 km west of Callantsoog at 03:48 hours. The crew are all commemorated on Runnymede Memorial. The Distinguished Flying Cross was announced in the London Gazette awarded to Pilot Officer Robert Cecil HOOPER (172176), Royal Air Force Volunteer Reserve, No. 630 Squadron-

'One night in April, 1944, this officer was the pilot of an aircraft detailed to attack Munich. On the outward flight the aircraft was engaged by fighters. Early in the fight the mid-upper and rear turrets were put out of action and the rear gunner was badly wounded. Pilot Officer Hooper manoeuvred his defenceless aircraft with great skill however, and eventually the attackers broke off the engagement. The bomber had sustained much damage but this did not deter Pilot Officer Hooper from continuing his mission. The target was far distant but he went on to execute a successful attack and afterwards flew the damaged bomber to base. This officer set a fine example of skill, courage and resolution'.

Wednesday 24th May 1944.

The Ford and General Motors factories in Antwerp were the target for the next raid in which 630 Squadron participated. 44 Lancasters with 7 Mosquito markers were despatched to bomb the Ford Motor factory at Antwerp. The bomb load was 11 x 1000lb AN-M and 4 x 500lb MC bombs.

24th/25th May 1944 : Night Bombing Attack on Antwerp

Take Off: at 22:45 hours LM537 flown by Kiwi Joe Lennon was the first to take off. Gordon Maxwell's crew were unable to take off in 'C-Charlie' which developed problems in both starboard engines.

ME739-D	F/L CW Rodgers RAAF	
ND531-K	F/O TG O'Dwyer	
ME650-B	F/O DG Gamble	
ND335-L	P/O DR Mallinson	
ME795-G	F/S LN Rackley RAAF	RD
LL972-T	F/L HW Hill	
ND797-W	F/L GR Joblin RNZAF	

ME782-N	F/O RC Hooper
ND527-O	F/O DE Hawker RNZAF
ME796-S	P/O AG Henriquez
LM537-X	P/O JW Lennon RNZAF

The attack opened on time although the markers apparently targeted the neighbouring dockyard buildings which were damaged. A particularly large explosion was reported at 00:49 hours. Crews in the early stages of bombing saw bombs exploding across the buildings but quickly the target was shrouded by smoke. The red spot flares were clearly visible at all times. Ground defences were reportedly light at the target but considerably more light flak was encountered than had anticipated. Some fighters were seen in the target area but no combats reported. The force attacked from 00:40 to 00:51 hours with 630 Squadron crews bombing between 00:42 and 00:49 hours from 6,350 to 7,850 feet. Doug Gamble in ME650 was the last to land back at East Kirkby at 02:19 hours. Northampton born Harold Hill's crew became the third crew to join Six-thirty from training and survive a full tour of ops, Antwerp was their 31st and last. Their captain was awarded a DFC and Canadian bomb aimer Doug Allen a DFM. Maurice Stancer, navigator for the first half of their tour had been posted to 44 Squadron after the Nuremburg attack of 30/31st March 1944 but completed his tour a shortly before and was awarded a DFM and commissioned, sadly though he died in 1973 aged only 49. Stan Davies flew every one of the 31 ops with Hill's crew as wireless operator and was commissioned before commencing an instructing tour. At the end of November 1945 he was killed while serving as a Flying Officer (Wireless Operator) with 525 Squadron, Transport Command, ferrying troops to and from India.

Saturday 27th May 1944.

Six-thirty next carried out an attack on the coastal gun batteries at St Valery-en-Caux, it was one of five such raids carried out that night along the French coastline. The squadron's Lancasters were each bombed up with 11 x 1000lb AN-M and 4 x 500lb MC (025) bombs.

27th/28th May 1944 : Night Bombing Attack on St Valery-en-Caux

Take Off: at 23:36 hours the first Lancaster airborne was Cliff Roger's ND531.

JB290-C	P/O DG Gamble	
ME739-D	F/L CW Rodgers RAAF	(P/O BW Brittain)
LL949-E	Sgt EP Mitchell	
ME795-G	F/S LN Rackley RAAF	
ND531-K	F/O HC Rogers	
ND335-L	F/O TG O'Dwyer	
ME650-B	P/O DR Mallinson	
ME782-N	P/O RC Hooper	
ND527-O	P/O DE Hawker RNZAF	
ND685-Q	P/O GE Maxwell RAAF	
ME796-S	P/O AG Henriquez	
LL972-T	W/C WI Deas	(G/C RT Taaffe)
ND797-W	F/L GR Joblin RNZAF	
LM537-X	P/O JW Lennon RNZAF	

At 01:22 hours flying at 7,200 feet Bob Hooper put ME782 'N-Nan' into a corkscrew to port to evade a JU88 night fighter as 19 year old Sergeant Danny Synnot shouted a warning before opening fire at it with a 400 round burst. The fighter also dived away and was lost in the darkness. Unsighted the Mid-upper gunner, Flying Officer Dave Timmins (Gunnery Leader) was unable to open fire. Initial flares went down at H+7 but were misplaced out to sea north west of the gun batteries. Minutes later flares were over the target but final marking was not completed till H+15. Bombing instructions were broadcast by W/T at 01:52

and at 01:53 hours the Controller ordered to attack. Crews of 630 Squadron attacked between 01:53 and 02:02 hours from 6,500 to 7,400 feet the single exception being ND685 (Gordon Maxwell) as Bill Griffiths the bomb aimer couldn't get the bomb load to release due to a technical fault. At 02:09 hours all aircraft were ordered to return to base. Six-thirty's crews reported that the bombing was well concentrated north west of the red spot flare. R/T was noticeably poor in the area. Two or three heavy guns fired from a mile or so south-west of the town but caused no problems and fighter activity was on a small scale in the target area resulting in 2 inconclusive combats. 630 Squadron aircraft bombed between 01:53 and 02:03 hours. Doug Gamble was last to land back at base at 03:51 hours. The logbook of Sergeant Len Page 19 year old mid-upper gunner in Wing Commander Deas' crew noted that Group Captain Taaffe flew with the crew on this op.

June 1944

The first two attacks of June 1944 included a large number of crews newly posted to 630 Squadron. Few of their pilots had the opportunity of flying as a Second Dickie and all were just thrown in at the deep end. One such crew from 16 OTU. and 1654 HCU was captained by a USAAF pilot, Technical Sergeant Bill Adams USAAF (ASN.10601540) a larger than life 'Yank' from Lexington, Massachusetts who had a USAAF mid-upper gunner in his crew, Staff Sergeant Jonny Kiesow USAAF (ASN.10601615) originally of Hertford County, Connecticut who had been working in Saskatchewan/Canada since his teens. Several bomber squadrons had USAAF airmen attached for complete tours of duty.

Bill Adams USAAF (Kiesow family)

Also trained at 16 OTU. and 1654 HCU alongside the Adams crew were the mainly Canadian crew captained by 30 year old Hazen Long[xvii] from Gibbon Mountain, New Brunswick and from 14 OTU. and 1654 HCU, 21 year old Ron Hayes'[xviii] with his all NCO crew. Arriving at Six-thirty from 17 OTU. and 1660 HCU was a crew captained by Aussie Bruce Brittain[xix], from 17 OTU. and 5 LFS came the former flying instructor 29 year old ex-journalist Flight Sergeant Claud Houghton[xx] of Bury St. Edmunds who had finally been granted his wish to fly on Ops after a long and distinguished Instructional tour at No. 10 Advanced Flying Unit (Dumfries) training pilots, Canadians Doug Simpson[xxi], with his all British crew and 28 year old Harold Wilson[xxii] from Birtle, Manitoba, still awaiting his commission although both his navigator and bomb aimer, fellow Canadians, were already Flying Officers and from 29 OTU. and 1661 HCU came the all British crew of 24 year old Windsor man Alan Kerr[xxiii] the son of an Army officer decorated for bravery in WW1.

Tour expired Squadron Leader Edward Butler DFC and Bar was posted to HQ Bomber Command at High Wycombe and replaced as A-Flight Commander by Flight Lieutenant (Acting Squadron Leader) Arthur Foster DFC[xxiv]. Although aged only 23 the popular Chertsey man was already a highly experienced bomber pilot who had been awarded a DFC with 61 Squadron after his first tour of 30 ops. Unsurprisingly his crew also included veterans embarking on their second or third tours. Rear gunner Flying Officer Len Davies DFM had served with 61 Squadron as had flight engineer Len Lawrence DFM and Flying Officer Fred Stone their wireless operator.

Left: Bruce Brittain RAAF (Bruce Brittain) Right: Claud Houghton (S Skinner/Houghton)

Harold Wilson RCAF (Michael Wilson)   *Arthur Foster (Martin Allen)*

Thursday 1st June 1944.

Target was to be the marshalling yards at Saumur, likely to be one of the vital lines of communication for German forces after the D-Day landings. Fifty-eight Lancasters of 5 Group attacked the Saumur railway junction, each of 630 Squadron's Lancasters delivered 10 x 1000lb MC and 4 x 500lb MC bombs.

1st/2nd June 1944 : Night Bombing Attack on Saumur

Take Off: at 21:58 hours ME650 flown by recently arrived Canadian pilot Hazen Long was first away. Six brand new crews from Six-thirty participated in the attack.

ME650-B	F/O HH Long RCAF
JB290-C	P/O DG Gamble
ME739-D	P/O DH Simpson RCAF
LM117-J	P/O BW Brittain RAAF
ND531-K	F/O HC Rogers
ND335-L	F/O TG O'Dwyer
ME795-G	F/S CM Houghton
LL949-E	F/S EP Mitchell
LL972-T	F/S HE Wilson RCAF
ME782-N	P/O RC Hooper
ND527-O	P/O DE Hawker RNZAF
ND685-Q	P/O GE Maxwell RAAF
ME796-S	P/O AG Henriquez
ND797-W	T/S W Adams USAAF
LM537-X	P/O JW Lennon RNZAF
LM118-V	P/O DR Mallinson

Amongst the attacking bombers were Bill Adams and crew on their first Op. The attack opened punctually with accurate flare marking and bombing commenced at 01:15 hours. Crews of 630 Squadron attacked between 01:15 to 01:20 hours when the controller ordered all remaining aircraft to stand by as the flares had either burned out or been bombed out. Cliff Rogers crew didn't receive the order and attacked at 01:26 hours after making a dummy bombing run to ensure accuracy. At 01:29 hours the Controller gave the order to continue the attack based on a red spot flare supported by a green TI and the remaining crews of Six-thirty (Wilson, Adams, Brittain and Houghton) attacked between 01:32 to 01:35 hours each having to make 2 dummy bombing runs before attacking. At de-briefing all crews reported a clear visual on the target and accurate bombing. Two very large explosions were noted at 01:22 and 01:35 hours. Only light ground defences formed an opposition although 9 combats took place within the target area. Bombing photos show a large gap in the bridge across the tracks at 01:17 hours. All bombing was accomplished from 6,350 to 8,100 feet. Doug Gamble was the last pilot to land at East Kirkby at 04:36 hours.

At 01:33 hours as they were preparing to bomb Doug Percy, the bomb aimer aboard ME795 'G-George' flown by Claud Houghton sighted a FW190 on their port bow closing quickly to attack. His prompt warning enabled Houghton to throw the bomber clear of the cannon and machine gun shells whilst both gunners, Sergeants Russ Dennis (Mid Upper) and Roland Locke (Rear Gunner) had the opportunity to return fire. The fighter disappeared and was not seen again. Photo reconnaissance results showed 'severe damage to junction, main lines torn up'. Cliff Rogers crew were congratulated on their return, they had completed 30 ops and were duly 'screened'. Cliff Rogers was recommended for a DFC and his flight engineer Bill Cox for a DFM, both awards were eventually confirmed and the crew split up to take up new postings. Postwar Rogers would become Chief Test Pilot for Rolls Royce having his work recognised by the award of an OBE in June 1968. Bill Cox DFM was sadly killed in the crash of a 1654 HCU Stirling in August 1944, Patrick Gillespie their RAAF rear gunner was commissioned and Mentioned in Despatches in January 1945 for his work as an instructor, Rogers' crew were only the fourth to fly a complete tour with 630 Squadron.

HC "Cliff" Rogers (bottom rt) with most of his crew at a wedding (Rogers family)

4th June 1944.

As the hour of the D-Day landings grew closer more and more resources were committed to give every possible chance to the Naval and ground forces. Gun emplacements and Coastal batteries were prime targets. Most of the 259 attacking aircraft were sent to bomb three targets in the Pas-de-Calais to continue to foster the German belief that the landings would be there at the narrowest point of the English Channel. Six-thirty however participated in a small attack on gun batteries in massive concrete emplacements at Maisy which overlooked what would be called 'Omaha' and 'Utah' beaches on 6th June 1944. 630 Squadron Lancasters were each armed with 18 x 500lb MC.

4th/5th June 1944 : Night Bombing Attack on Maisy
Take Off: at 01:20 hours 'Blue' Rackley in ME795 led the squadron into the air.

ME650-B	F/O HH Long RCAF
ND335-L	F/O TG O'Dwyer
ME739-D	P/O DH Simpson RCAF
ME795-G	P/O LN Rackley RAAF
LM117-J	P/O BW Brittain RAAF
LL949-E	F/S HE Wilson RCAF
ND531-K	F/S CM Houghton
ME782-N	P/O BB Lindsay RAAF
ND527-O	P/O DE Hawker RNZAF
LL966-P	P/O GD Gamble
ND685-Q	P/O AW Wilson RAAF
LM118-V	P/O DR Mallinson
LM537-X	P/O JW Lennon RNZAF
PA992-Y	P/O AR Kerr
LL972-T	T/S W Adams USAAF
ND797-W	Sgt RT Hayes
ME796-S	P/O RC Hooper

Owing to solid cloud the target was bombed based on Oboe sky markers and little could be seen of the result with most crews only noting the glow of red or green TIs through the cloud. Little heavy flak was encountered although 4 night fighters reported. Wing Commander JF Grey DSO DFC[i] of 207 Squadron was Controller and he found on landing that his Lancaster's W/T aerial had been carried away thus explaining why many crews had difficulty in receiving his instructions. The squadron's crews bombed between 03:38 and 03:45 hours from 5,000 to 8,850 feet and the attack was reportedly successful. Having descended to 5,000 feet seeking a target indicator or any description Alan Wilson's bomb aimer Frank Roche finally bombed at 03:45 using H2S as a last resort. At 03:13 hours in ME650 'B-Baker' flown by Hazen Long, rear gunner Sergeant Ed Browne sighted a JU88 on their starboard beam slightly below and called for a corkscrew before the night fighter was able to open fire, both he and Sergeant Frank Houston in the mid-upper turret fired bursts at the German before it was lost to sight. Harold Wilson brought LL949 home safely at 05:50 hours, the last to return.

Monday 5th June 1944.
On the eve of D-Day Bomber Command provided 1,012 bombers to attack coastal batteries at Fontenay, Houlgate, Maisy, La Pernelle, Merville, Mont-Fleury, Pointe-du-Hoc, Ouistreham and St.Martin-de-Varreville and 5,000 tons of bombs were dropped on the German defenders. Six-thirty made a maximum effort and 16 Lancasters took off each with a payload of 11 x 1,000 lb MC and 4 x 500 lb GP (.025) bombs.

5th/6th June 1944 : Night Bombing Attack on La Pernelle
Take Off: at 01:14 hours Doug Simpson and crew were the first off the deck.

ME739-D	F/L CW Rodgers RAAF
ME650-B	P/O HH Long RCAF
ME795-G	P/O DH Simpson RCAF
LM117-J	P/O BW Brittain RAAF
JB290-C	P/O GD Gamble
LL949-E	F/S HE Wilson RCAF
ND531-K	F/S CM Houghton
ND335-L	Sgt RT Hayes
LL972-T	F/L GR Joblin RNZAF
ME782-N	P/O BB Lindsay RAAF
ND527-O	P/O DE Hawker RNZAF
ND685-Q	P/O AW Wilson RAAF
ME796-S	P/O RC Hooper
LM118-V	P/O DR Mallinson
PA992-Y	P/O AR Kerr
LM537-X	T/S W Adams USAAF

The red TIs were slightly late but at 03:39 hours the Controller issued his order to attack. The squadron bombed between 03:40 and 04:03 hours from 6,800 to 11,850 feet. Negligible ground defences were in action and no fighters. This was the last attack before the invasion began and it was extremely successful. Mindful of possible civilian casualties Ron Hayes crew were ordered not to attack as markers were obscured by clouds of smoke and dust so the crew couldn't be certain of bombing accurately. The bombers flew homeward over the cloud masked invasion armada. ND335 'L-Love' was the last to land back at base at 06:26 hours. The D-Day landings commenced at 06:30 hours that morning. In his excellent memoir 'There's No Future in It' completed shortly before his death in 1988 Wade Rodgers recalled-

' In the early hours a thousand bombers flew carefully in a wide arc around the cross-channel invasion fleet and knocked out all ten coastal defence heavy gun batteries ahead of them, so relieving the incoming

boats of a lot of resistance. Of course we were almost certain that this was It and had confirmation when we flew back empty and, still in the dark, had a look at the H2S cathode plan indicator showing the immense spread of shipping on its way south. It was an historic day and we felt we were doing our bit in the monumental task of getting the troops ashore. But we hadn't finished yet. Late that evening we were back again to bomb rail and road intersections in the Caen area ahead of the invasion, to prevent the arrival of German heavy armoured vehicles and tanks. Our attack was made under cloud from about 2500 feet for accuracy, too low for photos'.

Tuesday 6th June 1944.

In support of the Allied Bridgehead in Normandy Bomber Command sent 1,065 aircraft to attack railway and road junctions, lines of communication and known German troop concentrations. Six-thirty were detailed to attack the Caen bridges just ahead of our advancing forces. Lancasters were each bombed up with 18 x 500lb GP bombs.

6th/7th June 1944 : Night Bombing Attack on Caen
Take Off: at 00:18 hours Wing Commander Deas led his squadron into the air.

ED531-K	S/L AE Foster
ME650-B	F/L JCW Weller
ME739-D	F/L CW Rodgers RAAF
LL949-E	F/O TG O'Dwyer
ME795-G	P/O LN Rackley RAAF
LL972-T	W/C WI Deas
ME782-N	P/O BB Lindsay RAAF
ND527-O	F/L GR Joblin RNZAF
ND685-Q	P/O AW Wilson RAAF
ME796-S	P/O RC Hooper
LM118-V	P/O DR Mallinson
PA992-Y	P/O JW Lennon RNZAF
JB290-C	P/O GD Gamble

The cloud base over the target was higher than expected and the aircraft had to orbit whilst accurate marking was achieved, the Controller then ordered bombing to be carried out at about 3,000 feet. It was low level for Lancasters. The squadron's crews attacked between 02:44 and 02:58 hours from 2,500 to 6,000 feet and de-briefing reports mentioned that the markers were well placed and bombing appeared to be concentrated on the markers until smoke blocked visibility of the target. Flying in so low over front line troops naturally attracted considerable light flak in the target area and across the Cherbourg peninsular on return. ME782 was the last to return to East Kirkby at 05:28 hours. Leaving the target area ND527 'O-Oboe' flown by George Joblin encountered a JU88 night fighter, Harold Spendelow in the rear turret sighted it first on their port quarter, down, and opened fire at 600 yards as the fighter moved to engage, hits were observed on the German aircraft followed by two small explosions from its fuselage before it broke away into a dive. The enemy aircraft was rated as Poss-Damaged. Not long afterwards at 02:58 hours at only 1,000 feet Joblin's mid-upper, 19 year old Robert Cousin sighted a JU88 at 600 yards off the port bow above, attacking another Lancaster. He fired several long bursts totalling 700 rounds and George Joblin and Bill Butcher the flight engineer sitting beside him both reported that he had scored numerous hits, the fighter broke off its attack with smoke trailing from the starboard engine. The enemy aircraft was rated as Damaged. The 5 Group force attacking Caen lost six Lancasters including one of 630 Squadron.

Lancaster III, ND685 (Codes LE – Q)

Pilot	– P/O Alan William Wilson RAAF. Age 22	Killed
Flight Eng	– Sgt George Bellman. Age 33	Prisoner
Navigator	– F/O Jack RG Morschel RAAF. Age 23	Prisoner
Bomb Aimer	– Sgt Frank James Roche RAAF. Age 19	Prisoner
Wireless Op	– P/O Reginald Charles H Wakely. Age 21	Killed
Mid Upper	– F/S Alastair Millar Henderson. Age	Killed
Rear Gunner	– Sgt James Hanna. Age 21	Killed

ND685 had encountered the night fighter of Oberleutnant (Flying Officer) Heinz Rökker of 2/NJG 2 (2nd Squadron/ Night Fighter Group 2) who had possibly shot down squadron mate 'Bob' Jackson on 11th/12th May. Rökker claimed his 28th Victory of the war at an altitude of 1,000 metres, south-west of Caen at 02:42

> Where did aircraft cross.
> Just on bombing run when aircraft was hit very solidly (only seemed to be one hit so assumed it was flak) height 2,300 ft. as briefed. Intercom went U/S almost immediately. Only heard B/A say to skipper jetison bombs. Very soon saw a glow coming through the door behind WOP then choking fumes, together with sound of exploding ammunition. Aircraft went into slight dive at first but skipper soon righted it. By the time I had fixed my chute and pulled back the curtain the B/A. Sgt. Roche had gone closely followed by the Engineer Sgt. Bellman. Never noticed the call light flashing. The skipper P/O. Wilson and W/Op. Sgt. Wakely were both O.K. when I left – the WOP was right behind me. There seemed to be an extensive fire in the tail of the aircraft, so am afraid the two gunners did not have much of a chance – MUG Sgt. Henderson, IG Sgt. HANNAH. Estimate height at 10,000 feet at the most. Aircraft still under control though difficulty when I left. Landed on a quarry so I don't know whether aircraft crashed immediately or not.

Jack Morschel's account of the loss of ND685 (Jack Morschel)

Jack Morschel (2nd left), Alan Wilson (centre) and crew (Geoff Vigar)

Jack Morschel RAAF (Jack Morschel) Alan Wilson RAAF (Wilson family collection)   George Belman (G. Belman)

hours. Wade Rodgers witnessed 'Happy Jack' Wilson's loss as flames streamed back from his Lancaster. He recalled, *'not knowing who it was then, we watched the flames and saw the parachutes open one by one. 'Jack' stayed at the controls and saw his crew out safely not being able to get out himself before he ploughed in'.*

Jack Morschel landed in a quarry amidst several German artillery batteries and despite a sprained ankle managed to crawl to cover and hide for five days avoiding the German patrols. Eventually desperate for water he had to ask local Frenchmen for help, water was provided to him along with a little food but Morschel was disgusted when within three hours a German patrol came directly to his hiding place to take him into captivity. Three members of the crew survived and were taken Prisoner of War but their captain, wireless op and both gunners were buried near Authie although they were later reburied at Bayeux War Cemetery. Flight Engineer George Bellman, a Joiner from Stockport spent the next year between Stalag Luft 7, Stalag 344 and Stalag Luft 7A. He was joined at Stalag Luft 7 by Frank Roche of Sydney. Alastair Henderson of Creif had only married his sweetheart Betty in Perth on 17th February.

Wednesday 7th June 1944.

Support of Allied ground forces was obviously of maximum importance and amongst the targets selected for the next night was a vital 6-way road junction halfway between Bayeux and St. Lo. The surrounding woodlands were reported as hiding a tank park of 7th and 21st Panzer Divisions containing both tanks and self-propelled assault guns (Sturmartillerie), their fuel and ammunition supplies. A counterattack was being prepared.112 Lancasters and 10 Mosquitoes were despatched to the target which was recorded as the Foret de Cerisy near Balleroy. 630 Squadron's Lancasters were each armed with 18 x 500 GP bombs.

The Wilson crew graves (Wilson family collection)

7th/8th June 1944 : Night Bombing Attack on Foret de Cerisy
Take Off: at 23:00 hours 'Pancho' O'Dwyer's LL949 was the first off the ground.

ND797-W	S/L AE Foster
JB290-C	F/O HH Long RCAF
LL949-E	F/O TG O'Dwyer
MD650-B	P/O DH Simpson RCAF
ME795-G	P/O LN Rackley RAAF
LM117-J	P/O BW Brittain RAAF
ND335-L	Sgt RT Hayes
ND527-O	P/O DE Hawker RNZAF
LM118-V	P/O AR Kerr
PA992-Y	P/O JW Lennon RNZAF
ME796-S	F/S HE Wilson RCAF
ME782-N	F/S CM Houghton
LL972-T	T/S W Adams USAAF

Summarised de-briefing reports noted that after the Controller had the Target Indicators corrected the bombing was concentrated and on target. Crews reported a very large explosion at 01:44 hours amidst a series of smaller explosions. Black smoke rising into the night sky was repeatedly reported. Very few fighters were encountered. The squadron attacked between 01:40 and 01:50 hours from 5,350 to 7,100 feet.

At 00:11 hours LM117 'J-Jig' (Bruce Brittain) was fired on by a twin engined night fighter and corkscrewed out of trouble as its gunners, Flight Sergeant Harry Wells and Sergeant Don Grant fired back from 600 yards before the fighter was lost to view. JB290 'C' (Hazen Long) was the last to return to East

Hazen Long RCAF and crew (RD Gale)

Kirkby landing at 05:58 hours. They were fortunate to make it home that night having been attacked before reaching the target by a JU88 which Sergeant Frank Houston (mid-upper gunner) fought off when the rear turret machine guns jammed and again over the target area at 01:44 hours by a pair of FW190's, the first came in firing as the second held clear. Hazen Long launched the Lancaster into a corkscrew to starboard as Sergeants Browne and Houston opened fire and scored some hits on the fighter. In the rear turret Ed Browne again had a stoppage on his four .303 browning machine guns after only firing 200 rounds and was thankful that the FW190 did not try to chase them.

Ron Hayes' crew aboard ND335 had also been set up for attack by a single engined fighter but it had aborted the attack when Sgt Walter Stead (mid upper) got in the first burst of machine gun fire.

On 8th June 1944 the London Gazette announced the award of the Air Force Medal to former flying instructor Flight Sergeant Claud Morley Houghton who had eventually been granted his wish to fly on ops and who had just brought his crew back aboard ME782. The AFM had been awarded in recognition of his guts and determination during a long tour of instruction at No. 10 Advanced Flying Unit (Dumfries) training pilots who were progressing towards operational flying. The counterpart of the DFM for gallantry in the face of the enemy, it was awarded for sustained courage away from the front line.

Friday 9th June 1944.

Further attacks were carried out to deprive German forces of supplies and reinforcements necessitating attacks on targets such as the railway yards and junction at Etampes. 5 Group provided 108 Lancasters and 4 Mosquitoes supplemented by 5 Pathfinder Mosquitoes. Six-thirty's Lancasters were each armed with 16 x 500lb GP bombs.

9th/10th June 1944: Night Bombing Attack on Etampes

Take Off: at 21:47 hours JB290 (Ron Hayes) was the first airborne.

ME650-B	F/O JCW Weller	
ME739-D	F/L CW Rodgers RAAF	
ME795-G	F/O HH Long RCAF	
ND335-L	F/O TG O'Dwyer	
JB290-C	P/O RT Hayes	
LM117-J	P/O BW Brittain RAAF	
ND531-K	P/O DH Simpson RCAF	
LL949-E	F/S HE Wilson RCAF	
PB121-F	F/S CM Houghton	
ND797-W	F/L GR Joblin RNZAF	
ME782-N	P/O BB Lindsay RAAF	
ND527-O	P/O DE Hawker RNZAF	RD
ME796-S	P/O RC Hooper	
LM118-V	P/O DR Mallinson	RD
LM537-X	P/O JW Lennon RNZAF	
PA992-Y	P/O AR Kerr	
LL972-T	T/S W Adams USAAF	

Yellow TIs were placed at the Datum Point, proximity markers and initial red spots were 400 yards north east of the aiming point resulting in some early crews bombing wide but at 23:59 and at 00:01hours the Controller ordered 'Stop bombing'. Markers were reset in green and based on the instruction to undershoot slightly when aiming the target was received concentrated bombing. Reports by the retuning crews report that they attacked as detailed in the third wave of bombers, between 00:09 hours and 00:24 hours from 4,500 to 7,400 feet. The controller issued the order to 'Cease bombing and return to base' at 00:20 and 00:21 hours. Some light flak was experienced in the target area. Bombing photos showed explosions in and amongst the railway tracks. Two combats with night fighters took place on the return flight. Don

Mallinson's LM118 'V-Victor' had its hydraulics shot away by cannon shells in an attack by a JU88 attacking from below and behind, he threw the Lancaster into a corkscrew as his gunners (Sergeants John McCartan and Don 'Taffy' Cross) returned fire. The JU88 was hit and its starboard engine cowling flew off. Both damaged in the engagement they lost contact with each other. Enemy aircraft confirmed damaged.

At 00:30 hours at 8,000 feet a JU88 which must have been in their port quarter up, fired at Alan Kerr's PA992 'Y-Yoke'. Sergeants Peter Yorston (mid upper) and Terry Noble (rear gunner) returned fire immediately as evasive action was taken, the fighter stayed with them and began to make a second attack from the starboard quarter down. Surprised that he kept closing on them the Lancaster's gunners fired long bursts into the fighter until it burst into flame and dived on fire into the ground. Enemy aircraft confirmed destroyed. Over the target at 5,600 feet Bill Adams' mid-upper gunner aboard LL972 'T-Tare', John

Jonny Kiesow USAAF (Debbie Guzman) *Ross Lough RCAF (G Lough (Canada))*

Kiesow USAAF sighted a single engined fighter possibly a Messerschmitt Bf109 at 400 yards range and called for a corkscrew to port as he and Ross Lough the rear gunner opened fire. The German dived away and was not seen again.

Queenslander Brian Lindsay's gunners in ME782 'N-Nan' were Sergeants Phil Lieberman and Tony Rainford who had joined the Southern Rhodesian Reserve together and trained together. They sighted a JU88 closing to attack and hit it with several bursts of fire, a 'damaged' was credited. ND531 (Simpson) was the last of the Lancasters to land at East Kirkby at 02:57 hours and the recently decorated Claud Houghton AFM and his crew Failed To Return.

Lancaster III, PB121 (Codes LE – F)

Pilot	– F/S Claud Morley Houghton AFM. Age 29	Killed
Flight Eng	– Sgt Horace Ison. Age 23	Killed
Navigator	– Sgt John Charles Cameron . Age	Killed
Bomb Aimer	– F/O Douglas Charles Percy. Age 24	Prisoner
Wireless Op	– Sgt William James Bott. Age 28	Killed
Mid Upper	– Sgt Russel Edward Dennis RCAF. Age 20	Killed
Rear Gunner	– Sgt William John Barr RCAF. Age 20	Killed

The post-war de-briefing of F/O DC Percy records that they were engaged by a night fighter whose second firing pass left PB121 engulfed in flames before its fuel tanks exploded. The bomber crashed at Omerville (Val d'Oise) a hamlet west of Magny-en-Vexin and the six members of the crew who died are buried at Omerville. Doug Percy a regular RAF airman from Wales landed unhurt and assisted by French civilians evaded capture. He was on the loose in Paris on 29th July 1944 when captured by German forces and locked up in the Gestapo prison at Fresnes for two weeks before being moved to Buchenwald Concentration Camp for two months. Eventually he was accepted as an RAF prisoner of war and transferred to Stalag Lift III (Sagan). Night fighter pilots made several claims that night but the most likely claimant for PB121 was Oberleutnant Johannes Werth of the Staff Flight of NJG2 at 00:42 hours. After flying 18 ops Don Mallinson and his crew were posted away for five weeks, they would however return to Six-thirty to complete their tour. Another 'sprog crew' posted to 630 Squadron were to fly their first op on 12th June but in common with virtually every new arrival during May and June there had not been time for their captain to gain operational experience flying on an attack with an

Alec Swain (Peter Swain)

experienced crew, as Second Dickie. 22 year old Matthew 'Alec' Swain[ii] from Southport headed an enormously loyal and committed young crew who were never to miss an op together during their service with the squadron. Swain's rear gunner 21 year old Geoff Bate from Aston, Birmingham was on his second tour (having flown previously with 61 Squadron from February to September 1943) and his experience coupled with their pilot's unflappable nature gave the crew enormous confidence.

Monday 12th June 1944.

Further attacks followed in support of ground forces as they desperately battled against an utterly determined combined force of German Army, Luftwaffe field troops and Waffen-SS to increase the Normandy Bridgehead. Six-thirty Lancasters were each bombed up with 13 x 1000lb ANM bombs for the attack.

12th/13th June 1944 : Night Bombing Attack on Caen Bridges
Take Off: at 23:34 hours Gordon Maxwell's PA992 was the first off the deck.

ND531-K	S/L AE Foster
ME650-B	F/O HH Long RCAF
JB290-C	P/O MA Swain
ME739-D	P/O DH Simpson RCAF
ME795-G	P/O LN Rackley RAAF
LM117-J	P/O AR Kerr
ND554-A	F/S HE Wilson RCAF
LL949-E	F/S EP Mitchell
LL972-T	S/L RO Calvert RNZAF
ME782-N	P/O BB Lindsay RAAF
LM118-V	P/O RC Hooper
ME796-S	P/O AG Henriquez
LM537-X	P/O JW Lennon RNZAF
PA992-Y	P/O GE Maxwell RAAF
ND797-W	T/S W Adams USAAF

Ron Hayes crew had problems with their aircraft and were unable to take off. The attack was rated 'Far below usual standard', only 7 of 15 squadron aircraft could attack (Wilson, Kerr, Calvert, Lindsay, Long, Lennon, Hooper all bombed between 02:22 and 02:29 hours from 6,000 to 9,600 feet) due to cloud cover and the Controller's instructions were unclear resulting in some aircraft attacking from below cloud level and others not bombing at all. Some target photos show bombing in the vicinity of the bridges and immediately north of the river. Ground defences slight and fighters were only seen in the target area. JB290 (Swain) was the last to land back at East Kirkby at 05:40 hours. At 02:02 hours Alan Kerr's LM117 'J-Jig' at 9,600 feet was attacked by a FW190 from 500 yards range but took violent evasive action just as the enemy aircraft opened fire and that coupled with the timely return fire from Alan Kerr's gunners, Sergeants Terry Noble and Peter Yorston, enabled the Lancaster to lose the fighter and return undamaged.

The night of 12th/13th June 1944 witnessed the start of the V-1 flying bomb (doodlebug) campaign against England. A small number of incidents were confirmed in London and its outskirts in Essex and Kent. The 'sprog' crews of 22 year old Edward 'Peter' Docherty[iii] and 21 year old Canadian Tom Hart[iv] had been assessed and cleared to make their operational debut as had the crew of 21 year old John Smith[v] from Witney, Oxfordshire, which had arrived in early May but for reasons unknown had not been operational although their pilot had been amongst the last to fly as a Second Dickie. A regular RAF serviceman 25 year old Dublin born pilot Thomas 'Paddy' Fenning[vi] and 22 year old Londoners John Bolton[vii] and Ralph Taft[viii] arrived from training with their crews and immediately commenced the set series of flying exercises in preparation for operations. Peter Docherty had inherited a complete crew who had been about to commence ops with 57 Squadron when their pilot (P/O Ron Culliford RAAF) made a 'second Dickie' trip aboard ND475 which crashed and exploded near Whittlesey, Cambridgeshire with the loss of all aboard. Without a captain and facing being split up they welcomed Peter with open arms and wouldn't hear of him making his operational debut without them.

Wednesday 14th June 1944.
Reports from the Military Liaison of major and concentrated German troop and armoured vehicle build-ups at Aunay-sur-Odon and Evrecy near Caen required a very fast response before they were able to deploy against Allied front lines in the vicinity. 337 aircraft were detailed to attack. In great haste the squadron's Lancasters were each armed with 11 x 1000lb AN-M and 4 x 500lb GP bombs.

14th/15th June 1944 : Night Bombing Attack on Aunay sur Odon
Take Off: at 22:15 hours ME650 flown by Hazen Long was the first to take off.

ME650-B	F/O HH Long RCAF
ME739-D	P/O DH Simpson RCAF
ME795-G	P/O LN Rackley RAAF
ND531-K	P/O MA Swain
ND335-L	P/O RT Hayes
ND554-A	F/S HE Wilson RCAF
LM117-J	Sgt EP Mitchell
ME796-S	P/O AG Henriquez
ME845-Q	P/O AR Kerr
ME843-U	P/O RC Hooper
LM118-V	P/O JHG Smith
ND797-W	P/O E Docherty
PA992-Y	P/O GE Maxwell RAAF
LM537-X	P/O BB Lindsay RAAF
LL972-T	T/S W Adams USAAF
ND527-O	P/O TG Hart RCAF

Low cloud was present in the target area but visibility was good. The markers and Red and green TIs were reportedly punctual and accurate and before it was obliterated some of the early crews clearly saw the road junction around which the deployments were reported, in the light of bomb bursts which were very accurate and concentrated. After 5 minutes the markers were obscured by smoke or went out and Controller had the target remarked accurately at 00:43 hours, recommencing the attack from 00:53 to 01:06 hours when he ordered 'stop bombing and return to base'. Six-thirty squadron crews attacked between 00:55 and 01:03 hours from 6,300 to 10,100 feet. Aboard LM117 'J-Jig' the crew of Sgt Eugene Mitchell had attacked and were heading for home when they found themselves in combat. At 01:21 hours in moonless conditions but with good visibility at 5,000 feet they were surrounded by fighter flares when bomb aimer P/O Ernie Roddis manning the nose gun turret sighted a twin engined fighter at 200 yards range port bow down, it opened fire and he let off an 80 round burst as it passed at 150 yards breaking to starboard. Two minutes later Sergeant Norman Longbottom in the rear turret saw what he believed to be same fighter passing from starboard to port below and both he and Sergeant Geoff Burt in the mid upper turret fired three second bursts causing the fighter to dive away into cloud. Twenty heavy anti-aircraft guns near the target area and some light flak four miles to the north had presented opposition along with fighter activity from crossing the French coast and then across the Channel Islands on their return. Alec Swain landed ND531 at 03:40 hours, the last of the squadron's aircraft to return.

Friday 16th June 1944.
Commencing a new campaign against the flying-bomb launching sites in the Pas-de-Calais Bomber Command marked four targets successfully with Oboe Mosquitoes and destroyed them with 385 heavy bombers. The Lancasters of 630 Squadron were each armed with 16 x 500lb GP and 2 x 500lb (36 hour delay) bombs.

"Pete" Docherty and crew, the "Breeze Boys" with LL966 (Bill Horsman)

Tom Hart RCAF (Library and Archives Canada)

John Bolton (Chris Bolton)

16th/17th June 1944 : Night Bombing Attack on Beauvoir

Take Off: at 22:30 hours a newly arrived crew aboard ND527 captained by Tom Hart took off first from East Kirkby.

ME650-B	F/L JCW Weller
LM117-J	F/O HH Long RCAF
ME739-D	P/O DH Simpson RCAF
ME795-G	P/O LN Rackley RAAF
ND531-K	P/O MA Swain
ND335-L	P/O RT Hayes
ND554-A	F/S HE Wilson RCAF
LL949-E	Sgt EP Mitchell
LL972-T	W/C WI Deas
ME782-N	P/O BB Lindsay RAAF
ME845-Q	P/O AR Kerr
ME796-S	P/O AG Henriquez
ME843-U	P/O RC Hooper
LM118-V	P/O JHG Smith
ND797-W	P/O E Docherty
LM537-X	P/O JW Lennon RNZAF
PA992-Y	P/O GE Maxwell RAAF
ND527-O	F/S TG Hart RCAF
ME729-I	T/S W Adams USAAF

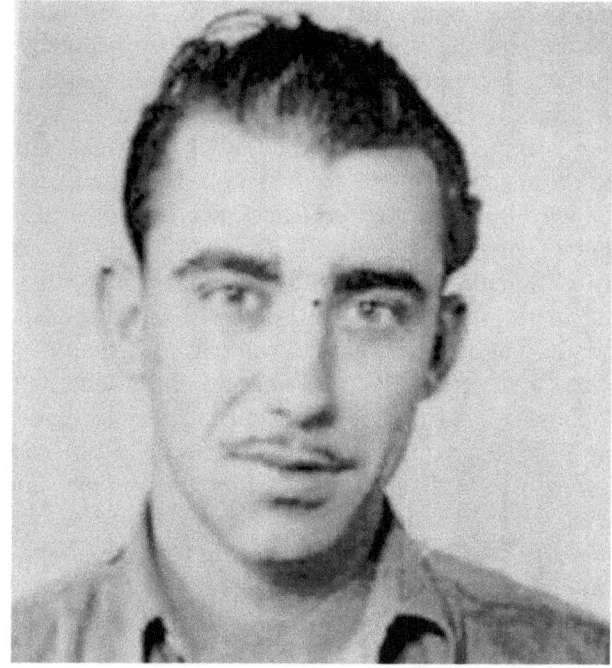

Brian Lindsay RAAF. This was his photo carried to aid evasion if he was shot down (Brian Lindsay)

ME782 'N-Nan' flown by Brian Lindsay was unable to attack as their bomb sight went un-serviceable. Target marking was reported as punctual and accurate. Six-thirty's aircraft attacked from 10,350 to 13,350 feet between 00:39 and 00:46 hours meeting no real opposition from ground defences although fighters were present in the target area and on the homeward route. ND335 (Ron Hayes) was the last to land back at base at 03:05 hours. The next raid however was to be a 'hairy-do'. For Brian Lindsay's crew it has been a frustrating 11th and last Op with 630 Squadron, they transferred out to 97 Squadron 'Straits Settlements' to complete their tours as Pathfinders and surviving the full tour their captain was later awarded a DFC.

Wednesday 21st June 1944.

133 Lancasters and 6 Mosquitoes were detailed to attack the synthetic oil refineries at Wesseling. Hitler's Panzer's were desperate for fuel in the fighting in Normandy and unless sufficient could be produced they would be helpless. Six-thirty were instructed to bomb-up with 1 x 4000lb HC and 6 x 500lb GP inst and 6 x 500lb (025) and 4 x 500lb GP (2 hour delay) aboard each Lancaster.

21st/22nd June 1944 : Night Bombing Attack on Wesseling
Take Off: at 23:13 hours ME845 (Alan Kerr) was the first airborne.

ND531-K	S/L AE Foster	
ME650-B	F/L JCW Weller	
JB290-C	P/O HH Long RCAF	
ME739-D	P/O DH Simpson RCAF	
ME795-G	F/O LN Rackley RAAF	
LM117-J	P/O MA Swain	RD
ND335-L	P/O RT Hayes	
ND554-A	F/S HE Wilson RCAF	
LL949-E	Sgt EP Mitchell	
ME782-N	P/O TG Hart RCAF	
ND527-O	P/O DE Hawker RNZAF	
ME845-Q	P/O AR Kerr	
ME796-S	P/O AG Henriquez	
ME843-U	P/O RC Hooper	
LM118-V	P/O JHG Smith	
ND797-W	P/O E Docherty	
LM537-X	P/O JW Lennon RNZAF	RD
PA992-Y	F/O GE Maxwell RAAF	
LL972-T	T/S W Adams USAAF	

The weather forecast of clear skies in the target area was incorrect and 5 Group attackers found 10/10ths cloud and had to revert to bombing on H2S. All aircraft pressed home this attack in the face of fierce resistance both from ground and from fighters. Markers were punctual and H2S confirmed their accuracy. The Controller's orders to bomb the red TIs and green TIs were received but some of the earliest to attack could only see red markers and later green and yellow were seen. The squadron's crews attacked between 01:43 and 01:48 hours from 17,600 to 19,850 feet. A large explosion was recorded at 01:45 hours. The German reaction was strong and sustained. Fighter interceptions had begun at the coast on the route in and continued all way round and out over the sea on the way back. Heavy and accurate flak was also experienced. Wesseling was a massacre of the heavy bombers. Bringing home ME739 at 04:02 hours Doug Simpson was the last to land. Six Lancasters were lost by 44 Squadron, six by 49 Squadron including their CO, Wing Commander Malcolm Crocker DFC and Bar formerly of 630 Squadron, six by 57 Squadron, six by 619 Squadron, five by 207 Squadron, five by 630 Squadron and so on went the roll call of casualties – approaching one third of the attacking bombers were shot down or crippled and fated to crash. Combats with fighters had taken place regularly throughout. Doug Hawker's recollection of events after crossing the French coast illustrate the situation vividly, *'Immediately fighter flares began to light up the sky and bombers began to go down in flames. We were supposed to record the positions of aircraft we saw shot down. Normally I would tell Jack (navigator) where a stricken aircraft should be seen relative to our position on his chart. At that precise time I was reporting the positions of aircraft going down in flames faster than he could plot the positions on his chart. I soon ceased to mention them because I felt such a devastating spectacle would be demoralising for the rest of our crew. All the way to the target and all the way back, aircraft were going down in flames'.*

At 01:12 hours flying on track at 18,850 feet with no moon but fair visibility in ND335 'L-Love' Ron Hayes' crew were alerted by their rear gunner Sgt Bernie Graves that three Me109's were in formation on a parallel course to port. A fighter flare suddenly lit up the sky and a fourth 109 commenced an attack for the port quarter up. He was caught out as the Lancaster corkscrewed to port before he could open fire and both gunners fired bursts which Sergeants Graves and Wally Stead in the mid upper turret saw strike home. The 109's were not seen again. Me109 claimed as damaged. In reasonable visibility at 01:18 hours Alan Kerr's mid-upper gunner Sergeant Peter Yorston aboard ME845 'Q' sighted a single engined fighter 500 yards ahead on the port bow firing on another Lancaster at 19,000 feet. He ordered a corkscrew to port and fired off a burst of 200 rounds at the German, if he was lucky he might damage the fighter but at the least he'd spoil his attack. Aboard Canadian Hazen Long's JB290 'C' his countryman and rear gunner Ed Browne shouted a warning at 01:54 hours when he saw a JU88 port up moving across to starboard level to commence an attack. Long dived into a corkscrew to port as the fighter opened fire and Ed Browne got off only 50 rounds and mid-upper gunner Sgt Frank Houston 150 rounds before their guns jammed. Fortunately the German did not stay with the Lancaster to continue the attack. At 02:23 hours flying homeward at 6,000 feet Alfred Henriquez's crew in ME796 'S-Sugar' came under attack from a Me210 sighted just astern and below by rear gunner Alan McKenzie. Henriquez made a corkscrew to port evading the cannon and machine gun fire as both McKenzie and Charles Henderson (mid-upper) opened up on the night fighter. Their Lancaster wasn't damaged and no results of their own return fire could be observed. At 02:25 hours New Zealander Joe Lennon in LM537 'X' was heading for home at 7,000 feet when Flight Sergeant Joe Pollard his Aussie rear gunner shouted a warning of a JU88 moving astern to the starboard quarter down. LM537 was thrown into a corkscrew as the night fighter opened fire and broke away. He and Phil Dixon-Burt in the mid upper turret returned fire, Joe Pollard reportedly turning the air blue as his guns jammed. He cleared the stoppage but the night fighter had been lost in their wake. Both gunners saw hits on the fighter. The JU88 was claimed as damaged. Harry Parkins (flight engineer) was convinced it had been destroyed.

The four missing from 630 Squadron were ND531 'K-Kitty' flown by flight commander Squadron Leader Foster, ME782 'N-Nan' by Hart, LM118 'V-Victor' by Smith and ME843 'U-Uncle' by Bob Hooper DFC and 'Blue' Rackley's ME795 'G-George' crashed in England on its return.

Lancaster III, ME795 (Codes LE – G)

Role	Name	Fate
Pilot	– F/O Lionel Norman Rackley RAAF. Age	Injured
Flight Eng	– Sgt Stanley Jones. Age	Survived
Navigator	– F/O Ian Stuart Gow. Age 23	Survived
Bomb Aimer	– F/S Douglas Stewart Morgan RAAF. Age 20	Survived
Wireless Op	– F/S Phillip Raymond Carroll. Age 19	Survived
Mid Upper	– F/S Jack D Jones Age	Survived
Rear Gunner	– F/S William Alfred Cecil Davis. Age 23	Killed

'G-George' was attacked by a fighter on approaching the target but despite his aircraft being badly damaged 'Blue' Rackley pressed on to bomb. On the way home the control column had to be locked back and the rudder bar locked over to starboard in order to fly straight and level. At 03:38 hours near Henlow in Buckinghamshire the crew had to abandon 'G-George' as it became more and more unmanageable and a tandem jump was necessary for Bill Davis the rear gunner as his parachute had been damaged by one of the night fighters cannon shells. Flight Sergeant Doug Morgan RAAF the bomb aimer volunteered to try and their harnesses were intertwined and clipped together but unfortunately the rear gunner's harness broke with the force of the canopy opening and he fell to his death. 'Blue' Rackley was badly injured when about to land his parachute was snagged by a speeding express train and he was dragged for some distance. Ian Gow was also seriously injured. In his rear turret Bill Davis had been sole survivor of the massive take off crash and explosion in February 1944. Stan Jones takes up the story- *'I am afraid old 'G-George' caught a packet over enemy territory, a JU-88 got us from underneath, shot away a lot of the rear turret, two thirds of the port elevator, blew a great hole in the fuselage opposite the entrance door, blew up some radio equipment, hit the mid-upper turret and damaged the aileron controls. It was a wonder that no one was hurt, we dropped our bombs, turned round and belted for home, but the aircraft was in a pretty bad state and 'Blue' (Flying Officer L. Rackley, DFC) did a wonderful job in flying it straight and level, but with Doug and I, in turn, hauling back on the stick, which developed a very heavy tendency and was hard to work. We managed it eventually and we reached England at about 15,000 feet. We could not turn the aircraft or make any attempt to land so 'Blue' said 'Bale out'. First of all I lashed the stick to the back of*

Left: "Blue" Rackley RAAF, his wound stripe visible on his sleeve (Blue Rackley) Right: "Ray" Carroll (Andy Carroll)

'Blue's' seat with wire, and then tied up the rudder controls. Doug and Taffy made their effort first with fatal results to poor old Taffy [one parachute was used between them]. I went sixth and 'Blue' followed.

It was a momentary effort to go through the front escape hatch, head first, with cloud rushing by so far below, but after a second or so, and the ripcord pulled, it was a wonderful sensation to be floating gently in space, and not a sound to break the stillness of the night. After a while, 'G' George came round in a great diving circle and disappeared through the clouds, a few seconds later a great glare went up as it crashed to earth. A little later I dropped through the clouds, the cloud base was so low I was rather taken by surprise and I hardly had time to get into some sort of position before I hit the deck. I could see the aircraft blazing merrily and, to my great relief, out in the wide open spaces. I made a fruitless trip across the field to what looked like a house but was only trees. However, I found a nice haystack and sat down for a welcome smoke. After a while something ran over me, probably a frog, so I set off to find a way out of the field, drew two blanks but at the third attempt I reached a road with telegraph wires which seemed hopeful. I struck off to the right, which looked more interesting and, after a minute or two, came across a couple of derelict looking caravans, and to my surprise as I went past a voice said, 'Who's there?' I asked the way to the nearest house and the old boy inside came to the door of the caravan and gave me the necessary directions and, as an afterthought, said 'Are you English?' which rather amused me.Five minutes' walk and I landed at a small pub and knocked up the owner who was downstairs in a moment and gave me a whisky. They had a phone so I was on to our own aerodrome immediately, and then to the nearest one here. The innkeeper gave me tea until the R.A.F. rolled up. We picked up Jack and 'Curly' on the way and found Ian already there, Doug had landed near a Yankee aerodrome and came on later in the morning. They dumped us all in the sick bay, gave us breakfast and then off to sleep.'

Stan Jones was unaware at the time that his Australian skipper, Flying Officer Blue. Rackley, had also survived, but with a fractured shoulder – he had the misfortune to get his parachute caught on the carriage of a London-bound express train and was dragged along the railway track for some distance before breaking free. Back in action in early August, Jones went on to complete his tour of operations with eight more sorties that month, most of them against German targets, and he was transferred to instructional duties in October 1944. Doug Morgan was awarded the British Empire Medal (Military Division) - Aus.413786 Flight Sergeant Douglas Stewart Morgan, Royal Australian Air Force.

'One night in June, 1944, Flight Sergeant Morgan was the air bomber in an aircraft which attacked an objective in the Rhineland. Whilst over the target the bomber was attacked by an enemy fighter and serious damage was sustained. Course was set for home but the aircraft was so difficult to control that Flight Sergeant Morgan was required to assist the pilot and flight engineer to keep the aircraft on its course. When this country was reached all attempts to turn the bomber on to its course for base were unavailing and it was impossible to attempt a landing. The pilot ordered the crew to escape by parachute and, as the rear gunner's parachute had been destroyed by cannon fire from the enemy fighter, Flight Sergeant Morgan volunteered to share his own parachute with the rear gunner. Unfortunately, the rear gunner was dislodged when the parachute opened but Flight Sergeant Morgan landed safely. He displayed complete disregard of his own safety, knowing that he faced the risk of serious injury in his gallant attempt to save the life of his companion'.

Rackley himself gave his thoughts in Lancaster at War, Garbett and Goulding, p.99-100: 'Caterpillars Extraordinaire' 'Soon after we crossed the Dutch coast we began to see aircraft exploding, so many in fact that I was almost convinced they were spoofs until suddenly it was our turn. I had just brought the kite to a straight and level attitude after a banking search when there was a terrific explosion aft, coupled with a muffled cry from one of my gunners. Eventually, I reached the clouds. The base must have been quite low because no sooner had I passed through than I realised that I was being dragged along at a terrific rate and I became aware of the distinctive sound made by train wheels, rattling beside my ear ... I remember finding myself beside a railway line. My second flying boot had gone, as had my watch. My chute was also gone. I found later that it had got caught up in the train, causing quite a stir on its arrival in London, when a search party was sent back up the line.'

Damage sustained by Blue Rackley's Lancaster was summarised as – 'Rear gunners intercom out of action, rear gunners turret smashed by cannon fire, port elevator out of action, large hole in fuselage caused by cannon fire, scanner shot away, entrance door jammed 6 inches open, hydraulics damaged, small hole in tip of fuselage, astern controls damaged'.

Lancaster III, ND531 (Codes LE – K)

Pilot	– S/L Arthur Edgar Foster DFC . Age 23	Killed
Flight Eng	– F/S Leonard Lawrence DFM . Age 22	Killed
Navigator	– F/L Robert Adams DFC . Age 32	Killed
Bomb Aimer	– F/O Frank Leonard Hewish. Age 23	Killed
Wireless Op	– F/O Frederick Richard Stone MID . Age 26	Killed
Mid Upper	– Sgt Dennis George Bradd. Age 20	Killed
Rear Gunner	– F/O Leonard George Davis DFM . Age 24	Killed

Many of the crew were on their second tours having completed a first tour with 61 Squadron, Squadron Leader Foster was awarded a DFC (London Gazette 9th March 1943, 61 Squadron). Leonard Lawrence had been awarded a DFM (London Gazette 14th October 1943, 61 Squadron), Leonard Davis a DFM (London Gazette 12th November 1943, 61 Squadron) and Squadron Navigation Leader Robert Adams a DFC (London Gazette 8th June 1943, 61 Squadron). Dick Stone was Mentioned in Despatches in the King's Birthday Honours List (London Gazette 2nd June 1944). The entire crew are commemorated on Runnymede Memorial to the Missing and they were possibly lost over the sea.

'Blue' Rackley (4th from left) Stan Jones (4th from rt). Ian Gow (3rd from rt) (Geoff Copeman/IWM)

This Lancaster was shot down by either Oberleutnant Walter Riedlberger of 1/NJG4 or Hauptmann Heinz Struning of 3/NJG1 over the sea north west of Schouwen as ND531 of 630 Squadron and ND695 of 49 Squadron fell within minutes of each other at 0224 and 0230 hours in this area.

Left: Len Davies (Patti Kellaway) Right: Robert Adams after the presentation of his DFC (J Bentley and C Young)

Lancaster I, ME782 (Codes LE – N)

Pilot	– P/O Thomas George Hart RCAF. Age 21	Killed
Flight Eng	– Sgt Ronald Merrick Jordan. Age 26	Killed
Navigator	– Sgt Michael John Macnaughton-Smith . Age 20	Killed
Bomb Aimer	– F/O John Joseph Scully RCAF. Age 21	Killed
Wireless Op	– F/S Raymond Guy Harwood . Age 20	Killed
Mid Upper	– P/O Richard John Walton RCAF . Age 20	Killed
Rear Gunner	– P/O Archie Harry Siemens RCAF . Age 22	Killed

Shot down by a night fighter, probably flown by Hauptmann Eckart-Wilhelm von Bonin of II/NJG 1 (2nd Wing of Night Fighter Group 1) at 01:14 hours. Von Bonin claimed a Lancaster at 5,400 metres 18 km east-south-east of Turnhout and ME782 crashed into open countryside 4km north-east of Turnhout (Antwerp). Alternatively Leutnant Manfred Scheunpflug of Stab I/NJG3 might have attacked it. Michael

Archie Siemens RCAF
M and J Siemens (Canada)

Dicky Walton RCAF
(Library and Archives Canada)

Fred Dewis RCAF.
(D Jadot/Morgana)

Macnaughton-Smith was a student of St.Johns College, Oxford. All of the crew were buried on 24th June in the cemetery of Antwerpen-Deurne and now lie in Schoonselhof Cemetery.

Lancaster I, ME843 (Codes LE – U)

Pilot	– P/O Robert Cecil Hooper DFC. Age 22	Killed
Flight Eng	– Sgt Thomas Dudley Fraser. Age 24	Killed
Navigator	– WO2 Frederick Sayre Dewis RCAF . Age 20	Killed
Bomb Aimer	– F/S John Leo McKenna RAAF. Age	Killed
Wireless Op	– Sgt Peter Hogan Kano. Age 21	Killed
Mid Upper	– F/L Thomas Neison DFC . Age 31	Killed
Rear Gunner	– Sgt Daniel Felix Oliver Synnott. Age 19	Killed

ME843 was attacked by the most successful night fighter pilot in history, Hauptmann Heinz-Wolfgang Schnaufer of IV/NJG1 (4th Wing of Night Fighter Group 1) at 02:04 hours 2,900 metres over Hamont-Achtel. Bob Hooper's Lancaster crashed in flames between Hamont (Limburg) and Bocholt. The crew are buried at Heverlee War Cemetery. Tom Neison DFC, Squadron Gunnery Leader was flying with the crew as Mid-Upper Gunner that night. Schnaufer was killed in a motor accident soon after the war but Fritz Rumpelhardt who was a member of his crew retained a copy of his 'leistungsbuch' (combat log) showing details of all 121 aircraft he shot down and the entry for Victory No. 84 at 02:04 hours on 22nd June 1944 records that he fought against intense return fire in his attack on ME843.

Lancaster III, LM118 (Codes LE –V)

Pilot	– P/O John Henry George Smith. Age 21	Killed
Flight Eng	– Sgt Ian Alistair Place. Age 19	Killed
Navigator	– Sgt Robert Edward Duck . Age 29	Killed
Bomb Aimer	– F/O Norman Bunker Wilcock. Age 30	Killed
Wireless Op	– Sgt John Kenneth Kimberley . Age 21	Killed
Mid Upper	– Sgt Eric Stanley Worden. Age 19	Killed
Rear Gunner	– Sgt Henry George Kember. Age 19	Killed

> **ROYAL AIR FORCE**
>
> WING COMMANDER MALCOLM CROCKER, D.F.C., previously reported missing, now presumed killed in action, was born in Massachusetts, United States, in 1917. He was educated at Trinity College, Hartford, Connecticut, and came from Washington to take up a commission in the R.A.F.V.R. in 1942. In October, 1943, as an acting squadron leader with No. 57 Squadron, he was awarded the D.F.C. after completing a number of sorties, including seven missions to the Ruhr and the raid on Friedrichshafen when Spezia was attacked on the return flight from North Africa. Three months later he gained a Bar to the D.F.C. for further skill, determination, and courage in attacks on many strongly defended German targets in command of No. 630 Squadron. He had always displayed the utmost keenness for operational work.

Malcolm Crocker's obituary (Mike Glenn)

LM118 was shot down by a night fighter, possibly Oberfeldwebel Heinrich Kuesling of 12/NJG3 and fell west of Eindhoven at 0212. The crew lie together in Eindhoven (Woensel) General Cemetery. Wesseling was a sad chapter in the history of 630 Squadron

Immediately after the fateful night Wade Rodgers recalled being nominated by Wing Commander Deas to lead 21 aircraft of the squadron in a formation parade around Lincolnshire, as he said it must have surprised a few pairs of eyes on the other bomber airfields and in civilian life. He was later complimented by the OC and also the Station Commander on the show.

Saturday 24th June 1944.
Continuing the campaign against flying bomb launch sites, the night of 24th/25th June saw 739 aircraft of all groups detailed to attack 7 sites in northern France. Due to sustained raids by the RAF and USAAF these sites were becoming so cratered that it was almost impossible to identify the latest results. Lancasters of Six-thirty were each armed with 16 x 500lb MC (025) and 2 x 500lb MC (6 hours delay) bombs.

24th/25th June 1944 : Night Bombing Attack on Pommerval
Take Off: at 22:21 hours the squadron took off following LL966 (Edward 'Peter' Docherty).

ME739-D	F/L CW Rodgers RAAF
ND335-L	F/O TG O'Dwyer
ND554-A	P/O MA Swain
ME796-S	P/O DG Gamble
ME650-B	P/O JH Bolton
LM117-J	P/O BW Brittain RAAF
LL949-E	Sgt EP Mitchell
ND797-W	F/L GR Joblin RNZAF
ND527-O	F/L DE Hawker RNZAF
LL966-P	P/O E Docherty
ME845-Q	P/O RN Taft
LM537-X	P/O JW Lennon RNZAF
PA992-Y	P/O GE Maxwell RAAF

The outward trip was uneventful and the attack commenced 2 minutes late as the first red spot flares were inaccurately placed but at 00:05 the controller ordered crews to attack the green TIs, 630 Squadron crews attacked between 00:07 and 00:17 hours from 6,350 to 9,200 feet. An excellent concentration of bombing took place around the green TIs. The bombing ceased at 00:17 hours. Ground defences were less than expected but fighters were active in the target area and also on the route home. Eight combats took place with night fighters and photos confirm that the target was bombed accurately. Soon after attacking the target John Bolton's ME650 'B-Baker' had a hairy moment when at 00:20 hours flying at 10,000 feet and in good visibility a single engine night fighter began to attack from 500 yards starboard quarter down. With tracer fire coming in Bolton corkscrewed starboard and both gunners returned fire each expending about 400 rounds, the number 2 gun in the mid upper turret jammed and as Sergeant John Gurney fought to clear the stoppage Sergeant Len Page in the rear turret continued to fire. Fortunately the German was lost in the darkness. At 02:13 hours Aussie Bruce Brittain landed LM117, the last to return to East Kirkby. After training at 29 OTU. and 1660 HCU the crew of 20 year old Arthur Kemp[ix] from Winnipeg joined Six-thirty

Wade Rodgers RAAF (Wade Rodgers)

followed by the unusually all British crew of 22 year old William McNeil[x] and were soon completing a series of pre-operations exercises. Both captains would fly as Second Dickies on 4th/5th July 1944 before commencing their tours simultaneously on the night of 7th/8th July. With 13 ops already under their belts in their first tour with Squadron Leader Blome-Jones' flight in 207 Squadron, Flight Lieutenant (Acting Squadron Leader) Roy Millichap[xi] and his crew were posted to 630 Squadron, replacing the recently missing flight commander Squadron Leader Foster. One month short of his 28th birthday, Plymouth-born 'Millie' Millichap was an experienced bomber pilot noted for his steadiness and reliability.

'Gem' Jewell (Wireless Op), Roy Millichap, Dave Schwab (Rear Gunner) (Roy Millichap)

Tuesday 27th June 1944.

The German Military V-bomb construction depot at Mimoyecques had been attacked by 104 Halifaxes of 4 Group during the day of 27th June and what had survived was the target for the night raid. The Lancasters of 630 Squadron were armed with 11 x 1000lb MC and 4 x 500lb GP bombs.

27th/28th June 1944 : Night Bombing Attack on Marquise

Take Off: at 22:58 hours ND545 (Alec Swain) was the first to take off.

ME739-D	F/L CW Rodgers RAAF
ND335-L	F/L TG O'Dwyer
ND554-A	P/O MA Swain
ME650-B	P/O JH Bolton
JB290-C	P/O DG Gamble
LM117-J	P/O BW Brittain RAAF
LL949-E	Sgt EP Mitchell
ND797-W	F/L GR Joblin RNZAF
ND527-O	F/L DE Hawker RNZAF
ME845-Q	P/O RN Taft
LL966-P	P/O E Docherty
LM537-X	P/O JW Lennon RNZAF
PA992-Y	P/O GE Maxwell RAAF
ME796-S	F/S TS Fenning

No fighters were airborne to attack the bomber stream and in the target area visibility was excellent. The squadron's crews attacked between 00:48 and 00:59 hours from 16,000 to 19,100 feet. Well placed red TIs were seen clearly and the bombing was concentrated near the TIs. The Luftwaffe mounted no opposition and light ground defences did not present serious opposition. This was assessed as a very successful attack. At 02:09 hours Doug Gamble's crew aboard 'C-Charlie' were the last to return, they had been last to bomb, eight minutes behind the remainder of the squadron, attacking only after doing a second bombing run at the insistence of Frank Burn their Scots bomb aimer.

On 30th June 1944 the London Gazette carried the announcement of the award of a Bar to the Distinguished Flying Cross for Flight Lieut. Ken Ames in respect of his service with No. 630 Squadron.

July 1944

Three recently arrived crews were completing their training preparing for Ops with 630 Squadron, the all NCO crew of 22 year old Flight Sergeant George Bowers[i] from Malvern Link, Worcestershire and the all NCO crew of 21 year old Flight Sergeant Peter Dennett RAAF[ii] of Toorak, Victoria who had known each other at 16 OTU. and 1654 CU and an all British crew captained by 22 year old Londoner Alex Sargent[iii] who had trained at 29 OTU.'Peter' Docherty's crew were by now fully established amongst their peers as the 'Breeze Boys' after the front escape hatch of their Lanc came loose in flight jamming open causing a

The Bowers crew. Back row l to r: Stott, Langridge, Carrier, Thompson.
Front row l to r: McLaughlin, Bowers, Fingland   (LAHC Archive)

Alex Sargent
(Sargent family album)

Peter Dennett RAAF
(Marjorie Smith)

David 'Robbie' Roberts DFC received congratulations on the DFC awarded for his tour (Jeff Manning and the Roberts family)

howling gale to blow through the fuselage of their Lancaster until it could be refitted. Navigator Francis Bailey's maps were retrieved, very gingerly indeed, from the Elsan chemical toilet.

Tuesday 4th July 1944,
307 Halifaxes of 4 and 6 Groups attacked the German Flying bomb storage depot which was sited in a large cave at St. Leu d'Esserent, north of Paris. 5 Group continued the attack with Six-thirty participating fully bombed-up with 11 x 1000lb MC, 2 x 500lb GP (025) and 2 x 500lb LD (8 hours) bombs.

4th/ 5th July 1944 : Night Bombing Attack on Creil (St. Leu d'Esserent)
Take Off: at 23:01 hours 'Sam' Weller in ME650 was the first off, behind him two of the experienced crews had Second Dickies aboard.

ND688-R	S/L RO Calvert RNZAF	(P/O AF Kemp RCAF)
ND797-W	F/L GR Joblin RNZAF	(P/O WA McNeil)
ME867-N	P/O RN Taft	
LL966-P	P/O E Docherty	
ME845-Q	P/O AR Kerr	
ME796-S	P/O AG Henriquez	
LL972-T	T/S W Adams USAAF	RD
PA992-Y	P/O GE Maxwell RAAF	
ND949-Z	F/S TS Fenning	RD
ME650-B	F/L JCW Weller	
ME739-D	F/L CW Rodgers RAAF	
ND335-L	F/L TG O'Dwyer	
PB236-F	F/O HH Long RCAF	
JB290-C	P/O DG Gamble	
LM216-K	P/O DH Simpson RCAF	
LM637-V	P/O RT Hayes	
ND527-O	P/O HE Wilson RCAF	
LM117-J	P/O BW Brittain RAAF	RD
LM537-X	P/O JH Bolton	
LL949-E	Sgt EP Mitchell	

Over the target there were small amounts of cloud but it was mainly clear and the marking was punctual and seemed accurate. The original markers were well backed up and bombing seemed concentrated on red TIs picked out by green TIs. 630 Squadron attacked between 01:32 and 01:39 hours from 14,350 to 18,100 feet. Ground defences were less than expected but there was considerable evidence of fighter activity with combats on both outward and homeward routes and also through the target area. The main force lost 10 Lancasters, one of them from Six-thirty. Bombing photos show that the marker was probably accurate and ensuing bombing was around the marker. At 01:52 hours in patchy cloud under a full moon at 9,000 feet a fighter flare lit up ME845 'Q' and a JU88 was sighted at 1000 yards on the starboard quarter down moving across to port quarter up as he tried to get into position. Alan Kerr immediately flung 'Queenie' into a corkscrew as Sergeant Peter Yorston in the mid upper turret began hosing .303 rounds at the German joined by Sergeant Terry Noble the rear gunner after he cleared an early stoppage. The German pilot followed Kerr's Lancaster in its violent manoeuvre and staying with the bomber he opened fire at 200 yards but receiving numerous hits from the gunners' return fire the night fighter broke off his attack. Sergeant John Fraser the flight engineer saw pieces breaking off the JU88 between its fuselage and port engine and it dived away not to be seen again. 1,800 rounds were fired by the two gunners during the combat. The authorities rated this as Confirmed Damaged. Aboard 'Paddy' Fenning's ND949 'Z-Zebra' mid upper gunner Sergeant Jim O'Leary and rear gunner Jimmy Brown had been in combat with a JU88 which was recorded as damaged and an Me109. No combat report appears to have survived. Ron Hayes gunners found themselves in action again, this time aboard 'V-Victor' (LM637) and they also fought back when a JU88 attacked and claimed it damaged. Sergeant Walter Stead was mid-upper and Sergeant Bernie Graves rear gunner. Technical Sergeant Bill Adams USAAF flying LL972 'T-Tare' returned thanks to alert gunners Sergeant Ross Lough (rear gunner) and Sergeant Johnnie Kiesow (mid upper) who fought off a night fighter shooting it down. A Do217 destroyed was officially confirmed. A Ju88 which manoeuvred to attack Gordon Maxwell's PA992 'Y-Yoke' also came off worst when their new rear gunner 'Paddy' Leary, who had recently joined the crew to replace Ron Peake after he'd been wounded in an attack by a night fighter in late May, displayed his rumoured superior night vision and 'clobbered it' before it could open fire, the JU88 was rated probably destroyed. The last to return safely to East Kirkby was Doug Simpson's LM216 at 04:44 hours. One crew Failed To Return.

Lancaster III, ME867 (Codes LE – N)

Pilot	– P/O Ralph Norman Taft. Age 22	Killed
Flight Eng	– Sgt William John Goodyear. Age 34	Killed
Navigator	– Sgt Harold Bradley. Age 20	Killed
Bomb Aimer	– Sgt Frank Hartley. Age 20	Killed
Wireless Op	– Sgt Eric Charles Day. Age 21	Killed
Mid Upper	– Sgt Frederick Hubert Hard. Age 19	Killed
Rear Gunner	– Sgt George Herbert Tyler. Age 22	Killed

Ralph Taft's Lancaster crashed at Lannoy-Cuillere (Oise), 4 km north-west of Abancourt, it was quite possibly shot down at 0203 hours by Oberleutnant Rold Klages who claimed a bomber 5km south of Aumale flying at 2100m altitude. Sgt Hard is buried in Lannoy-Cuillere Cemetery but the remainder of his crew lie for reasons unknown at Poix-de-la-Somme Churchyard.

Ralph Taft and crew (LAHC Archive)

Friday 7th July 1944.

208 Lancasters of 5 Group following Mosquito markers again attacked St. Leu d'Esserent storage cave and an associated network of tunnels formerly used for mushroom farming in which the Germans had stored V-1's and essential parts. 'Six-thirtys' Lancasters carried bomb loads of 11 x 1000lb AN-M and 4 x 500lb LD (6 hours) bombs.

7th/ 8th July 1944 : Night Bombing Attack on Creil (St. Leu d'Esserent)

Take Off: at 22:28 hours Arthur Kemp in ND797 (incorrectly shown as Kerr in ORB) led the take-off from East Kirkby.

ND688-R	W/C WI Deas
ME650-B	F/L JCW Weller
ND335-L	F/L TG O'Dwyer
PB236-F	F/O HH Long RCAF
JB290-C	P/O DG Gamble
LL949-E	P/O BW Brittain RAAF
ND554-A	P/O HE Wilson RCAF
LM216-K	P/O DH Simpson RCAF
ME739-D	P/O JH Bolton
ND797-W	P/O AF Kemp
ND527-O	P/O WA McNeil
ME796-S	P/O AG Henriquez
PA992-Y	P/O GE Maxwell RAAF
LL966-P	P/O E Docherty
ME845-Q	P/O AR Kerr
LM537-X	P/O RT Hayes
LM637-V	F/S TS Fenning

Small amounts of cloud were present but visibility in the target area was excellent. Marking was completed aided by flares and at 01:16 hours the main force received orders from the Master Bomber to bomb the Red TI overshooting by 1 second. The squadron's crews attacked from 01:19 to 01:29 hours from 11,350 to 15,000 feet. Bombing appeared well concentrated and there was soon a large fire burning 400 yards south of the markers. Ground defences were considerably stronger than previously and fighter activity was intense. Six combats were recorded by returning crews. Accurately placed marking and bombing closed off the mouths of the tunnels and destroyed the approach roads denying the German's access to the site. John Bolton's crew was the last to return to East Kirkby at 03:55 hours. It was soon obvious that the C.O. W/Cdr Deas had Failed To Return. Wing Commander Deas was flying his 69th operation. Squadron records contradict themselves in places where his first tour(s) is counted variously as 50, 56 or 58 ops, plus the number flown on his current tour. The record of the attack on Brunswick on 22nd/23rd May recorded that he had already completed 56+9 (ie: 56 ops on previous tours and 9 during his current tour), St.Valery-en-Caux on 27th/28th May recorded 58 + 10, Caen on 6th/7th June showed 50+11, Beauvoir on 16th/17th June stated 58+12 and his final op recorded 58+13. Since all of these numbers are handwritten it seems likely that human error has played a part. The op against Creil was actually his 14th with 630 Squadron.

Left – Right: W/Cdr Bill Deas, Wally Upton, George Farara. Joe Taylor (all LAHC Archive/Patti Kellaway)

Lancaster III, ND688 (Codes LE – R)

Pilot	– W/C William Inglis Deas DSO DFC and Bar. Age 29	Killed
Flight Eng	– F/O Joseph Thomas Taylor DFC[iv].	Killed
Navigator	– P/O Charles Norman Wright. Age 29	Killed
Bomb Aimer	– F/L George Grafron Haig Farara DFC DFM. Age 26	Killed
Wireless Op	– F/O Walter Thomas Upton DFM[v]. Age 23	Prisoner
Mid Upper	– Sgt Leonard Augustus Alfred Page. Age 19	Killed
Rear Gunner	– F/S Roland James Locke. Age 24	Killed

ND688 crashed at circa 01:30 hours just south east of Villers-en-Arthies (Val d'Oise) very probably the first night fighting victory of Oberfeldwebel (Flight Sergeant) Manfred Gromoll of 3/JG301 who claimed a Lancaster at 01:36 hours at Bray/Gasny to the east of Vernon. The dead lie in Omerville Communal Cemetery alongside 6 of the crew of Claud Houghton AFM who had been lost a month previously.

The records of the squadron clearly state the feeling of sadness at the loss of a *'most popular and efficient Commanding Officer a squadron could have'* which was described as *'the saddest blow and most grievous loss'*. Adding to the loss was the fact that aboard the CO's Lancaster were the Deputy Squadron Engineer Leader, the Squadron Bombing Leader and Squadron Signals Leader.

Former accountant's clerk Wally Upton DFM from Eythorne near Dover, who had already completed a tour with 61 Squadron in 1942 (awarded the DFM London Gazette 29th December 1942), survived the loss of the bomber to be captured on landing by parachute. Wounded he was denied treatment and interrogated at a local Military barracks before being handed over to the SS and Gestapo and imprisoned at Fresnes Gestapo prison near Paris where he was kicked, punched and knocked to the floor. Passed next to the Wiesbaden Gestapo on 2nd September he was again illtreated and threatened with transfer to a Concentration Camp still being denied proper medical attention until he arrived at Stalag Luft I (Barth) on 10th September. Upton settled in Australia post-war and became a world recognised Orchid authority lecturing to fellow enthusiasts in most English speaking countries across the globe, he completed over 500 botanical drawings of orchids and registering over 165 orchid hybrids. Awarded the Medal of the Order of Australia Wally Upton died in 2012.

Squadron leader Roy Calvert RNZAF serving as B-Flight commander assumed command of 630 Squadron temporarily with his deputy, Flight Lieutenant Doug Hawker, taking over B-Flight. Twenty-six year old Flying Officer Tom Cass DFM[vi] arrived to take up the role of Squadron Gunnery Leader, the married man from Lincoln was the proud father of a baby girl. He had enlisted in the RAF pre-war as an Air Gunner and flown a previous tour with 61 Squadron ending in late 1942 after which he'd been awarded the DFM and commissioned before being appointed Gunnery Leader at 5 LFS Syerston. Flying Officer George Arkieson[vii] 21 year old bomb aimer from Edinburgh became Squadron Bombing Leader he would join 'Pancho' O'Dwyer's crew after Stan Pinches was posted.

Tom Cass (Gunnery Leader) and standing beside the tools of his trade (Cass family album)

After flying their 10th op with Six-thirty Doug Gamble and crew transferred to 83 Squadron becoming Pathfinders. This crew survived their extended tour at the end of which their captain received a DFC, navigator Bill Hallam a DFC and 35 year old Scots bomb aimer Frank Burn, a DFM. Burn was a married man, much older than the average aircrew and was lucky to return to his native Scotland, his wife and three small children.

Monday 10th July 1944.
It appears that an op was planned to bomb St. Philibert Ferne but that it was scrubbed in the early stages. In response to Naval requests for sea mining in the area code named 'Silverthorne', a section of Kattegat Bay, regularly used in U-boat training and a known U-boat transit area. Three aircraft of the squadron were detailed and the load for the night was 9 x Mk.VI and 2 x Mk.IV mines.

10th /11th July 1944 : Night Mine laying in Kattegat Bay
Take Off: at 22:17 hours Ron Hayes in LM216 was the first away.

PB236-F	P/O BW Brittain RAAF
LM216-K	P/O RT Hayes
ME796-S	P/O AG Henriquez

Alfred Henriquez Lancaster had engine problems and had to return early. The weather remained fair and with Datum Points established mining was carried out successfully. When Ron Hayes landed LM216 at 04:30 hours his crew were the last home.

Wednesday 12th July 1944.

Squadron Leader (Acting Wing Commander) Leslie Blome-Jones[viii] arrived to take command of 630 Squadron. An experienced flight commander who had completed a 32 op first tour and had already flown 10 ops of his second tour with neighbouring 207 Squadron, he was more of 'stickler for the book' than his predecessor had been. A pre-war regular officer commissioned in April 1936 at the age of twenty-four, Blome-Jones's father and uncles were both Sheerness solicitors, his uncle also a Lieutenant-Colonel in the Kent Volunteers, Royal Garrison Artillery. In Blome-Jones' crew was an outstanding navigator, Flight Lieutenant Jimmy Martin[ix], who quickly became Squadron Navigation Leader on arrival at Six-thirty. Martin had flown a tour of 32 ops from bases in Malta and the Middle East and then commenced a second tour with 207 Squadron.

Railway junctions received the renewed attention of the heavy bombers. As part of the attacking force Six-thirty despatched Lancasters armed with 8 x 1000lb GP and 4 x 500lb GP bombs.

12th/13th July 1944 : Night Bombing Attack on Culmont-Chalindrey
Take Off: at 21:42 hours Australian Wade Rodgers (ME739) led the take-off, two of the Lancasters had Second Dickies aboard, newly arrived pilots Alex Sargent and Pete Dennett.

LM216-K	S/L RE Millichap	
ME739-D	F/L CW Rodgers RAAF	(F/O AJ Sargent)
LM637-V	F/O DH Simpson RCAF	
PB236-F	F/O HH Long RCAF	
ND554-A	P/O HE Wilson RCAF	
LL949-E	F/S EP Mitchell	
ND527-O	F/L DE Hawker RNZAF	(F/O PB Dennett RAAF)
LL966-P	P/O MA Swain	
ND797-W	Flt/O W Adams USAAF	
LM537-X	F/O JW Lennon RNZAF	
PA992-Y	F/O GE Maxwell RAAF	

One or 2 fighters were seen at the French coast en-route to the target area. The weather on the outward journey and in the TA was good and clear but on the return flight it turned foul and squadron aircraft landed at airfields across England, but all returned safely. Marking was punctual and accurate and all crews received the Controller's instructions clearly, 630 Squadron attacked between 01:51 and 01:58 hours from 5,400 to 7,150 feet. With virtually no opposition a successful attack was delivered. Landing at 06:30 hours the recently promoted Flight Officer Bill Adams USAAF and crew in ND797 were the last to return. Records are unclear about the Lancaster flown by Doug Simpson and crew, the majority however state that it was LM637 'V-Victor'.

Friday 14th July 1944.
242 Lancasters were despatched to bomb the railway marshalling yards at Revigny and Villeneuve-St. George. 630 Squadron aircraft were each armed with 16 x 500lb GP (025) and 2 x 500lb GP LD (72 hours) bombs.

14th/15th July 1944 : Night Bombing Attack on Villeneuve-St. George
Take Off: at 21:56 hours the squadron followed ND554 (Alec Swain) into the air.

LL966-P	W/C LM Blome-Jones
ME650-B	F/L JCW Weller
ND554-A	P/O MA Swain
JB290-C	F/O BW Brittain RAAF

PB236-F	F/O HH Long RCAF
PB211-H	P/O RT Hayes
ME845-Q	P/O AR Kerr
PB244-N	P/O AF Kemp RCAF
LM637-V	P/O WA McNeil

Excellent Weather conditions in the Target Area enabled bombing altitude to be maintained instead of attacking at low altitude as with some recent targets. The Controller ordered the attack to commence at 01:35 hours but ordered 'stop bombing' at 01:38 hours and then at 01:45 hours ordered crews to attack the concentration of red and green TIs, this was confirmed at 01:48 and bombing was accurate based on visuals of the nearby river. The squadron attacked between 01:44 and 01:56 hours from 6,000 to 7,650 feet. Ground defences were negligible but some fighters were seen in the TA. The railways were hit and the German lines of communication further disrupted. ME845 (Alan Kerr) was the last of the squadrons aircraft to land, at 05:18 hours.

Completing a tour of 35 ops the crew of 'Sam' Weller were screened from Ops, they had more than 'done their bit' and set a superb example to their fellow crews of 'unflappability'. Already awarded the DFC in April for his spirit (London Gazette 11th April 1944) it is surprising that from the crew only Weller's Canadian bomb aimer Andy Kuzma[x] was awarded a DFC (London Gazette 19th September 1944) suggesting perhaps that the highly restrictive 'quota system' had prevented some well-earned awards to other crewmen. After a well-earned leave most were posted as instructors, 'Sam' Weller to 1661 Heavy Conversion Unit where he was injured in the crash of Stirling KF266 on 4th November 1944, Andy Kuzma later to return to East Kirkby in a staff role. On July 15th one of 57 Squadron's ground crew was found dead at East Kirkby's No.4 Living Site Picket Post, a post mortem revealed that 18 year old AC2 Aubrey

JCW "Sam" Weller (Patti Kellaway)

Roy "Milly" Millichap (Bob Millichap)

Nigel Gurney of Headington had died of natural causes. His funeral was at Oxford Wolvercote Cemetery. 'B' Flight of 2785 (Anti-Aircraft) Squadron under Flight Lieutenant Ian MacDougall[xi] which protected RAF East Kirkby transferred to RAF Hawkinge in Kent on 15th July. The remaining members of 2785 Squadron were dispersed to other units.

Saturday 15th July 1944.

Attacks on railway junctions continued and 222 Lancasters attacked marshalling yards at Chalons-sur-Marne and Nevers. Each of Six-thirty's Lancasters were bombed up with 9 x 1000lb MC and 4 x 500lb GP bombs.

15th/16th July 1944 : Night Bombing Attack on Nevers
Take Off: at 21:53 hours in ME650, Terence O'Dwyer led the take-off.

LM216-K	F/L CW Rodgers RAAF
ME650-B	F/L TG O'Dwyer
PB211-H	P/O DH Simpson RCAF
LL949-E	P/O EP Mitchell
ME796-S	F/L DE Hawker RNZAF
LM537-X	F/O JW Lennon RNZAF
PA992-Y	F/O GE Maxwell RAAF
ND797-W	Flt/O W Adams USAAF

The weather was very clear with good visibility despite a slight haze over the river. The initial two red spot flares were inaccurate and yellows had to be dropped on them as a cancellation measure. Some bombing was however observed the result of contradictory instructions from the Controller at 01:58 and 01:59 hours. After re-marking properly the Controller ordered the main force to attack at 02:05 hours. 630 Squadron's crews attacked between 01:59 and 02:14 hours from 4,300 to 5,050 feet. As bombers ran in and bombed a very large explosion seen at 02:09 hours. Tall trees in the target area could be seen and the bombs were landing well in relation to them. Enroute home Stan Pinches, bomb aimer in 'Pancho' O'Dwyer's ME650 'B' had to jettison a 1000lb bomb at 03:48 hours as it had hung-up over the target just as the large explosion occurred, Stan had struggled in vain determined to release it over the target. Bill Adams crew aboard ND797 were the last to land at 06:10 hours.

Tuesday 18th July 1944.

A daylight Op was ordered, the first by 630 Squadron. In preparation for 'Operation Goodwood' – the planned push by the armoured forces of the British 2nd Army through the Caen area – 942 aircraft attacked fortified villages and the fortified steel works near Caen. 630 Squadron participated in the attack on the steel works at Mont Evelle all aircraft armed with 11 x 1000lb AN and 4 x 500lb AN bombs.

18th July 1944 : Daylight bombing Caen
Take Off: at 03:27 hours in ND554 Harold Wilson and crew were the first airborne.

LL966-P	W/C LM Blome-Jones	
LM216-K	S/L RE Millichap	
ME650-B	F/L TG O'Dwyer	
ME739-D	F/L CW Rodgers RAAF	
ND554-A	F/O HE Wilson RCAF	
JB290-C	P/O DH Simpson RCAF	RD
LD949-E	P/O EP Mitchell	
PB236-F	F/O HH Long RCAF	
PB211-H	F/O RT Hayes	

LM117-J	P/O BW Brittain RAAF	
ND797-W	F/L GR Joblin RNZAF	
ND527-O	F/L DE Hawker RNZAF	
PB244-N	F/O AF Kemp RCAF	
ME845-Q	F/O AR Kerr	
ME796-S	F/O GE Maxwell RAAF	
LM537-X	F/O JW Lennon RNZAF	
LM637-V	Flt/O W Adams USAAF	RD

Commencing at dawn in clear conditions the Oboe marking was practical and accurate on both targets and very well controlled by the Master Bomber, Squadron Leader Keith Creswell DSO DFC[xii]. Crews in the early stages of attack could identify the River Orne and the steel works before smoke and dust lifted. The bombers attacked from 5,000 to 9,000 feet after Army batteries and Naval guns worked to suppress the flak batteries which would otherwise decimate the main force. Remaining flak was light and no fighters were seen. The squadron attacked between 05:43 and 06:13 hours from 6,000 to 9,800 feet. USAAF bombers also attacked and 6,800 tons of bombs were dropped in total, more than 5,000 tons by the RAF. The 16th Luftwaffe Field (Infantry) Division and the 21st Panzer Division both sustained serious numbers of casualties and fighting vehicles. At East Kirkby ME845 (Alan Kerr) was last to land at 07:46 hours.Tuesday

18th July 1944.

A second op was ordered within 24 hours and 630 Squadron were participating. The railway junctions at Aulnoye and Revigny were high on the priority list of targets and were next attacked by 1, 3, 5 and 8 Groups. Lancasters of Six-thirty bombed up with 11 x 1000lb AM and 4 x 500lb GP (36 hours delay) bombs.

18th/19th July 1944 : Night Bombing Attack on Revigny

Take Off: at 22:36 hours New Zealander George Joblin was the first off.

ND554-A	F/O HE Wilson RCAF	
ME650-B	F/O MA Swain	RD
PB211-H	F/O RT Hayes	
ND797-W	F/L GR Joblin RNZAF	
PB244-N	F/O AF Kemp RCAF	
ME845-Q	F/O AR Kerr	
PB236-F	P/O AJ Sargent	
LM117-J	P/O BW Brittain RAAF	
ME796-S	P/O GE Maxwell RAAF	
LM537-X	P/O PB Dennett RAAF	

Arriving in the Revigny area the attacking force found conditions clear with a slight ground haze. After some delay in getting the target marked and after the Controller had ordered the force to 'stand by' he finally gave the instruction to attack the red spot flare at 01:43 hours. Some crews noted that it was actually on the railway tracks and bombing commenced with a major explosion seen 1 minute later. 630 Squadron crews attacked 01:44 and 01:54 hours from 7,300 to 9,300 feet. Defences were light but fighter activity on outward route and in the TA were intense and did not decrease until part way home. 24 of the force of 253 Lancasters were shot down by night fighters and several combats took place. At 01:10 hours in hazy conditions whilst 6 miles to port of the main track the crew of PB244 'N-Nan' (Arthur Kemp) had observed a flare below them on the starboard bow just as the 'Fishpond' early warning system plotted a fighter 1000 yards off their port quarter and almost immediately a second one on their starboard quarter. Kemp instantly began a banking manoeuvre to port and then back to starboard to provide his gunners with the best possible chance of locating the enemy. As the Lancaster levelled out a twin engined night fighter opened fire from below on the port quarter and Sergeant James Stirling RCAF the rear gunner fired a 600 round burst, strikes were seen across the starboard wing of the night fighter which caught fire. The German dropped back but went into a spin and dived into the ground where it exploded, several members of the crew witnessed the crash. Immediately tracer was seen coming in on the starboard quarter but the fighter was lost as the Lancaster dropped into a corkscrew. Claimed as Destroyed. Bombing destroyed the railway lines to the battlefront and reinforcements and supplies were denied to the German front lines. The last of the 630 Squadron Lancasters to touch down at East Kirkby was PB244 at 04:10 hours. One Lancaster failed to return.

Lancaster III, LM117 (Codes LE – J)

Pilot	– F/O Bruce William Brittain RAAF. Age 21	Evaded
Flight Eng	– Sgt Ronald Francis Gannon. Age 21	Prisoner
Navigator	– F/S Stanley Robert Ashton. Age 20	Prisoner
Bomb Aimer	– F/S Ernest (Joe) Couchman. Age 23	Evaded
Wireless Op	– F/S Gordon Edwin Beckhouse RAAF. Age 20	Killed
Mid Upper	– Sgt Donald Andrew Grant RCAF. Age 19	Evaded
Rear Gunner	– F/S Ernest Harold Wells . Age 22	Prisoner

Homebound, LM117 was hit by flak near Vitry and crashed about 02:04 hours near Togny-aux-Boeufs (Marne) 13km south east of Chalons-sur-Marne. A German night fighter flown by Hauptmann Heinz-Horst Hissbach of 5/NJG2 had also attacked LM117.

The entire crew baled out but Gordon Beckhouse, their RAAF Wireless Op, landed safely only to be shot by the German sentry guarding railway line beside which he landed. His death was reported to his father in an official letter (excerpt above).

22 year old Leicester Insurance clerk Harry Wells and 20 year old Stan Ashton from Hackney were captured near Sogny and saw out the war together in Stalag Luft 7 and Stalag IIIA. A local family helped Ernest Couchman to evade captivity and assisted by local resistance fighters nineteen year old Sergeant Don Grant of Lake Cowichan, British Columbia also evaded.

Bruce Brittain RAAF (Bruce Brittain)   *Ron Gannon (Mark and Phil Gannon)*

Left: RAAF official records of the loss confirm the crew parachuted to safety, including Gordon Beckhouse (National Archives of Australia). Right: The fate of Gordon "Ted" Beckhouse (B Moorcroft)

Lancaster III, ME796 (Codes LE – S)

Pilot	– F/O Gordon Edward Maxwell RAAF. Age 27	Killed
Flight Eng	– Sgt James Napier Howie. Age 31	Killed
Navigator	– F/O John Francis Bush RAAF. Age 26	Killed
Bomb Aimer	– Sgt William Edward Griffiths. Age 20	Killed
Wireless Op	– F/S Stanley Arthur Hawken RAAF. Age 27	Evaded
Mid Upper	– Sgt Albert Ernest DeBruin. Age 22	Evaded
Rear Gunner	– F/S William Leary. Age	Evaded

Left to Right: Gordon Maxwell RAAF (Patti Kellaway); Stan Hawken RAAF (Stan Hawken); Johnny Bush RCAF (David Bush); Bert DeBruin (DeBruin collection)

Gordon Maxwell's crew were ordered to delay attacking by 5 minutes and to orbit to port. Whilst stooging around over the target and waiting for permission to attack 'S-Sugar' was acquired by several searchlights, shot up by a night fighter flown by Hauptmann Hubert Rauh of Stab II/NJG4 which made a head on attack and may have been hit by the return fire of Paddy Leary but the bomber was then almost immediately hit by flak. Although the Lancaster was blazing furiously Maxwell held the aircraft steady for his crew to bale out and then steered away from the village below for his bomb aimer to jettison their bomb load. The Lancaster crashed after 01:30 hours at Villers-le Sec (Marne) in which churchyard the four dead were buried. Rear gunner Bill Leary, Wireless Op Stan Hawken and Mid-Upper gunner Bert DeBruin all parachuted to safety and were hidden by French patriots.

Telegram to the Hawken family (Stan Hawken)

Stan Hawken[xiii] wrote his story down in 'Missing Presumed Dead' (published 1989 by Hill of Content, Melbourne). He and Leary were sheltered by a local family and later hid in forests with a resistance group. Bert DeBruin was unfortunate in landing in a forest beside the River Marne where after several days of dodging the frequent German patrols and living off the land primarily on berries he met a French Resistance group as they returned from a rendezvous with an RAF aircraft which had just flown in weapons and explosives to a secret landing ground. He had narrowly 'missed the bus' and spent several months with the resistance before US troops liberated the district.

Lancaster III, LM537 (Codes LE – X)

Pilot	– F/O Peter Buck Dennett RAAF. Age 21	Killed
Flight Eng	– Sgt George Armstrong Alexander. Age 35	Prisoner
Navigator	– F/S Cedric Raymond Jerwood . Age 21	Killed
Bomb Aimer	– Sgt Hume Paul Ritchie RCAF . Age 23	Evaded
Wireless Op	– Sgt William John Jarman. Age 20	Killed
Mid Upper	– Sgt Reginald Arnold Hilborne. Age 35	Evaded
Rear Gunner	– Sgt Joe 'Geordie' Stones. Age	Evaded

Peter Dennett's crew were on their first op when they were attacked by a fighter flown by Oberfeldwebel Reinhard Kollak of 8/NJG4 and also struck by flak over Margerie Hancourt. The Lancaster's fuel tanks caught fire causing great streams of flame to trail behind the stricken bomber until it suddenly exploded as the crew were baling out. The remains of LM537 crashed circa 02:00 hours at Chassericourt (Aube) where the dead were buried in Chassericourt Churchyard. George Alexander a 35 year old motor engineer from Belfast evaded capture until 10th August when he fell into German hands near Troyes ending up in Stalag Luft 7. Shoe repairer Reg Hilborne also 35 years old, from Mitcham fortunately landed near Margerie-Hancourt in one piece despite fire damage to his parachute canopy and burned gloves but his face was quite badly burned. He evaded capture and a week or so later joined an SAS patrol operating behind enemy lines in 'Operation Hardy'. He recalled later that his time with the SAS was *'not for the faint hearted or for those with a weak stomach'*. 'Geordie' Stones also suffered burns.

(L to r) Ron Gannon, Bruce Brittain RAAF, Ted Beckhouse RAAF (top), possibly Harry Wells, Don Grant RCAF (Mark and Phil Gannon)

Lancaster III, PB236 (Codes LE – F)

Pilot	– P/O Alexander James Sargent. Age 22	Killed
Flight Eng	– Sgt David Drylie Moffatt. Age 23	Killed
Navigator	– Sgt Kenneth Adams. Age 22	Killed
Bomb Aimer	– Sgt Kenneth Nelson . Age 22	Killed
Wireless Op	– Sgt David Withers. Age 20	Killed
Mid Upper	– Sgt John Rae. Age 23	Killed
Rear Gunner	– Sgt Norman Barker. Age 35	Killed

Peter Dennett RAAF (Marjorie Smith)

Before reaching the target Alex Sargent's crew on their first op were shot down by a night fighter flown by Oberfeldwebel Herbert Altner of 8/NJG5 in Luftwaffe night fighter Quadrant BH at 2500m altitude and crashed at 01:21 hours at Neuvy (Marne) 15km west of Sezanne. Sargent and his crew lie together in Neuvy Communal Cemetery. The attack is covered in great detail by Oliver Clutton-Brock in his 'Massacre Over The Marne' (published by PSL).

During July the crew of F/O William 'Peter' Sparks[xiv] arrived from Conversion Unit and began the program of cross-country, navigation and night bombing exercises to be completed by all new crews arriving with Six-thirty. Sparks was a 25 year old former Territorial Army soldier who had transferred from the Army volunteering for aircrew training.

At 22:04 hours on the night of 18th July the Sparks crew took off for a navigation exercise in 'I-Item' (ME729; previously 'T-Tare') an aircraft which had been grounded for some weeks due to recurrent technical problems. At 00:59 hours near Ayr in Scotland with two engines failing the crew baled out abandoning their Lancaster which crashed in the fields of Mossdale farm at Dalmellington. It is unclear how three of the crew came to be killed but the two Canadians are buried at Dunure Cemetery and 38 year old Sergeant Helliwell in his hometown of Lancaster.

Lancaster I, ME729 (Codes LE – I)

Pilot	– F/O William Angus Sparks. Age 25	Injured
Flight Eng	– Sgt Frank Helliwell. Age 38	Killed
Navigator	– Sgt Wilton Garnet Armour RCAF. Age 22	Unhurt
Bomb Aimer	– Sgt Frederick George Brezina RCAF. Age 26	Killed
Wireless Op	– Sgt Wilfred Shillito. Age 20	Unhurt
Mid Upper	– Sgt James Alexander Calder RCAF. Age 21	Killed
Rear Gunner	– Sgt. George Rye. Age 19	Unhurt

After medical treatment the crew were reformed under 'Peter' Sparks and shortly afterwards transferred out to 207 Squadron although they did return once to 630 Squadron in late September to help make up the numbers on a night when the squadron had more Lancasters serviceable than crews to fly them. Sadly when returning to base after an attack on Harburg on 11th November 1944 their 207 Squadron Lancaster (PB428)

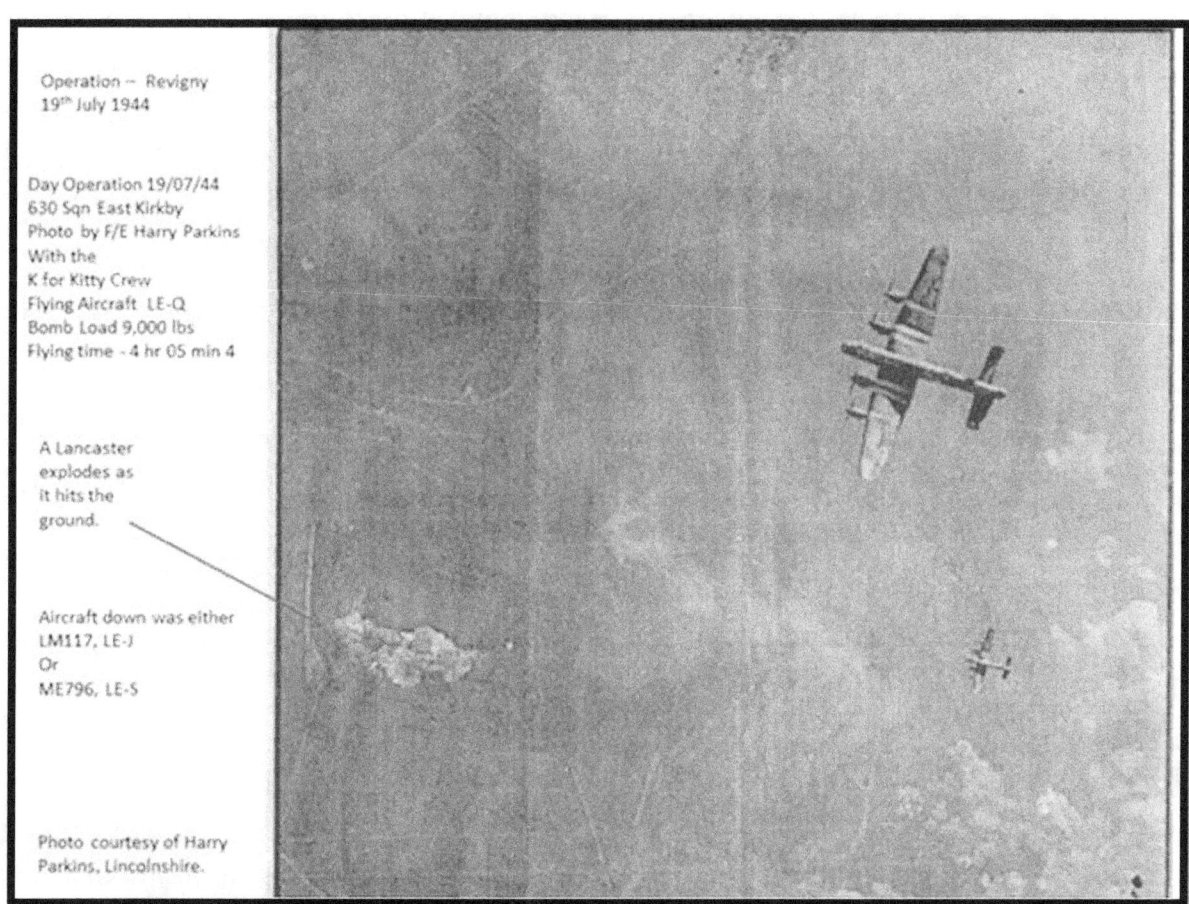

Top: A 630 Squadron Lancaster explodes (Harry Parkin) Bottom : "Peter" Sparks and crew (Christie Clark)

The ID card of Fred Brezina RCAF (Library and Archives Canada)

collided in circuit over Spilsby with 44 Squadron's LM648 (P/O PAC Caryer) and all 14 airmen were killed in the crashes which followed.

Wednesday 19th July 1944.
Attacks on flying bomb sites continued and a raid was detailed against 2 launching sites and a supply dump. Each 630 Squadron Lancaster was armed with 10 x 1000lb MC and 4 x 500lb GP long delay bombs.

19th July 1944 : Daylight Bombing Attack on Creil
Take Off: at 19:20 hours Flight Commander, S/L Roy Millichap took off first LM216.

LM216-K	S/L RE Millichap	
ME739-D	F/L CW Rodgers RAAF	(extra Nav = F/S Fingland RCAF) RD
ND554-A	F/O HH Long RCAF	
PB211-H	P/O DH Simpson RCAF	
ND527-O	F/L DE Hawker RNZAF	RD
ME845-Q	F/O JW Lennon RNZAF	RD
ND797-W	F/O MA Swain	
PA992-Y	Flt/O W Adams USAAF	RD
PB244-N	F/S EGW Bowers	(W/C GP Gibson VC DSO*DFC*)

The Oboes and Red TIs were reportedly late and somewhat inaccurate so the main force arrived at the target to find no markers in place, the target areas were partly cloud covered but, some crews orbited and bombed on target but bombing was generally scattered – the primary targets were believed to have been destroyed. 630 Squadron attacked between 21:20 and 21:38 hours from 14,300 to 18,000 feet. Moderate heavy flak was experienced from 30-40 guns but no enemy fighters were seen. Wade Rodgers 'D-Dog', Doug Hawkers 'O-Oboe' and Joe Lennon's 'Q-Queen' both received more flak damage Hawker recalled that 'Griff' Griffin his bomb aimer was shaken when the bombsight was struck by a piece of flak as he looked through it. The crew of Flight Officer Bill Adams USAAF aboard PA992 'Y-Yoke' were the last to return at 23:38 hours in another damaged Lancaster.

Bill Adams USAAF (Kiesow family)   *Guy Gibson VC DSO DFC (Crown Copyright)*

It is little known that Wing Commander Guy Gibson VC DSO and Bar DFC and Bar flew his very last Lancaster sortie with 630 Squadron before his loss in September 1944 flying a Mosquito. Gibson, who had led 617 Squadron on the famous Dams raid had been grounded permanently by Bomber Command HQ and was flying a desk as Base Operations Officer, utterly forbidden to fly on Ops. After the loss of Wing Commander Bill Deas, Gibson used his rank and position to wrangle an op and joined the 'sprog crew' of Flight Sergeant George Bowers aboard PB244 'N-Nan' on their first op. The Station Navigation Officer Squadron Leader Alex St.Clair-Miller DFC (formerly of 44 Squadron) flew as navigator for the attack. The entry below shows Gibson's own log book entry. He recorded himself as pilot in place of Bowers. Wade Rodgers later wrote that Gibson asked him to take Bowers as Second Dickey aboard 'D-Dog' and to keep it to himself. The Squadron Ops Record shows Gibson as pilot although the Operations Record Book' shows Bowers as pilot.

Roy Millichap's bombing photo (Bob Millichap)

189

Guy Gibson's logbook entry (RAF Museum Hendon)

Thursday 20th July 1944.

Maintaining the pressure on vital railway lines being used for bringing up reinforcements and materiel more railway yards were to be attacked. 302 Lancasters and 15 Mosquitoes of 1, 5 and 8 Group bombed the marshalling yards and a 'triangle' railway junction at Courtrai. With its aircraft armed with 11 x 1000lb AN-M, 2 x 500lb GP (025) and 2 x 500lb GP long delay bombs 630 Squadron participated in the attack.

20th/21st July 1944 : Night Bombing Attack on Courtrai

Take Off: at 23:01 hours aboard ND527 (Kiwi Doug Hawker) and JB290 (Terence O'Dwyer) led the squadron into the air from East Kirkby.

JB290-C	F/L TG O'Dwyer
ND554-A	F/O HE Wilson RCAF
ME739-D	F/O HH Long RCAF
LL949-E	P/O EP Mitchell
PB211-H	F/O RT Hayes
LM216-K	F/O DH Simpson RCAF
ND527-O	F/L DE Hawker RNZAF
PB244-N	P/O AF Kemp RCAF
LM637-V	F/O JW Lennon RNZAF
ND797-W	F/O AR Kerr
PA992-Y	Flt/O W Adams USAAF

The weather conditions were quite clear over the target and visibility excellent. Green TIs were punctually placed within 100 yards of the aiming point by the Mosquitoes. The Oboe Red TI was also considered accurate. The resulting bombing was well concentrated on the Green TIs and several large explosions reported by returning crews including a large oil fire near the end of the attack. The squadron attacked between 00:56 and 01:03 hours from 10,000 to 13,900 feet. PB244 (P/O Kemp) was the last of the squadron's Lancasters to return to East Kirkby at 02:38 hours. Buffeted by heavy flak at 13,500 feet while orbiting the target at 01:05 hours Gerald Benson the Wireless Op of PB244 'N' shouted that 'Fishpond' was warning of a fighter closing to attack. In a fraction of a section Arthur Kemp the Canadian pilot launched the Lancaster into a corkscrew to port just as fellow Canadian Sergeant George Cameron in the mid upper turret called that tracer was coming in from the port quarter down and Sergeant Jim Stirling in the rear turret returned fire in that direction. The German fighter was lost in the evasive action and not seen again. At 01:17 hours as they left the brightly lit target area F/L Doug Hawker's ND527 'O' came under attack from an enemy they never saw, 'Shortie' Adams in the mid upper turret instructed a 'corkscrew port now' as tracer closed on the Lancaster from the port quarter up and as they dropped away he and 'Dusty' Miller (rear gunner) returned fire at about 800 yards into the darkness and although the German followed them into the corkscrew and fired again he was unable to stay with the Lancaster and was lost into the night.

With the benefit of photo reconnaissance Bomber Command reported this attack to have been 'devastating' to the railway target.

Sunday 23rd July 1944.

In the first major raid on a German city for two months 629 bombers including six aircraft of 630 Squadron were detailed to participate in an attack on the town of Kiel. Elaborate deception in form of minor diversionary and training sweeps by 180 aircraft over the North Sea, 27 Mosquitoes bombing Berlin, the surprise of a return to a German target and Radio Counter Measures (RCM) combined to confuse the German controllers who unable to get their forces in place so casualties were light. The six participating Lancasters of Six-thirty were each armed with 11 x 1000lb AN-M and 4 x 500lb GP long delay bombs.

23rd/24th July 1944 : Night Bombing Attack on Kiel

Take Off: at 22:45 hours Terrence 'Pancho' O'Dwyer's ND335 was first to lift off, they had a Second Dickie aboard to gain operational experience.

ND335-L	F/L TG O'Dwyer	(F/S EGW Bowers)
JB290-C	F/O JH Bolton	
ME739-D	P/O MA Swain	
ND797-W	F/L GR Joblin RNZAF	
LM637-V	F/O TS Fennng	
LL966-P	F/O E Docherty	RD

The main force of 612 heavy bombers appeared suddenly from behind a 'Mandrel' jamming screen which the local ground defences had assessed as a small force of mine laying aircraft. Pathfinder marking was punctual and the attack well controller by the Master Bomber whose instructions were clear and precise. In an attack lasting 25 minutes some bombing was believed to be scattered however several large fires were burning by the end of the attack and the glow from these fires could still be seen 100 miles into the return flight. The squadron attacked between 01:27 and 01:32 hours from 16,300 to 19,300 feet. Moderate heavy flak was encountered over the target and no fighters were seen although some horizontal tracer fire was observed. German records show that all districts of Kiel were hit with particularly heavy damage in the port area, the important U-boat building yards and naval installations. Kiel suffered heavily in its first RAF raid since April 1943 and what would be its heaviest RAF raid of the war. The 500 plus 'Long Delay' bombs, some set for 36 hours or more, coupled with unexploded duds paralysed the area for some days, there was no water for 3 days, busses and trains were out of action for 8 days and there was no gas for cooking for 3 weeks. Tom Fenning and crew aboard LM637 were the last to land at 04:13 hours.

Three more of Six-thirty's aircraft formed half of force minelaying in Kiel Bay across transit routes believed to be used by surface patrol craft and new and repaired U-boats doing their sea trials. Each of Six-thirty's three aircraft tasked for mine-laying carried 3 x Mk.3 and 3 x Mk 4 mines.

23rd/24th July 1944 : Mine laying in Kiel Bay

ND527-O	F/L DE Hawker RNZAF	
PB244-N	F/O JW Lennon RNZAF	RD
PB211-H	F/O RT Hayes	

All of the mines were laid successfully after the Datum Point was established. Opposition from flak ships and shore was heavy. Ron Hayes' PB211 Failed to Return.

Lancaster III, PB211 (Codes LE – H)

Pilot	– F/O Ronald Thomas Hayes. Age 21	Killed
Flight Eng	– Sgt William Wallace. Age 20	Killed
Navigator	– WO Winston Kimberley Goodhew RCAF Age 27	Rescued
Bomb Aimer	– Sgt James Francis Joseph Murray. Age 22	Killed
Wireless Op	– Sgt John Alfred Helliwell. Age 22	Killed
Mid Upper	– Sgt Walter Stead. Age	Killed
Rear Gunner	– Sgt Bernard Norton Graves. Age 28	Rescued

For reasons unknown 'H-How' crashed into the sea just off Cromer on the North Norfolk coast when almost home. Two of the crew survived, W/O Goodhew and Sgt Graves were rescued by the RN minesweeper Courser after 7 hours adrift in a rubber dinghy. The bodies of the dead were not apparently recovered and therefore may lie in or near the wreckage of their aircraft, they are commemorated on the Runnymede Memorial to the Missing. Winston 'Goodie' Goodhew was recommended for a DFC after flying on 29 ops and his recommendation includes :

'On the 23/24th July, this officer was navigator of an aircraft detailed for mining operations over Kiel Bay. In the return flight, while flying low, the aircraft hit the sea. Pilot Officer Goodhew at once released the upper escape hatch, climbed out and helped the wireless operator to follow. When they got into the dinghy it was found that as it was not properly inflated it would not carry their combined weight. Pilot Officer Goodhew left the dinghy to the wireless operator and swam back to the aircraft. He clung to the wreckage with the pilot and air bomber until it started to sink. He then cut the painter of the dinghy by rubbing it against a jagged edge of the main plane, and the dinghy started to drift away.
Pilot Officer Goodhew, accompanied by the pilot and air bomber, started to swim to the dinghy, but he was the only one to reach it. Despite his exhausted condition, Pilot Officer Goodhew went back to the aircraft three times, which had not yet disappeared, in an endeavour to find the pilot and air bomber, but without success. On the fourth attempt he was seized by cramp and started to sink, but he managed to return to the dinghy. Holding onto a rope from the dinghy with one hand to keep afloat, Pilot Officer Goodhew worked continuously for two hours trying to open the pack. This he accomplished, extracted the Verey pistol, and fired Verey lights to attract attention. While he was doing this the wireless operator died and disappeared under the sea. Pilot Officer Goodhew was rescued by H.M. Minesweeper Courser seven hours after the aircraft hit the sea. This officer displayed great courage, resource, tenacity and disregard for his own safety from the time the aircraft hit the sea until he was rescued. His conduct has set a most praiseworthy example to all other aircrew on the station. Pilot Officer Goodhew is a first-class navigator, and he has shown marked enthusiasm to operate on every possible occasion. He takes a keen interest in the training of new navigators in the squadron, and by his efforts he has raised the standard of navigation considerably. He is strongly recommended for the non-immediate award of the Distinguished Flying Cross'.

An RCAF official photo PL-33991 (dated 10 November 1944) is captioned: 'Pilot Officer W. 'Goodie' Goodhew of Saskatoon, Saskatchewan, a former shift boss with International Nickel at Sudbury, was one of two who survived when his RAF Lancaster crashed in the English Channel at 200 mph. His perseverance in opening Very cartridges with his teeth and firing the signal pistol while bobbing about in the water is credited with saving the life of Pilot Officer Bernard Graves, an RAF rear gunner. The signals were sighted by a British mine sweeper and the weakened and numbed airmen taken aboard.

Monday 24th July 1944.
5 Group continued to split Six-thirty's available aircraft and next tasked part of the squadron to participate in a general attack by over 600 bombers on a German target and the remainder to join a 5 Group 'bash' on the oil depot at Donges (St. Nazaire) probably a part of the fuel supply network for the major U-boat bunkers

nearby. Attackers for the Stuttgart raid were bombed up with 1 x 2000lb HC and 12 x 500lb J type cluster incendiary bombs.

24th /25th July 1944 : Night Bombing Attack on Stuttgart
Take Off: at 21:31 hours LM216 (Roy Millichap) was the first to get off the deck.

LM216-K	S/L RE Millichap
ND554-A	F/O HE Wilson RCAF
JB290-C	F/O JH Bolton
LL949-E	F/O DH Simpson RCAF
LM259-F	F/O HH Long RCAF
LL966-P	F/O E Docherty
ME845-Q	P/O AR Kerr
PA992-Y	Lt W Adams USAAF

John Bolton returned early when his mid-upper gunner Sgt John Gurney) was taken ill, landing 'C-Charlie' at 01:34 hours. Fighter activity mounted as the bombers closed on Stuttgart. Cloud over the target prevented marking with red TIs and Wanganui flares were used. The squadron's crews attacked between 01:56 and 02:02 hours from 18,300 to 20,300 feet. Crews bombing later in attack found the sky markers were extinguished and bombed on the glow of the markers from beneath the cloud, fires which seemed to be grouped around the ground markers. Ground defences put up moderate heavy flak in loose barrage form up to 21,000 feet, diminishing as the raid continued. Arriving back at East Kirkby, 'Millie' Millichap was the last of the Stuttgart raiders to land, at 06:01 hours. The attack was the first of three large raids in 5 nights on Stuttgart by the end of which central Stuttgart which lay along three narrow valleys and as such had escaped most previous attacks, was devastated. Virtually all public, bureaucratic and major buildings were destroyed.

630 Squadron had lost its 'Yank' crew, only recently commissioned as Flight Officer by the USAAF, Adams survived but his USAAF mid-upper gunner John B. Kiesow of Hartford County, Connecticut but more recently of Saskatchewan/Canada, died.

Lancaster III, PA992 (Codes LE – Y)

Pilot	– Lt William Adams USAAF . Age 23	Evaded
Flight Eng	– Sgt Trevor William Tanner. Age 21	Evaded
Navigator	– Sgt Reginald Arthur 'George' Toogood. Age 21	Evaded
Bomb Aimer	– F/O Edward Kennison Wood RCAF . Age 21	Evaded
Wireless Op	– F/O Arthur Sidney Woolf . Age	Prisoner
Mid Upper	– Tech/Sgt John B Kiesow USAAF. Age 19	Killed
Rear Gunner	– Sgt Ross William Lough RCAF. Age 23	Killed

Shot down by Leutnant Johannes Strassner of 2/NJG2 Lancaster PA992 crashed between Tramont-Emy and Tramont-Lassus where Sgt Ross Lough lies in the Communal Cemetery. Johnny Kiesow was originally buried beside his Canadian crewmate but his body was exhumed on 28th January 1945 for repatriation across the ocean by American authorities for a private burial by his family.

Adams later recalled that hurtling towards the ground he couldn't get to the escape hatch so he opened the cockpit side windows and dived out luckily not being hit by the propellers. It is possible that Bill Adam's Lancaster was the bomber claimed over the Nancy area 3,300 metres by Oberleutnant Hans-Heinrich Breitfeld of Stab I/NJG 5 flying from St.Dizier although he recorded his attack at 02:31 hours. Twenty-one year old Cardiff lad Trevor Tanner a former Merchant Navy boy seaman evaded the Germans and hid up until Allied forces arrived in the area. Postwar he returned to Wales and joined the police force serving

| AS "Syd" Woolf | Trevor Tanner | Arthur "George" Toogood | EK Wood RCAF |
| (AS Woolf) | (LAHC Archive) | (M Toogood) | (EK Wood (Canada)) |

several years before enlisting with the RCAF in 1949 and migrating to Canada with his wife and young family.

The seven of Six-thirty's Lancasters detailed to participate in the 5 Group 104 Lancaster attack on Donges (St. Nazaire) were each armed with 11 x 1000lb AN-M and 4 x 500lb GP (long delay) bombs.

24th /25th July 1944 : Night bombing attack on Donges/St.Nazaire
Take Off: at 22:00 hours Doug Hawker (ND527) was first off.

ME739-D	F/L CW Rodgers RAAF	RD
ND335-L	F/L TG O'Dwyer	RD
ND527-O	F/L DE Hawker RNZAF	
ND797-W	F/L GR Joblin RNZAF	RD
PB344 -R	F/O TS Fenning	
PB244-N	F/O JW Lennon RNZAF	
LM637-V	F/O MA Swain	RD

Arriving unopposed over the target the force suddenly encountered moderate to intense light and heavy flak bursting at 8,000 to 11,000 feet vertically into search light cones. There is also a report of rockets firing up search light beams with 15-20 search lights in action. All of 630 Squadron's aircraft attacked between 01:45 and 01:48 hours from 8,300 to 10.700 feet and returned safely from Donges, George Joblin landed the last of them (ND797) at East Kirkby at 04:20 hours. Photo reconnaissance results shortly afterwards enabled the result of the attack to be rated as devastating.

Tuesday 25th July 1944.

Continuing the onslaught on Stuttgart 412 Lancasters and 138 Halifaxes attacked. Six-thirty's Lancasters participated and were each armed with 1 x 2000lb HC and 12 x 500lb J type cluster incendiary bombs.

25th /26th July 1944 : Night Bombing Attack on Stuttgart
Take Off: at 21:20 hours ND335 (Terence O'Dwyer) was the first airborne.

ND335-L	F/L TG O'Dwyer
ND554-A	F/O HE Wilson RCAF
JB290-C	F/O JH Bolton
LL949-E	F/O MA Swain
LM259-F	F/O HH Long RCAF

LM216-K	F/O DH Simpson RCAF	RD
PB344-R	S/L RO Calvert RNZAF	(F/O WH Gordon)
ND527-O	F/L DE Hawker RNZAF	
PB244-N	F/O DR Mallinson	
LL966-P	F/O E Docherty	
ME845-Q	F/O AR Kerr	
NN703-X	F/O TS Fenning	

Having re-joined 630 Squadron after their six week posting, the crew of Don Mallinson were back on the Battle Order for the next night attack. 'Pancho' O'Dwyer returned on three engines at 03:30 hours after 'L-Love'' suffered port inner engine failure and 'X-X ray' – F/O Tom Fenning also returned early, due to oxygen system leaks. Broken cloud in various forms hung above the target but all crews saw red and green TIs and heard the Master Bomber's instructions. 630 Squadron's crews attacked between 01:55 and 02:10 hours from 17,200 to 19,400 feet. Fires were started over an area of several square miles with a concentration around the aiming point. The glow of fires was still visible 100 miles into the return flight. Fighter activity was only encountered during the mid portion of the flight and ground defences were only moderate in the target area. Several crews expressed concern at being required to climb over enemy territory during the outward route as the increased exhaust flames were very visible for miles. At 06:27 hours John Bolton was the last to land back at base. After flying 18 ops in 8 weeks the crew of Canadian Doug Simpson transferred to 97 Squadron Pathfinders to complete an extended tour which they were fortunate to survive. At the end of the tour DFCs were awarded to their captain and to John Mollison their navigator.

Wednesday 26th July 1944.
Returning to the mission of denying the German forces their ammunition, supplies and reinforcements 5 Group raided Givors South Marshalling Yards with 178 Lancasters and Mosquito markers. 630 Squadron aircraft were each bombed up with 7 x 1000lb AN-M65, 3 x 500lb GP (025) and 1 x 500lb GP LD (36 hours) bombs.

26th /27th July 1944 : Night Bombing Attack on Givors
Take Off: at 21:05 hours Wing Commander Blome-Jones led his squadron in NN702.

NN702-J	W/C LM Blome-Jones
LM216-K	S/L RE Millichap
ND527-O	F/O HE Wilson RCAF
LL949-E	F/O HH Long RCAF
ND797-W	F/L GR Joblin RNZAF
NN703-X	F/O JW Lennon RNZAF
PB244-N	F/O DR Mallinson
PB344-R	F/O EGW Bowers

From approximately position 0200E almost as far as the target severe electrical storms and driving rain was encountered in cloud, entailing pilots flying for 3 hours through storms of torrential raid and lightning. Weather in the target area was quite clear despite some haze and cloud just short of the target at 8,000 feet. The long delay in marking the target made the attack late and at 01:56 hours crews were ordered to stand by. Lancasters orbited in the TA with navigation lights on until 02:12 hours when the Red force was ordered to attack the Green TIs and 02:15 hours when Green Force were also ordered to attack. The squadron's crews attacked between 02:14 and 02:26 hours from 5,600 to 7,550 feet. Wing Commander Blome Jones orbited the target for 32 minutes until Bob Foulkes his bomb aimer was satisfied with conditions and 'hit the tit'. There was little fighter activity on the outward route and no enemy activity at the target but two bombers were seen to collide at 02:05 hours. George Bowers and crew were the last to return to East Kirkby

Lancaster ND527 "O" (Geoff Copeman)

at 06:40 hours. Serious concerns over the fate of 'J-Jig' (Wing Commander Blome-Jones) were harboured until it was learned that he had landed at Harwell short of fuel and returned to base after refuelling. However one of Six-thirty's crews did Fail To Return.

Lancaster III, ND527 (Codes LE – O)

Pilot	– F/O Harold Earl Wilson RCAF. Age 28	Killed
Flight Eng	– Sgt Frederick Robert Arnold. Age 31	Killed
Navigator	– F/O Ambrose Bain RCAF. Age 29	Killed
Bomb Aimer	– F/O Alexander Lindsay RCAF. Age 26	Killed
Wireless Op	– Sgt Percy Arthur Gilliatt. Age 27	Killed
Mid Upper	– Sgt John Reginald Cecil Gutcher RCAF. Age 27	Killed
Rear Gunner	– Sgt David Jack Irvin Fontaine. Age 22	Killed

Having successfully flown approximately 50 ops ND527 crashed at 02:45 hours at St. Ignat (Puy-de-Dome) 14 km east of Riom. The entire crew were buried on 27th July in Clermont-Ferrand (des Carmes-Dechaux) Communal Cemetery. Their Lancaster came down almost simultaneously with an 83 Squadron Lancaster ND856 which is reported to have exploded in the air near Surat killing Squadron Leader RK Eggins DFC and crew (with Wing Commander GF Georgeson DSO DFC aboard). ND527 crash landed near the neighbouring village of St. Ignat but hit a row of trees including a large oak and caught fire, the entire crew were killed. This may have been a mid-air collision. A nephew of the 630 Squadron pilot said – *'F/O Harold Wilson was my father's brother, the oldest of four siblings. The 'one who had it all', as my father has said, meaning he was smart, athletic and good looking. My father, the youngest sibling – now 90 years old still lives on the farm where he and his family grew up. My brother now farms there. Harold's sister, 92 years old is also still living, in Toronto. A portrait of Uncle Harold, having receiving his pilot's wings, still hangs on the wall of the farmhouse'.*

Returning 5 Group crews reported one or even possibly two collisions in the target area whilst orbiting in filthy weather conditions, one at 02:05 hours (British time). It is recorded that inhabitants of Surat reported that during the fierce storm both aircraft were flying very low, one jettisoning flares when the aircraft collided as they simultaneously emerged from low cloud. The 83 Squadron aircraft exploded in flight with

Harold Wilson RCAF and John Gutcher RCAF (both photos Michael Wells)

George Patterson RNZAF and Athol Thomas RNZAF (both photos Gillian Thomas)

wreckage continuing on the flight path before it fell to earth cutting a trench across the road to Pagnant finally coming to rest in a field some distance further on. Harold Wilson's Lancaster was crash landed with considerable skill near St. Ignat but unfortunately hit a belt of trees and caught fire, there were no survivors from either Lancaster.

Friday 28th July 1944.

George Patterson[xv] and crew joined Six-thirty. They had progressed from Wellington's at 16 OTU. to Stirlings at 1660 HCU and finally Lancasters at 5 LFS and before joining the squadron. Born in Levuka/Fiji in 1921 George Patterson had spent 3 years in the 1st Auckland Regiment of the NZ Army before volunteering for aircrew duty and training in Canada. His elder brother Tom had died on Ops with 99 Squadron (Wellingtons) on 15th November 1941. His navigator was fellow Kiwi Atholl Thomas of Auckland/New Zealand.

Participating in the third of the series of attacks on Stuttgart Six-thirty joined a force of 494 Lancasters heading to southern Germany. Each of the squadron's Lancasters were armed with 1 x 2000lb HC and 12 x 500lb J type cluster incendiary bombs.

28th/29th July 1944 : Night Bombing Attack on Stuttgart

Take Off: at 21:51 hours S/L Roy Calvert was the first off followed by a crew on-loan from 57 Sqdn.

PB344-R	S/L RO Calvert RNZAF	
ND797-W	F/L GR Joblin RNZAF	
PB244-N	F/O DR Mallinson	RD
LL966-P	F/O E Docherty	RD
LL972-T	F/O AR Kerr	
NN703-X	F/O JW Lennon RNZAF	
ND335-L	F/L TG O'Dwyer	RD
ND554-A	F/O EGW Bowers	
LM259-F	F/O HH Long RCAF	
LL949-E	F/O TS Fenning	RD
NN702-J	F/O MA Swain	RD
LM216-K	F/O LA Shamback (57 Sqdn)	

The forecast heavy cloud cover on the outward route was not as expected and intense fighter activity took place from 0500East to the target where moderate heavy flak became the opposition. Pathfinder marking was punctual and the majority of Green TIs rated as accurate according to H2S. The Master Bomber ordered the main force to attack the Green TIs and the main concentration of fires seemed to be underneath the clouds in that area. 630 Squadron attacked between 01:54 and 02:07 hours from 14,600 to 17,900 feet and the centre of Stuttgart was devastated with virtually all major buildings destroyed in the three attacks. At 06:17 hours Terence O'Dwyer's ND335 landed at East Kirkby and it was soon obvious that ND797 (George Joblin and his veteran crew) had Failed To Return.

Lancaster III, ND797 (Codes LE – W)

Pilot	– F/L George Russell Joblin DFC RNZAF. Age 24	Killed
Flight Eng	– F/S William Albert (Ken) Butcher. Age 22	Killed
Navigator	– F/O Donald Bell Lambton. Age 28	Killed
Bomb Aimer	– F/O Williamson Charles John Beeson. Age 32	Prisoner
Wireless Op	– F/S George Edward Stenner . Age 23	Killed
Mid Upper	– Sgt Robert Frederick Cousin. Age 19	Killed
Rear Gunner	– Sgt Harold Raymond Spendelow. Age 19	Killed

George Joblin RNZAF (LAHC Archive)   *WCJ Beeson (Helen Wilson)*

George Joblin's crew on their 29th op (their captain's 30th) were caught by a night fighter and shot down about 02:00 hours between Magstadt and Sindelfingen just outside Stuttgart. It is possible that this is the bomber which was claimed by Unteroffizier Benno Kratz of 2/NJG6 at 01:47 hours. Three members of the crew managed to bale out of the stricken bomber but sadly only F/O Bill Beeson survived, the former Transport Contractor from Radyr, Cardiff survived the war having spent time in Stalag Luft 3 (Sagan) and Stalag IIIA (Luckenwalde). Ken Butcher left behind a young widow and baby daughter Shirley. Originally buried at Magstadt the dead were later moved to Durnbach War Cemetery.

Already recommended for a DFC and right at the end of his tour George Joblin's parents were later notified that their son had been awarded the Distinguished Flying Cross and it was recorded in the London Gazette 18 September 1945, the award to be dated from 27th July 1944. Roy Calvert's tour was almost over, he would fly his last Op with the squadron but remain in place as B-Flight Commander until his replacement arrived. His bravery and commitment was rewarded with the award of a 2nd Bar to his DFC, one of only sixty airmen to be so decorated. His French Canadian navigator Joseph Beaudoin[xvi], flight engineer Bill Mooney DFM[xvii] and wireless operator Alan Connor DFM[xviii] all received DFCs for their service. Gordon Cruickshank DFM had also completed his second tour having received the DFM with 50 Squadron in November 1942.

Bill Mooney DFC DFM having completed two tours with Bomber Command was sadly murdered by a gang of thieves and highway robbers in India in December 1945 traveling to the wedding of a friend.

Sunday 30th July 1944.
Back in support of the Allied ground forces in Normandy 692 heavy bombers attacked 6 German positions along a front about to be assaulted by American troops in the Villers Bocage-Caumont area. The target of 630 Squadron was to be Cahagnes – Aunay-sur-Odon with all of their Lancasters armed with 20 x 500lb MC (No.4 pistol fuse 2) bombs.

30th July 1944 : Daylight Bombing Attack on Aunay-Sur-Odon
Take Off: at 11:20 hours Canadian Hazen Long (LM259) was first off the deck.

WA "Ken" Butcher and his commemorative scroll (Shirley Moulsley

George Cruickshank (George Cruickshank)   *Bill Mooney (LAHC Archive)*

ND554-A	F/O EGW Bowers
ME739-D	F/L CW Rodgers RAAF
LM259-F	F/O HH Long RCAF
NN702-J	F/O MA Swain
LM216-K	F/O JH Bolton
ND335-L	F/L TG O'Dwyer
PB244-N	F/O DR Mallinson
ME845-Q	F/O AR Kerr
PB344-R	S/L RO Calvert RNZAF
LM260-S	F/O E Docherty
LL972-T	F/L DE Hawker RNZAF
NN703-X	F/O JW Lennon RNZAF

Dense cloud masked the target on arrival. The raid was assessed as a 'most unsuccessful mission owing to bad and unexpected weather'. All aircraft returned to base with full bomb loads after the Master Bomber instructed 'abandon mission' at 07:58 hours. The last of the squadron to return were Wade Rodgers and crew in ME739 at 05:31 hours. About to commence their tours were the crews of Pilot Officer Bill Gordon[xix] which included as navigator Sergeant John Langston (later Air Commodore, CBE), that headed by 33 year old Pilot Officer Charles Faulkner[xx] a married man from Lambeth who had served in the Army before volunteering for aircrew duties and the all British all NCO crew of 23 year old Warrant Officer Steve Nunns[xxi] from Pontefract.

Monday 31st July 1944.
Nine aircraft of Six-thirty were detailed to participate in a 127 Lancaster raid by 1 and 5 Groups on railway yards at Joingy-La-Roche all armed with 10 x 1000lb AN-M LD and 4 x 500lb LD bombs, with three more (NN702, ND335 and LM260) to join a force of 97 Lancasters of 5 Group in an attack on flying bombs sites at Rilly La Montague.

31st July 1944 : Daylight Bombing Attacks Joingy-La-Roche and Rilly
Take Off: at 17:20 hours George Bowers (ND554) was the first away.

ND554-A	F/O EGW Bowers	
ME739-D	F/O JH Bolton	
LM259-F	F/O HH Long RCAF	
NN702-J	F/O MA Swain	RD
LM216-K	S/L RE Millichap	
ND335-L	F/L TG O'Dwyer	
PB244-N	F/O DR Mallinson	
ME845-Q	F/O AR Kerr	
PB344-R	F/O WH Gordon	
LM260-S	F/O E Docherty	
LL972-T	F/L DE Hawker RNZAF	
NN703-X	F/O JW Lennon RNZAF	

Both targets were clearly seen and were bombed visibly with good results despite moderate flak defences but neither had fighter cover. The Joigny railway yards were classified as successfully bombed and at Rilly 617 Squadron used Tallboy bombs to cave in both ends of the tunnel whilst the main force cratered the approach areas to ensure that repairs were extremely difficult. 630 Squadron aircraft on the Joigny raid attacked between 20:26 and 20:27 hours from 12,750 to 15,750 feet and the three bombing Rilly (O'Dwyer, Long and Swain) attacked between 20:19 and 20:21 hours from 16,500 to 17,500 feet. The return flight was very difficult due to filthy weather and the squadron's crews landed mostly at Syerston but other stations too. Two Lancasters were lost one being flown by F/L Bill Reid VC of 617 Squadron. John Bolton brought back the last of 630 Squadron's aircraft to East Kirkby at 23:26 hours.

Steve Nunns and crew (Steve Nunns)

Waiting to go (Russell brothers)

August 1944

Tuesday 1st August 1944.

Attacks against flying bomb launch and storage sites continued when 777 bombers were despatched to attack numerous targets but only 79 aircraft were able to bomb. Six-thirty were detailed to provide 4 aircraft armed with 8 x 1000lb AN-M59 bombs.

1st August 1944 : Daylight Bombing Attack on La Breteque/Siracourt
Take Off: at 16:27 hours LM259 (Eugene Mitchell) was first to take off almost simultaneously with Tom Fenning in ND949.

LM259-F	F/O EP Mitchell
NN702-J	F/O AF Kemp RCAF
ND949-Z	F/O TS Fenning
NN703-X	F/O WA McNeil

The mission was abandoned in poor weather on the orders of the Controller by R/T at 18:30 hours and all returned to base. LM259 (Mitchell) being the last to land, 20:45 hours.

Wednesday 2nd August 1944.

Three hundred bombers attacked a V-1 launching site and 3 supply depots. 12 aircraft of the squadron were detailed to attack, each being bombed up with 9 x 1000lb ANM 59 and 4 x 500lb GP LD bombs.

2nd August 1944 : Daylight Bombing Attack on Trossy-St-Maximin
Take Off: at 14:27 hours John Bolton (ME739) was the first airborne.

ND554-A	F/O CR Faulkner	RD
ME739-D	F/O JH Bolton	RD
LM262-G	F/O EGW Bowers	
NN702-J	F/O MA Swain	RD
ND335-L	W/O SA Nunns	
LM269-I	F/O HH Long RCAF	
LM287-O	F/L DE Hawker RNZAF	RD
ME845-Q	F/O AR Kerr	RD
PB344-R	F/O WH Gordon	RD
LL972-T	F/O AF Kemp RCAF	RD
NN703-X	F/O WA McNeil	RD
ND949-Z	F/O TS Fenning	RD

In fine weather and with good visibility over the target all crews attacked the punctual and accurate Red TIs or bombed the target visually. The squadron bombed between 17:00 and 17:03 hours from 15,250 to 18,000 feet over half visually. An excellent concentration of bombs was reported and no fighters appeared but quite accurate heavy flak was encountered in the target area with many aircraft damaged. Rated as a highly successful mission. Bill McNeil was last to land at 19:11 hours.

Thursday 3rd August 1944.

1,114 bombers carried out major raids on the Bois de Cassan, Foret de Nieppe and Trossy St Maximin flying bomb sites. Six-thirty had 10 aircraft detailed for Trossy St-Maximin each armed with 11 x 1000lb ANM (fused 025) bombs.

3rd August 1944 : Daylight Bombing Attack on Trossy-St-Maximin
Take Off: at 11:41 hours Flight Commander Roy Millichap led the formation off.

LM259-F	F/O CR Faulkner	
LM262-G	F/L TG O'Dwyer	RD
LM269-I	F/O JH Bolton	
NN702-J	W/O SA Nunns	
LM216-K	S/L RE Millichap	RD
PB244-N	F/O AF Kemp RCAF	RD
ME845-Q	F/O AR Kerr	RD
PB344-R	F/O WH Gordon	
LL972-T	F/O WA McNeil	
NN703-X	F/O JW Lennon RNZAF	RD

The weather conditions were not as good as on the previous day but the Red TIs were again punctual and accurate and all crews attacked them or bombed the target visually although smoke handicapped the later crews. 630 Squadron crews attacked between 14:32 and 14:33 hours from 16,200 to 17,000 feet. Bombing was not as concentrated as in the previous attack. No fighters were encountered but moderate heavy flak engaged the attackers over the target and on track in the Rouen area. Landing LL972 Bill McNeil and crew were the last to return to East Kirkby at 16:36 hours.

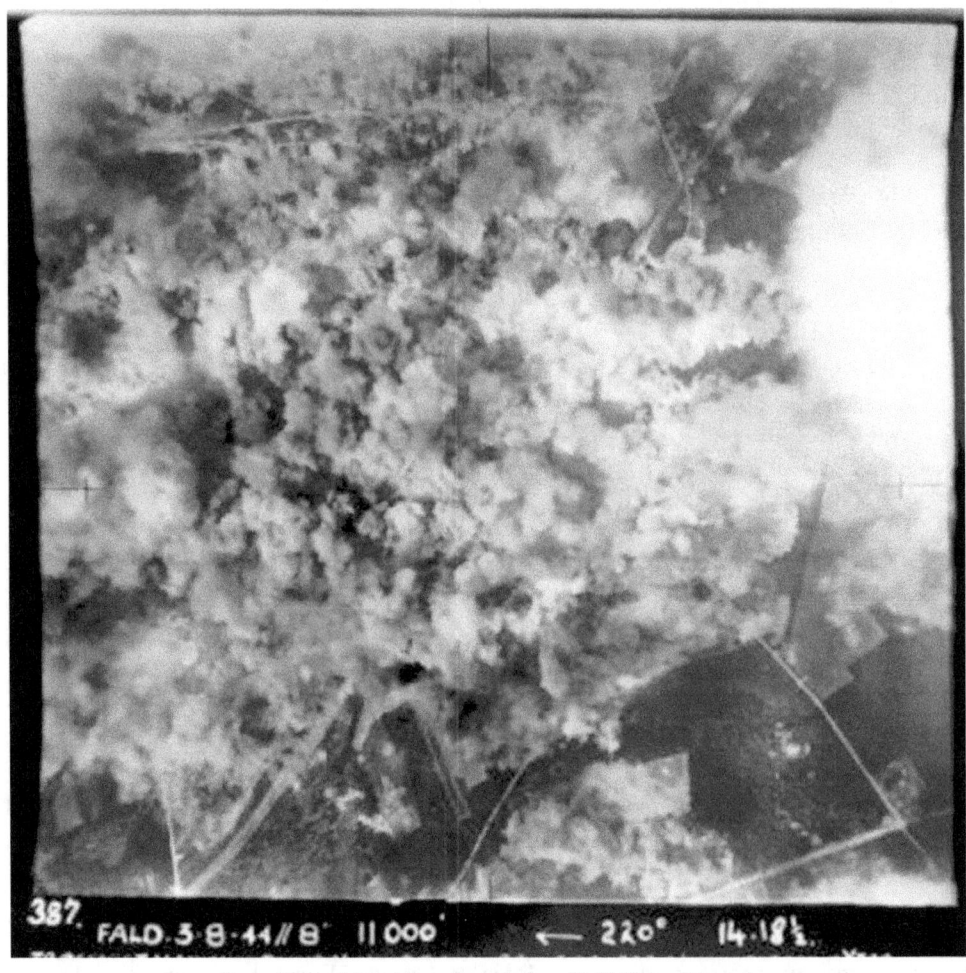

Steve Nunns' bombing photo 3 Aug 1944 (Steve Nunns)

Saturday 5th August 1944.

742 bombers participated in attacks on flying bomb sites at Foret de Nieppe and St-Leu-d'Esserent. 12 aircraft of 630 Squadron were detailed – each was bombed up with 11 x 1000lb ANM (fused 025) bombs.

5th August 1944 : Daylight Bombing Attack on St. Leu-d'Esserent

Take Off: at 10:52 hours Roy Millichap, A-Flight Commander, again led the formation off from East Kirkby.

LM259-F	F/O HH Long RCAF	
LM262-G	F/O EP Mitchell	
LM269-I	F/O JH Bolton	
NN702-J	F/O MA Swain	
LM216-K	S/L RE Millichap	
ND335-L	F/L TG O'Dwyer	
PB244-N	F/O AF Kemp RCAF	
LM287-O	F/L DE Hawker RNZAF	
ME845-Q	F/O AR Kerr	
PB344-R	F/O WH Gordon	RD
LL972-T	F/O WA McNeil	
NN703-X	F/O JW Lennon RNZAF	

'X-X ray' – Joe Lennon had engine trouble and had to abandon, limping back to East Kirkby but landing there safely. De-briefing reports were to the effect that the leading formation was well to starboard of track for most of the outward leg of the flight only making the necessary correction in the last 25 miles. This made the task of 630 Squadron considerably more difficult in making a good bombing run between 13:33 and 13:35 hours from 16,250 to 17,000 feet. Bombing generally seemed scattered on arrival in the target area and moderate heavy flak was present but no fighters were seen. Back at East Kirkby the last to land, almost simultaneously at 15:42 hours were Eugene Mitchell and John Bolton.

LM259 "Spirit of Canada" the favourite of Hazen Long RCAF and crew (RD Gale)

Sunday 6th August 1944.
222 aircraft were despatched to attack the flying bombs sites in the Bois de Cassan, L'Isle Adam, Foret de Nieppe area. Six-thirty provided the requested 6 aircraft each armed with 11 x 1000lb ANM and 4 x 500lb GP bombs.

6th August 1944 : Daylight Bombing Attack on Boise de Cassan, L'Isle Adam
Take Off: at 09:29 hours the first airborne was NN702 (Eugene Mitchell).

NN702-J	F/O EP Mitchell
LM259-F	F/O CR Faulkner
PB344-R	F/O AG Henriquez
LM269-I	F/O WH Gordon
ME845-Q	F/O E Docherty
NN703-X	F/O TS Fenning

Twenty-five miles from target the bomber stream met dense cloud in which severe icing was quickly experienced. Approaching the cloud wall and whilst in cloud conflicting orders were given on the R/T and VHF (1) to split up the formation, (2) to go down beneath the cloud, (3) to climb above the cloud and return to base, (4) to maintain course through the cloud. Static conditions in the cloud made radio reception problematic to add to the confusion. Gunners witnessed small flashes of blue lightning between the barrels of their .303 Browning machine guns. The bombers which continued to the target were able to bomb visually although virtually without fighter cover as the fighters had returned to base. This left enemy fighters almost unopposed and fighters quickly appeared in numbers. 'J', 'I' and 'F' were ordered to RTB at 12:02 hours and each jettisoned parts of its bomb load over the sea on course for home. The crews of Alfred Henriquez, 'Peter' Docherty and Tom Fenning attacked between 12:14 and 12:17 hours from 13,500 to 16,000 feet. The bombing was concentrated and smoke and fires were seen on target. 630 Squadron Ops Record states that Bill Gordon and crew flew 'I-Item' rather than Steve Nunns and his crew, this is

Frank Millar RNZAF (2nd from left) with his crew at HCU (Richard Millar)

Ian Herbert RNZAF (Ian Herbert (NZ)) Frank Millar RNZAF (Richard Millar)

Matt Miller and crew ("Flash" Love at rear right). Joyce Boldero

confirmed by former members of both crews and the absence of his attack from the list in the recommendation for Steve Nunns' DFC. The last of the squadron's aircraft to land at base was LM254 (Chas Faulkner) at 14:48 hours. On its bomb run at 12:14 hours the Jamaican pilot of PB344 'R-Robert' (Alfred Henriquez) saw a Fw190 fighter commence a head-on attack and dropped into a steep diving turn to starboard to avoid the cannon and machine gun fire. He pulled out 2,000 feet lower coming back on course so that his Canadian bomb aimer Danny Carter could make their attack as a Mosquito fighter latched onto the Fw190 and the hunter became the hunted.Recently arrived crews about to make their operational debut were those of two 21 year old New Zealanders Ian Herbert[i] a former dairyman from Taranaki and

Jerry Monk and crew, with Joe Baldwin 2nd from left (Bob Baldwin)

from 1660 HCU Frank Millar[ii] of Kaukapakapa who had both trained in New Zealand and South Africa before arriving in the UK, Henry Archer[iii] the 21 year old son of a Canon who had trained with his crew at 1661 HCU., the all NCO crew of Sergeant Matthew Miller[iv] and that of 21 year old Eric 'Jerry' Monk[v] from Harlow.

When some of the recent arrivals were presented to their flight commanders, 'A' Flight's Squadron Leader Roy Millichap kidded Steve Nunns and Jerry Monk, *'they send me a Monk and Nunns ? That's all we need – a Holy War !'*

Monday 7th August 1944.

In support of ground operations Bomber Command despatched 1,019 bombers in a night attack on five German strong points ahead of Allied troops. The attack was to be very carefully controlled to avoid collateral damage. 14 aircraft from Six-thirty participated in the attack, each armed with 11 x 1000lb ANM and 4 x 500lb GP bombs.

7th/8th August 1944 : Night Bombing Attack on Secqueville
Take Off: at 21:04 hours the first to take off was Chas Faulkner in LM254.

LM259-F	F/O CR Faulkner
LM262-G	F/S GVB Patterson RNZAF
LM269-I	W/O SA Nunns
NN702-J	F/O MA Swain
LM216-K	F/S SID Herbert RNZAF
ND335-L	F/L TG O'Dwyer
PB244-N	F/O AF Kemp RCAF
LM287-O	F/S FE Millar RNZAF

ME845-Q	F/O AR Kerr
PB344-R	F/O WH Gordon
LL972-T	F/O WA McNeil
LM637-V	F/O AG Henriquez
NN703-X	F/O HD Archer
ND949-Z	F/O TS Fenning

Weather conditions were clear with some ground haze Red TIs had landed punctually and on target, the squadron attacked between 23:21 and 23:23 hours from 6,000 to 9,000 feet and an excellent bombing concentration by those crews who attacked had achieved the purpose of the mission. Most of the later arrivals in the target area including three of 630 Squadron (Nunns, Millar and McNeil) received orders from the Master Bomber to abandon the mission at 23:25 hours. Henry Archer's crew in NN703 'X' had three encounters with night fighters at 9,000 feet, at 23:30 they were shadowed by a fighter which remained out of range and did not attack when the bombers alert mid-upper gunner Sergeant Ron Crowhurst ordered a corkscrew but at 23:37 in bright moonlight a Fw190 was spotted at 800 yards on the starboard beam. He opened fire as the Lancaster corkscrewed away to starboard and the rear gunner Sgt Perce Davis let rip a 100 round burst. Archer continued violent evasive action for 10 minutes before they were satisfied that they have evaded the fighter. Almost immediately at 23:47 hours another night fighter was seen holding off the starboard quarter, it didn't have time to attack before NN703 was thrown into another corkscrew which lost the German. No claims were made of damaging the enemy fighters. Arthur Kemp flying PB244 'N' was the last to land at 01:40 hours, they had been attacked by a night fighter at 23:24 hours. Fortunately the

Left: Henry Archer (Matthew Archer) Right: George Patterson RNZAF, Athol Thomas RNZAF and crew with LM262/G (Gillian Thomas)

German pilot opened fire at extreme range and as the Canadian rear gunner Sgt James Stirling shouted for an evasive corkscrew to port he noted the tracer shells burning out as they fell short. The fighter followed them into the corkscrew but after 5 minutes of violent evasive action it was not seen again. Sergeant George Cameron the mid-upper was unsighted. No claim was made by the gunners. One crew Failed To Return –

Lancaster I, LM262 (Codes LE – G)

Pilot	– F/S George Vernon Bentley Patterson RNZAF. Age 23	Killed
Flight Eng	– Sgt Raymond Arthur White. Age 22	Prisoner
Navigator	– F/O Athol Albert Thomas RNZAF. Age 22	Prisoner
Bomb Aimer	– Sgt Leslie Bertram Hewitt. Age	Killed
Wireless Op	– Sgt Thomas Henry East. Age 20	Evaded
Mid Upper	– Sgt Ernest Nelson Watson. Age 21	Killed
Rear Gunner	– Sgt Dennis Wilkinson. Age 19	Killed

Lost on their first op with 630 Squadron the crew had three survivors. The Lancaster exploded when it hit the ground on the farm of the Cholet family at Montreuil-en-Auge. Under German instruction the three airmen found dead in the wreckage were originally wrapped in a sheet by a French forced-labourer Robert Balet from Beauvron-sur-Auge and buried at the local churchyard near the crash site. They were moved later to St.Valery-en-Caux Cemetery by a Graves Registration Unit. Reportedly injured Sergeant Hewitt landed by parachute in a field known as 'Les Bryeres' at La Roque Baignand on the estate of the David family and according to a Monsieur Maertent the estate gamekeeper was murdered overnight by a German patrol and buried by them near where he fell, on the edge of the field, he is now buried at St.Desir War Cemetery. Landing by parachute near Bonnesbosque the Auckland accountancy student Athol Thomas and North Ockenden mechanical fitter Ray White were captured, Thomas suffering from wounds to his head and nose. They spent much of the remainder of their war at Stalag Luft I (Barth) and Stalag Luft 7 respectively. It has been established that in a matter of minutes around midnight four Lancasters were shot down over the LeHavre region of Nord France, two by Hauptmann Heinz Rökker and one by Leutnant Johannes Strassner (both pilots of 2/NJG2) and the other by Unteroffizier Rolf Koch of 4/NJG4. It will almost certainly remain impossible to positively identify which fighter shot down LM262.

Headstones of Sgts. Wilkinson, Watson, and F/S Patterson (R Biaux)

Athol Thomas wrote home to New Zealand – *'At 2322 Les says, 'Bombs gone'. At 2333 under attack along the fuselage, by a Night Fighter which was unsighted. The gunners hadn't seen it until they were both dead. Second wave of bullets hit starboard wing. George called out the emergency bailout signal 'Jump Jump Jump' which means to get out as quickly as possible, every man for himself'.*

Bill McNeil's crew had flown their 7th and last op with 630 Squadron and were transferred to another 5 Group Squadron to complete their tour.

Athol Thomas RNZAF, German PoW mugshots (Gillian Thomas)

Wednesday 9th August 1944.

630 Squadron participated in an attack by 176 Lancasters and 14 Mosquitoes against a Fuel depot at Foret de Chatelleraullt. 15 aircraft were detailed all bombed up with 10 x 1000lb ANM.59 and 4 x 500lb GP (instant fuse) bombs.

9th/10th August 1944 : Night Bombing Attack on Chatellerault
Take Off: at 20:39 hours PB344 (Bill Gordon) was first to take off.

LM259-F	F/O HH Long RCAF
ND412-H	W/O SA Nunns
LM269-J	F/O JH Bolton
NN702-J	F/O EP Mitchell
LM216-K	F/S SID Herbert RNZAF
ND335-L	F/O CR Faulkner
PB244-N	F/O AF Kemp RCAF
LM287-O	F/L DE Hawker RNZAF
ME845-Q	F/O AR Kerr
PB344-R	F/O WH Gordon
LL972-T	F/O HD Archer
LM637-V	F/O AG Henriquez
NN703-X	F/O JW Lennon RNZAF
ND949-Z	F/S FE Millar RNZAF
ND982-Y	F/O E Docherty

The markers were late with the first flare dropped slightly inaccurately at 23: 52 hours so the Controller did not order an attack, instructing his main force to 'stand by' at 23:55 hours. At 00:04 the Controller ordered the main force to *'attack Green TI overshooting by 7 seconds'*. The squadron attacked between 00:03 and 00:09 hours. It is reported this had gone out over VHF up to 3 minutes earlier. At 00:10 he ordered *'stop bombing'* although the instruction was received by Alfred Henriquez's crew who did not attack, it wasn't heard by Chas Faulkner or Doug Hawker who both attacked at 00:16 hours or by Frank Millar's crew who bombed at 00:26 hours. The Green TI had gone out most likely due to bombing. The initial wave of bombing was scattered, the second wave was better, large fires were by then giving off volumes of black smoke and were visible from 50 miles on the return flight. All aircraft attacked except one which was ordered not to bomb after markers had been obscured by smoke. Virtually no opposition was encountered but 2 Lancasters(one each of 50 and 619 Squadrons) were seen to collide and go down breaking up. Steve Nunns' crew were the last to land back at East Kirkby at 03:47 hours.

New Zealander Joe Lennon and crew had completed their 33rd op and were screened, tour expired – they were posted to bases across the UK as Instructors and eventually Lennon would learn that the recommendation for a DFC submitted in his name had been approved. Doubtless he waited with bated breath for 24 hours as the crew of his great friend and fellow countryman Doug Hawker completed their 34th and final op. Hawker's crew would also be screened and their pilot recommended for a well-deserved DFC, his crew had flown every single op together and none had ever missed. The New Zealanders in the crews were posted together to a NZ OTU based in Oxfordshire. Late in 1945 after his return home Hawker was called to receive his DFC from the Governor-General of New Zealand, standing beside him and holding the cushion on which the medal lay was his ADC, Squadron leader David Roberts DFC with whom Hawker had made his initial Second Dickie flights at 630 Squadron. During the day of the 10th of August a new crew arrived at 630 Squadron, that of New Zealander Doug Twidle[vi] a former saw mill hand from Hokitika. They had progressed via the usual route from Wellington's at OTU. (in this case 16 OTU.) then to Stirlings at HCU (it was 1654 HCU) and finally Lancasters at 5 LFS and before joining the squadron. Replacement crews were continually arriving through mid-August and included from 1661 HCU the crew of 23 year old Liverpudlian John Davies[vii], including 39 year old flight engineer John Leslie originally from Alnwick but then living in Tooting, SW London and the crew of Cyril Peters[viii] a 21 year old from Point Clear, Essex. Wing Commander Blome-Jones had recommenced the practice of newly arrived captains flying an Op as Second Dickie with an experienced crew and these pilots would all have that opportunity. Walter Filby[ix] a 21 year old from Weymouth, a regular RAF serviceman, arrived with his crew in early August and was quickly scheduled for a trip as Secon Dickie.

Thursday 10th August 1944.
215 bombers were despatched to attack oil storage depots at Bordeaux. 5 aircraft of 630 Squadron were detailed, each with 5 x 2000lb API 1 sec fuse, 1 x 1000lb AN-M59 (025) bombs.

10th/11th August 1944 : Night Bombing Attack on Bordeaux
Take Off: at 18:38 hours LM216 (Squadron Leader Roy Millichap) was the first off.

LM259-F	F/O HH Long RCAF
NN702-J	F/O MA Swain
LM216-K	S/L RE Millichap
PB244-N	F/O AF Kemp RCAF
LM287-O	F/L DE Hawker RNZAF

The weather at the target was clear with a slight haze and the town and river were seen clearly by most crews. At 22:32 hours the controller ordered the main force to attack the concentration of red and green TIs after this compact group of 6 markers were seen to be accurately placed. The squadron bombed between 22:32 and 22:35 hours from 16,600 to 19,000 feet all reporting successful attacks. At 22:41 the controller ordered crews to attack the green TIs. Black smoke was rising from the depot after the attack, there was no fighter activity and slight ground defences. Back at East Kirkby the last Lancaster to land was Alec Swain's NN702 at 01:46 hours. Douglas Hawker and crew had completed their tour and were screened, their pilot later received a well-earned DFC and returned to New Zealand where in later years he wrote his experiences for publication.

Friday 11th August 1944.
The squadron were to participate in two attacks. The first was an operation mounted by 5 Group with 52 Lancasters and 3 Mosquitoes against the U-boat bunkers at Bordeaux which had been built to provide safety for the 12th U-boat Flotilla who operated large long-range U-boats into distant waters including the South

Doug Hawker RNZAF and crew at HCU (Geoffrey Meace)

Atlantic, Indian Ocean and to the Far East. 5 Lancasters of Six-thirty armed with 5 x 2000lb AP and 1 x 1000lb AN-M59 (025) bombs joined the force.

11th August 1944 : Daylight Bombing Attack on Bordeaux
Take Off: at 12:01 hours Alan Kerr (LL972) was first airborne.

PD253-D	W/O SA Nunns	RD
ND335-L	F/O CR Faulkner	
ND949-Z	F/O TS Fenning	RD
LL972-T	F/O AR Kerr	RD
ND982-Y	F/O E Docherty	

Over the target the weather was clear and visibility excellent. The aiming point and entire dock system was clearly seen from miles away and aircraft were able to make steady bombing runs. 630 Squadron attacked between 16:32 and 16:33 hours from 17,050 to 17,900 feet. Entire sticks of bombs could be clearly seen landing across the submarine pens. Although there was no enemy fighter activity approximately 12 heavy anti-aircraft guns engaged the bombers and 6 aircraft sustained minor damage. When the bunkers were captured by ground forces a few weeks later it was discovered that even the 2,000lb Armour Piercing bombs had been unable to smash their way through the depth of steel reinforced concrete which the Germans had used for the roof of the complex. At 19:47 hours LL972 (Alan Kerr) was the last to touch down at East Kirkby.

On that evening as part of a force of 179 Lancasters and Mosquitoes, crews of 630 Squadron attacked the railway marshalling yards at Givors next. 10 aircraft were detailed and all were armed with 7 x 1000lb AN-M59, 3 x 500lb GP (025) and 1 x 500lb GP (72 hour LD) bombs.

11th/12th August 1944 : Night Bombing Attack on Givors
Take Off: at 20:22 hours Hazen Long in LM259 were the first off the deck, Wade Rodgers' crew were joined by a Second Dickie.

LM259-F	F/O HH Long RCAF
ND412-H	F/S SID Herbert RNZAF
LM269-I	F/O JH Bolton
NN702-J	F/O MA Swain

PB244-N	F/O AF Kemp RCAF	
LM287-O	F/O FE Millar RNZAF	
ME845-Q	F/O EP Mitchell	
PB344-R	F/L CW Rodgers RAAF	(F/O EJ Monk)
LM637-V	F/O DR Mallinson	
NN703-X	F/O AG Henriquez	

'W-William' manned by Henry Archer's crew went unserviceable at the last moment and was unable to take off. Weather conditions were clear over the target with some ground haze. Problems were experienced with the marking which delayed the main attack an eventually at 01:14 hours the controller ordered *'attack concentration of red TIs'* over the R/T. No concentration could be seen by the main force although a crescent of red TIs was spread across the railway yard. On VHF the controller ordered *'attack the most easterly red TI'* and later to *'attack the centre of the TIs'*. The orders were not confirmed and were not heard by some crews, other crews could see Red TIs on the railway yard and they promptly bombed them. 630 Squadron crews attacked between 01:10 and 01:19 hours from 6,600 60 8,800 feet. Returning crews reported sticks of bombs falling in the railway yards and at 01:16 hours a large petrol explosion was widely reported. No fighters were active and the only ground defences were from a neighbouring installation. LM287 flown by New Zealander Frank Millar was the last to return to East Kirkby at 05:23 hours. Post attack assessments rated this *'an exceptionally accurate attack'*.

Saturday 12th August 1944.

In an experimental raid Bomber Command attacked Brunswick without Pathfinder or any other form of marking, the concept being to gauge the accuracy of allowing each individual aircraft to attack based on its own H2S set. Part of the squadron participated in the experiment whilst the remainder joined an attack on German military positions in Normandy. 8 Lancasters were detailed to attack Brunswick, they were bombed up with 1 x 2000lb HC and 12 x 500lb J-type incendiary clusters.

12th/13th August 1944 : Night Bombing Attacks on Brunswick

Take Off: at 21:29 hours the flight from Six-thirty attacking Brunswick was led by Wade Rodgers in PD253.

PD253-D	F/L CW Rodgers RAAF	
LM259-F	F/O MA Swain	
LM269-I	F/O JH Bolton	
ND335-L	F/O EP Mitchell	RD
ME845-Q	F/O AR Kerr	
LM637-V	F/O DR Mallinson	
ND982-Y	F/O E Docherty	
ND949-Z	F/O TS Fenning	

10/10ths cloud covered Brunswick when the bombers arrived and as expected crews bombed based on their H2S. The squadron's crews attacked between 00:03 and 00:05 hours from 19,500 to 22,800 feet. Larges fires were evident beneath the clouds, spread over a wide area but with greater concentration in the centre. Less enemy fighter activity was in the air than had been expected but heavy flak was active and searchlights were numerous but ineffective due to the clouds. The last to land at East Kirkby was LM259 (Alec Swain) at 02:55 hours. ND335 'L-Love' (Eugene Mitchell) landed at Woodbridge with battle damage. At 00:25 hours when he'd just got away after being coned by searchlights and damaged by flak bomb aimer Ernie Roddis sighted a JU88 night fighter on their beam and slightly up, he opened fire with a 75 round burst from the nose turret and saw several tracer strikes on the enemy aircraft. As Mitchell broke into a diving turn to port to evade the enemy Sergeant Geoff Burt in the mid-upper turret opened up with a 300 round burst and his tracer was observed hitting the German who was manoeuvring towards the port outer position where rear gunner Sergeant Norm Longbottom fired 400 rounds at the enemy and saw flames pouring from the fighter before it was suddenly engulfed in flame, went into a spin and hit the ground. The crew saw the burning fighter crash before further evasive action was necessary to avoid concentrated flak which holed ND335 repeatedly. Claim : Destroyed.

Bomber Command regarded the raid as unsuccessful as there was no firm evidence of a concentration of bombing. German reports regarded it as a 'heavy raid' with damage in the Central and Stadtpark districts. Neighbouring towns up to 20 miles distant were mistaken for Brunswick by some inexperienced crews and also bombed. Meanwhile 3 Lancasters were detailed to join the force bound for a German troop concentration around a Falaise road junction, all had been bombed up with 11 x 1000lb MV (025), 3 x 500lb GP (035) and 1 x 500lb GP L/D (1 hour) bombs.

12th/13th August 1944 : Night Bombing Attack on Falaise
Take Off: at 00:12 hours Roy Millichap took off in LM216.

NN703-X	W/C LM Blome-Jones
LM216-K	S/L RE Millichap
LM287-O	F/O HD Archer

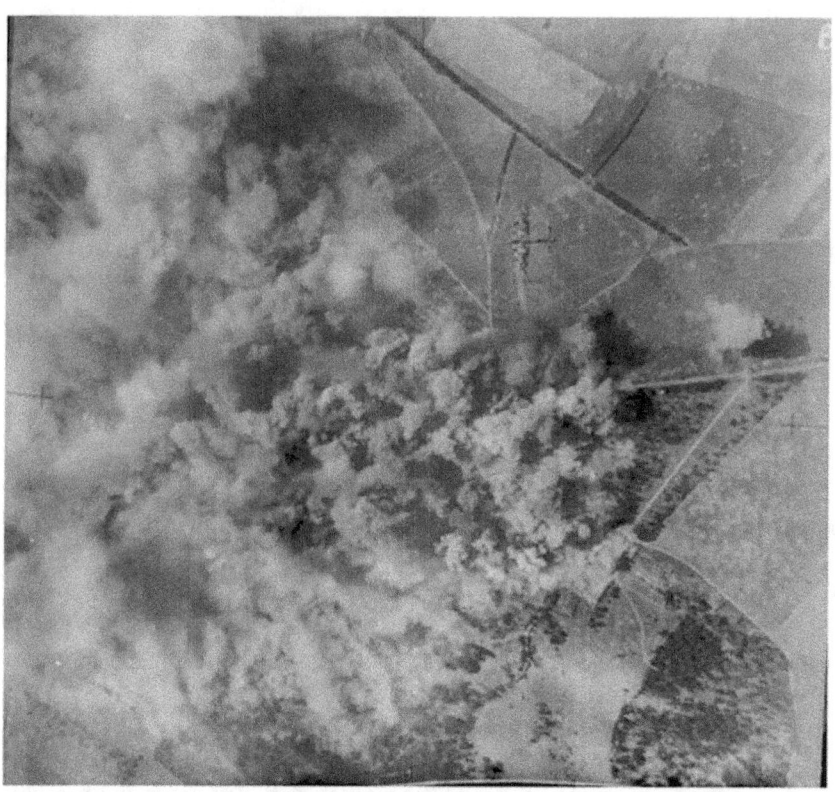

Don Mallinson's bombing photo (note Lanc in top right quarter) (Richard and Barry Mallinson)

On their return the crews reported an excellent attack following the concise instructions of the Controller to ignore the red TIs but bomb the greens which were well concentrated and clearly seen. The three from 630 Squadron attacked between 02:18 and 02:20 hours from 5,800 to 8,000 feet. Several large explosions occurred at the target and bomb bursts were observed straddling the markers. Some fairly accurate flak came up in the TA but no fighters were seen. Reports stated that the bombing was highly effective and had caught a German unit before it had chance to disperse. LM287 (Henry Archer) was the last of the three to touch down at 04:08 hours.

Monday 14th August 1944.
In support of military operations part of the squadron participated in a raid 805 bombers attacking German troop positions facing the 3rd Canadian Division as it advanced on Falaise whilst four aircraft joined a 5 Group 'bash' comprising 155 Lancasters and 4 Mosquitoes attacking warships in the harbour at Brest. Each of the 8 aircraft detailed for Normandy attacked German positions at Quesnay Wood with 11 x 1000lb MC and 4 x 500lb GP bombs.

14th August 1944 : Daylight Bombing Attack on Quesnay Wood
Take Off: at 12:20 hours LL972 (Alfred Henriquez) and LM637 (Don Mallinson) both took off from East Kirkby.

ND412-H	F/O CR Faulkner	
LM269-I	F/O SA Nunns	
NN702-J	F/O EJ Monk	
LM287-O	F/S FE Millar RNZAF	
LL972-T	F/O AG Henriquez	
LM637-V	F/O DR Mallinson	
NN703-X	F/O HD Archer	
ND982-Y	F/O M Miller	
ND949-Z	F/O TS Fenning	

In cloudless weather with a slight haze at target the long straight road west of the target proved to be a good navigational aid. 630 Squadron rated the Master Bomber's instructions as very clear and all crews followed them overshooting the Yellow TI by 1 second as instructed. A lot of smoke rose from the aiming point and sometimes obscured the marker. Bombing was very well concentrated on the German lines. No enemy fighters were seen and ground defences were negligible but present. At 16:09 hours the last two Lancasters returned to East Kirkby, LM269 and NN702.

The 630 Squadron Operations Record Book at the National Archives does not record Henry Archer's crew participating in the attack however the Ops Record held at the RAF Museum does show (and detail) their participation, the fact being confirmed by his DFC recommendation. Meanwhile the 4 aircraft and crews detailed for an attack on a Battleship reported to be in harbour at Brest took off following the C.O.

14th August 1944 : Daylight Bombing Attack on Brest Harbour
Take Off: at 17:30 hours Wing Commander Blome-Jones was first off.

PB253-D	F/S SID Herbert RNZAF	RD
LM216-K	W/C LM Blome-Jones	RD
ME845-Q	F/O E Docherty	RD
PB344-R	F/O JH Bolton	RD

PB253 returned early with technical problems, landing at 18:36 hours. Over the target the weather was clear and ships could be seen in the harbour. 630 Squadron crews attacked in the face of intense flak of both heavy and light calibre, between 20:23 and 20:26 hours from 17,300 to 19,600 feet. A large ship reportedly a battleship was hit by 3 or more sticks of bombs some being seen to explode. A tanker was also hit and one Rear Gunner reported that it sank as they left the target area. No enemy fighters were seen but flak was moderate to intense in barrage form and all aircraft were hit by flak but returned safely, the last being ME845 ('Peter' Docherty) at 22:27 hours. Intelligence showed that the incomplete Vichy French collaborationist naval forces battleship 'Clemenceau' and cruiser 'Gueydon' were hit and left sinking in a 'safe' position, ie: one which would not hinder Allied use of the port once it was captured.

On the 15th August a silver P51B Mustang fighter of 8th USAAF crash landed at RAF East Kirkby, the pilot (O-826517 2nd LT. JR Ryan USAAF) already clambering out of the fighter as it slid down the runway on its belly. Fortunately he was unhurt and was collected by aircraft that evening for return to his unit after being hosted royally in the officer's mess. It transpired that he'd incorrectly believed that he was almost out of fuel and had forgotten to lower his landing gear before touching down.

Tuesday 15th August 1944.
The invasion of Southern France commenced in the early hours. Back in North West Europe Bomber Command took the battle to their own enemy with 1,004 aircraft attacking Luftwaffe night fighter airfields next, targeting 9 airfields in Holland and Belgium hoping to reduce fighter activity when the bombing campaign against German resumed. The campaign against the night fighter bases played a material part in the Luftwaffe moving its night fighters eastwards, back to airfields within the German homeland. Deelen

Luftwaffe night fighter control centre at Deelen (Emil Nonnenmacher)

housed the regional fighter control command and communications centre and based there was an 'ace' night fighter unit, II /NJG 1 (2nd Wing of Night Fighter Group 1) accompanied by III/KG 3 (3rd Wing of Bomber Group 3) and the entire KG6 (Kampfgeschwader – Bomber Group 6) the latter unit undergoing conversion training to night fighting. 11 Lancasters of Six-thirty were detailed to join the attack each armed with 11 x 1000lb AN-M59 and 4 x 500lb GP LD bombs.

15th August 1944 : Daylight Bombing Attack on Deelen Airfield
Take Off: at 10:03 hours Wade Rodgers (LL972) was first off the deck.

PD253-D	F/S SID Herbert RNZAF	
ND412-H	F/O EJ Monk	
NN702-J	F/O MA Swain	
LM216-K	F/O EP Mitchell	
PB244-N	F/O DR Mallinson	
LM287-O	F/S FE Millar RNZAF	
LL972-T	F/L CW Rodgers RAAF	
ME845-Q	F/O HD Archer	
ND982-Y	F/O M Miller	RD
ND949-Z	F/O TS Fenning	
LM269-I	F/O EGW Bowers	

In the target area the weather was clear and the visibility excellent. All crews saw the airfield clearly from a long way off and bombed visually assisted by Yellow TIs which were on the airfield to the south east of the aiming point. 630 squadron attacked between 12:08 and 12:10 hours from 16,200 to 18,000 feet. Bombing was very good and the airfield was covered with bomb bursts. When the smoke cleared the obvious results were an airfield and runways pitted with craters, bombing photographs confirm this assessment. No enemy fighters were seen although accurate flak was encountered from 15-20 guns. At 14:03 hours PD253 flown by Kiwi Flight Sergeant Ian Herbert was the last to touch down at East Kirkby after the attack. The airfield was comprehensively pock marked and thousands of labourers were shipped in by the Germans to repair the damaged runways. The Dutch labourers re-filled the bomb craters with any available debris and purposely covered over unexploded bombs in the hope that they would later explode.

Wednesday 16th August 1944.
Returning to targets in Germany, Bomber Command despatched 461 Lancasters to attack port and industrial districts of Stettin. 14 aircraft of Six-thirty were detailed for ops each armed with 1 x 2000lb HC, 12 x 500lb J-type incendiary clusters.

16th/17th August 1944 : Night Bombing Attack on Stettin
Take Off: at 20:56 hours Wing Commander Blome-Jones was the first off.

PB253-D	F/O SA Nunns	
ND412-H	F/O CR Faulkner	
NN702-J	F/O MA Swain	(F/O JO Davies)
LM216-K	W/C LM Blome-Jones	
LM259-F	F/O EP Mitchell	(F/O CET Peters)
PB244-N	F/O AF Kemp RCAF	
LM287-O	F/O FE Millar RNZAF	
ME845-Q	F/O M Miller	
LL972-T	F/O AG Henriquez	(F/O WGF Filby)
NN703-X	F/O HD Archer	
ND982-Y	F/O E Docherty	(F/O DG Twidle RNZAF)
ND949-Z	F/O TS Fenning	
PB344-R	F/O EJ Monk	
LM637-V	F/S SID Herbert RNZAF	

Weather encountered was 8/10th to 10/10ths cloud with some breaks in the target area. Most crews reported a fair concentration of Red and Green TIs but these were wide of the target to the north and west. Considerable interference prevented clear instructions from the Master Bomber and bombing was scattered causing some large fires near the Target Indicators. The squadron's crews attacked between 01:03 and 01:10 hours from 17,300 to 19,800 feet. Flak was reported as moderate with the ever present search lights ineffective due to the clouds, few fighters were seen in the target area but they were present over Denmark on the return. The German assessment of the raid stated that over 1,500 houses and 29 industrial premises were destroyed and 1,000 houses and 26 industrial plants badly damaged. 5 ships in the harbour totalling 5000 tons were sunk and 8 ships (15,000 tons) seriously damaged. Recently commissioned Eric 'Jerry' Monk was the last to land at East Kirkby at 05:32 hours. One of Six-thirty's aircraft was missing.

Steve Nunns crew (bottom row) Keith Nelson, Steve Nunns, Reg Fletcher (Steve Nunns family).

Lancaster III, LL972 (Codes LE – T)

Pilot	– F/L Alfred George Henriquez. Age 28	Killed
2nd Pilot	– F/O Walter George Frederick Filby. Age 21	Killed
Flight Eng	– Sgt Philip Donald Secretan. Age 20	Killed
Navigator	– Sgt Peter Woolvin Jarvis. Age 22	Killed
Bomb Aimer	– WO2 Daniel Newton Carter RCAF. Age 28	Killed
Wireless Op	– F/S Thomas George Nottingham. Age 23	Killed
Mid Upper	– Sgt Ronald Ernest Williams. Age 20	Killed
Rear Gunner	– Sgt Alan McKenzie. Age not stated	Killed

LL972 is likely to have fallen victim to either Oberfeldwebel Martin Kramer of Stab/NJG 3 or otherwise to Oberleutnant Arnold Brinkmann, both reporting attacking bombers over the Kiel area between 00:06 and 00:15 hours, the Lancaster crashed near Medewitz, south-east of Wollin in what is now Poland. Originally buried at Rissnow Cemetery the crew were moved to Poznan Garrison Cemetery in Poland. Alfred Henriquez was a Jamaican of Jewish faith from Buff Bay/Jamaica.

Friday 18th August 1944.
Military supply dumps in Forest L'Isle Adam and Bordeaux were next on the list of priority targets. 5 of the squadron's Lancasters were detailed to join the 5 Group attack on L'Isle Adam – each was armed with 11 x 1000lb MC (30min delay) and 4 x 500lb GP (30 min delay).

Alfred Henriquez (thejewsofbombercommand.com) *Alan McKenzie (LAHC Archive)*

18th August 1944 : Daylight Bombing Attack on Forest of L'Isle Adam
Take Off: at 12:04 hours Wade Rodgers (PB344) was the first off the deck.

LM259-F	F/O EP Mitchell	
ND412-H	F/O CR Faulkner	RD
PB244-N	F/O AF Kemp RCAF	
ME845-Q	F/O EJ Monk	
PB344-R	F/L CW Rodgers RAAF	

Considerable difficulty was experienced in making up the formation and the planned waves of attackers did not arrive in the correct order. The target area was visually identified and the smoke marker at the last turning point was seen. 630 Squadron's crews attacked at 14:11/14:12 hours from 9,500 to 10,000 feet. Smoke from bomb bursts soon covered the area but the aiming point was identified from nearby landmarks, the bombing was reported to be well concentrated. Enemy fighters were sighted north of Rouen but they did not engage. One of the squadron's Lancasters Failed to Return.

Lancaster III, PB244 (Codes LE – N)

Pilot	– F/O Arthur Frederick Kemp RCAF. Age 20	Evaded
Flight Eng	– Sgt Reginald Douglas Larritt. Age 27	Evaded
Navigator	– F/O William Joseph Shearstone RCAF. Age 21	Killed
Bomb Aimer	– F/O William Francis Jones RCAF. Age 27	Evaded
Wireless Op	– Sgt Gerald Edward Benson. Age 23	Prisoner
Mid Upper	– Sgt George Cameron RCAF. Age 30	Killed
Rear Gunner	– Sgt James Wilson Stirling RCAF. Age 20	Evaded

The Kemp crew. Back row l to r: Cameron, Larritt, Benson, Stirling. Front row l to r: Jones, Kemp, Shearstone. (LAHC Archive)

Having been hit by flak about 14:00 hours PB244 crashed at Rouvray-Catillon and both of the dead are commemorated on the Runnymede Memorial to the missing. Gerald Benson a Wholesale Outfitter from Norwich was captured on landing by parachute and his wounds were treated at Beauvais Hospital and later Amiens Hospital until 26th August when he was transferred to the hospital at Stalag XIIA (Limburg) for 3 further weeks before undergoing a brief visit to Dulag Luft Interrogation Centre. Benson entered Stalag Luft 7 (Bankau) in the last week of September 1944 and from February 1945 was held at Stalag IIIA (Luckenwalde). James Stirling RCAF baled out and landed at about 14:05 hours in a wood called Bois Guilbert 5km west of Buchy, he was fortunate to be a fluent French speaker as a former repair man with the Bell Telephone Company based in French speaking Montreal, Quebec. He hid his parachute and clothing and headed south-east stopping to sleep in a haystack. Caught hiding in bushes near a chateau on 19th August Stirling was dragged into the chateau and interrogated but speaking fluently he bluffed he was way through it and was released to go back to work on a fictitious farm. Aided by the resistance he hid on a farm until 15th August when SS troopers arrived to requisition food. After 5 days hiding in the woods during which time local people fed him, he was able to return to the farm and lay low until the Canadian Army arrived to liberate the district. Eugene Mitchell and crew in LM259 were last of this flight to return to East Kirkby at 16:22 hours.

9 aircraft of 630 Squadron were detailed to participate in a 64 Lancaster and 5 Mosquito attack on oil storage plants at Bordeaux, each was armed with 6 x 1,900lb SAP fused .025 seconds, a bomb which had not been used for a considerable time and caused some surprise and interest when seen again.

18th August 1944 : Daylight Bombing Attack on Bordeaux
Take Off: Frank Millar and crew were the first of this flight to take off.

PD253-D	F/O SA Nunns	
LM269-I	F/O JH Bolton	
NN702-J	F/O MA Swain	RD
LM216-K	S/L RE Millichap	
LM287-O	F/O FE Millar RNZAF	RD
LM637-V	F/O SID Herbert RNZAF	
PD254-W	F/O EGW Bowers	RD
NN703-X	F/O HD Archer	
ND982-Y	F/O E Docherty	

Weather was clear with a slight haze, most crews reported seeing the town and docks clearly from some distance away and identified the aiming point. 630 Squadron crews attacked between 20:09/20:10 hours from 14,000 to 16,000 feet. Bomb bursts were seen all around the aiming point and smoke was rising as the aircraft turned for home. George Bowers touched down in PD254 the last to land at 23:38 hours, flak holes through his windscreen. 'I – Item' bombed with the formation but was hit by flak and seen leaving the target area in a north easterly direction losing height.

Lancaster I, LM269 (Codes LE –I)

Pilot	– P/O John Herbert Bolton. Age 22	Evaded
Flight Eng	– Sgt Charles Edward Goodman. Age 20	Evaded
Navigator	– WO2 Gordon Alan Bullock RCAF. Age 20	Killed
Bomb Aimer	– F/S Ronald William Bishop. Age 22	Killed
Wireless Op	– Sgt William Edgar Durber. Age 22	Evaded
Mid Upper	– Sgt John Leslie Gurney. Age 22	Evaded
Rear Gunner	– Sgt Walter Hunt. Age 19	Evaded

Soon after leaving the target LM269 started to break up with debris falling at St. Crepin. F/S Bishop is buried in St. Crepin Communal Cemetery but WO2 Bullock was found near the village of Muron, his parachute unopened and he was buried in the Communal Cemetery there. Bill Durber landed safely and successfully evaded capture but sadly after his return to the UK he was killed in the crash of a Domini of No.1 Radio School on 20th March 1945 serving as a Wireless Operator Instructor. John Bolton and three of his crew evaded capture and returned to the UK. Sadly John Bolton died in 1951 in a crash, still serving as an RAF pilot. Hazen Long's crew having adopted 'F-Fox' as their own had the 'figure of a lovely lass' painted on her nose along with the wording 'The Spirit of Canada' beside the bomb silhouettes which recorded her sorties.

Above : John Bolton and crew survivors with French helpers. Below: Wreckage of the Bolton crew's 'I-Item' (both photos Chris Bolton)

Hazen Long RCAF aboard 'The Spirit of Canada' (LAHC Archive)

On 22nd August during a lull in Ops more new crews arrived including that of rugger playing Ross Flood[x] from Otahuhu in NZ who had volunteered for aircrew duty and trained in the UK. The crew had progressed via the usual route from Wellington's at OTU. (in this case 17 OTU.) then on to Stirlings at HCU (in this case 1661) and finally Lancasters at 5 LFS before joining the squadron.

Posted in to the squadron at about the same time were the crews of Irishman Deryck 'Cliff' Clifford[xi] from 5 LFS at Syerston (and previously 1660 HCU), those captained by 22 year old RNZAF pilots Ron Stone[xii] and Eric Harris[xiii] who had sailed to the UK together aboard the 'Akaroa' in July 1943. Eric Harris was coming back to England as he'd been born in Redruth Cornwall, his bomb aimer was 23 year old Dave Cole from Wanganui, NZ who would at some stage be releasing his bombs based on markers named after his home town.

The Stone crew had trained at 1660 HCU and arriving directly on their tail were another crew from 1660 HCU captained by 25 year old Eric Britton[xiv] a married man from Dorking who had been a soldier before volunteering for duty as aircrew. Shortly afterwards and also from 1660 HCU came Arthur Bates[xv] and crew, unusually Bates would make two trips as Second Dickie before his crew commenced their tour.

Ross Flood RNZAF and WR Ingram RNZAF (Flood family (NZ))

*'Cliff' Clifford and crew. Back row l to r: RH Mott (MU/G), LTC Matthews (Nav), FGH Tavner (R/G), PWA Sharp (WOp)
Front row l to r: JC Thomson (A/B), DA Clifford (Pilot), RG Wood (F/E) (LAHC Archive)*

Ron Stone RNZAF and crew (Frank Cummings)

After a major party in the officer's mess B-Flight commander Squadron Leader Roy Calvert left the squadron on Thursday 24th August to spend a few days at No. 5 Lancaster Finishing School as his passage home to New Zealand was arranged. Moving over to B-Flight for his last few ops Wade Rodgers was promoted Temporary Flight Commander pending the arrival of the new permanent CO, Squadron Leader Malcolm Eyre[xvi] a 23 year old Londoner from Willesden who had trained in Canada and successfully completed a 31 op first tour. Shortly afterwards Eyre was posted in with his crew of 'second tour men' including rear gunner Warrant Officer Bill Atkins DFM (formerly of 61 Squadron) and mid-upper George Arrowsmith (formerly of 467 Squadron).

Friday 25th August 1944.
630 Squadron participated in the third wave of the 190 Lancaster and 6 Mosquito attack by 5 Group on Darmstadt, a target which had not been seriously attacked by Bomber Command previously. 15 of the squadron's aircraft were detailed and each was bombed up with 1 x 4000lb HC, 10 x No.14 Mk.I incendiary clusters.

25th/26th August 1944 : Night Bombing Attack on Darmstadt
Take Off: at 20:40 hours LL949 (Eugene Mitchell) and LM216 (Terence O'Dwyer) were the first airborne. Four of the Lancasters carried Second Dickies that night.

ME650-B	F/O EGW Bowers	
PD253-D	F/O EJ Monk	
LL949-E	F/O EP Mitchell	(F/O DA Clifford)
LM259-F	F/L HH Long RCAF	
ND412-H	F/O JO Davies	
NN702-J	F/O CET Peters	
LM216-K	F/L TG O'Dwyer	
LM287-O	F/O AR Kerr	(F/O EI Britton)
LL966-P	F/O E Docherty	
PB344-R	F/O WH Gordon	
LM637-V	F/L DR Mallinson	(F/S RA Stone RNZAF)
PD254-W	F/O M Miller	
NN703-X	F/L CW Rodgers RAAF	(F/O EC Harris RNZAF)
ND982-Y	F/O DG Twidle RNZAF	
ND949-Z	F/O TS Fenning	

No cloud was encountered in the target area but there was considerable ground haze. Arriving over Darmstadt crews observed the illuminating flares spread over a wide area but at 01:19 hours they were ordered to postpone attacking by 5 minutes. The flares burned out before the precise aiming point was established and some red spot flares were placed although the Deputy Controller was unsure of their accuracy and at 01:35 ordered crews to attack using H2S. After orbiting for 20 minutes most crews found it impossible to make a satisfactory run in over the target using H2S and bombed concentrations of fire near the markers. No instructions were received from the Controller during the entire attack as he had had to turn for home with engine problems and both of his Deputies had been shot down. The squadron's crews attacked between 01:34 and 01:48 hours from 6,000 to 10,000 feet. A lone straggler, John Davies' crew, bombed at 02:04 hours. Ground defences were light and some fighters were seen in the target area. Cyril Peters and crew were the last to return to East Kirkby, landing at 05:56 hours.

Saturday 26th August 1944.
175 Lancasters of 5 Group attacked Königsberg which was a vital port and railway hub in the supply route for the Eastern Front. The outward flight was 950 miles across the North Sea and the Baltic. The squadron contributed 15 aircraft each armed with 1 x 2000lb HC and 12 x J-type incendiary clusters.

26th/27th August 1944 : Night Bombing Attack on Königsberg
Take Off: at 19:53 hours LL949 (Eugene Mitchell) was the first airborne.

ME650-B	F/O EGW Bowers	
PD253-D	F/O EJ Monk	
LL949-E	F/O EP Mitchell	RD
LM259-F	F/L HH Long RACF	
NN702-J	F/O CET Peters	
LM216-K	F/L TG O'Dwyer	
ND412-H	F/O JO Davies	
LM287-O	F/O AR Kerr	
LL966-P	F/O E Docherty	
PB344-R	F/O WH Gordon	
LM637-V	F/L DR Mallinson	(F/O A Bates)
PD254-W	F/O M Miller	
NN703-X	F/L CW Rodgers RAAF	(F/S GR Flood RNZAF)
ND982-Y	F/O DG Twidle RNZAF	
ND949-Z	F/O TS Fenning	

Very bad weather was encountered on the route out, over the target and on the route homeward. The target was well marked, the squadron attacked between 01:16 and 01:20 hours from 10,200 to 11,500 feet and all bombs seemed to have been dropped satisfactorily although later photo recce pictures showed that most of the bombing fell in the eastern districts of the town. Most crews faced considerable well directed flak both going in and leaving the target and determined fighter activity was encountered during bombing runs and over the target area. Search light activity was intense. Some light flak came from Denmark and Sweden. A note in the Ops Record of 630 Squadron held at the RAF Museum suggests that the O'Dwyer crew aboard LM216 dropped mines in the area from 12,000 feet at 01:16 hours rather than bombing. Weather conditions prevented any aircraft landing at East Kirkby on their return but all except 'B' which Failed To Return, landed at stations across the North, the last home safely being PD253 ('Jerry' Monk) at 07:16 hours.

<u>Lancaster III, ME650 (Codes LE –B)</u>

Pilot	– F/O Evelyn George William Bowers. Age 22	Killed
Flight Eng	– Sgt Guy Raymond Stott. Age 21	Killed
Navigator	– Sgt Wilfred James Fingland RCAF. Age 30	Killed
Bomb Aimer	– F/S Burton McLauchlin RCAF. Age 23	Killed
Wireless Op	– Sgt Leslie Thompson. Age 22	Killed
Mid Upper	– W/O William John Carrier RAAF. Age 22	Killed
Rear Gunner	– Sgt Alan Ambrose Michael Langridge. Age 19	Killed

On its flight homewards ME650 was attacked by a night fighter of 8/NJG 3 flown by Oberleutnant Arnold Brinkmann 10 km north west of Hörnum, eye witnesses recorded that the bomber flew on course streaming flames for some considerable distance before it crashed at approximately 04:15 hours in a field belonging to Farmer Peter Petersen at Sønder Grene near Skarrild (Denmark) with the loss of the entire crew. Six bodies were found in the burning wreck and one dead flyer was found in a field a couple of hundred metres away. The Germans left the bodies in the field until 14:30 hours on the afternoon of 29th August when four labourers sent from the Military Airfield at Vandel started digging a hole at the side of the field to bury the airmen. Rural Constable Egon Christensen approached the German in command and persuaded him to let the local Police arrange for the bodies to be buried at Skarrild cemetery. The German happily accepted to

Left: The original graves of the crew maintained by Danish locals (Airwar Over Denmark) - Bill Carrier RAAF (Marc Lilley)

Eric Harris and crew (Tom Lockett)

pass the responsibility to the Police on the basis that there would be no expenses for the Luftwaffe to pay. The constable borrowed a horse drawn carriage from the nearby 'Clasonborg' manor and placed the bodies on it covering them with the Danish flag. In the Skarrild cemetery a grave was prepared and two large coffins had been placed in it. The carriage was parked next to it and Constable Christensen climbed down in the grave. One at a time the seven bodies were handed down to him and placed in the coffins. When this was done, the local churchman Henrik Ingerslev officiated at the graveside ceremony. The Germans allowed the 40-50 attending Danes to sing one hymn. Before the end of the day the grave was covered with flowers. Sergeant Stott was a pre-war RAF regular serviceman and had been a Halton Aircraft Apprentice. Some superb research has been done by the highly recommended 'Airwar over Denmark' website team who have a wonderful commemoration of this No. 630 Squadron crew.

The 630 Squadron Operations Record Book at the National Archives does not record Matt Miller's crew participating in this operation although the 630 Squadron Ops Record held at the RAF Museum confirms the statement of Des Brunwin (Miller crew Wireless Op) that they did fly that night, attacking the Red TIs on target at 01:19 hours from 10,200 feet on a course of 259°.

Wilf Fingland RCAF (Troy Krawczyk)

Wreckage of Lancaster ME650 (Airwar Over Denmark)

The Königsberg op was Wade Rodgers' and crew 31st and last Op, they had survived and were screened – tour expired. The crew had welded into an utterly loyal unit and had an almost impeccable record of availability for ops. Their Aussie captain Wade Rodgers was awarded a DFC and navigator Jim Campnett[xvii] was Mentioned in Despatches. Rodgers' services were retained at RAF East Kirkby as a Staff Pilot, later test pilot to 55 Base Major Servicing Section, and he often flew as the Base Commander's personal pilot. Recently arrived from 1661 HCU twenty-three year old Lewisham man George 'Billy' Billing[xviii] and his all NCO crew were commencing the series cross-country navigation and high level bombing exercises. In his crew was 27 year old London born mid-upper gunner Denis Holloway who had married and settled in Coventry. Holloway made no secret of his determination to deliver some payback for the Blitz on Coventry in the wake of which his first wife Marion had died.

Tuesday 29th August 1944.

630 Squadron participated in a 189 Lancaster attack on Konigsberg, one of the most successful 5 Group attacks of the war despite the extreme range which allowed only 480 tons of bombs to be carried. 12 aircraft of the squadron participated each armed with 1 x 2000lb HC and 13 x 500lb No.14 Mk.I Incendiary Clusters. A minelaying mission was also carried out 'gardening' in Danzig Bay.

29th/30th August 1944 : Night Bombing Attack on Königsberg

Take Off: at 20:08 hours Kiwi Ross Flood was the first airborne and coincidentally also the last to land at 07:52 hours.

ND554-A	F/O DA Clifford	
PD253-D	F/O EJ Monk	
ND412-H	F/S RA Stone RNZAF	RD
NN702-J	F/O CET Peters	
LM216-K	F/O EC Harris RNZAF	
LM260-S	S/L MA Eyre	
LM637-V	F/L DR Mallinson	
PD254-W	F/O M Miller	
NN703-X	F/O JO Davies	
ND982-Y	F/O DG Twidle RNZAF	
ND949-Z	F/O TS Fenning	
LL949-E	F/S GR Flood RNZAF	

Wade Rodgers RAAF crew. Back row l to r: Jack Butters, Wade Rodgers, Tom Bourke. Front row l to r: Fred Mottershaw, Jim Campnett, Frank Mason, Bert Taylor (Wade Rodgers)

Weather over the target was clear once the Lancasters descended through 9/10ths cloud at 10,000 to 11,000 feet. Crews arriving on time had to orbit the target for over 40 minutes before permission was given to bomb due to the original un-supported markers burning out and marking having to be done a second time to satisfy the Pathfinder legend John Woodroffe who was Master Bomber.. A clear concentration of red and green TIs was then placed and the Controller instructed crews to attack. 630 Squadron's crews attacked between 01:40 and 01:50 hours from 9,000 to 11,900 feet. Large fires in several parts of the town were obvious to all although bombing was probably scattered and some aircraft attacked before permission had been given. Post raid assessment of damage showed that 41 of all housing and 20% of industry in the town were destroyed with large amounts also damaged. Batteries of search lights worked to cone bombers for intense light flak which was effective particularly at 9,000 – 11,000 feet over the target. Light flak also caused trouble over the west coast of Denmark on the return and fighters were seen from the target to Denmark. Sadly one of Six-thirty's crews Failed To Return.

Lancaster III, ND982 (Codes LE – Y)

Pilot	– F/L Douglas George Twidle RNZAF. Age 24	Killed
Flight Eng	– Sgt Charles William Garner. Age 31	Killed
Navigator	– Sgt John Archer Akers. Age	Killed
Bomb Aimer	– Sgt Samuel Stanton. Age 21	Killed
Wireless Op	– F/S Leonard Prior. Age	Killed
Mid Upper	– Sgt Edward John Walton. Age	Killed
Rear Gunner	– Sgt Harold Walter Wickenden. Age 19	Killed

Douglas Twidle RNZAF (New Zealand official)   *Ted Walton (LAHC Archive)*

ND982 was shot down at 01:48 hours by Feldwebel Schäfer of NJG102, 25km south-east of the target at (Gross Haferbeck) Gross Waldeck (renamed Ossokino by the Russians), east of Underwangen (renamed Tschechowo). Official records state that the Germans buried the crew in the local cemetery at Underwangen but post-war Graves Registration Units were refused permission to visit the area by the Russian Army in occupation. Although they do have graves the entire crew are named on Runnymede Memorial in accordance with Air Ministry instructions. The question of their graves being official recognised has been raised with the authorities, access is currently still denied by the Russians.

Following their safe return from their 19th Op 'Paddy' Fenning and crew readied themselves for transfer to 83 Squadron Pathfinders. In December they would later transfer again to the newly formed 189 Squadron where on completion of their tour their captain was awarded a DFC.

The 4 aircraft which were detailed for mining in the area code named 'Tangerine (off the important port of Danzig) were armed with 4 x Mk.VI mines per aircraft.

29th/30th August 1944 : Night Minelaying in Danzig Bay

LM259-F	F/L HH Long RCAF
LL966-P	F/O E Docherty
ME845-Q	F/O AR Kerr
PB344-R	F/O WH Gordon

Ross Flood RNZAF (Flood family (NZ))

Mines were 'planted' successfully in the vegetable patch using H2S. Little opposition was reportedly encountered despite good visibility. The 630 Squadron Operations Record Book at the National Archives and the squadron 'Ops Book' held at the RAF Museum contradict each other on this night, the 'Ops Book' detailing a bombing attack on Konigsberg by Ross Flood's crew and recording a mining attack by Bill Gordon's crew, the ORB states the opposite. The record here follows the 'Ops Book' which records that Flood bombed based on the Red TIs at 01:48 hours from 11,000 feet on a course 110°T.

At 02:45 hours that night as the bombers closed in to attack their target, back at RAF East Kirkby frantic work commenced to deal with a Wellington bomber (LN895) of 21 OTU damaged by 'friendly' anti-aircraft fire off Cromer, which had just crash landed on the airfield wrecking a flight hut and injuring two members of the ground staff. They and the aircraft's pilot and rear gunner were admitted to RAF Hospital Rauceby while the remaining four crew members were detained in Station Sick Quarters for 24 hours 'for observations'.

Thursday 31st August 1944.

601 bombers attacked storage areas in Northern France believed to be primary sites for V-2 rockets. Eight sites were found and attacked. 15 Lancasters of Six-thirty were detailed, all armed with 11x 1000lb AN-M65 (.025) and 4 x 500lb GP (1 hour delay) bombs.

31st August 1944 : Daylight Bombing Attack on Bergueneuse
Take Off: at 16:00 hours LL949 (Eugene Mitchell) was first off.

ND554-A	F/O DA Clifford
PD253-D	F/S GR Flood RNZAF
LL949-E	F/O EP Mitchell
LM259-F	F/L HH Long RCAF
PD283-G	F/O CR Faulkner
NN702-J	F/O CET Peters
LM287-O	F/O EC Harris RNZAF
LL966-P	F/O E Docherty
ME845-Q	F/O AR Kerr
PB344-R	F/O WH Gordon
LM260-S	S/L MA Eyre
LM637-V	F/O JO Davies
PD254-W	F/O M Miller
NN703-X	F/O HD Archer
ND949-Z	F/S RA Stone RNZAF

At 18:00 hours, the planned H-Hour, as a bank of cloud covered the target area drifting slowly, the Controller ordered crews to orbit while he dropped below the clouds at 6,000 feet to check the marking. Target Indicators were well placed and he ordered the attack. Cloud had moved by 18:14 hours and crews were able to bomb visually achieving a good concentration of bombs on target. The squadron's crews attacked between 18:18 and 18:36 hours from 10,000 to 13,000 feet. No enemy fighters were seen and flak was light. LL949, which had been the first to take off was also the last to land at 21:09 hours. The Ops Record of 630 Squadron held at the RAF Museum states that Eugene Mitchell's crew 'did not bomb' but offers no explanation, nor is there anything in the Operations Record Book.

September 1944

Saturday 2nd September 1944.
Shipping in the dry dock facility at the harbour of Brest was the next target, when the squadron formed a part of the 67 Lancaster attack by 5 Group. 11 aircraft of the squadron were detailed to participate, each with a bomb load of 11 x 1000lb AN-M fused .025 sec plus 4 x 500lb AN-M64 (.025).

2nd September 1944 : Daylight Bombing Attack on Brest
Take Off: at 11:07 hours Terence O'Dwyer (LL966) and John Davies (LM637) took off from East Kirkby at the head of the squadron.

LL949-E	F/S GR Flood RNZAF
LM259-F	F/O DA Clifford
NN702-J	F/O CET Peters
LM287-O	F/O EC Harris RNZAF
LL966-P	F/L TG O'Dwyer
ME845-Q	F/O AR Kerr
PB344-R	F/O WH Gordon
LM637-V	F/O JO Davies
PD254-W	F/O M Miller
NN703-X	F/O HD Archer
ND949-Z	F/S RA Stone RNZAF

Chas Faulkner and crew had to stay behind when 'G-George' went unserviceable at take-off. Weather at the target was clear throughout the attack and ships under repair were clearly seen in the docks before the attack. Crews of the squadron all attacked visually between 14:35 and 14:56 hours from 10,800 to 13,500 feet. The scene afterwards was of flooded docks and ships with their decks awash as the bombing had been concentrated on the dry docks and the dockside to the east. No opposition made undisturbed bombing runs possible with many crews going round again for a repeat run before bombing to ensure accuracy. Cloud began to drift in and at 14:14 hours the Controller ordered 'stop bombing' for five minutes to allow it to clear. Photographs taken at 14:47 show the docks flooded and both ships sunk. NN702 was the last to return at 17:36 hours.

Sunday 3rd September 1944.
675 bombers were despatched to make a second attack on Luftwaffe Night fighter stations in the Netherlands. 17 aircraft of Six-thirty were detailed with bomb loads of 11 x 1000lb MC LD (1 hour) plus 4 x 500lb MC LD (1 hour).

3rd September 1944 : Daylight Bombing Attack on Deelen
Take Off: the Lancasters took off from East Kirkby from about 15:15 hours.

ND554-A	F/O DA Clifford	
JB290-C	F/O EI Britton	
PD253-D	F/O EJ Monk	
LL949-E	F/O EP Mitchell	RD
LM259-F	F/L HH Long RCAF	
PD283-G	F/O CR Faulkner	
NN702-J	F/O CET Peters	
LM216-K	F/S GR Flood RNZAF	

NF961-L	F/L TG O'Dwyer	RD
LM287-O	F/O EC Harris RNZAF	RD
LL966-P	F/O E Docherty	RD
ME845-Q	F/O AR Kerr	RD
PD344-R	F/O WH Gordon	RD
LM260-S	S/L MA Eyre	RD
LM637-V	F/O JO Davies	RD
PD254-W	F/O M Miller	
NN703-X	F/O HD Archer	
ND949-Z	F/S RA Stone RNZAF	

The weather conditions on the outward flight made formation flying difficult and to the north of the planned track. The proximity marker was however well placed and crews had no difficulty in identifying their aiming points although some had to make a second bombing run to catch a break in the clouds. 630 Squadron crews attacked between 17:30 and 17:33 hours from 14,000 to 16,500 feet. Accurate and heavy flak was encountered over Utrecht and over the target area with 9 aircraft reporting flak damage although only 1 of the 675 raiders was lost. Ross Flood landed LM216 at 20:38 hours, the last of the squadron's Lancasters to touch down. Fliegerhorst Deelen was again badly torn up and its runways badly damaged. The Luftwaffe obviously decided that enough was enough and beginning on the following day

Desmond Reynolds SAAF and crew (front row) Paddy Walsh (rear gunner), Desmond Reynolds (Skipper), Bill Brentnall (bomb aimer). (back row) Alan Ellis (flight engineer), unknown, Noel Coster (Navigator), Ed Burnand (wireless op). Photo: Kay Rowland

transferred all of its units and aircraft further back into the Fatherland, effectively pulling out of Deelen by 11th September. Cyril Peters crew had completed their 6th Op, their last with Six-thirty as they transferred to 97 Squadron Pathfinders where sadly they would all be lost on the night of 10th November 1944 on a night training exercise using LORAN over liberated France. Their Lancaster (PB200) dived into marshes and they were buried at Clichy New Communal Cemetery. Two 97 Squadron aircraft on that exercise were lost, the other disappeared without trace. Between 3rd and 6th September the 'Coastal types' (154 Wing) lodging at Strubby moved out, 144 and 404 Squadrons to RAF Banff and 280 Squadron to RAF Langham. The Base was expanded to 5 Lancaster squadrons with the arrival of 619 Squadron at RAF Strubby and 44 Squadron at RAF Spilsby on 28th and 30th of the month respectively. The administration of the Wainfleet bombing ranges was also transferred from RAF Coningsby to RAF Spilsby during the month. Group Captain John R Jeudwine DSO OBE DFC (formerly CO No. 619 Squadron) took command of RAF Strubby from 7th October.

A number of newly arrived crews were preparing for operations at the time, two were captained by officers of the South African Air Force, 26 year old Lieutenants Desmond Reynolds[i] from Breyten and 25 year old Douglas Turner[ii] from Natal who had trained at 1660 HCU, one was headed by Australian 'Olly' Atkinson[iii] of Beenleigh, Queensland, another by New Zealander Tony Wilson[iv] from Wellington who had trained in South Africa before coming to the UK and three crews headed by British pilots, 21 year old

Doug Turner SAAF and crew. Back row l to r: Bell, Laight, Moorcroft and Hughes. Front row l to r: Key, Turner and Phillipson (Paul and John Key)

Henry Thompson and crew, Ken Arscott in the centre of the rear row (Keith Arscott)

recently married Geoff Daggett[v] from Ilford, Northfleet innkeepers son Geoff Stemp[vi] just days passed his 21st birthday and recently commissioned Henry Thompson[vii] from Harrogate (originally from Aspatria in Cumberland), who was a 28 year old RAF regular serviceman.

Saturday 9th September 1944.
113 Lancasters and 24 Mosquitoes of 5 and 8 Group were tasked to attack a German target next. 16 aircraft of 630 Squadron were detailed for Ops, each with 1 x 4000lb HC and 2,000 x 4lb incendiaries.

9th/10th September 1944 : Night Bombing Attack on Mönchen Gladbach
Take Off: at 02:35 hours Eric Harris and crew in PD254 were the first airborne. Five of the crews were accompanied by Second Dickies, the most ever carried on Ops by Six-thirty.

ND554-A	F/O DA Clifford		
PD253-D	F/O SA Nunns		
LL949-E	F/O EP Mitchell		
LM259-F	F/L HH Long RCAF	(P/O GE Billing)	
PD283-G	F/O CR Faulkner	(F/S DA McGillivray RNZAF)	
LM216-K	F/O SID Herbert RNZAF		
NN702-J	F/O MA Swain	(F/O GE Stemp)	
ND412-H	F/S GR Flood RNZAF	RD	
NF961-L	F/O A Bates		
LM287-O	F/O FE Millar RNZAF		
LL966-P	F/S RA Stone RNZAF		
PB344-R	F/O WH Gordon	(F/S OJS Atkinson RAAF)	
LM260-S	F/O EI Britton		
PD254-W	F/O EC Harris RNZAF		
NN703-X	F/O HD Archer	(F/O AJR Wilson RNZAF)	RD
ND949-Z	F/O JO Davies		

Weather conditions were good with no cloud although there was a little haze or smoke in the target area. Two red TIs were dropped by the marker force and the Controller gave instructions to attack the southerly one. The squadron's crews attacked between 05:19 and 05:27 hours from 17,000 to 17,500 feet. Bombing was very concentrated and some major explosions were seen by multiple crews with the first still visible from the Dutch coast on the return. Ground defences were lighter than usual. At 05:27 hours flying at 17,000 feet with a clear moon to starboard of PB344 'R-Robert' Bill Gordon's mid upper gunner Sergeant Fred 'Dobbie' Dobson sighted a twin engined night fighter on their starboard beam up, at about 400 yards range and ordered a corkscrew to starboard opening fire himself with a burst of 200 rounds. The German continued to dead astern and broke away to port being lost in the darkness. Their rear gunner Sergeant Vic Cardwell didn't get a chance to open fire and 'Dobbie' Dobson later complained that there was little or no tracer amongst his ammunition which prevented him from correcting his sighting. Echoing the thoughts of Sergeant Dobson on the lack of tracer rounds was Sergeant Bernie Edwards, John Davies' mid-upper aboard ND949 'Z-Zebra'. Flying at about 17,000 feet at 05:35 hours immediately after bombing the target he sighted a fighter on the port quarter at about 250 yards. Davies carried out a banking search to starboard and the fighter passed about 200 feet above the Lancaster between the mid-upper and rear turrets. Bernie Edwards fired a 100 round burst at point blank but without tracer was unable to correct his aim or observe hits. The fighter broke off and disappeared never presenting itself as a target for Sergeant Ted Dodge in the rear turret as their pilot threw the Lancaster into a port corkscrew. No claim could be made. At 07:47 hours Henry Archer (NN703) was the last to return. The assessment of the raid matched German reports, it was a devastating attack and the centre of the town was destroyed.

Monday 11th September 1944.
In support of ground operations German defensive positions at Le Havre were pounded by 218 bombers. 15 aircraft were detailed to join the force each armed with a bomb load of 10 x 1000lb AN-M65 fused .025.

11th September 1944 : Daylight Bombing Attack on Le Havre
Take Off: at 05:38 hours Don Mallinson (LL966) was the first off the deck.

ND554-A	F/O DA Clifford
PD253-D	F/O SA Munns
LL949-E	F/O EP Mitchell
LM259-F	F/L HH Long RCAF
PD283-G	F/O CR Faulkner
NN702-J	F/O GE Billing
ND412-H	F/O A Bates
LM216-K	S/L RE Millichap
NF961-L	F/O SID Herbert RNZAF
LM287-O	F/O FE Millar RNZAF
LL966-P	F/L DR Mallinson
PB344-R	F/O WH Gordon
LM260-S	F/O AR Kerr
PD354-W	F/O EC Harris RNZAF
ND949-Z	F/O JO Davies

Weather at the target was clear with very good visibility. 5 Group's target had no markers at H-hour (07:30) but the other target further south was being marked. The squadron's crews attacked between 07:33 to 07:42 hours from 10,200 to 13,000 feet. No instructions were received from the controller until he called 'Cease bombing' and Return to Base as the targets had been destroyed. British Ground forces led by 2 British divisions stormed Le Havre and a few hours later the Germans surrendered. Steve Munns and crew in PD253 were the last to return to East Kirkby at 09:27 hours

The Mitchell crew lined up behind the CO (Bill Deas) Flight Commander and senior officers, (l to r) Ernie Leese, Walt Scott, Norm Longbottom, Geoff Burt and Eugene Mitchell (LAHC Archive).

Returning safely from Le Havre Eugene Mitchell's crew heaved a sigh of relief, they had completed their last op, were classified 'tour expired' and screened. They had lost their original navigator Ken Chamberlain who with previous operational experience had completed his tour six weeks earlier and been posted as an instructor with a recommendation that he be awarded a DFC (it was later confirmed). His seat was filled by flight commander Roy Calvert's own navigator French-Canadian Joe Beaudoin for the next six ops until they were permanently allocated the Canadian 'Goodie' Goodhew DFC who had just survived the ditching which claimed the lives of all of his former crew (his pilot was Ron Hayes) except himself and the rear gunner. Goodie became their navigator through till the tour end. Eugene Mitchell was duly recommended for a DFC and the crew were split up and posted away in instructional roles.

In the second raid of the day undertaken by the squadron, Six-thirty formed a part of a 226 Lancaster and 14 Mosquito force despatched by 5 Group to Darmstadt in what would be a 'night of fighters' for 630 Squadron. 17 aircraft were detailed each with 1 x 4000lb HC and 14lb incendiary clusters.

11th/12th September 1944 : Night Bombing Attack on Darmstadt

Take Off: at 20:39 hours flying LM216 Wing Commander Blome Jones led the squadron from East Kirkby.

ND554-A	F/O DA Clifford	
PD253-D	F/O SA Nunns	
LL949-E	F/S GR Flood RNZAF	
LM259-F	F/L HH Long RCAF	
PD283-G	F/O CR Faulkner	
ND412-H	F/O SID Herbert RNZAF	
NN702-J	F/O GE Billing	
LM216-K	W/C LM Blome-Jones	
NF961-L	F/L TG O'Dwyer	RD
LM287-O	F/O FE Millar RNZAF	
NG125-N	F/L DR Mallinson	
PB344-R	F/O WH Gordon	
LM260-S	F/O A Bates	
ME739-T	F/S RA Stone RNZAF	
PD254-W	F/O EC Harris RNZAF	
NN703-X	F/O HD Archer	
ND949-Z	F/O JO Davies	

It is possible that Don Mallinson actually flew LL966 'P-Peter' attacking Darmstadt, records are contradictory. No cloud and good visibility in the Target Area aided the attackers and the target was punctually and accurately marked so the bombing started immediately, before H-Hour on instructions from the Controller. 630 Squadron's crews attacked between 23:58 and 00:03 hours from 12,000 to 13,700 feet. Bombing was regarded as extremely concentrated. Several large explosions were seen in the city centre and one particularly large one was reported by several crews at 00:45 hours after they had left the TA. Some of the later arrivals at the target found bombing less easy due to the heavy pall of smoke which was then at 10,000 feet. Ground defences were slight around Darmstadt but the searchlight belt between Mannheim and Frankfurt was very active. Fighter activity in the TA was intense and several combats resulted. The glow from the fires was obvious from 180 miles away on the return flight. Over the target at 00:02 hours at 13,100 feet the rear gunner aboard NN702 'J-Jig' (George 'Billy' Billing) Flight Sergeant Dave Todd RAAF sighted two FW190's dead astern and slightly up, as they came into attack he instructed a corkscrew to port and got off a 100 round burst just as the enemy fired, before his guns jammed and he lost sight of the fighters as he struggled to clear the stoppages. Fortunately he was successful before the next attack on 'J' which would follow shortly.

Also over the target moments later Hazen Long's 'Spirit of Canada' LM259 'F-Fox' (the ORB states LM260 but the Combat Report and Ops Record both give LM259 which he'd flown on the earlier raid on Le Havre) was sandwiched between two twin engined fighters. Sergeant Eddie Browne RCAF in the rear turret monitored one fine on the port quarter, down while Sergeant Frank Houston (mid upper) maintained a watch on its mate starboard quarter, up. Turning in to attack from starboard the first opened fire at 400 yards, his aim was off and his shells and bullets passed over the starboard wing. As Hazen Long threw the Lancaster into a port corkscrew Eddie Browne gained a visual on the fighter and fired a 400 round burst firing into it at 200 yards in the roll. The strikes were obvious and the fighter went into a spiral dive with its starboard engine on fire, spreading to the starboard wing. Both rear gunner and bomb aimer (F/O Joe Perreault RCAF) saw the enemy aircraft hit the ground with a bright explosion. Claim was made for a twin engined fighter destroyed. At 00:05 hours at 12,700 feet a JU88 passed from starboard to port astern the rear turret of Ross Flood's LL949 'E' probably in pursuit of another Lancaster. With amazingly quick reactions Sergeant Maurice Henley fired a 400 round burst at it before it was lost to sight. Mid Upper gunner Fred Hughes was searching the sky on the port side. Henley's report states a preference for tracer amongst his ammunition, a complaint which would be repeated many times that night.

LM260 'S-Sugar' flown by Arthur Bates was on its bombing run over the target just after midnight when his rear gunner Warrant Officer Walter Bowman sighted a JU88 coming in to attack on the port quarter up. He watched the unsuspecting fighter close to 600 yards and fired off a burst of 1,000 rounds as the German aircraft broke away to the starboard quarter down, continuing his burst as it belched smoke. Sergeant John Jenkins (mid-upper gunner) wasn't in a position to fire. Strikes were seen on the enemy fighter but at his debriefing Bowman complained that the lack of tracer amongst his ammunition made initial sighting very difficult. Leaving the target at 00:06 hours a JU88 attacked ME739 'T-Tare' flown by Kiwi Ron Stone. His mid-upper gunner Sergeant Les Moore sighted the fighter just as it fired and he returned fire as he called for a corkscrew to port. As the fighter closed to 100 yards Sergeant Alf Sherringham in the rear turret got in a 100 round burst before it broke off suddenly to starboard and disappeared. Both gunners later complained the difficulty in aiming due to the lack of tracer amongst their ammunition. Just moments later at 00:08 hours New Zealander Frank Millar's LM287 'O-Orange' was the target of cannon and machinegun fire from an unseen night fighter on their port quarter at 13,200 feet. Millar dived to port as his gunners Sergeant's Pete Wooller (mid upper) and Frank Whatling (rear gunner) returned fire, 200 and 400 round bursts respectively.

Squadron Bombing Leader Flight Lieutenant George Arkieson persuaded his pilot (Terence O'Dwyer) to stooge around over the target for 15 minutes in order for him to get a good bombing run despite suffering severe flak damage, an engine put out of action and some hydraulics shot away then at 00:09 hours nine minutes after they had bombed NF961 'L-Love' was trapped between searchlights to port and to starboard which had enthusiastically coned enemy fighters in some cases. A JU88 was sighted on their starboard quarter by Sergeant Stew Somerville (mid-upper) who instructed a corkscrew to starboard opening fire with a 200 round burst as Sergeant Jack Cumming (rear gunner) acquired the target and delivered a burst of 400 rounds. The gunners both saw the starboard engine of the JU88 on fire as it dived apparently out of control. NF961 had to land at an emergency airfield on its return. The gunners claimed a JU88 Damaged.

NF961 flown by 'Pancho' O'Dwyer's crew was so seriously damaged (as above) that L-Love was categorised AC requiring extensive repairs beyond the resources of the squadron. A specialist team worked on the Lancaster for two weeks at East Kirkby before it could be accepted back into service on 26th September 1944 (thanks to Karen Shortland for this information). It is believed that the JU88 fighter of Leutnant Bruno Lange of 4/NJG6 made this devastating attack. At 00:16 hours at 13,100 feet as NN703 'X' flown by George 'Billy' Billing left the target area his rear gunner Aussie Flight Sergeant Dave Todd sighted a Me210 or 410 coming in to attack on the port beam, it was banking and firing as it came in. Todd opened fire with a burst of 600 rounds as the mid-upper gunner Sergeant Denis Holloway instructed a corkscrew to port. No hits were observed on the enemy fighter due to lack of tracer. They also fought off two Fw190 fighters.

German records confirm that the raid was devastating and suggest 12,300 casualties including over 1,000 servicemen. All aircraft attacked and returned to base ahead of ND554 ('Cliff' Clifford) which touched down at 02:38 hours, except 'G-George' (F/O CR Faulkner) which was missing

Lancaster III, PD283 (Codes LE – G)

Pilot	– F/O Charles Robson Faulkner. Age 33	Killed
Flight Eng	– Sgt Robert Arthur Godwin Cranefield. Age 20	Killed
Navigator	– Sgt George Law Lawrie. Age 22	Killed
Bomb Aimer	– Sgt Donald McMillanBoyd RCAF. Age 20	Killed
Wireless Op	– Sgt Leslie Alfred Broomfield. Age 22	Killed
Mid Upper	– Sgt Thomas Richard Riley. Age 20	Killed
Rear Gunner	– Sgt Ronald Charles Quinn. Age 21	Killed

The crew crashed at Schmidthachenbach and were all killed, they are buried at Rheinberg War Cemetery. PD283 may have been the bomber claimed by Hauptmann Kurt Fladrich of 9/NJG 4 at 4,200 metres altitude above Hunsrück, north-east of Trier at 00:21 hours. It was his 14th victory. Charles Faulkner left behind a widow in south-east London.

Left to right: Lawrie, Faulkner, unknown (LAHC Archive). Don Boyd RCAF. S Boyd (Mass). A letter to George Lawrie, returned due to his death in action. Source unknown

Aboard 'F-Fox' it had been a 'hairy' night for Canadian Hazen Long and his crew, it was the 35th and last op of their tour and they had been sandwiched between two night fighters and shot one of them down. They were remembered as another 'tight crew' who were careful about their operational training and didn't cut corners. Their captain was recommended for a DFC as was Richard McCann[viii] (navigator) and Hazen Long pushed for a DFM for Eddie Browne[ix] his rear gunner, all of the awards were approved. The four Canadians in the crew were promptly repatriated to Canada, John Studholme their flight engineer was posted as an instructor and the two other British lads remained attached non-operationally to Six-thirty until January 1945. That night the CO flew his 7th Op with Six-thirty which also completed the tour which he'd started as a flight commander with 207 Squadron, Wing Commander Leslie Blome-Jones was recommended for a DFC and would remain in command until his successor arrived. He and his crew were fortunate to survive this attack when a bomb from an aircraft above tore a great hole in the mainplane of his Lancaster on their bombing run. His wireless op, Warrant Officer Arthur Murphy, was posted as an instructor as was navigator Jim Martin[x] who was recommended for a DFC, but 28 year old Bob Foulkes[xi] bomb aimer and former soldier from Beckenham, 'Swannee' Swann their flight engineer and both gunners were only part way through their own tours and would quickly form the nucleus of a new crew for pilot Bill Adams, 'the Yank' was about to return to Six-thirty after being shot down over France but successfully evading capture. Together they continued to operate with Six-thirty until the gunners and

'Swannee' completed their tours but Bob Foulkes remained with Bill Adams and they transferred together to 617 Squadron. Post-war Foulkes became a widely recognised and respected horologist and a published author on the subject.

Tuesday 12th September 1944.
5 Group mounted another attack, supported by 1 Group, totalling 204 Lancasters and 13 Mosquitoes on Stuttgart. 14 of 630 Squadron's aircraft and crews were detailed, they were bombed up with1 x 4000lb HC and 14 x Mk.14 incendiary clusters.

12th/13th September 1944 : Night Bombing Attack on Stuttgart
Take Off: at 18:53 hours LM260 (Eric Britton) was the first away.

ND554-A	F/O DA Clifford	RD
PD253-D	F/O SA Nunns	
LM259-F	F/O SID Herbert RNZAF	
ND412-H	F/O A Bates	
NN702-J	F/O MA Swain	
LM216-K	F/S GR Flood RNZAF	
NG125-N	F/L DR Mallinson	
LM260-S	F/O EI Britton	
ME739-T	F/O RA Stone RNZAF	
NG123-U	F/O WH Gordon	
PD254-W	F/O EC Harris RNZAF	
NN703-X	F/O HD Archer	
ND949-Z	F/O JO Davies	

Two Lancasters failed to take off due to technical defects. Weather was clear at the target and visibility good so the first crews saw the town clearly in the light of the flares and reported that the green and red TIs were pretty accurate. The Controller's orders were simple and were followed. Early bombing was split between the red TIs and the town centre. 630 Squadron's crews bombed between 23:11 and 23:18 hours from 17,000 to 17,900 feet. One crew reported hearing a suspicious voice over the 1169 frequency giving spurious instructions, they had the main force call sign but did not have the Controllers Call Sign. A very large explosion was noted at 23:28 hours in the target area. On the return flight fires could be seen from 100 miles away both at Stuttgart and at Frankfurt. No searchlights were in operation and only light ground defences. Fighters began to arrive west of Karlsruhe but seemed to target the force which had attacked Frankfurt. No activity was seen after crossing the Rhine and although there were 6 combats no claims were made. Eric Britton's crew in LM260 'S-Sugar' suffered the persistent attentions of the Luftwaffe night fighters but were fortunate to escape. In clear conditions and in the light of the target an initial attack was made shortly after 23:10 hours by a FW190 while flying at 17,000 feet. Sergeant Blair Wood in the rear turret sighted the fighter closing fast from 1000 yards dead astern and called for a corkscrew to port at 700 yards range opening up with a burst of 160 rounds before all four machine guns jammed due to spent cartridges piling on top of the servo feed. Flight Sergeant Les Fairhead RAAF in the mid-upper turret was doubtlessly cursing his guns which wouldn't open fire due to a stuck solenoid. The fighter broke off without opening fire. Minutes later though another single engined fighter, possibly the same FW190, commenced an attack from their starboard quarter up. He was defeated by a prompt corkscrew to starboard as both gunners fought to get their weapons back into action. Regaining altitude after the evasion tactic Eric Britton levelled out at 17,350 feet only to be lit up by fighter flares. Blair Wood called a warning of a twin engined night fighter at 900 yards on the port quarter above, instructing a corkscrew to port before the German pilot was able to open his attack. Ammunition was piled up in the rear turret and the mid-upper guns wouldn't elevate sufficiently for Les Fairhead to open fire. The night fighter followed the Lancaster into the corkscrew but was lost only to apparently re-acquire its target at 23:25 hours at 16,000 feet. Blair Wood kept a watching vigil on the fighter which was 900 yards off their port quarter and he instructed a port corkscrew as it closed to 700 yards. The German pilot followed without firing but again lost the Lancaster. At 23:27 hours Les Fairhead in the mid-upper turret sighted a JU88 fighter at 700 yards to starboard and instructed a corkscrew to starboard at 600 yards, neither gunner had managed to get their guns back into firing condition and there must have been a huge sigh of relief when the JU88 following them stood off during the corkscrew and did not attack.

Deryk 'Cliff' Clifford and crew aboard ND554 'A-Able' were fortunate to return at all, their flight engineer Gerry Wood badly injured and their port engines and props badly damaged. Lancaster 'Z' of 207 Squadron had slammed into their underside while taking violent evasive action to avoid a night fighter attack. Gerry Wood was evacuated in an ambulance on return and later discharged. German sources state that the northern and western sections of the town centre were completely destroyed by the bombing and the firestorm which followed. Property damage in neighbouring districts was extensive. Ian Herbert and crew in 'F-Fox' were the last to return to base, landing at 02:08 hours. During September further replacement crews arrived at East Kirkby for 630 Squadron the first captained by 29 year old Rendel Lewis[xii] a Barrister in civil life and member of the Territorial Army who had until recently been a navigation instructor at the RAF College Cranwell, his own navigator was 18 year old Lambeth lad Ken Lenton. Aussie Henry Ryan[xiii] arrived with his crew of 4 Aussies and 3 British boys, 22 year old Leslie (Jim) Ovens[xiv] from West Ham was posted in with his crew along with New Zealander Don McGillivray[xv] and crew and finally 22 year old George Cowan[xvi] from Larkhall, Lanarkshire who had been living in Newcastle on Tyne.

'Jim' Ovens crew. Back row l to r: Mather, Midgley, Cooper and Dawson. Front row l to r: Howley, Ovens, Maconachie RAAF. (Stuart Hablethwaite)

Sunday 17th September 1944.

762 bombers were despatched with over 3,000 tons of bombs to attack German fortifications at Boulogne in preparation for an attack by Allied ground forces. 17 aircraft of Six-thirty participated, each with a bomb load of 12 x 1000lb AN-M65 fused .025 and 4 x 500lb AN-M64 (.025).

17th September 1944 : Daylight Bombing Attack on Boulogne
Take Off: at 06:44 hours 'Pancho' O'Dwyer led the formation from East Kirkby.

PD253-D	F/O SA Nunns
LL949-E	F/O GE Billing
LM259-F	F/O SID Herbert RNZAF
PD317-G	Lt DCB Reynolds SAAF
ND412-H	F/O A Bates
NN702-J	F/O MA Swain
LM216-K	F/L TG O'Dwyer
NG125-N	F/O EI Britton
LM287-O	F/O FE Millar RNZAF
LL966-P	F/O E Docherty
PB344-R	F/O H Thompson
LM260-S	F/L DR Mallinson
ME739-T	F/S OJS Atkinson RAAF
NG123-U	F/O GE Stemp
PD254-W	F/O M Miller
NN703-X	F/O HD Archer
ND949-Z	F/O AR Kerr

Low cloud was encountered in the TA with thin low stratus over the target. Green and Red TIs were seen and considered well placed but as the attack progressed bombing obscured the TIs and they had to be renewed. The squadron's crews attacked between 08:30 and 08:32 hours from 8,000 to 8,900 feet. Over the aiming point Don Mallinson's bomb aimer Sergeant Frank Pomeroy aboard 'S-Sugar' 'hit the tit' but their bombs did not release due to a technical defect, their photo was triggered and showed the aiming point from 8,300 feet altitude.. No opposition was encountered. On return to East Kirkby the Lancasters found poor conditions and low visibility which gave for some hairy landings, NG123 (Geoff Stemp) was the last to set down safely, at 10:57 hours. 630 Squadron were particularly pleased with their effectiveness and accuracy in comparison with some other units bombing especially when the German forces surrendered just hours later.

Monday 18th September 1944.

To continue the series of highly successful attacks 5 Group sent 206 Lancasters and 7 Mosquitoes to Bremerhaven supported by a Radio Counter Measures mission flown by 100 Group. 16 Lancasters of 630 Squadron were detailed. NN702, ND949, LM260 and LM269 carried 1 x 2000lb HC and 12 x 500lb J-type incendiary clusters, NG123 carried 2,500 x 4lb incendiaries and all other aircraft carried 3000 x 4lb incendiaries.

18th/19th September 1944 : Night Bombing Attack on Bremerhaven
Take Off: at 18:26 hours Alan Kerr and crew in ND949 were the first off.

LM673-B	F/O GE Stemp
PD253-D	F/O SA Nunns
LL949-E	F/O GE Billing
LM259-F	F/O SID Herbert RNZAF

PD317-G	F/O H Thompson	
ND412-H	F/O A Bates	
NN702-J	F/O MA Swain	(Lt DS Turner SAAF)
LM216-K	S/L RE Millichap	(Lt DCB Reynolds SAAF)
LM287-O	F/O M Miller	RD
LL966-P	F/O E Docherty	(F/O GW Daggett)
PB344-R	F/O WH Gordon	RD
LM260-S	F/O OJS Atkinson RAAF	
NG123-U	F/O AJR Wilson RNZAF	
NG125-N	F/O EI Britton	
NN703-X	F/O HD Archer	
ND949-Z	F/O AR Kerr	

At the target the weather was clear and all crews saw the estuary and the town. 630 Squadron crews attacked between 21:02 and 21:08 hours from 13,000 to 13.600 feet. Very large fires were started in several districts of Bremerhaven which were visible 150 miles into the trip home. Light flak was intense and heavy flak was moderate, search lights were active and accurate. Fighters arrived after the attack had started and persisted in their attacks until about 0500East on the return route. 630 Squadron were involved in two combats with JU88's that night. Bremerhaven had not been seriously attacked by the RAF previously and required a single knock-out blow by a relatively small force with only 900 tons of bombs to devastate the ship building centre. Olly Atkinson flying LM260 'S-Sugar' had to abandon his sortie and jettison part of his bomb load after combat with a JU88, he jettisoned some but brought back the remainder safely landing at 23:40 hours, after all of the other aircraft had touched down. Alan Kerr and crew had completed their tour of 35 ops and were screened, another crew with exceptional team spirit had beaten the odds. Their captain was recommended for a DFC and over the next few weeks his crew were dispersed to new postings across the country. A similar crew, that of Peter Docherty were about to fly their 28th and last mission although on completion several of the crew, pilot included, remained attached to the squadron in various roles and Docherty himself wasn't posted away until six months later.

Tuesday 19th September 1944.
227 Lancasters and 10 Mosquitoes of 1 and 5 Groups made the attack. 630 Squadron had 17 Lancasters and crews detailed, each armed with 2000lb HC's and 12 x 500lb J-type cluster incendiaries.

19th/20th September 1944 : Night Bombing Attack on Mönchen Gladbach
Take Off: at 18:44 hours Flight Commander, Squadron Leader Malcolm Eyre flying LM260 took off almost simultaneously with Arthur Bates crew in ND412.

LM673-B	F/O GE Stemp
PD253-D	F/O SA Nunns
LL949-E	F/O GE Billing
LM259-F	F/O SID Herbert RNZAF
PD317-G	F/O EJ Monk
ND412-H	F/O A Bates
NN702-J	Lt DCB Reynolds SAAF
NG125-N	F/O EI Britton
LM287-O	F/O FE Millar RNZAF
LL966-P	F/O E Docherty
PB344-R	F/O WH Gordon
LM260-S	S/L MA Eyre
ME739-T	F/O OJS Atkinson RAAF
NG123-U	Lt DS Turner SAAF

PD254-W	F/O GW Daggett
NN703-X	F/O HD Archer
ND949-Z	F/O H Thompson

Jerry Monk aboard 'G-George' had to return early with engine problems and landed at East Kirkby at 21:15 hours. The Master Bomber on this attack flying a 627 Squadron Mosquito was Wing Commander Guy Gibson VC DSO and Bar DFC and Bar now serving as Base Operations Officer at RAF Coningsby, who had never flown in this role previously. At the target the weather was clear with some ground haze, the aiming point was punctually and accurately marked and Guy Gibson's voice was heard clearly through the attack. Crews were instructed to bomb the Yellow TIs and 630 Squadron attacked between 21:45 and 21:52 hours from 11,000 to 13,000 feet. Bombing was reportedly accurate and well concentrated although some of the later crews noted difficulties due to smoke rising. Opposition was slight although some fighters were seen in the TA and several combats took place, one including one of Six-thirty's Lancs although it suffered no damage and the enemy aircraft wasn't hit. At 00:19 hours LM673 (Geoff Stemp) was the last of 630 Squadron's Lancasters to land back at East Kirkby. Sadly on the homeward route the Mosquito flown by Gibson and his navigator Squadron Leader James Brown Warwick DFC crashed. In the absence of a German claim engine failure had been considered although more recently a story was published in the 'Daily Mail' (11th October 2011) based on a letter left by Lancaster rear gunner Sergeant Bernard McCormack of 227 Squadron who died in 1992, in which he had stated his belief that the night fighter which he'd fired at and believed shot down might had been Gibson's Mosquito. The 600 rounds which he had fired had hit an aircraft which crashed in the exact area of Gibson and Warwick's Mosquito. In the Station the water supply failed again on 20th September, due to a mains supply leak on this occasion and again the supply was not restored until the following day. The 'sprog crew' of recently arrived 26 year old Flight Sergeant E Ainsley Thomas[xvii], a married former Taunton police officer and county rugby players were on the Battle Order for the night's op.

Saturday 23rd September 1944.

Six-thirty participated in an attack on Handorf night fighter airfield near Munster in support of a 5 Group raid on the nearby Dortmund-Ems canal at Ladbergen. 21 aircraft and crews were detailed, each armed with 12 x 1000lb AN-M and 4 x 500lb AN-M bombs.

23rd /24th September 1944 : Night Bombing Attack on Handorf Airfield
Take Off: 18:33 hours LM259 flown by Kiwi Flight Sergeant Herbert took off first.

LM673-B	F/O GE Stemp	
JB290-C	F/S EA Thomas	
PD253-D	F/O SA Nunns	
LL949-E	F/O H Thompson	
LM259-F	F/O SID Herbert RNZAF	
PB317-G	F/O EJ Monk	
ND412-H	F/O A Bates	
NN702-J	F/O MA Swain	
LM216-K	S/L RE Millichap	
NG125-N	Lt DCB Reynolds SAAF	
LM287-O	F/O FE Millar RNZAF	
LL966-P	F/O AJR Wilson RNZAF	
LM260-S	S/L MA Eyre	
ME739-T	F/O OJS Atkinson RAAF	
NG123-U	Lt D Turner SAAF	
LM637-V	F/L DR Mallinson	(F/S TB Baker RAAF)
PD254-W	F/O M Miller	

NN703-X   F/O HD Archer
ND949-Z   F/O GW Daggett
PD327-Y   F/O GE Billing
PB344-R   F/O WH Gordon

Running in over the target area the first crews saw the illuminating flares covering a wide area, they orbited awaiting green TIs but none were seen. Crews received orders to bomb Yellow markers but in the meanwhile Green TIs were placed in the vicinity of the airfield and crews bombed them. The squadron's crews attacked between 21:53 and 22:06 hours from 16,200 to 17,000 feet. VHF and TR1196 reception was very poor and back up of orders by W/T too slow. Results of the bombing which took place between 21:41 and 22:10 hours were not observed due to cloud. Ground defences were very active and fighters were active from 0400E outward until Arnhem. Three combats took place but the only conclusive one was that of Bill Gordon's gunners aboard PB344 'R-Robert', Sergeants Vic Cardwell and Fred 'Dobbie' Dobson who shot down a night fighter. Sadly the combat report cannot now be traced. The claim was rated – Confirmed Destroyed. LM260 (Eyre), LL966 (Wilson) and PD253 (Nunns) did not attack as the markers were unidentifiable. NN703 (Henry Archer) was he last to return, at 00:55 hours. After only 2 ops with Six-thirty the crew of Geoff Daggett transferred to 44 Squadron where they completed a full tour which culminated in an award of the DFC for their captain.

The newly arrived crew of 22 year old Mancunian Reg Waterfall[xviii] were listed on the Battle Order for the next attack, they had flown 5 ops with 106 Squadron prior to joining Six-thirty. The ground crews had achieved wonders having two more aircraft serviceable than there were crews available to fly them so 207 Squadron loaned two crews to the squadron to fly the aircraft, one captained by George Stenhouse, the other of 'Peter' Sparks had been members of the squadron before their accident in July. Tom Baker[xix] a 23 year old RAAF pilot from South Perth, Western Australia announced to his all NCO crew that they were now operational and would be listed on one of the next Battle Orders. His crew included four Australians, the navigator being 21 year old Ken Taeuber who in later life held numerous senior positions in local

Left: Reg Waterfall. David Johnson. Above : Tom Baker RAAF (RAAF official)

government for South Australia. Harry Grayson[xx] and his all British crew were commencing the series of exercises to be completed by all new crews prior to starting their tour.

Tuesday 26th September 1944.
Combining forces, 1 and 5 Group despatched 226 Lancasters and 11 Mosquitoes to attack Karlsruhe. 20 Lancasters of Six-thirty were detailed, PD253 carried 1 x 4000lb HC and 8 x 1000lb MC bombs but the remainder were armed with 2,700 x 4lb incendiaries.

26th September 1944 : Daylight Bombing Attack on Karlsruhe
Take Off: at 00:22 hours NG145 (Terence O'Dwyer) and ND412 (Peter Sparks) lifted off.

LM637-B	F/O H Thompson	
PD253-D	F/O SA Nunns	
PD317-G	F/O EJ Monk	
ND412-H	F/O WA Sparks (207 Squadron crew)	RD
NG145-I	F/L TG O'Dwyer	
NN702-J	F/O MA Swain	
LM216-K	S/L RE Millichap	
NF961-L	F/O SID Herbert RNZAF	
NG125-N	Lt DCB Reynolds SAAF	
LM287-O	F/O FE Millar RNZAF	
LL966-P	F/S EA Thomas	
PB344-R	Lt DS Turner SAAF	
LM260-S	F/O G Stenhouse (207 Squadron crew)	
ME739-T	F/O RA Stone RNZAF	
NG123-U	F/O OJS Atkinson RAAF	
LM637-V	F/L DR Mallinson	
PD254-W	F/O M Miller	
NN703-X	F/O RG Waterfall	
PD327-Y	F/O AJR Wilson RNZAF	
ND949-Z	F/O JO Davies	RD

Don Mallinson (Richard and Barry Mallinson)

John Davies in ND949 'Z-Zebra' had to return early (at 02:35 hours) after their escape hatch blew off and the mid-upper turret went unserviceable and Ian Herbert's crew in NF961 returned at 04:15 hours with W/T failure and the electrical system for their mid-upper turret unserviceable. The attack opened punctually with crews instructed to bomb the concentration of red and green TIs. 630 Squadron's crews bombed between 04:00 and 04:07 hours from 10,000 to 10,700 hours. Heavy cloud made identification of the aiming point and assessment of bombing results difficult. Some crews reported fires burning in a built up area and visible for 100 miles into their return flight. Fighter activity was on a small scale in the target area and ground defences were not troublesome although three crews of the squadron did have brief combats with enemy aircraft, none of which involved any known hits or damage caused. Damage was caused throughout Karlsruhe according to German records. Desmond Reynolds, who did not bomb, was the last to return to base at 08:12 hours. For Don Mallinson's crew it was a landmark op, they had completed their tour, Mallinson was recommended for a DFC and the crew dispersed over the next fortnight or so to their new postings.

Wednesday 27th September 1944.
In the only raid of the war against Kaiserslautern, 1 and 5 Groups despatched 217 Lancasters and 10 Mosquitoes with 909 tons of bombs. 19 of Six-thirty's Lancasters were detailed – 9 armed with 1 x 2000lb HC and 12 x 500lb J type clusters, the other 10 carried 2,700 x 4lb incendiaries.

27th/28th September 1944 : Night Bombing Attack on Kaiserslautern
Take Off: Steve Nunn's crew in PD253 were the first airborne at 21:55 hours.

LM673-B	F/O H Thompson	
PD253-D	F/O SA Nunns	RD
LL949-E	F/O GR Flood RNZAF	
PD317-G	F/O EJ Monk	
NG145-I	F/L TG O'Dwyer	
NN702-J	F/O MA Swain	
LM216-K	F/S EA Thomas	
NF961-L	F/O SID Herbert RNZAF	
NG125-N	Lt DCB Reynolds SAAF	
LM287-O	F/O FE Millar RNZAF	
LL966-P	F/O JO Davies	
PB344-R	F/O Wells (207 Squadron crew)	
LM260-S	F/S TB Baker RAAF	
ME739-T	F/O RA Stone RNZAF	
NG123-U	F/O OJS Atkinson RAAF	
LM637-V	F/O RG Waterfall	
PD254-W	F/O M Miller	
NN703-X	Lt DS Turner SAAF	
PD327-Y	F/O AJR Wilson RNZAF	
LM259-F	F/S L Baush (57 Squadron crew)	

The attacking force encountered 8/10ths cloud. Marking was punctual and accurate on both targets although the cloud conditions made it difficult for some crews to see the markers in time to make good bombing runs. The squadron's crews attacked between 01:03 and 01:17 hours from 4,000 to 5,600 feet. Most crews bombed as ordered and others bombed the fires in the town as they did not see the markers in time. There was possibly some confusion in the attack on the railway yards as there were 2 pairs of red spot flares and although the Controller gave instructions which to bomb they may not have been clearly understood by all crews. A few fighters were in the target area and only moderate light flak which was accurate, there were no search lights. Sergeants Ken Arscott (mid-upper) and Jim Durney (rear gunner) aboard Henry Thompson's LM673 'B-Baker' sighted a Fw190 before it could attack them and delivered several bursts of fire which damaged the fighter driving it off.

Flying PD253 'D-Dog' Steve Nunns ordered his crew to jettison their bomb load after the port outer engine caught fire without warning and burned despite the attention of flight engineer Colin Batcup using the fire extinguisher system, it gained a hold even after Nunns increased revs hoping to blow it out. Mid Upper gunner Keith Nelson manually released Jim Elliott the rear gunner as with the turret's hydraulics unserviceable, the result of the fire in the port outer, he was trapped. At 00:10 to 00:12 hours the crew baled out responding to their captain's urgent gesticulating and as Nunns was about to abandon the aircraft himself the fires apparently finally burned out, so he returned to the controls. Within moments the flames were streaming back again so he again moved towards the escape hatch and looking back saw that the fire had died down considerably just in a matter of seconds. Steve Nunns decided to stick with it and back at the controls watched with relief as the flames died. Activating the autopilot he dashed back to the Navigator's

Ken Arscott (Keith Arscott)

table and using the flight plan and beacon schedule to work out a course. His crew landed safely in their chutes near St Quentin and the pilot returned to base alone, having several times used 'George' to fly the Lancaster while he checked his course before touching down safely at 03:35 hours. His crew were flown back to East Kirkby in the days which followed, Jim Elliott having dodged German patrols and some quite hostile French farm hands, swum a river and been handed over by the French Resistance to US troops.

Wireless op Philip 'Ray' Carroll was becoming an old hand at parachute jumping having baled out over Bedfordshire from 'Blue' Rackley's Lancaster which had been shot to pieces over Wesseling in June and now a second descent. SAAF pilot Desmond Reynolds landed NG125 at 05:38 hours, the last to return. The post-war British Bombing Survey estimated that 36% of the town's built up area was destroyed including many factories and public buildings.

Friday 29th September 1944.
630 Squadron took part in minelaying operations near Wilhelmshaven Naval base. 5 aircraft were detailed each probably armed with Mark IV or Mark VI mines.

29th/30th September 1944 : Night Minelaying 'Rosemary Garden'

Take Off: at 18:59 hours New Zealanders Frank Millar and Ian Herbert took off almost simultaneously leading the five.

LM259-F	F/O SID Herbert RNZAF
NN702-J	F/O MA Swain
LM287-O	F/O FE Millar RNZAF
LM260-S	F/O JO Davies
PD254-W	P/O M Miller

Weather conditions were 10/10ths cloud at 5,000 – 6,000 feet. Crews successfully identified their aiming points by H2S and their cargo of mines were laid as required between 20:51 and 21:04 hours, Herbert being the last to return to East Kirkby at 23:19 hours. .

Philip 'Ray' Carroll (Andy Carroll)   *Keith Nelson (Gemma Nelson)*

Steve Nunns (centre) with Carroll and Nelson after their return (Brian Lunn)

October 1944

In the early days of October an 8th USAAF B-17 Flying Fortress landed at RAF East Kirkby returning from an attack during which its Ball-Turret gunner had sustained wounds to his leg caused by flak, he was evacuated to RAF Hospital Rauceby before the Americans flew on to their base.

Thursday 5th October 1944.
227 Lancasters and 1 Mosquito of 5 Group were despatched to bomb the important Naval and shipbuilding own of Wilhelmshaven on the north German Baltic coast. 21 Lancasters of 630 Squadron were detailed – all armed with 10 x 1000lb ANM65 (.025) and 4 x 500lb J type clusters.

5th October 1944 : Daylight Bombing Attack on Wilhelmshaven
Take Off: at 07:43 hours Malcolm Eyre was the first airborne.

LM673-B	F/O GE Stemp
LL949-E	F/O GR Flood RNZAF
LM259-F	F/O SID Herbert RNZAF
PD317-G	F/O LF Ovens
NG145-I	F/O DA Clifford
NN702-J	F/O MA Swain
LM216-K	F/O H Grayson
NF961-L	F/S EA Thomas
ND412-H	F/O A Bates
NG125-N	F/O EI Britton
LM287-O	F/O FEH Millar RNZAF
LL966-P	F/S TB Baker RAAF
ME845-Q	F/O RG Waterfall
PB344-R	F/O JO Davies
LM260-S	S/L MA Eyre
ME739-T	F/O RA Stone RNZAF
NG123-U	F/O EC Harris RNZAF
LM637-V	F/L RF Lewis
PD254-W	F/O M Miller
NN703-X	F/O HD Archer
ND949-Z	W/O HT Ryan RAAF

Arriving over Wilhelmshaven the force encountered 10/10ths cloud which only permitted fleeting glimpses of the coastline to the north of the town. All but seven of the squadron's crews bombed using H2S although crews unable to get a decent fix attacked ships which could be seen in the harbour. Five attacked by holding formation with other crews and bombing simultaneously. Experienced crews believed bombing might have been to the east of Wilhelmshaven. They attacked between 11:03 and 11:07 hours from 15,000 to 18,000 feet. No fighters were encountered and the flak was reported to be inaccurate and short. Unable to identify the primary target both 'U' bombed Leeuwarden and 'K' bombed Jever. NF961 (Ainsley Thomas) landed at 13:47 hours, the last to touch down.

The 630 Squadron Operations Record Book at the National Archives records 'Billy' Billing and crew flying 'G-George' however this is contradicted by the RAF Museum's 630 Squadron Ops Record and East Kirkby 'Raid Book' which both state that 'Jim' Ovens and crew flew 'G-George', both providing precise

Lancaster LM259 "F-Fox" (RD Gale)

detail of their attack, bombing time, height course, etc and this is also supported by the listing of ops flown by Ovens in the recommendation for his DFC. It has been suggested that it was a last minute change.

Alec Swain and his crew had flown the last op of their tour and were promptly screened from ops as he was recommended for a DFC. Their rear gunner 21 year old Geoff Bate from Aston in Birmingham who had flown a tour before joining the crew had finished his tour and been posted away in August having been recommended for a DFC, the remainder of the crew broke up as they were posted away.

Friday 6th October 1944.

In the last of 32 major attacks against Bremen 246 Lancasters and 7 Mosquitoes of 1 and 5 Groups set out again for the north German coastline. 18 of Six-thirty's Lancasters were detailed for the mission – 2 armed with 1 x 4000lb HC and 9 x 1000lb ANM59, each of the others with 3,000 x 4lb incendiaries. A minelaying operation was also detailed.

6th /7th October 1944 : Night Bombing Attack on Bremen
Take Off: at 17:34 hours New Zealander Ross Flood was the first of 630 Squadron to take off.

LM673-B	F/O GE Billing	RD
LL949-E	F/O GR Flood RNZAF	
PD317-G	F/O SA Nunns	(W/O HT Ryan RAAF)
NG145-I	F/O DA Clifford	
NN702-J	F/S EA Thomas	
LM216-K	F/O M Grayson	
NF961-L	F/O TB Baker RAAF	
NG125-N	F/O EI Britton	RD
LM287-O	F/O FEH Millar RNZAF	(F/O LF Ovens)
ME845-Q	F/O RG Waterfall	
JB290-C	F/O A Bates	
ME739-T	F/O RA Stone RNZAF	
NG123-U	F/O GE Stemp	
LM637-V	F/L RF Lewis	RD

PD254-W	F/O M Miller	
NN703-X	F/O HD Archer	
PD327-Y	F/O EC Harris RNZAF	
LM260-S	S/L MA Eyre	RD

Ross Flood in 'E' had to jettison his bomb load over the North Sea and return early with their pitot head unserviceable. Over the target weather conditions were clear with excellent visibility and crews believed that the markers were accurately placed, 1,021 tons of bombs were dropped of which 868 tons were incendiaries. 630 Squadron's crews attacked the green target indicators between 20:25 and 20:32 hours from 17,750 to 18,500 feet. The attack went as planned aside from serious interference on VHF. Joe Barton, Eric Britton's bomb aimer aboard 'N-Nan' encountered technical problems and the crew jettisoned their bomb load in the target area. A large area of fire was seen on both banks of the river and flak defences were strong, active and accurate with several aircraft sustaining damage, search lights were also reported numerous and active. Several fighters were in position over the town and 'V-Victor' flown by Rendel Lewis was in combat with a JU88 which was claimed as damaged by his gunners Sergeants Reg Bennett (mid-upper) and Joe Morgan (rear gunner). No combat report had been located. George 'Billy' Billing in LM673 was the last of Six-thirty to land at 23:10 hours. Serious damage was caused in this attack to the AG Weser ship building yards where U-boats and other warships were built, to two Focke-Wulf aircraft factories, the Siemens-Schuckert electrical works and several associated war industries. A German report states that the transport network was seriously disrupted. On the same night 3 aircraft were detailed to participate in an operation to lay mines in the 'Young Yams' area, two carried 6 x G718 mines and one carried 1 x D46, 1 x 406.B230, 1 x G716 variant, 1 x B230, 1 x D406 and 1 x G716.

6th /7th October 1944 : Night Minelaying in 'Young Yams'
Take Off: at 17:48 hours Bill Gordon (PB344) was the first of the minelayers to take off and Kiwi Ian Herbert the last of them to return at 22:01 hours.

LM259-F	F/O SID Herbert RNZAF
LL966-P	F/O JO Davies
PB344-R	F/L WH Gordon

Weather was fine with excellent visibility and coastal features were clearly identified. There was no opposition and between 20:14 and 20:27 the mines were dropped as required from 1,500 feet. At Bardney on 7th October No.5 Group formed another new Lancaster squadron, actually reforming 227 Squadron which had earlier operated Beaufighter's in anti-shipping operations in the Mediterranean and Aegean. The new 227 Squadron was to be immediately operational and as such received 9 Squadron's 'A' Flight and 619 Squadron's 'B' Flight supplemented by experienced crews from elsewhere within the Group. Six-thirty contributed the crews of New Zealanders Tony Wilson (4 ops) and Ian Herbert (21 ops) accompanied by those of Arthur Bates (11 ops) and Eric Britton (8 ops). Both the Britton and Herbert crews were shot down on 4th December and Tony Wilson was shot down on 18th December whilst flying with another crew.

Saturday 7th October 1944.
121 Lancasters and 2 Mosquitoes of 5 Group attacked the sea wall east of Flushing as a part of a tactic to flood the surrounding land which was below sea-level and had been recovered from the sea. 630 Squadron had 16 Lancasters detailed for the operation – all armed with 14 x 1000lb (1 hours).

7th October 1944 : Daylight Bombing Attack on Walcheren Dykes
Take Off: at 11:47 hours the first airborne was Henry Archer in NN703.

NG123-U	F/O GE Billing	
LL949-E	F/O GR Flood RNZAF	
PD317-G	F/O SA Nunns	RD
ME739-T	W/O HT Ryan RAAF	
NG145-I	F/O H Grayson	RD
NN702-J	F/S EA Thomas	
LM637-V	F/L RF Lewis	RD
NN703-X	F/O HD Archer	RD
LL966-P	F/O JO Davies	RD
ME845-Q	F/O LF Ovens	RD
PD327-Y	F/O EC Harris RNZAF	RD
PB344-R	F/O FE Millar RNZAF	
NF961-L	F/O A Bates	
LM260-S	S/L MA Eyre	RD
LM216-K	F/O SID Herbert RNZAF	RD
PD254-W	F/O M Miller	RD

Conditions for the attack were perfect, the weather was clear and visibility excellent, red TIs were accurately placed in the middle of the Dyke on the seaward side. After a first run up the wind estimation was adjusted and later sticks of bombs fell directly across the dyke. Some bombs exploded immediately despite their long delay settings and caused obvious damage, holes could also be seen where LD bombs had gone into the dyke. 630 Squadron's crews attacked between 12:32 and 12:39 hours from 6,900 to 8,500 feet virtually all making a visual attack. Accurate flak defensive fire came from Flushing and Breekobs, and 16 aircraft showed flak damage. The sea walls were successfully breached. Ainsley Thomas and crew were the last to return at 14:51 hours.

Wednesday 11th October 1944.
160 Lancasters and 20 Mosquitoes of 1 and 8 Group attacked Fort Frederik Hendrik gun batteries at Breskens on the south bank of the Scheldt whilst 115 more 5 Group Lancasters attacked guns near Flushing on the north bank. 61 more 5 Group Lancasters and 2 Mosquitoes attacked the seawalls at Veere on he north-east coast of the Island. 15 of Six-thirty's aircraft and crews were detailed for the operations, 9 to attack Flushing Docks and 6 to attack the sea wall north of Veere – all were armed with 12 x 1000lb AN-M59 and 14 x 500lb ANM64 (.025) bombs.

11th October 1944 : Daylight Bombing Attack on Walcheren (Docks and Veere)
Take Off: At 13:00 hours Steve Nunns crew in PD253 were the first airborne.

PD253-D	F/O SA Nunns
ND412-H	F/O EJ Monk
NN702-J	F/O HT Ryan RAAF
LL966-P	F/O TB Baker RAAF
ME845-Q	F/O DA McGillivray RNZAF
LM260-S	S/L MA Eyre
ME739-T	F/O RA Stone RNZAF
NG123-U	F/O EC Harris RNZAF
PD254-W	F/O M Miller
NG145-I	F/O DA Clifford
PB344-R	F/L WH Gordon

LM287-O	F/L RF Lewis	
PD327-Y	F/O GE Billing	
ND949-Z	F/O JO Davies	RD
LL949-E	F/O GR Flood RNZAF	

5/10ths cloud hung over the primary target at 3,000 feet but visibility was good. The squadron's crews identified the target visually and bombed the sea wall north of Veere from 14:41 to 14:43 hours from 6,000 to 6,800 feet and the sea wall at Flushing between 14:47 and 14:54 hours from 6,800 to 7,800 feet. A good concentration of bomb bursts were evident in the northern part of the dockyards and towards the end of the attack the aiming point was no longer visible due to bomb bursts. Flak was negligible and no fighters were seen. 630/E didn't see the markers until too late and bombed the dyke visually, south of the canal mouth at Veere. ND412 ('Jerry' Monk) was the last aircraft back to East Kirkby at 16:20 hours.

On 14th October 1944 Wing Commander John Grindon[i] took command of 630 Squadron. A 27 year old from Newquay in Cornwall, Grindon's father had been killed at Ypres, he graduating from RAF Cranwell in 1937 joining 98 Squadron flying Hawker Hinds and shortly before the outbreak of war 150 Squadron flying Fairey Battles. Serving in France during the Blitzkrieg he was posted to the UK on a Navigation course shortly before the Fairey Battle equipped squadrons were annihilated and following that to Canada as an instructor with 34 OTU at Pennfield Ridge, New Brunswick. John Grindon maintained a barrage of requests to return to operational flying until July 1944 when he was posted to 106 Squadron to replace a Flight Commander who had just failed to return. Having flown 13 ops with 106 Squadron and proven himself a very able flight commander he had gained sufficient operational experience to take command of 630 Squadron. Wing Commander Blome-Jones left the station to take up a staff position.

"Jim" Ovens   *W/Cdr John Grindon. (J Grindon)*   *Len Barnes (Gill Meredith)*

Eric Harris' crew were allocated NG123 'U-Uncle' as 'their own' and immediately commissioned nose art worthy of an 8th USAAF B-17. Adorned with a reclining blonde nude beneath 'Oh U Beauty' their Lancaster is recognisable on many photos from that stage onwards.

Welcomed back at East Kirkby with a 'bash' in the mess celebrating their successful evasions and time with the French Resistance after being shot down over France in mid-March and late July respectively, Len Barnes and Bill Adams USAAF arrived back with 630 Squadron. Both quickly re-formed crews from available bods and were soon back on Battle Orders to complete their tours, Barnes immediately opted to make another trip as Second Dickie to 'get his hand in' in the light of the changes to ops since he'd last flown. Quickly making friends with Flying Officer John Black[ii] a senior air gunner about to commence his second tour, having no mid-upper gunner for his new crew Barnes was delighted to have Johnny Black join him.

Saturday 14th October 1944.
5 Group tried to destroy Brunswick 4 times in 1944 and finally accomplished that aim in its coming operation mounted by 233 Lancasters and 7 Mosquitoes. 20 of the squadron were detailed to participate, all armed with 2 x 1000lb MC and 16 x No.14 Mk.I clusters.

14th/15th October 1944 : Night Bombing Attack on Brunswick
Take Off: at 22:25 hours SAAF pilot Desmond Reynolds in NF961 was first to take off from East Kirkby. Ross Flood apparently flew 'J' borrowed from 57 Squadron.

PD253-D	F/O GE Billing
ME626-57	F/O GR Flood RNZAF
PD317-G	F/O EJ Monk
ND412-H	F/O H Thompson
NG145-I	F/O GE Stemp
NN702-J	F/S EA Thomas
LM216-K	Lt DS Turner SAAF
NF961-L	Lt DCB Reynolds SAAF
LM287-O	F/O LF Ovens
LL966-P	F/O HT Ryan RAAF
ME845-Q	F/O RG Waterfall
PB344-R	F/L WH Gordon (F/O LA Barnes)
LM260-S	S/L MA Eyre
ME739-T	F/O RA Stone RNZAF
NG123-U	F/O EC Harris RNZAF
LM637-V	F/L RF Lewis
PD254-W	F/O M Miller
NN703-X	F/L HD Archer (F/S GH Cowan)
PD327-Y	F/O TB Baker RAAF
ND949-Z	F/O JO Davies

The marking was punctual and red TIs were assessed as 200 yards west of the aiming point so crews were ordered to bomb the eastern edge of the grouping of red TIs. A good concentration of bombing resulted in the town being well ablaze by the time the attack ended. Crews of 630 Squadron attacked between 02:26 and 03:38 hours from 18,200 to 19,000 feet and on their return complained that some squadrons had jettisoned considerable quantities of incendiaries along the route home for the first 50 miles which gave great assistance to enemy fighters and ground defences. Two aircraft sustained flak damage over the target and there were 4 combats with enemy fighters but no claims or damage. Ainsley Thomas landed NN702 at 07:41 hours, the last to touch down. The centre of Brunswick was gutted and German reports state that 150 hectares of the town were hit.

Sunday 15th October 1944. 630 Squadron were detailed to contribute 2 Lancasters and crews to a minelaying operation in the 'Silverthorn' area. Each carried 6 x Mk.IV mines.

15th/16th October 1944 : Night Minelaying in the Kattegat
Take Off: at 18:40 hours Henry Archer was the first away, he landed at 01:00 hours at Syerston, shortly after Bill Gordon touched down at Strubby.

LL966-P	F/L WH Gordon
NN703-X	F/L HD Archer

Lancaster LM216 "K-Kitty" (WL Goodwin)

An unsuccessful sortie as both aircraft had H2S failures and couldn't identify landmarks visually in 7/10ths cloud cover so returned with their loads intact. One source states that the Archer crew flew 'I-Item' on this night. Twenty-four year old Dennis Brammer[iii] from Stone in Staffordshire and his crew who had recently joined the squadron from training were in the early stages of operational readiness exercises.

Tuesday 17th October 1944.
5 Group returned to the sea wall at Walcheren despatching 47 Lancasters and 2 Mosquitoes. 5 aircraft of Six-thirty were detailed, each armed with 14 x 1000lb MC (Delayed fuse).

17th October 1944 : Daylight Bombing Attack on West Kapelle Sea Dykes
Take Off: at 12:42 hours Rendel Lewis and crew in NN703 were the first airborne.

JB290-C	F/O LA Barnes
NG145-I	F/O DA Clifford
LM216-K	F/O GE Billing
NG123-U	F/S GH Cowan
NN703-X	F/L RF Lewis

The weather was clear, cloudless and visibility very good. A red TI was accurately placed and crews were able to identify the target visually between 14:00 and 14:15 hours. 630 Squadron attacked promptly between 14:00 and 14:01 hours from 5,000 to 5,700 feet. The majority of bombs fell between the existing breach in the sea dyke and the red TI with several sticks of bombs straddling the dyke. Flak at the target was negligible with only a few light guns and one heavy gun firing from positions north of the town, one aircraft received flak damage, no enemy fighters were seen. 'Billy' Billing was the last to touch down at 15:23 hours.

That night on a routine night cross country navigation exercise the newly arrived crew of Dennis Brammer crashed and sadly were all killed

Lancaster I, NF961 (Codes LE – L)

Pilot	– F/O Dennis Archibald Brammer. Age 24	Killed
Flight Eng	– Sgt Leonard George Cook. Age 20	Killed
Navigator	– W/O Gerald Joseph Davies. Age 34	Killed
Bomb Aimer	– Sgt William Albert White. Age 21	Killed
Wireless Op	– Sgt Dennis Gordon Holyoak. Age 21	Killed
Mid Upper	– Sgt John Christopher Fitzpatrick. Age 21	Killed
Rear Gunner	– Sgt Clifford John Evans. Age 35	Killed

Dennis Brammer and crew (LAHC Archive)

NF961 crashed at approximately 02:35 hours possibly due to icing, on Harfa Bank near Osmotherly about 6 miles north-east of Northallerton. Four of the crew are buried at Harrogate (Stonefall) Cemetery, the pilot was buried at Stone Cemetery in Staffs, the wireless operator at Birmingham (Yardley) Cemetery and the rear gunner at Bridgend Cemetery in Wales.

Thursday 19th October 1944.
263 Lancasters and 7 Mosquitoes of 5 Group returned to Nuremburg to attempt the knockout blow on the city which had avoided total destruction on several previous raids. 20 aircraft of 630 Squadron were detailed each armed with 1 x 2000lb HC and 12 x 500lb J-type clusters.

19th/20th October 1944 : Night Bombing Attack on Nuremburg
Take Off: 17:18 hours Ross Flood and crew took off in LL949 'E'.

JB290-C	F/O HT Ryan RAAF		
PD253-D	F/O GE Billing		
LL949-E	F/O GR Flood RNZAF	(W/O JW Langley)	
PD317-G	F/O EJ Monk		
ND412-H	F/O H Thompson		RD
NG145-I	F/O DA Clifford		
NN702-J	F/O GE Stemp		
LM216-K	Lt DS Turner SAAF		
LM287-O	F/O LF Ovens		
LL966-P	Lt DCB Reynolds SAAF		
ME845-Q	F/O RG Waterfall		
PB344-R	F/L WH Gordon	(F/O A McGuffie)	RD
LM260-S	Lt W Adams USAAF		
ME739-T	F/O RA Stone RNZAF		
NG123-U	F/O EC Harris RNZAF		RD
LM637-V	F/L RF Lewis		
PD254-W	F/O LA Barnes		
NN703-X	F/L HD Archer	(F/O JW Hoare RAAF)	
PD327-Y	F/S GH Cowan		RD
ND949-Z	F/O JO Davies		

The aiming point had not been marked, almost total cloud cover was over Nuremberg, so the controller ordered the Back Up markers and green and red TIs, the crews could see the markers clearly and after a 200 yard correction was ordered, a good concentration developed, fires covering a large area. VHF reception was good and the controller's orders were clear. The squadron attacked between 20:56 and 21:04 hours from 15,600 to 19,000 feet. Ground defences were not strong and light fighter activity was reported over the target. There were combats but no claims and flak engaged several aircraft over France on the return flight. On the return journey jet propelled fighters were reported south of Stuttgart and one crew identified an Me262. A German report confirmed that bombing destroyed 41 industrial buildings and almost 400 houses in the industrial southern districts. For three crews it was their last op with 630 Squadron, John Davies' crew (19 ops) and Aussie Henry Ryan (5 ops) to the newly formed 189 Squadron on 22nd October and actually went on the 23rd, almost a week later on 29th they were followed by Flight Lieutenant Bill Gordon's crew who had flown 24 ops with 630 Squadron, on arrival Gordon was promoted Squadron Leader and became a flight commander. A week later two more of Six-thirty's crews would be joining them. On 22 October Flight Lieut. Freddie Spencer, Squadron Flight Engineer Leader recently awarded the DFC after almost 60 Ops flown during two tours was posted to Instructional Duties. He had survived Ops with 630 Squadron from 1 January 1944 through until 17 Sep 1944

Monday 23rd October 1944.

112 Lancasters of 5 Group were despatched to attack the Flushing coastal gun batteries. 6 aircraft of Six-thirty were detailed, they were bombed-up with 14 x 1000lb AN-M65 (.025) bombs.

23rd October 1944 : Daylight Bombing Attack on Flushing

Take Off: at 15:11 hours Lieutenant Bill Adams USAAF was the first off the deck followed almost immediately by George Cowan.

PD317-G	F/O EJ Monk
NG145-I	F/O GE Stemp
NN702-J	Lt DCB Reynolds SAAF
LM287-O	F/O LF Ovens
LM637-V RD	Lt W Adams USAAF
PD327-Y	F/S GH Cowan

Visibility at the target was poor and most crews had to make several orbits before they could identify the aiming points in order to make a satisfactory bombing run. The Controller gave orders to abandon the mission after he had failed to identify the target. The majority of crews did however to make

Freddie Spencer - Flight Engineer Leader (Jane Spencer)

bombing runs and bombs were seen straddling the gun emplacements. All of 630 Squadron crews involved in the attack did bomb between 16:29 and 16:38 hours from 4,000 to 4,800 feet. Some heavy and light flak was encountered on the approach and over the target and 6 aircraft were slightly damaged. No enemy fighters were seen. The last to return to base was PD237 (George Cowan) at 17:51 hours.

Tuesday 24th October 1944.

4 aircraft were detailed for minelaying along the established U-boat transit routes of the Kattegat. 6 x Mk.IV mines were delivered by each of the squadron's Lancasters.

24th/25th October 1944 : Night Minelaying in the Kattegat

Take Off: at 17:25 hours ME845 (Henry Archer) lifted off from East Kirkby first.

PD253-D	F/L TG O'Dywer
ME845-Q	F/L HD Archer
PB344-R	F/O FEH Millar RNZAF
LM260-S	Lt W Adam USAAF

Millar and O'Dwyer's mines were released at 21:41 and 21:54 hours both at 7,000 feet and Adams and Archer's at 21:14 and 21:53 hours both from 12,000 feet. The gardening operation was classified successful. LM260 (Bill Adams) was the last to land at 01:50 hours. On that minelaying sortie 'Pancho' O'Dwyer's crew completed the last op of their tour, their captain was recommended for a DFC, as was George Arkieson (Bombing Leader) who had regularly flown with the crew. The wireless op Len Wood had completed his tour some weeks earlier and had been recommended for a DFC before being transferred as an instructor. Flight Lieutenant Herbert Graham Cawdron DFM, Squadron Signals Leader, who took his place on a

HG Cawdron (Cawdron family)

regular basis had been awarded his DFM with 9 Squadron in August 1942 on completion of his first tour. Several of the crew including George Arkieson and navigator Tom Collins subsequently joined 617 Squadron in January. The next Battle Order featured the CO Wing Commander Grindon and three recently arrived crews were making their operational debuts after their captain's had made their flights as Second Dickies. The crews were captained by Australian Jack Hoare[iv] from Shenton Park, Western Australia, John Langley[v] from Eltham in Kent with his all NCO crew and the Scots/English crew of former soldier Alex McGuffie[vi].

Saturday 28th October 1944.
Not having flown operationally for several days it seems likely that 5 Group had been awaiting suitable weather conditions to attack the U-boat bunkers at Bergen in Norway. 237 Lancasters and 7 Mosquito markers were despatched. 19 aircraft of 630 Squadron participated all armed with 11 x 1000lb AN-M65 bombs.

28th/29th October 1944 : Night Bombing Attack on U-boat base at Bergen
Take Off: at 22:15 hours Wing Commander John Grindon flying his first Op with the squadron was the first off the deck.

PD253-D	F/L SA Nunns	(F/O PS Weston)
LL949-E	F/O GR Flood RNZAF	
PD317-G	F/O H Grayston	
ND412-H	F/O H Thompson	
NG145-I	F/O DA Clifford	
NN702-J	F/O GE Stemp	RD
LM216-K	Lt DS Turner SAAF	
LM287-O	F/O FEH Millar RNZAF	
LL966-P	F/O OJS Atkinson RAAF	
ME845-Q	F/O RG Waterfall	
PB344-R	W/C JE Grindon	
LM260-S	F/O JW Langley	
ME739-T	F/O A McGuffie	
NG123-U	F/O EC Harris RNZAF	
LM637-V	F/L RF Lewis	
PD254-W	F/O TB Baker RAAF	
NN703-X	F/O JW Hoare RAAF	
PD327-Y	F/O DA McGillivray RNZAF	
ND949-Z	F/S GH Cowan	

Clear conditions were expected but cloud covered the target on arrival. The concrete submarine pens were punctually marked and at 02:00 hours the Controller ordered crews to attack from between 5,000 and 8,000 feet and bombing took place between 02:03 and 02:13 hours. Crews made two or three bombing runs but in most cases couldn't see the red TIs due to filthy weather. At 02:10 controller ordered *'return to base'*.

The Operations Record Book of 630 Squadron indicates that only one crew of the squadron were able to attack but bombing records show positively that Don McGillivray's crew bombed Red target indicators at 02:07 hours from 6,000 feet and suggest that Tom Baker and Geoff Stemp's crews also attacked at 02:05 and 02:15 hours from 5,000 and 5,200 feet as all other crews are clearly marked 'did not bomb'. Ground defences in the area of the U-boat bunkers were light but some fighters were seen. All aircraft were diverted to alternative stations on their return and landed all across Yorkshire. Jack Hoare and crew were apparently the last to land safely at 05:59 hours when they touched down at Snaith. D, I, K, Q and T landed at Burn, E, H, J, O, R, S, U, V, N, W, Z and X landed at Snaith, P landed at Carnaby, G and Y landed at base.

Monday 30th October 1944.
102 Lancasters and 8 Mosquitoes of 5 Group attacked the southern West Kapelle gun batteries in support of the Walcheren campaign and the Opening of the River Scheldt. 12 Lancasters of Six-thirty were detailed for the mission, which were bombed up with 14 x 1000lb MC (1 hour delay) bombs.

30th October 1944 : Daylight Bombing Attack on Walcheren
Take Off : at 10:17 hours ME845 Reg Waterfall took off at the head of 630 Squadron.

PD253-D	F/O GE Billing
LL949-E	F/O GR Flood RNZAF
PD317-G	F/O H Grayson
NG145-I	F/O DA Clifford
NN702-J	Capt DCB Reynolds SAAF
LM216-K	S/L RE Millichap
LL966-P	F/O OJS Atkinson RAAF
PB344-R	Lt DS Turner SAAF
LM260-S	F/O JW Langley
LM637-V	F/O JW Hoare RAAF
PD327-Y	F/O DA McGillivray RNZAF
ME845-Q	F/O RG Waterfall

Weather was clear and visibility good in the target area when the attackers arrived. The red Target Indicators were assessed as accurate by the Controller and most of the bombing was concentrated on these TIs. 630 Squadron crews attacked between 12:14 and 21:21 hours from 3,000 to 4,000 feet. Crews reported that the TIs landed in sand dunes and could be difficult to see. No opposition of any kind was met. The following day Canadian and Scottish troops accompanied by Commandos sailed their landing craft into the breaches which Bomber Command had created in the sea walls and after a week of fighting the island fell. The last to return to East Kirkby was PD253 flown by 'Billy' Billing at 13:51 hours.

For the crew of Roy 'Millie' Millichap who had joined the squadron mid-tour when the services of an experienced senior pilot were required as flight commander, they had flown their last op with the squadron. All of their recent 16 ops had been carried out aboard LM216 'K' and they were now split up. Tom Scrivener, navigator and mid upper and rear gunners Eric Darton and David Schwab were promptly posted as instructors, the remainder of the crew trickled away from East Kirkby gradually, their captain's DFC was announced in early December and finally in January Roy Millichap handed over his position as flight commander and was himself posted. Millichap remained in aviation and post-war attained the position of Flight Superintendent for BOAC's fleet of Constellations receiving a Queens Commendation for Valuable Service in the Air in the 1957 New Years Honours List for his work in that capacity. At the end of October 1944 the mixed Australian, Canadian and British crew of 20 year old Flying Officer Richard Scott RAAF were posted to 630 Squadron having been cleared for ops by S/Ldr Lawrence Pilgrim DFC at No.5 Lancaster Finishing School, he followed them to the Squadron six months later to commence another tour of ops as Flight Commander.

Richard Scott RAAF (RAAF official)

Jack Hoare RAAF (J Hoare (Australia))

November 1944

Roy Millichap and crew with LM216 "K-Kitty" (Bob Millichap)

Wednesday 1st November 1944.
226 Lancasters and 2 Mosquitoes of 5 Group supported by 8 Mosquitoes of 8 Group attacked the Meerbeck Synthetic oil plant at Homberg. 19 aircraft of Six-thirty were detailed for Ops, each armed with 11 x 1000lb AN-M65 (.025) and 4 x 500lb AN-N64 (.025) bombs.

1st November 1944 : Daylight Bombing Attack on Homberg
Take Off: at 13:26 hours in LM260 Wing Commander Grindon was first away.

PD253-D	F/O SA Nunns	RD
LL949-E	F/O GR Flood RNZAF	RD
ND412-H	F/O H Thompson	RD
NG145-I	F/O DA Clifford	RD
NN702-J	F/O GE Stemp	RD
LM216-K	Lt DS Turner SAAF	RD
LM287-O	F/O FE Millar RNZAF	RD
LL966-P	F/O OJS Atkinson RAAF	
ME845-Q	F/O JW Langley	RD
PB344-R	F/O GE Billing	RD
LM260-S	W/C JE Grindon	RD
ME739-T	F/O A McGuffie	RD
NG123-U	F/O EC Harris RNZAF	RD
LM637-V	F/L RF Lewis	RD
PD254-W	F/O TB Baker RAAF	RD
NN703-X	F/O JW Hoare RAAF	RD
PD327-Y	F/O DA McGillivray RNZAF	RD
ND949-Z	F/S GH Cowan	
PD317-G	F/O H Grayson	RD

Arriving in the target area heavy cloud hung over the synthetic oil plant. The early wave of the main force bombed before the markers went down, others arrived just as the markers were dropped directly in front of them. The force leaders were east of the track approaching the target area and the majority of crews reported attacking the markers between 16:08 and 16:12 hours from 17,000 to 18,000 feet. Four crews of 630 Squadron bombed Mors, the built up area south of the target, as they could not identify the primary and 'D-Dog' (Steve Munns) bombed Krefeld for the same reason. Moderate to intense accurate flak was encountered over the target and many aircraft returned with flak damage, Wing Commander Grindon's aircraft was holed in 33 places by flak, the hydraulics were shot away, the main rudder controls and elevator controls were damaged. Some like Henry Thompson's crew found their aircraft to be 'like a sieve' when they inspected it later, Jack Hoare's 'X-Xray' was quite badly damaged by flak but no enemy fighters were seen. ME739 (Alex McGuffie) was the last to return to base at 18:50 hours.

Thursday 2nd November 1944.
Bomber Command launched its last major attack of the war against Dusseldorf with 992 bombers. 14 Lancasters of Six-thirty participated, each bombed up with 1 x 4000lb HC, 6 x 1000lb AN-M59, 4 x 500lb GP (.025) and 2 x 500lb GP 53 (LD ½ hour) bombs.

2nd/3rd November 1944 : Night Bombing Attack on Dusseldorf
Take Off: at 16:21 hours the recently promoted Captain Desmond Reynolds of the SAAF took off ahead of the squadron.

PD253-D	F/O H Thompson	
LL949-E	F/O GR Flood RNZAF	(F/S GR Scott RAAF)
NG125-F	Capt DCB Reynolds SAAF	
PD317-G	F/O H Grayson	
LM287-O	F/O FE Millar RNZAF	(F/O RJ Sassoon)
LL966-P	F/O OJS Atkinson RAAF	
ME845-Q	F/O JW Hoare RAAF	

PB344-R	F/O JW Langley	
NG123-U	F/O EC Harris RNZAF	
LM637-V	Lt W Adams USAAF	(F/O AM MacLean RCAF)
PD254-W	F/O A McGuffie	
NN703-X	F/L HD Archer	(Lt MT Ackerman SAAF)
PD327-Y	F/O TB Baker RAAF	
ND949-Z	F/S GH Cowan	

Weather conditions were clear at the target with good visibility and ground defences were not troublesome with flak bursting clear of the bombers and the searchlights ineffective in the moonlight. The target was marked punctually with Red TIs which were quickly assessed as accurate when compared with the bends in the River Rhine and the inland waterway dock yards. Minutes later the reds were backed up with green TIs which fell slightly to the east. The squadron attacked between 19:17 and 19:36 hours from 17,400 to 21,000 feet. Throughout the attack the ground markers were clearly seen and experienced crews rated the concentration of bomber as excellent. The Germans set some decoy red TIs 3 – 4 miles north west of the target and a slight delay in setting the green markers might have caused some confusion. Large fires were soon burning with a thick pall of smoke over the town, the fires could be seen for 100 miles on the return flight. Fighters began to appear over the target about halfway through the attack and continued to attack the main force as it flew home until about 0430East. 6 combats took place with night fighters. PD254 'W' arrived 12 minutes late and did not attack. The bombing fell mainly on the northern half of the city where more than 5,000 houses were destroyed or badly damaged and 7 factories were destroyed and a further 18

The MacLean crew. Back row l to r:Joe Cook (R/G), JH 'Mick' Mitchell (F/E), S 'Jock' Cruickshank (WOp), SCH 'Titch' Priest (MU/G). Front row l to r: EHO 'Sandy' Saunders (Nav), AM 'Mac' MacLean RCAF, Ron Norgrove (A/B) (LAHC Archive)

seriously damaged including some steel production plants vital to the German war effort. Bill Adams and crew were the last to return to base at 22:04 hours in LM637. On 4th November Harry Grayson's crew (7 ops) and that of New Zealander Don McGillivray (4 ops) were posted to 189 Squadron to provide further crews with some operational experience amongst a squadron which had been formed mainly from sprog crews directly from training. A number of crews recently arrived from training were preparing for ops in early November, they included Canadian Albert 'Mac' MacLean's[i] crew of British lads from 1654 HCU, 21 year old Richard Sassoon[ii] the son of a retired Army officer from Roehampton and his all British crew, Aussie George Scott[iii] with a mixed Australian, Canadian and British crew, the crews of 26 year old New Zealander Harry Ramsey[iv] from Auckland, his countryman Phil Weston[v] from Hunterville, NZ and Australian Neil Roberts[vi] from Healesville, Victoria. Arnold Stockill[vii] and crew were amongst the most recent arrivals, their captain was a 31 year old married man with two small children, originally from Darlington but resident in Wallasey.

Neil Roberts RAAF and crew (Kay Rowland)

Arnold Stockill (Geoff Copeman)

Phil Weston RNZAF (P Weston)

Harry Ramsey RNZAF and crew at 5 LFS with Les Duck, 1st right (Les Duck and Richard Gold)

Saturday 4th November 1944.

174 Lancasters and 3 Mosquitoes of 5 Group were despatched to bomb the section of the Dortmund-Ems Canal near Ladbergen, north of Munster, just repaired by the Germans. 13 Lancasters of 630 Squadron participated in the attack, each armed with 14 x 1000lb AN-M (.025) bombs.

4th/5th November 1944 : Night Bombing Attack on Ladbergen

Take off: at 17:34 hours in sequence behind Desmond Reynolds (NG125). One of the aircraft carried Neil Roberts RAAF a new pilot making a Second Dickie trip, sadly the ORB does not show which aircrew he flew with, but the logbook of F/O FEH Millar DFC records that he was accompanied by Neil Roberts on this op.

LL949-E	F/O GE Billing	
NG125-F	Capt DCB Reynolds SAAF	
PD317-G	F/O EJ Monk	
LM216-K	Lt DS Turner SAAF	
LM287-O	F/O FEH Millar RNZAF	(P/O NG Roberts RAAF)
LL966-P	F/S EA Thomas	
ME845-Q	S/L MA Eyre	
PB344-R	F/S GH Cowan	
NG123-U	F/O LA Barnes	
LM637-V	F/O A McGuffie	
NN703-X	Lt W Adams USAAF	
PD327-Y	F/O TB Baker RAAF	
ND949-Z	F/O LF Ovens	

Weather at the target was clear and visibility good and the marking was punctual and accurate after which the controller ordered the force to bomb the southern of the two lots of red TIs. The distance between both lots was less than 150 yards and both lay between the two branches of the canal junction. The squadron's attack took place from 10,200 to 13,000 feet between 19:30 and 19:34 hours and bombing was reported to be very concentrated with multiple sticks of bombs straddled the canal junction. Ground defences were negligible although fighter flares were seen repeatedly between the Dutch coast and the target but few fighters were seen. German decoy interference included W/T messages such as 19:32 hours *'Return to Base'*, repeated at 19:34 hours and at 19:35 hours *'Flare force return to base'* but as crews had satisfactory VHF reception they followed the Controllers orders and ignored the interference. The banks of both branches of the inland waterway were breached again letting the water drain off and leaving large cargo carrying barges stranded. Post war a report by Industry Production Minister Speer which had been prepared for Hitler recorded that the bombing of the canal prevented delivery of smelting coke from the Ruhr to 3 important steelworks, 2 near Brunswick and 1 near Osnabruck. In post-war interrogations Speer revealed that these raids on the Dortmund-Ems Canal together with attacks on the German railway system produced more serious setbacks to German war production than any other bombing. At 22:23 hours Len Barnes flying 'U-Uncle' was the last of the squadron to land back at base. Records contradict themselves as to whether the Adams crew or the McGuffie crew flew 'V' or 'X' respectively.

Wednesday 6th November 1944.

Continuing the campaign, 235 Lancasters and 7 Mosquitos of 5 Group attempted to cut the Mittelland Canal at its junction with the Dortmund Ems Canal near Gravenhorst. Detailed to participate were 17 aircraft of Six-thirty each with a load of 13 x 1000lb AN-M65 bombs.

6th/7th November 1944 : Night Bombing Attack on Gravenhorst

Take Off: at 16:08 hours NG125 (Desmond Reynolds) and his SAAF colleague Douglas Turner (flying LM216) were the first away. Frank Millar (LM287) had another recently arrived SAAF pilot (Gordon Lacey) aboard as Second Dickie.

PD253-D	F/O GR Scott RAAF	
LL949-E	F/O GE Billing	
NG125-F	Capt DCB Reynolds SAAF	
PD317-G	F/O EJ Monk	
NN702-J	W/O EA Thomas	
LM216-K	Lt DS Turner SAAF	
LM287-O	F/O FE Millar RNZAF	(Lt GR Lacey SAAF)
LL966-P	F/O OJS Atkinson RAAF	
ME845-Q	F/O H Thompson	
PB344-R	W/O GH Cowan	
ME739-T	F/O A McGuffie	
NG123-U	F/O GE Stemp	
LM637-V	F/O RJ Sassoon	
PD254-W	F/O LA Barnes	
NN703-X	F/O AM MacLean RCAF	
PD327-Y	F/O TB Baker RAAF	
ND949-Z	F/O LF Ovens	

Weather over the target was clear with some slight haze but the flares were so accurately placed by the Mosquito low-level marker (Flight Lieutenant LCE DeVigne) that they fell into the canal and so were almost immediately extinguished. The Controller ordered the force to stand-by but was unable to get adequate illumination of the target and at 19:38 hours after only 31 aircraft had bombed gave the order to abandon the attack and return to base. None of the squadron's crews were able to attack. Ground defences were negligible but some fighters were observed. Sergeants Jim Sloan and Jim Porter the gunners aboard George Cowan's PB344 'R-Roger' destroyed a Fw190 fighter which engaged their Lancaster. The MacLean crew in 'X-X ray' were the last to return at 22:35 hours.

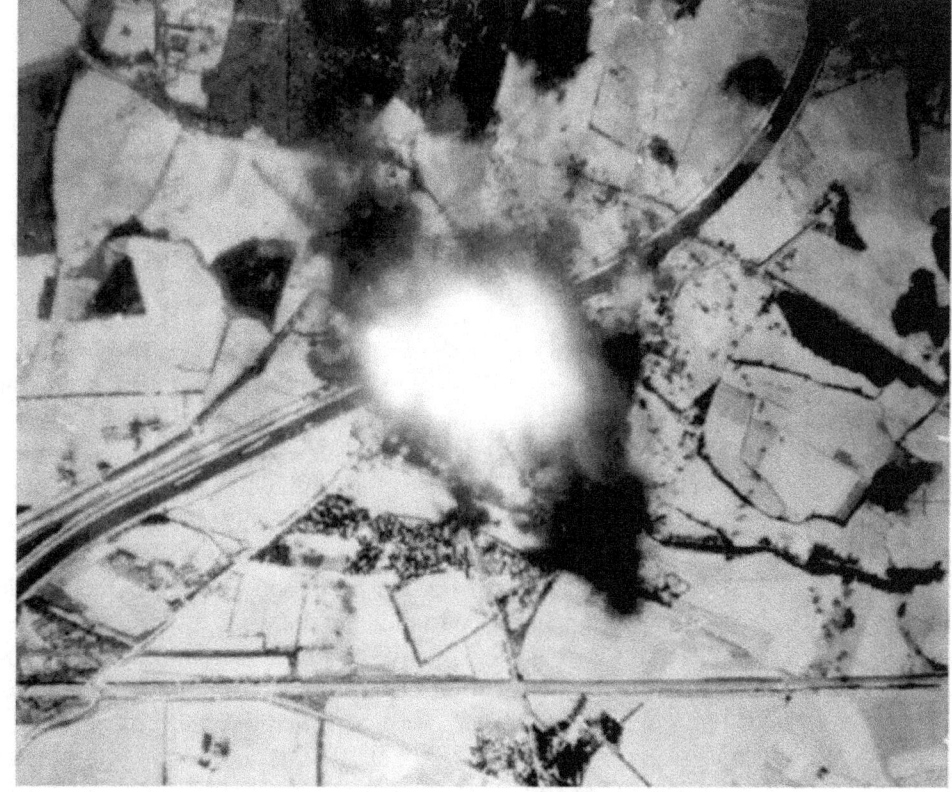

Mittelland canal attack (Geoff Copeman)

Tuesday 7th November Flying Officer Bill Horsman[viii], who had flown as bomb aimer in Peter Docherty's crew until they completed their tour some weeks earlier, was welcomed back when he joined the staff of RAF East Kirkby as Station Air Sea Rescue officer but was immediately waved off again as he was despatched on a 3 week specialist ASR course at Blackpool.

Saturday 11th November 1944.

The squadron participated in two simultaneous missions next as 5 Group attacked Harburg with 237 Lancasters and 8 Mosquitoes and also laid mines off Oslo, in the Kattegat and in the estuary of the River Elbe. 17 aircraft from Six-thirty were tasked to attack the Rhenania-Ossag oil refinery at Harburg, each bombed up with 1 x 4000lb HC and 14 x No.14 incendiary clusters.

11th/12th November 1944 : Night Bombing Attack on Harburg and Minelaying

Take Off: at 16:12 hours the recently arrived Flight Commander Squadron Leader Malcolm Eyre led the formation out from North Kirkby.

ME312-A	F/O LA Barnes	
NG258-B	F/O GE Stemp	
PD253-D	F/O PS Weston RNZAF	
NG125-F	Capt DCB Reynolds SAAF	
PD317-G	F/O HA Ramsey RNZAF	
NN702-J	W/O EA Thomas	
LM216-K	F/O GE Billing	
NG259-N	F/O H Thompson	
LL966-P	F/O OJS Atkinson RAAF	
ME845-Q	F/O RG Waterfall	
PB344-R	F/O GR Scott RAAF	
ME739-T	F/O A McGuffie	
NG123-U	F/O AM MacLean RCAF	
LM637-V	S/L MA Eyre	RD
PD254-W	F/O TB Baker RAAF	
ND949-Z	F/O LF Ovens	
PD237-Y	F/O RJ Sassoon	

ME312 'A-Able' (Len Barnes) returned early landing at 19:17 hours after his bomb aimer (F/O Derrek Simons) was taken ill and LL966 'P' (Olly Atkinson) had returned early at 18:11 hours when the W/T receiver failed and couldn't be repaired. Ground defences lit fighter flares from the coast near Heligoland onwards to the target to draw fighters in to the bomber stream, along the route to the target and even on the homeward route. Marking at the target was a few minutes late but appeared to be accurate and the Controller's clear instructions avoided confusion when the Germans lit a decoy flare. The squadron attacked between 19:18 and 19:31 hours from 16,250 to 19,000 feet. Smoke from the burning oil tanks obscured the markers later during the attack, several large explosions were seen at 19:18, 19:22 and 19:25 hours and heavy black smoke was rising from the oil depot. Ground defences died down as the attack commenced and search lights were being used to indicate the track of the bombers to night fighters. Few enemy aircraft were seen but there were 2 inconclusive combats with night fighters. Realising that they would not make it to the target in time after hearing the Controllers instruction cease bombing and return to base the crew of PD237 'Y-Yoke' (Richard Sassoon) jettisoned their bombs on a concentration of search lights and anti-aircraft guns situated at 5340Nx0900E at 19:50 hours from 17,750 feet. Formation leader Squadron Leader Eyre was the last of the squadron's Harburg force to return to base at 22:08 hours.

On the same night two of the squadron's Lancasters were involved in a gardening operation each armed with 6 Mark VI mines.

11th/12th November 1944 : Minelaying in the 'Young Eglantines' area

Take Off: at 16:33 hours Frank Millar was the first off the deck, he was also the last to return to base at 21:05 hours.

LM287-O	F/O FE Millar RNZAF
NN703-X	F/L HD Archer

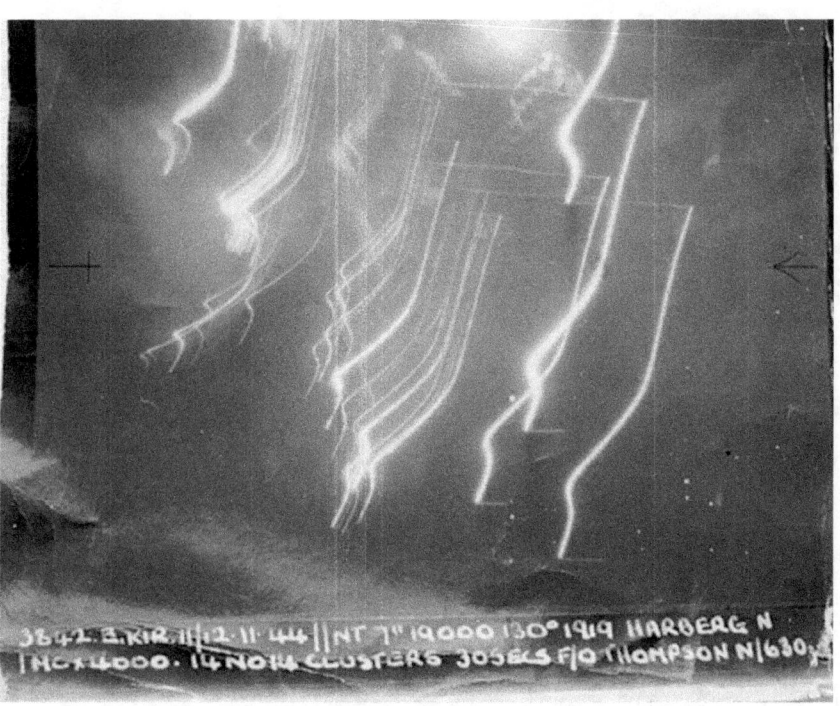

Henry Thompson in "N-Nan" bombing photo (Keith Arscott)

The two aircraft and crews designated for 'gardening' duties planted their 'vegetables' at 19:02 and 19:15 hours in the allotted positions using H2S without serious difficulty although some heavy flak was experienced from Heligoland. No enemy fighters were seen but fighter flares were observed near Cuxhaven.

Next, Bomber Command joined the 8th USAAF to attack targets at Düren, Jülich and Heinsberg in preparation for an attack by the American 1st and 9th Armies. Thursday 16th November 1944. The RAF despatched 1,188 bombers to destroy lines of communication and the USAAF sent 1,239 bombers to raid troop positions. 19 aircraft of Six-thirty were despatched to join the force attacking Düren each bombed-up with 11 x 1000lb AN-M65 and 4 x 500lb AN-M64 (.025) bombs.

16th November 1944 : Daylight Bombing Attack on Düren

Take Off: at 12:24 hours South African Doug Turner was the first away.

ME312-A	F/O DA Clifford
NG258-B	F/O GR Scott RAAF
LL949-E	F/O JW Langley
NG125-F	F/O A Stockill
PD317-G	F/L SA Nunns
NN702-J	W/O EA Thomas
LM216-K	Lt DS Turner SAAF
NG259-N	F/O JW Hoare RAAF
LM287-O	F/O FE Millar RNZAF
LL966-P	F/L RF Lewis
ME845-Q	F/O RG Waterfall
PB344-R	F/O HA Ramsey RNZAF
ME739-T	F/O RA Stone RNZAF
NG123-U	F/O EC Harris RNZAF
PD254-W	F/O AM MacLean RCAF
NN703-X	F/O NG Roberts RAAF
PD327-Y	F/O RJ Sassoon

ND949-Z   F/O LF Ovens
LM637-V   F/O TB Baker RAAF

Steve Nunns and crew (Brian Lunn)

In a rare moment of awkwardness Steve Nunns' 'D-Dog' went unserviceable at the last moment, Jerry Monk's crew were taken off the Battle Order making 'G-George' available for the Nunns crew. Although there was a thick haze and dense smoke covering the town the immediate target area was clear and visibility was good. The Controller was considered by the main force to be excellent, giving clear precise instructions although W/T reception was poor at times. He ordered the force down to 10,000 feet, the squadron attacked between 15:34 and 15:39 hours from 9,800 to 12,400 feet and bombing was reported to be very concentrated on the target. One very large explosion was seen at 15:37 hours although no fighters were seen and the flak was moderate. An Air Gunner reported that the Lancaster seen to go down in flames at 15:33 hours was hit in the starboard wing by a Lancaster with a fin and rudder painted yellow. The casualty had a red letter painted on a black fin but its squadron letters could not be seen. Tom Baker was the last to return at 18:38 hours. John Langley's crew aboard LL949 'E-Easy' could not attack as their bombs hung-up when the distributor failed to move, the crew managed to jettison two 1000lb bombs over the North Sea but brought the remainder home. The three towns attacked by the RAF were virtually destroyed. Many aircraft had to divert to Strubby due to very poor conditions over base on their return. The weather remained very poor and an attempt to return on the following day had to be aborted again due to conditions over East Kirkby.

Left: Lieut's Lacey and Ackerman SAAF. Right: S/L Cuelenaere RCAF, W/Cdr Grindon, S/L Eyre (both LAHC Archive)

After a heavy rain storm in the early hours of Sunday 19th November a preliminary warning of Ops was received at 10:05 hours – an early take-off was planned and the station put in maximum effort to be ready however the order was later cancelled. The same thing happened the very next day with an 09:40 hours warning, everything was ready for the planned 13:15 hours take off but it was delayed until 16:25 hours and finally scrubbed at 16:45 hours. With their pilots each having completed an op as Second Dickie the crews captained by South Africans Gordon Lacey[ix] and Marthinus Ackerman[x] were to be detailed for ops on the next Battle Order.

Tuesday 21st November 1944.
5 Group maintained the pressure on the German inland water transport system returning to the Mittelland Canal near Gravenhorst with 138 Lancasters and 5 Mosquitoes. 21 Lancasters of Six-thirty were bombed with 1000lb GP (.025) bombs.

21st/22nd November 1944 : Night Bombing Attack on Gravenhorst
Take Off: at 17:22 hours Squadron Leader Malcolm Eyre in PD254 was first away.

ND949-Z	Lt W Adams USAAF
JB290-C	F/O TB Baker RAAF
ME312-A	F/O DA Clifford
NG258-B	F/O GR Scott RAAF
PD253-D	F/O A Stockill
LL949-E	F/O GR Flood RNZAF
NG125-F	Capt DCB Reynolds SAAF
NN702-J	W/O EA Thomas
PD317-G	F/O HA Ramsey RNZAF
LM216-K	Lt DS Turner SAAF
NG259-N	F/O LA Barnes
LM287-O	Lt MT Ackerman SAAF

LL966-P	Lt GR Lacey SAAF
PD254-W	S/L MA Eyre
ME845-Q	F/O RG Waterfall
ME739-T	F/O RA Stone RNZAF
PD344-R	F/O JW Hoare RAAF
NG123-U	F/O EC Harris RNZAF
LM637-V	F/L RF Lewis
NN703-X	F/O NG Roberts RAAF
PD327-Y	F/O RJ Sassoon

The marking was punctual but some of the Controllers orders were considered to be confusing. At 20:59 hours some crews were ordered by W/T to descend to 4,000 ft and attack but then received a message by VHF to attack as planned and had to climb back to their original bombing height. 630 Squadron attacked between 21:03 and 21:12 hours from 3,500 to 9,800 feet and was reported as well concentrated, only a small amount of light flak was experienced and no search lights. Small scale fighter activity and only in the target area and start of the route homeward. There were five combats with fighters in the target area and one on the route home but none were conclusive. The canal banks were successfully breached and later photographs showed that the water drained off over a 30 miles stretch leaving 59 barges stranded in one short section alone. George Scott and crew aboard NG258 were the last to land at 00:11 hours.

The Squadron Adjutant, Flight Lieutenant Charles Martin, MM was posted out to a training unit, he was later cashiered by sentence of a General Court Martial (17th September 1945) having been found guilty of historically allowing crews access to service vehicles and fuel for occasional recreational outings or brief

Ted Watson and Lancaster NG123-U "Oh U Beauty" (Ted Watson)

Charles Martin (Patti Kellaway). *Alf Britton (Adjutant) (LAHC Archive)* *Marcel Cuelenaere RCAF (Cuelenaere family)* *Bob Corkill (LAHC Archive)*

periods of leave between Ops. An Ealing man, thirty-nine year old former insurance official Flight Lieutenant Alfred Henry Lionel Britton quickly arrived to replace him.

In the second half of the month a new flight commander was posted in to replace A-Flight's Squadron Leader Millichap. Squadron Leader Marcel Cuelenaere DFC RCAF[xi] was a French-Canadian who had completed a tour of 30 ops with 97 Squadron between October 1942 and March 1943 which included some of the very long range missions to bomb Italy (awarded a DFC, London Gazette 15th June 1943). He had been presented with his DFC at Buckingham Palace by HM King George VI at an investiture on 21st March 1944. During a long Instructing tour at 1654 and 1660 HCU he survived injury when the Lancaster (W4937) in which he was instructor swung and crashed on landing at Swinderby on 26th September 1943, he instructed further at 1668 HCU and finally 5 LFS before joining 630 Squadron. Not surprisingly his crew included second tour veterans such as navigator 36 year old Manx postal telegraphist Bob Corkill DFC formerly of 9 Squadron and wireless op 31 year old Wil MacDonald DFC who had completed his previous tour with 61 Squadron. Both of these two men would go on to have distinguished careers post-war in the Colonial Service, Bob Corkill in the West African Postal Administration and Wil MacDonald as a Superintendent of Police in Kenya.

Wednesday 22nd November 1944.

171 Lancasters and 7 Mosquitoes of 5 Group were despatched to attacked the U-boat pens at Trondheim. The squadron records do not indicate what bomb load was carried by its 12 Lancasters however LL949 which was lost is reported to have had 17 x 500lb MC (.025) aboard.

22nd/23rd November 1944 : Night Bombing Attack on Trondheim
Take Off: at 15:38 hours Desmond Reynolds (NG125) was first to get airborne.

LL949-E	F/O GR Flood RNZAF
NG258-B	P/O GR Scott RAAF
ME312-A	F/O JW Hoare RAAF
PD253-D	F/O A Stockill
PD317-G	F/O EJ Monk
NG125-F	Capt DCB Reynolds SAAF
LM216-K	F/O HA Ramsey RNZAF
NN702-J	W/O EA Thomas
PD254-W	F/O RJ Sassoon

Doug Turner SAAF and crew (Paul and John Key)

ME739-T	F/O RA Stone RNZAF
LM637-V	F/L RF Lewis
PD327-Y	Lt W Adams USAAF
NG259-N	F/O LA Barnes

NG259 'N-Nan' (Len Barnes) returned early 20:59 hours as their bomb aimer was ill. On the outward journey a weather front forecast for 5758N was encountered at 56N and spread over 5° of latitude. At 61N there were breaks in the cloud and the target area visibility was very good. The green proximity marker was clearly seen and the first flares dropped at H -13. Fairly intense light flak came up from the target area and the line of fire gradually lowered to converge at about 1000 feet. The Controller ordered crews to return to base at 21:08 hours. Ten searchlights were active and maintained a steady beam to track aircraft leaving the target area. B, F, G. J. K, T, V, W and Y all returned immediately as instructed. The return flight included 5 hours in solid cloud. Arnold Stockill in 'D-Dog' landed at Thornaby short of fuel and Ainsley Thomas flying 'J-Jig' was the last to return landing at 03:36 hours. One crew Failed To Return.

Lancaster I, LL949   (Codes LE – E)

Pilot	– F/O George Ross Flood RNZAF. Age 21	Killed
Flight Eng	– Sgt Leslie Thomas Woodward. Age 20	Died
Navigator	– F/S Charles Agnew RNZAF. Age 25	Killed
Bomb Aimer	– F/S Kenneth James Aspell. Age 26	Killed
Wireless Op	– F/S William Richie Ingram RNZAF. Age 22	Killed
Mid Upper	– Sgt Frederick Hughes. Age	Killed
Rear Gunner	– Sgt Maurice Benjamin Henley. Age 22	Killed

Nothing was heard of the aircraft or crew until 26th November when wreckage was found by a farmer on a sandbank near the north bank of Humber off Sunk Islands Sands and reported to Withernsea Police Station. Six members of the crew were found dead but the flight engineer was still alive. Twenty year old Leslie Woodward, a married man from London had survived the crash but was injured and suffering terribly from exposure, sadly he died of his injuries on 1st December. LL949 appeared to have flown into the ground at a shallow angle in a north to south direction while returning from a long distance attack. The crew had operated on the previous night and the Head of the Court of Enquiry believed that fatigue had been a leading factor in the accident after a long range mission flown at low altitude. Amongst the crew was Scots born Charlie Agnew who had emigrated 'down under' with his family to Australia as a young child he grew up in Perth, WA, he moved to New Zealand in 1937 and joined the New Zealand Army Department as a Signwriter. The three Kiwis and Sgt Henley are buried in Harrogate (Stonefall) Cemetery, Sgt Woodward is buried at Hampstead Cemetery, Sgt Hughes at Moston (St Josephs) RC Cemetery and Sgt Aspell at Coventry (St Paul's) Cemetery. Several days of filthy weather followed and the Station was stood down.

Sunday 26th November 1944.
270 Lancasters and 8 Mosquitoes of 5 Group attacked Munich with aiming points in several railway centres. 20 Lancasters of 630 Squadron but 2 returned early. The bomb loads are not recorded however it is known that they comprised 1000lb MC and 4lb incendiaries.

26th/27th November 1944   Night Bombing Attack on Munich
Take Off: at 10:35 hours LM216 (Phil Weston) took off from East Kirkby leading the squadron.

ME312-A	F/O JW Langley
NG258-B	F/O GE Stemp
PD253-D	F/O H Thompson
NG125-F	F/O GE Billing

PD317-G	F/O EJ Monk	
NG145-I	F/O DA Clifford	
LM216-K	F/O PS Weston RNZAF	
NG259-N	F/O HA Ramsey RNZAF	
LM287-O	F/O A McGuffie	
LL966-P	F/O OJS Atkinson RAAF	
ME845-Q	W/O GH Cowan	
LM260-S	Lt W Adams USAAF	
ME739-T	F/O RA Stone RNZAF	
NG123-U	F/O EC Harris RNZAF	
LM637-V	F/L RF Lewis	
PD254-W	F/O M Miller	
NN703-X	F/O NG Roberts RAAF	
ND949-Z	F/O LF Ovens	
JB290-C	F/O RJ Sassoon	
PB344-R	F/O JW Hoare RAAF	RD

John Langley's 'A-Able' returned early after its starboard inner failed, landing at Manston at 01:50 hours and Billy Billing's 'F-Fox' landed back at base at 03:59 hours with navigational aids, intercom and bomb sight all unserviceable. The target marking was accurate and all crews saw the concentration of TIs clearly. To the north there was a single Red TI cancelled by a Yellow and to the west were decoy TIs set by the Germans which do not seem to have deceived any of the attackers. Large areas of the town were seen to be on fire and the conflagration could be seen 100 miles away. The squadron's attack took place between 05:00 and 05:24 hours from 15,200 to 17,500 feet and a very large explosion was seen at 05:07 hours just north of the eastern end of the marshalling yards. Ground defences and searchlights were surprisingly light and ineffective. Some fighters attacked and there was 1 combat before reaching the target and 2 combats in the target area. Rendel Lewis brought LM637 in to land at 23:18 hours, the last of the squadron to return to base. On Thursday 30th November Group Captain Taaffe OBE relinquished command of RAF East Kirkby to Group Captain Bernard Casey OBE[xii] who would remain in command for the next 12 months.

Ross Flood RNZAF and Charles Agnew RNZAF (Agnew family)

G/Capt Bernard Casey (J Casey)

December 1944

At 10:15 hours on 2nd December a night operation was announced and with all aircraft airborne on exercises the Station pulled out all of the stops to prepare. By 13:00 all aircraft were ready and crews briefed. At 15:45 hours with twenty crews in their aircraft, engines running and ready for take-off, the Op was cancelled.

Monday 4th December 1944.
Sited on the main north-south railway line Heilbronn had little other importance and as such escaped a serious attack until the railway network in the area increased in priority as a target and 5 Group despatched 282 Lancasters and 10 Mosquitoes. 20 aircraft and crews of 630 Squadron armed with 1 x 4000lb HC and Mk.14 Incendiary clusters.

4th/5th December 1944 : Night Bombing Attack on Heilbronn
Take Off: at 16:04 hours Wing Commander Grindon and crew in NG259 were first away.

ME312-A	F/O JW Langley
NG258-B	F/O GE Stemp
PD253-D	F/O A Stockill
NG125-F	Capt DCB Reynolds SAAF
PD317-G	F/O GE Billing
ND412-H	F/O GR Scott RCAF
NN702-J	F/O H Thompson
LM216-K	Lt DS Turner SAAF
NG259-N	W/C JE Grindon
LM287-O	F/O A McGuffie
ME845-Q	F/O RG Waterfall
PB344-R	W/O GH Cowan
LM260-S	Lt W Adams USAAF
ME739-T	F/O RA Stone RNZAF
NG123-U	F/O EC Harris RNZAF
LM637-V	Lt GR Lacey SAAF
PD254-W	F/O OJS Atkinson RAAF
NN703-X	F/O AM Maclean RCAF
PD327-Y	F/O TB Baker RAAF
ND949-Z	F/O LF Ovens

The target was punctually and accurately marked and the attack went as planned between 19:30 and 19:40 hours from 11.000 to 12,000 feet. Massive areas of fire were seen across the town with heavy explosions between them. On the homeward track incendiaries were again reported being jettisoned aiding enemy fighters searching for the bombers. Considerable fighter opposition was encountered mainly within 25 miles of the target. Aboard Eric Harris' NG123 'U-Uncle' mid-upper gunner Sergeant Tom Lockett and rear gunner Sergeant Bert Lewis were involved in two decisive combats with both resulted in JU88's being damaged. Sadly the combat reports can no longer be traced. (Note: the Station ORB records the Lancaster as 'G-George' but that is considered to be a typing error). Severe icing in thick cloud was encountered on the homeward flight shortly after leaving the target and it proved hard to climb clear of the cloud. NN703 flown by the Canadian Albert Maclean was the last to return to base at 23:47 hours. The post war British Bombing Survey reported that after the 1,254 tons of bombs fell within just minutes the resulting fires destroyed 351 acres of the town, 82% of the built up area. It is likely that a true firestorm developed and

Lancaster NG125 "F-Fox" (Geoff Copeman)

burned the town. Records are contradictory on this night and it is possible that the aircraft flown by the Thompson and Scott crews have been transposed.

Wednesday 6th December 1944.
In 5 Group's next attack their 255 Lancasters and 10 Mosquitoes were split to attack two different aiming points, 168 aircraft bombing the town centre and 87 the railway yards. Six-thirty provided 16 Lancasters each armed with 1 x 4000lb HC and Mk.14 Incendiary clusters.

6th/7th December 1944 : Night Bombing Attack on Giessen
Take Off: at 16:46 hours Cliff Clifford and crew were first away from base.

ME312-A	F/O JW Langley
NG258-B	F/O GE Stemp
PD317-G	F/O PS Weston RNZAF
ND412-H	F/O JW Hoare RAAF
NN702-J	F/O DA Clifford
NG259-N	F/O GE Billing
LM287-O	F/O FE Millar RNZAF
LL966-P	F/O OJS Atkinson RAAF
ME845-Q	F/O RG Waterfall
PB344-R	F/O A McGuffie
LM260-S	S/L MA Eyre
ME739-T	F/O RA Stone RNZAF
NG123-U	F/O EC Harris RNZAF
LM637-V	F/L RF Lewis
PD254-W	W/O GH Cowan
NN703-X	Lt GR Lacey SAAF
PD327-Y	F/O TB Baker RAAF
ND949-Z	F/O LF Ovens

'G-George' flown by Phil Weston and 'H-How' by Jack Hoare took off but both abandoned their missions after engine failures, neither are listed in the 630 Squadron Operations Record Book but they are detailed in the 630 Squadron Ops Record held at the RAF Museum, Hoare jettisoned his complete bomb load over the North Sea while Weston jettisoned his Cookie and some incendiaries. Weather made the flying tricky for long stretches of both the outward and homeward routes and arriving over the target crews found patchy cloud but had clear visibility of the aiming point. The Controller had the markers placed accurately and on time and gave clear instructions for the attack. The squadron attacked from 20:15 until 20:19 hours from 9,800 to 12,000 feet and was well concentrated in the town with fires spread over a large area. Fighters were first encountered over the target and followed the home route for 15 minutes. 'V-Victor' flown by Rendel Lewis was in combat with a JU88 which was claimed as destroyed by his gunners Sergeants Reg Bennett (mid-upper) and Joe Morgan (rear gunner). No combat report has been located. That day several reports speak of jet propelled fighters operating and bombers were seen to be shot down. At 23:57 hours Geoff Stemp touched down at base, the last of the squadron's aircraft to return. Severe damage was caused at both targets, the raid being a total success.

Friday 8th December 1944.

Crews were called from their beds at 03:45 in the morning and briefings started at 05:00 hours. 14 aircraft of 630 Squadron were detailed for Ops and bombed up with 14 x 1000lbHC TD .025. They were part of a force of 205 Lancasters of 5 Group attacking the Urftdam as a previous raid by 8 Group had failed to destroy it. The Germans were using the dam to release substantial amounts of water when US Forces attempted to advance down river.

8th December 1944 : Daylight Bombing Attack on Heimbach-Urft Dam

Take Off: at 08:13 hours Squadron Leader Marcel Cuelenaere DFC RCAF, flight commander, led the squadron from East Kirkby.

ME312-A	F/O JW Langley
NG125-F	S/L MR Cuelenaere RCAF
NN702-J	F/O DA Clifford
LM216-K	Lt DS Turner SAAF
NG259-N	W/C JE Grindon
LM287-O	F/O A Stockill
LL966-P	F/O OJS Atkinson RAAF
PB344-R	W/O GH Cowan
LM260-S	Lt W Adams USAAF
ME739-T	F/O RA Stone RNZAF
LM637-V	F/L RF Lewis
PD254-W	Lt GR Lacey SAAF
PD327-Y	F/O TB Baker RAAF
ND949-Z	F/O GR Scott RAAF

Despite 9/10ths cloud all crews identified the target visually, the attack ran from 10:48 to 11:14 hours bombing from 8,000 to 10,000 feet and one stick of bombs was seen to straddle the aiming point, other bombs were seen in the right location but prevailing weather conditions prevented proper assessment. 630 Squadron crews attacked between 10:47 and 10:58 hours from 8,200 to 9,500 feet. There were no ground defences and no fighter opposition. One Lancaster was seen to lose its tail fin and rudder before diving into the ground after only two of its crew escaped by parachute, sadly it was a Six-thirty crew. All aircraft were diverted to Tarrant Rushton on return due to very poor weather conditions at base. Ron Stone landed at 13:56 hours, the last to return safely. Lieutenant Lacey in 'W-William' landed at Manston short of fuel. Crews were ordered to remain where they had landed until 09:30 on the 9th. The Squadron Bombing Leader F/L George Arkieson is reported to have flown on this attack, it is suspected that he flew as a supernumerary with a crew but was not recorded in the ORB. Rendel Lewis and crew had Failed To Return.

Lancaster III, LM637 (Codes LE – V)

Pilot	– F/L Rendel Forrest Lewis. Age 29	Killed
Flight Eng	– Sgt Leslie Oyston. Age 24	Killed
Navigator	– F/S Kenneth Frank Lenton. Age 18	Killed
Bomb Aimer	– F/O Reginald Harold William Usher. Age 21	Killed
Wireless Op	– Sgt Cyril Cook. Age 19	Killed
Mid Upper	– F/S Reginald Joseph Bennett. Age 25	Killed
Rear Gunner	– Sgt Joseph Anthony Morgan. Age 19	Prisoner

Cyril Cook (Bob Wilson) *Joe Morgan (Andy Morgan)*

Unfortunately LM637 was in collision with another Lancaster in the target area around 11:00 hours, losing its tail fin and rudder it crashed on the western bank of the Urftalsperre near Schleiden/Eifel. Those who died are buried at Rheinberg War Cemetery. F/L Rendel Lewis was a Barrister at Law and had been a Navigation Instructor at the RAF College Cranwell, his navigator Ken Lenton was only 18 years old. Joe Morgan the 19 year old Rear Gunner from Crook, Co. Durham suffered a broken leg due to flak splinters and parachuted into captivity in agony. His leg was not properly treated and was left to set itself as he passed through a succession of 6 different prison camps.

The post-war RAF investigation concluded that 'following collision Lancaster LM637 fell directly into the lake at a steep angle'. In 1959 the wreckage of the aircraft and remains of the crew were found when part of the Heimbach-Urft dam Schwammeauel lake scheme was drained. The aircraft was positively identified and the crew were buried at Rheinberg War Cemetery, previously they had been commemorated on Runnymede Memorial.

Sunday 10th December 1944. An early morning attack against the Heimbach-Urftdam was launched with 16 Lancasters of the squadron participating fully bombed up with 14 x 1000lbHC TD .025 bombs.

10th December 1944 : <u>RECALLED</u> - Daylight Bombing Attack on Heimbach-Urft Dam
They took off about 04:00 hours but were all recalled and returned to base at about 06:00 hours.

ME312-A	P/O A Stockill
NG258-B	F/O GE Stemp
JB290-C	F/O GR Scott RAAF
NG125-F	F/O JW Hoare RAAF
PD317-G	F/O PS Weston
ND412-H	F/O H Thompson
NN702-J	F/O DA Clifford
LM216-K	Lt DS Turner SAAF
NG259-N	F/O GE Billing
LL966-P	F/O OJS Atkinson RAAF
PB344-R	F/O A McGuffie
LM260-S	F/O AM Maclean RCAF
NG123-U	F/O EC Harris RNZAF
ME739-T	F/O RG Waterfall
PD327-Y	F/O TB Baker RAAF
ND949-Z	F/O LF Ovens

This was not counted as an attack and as such not recorded in the 630 Squadron Operations Record Book or permitted to count towards the number of ops required towards tour completion by the airmen.

Monday 11th December 1944.
5 Group were returning to the Urftdam with 233 Lancasters and 5 Mosquitoes of 8 Group. The squadron's aircraft were each bombed up with 14 x 1,000 lb T.D. (.025) bombs.

11th December 1944 : Daylight Bombing Attack on Heinbach-Urft Dam
Take Off: at 12:21 hours PD317 Phil Weston and crew were first airborne.

ME845-Q	P/O A Stockill	
NG258-B	F/O GE Stemp	
JB290-C	F/O GR Scott RAAF	
NG125-F	F/O JW Hoare RAAF	RD
PD317-G	F/O PS Weston	
ND412-H	F/O H Thompson	
NN702-J	F/O DA Clifford	
LM216-K	Lt DS Turner SAAF	
NG259-N	F/O GE Billing	
LL966-P	F/O OJS Atkinson RAAF	
PB344-R	F/O A McGuffie	
LM260-S	F/O AM Maclean RCAF	
NG123-U	F/O EC Harris RNZAF	
PD327-Y	F/O TB Baker RAAF	
ND949-Z	F/O LF Ovens	

Conditions were quite cloudy in the target area however bombing was generally reported as being in the correct location, the squadron's crews attacked between 14:45 and 14:56 hours from 8,000 to 10,000 feet several sticks of bombs were seen to straddle the spillway and an experienced crew reported craters on the spillway and the dam. Most crews had to make 2 or 3 bombing runs before they could get a clear enough view to attack the slipway due to drifting clouds and the smoke from bomb bursts. Attacking at 14:56 hours 'C-Charlie' had one bomb hang-up, it later dropped clear over France on the flight home. Some light flak was experienced from the dam and some heavy flak from the neighbouring village of Heinbach. 'Billy' Billing's crew in NG259 did not attack as the crew could not identify the target in the cloud and smoke. Aboard LM216 'K' the Squadron Bombing Leader Flight Lieutenant George Arkieson persuaded his pilot Lieutenant Doug Turner SAAF to orbit the target for 20 minutes until the cloud had drifted past enabling him to identify the dam and execute a pinpoint attack. All aircraft of the squadron had returned by the time that Jim Ovens and crew in ND949 touched down at 17:49 hours. Photo reconnaissance confirmed hits on the dam but still no major breaches. Tuesday 12th December 1944 – preparations were made for a daylight bombing attack with an expected take off at midday. At 11:25 hours with all crews in their Lancasters ready to take off the operation was scrubbed. At lunchtime a Lancaster (JA908) of 1668 Heavy Conversion Unit on a training sortie from Bottesford lost its port outer engine and was ordered to divert to East Kirkby. Arriving in a period of poor visibility they touched down but bounced back into the air losing their starboard main wheel in the process. The aircraft was unable to climb leaving F/O LJ Richer RCAF, its pilot, no alternative but to force land in the circuit at 13:09 hours. The Lancaster skidded to a halt and caught fire, seven of the eight aircrew aboard being slightly injured. The flight engineer had a fractured left leg.

On Wednesday 13th December 1944 preparations were made for a daylight bombing attack with an expected take off about midday for an attack at 15:00 hours. Briefings commenced at 09:00 and At 12:00 hours, just 15 minutes before take-off, with all crews in their Lancasters ready to take off the operation was scrubbed and carried forward for the next day. At 17:10 hours the squadron were advised that they should prepare for a morning take off and to attack at 13:00 hours.

Thursday 14th December 1944.
Preparations were made and crews stood by for briefing at 09:20 hours when word was received a one hour postponement. At 10:06 hours two crews of Six-thirty were detailed to join two of 57 Squadron in a minelaying operation. Nine minutes later the remainder of the crews were told that their mission was cancelled but to prepare for a night bombing attack that night. At 13:15 hours the night bombing attack was cancelled but the briefing for the minelaying crews went ahead at 13:30. Two Lancasters were detailed to plant mines in the U-boat passage routes of the Kattegat.

14th December 1944 : Night Minelaying Mission 'Silverthorne'
Take Off: at 15:27 hours Bill Adams (LL966) took off before Ainsley Thomas and returned after he had landed, at 22:05 hours. Both squadron aircraft had to be diverted to Spilsby on return.

NN702-J   W/O EA Thomas
LL966-P   Lt W Adams USAAF

In the 'Silverthorne' area visibility was good and from 15,000 feet the 2 Lancaster's planted their mines between 18:05 and 18:35 hours in the allotted positions without difficulty. Some heavy flak was encountered from a flak ship in the vicinity and a JU88 was seen but there were no combats. Preparations were made for an attack during Friday 15th but it was cancelled at 17:00 hours, put off until the following day when at 10:15 hours warning was received for a maximum effort raid. Full preparations were made, flight planning took place at 15:30 and aircrew briefing at 17:10 for a 22:00 hours attack. H-hour was delayed till 22:30 then 06:00 before the Op was scrubbed 45 minutes before take-off.

Sunday 17th December 1944.
At 10:30 a maximum effort attack was announced with flight planning commencing at 13:30 hours for an attack on the town centre and railways yards of Munich, 5 Group sent 280 Lancasters and 8 Mosquitos. 17 aircraft of Six-thirty were detailed each armed with 1 x 2000lb HC bombs and Mk.14 Incendiary clusters.

17th/18th December 1944 : Night Bombing Attack on Munich
Take Off: at 16:01 hours flight commander Squadron Leader Malcolm Eyre in LM260 and Bill Adams in ND949 were the first away.

ME312-A	F/O H Thompson
NG258-B	F/O A Stockill
LL949-E	F/O GR Scott RAAF
NG125-F	Capt DCB Reynolds SAAF
PD317-G	F/O PS Weston RNZAF
NN702-J	F/O LA Barnes
LM216-K	F/O HA Ramsey RNZAF
NG259-N	F/O GE Billing
LL966-P	F/O OJS Atkinson RAAF
ME845-Q	F/O RG Waterfall
PB344-R	Lt GR Lacey SAAF
LM260-S	S/L MA Eyre
ME739-T	F/O RJ Sassoon
NG123-U	F/O NG Roberts RAAF
PD254-W	Lt MT Ackerman SAAF
PD327-Y	F/O TB Baker RAAF
ND949-Z	Lt W Adams USAAF

En-route for the target all radio navigational aids aboard LM260 'S-Sugar' became unserviceable but Flight Lieutenant George Arkieson (Squadron Bombing Leader) aided Flight Lieutenant Bert Hewitt ensuring a successful attack. Arriving over the target the attacking force found the weather clear with some smoky haze low down. The markers were well concentrated and were believed to have been accurately placed. 630 Squadron attacked from 13,300 to 15,000 feet between 22:02 and 22:11 hours the target appeared well bombed. Again there were reports of incendiary clusters being dropped along the route home as far west as the Rhine. Heavy flak and search lights were active but there were no fighters in the TA. There was Intense light flak between Basle and Mulhaus. Neil Roberts RAAF flying MG123 was the last of the squadron to return at 02:17 hours. Bomber Command recorded severe and widespread damage in the city centre and in the marshalling yards.

Monday 18th December 1944.
The next attack involving the squadron was a 5 Group raid on Gdynia far across the Baltic Sea. The cruiser 'Lützow' was in port and was a prime target. 13 aircraft of 630 Squadron were detailed to participate in the attack and were bombed up with 9 x 1000lb HC. At the same time the squadron was instructed to provide aircraft and crews for a minelaying operation.

Henry Thompson's bombing photograph (Keith Arscott)

18th/19th December 1944 : Night Bombing Attack on Gdynia
Take Off: at 16:53 hours Steve Nunns and crew in NG125 were first away.

ME312-A	F/O PS Weston RNZAF	
JB290-C	F/O HA Ramsey	
LL949-E	F/O GR Scott RAAF	
NG125-F	F/L SA Nunns	
PD317-G	F/O EJ Monk	
LM216-K	Lt DS Turner SAAF	
LL966-P	Lt MT Ackerman SAAF	
ME845-Q	F/O RG Waterfall	
PB344-R	W/O GH Cowan	
LM260-S	F/O A McGuffie	RD
ME739-T	F/O RJ Sassoon	
NG123-U	F/O NG Roberts RAAF	
ND949-Z	Lt W Adams USAAF	

Lancaster PB344 "R-Roger" (Geoff Copeman)

'B-Baker' was unserviceable at the last moment leaving Geoff Stemp's crew unable to take off. In the target area over the harbour the warship designated as Six-thirty's aiming point was clearly seen in the expected position but it proved hard to get good bombing runs. Attacking from 11,600 to 14,000 feet between 22:01 and 22:08 hours, bombs were seen to straddle the ship and jetty and there was a large explosion on the jetty followed by an oil fire. George Radley, bomb aimer aboard Mathinus Ackerman's 'P-Prune' found at the critical moment that the bomb release 'tit' did not work and they had to orbit to make a second run effectively jettisoning their load over the red marker, 'U-Uncle' also had technical problems, Neil Roberts' bombs landed between the railway tracks and the docks. German records confirm damage to shipping, dockyard installations and housing in the town. Numerous searchlights were in action as were some single engined fighters over the target. Only Bill Adams and crew in 'Z-Zebra' landed back at base in thick fog, the Scott crew aboard 'E-Easy' landed at Strubby, all other crews landed at Woodbridge. South African Marthinus Ackerman was the last of the squadron to touch down at 03:59 hours.

Simultaneously three of the squadron's Lancasters planted mines, all 3 aircraft were armed with 6 x Mk.IV mines.

18th/19th December 1944 : Night Minelaying Mission 'Spinach South'
Take Off: at 03:02 hours NN703 (Frank Millar) was the first to take off.

NN702-J	W/O EA Thomas
PD254-W	F/L M Miller
NN703-X	F/O FE Millar RNZAF

Weather was clear and no opposition was encountered when mines were laid from 14,000 feet at 21:55 hours by Matt Miller's crew and 15,000 feet at 22:07 by Ainsley Thomas' crew. A JU88 was seen but it did not attack. NN703 'X-X ray' brought its mines back as their H2S failed and planting would not have been reliable. Thomas and Millar landed at Woodbridge on their return in very poor weather conditions Frank Millar being the last down at 03:02 hours. On Tuesday 19th December 1944 an op was planned to attack Kaiserslautern, with preparations nearing completion and the aircrew briefing in progress news was received at 14:05 hours to scrub the mission due to bad weather in the target area. Poor weather then descended on East Kirkby preventing any further flying.

Thursday 21st December 1944 – 207 Lancasters and 1 Mosquito of 5 Group attacked the Synthetic Oil Plant at Pölitz. 6 aircraft of 630 Squadron were detailed for the attack and bombed up with 1 x 4000lb HC Minol and 12 x 500lb (Tail Inst) bombs.

21st/22nd December 1944 : Night Bombing Attack on Pölitz
Take Off: at 16:55 hours NN703 (Henry Archer) took off from East Kirkby first.

NG258-B	F/O A Stockill
NG259-N	F/O GE Billing
LM287-O	F/O FE Millar RNZAF
PD254-W	F/O M Miller
NN703-X	F/L HD Archer
PD327-Y	P/O TB Baker RAAF

The attack was late to start as crews had to orbit whilst the placement of the markers was assessed. The red and green TIs were found to be 300 yards north of the target and with an adjustment for that the Controller ordered the attack to commence. The attack took place between 22:04 and 22:11 hours from 15,500 to 18,000 feet and some good fires and large explosions were seen. There were numerous searchlights but very little flak and very few sightings of enemy fighters. On return 'W-William' was diverted to Kinloss, 'X-X ray' to Carnaby, 'B-Baker' and 'Y-Yoke' to Strubby.

Lancaster I, NG258 (Codes LE – B)

Pilot	– F/O Arnold Stockill. Age 31	Killed
Flight Eng	– Sgt James Duffett. Age 21	Killed
Navigator	– F/O William McPherson James. Age 31	Killed
Bomb Aimer	– Sgt Raymond Athol Bruck. Age 22	Killed
Wireless Op	– Sgt James Stuart Bain. Age 20	Killed
Mid Upper	– Sgt John Henry Quinlivan. Age 20	Killed
Rear Gunner	– Sgt Leslie George Pooley. Age 19	injured

Harry Ramsey RNZAF (Peter and Gael Ramsey) *Jerry Monk (EJ Monk)*

Matt Miller and crew (Joyce Boldero)

Diverted to Strubby due to weather conditions at base 'B-Baker' crashed at 03:20 hours at Scrafield Farm between Scrafield and Mareham-on-the-Hill. The dead were buried near to their home towns or relatives across the country. Stockill was cremated at Darlington, Duffett buried at Colchester, James at Stockton-on-Tees (Oxbridge Road) Cemetery, Bruck at Tankersley (St Peter) Churchyard, Bain at Edinburgh (Liberton) Cemetery and Quinlivan Park Cemetery, London. Their teenage rear gunner Les Pooley from Wisbech survived injured and was taken to Woodhall Spa Hospital where he recovered.

Aircraft diverted to other stations were ordered to remain there until the weather cleared and due to persistent fog were away until after Christmas. Post raid photo reconnaissance showed that the chimneys of the power station serving the plant had collapsed and that other damage had been caused. The return to East Kirkby of 'O – Oboe' was certainly in filthy weather however her crew were elated, New Zealander Frank Millar's lads had never missed an op together and had completed their tour, they were screened and their pilot recommended for a DFC.

Tuesday 26th December 1944.

After several days of filthy weather the conditions suddenly improved and Bomber Command supported ground actions in the fighting in the Ardennes. A mixed group mission comprising 294 aircraft attacked Wehrmacht positions near St. Vith. Six-thirty were ordered to provide 2 aircraft armed with 14 x 1000lb bombs. It was decided to detail aircraft which had been waiting to return to base from stations which they had been diverted to.

Left: Ray Bruck serving as a police constable pre-war (LAHC Archive) Right: Jonny Quinlivan (Quinlivan family)

26th December 1944 : Night Bombing Attack on St. Vith
Take Off: at 13:15 hours LM287 was the first of the two to take off and also coincidentally would be the last to land at 18:10 hours.

NG259-N   F/O EJ Monk
LM287-O   F/O NG Roberts RAAF

Aircraft climbed to bombing height and encountered no flak until the target was reached where moderate flak came up. Crews were briefed to bomb the Red TIs and as the target was well marked and visibility good, a good concentration of bombing was observed. The 630 Squadron pair attacked from 13,200 to 13,900 feet at 15:31 and 15:33 hours. Jerry Monk later recalled that they attacked in brilliant sunshine beneath a formation of hundreds of Halifaxes which bombed from six thousand feet above, with thousand pounders and window falling all around. Both aircraft were diverted again on their return, this time to St. Eval a Coastal Command station in Cornwall where the visiting crews reported feeling less than welcome. Two days later when the weather cleared in Lincolnshire and they were able to escape, they roared off the end of St. Eval's cliff top runway and Jerry Monk turned back to 'beat up' the airfield before making a low run past the Flying Control with his crew all making the less polite V for Victory towards their former hosts. Back at East Kirkby Jerry was hauled before the CO who had received a bumpy telephone call from his opposite number at St. Eval. With hindsight it was speculated that this incident on an otherwise spotless operational record could be the reason that Jerry Monks did not receive a DFC on completion of his tour.

With training flights scheduled an order was received for an op and Six-thirty detailed aircraft X, Y, E and R which were on the deck at Strubby. The Lancasters were bombed up and their crews briefed at Strubby. As the day commenced the squadrons' aircraft which had been sitting on other bases all returned, N and O from St Eval, J from Spilsby, C, F, G, K, Q, T, P and U from Swinderby and Z from Woodbridge.

Thursday 28th December 1944.
5 Group mounted a raid comprising 67 Lancasters and 1 Mosquito to attack a 'large naval unit' – the cruiser 'Köln' and nearby shipping off Horten in Oslofjord. Four aircraft were detailed but only three took off each armed with 13 x 1000lb bombs. As mentioned above the crews took off from Strubby where they had been diverted.

28th/29th December 1944 : Night Bombing Attack on shipping in Oslofjord
Take off: at 19:39 hours Warrant Officer George Cowan and crew (PB344) led the section. 'E-Easy' (McGuffie) did not take off due to brake pressure problems.

PB344-R   W/O GH Cowan
PD327-Y   P/O TB Baker RAAF
NN703-X   F/L HD Archer

630 Squadron crews attacked between 23:49 and 23:59 hours from 7,500 to 8,000 feet bombing visually by moonlight but Wanganui and sea markers were used as proximity markers. A thin layer of cloud obscured the moon and made identification of the ships difficult. The Kriegsmarine cruiser 'Köln' could not be found and despite crews remaining over the target area in the face of intense light flak for 31 minutes it was impossible to gain any hits on the target vessels however U-735 was bombed and sunk, her commander and over half of her crew killed. Squadron aircraft landed back at East Kirkby, where Tom Baker (PD327) as the last to touch down at 02:51 hours.

Jerry Monk and crew (EJ Monk)

Friday 29th December 1944.
At 10:55 hours on 29th the squadron were warned of a minelaying Op and crews were briefed at 14:15. Two aircraft were despatched with mines.

29th /30th December 1944 : Night Minelaying 'Onions Area'
Take off: at 15:57 hours Matt Miller in PD254 was first away followed a minute later by Steve Nunns in NG125.

NG125-F   F/L SA Nunns
PD254-W   F/O M Miller

At 19:06 and 19:09 hours from 12,000 feet both crews planted their vegetables in position using H2S and available landmarks. Slight heavy flak emanated from Oslo and some light flak from ships in the fjord but thankfully no fighters were seen. At 22:45 hours NG125 touched down at base 4 minutes after PD254.

Saturday 30th December 1944.
Scheduled to participate in a daylight attack 630 Squadron carried out flight planning and aircrew briefings from 08:45 hours. Aircraft were taxying around the perimeter towards the runway to take off when the mission was cancelled at 11:23 hours. Just over an hour later orders were received to prepare for a night attack. At mid-day on Saturday 30th December a B-17 Flying Fortress of 8th USAAF crashed in flames at East Kirkby while trying to land in bad visibility, sadly the entire crew were killed. During the afternoon aircraft were prepared and their crews briefed at 22:10 hours. 5 Group carried out an attack using 154 Lancasters and 12 Mosquitoes against an identified German military supply bottleneck in a narrow valley at Houffalize. 12 aircraft of 630 Squadron were detailed to participate and were bombed up with 6 x 900lb and 12 x 1000lb.

30th /31st December 1944 : Night Bombing Attack on Houffalize
Take Off: at 02:12 hours Desmond Reynolds in NG125 was first off the deck.

NG125-F	Capt DCB Reynolds
NN702-J	F/O EJ Monk
LM216-K	F/O JW Hoare RAAF
NG259-N	F/O LA Barnes
LM287-O	F/O RJ Sassoon
LL966-P	Lt GR Lacey SAAF
ME845-Q	F/O NG Roberts RAAF
ME739-T	F/O RA Stone RNZAF
PD254-W	F/O AM Maclean RCAF
NN703-X	F/O HA Ramsey RNZAF
PD327-Y	F/O TB Baker RAAF
ND949-Z	W/O GH Cowan

The squadron's crews attacked between 05:00 and 05:05 hours from 5,000 to 11,500 feet. Solid cloud lay over the target with occasional breaks and crews who bombed saw the TIs cascading on the ground through patches of thin cloud and often only at the last minute. Jack Hoare's crew descended below the clouds to 5,000 feet and bombed in clear visibility observing that a good concentration of bombing was falling around the TIs. The crews of F, J, N T and Z did not bomb. No fighter opposition was fielded by the Luftwaffe. Len Barnes (NG259) was the last to return to base at 07:56 hours. The aircraft flown by the Ramsey and Cowan crews may have been transposed.

Sunday 31st December 1944.

At 10:40 hours an order was received for a minelaying mission, aircrew briefing commenced at 13:00 hours. 2 Lancasters of Six-thirty participated in a small scale mining operation, each carrying 6 x Mk.IV mines in u-boat transit channels in the Kattegat area.

31st December 1944/1st January 1945 : Night Minelaying in 'Yew Trees' area
Take Off: at 16:20 hours PB894 (Ainsley Thomas) was the first to take off.

PB894-A	W/O EA Thomas
LM287-O	F/O M Miller

Mines were planted at 20:24 hours from 15,000 feet by Matt Miller in LM287 which returned to base at 23:08 hours. Night fighters are known to have been active in the area and Ainsley Thomas' crew Failed To Return.

Lancaster I, PB894 (Codes LE – A)

Pilot	– W/O Edward Ainsley Thomas. Age 26	Killed
Flight Eng	– Sgt David Daniel Jones. Age 31	Killed
Navigator	– F/S William Henry McDonald Marshall. Age 23	Killed
Bomb Aimer	– F/S Eric Leese. Age 23	Killed
Wireless Op	– F/S Joseph Henry Jones. Age 23	Killed
Mid Upper	– Sgt Bernard John Phillips. Age 30	Killed
Rear Gunner	– Sgt George Rex Boden. Age 22	Killed

It is believed that PB894 was the Lancaster claimed by Hauptmann Eduard Schröder of 3/NJG 3 at 2,800 metres altitude over the sea 50 km north-west of Hanstholm at about 21:00 hours, it was his 18th victory. The Lancaster dived directly into the sea. Commemorated on Runnymede Memorial.

A former Police Constable and coroners officer in the West Somerset Constabulary, Ainsley Thomas had taken to flying as he had to rugby football, he was a natural being commissioned Pilot Officer in October 1942 when he completed pilot training. He had been a member of the then undefeated Somerset Police Rugby Football Club sometimes representing the county of Somerset at county level. A married man with two small children Ainsley Thomas had then been in trouble for extremely low flying over houses at his home town Caerau in Wales and been dismissed by the RAF. Unwilling to sit on the side-lines he re-enlisted and worked his way up through the ranks again. By the time of their loss he was a Warrant Officer and may not have known that his re-commission as Pilot Officer had actually come through.

George Boden (Andrew Swann)

January 1945

Monday 1st January 1945. 102 Lancasters and 2 Mosquitoes of 5 Group were despatched to attack the section of the canal near Ladbergen which had been recently repaired. Ten aircraft of 630 Squadron were bombed up with 14 x 1000lb MC (30 mins delay).

1st January 1945 : Daylight Bombing Attack on Dortmund-Ems Canal, Ladbergen
Take Off: following Henry Archer in NN703 at 07:45 hours.

PB880-B	F/O HA Ramsey RNZAF
NG125-F	Capt DCB Reynolds SAAF
NN702-J	P/O EJ Monk
LM216-K	F/O GR Scott RAAF
NG259-N	F/O LA Barnes
LM287-O	F/O A McGuffie
LL966-P	Lt GR Lacey SAAF
ME845-Q	F/O NG Roberts RAAF
PD254-W	F/O AM Maclean RCAF
NN703-X	F/L HD Archer

630 Squadron dispersal in Jan 1945 (Brian Garbett/Mike Goulding)

Weather at target area was clear with excellent visibility and all bomb aimers saw the target clearly and identified the aiming point. The Red TIs straddled the aiming point about 300 yards to the north and south. The squadron's crews attacked from 9,200 to 10,000 feet between 11:16 and 11:18 hours and the bombing was later assessed as very good with a very large number of bombs landing in the vicinity of the aiming point. Results were not observed due to the delayed action bombs. No fighters were seen but some heavy flak was accurate and some aircraft damaged. NN703 had been the first to take off and was also the last to land when it touched down at 13:45 hours. Post-raid photo reconnaissance showed that the canal had been breached again and was drained of water for some distance. One of the two 5 Group Lancasters lost was a 9 Squadron aircraft (Flying Officer RFH Denton) which was hit by flak shortly after bombing. The aircraft caught fire and the Wireless Operator Flight Sergeant George Thompson suffered severe burns as he rescued both gunners who were trapped by the blaze. Denton managed to crash land the aircraft but the Mid Upper gunner, Sgt Ernest John Potts, aged 30, died later due to his burns and three weeks later George Thompson died of burns, he was awarded a posthumous Victoria Cross.

That same evening a second attack was planned to maintain the pressure on the inland waterways system so vital to German war production 5 Group returned to the canals again that night attacking the Mittelland Canal at Gravenhorst with 152 Lancasters and 5 Mosquitoes. 6 Lancasters of Six-thirty participated, each armed with 14 x 1000lb (30 mins delay).

1st/2nd January 1945 : Night Bombing Attack on Mittelland Canal, Gravenhorst
Take Off: 17:03 hours PD253 and ND554 (Steve Nunns and Jack Hoare) were the first airborne.

PD253-D	F/L SA Nunns
ND554-E	F/O JW Hoare RAAF
PB344-R	W/O GH Cowan
ME739-T	F/O RJ Sassoon
PD327-Y	F/O TB Baker RAAF
ND949-Z	Lt MT Ackerman SAAF

Weather conditions at East Kirkby were very poor and the Lancasters took off from base into 600 feet of haze. Crossing the North Sea the conditions were better but at 18:38 the force had to climb at the Dutch Coast due to heavy cloud, reaching the pre-designated height for the wave at 9,600 feet they reached the target without opposition. Flares were already going down on arrival and a string of Red and Green TIs went down across the aiming point. At 19:03 hours the Controller confirmed that the markers were accurate and over the R/T ordered the main force to attack. 630 Squadron attacked between 19:14 hours and 19:20 hours from 9,600 to 12,000 feet and bombing appeared to be very accurate, some bombs exploded in the TA despite being set with delays. A few scattered bursts of heavy flak were encountered and heading for the French coast there were scattered concentrations of search lights which seemed unable to cone any of the bombers and finally heavy flak near the enemy front line. On return East Kirkby was still shrouded in haze and all aircraft landed at Kinross in Scotland, Steve Nunns landed the last at 00:14 hours. The attack was accurate, a half mile stretch of banks were badly pitted with bomb craters and there were some breaches which allowed the water to escape. On completion of repairs in late Nov 1944 ND554 was re-coded from 'A-Able' to 'E-Easy' ready to re-commence ops in January 1945.

At 09:15 hours the following morning all aircraft and crews were ordered to return to base from Scotland to land after midday, it was expected that they would be participating in an attack later that day. The first aircraft to return to East Kirkby landed at 13:30 hours with others touching down through the afternoon. At 17:30 the squadron was stood down. On Wednesday 3rd January with a westerly gale forecast all projected operations were cancelled however at 11:00 on the next morning preliminary warning was received for an operation that night with a projected H-hour of 04:00 on the morning of 5th January.

Thursday 4th January 1945.
At 17:00 hours flight planning commenced and aircrew briefings took place at 21:00 hours. Royan is a town situated at the mouth of the River Gironde which was well garrisoned with a strong force of German soldiers. Two Fortresses Gironde Mündung Nord (north, at Royan) and Gironde Mündung Süd (south, at La Point de Grave) were holding out long after the liberation of the remainder of the country and were besieged by 12,000 French Resistance fighters under control of the Free French Army under General de Laminat and General de Gaulle and without sufficient heavy artillery little progress was being made. Following a meeting between US and French military authorities a request for a heavy bomber attack was processed through SHAEF (Supreme HQ Allied Expeditionary Forces) and passed to Bomber Command.

347 Lancasters and 7 Mosquitoes of 1, 5 and 8 Groups attacked in the early hours of 5th January 1945 with 1,576 tons of high explosive bombs including 285 x 4,000lbers. Eighteen aircraft of 630 Squadron were detailed, each armed with 1 x 4000lb HC Minol and 16 x 500lb MC (.025),

4th/5th January 1945 : Night Bombing Attack on Royan

Take Off: at 00:42 hours South African Marthinus Ackerman was first away.

PB880-B	F/O GR Scott RAAF
PD253-D	F/O HA Ramsey RNZAF
ND554-E	F/O H Thompson
NG125-F	F/O JW Hoare RAAF
PD317-G	F/O EJ Monk
LM216-K	Lt DS Turner SAAF
NN702-J	F/O DA Clifford
NG259-N	F/O LA Barnes
LM287-O	F/O NG Roberts RAAF
LL966-P	Lt GR Lacey SAAF
ME845-Q	F/O RG Waterfall
PB344-R	Lt MT Ackerman SAAF
ME739-T	Lt W Adams USAAF
NG123-U	F/O EC Harris RNZAF
NG413-V	R/O RJ Sassoon
PD254-W	F/O M Miller
NN703-X	F/L HD Archer
PD327-Y	F/O TB Baker RAAF
ND949-Z	F/O LF Ovens

Henry Archer (Matthew Archer)

The weather was clear but with some haze or smoke in the later stages of the attack. The squadron attacked between 04:04 and 04:15 hours from 8,250 to 9,000 feet. Many aircraft had to make 2 bombing runs as the initial markers were found to be inaccurate and had to be re-done. Some crews evidently misunderstood the bombing instructions however a good spread of bombing was achieved. There was some flak in the target area but no fighters reported. Crews reported 'scarecrow flares' thought to be fired up to simulate the orange glow of burning bombers falling to earth. In fact the Germans had no such device and what the crews were seeing were actually bombers being shot down in flames. The last to return were Richard Sassoon and crew at 08:04 hours. The German garrison eventually surrendered on 18th April 1945. The starboard inner engine of Lieut. Ackerman's PB344 'R - Roger' failed in the outward flight however he and his crew were unwilling to turn for home and flew on to attack the target and then return home successfully on just 3 engines. After five straight months operational service with 630 Squadron deputy flight commander Henry Archer's crew landed to receive confirmation that their tour was completed, their captain was recommended for a DFC and he in turn strongly recommended Rees

Jerry Monk's crew with Lancaster PD317 'LE – G' (Bob Baldwin)

Rawlings his Welsh navigator just a week or two short of his 25th birthday and Stan Spencer his bomb aimer for awards, sadly the latter two did not apparently get through the system. Henry Archer's crew are not shown in the 630 Squadron 'Operations Record Book' as participating in the Royan attack however one of his gunners confirmed that they did fly and this is confirmed by the recommendation for Archer's DFC which lists this attack amongst the total of 30.

The attached USAAF pilot Bill Adams had completed 30 ops with 630 Squadron at this stage but rather than complete their tour and settle to instructing his crew opted to 'extend' and transferred to 617 Squadron (effective 16th January) continuing to fly operationally. During the day the new Chaplain, Squadron Leader The Rev. WJ Mulholland[i] arrived from 2 FIS at Montrose to take up his duties at RAF East Kirkby.

Friday 5th January 1945.
5 Group mounted another attack on the German supply bottleneck at Houffalize in the Ardennes, this time despatching 131 Lancasters and 9 Mosquitoes. At briefing the aircrew were told very clearly that due to the close proximity of Allied ground forces any crew who were unable to make a satisfactory identification of the target were not to make a second bombing run or orbit to await an opportunity, but they were to turn for home and bring their payload home. It is uncertain if 12 or 9 aircraft were scheduled to participate however 9 Lancasters and crews of the squadron were tasked and bombed up with 11 x 1000lb HC Minol (fused tail .025).

5th/6th January 1945 : Night Bombing Attack on Houffalize
Take Off: at 00:06 hours Squadron Leader Marcel Cuelenaere (Flight Commander) was first airborne in NG125.

PB880-B	F/O GR Scott RAAF
ND554-E	F/O H Thompson
NG125-F	S/L MR Cuelenaere RCAF
NN702-J	F/O EJ Monk
ME845-Q	F/O JW Hoare RAAF
NG259-N	F/O LA Barnes
PB344-R	F/O JW Langley
NN703-X	F/O NG Roberts RAAF
PD327-Y	F/O TB Baker RAAF

10/10ths cloud was encountered over the target but visibility above the clouds was good. The TIs were seen as expected cascading and glowing below the cloud, green TIs in close proximity to the red were the aiming point. A good concentration of bombing was reported when the squadron attacked between 03:01 and 03:06 hours from 9,750 to 12,000 feet. No fighters and little heavy flak were encountered but the flak which was active was very accurate and 2 aircraft were damaged. The attack was rated as very accurate. The last to return was Len Barnes (NG259) at 06:05 hours. Four additional crews did not take off for the attack, Matt Miller's (in 'P-Peter'), Eric Harris' (in 'U-Uncle'), Richard Sassoon's (in 'V-Victory') and Jim Ovens' (in 'Z-Zebra') the reason for these being scrubbed is not recorded.

Saturday 6th January 1945.
Notification of a mining mission was received at 10:10 hours, the details followed at 10:55 and crews were briefed at 13:45 hours, taking off at 16:05 only to be ordered to return to bases. Visibility over East Kirkby was very poor and crews had to divert to Strubby until base was again fit to land at 23:00 hours. The mining operation went ahead later that night and 3 Lancasters from Six-thirty participated each carrying 6 x Mk.IV mines.

6th/7th January 1945 : Night Minelaying in 'Spinach' area
Take Off: at 01:39 hours flying LL966 Reg Waterfall and crew were first away

NG125-F	F/L SA Nunns
PD317-G	Lt DS Turner SAAF
LL966-P	F/O RG Waterfall

There was no fighter opposition and little flak although fighter flares were seen over Denmark. Mines were laid in Danzig Bay off Gdynia between 20:41 and 20:53 hours all from 14.750 feet in allotted positions, crews able to be certain based on visual identification of Hel Point but backed up with H2S. Despite some considerable light flak of great accuracy fired from Sweden all three aircraft returned safely, Steve Nunns being the last to touch down at 10:01 hours.

Sunday 7th January 1945.
The last of the aircraft which had landed at Strubby were flown back to East Kirkby during Sunday 7th January in preparation for a night operation. At 13:00 hours the flight planning and navigation briefing commenced, followed 30 minutes later by the pilot's and crews briefing. At 15:30 hours a warning of expected snow during the next 24 hours was received. Bomber Command made its last major attack on Munich with 645 Lancasters and 9 Mosquitoes of 1, 3, 5, 6 and 8 Groups. 14 aircraft of Six-thirty were detailed for operations and each bombed up with 1 x 4000lb HC Minol and 10 x No.14 Cluster incendiaries.

7th/8th January 1945 : Night Bombing Attack on Munich

Take off: at 16:39 hours Wing Commander John Grindon (NG259) and John Langley (LM216) were the first airborne.

PB880-B	F/O DA Clifford
PD253-D	F/O HA Ramsey RNZAF
ND554-E	F/O LA Barnes
LM216-K	F/O JW Langley
NG259-N	W/C JE Grindon
LM287-O	Lt MT Ackerman SAAF
PB344-R	F/O NG Roberts RAAF
ME739-T	S/L MA Eyre
NG123-U	F/O EC Harris RNZAF
NG413-V	F/O RJ Sassoon
PD254-W	F/O M Miller
NN703-X	Lt GR Lacey SAAF
PD327-Y	F/O JW Hoare RAAF
ND949-Z	F/O LF Ovens
PD317-G	F/O GE Billing

Left: Gordon Lacey SAAF (B Jadot/Morgana) Above: The Billings crew crash summary (The National Archives)

Henry Thompson and crew in 'J-Jig' were unable to take off due to technical problems and Reg Waterfall in 'Q-Queen' had to abort their take off due to a burst tyre. Len Barnes in 'E-Easy' returned early when the rudder control bar seized solid and John Langley in 'K-King' with engine failure, both jettisoned their 4000 pounders at sea and returned with their load of incendiaries. Thin cloud was encountered over the target but it broke at 16,500 to 18,500 feet and some crews climbed above the cloud to bomb, all crews saw the green TIs and attacked as instructed. The squadron attacked between 20:31 and 20:40 hours from 15,700 to 18,000 feet. Bombing was well spread over the northern districts and at 20:52 hours when the last aircraft bombed, the north of the city seemed to be a mass of flames. A very large explosion was reported at 20:45 hours. Ground defences were negligible and few enemy aircraft seen. One combat took place over the target but was inconclusive. The last of the squadron to return safely was NN703 (Gordon Lacey) at 02:35 hours.

PD317 'G-George' took off at 16:45 hours but apparently lost its port inner engine almost immediately after take-off, the crew jettisoned their 4000lb HC(M) into the sea and arrived back over base at 17:45 hours. Making a circuit approach on 3 engines the Lancaster bounced badly and cartwheeled across the field onto its port wing tip, crashing.

Lancaster I, PD317 (Codes LE – G)

Pilot	– F/O George Ernest Billing. Age 24	injured
Flight Eng	– Sgt Sidney Harris. Age	injured
Navigator	– F/S Arthur Hobson. Age 23	Killed
Bomb Aimer	– F/O Leonard Knowles. Age	injured
Wireless Op	– Sgt John Williamson Duncan. Age	injured
Mid Upper	– Sgt Denis Albert Holloway. Age 27	Killed
Rear Gunner	– F/S David Gordon Todd RAAF. Age 20	injured

24 year old 'Billy' Billing was thrown clear of the wreckage still strapped into his seat but sustaining injuries which resulted in the loss of an arm, he also suffered a fractured skull and burns, Len Knowles and John Duncan had burns to their hands and faces and flight engineer Sergeant Harris had a lacerated scalp, all were transferred to RAF Hospital Rauceby by ambulance. Flight Sergeant David Todd sustained damage to the bones of his legs and left knee which resulted in him being hospitalised on 8th January. Sadly their navigator and mid-upper gunner were killed, they were later returned to their home towns of Barnsley and Coventry for burial and cremation respectively. The wounded all recovered from their injuries, some later returning to operations with 630 Squadron.

Bob Knight RNZAF (J Knight)

On Tuesday 9th January during a lull in Ops another new crew arrived, that of Bob Knight[ii] a keen deer stalker and fisherman from Waiuku, NZ where he'd grown up on his father's farm. He volunteered for aircrew duty and trained in New Zealand and the UK. Bob Knight had survived a mid-air collision at 3 EFTS (the junior pilot of the other Tiger Moth and his instructor were both killed). At 10 OTU the crew had survived when they crashed on take-off in Whitley (Z6499) at Stanton Harcourt on 31st July 1944 whilst flown by another pilot. On the night of 23rd August, still with 10 OTU, having been promoted Flight Sergeant, he was pilot of Whitley BD215 on a cross country training flight when he made a heavy landing on return to base. Attempting to go around again the port engine cut out and the bomber swung ending up in a quarry 200 yards beyond the runway. All of his crew escaped unhurt apart from the rear gunner (Sergeant Cameron) who was injured. The entire crew, plus their flight engineer, joined Six-thirty intact to commence their tour of Ops.

In a series of days marked by very poor weather the squadron was stood down day after day and maximum effort was given by the ground crews to ensuring the serviceability of every single aircraft and to various escape drills and trade proficiencies by the aircrews On 12th January the Station Dental Officer, Flying Officer JW Price took up his post.

Saturday 13th January 1945.
218 Lancasters and 7 Mosquitoes of 5 Group attacked the oil plant at Pölitz near Stettin. 15 Lancasters of Six-thirty were detailed for Ops, ten carrying 1 x 4000lb HC and 8 x 500lb M64 (.025) and 1 x 500lb MC LD 6 hours and five carried 1 x 4000lb HC and 11 x 500lb M64 (.025) and 1 x 500lb MC LD 6 hours. A mining operation was also carried out in the area code-named 'Geranium'.

13th/14th January 1945 : Night Bombing Attack on Politz
Take Off: at 16:04 hours Squadron Leader Marcel Cuelenaere (NG125) was the first away.

PD253-D	F/O HA Ramsey RNZAF
PB880-B	F/O JW Langley
NG125-F	S/L MR Cuelenaere RCAF
ND412-H	F/O H Thompson
NN702-J	F/O DA Clifford
LM216-K	F/O JW Hoare RAAF
NG259-N	S/L MA Eyre
LM287-O	Lt MT Ackerman SAAF
LL966-P	F/O OJS Atkinson RAAF
PB344-R	F/O LA Barnes
ME739-T	F/O RA Stone RNZAF
NG123-U	F/O A McGuffie
PD254-W	F/O NG Roberts RAAF
PD327-Y	F/O AM Maclean RCAF
ND949-Z	F/O LF Ovens

F/O Albert MacLean RCAF landed 'Y-Yoke' at Carnaby at 02:00 hours after their port outer engine failed. Expecting to carry out a blind bombing attack due to forecast weather conditions the force arrived over the target to find some visibility. Low level ground marking was carried out and crews instructed to bomb concentration of Red TIs ignoring the more isolated ones. The Controller was heard to comment on the accuracy of the bombing and the attack was a success. The squadron attacked between 22:15 and 22:25 hours from 14,500 to 18,250 feet. Several heavy explosions were noted particularly at 22:17 hours just as 'Olly' Atkinson and 'Cliff' Clifford's crews were bombing, it gave off thick dense smoke and the shock wave was felt by crews up to 18,000 feet. Clifford's crew attacked despite their bomb aimer being taken ill. 50-80 search lights were active but flak was slight. No fighters were found over the target but there were three combats which produced no claims. Photographs showed the oil plant reduced to scrap metal. 'Jim' Ovens (ND949) was the last to return ,at 03:30 hours. One 630 Squadron Lancaster Failed To Return.

Lancaster I, PB880 (Codes LE – B)

Pilot	– F/O John William Langley. Age 23	interned
Flight Eng	– Sgt Joseph R Thomas. Age	interned
Navigator	– F/S George Bernard Gaughan. Age 21	interned
Bomb Aimer	– F/S Ivor James Penglase RAAF. Age 24	interned
Wireless Op	– W/O Sydney Harold Potter RNZAF. Age 34	interned
Mid Upper	– W/O Ernest James Edwards. Age	Died
Rear Gunner	– F/S Thomas William Panting RCAF. Age 19	interned

On the outbound flight the starboard outer engine began to play up and whilst passing over Denmark at about 20:15 hours it caught fire. Despite great efforts the fire could not be put out nor the prop feathered so reaching the coast of Sweden the crew identified Bastad 20 miles north of Halsingborg and baled out at 8,000 feet . Sadly W/O Edwards hit the tail plane and suffered fatal head wounds, he died the following day and was buried at municipal cemetery Halsingborg (Palsjo). The remaining crew had all landed safely on the outskirts of the town and within an hour were mustered in the sitting room of a local home. By 01:00 hours they had been collected by the Swedish Army and taken to a local military camp ready to be moved again at 14:00 hours to a detention barracks at Halsingborg. They were quizzed by a Swedish Army officer and at 21:00 on the 15th of January moved to an Internment Camp at Falun (120 miles north of Stockholm). The crew remained there together until 13th March when they were taken to Stockholm and at 19:00 on the following day were flown back to the UK. On the same night as the attack on Pölitz the squadron provided three aircraft for a minelaying operation in the Pomeranian Bay off Swinemünde each carrying six MkIV mines.

13th/14th January 1945 : Night Minelaying in 'Geranium' garden
Take Off: at 16:11 hours ME845 (Reg Waterfall) was the first off the deck.

NG413-M	F/O GE Stemp
ME845-Q	F/O RG Waterfall
NN703-X	F/O M Miller

One fighter was seen in the area but there was no flak opposition and the mines were planted from 15,000 feet between 21:54 and 22:03 hours in their required positions despite some cloud. At 21:54 hours Geoff Stemp's crew in 'M-Mother' had to 'plant' their 'vegetables' without the benefit of Loran or H2S both of which failed. Her crew were the last of the three to return to base, landing at 02:42 hours. On returning Matt Miller's crew reported that two of the static lines for the mine parachutes were badly worn and frayed.

Sunday 14th January 1945.
At 09:54 hours warning was received from Group of a Maximum Effort attack, route planning and operational plans arrived at 10:37 and at 13:00 flight planning and Navigators briefing commenced, the Pilot's briefing was at 13:30 and main briefing at 14:00 hours. 573 Lancasters and 14 Mosquitoes of 1, 5, 6 and 8 Groups carried out 2 attacks separated by three hours on the Leuna synthetic Oil Plant near Merseburg. 13 aircraft of the squadron were detailed, briefing was at 13:30 hours and the Lancasters were armed with 1 x 4000lb MC M2 NInst and 11 x 500lb MC .025 and 1 x 500lb MC LD (12 hours).

14th/15th January 1945 : Night Bombing Attack on Leuna near Merseburg
Take Off: at 16:107 hours 'Jim' Ovens (ND949) was the first away.

JB290-C	F/O PS Weston RNZAF	
PD253-D	F/O LA Barnes	RD
NG125-F	F/O HA Ramsey RNZAF	
ND412-H	F/O H Thompson	
NN702-J	F/O EJ Monk	
NG413-M	F/O GE Stemp	
LL966-P	F/O OJS Atkinson RAAF	
ME845-Q	Lt MT Ackerman SAAF	
PB344-R	F/O A McGuffie	
ME739-T	F/O RA Stone RNZAF	
NN703-X	F/O NG Roberts RAAF	
NG123-U	F/O DA Clifford	
ND949-Z	F/O LF Ovens	

Leuna was reached without opposition, the marking was on time and assessed as very accurate and the resulting bombing very concentrated. The squadron attacked from 14,100 to 17,000 feet between 21:02 and 21:11 hours. A large concentration of search lights were active in the target area but they were ineffective although there was considerable flak opposition. Weather was very poor on returning to base and all aircraft were diverted to Tholthorpe. Len Barnes landed PD253 at 02:30 hours, the last of the squadron to touch down. Crews returned to East Kirkby throughout the day and were de-briefed for a second time on arrival. Albert Speer mentioned during his post-war interrogations that this raid was one of the most damaging of a series against the synthetic oil industry. On 16th January 1945 Lieutenant Bill Adams and his crew transferred to 617 Squadron after a party in the mess.

Bill Adams USAAF and crew (Deirdre, Gill Pratt's daughter)

Tuesday 16th January 1945.

The emphasis of Bomber Command was very much on oil and 1 and 5 Group despatched 231 Lancasters and 6 Mosquitoes to the synthetic oil plant at Brüx in western Czechoslovakia. 15 aircraft and crews of the squadron were detailed and each Lancaster bombed up with 1 x 4000lb HC N Inst M2 and 9 x 500lb MC TD 025.

16th/17th January 1945 : Night Bombing Attack on Brüx

Take Off: at 17:45 hours Squadron Leader Marcel Cuelenaere (NG259) was the first away.

JB290-C	F/O JW Hoare RAAF
PD253-D	F/O HA Ramsey RNZAF
ND554-E	F/O LA Barnes
NG125-F	F/O PS Weston RNZAF
ND412-H	F/O H Thompson
NN702-J	F/O DA Clifford
NG413-M	F/O GE Stemp
LM287-O	W/O GH Cowan
NG259-N	S/L MR Cuelenaere RCAF
LL966-P	F/O OJS Atkinson RAAF
ME845-Q	F/O RA Stone
NG123-U	F/O EC Harris RNZAF
PD254-W	F/O M Miller
NN703-X	F/O A McGuffie
ND949-Z	F/O LF Ovens

On arrival over the target the Controller instructed crews to hold for 2 minutes but at 22:31 hours gave the order to attack the green and red TIs. The latter being regarded as close to the chimneys at the southern end of the target. The squadron attacked between 22:31 and 22:37 hours from 14,200 to 16,750 feet. Bombing was reported to be concentrated and a pall of black smoke was seen above the cloud layer after the attack concluded. Moderate heavy flak was encountered in the TA and several fighters were seen some of which may have tried to follow the bombers on the route home. A FW190 was seen at 23:19 hours. There

Jimmy Wallace RNZAF and crew (Kay Rowland)

were 2 combats in the TA. Aboard Harry Ramsey's PD253 'D-Dog' which was making its bombing run the rear gunner Sergeant Hugh McDonald sighted a JU88 night fighter which both gunners poured fire into, Sergeant Matt Barry the mid-upper gunner commented that the German fighter staggered and fell away shedding pieces before it crashed in flames. It was claimed as destroyed and later confirmed. Albert Speer's interrogations post-war also specifically mention this attack as a particularly severe set-back to German oil production. NN703 'X-X ray' was the last to return to base at 04:04 hours.

Crews posted to 630 Squadron at around this time were those captained by Canadian trained New Zealander Jim Bathgate[iii] from Outram, arriving from No. 5 L F S were 24 year old Aussie Angus Cameron[iv] and 28 year old Belfast man Harold Kirkwood[v] who had returned to the UK from his studies in the USA just before the outbreak of war to join up. Warrant Officer Don Plumb[vi] a 22 year old married man from Norwich was posted in with his all NCO crew as were the crew of New Zealander Jimmy Wallace[vii]. Not long afterwards Flight Sergeant Richard Grange[viii] and crew joined the squadron. Application had been made for an official crest for the Six-thirty and on 18th January the Chester Herald of the College of Arms recorded *'630 Squadron wishing to include a Lancaster rose in its badge in refence to the aircraft with which it is equipped. The ogress has reference to night operations on which the unit is mostly engaged and may also be taken as symbolic of the bombs dropped. The argent (or white) fimbriation is indicative of the duties carried out in daylight. The motto may be translated as Death By Night'.*

The latter half of January 1945 was a period of inactivity for 630 Squadron and for East Kirkby generally, the squadron was repeatedly stood down and even training flying was not possible for several days. On the morning of Wednesday 24th January a mining operation was planned, from 13:15 hours mines were loaded aboard the aircraft and crew briefings planned but the operation was then scrubbed. On the next day a member of Station Staff, Flight Lieutenant Dave Timmins[ix], the Gunnery Analysis Officer at RAF East Kirkby (formerly with 630 Squadron flying with Roy Calvert and Bob Hooper) was despatched to No.1 CMB in London for a Medical Board. Attacks were planned for Sunday 28th, Monday 29th and Tuesday 31st January but on each occasion the squadron were stood down when preparations were well underway and briefings fully scheduled. A note in the records for January 1945 reveals that the highly popular Flight Lieutenant Peter Docherty who completed a tour as a pilot with 630 Squadron had returned to the Staff of RAF East Kirkby because he was mentioned as returning to duty at East Kirkby from RAF Hospital Loughborough.

Harry Ramsey RNZAF and crew with "D-Dog" (Peter and Gael Ramsey)

The Bathgate crew. Back row l to r: Pat Crowley, Reg Winson, Chris Christopher, Duncan Paterson. Front row l to r: Jim Doyle, Jim Bathgate, Chas Roper). (Pat Crowley - son)

February 1945

Thursday 1st February 1945.
5 Group despatched 271 Lancasters and 11 Mosquitoes to attack the railway marshalling yards at Siegen. 19 aircraft of the squadron were detailed and bombed up with 1 x 4000lb HC and 2,100 x 4lb incendiaries.

1st/2nd February 1945 : Night Bombing Attack on Siegen
Take Off: at 15:23 hours Reg Waterfall was the first away in ME845 'Q-Queenie'.

JB290-C	F/O HA Ramsey RNZAF		
ND554-E	F/O RB Knight RNZAF		
PD253-D	F/O PS Weston RNZAF		
NG125-F	Capt DCB Reynolds SAAF		
NN702-J	F/L H Thompson	(F/O JW Wallace RNZAF)	
LM216-K	Lt DS Turner SAAF		
NN774-L	F/O JW Hoare RAAF		
NG413-M	F/L GE Stemp	(F/L HF Kirkwood)	
NG259-N	F/O RJ Sassoon		
LM287-O	F/O A McGuffie		
LL966-P	F/O EJ Monk		
ME845-Q	F/L RG Waterfall		
PB344-R	W/O GH Cowan		
LM260-S	F/O AM Maclean RCAF		
NG123-U	Lt MT Ackerman SAAF		
PD254-W	F/O M Miller		
NN703-X	F/O NG Roberts RAAF		
PD327-Y	Lt GR Lacey SAAF		
ND949-Z	F/L LF Ovens	(F/O AV Cameron RAAF)	RD

Phil Weston's crew in PD253 'D-Dog' returned early when the starboard inner engine went unserviceable. Window was dropped from 7° East on the outward leg until 5° East on the return. On arrival the target area was covered with 10/10ths cloud and the Controller had difficulty marking so crews had to orbit the target 2 or 3 times waiting. Between 19:19 and 19:34 hours from 8,200 to 12,000 feet crews either bombed the glow of the TIs below the cloud or the glow of the fires below. Ground defences were quite low key although there was a little heavy flak to the starboard side over the target. Some fighters were seen and the Germans made an attempt to mark the direction of the homeward route for about 30 miles aided once again by jettisoned incendiaries. Flying at 6,000 feet at 19:45 hours aboard South African Doug Turner's LM216 'K' South Rhodesian mid-upper gunner F/Sgt Des Moorcroft saw a twin engined JU88 fighter on their port beam and called a warning as the fighter dived beneath the Lancaster. Moorcroft requested a banking search to port and then just as they changed to starboard South Rhodesian F/Sgt Arthur Bell in the rear turret sighted the fighter on the port quarter beam as it opened fire, he couldn't depress his guns far enough to return fire. Moorcroft was dazzled by the flash of the German's guns. Diving into a corkscrew to port Turner made to evade the fighter as Bell opened fire with a burst of 200 rounds. The JU88 backed off to starboard and wasn't seen again. No claim was made.

At 20:11 hours LM260 'S-Sugar' flown by Canadian Albert Maclean was attacked at 6,000 feet after leaving the target area against the backdrop of searchlights to starboard. Sergeant Joe Cook (rear gunner) sighted an unidentified twin engined fighter at about 250 yards range, starboard down and immediately opened fire instructing a corkscrew to port, continuing to fire as Sergeant 'Titch' Priest the mid-upper struggled to get his guns sighted. Coming out of the manoeuvre Joe Cook applied deflection to his shooting and the fighter flew straight through his fire before diving vertically down into the cloud and not being seen again. The rear gunner fired 800 rounds from 250 down to 100 yards range. At base a Gale Warning was received at 22:05 hours but all squadron aircraft landed safely. Touching down at 23:03 hours New Zealanders Bob Knight (ND554) and Phil Weston (PD253) were the last of the squadron's crews to return. Some damage was caused to the railway yards but a strong wind and German decoys caused some of the bombing to fall in the open countryside outside Siegen. Matt Miller and crew had flown the last op of their tour, they were screened. South Londoner Des Brunwin their wireless op who had celebrated his 21st birthday only days earlier recalled the relief of having 'made it through' and then of the crew being confounded at being asked if any of them would like to be commissioned. They all declined and over the next few weeks went on their separate ways still as Flight Sergeants. Fellow South Londoner Vic Larrett was then the 23 year old rear gunner who had married his sweetheart Joyce very shortly before they commenced their tour, had the same feelings at surviving his tour 'unbelievable luck'. Both men were baffled at the lack of a DFC for their captain. On Friday 2nd February, Flying Officer GD Thompson (Provost Marshal, Inspectorate) carried out an inspection of RAF Police at East Kirkby.

Friday 2nd February 1945.
The 5 Group attack on Karlsruhe was the last major attack of the war against the town and for the German's it was fortunate that the raid by 250 Lancasters and 11 Mosquitoes was a failure. 16 aircraft of 630 Squadron participated each armed with 1 x 4000lb HC and 2,100 x 4lb incendiaries except for ND554 and JB290 which both carried 1 x 4000lb HC and 1,800 x 4lb incendiaries.

2nd/3rd February 1945 : Night Bombing Attack on Karlsruhe
Take Off: at 19:56 hours South African Gordon Lacey in LM260 was away first.

JB290-C	F/O PS Weston RNZAF
PD253-D	F/O HA Ramsey RNZAF
ND554-E	F/O RB Knight RNZAF
NG125-F	F/L SA Nunns
NN702-J	F/O EJ Monk
LM216-K	Lt DS Turner SAAF
NN774-L	F/L HF Kirkwood
NG413-M	F/L GE Stemp
NG259-N	F/O RJ Sassoon
LM287-O	F/O A McGuffie
LL966-P	F/O OJS Atkinson RAAF
ME845-Q	F/O AV Cameron RAAF
LM260-S	Lt GR Lacey SAAF
NG123-U	W/O DI Plumb
NN703-X	F/O NG Roberts RAAF
PD327-Y	F/L TB Baker RAAF

Albert MacLean's crew in 'W-William' had last minute technical problems and couldn't take off. The plan called for crews to fly below 6,000 feet across the continent to a position 6° East then to climb through the cloud into the clear at 13,000 feet. Arriving in the target area they found 10/10ths cloud over Karlsruhe. The Controller ordered sky marking and instructed the crews to bomb the southern end of the glow from the floating green TIs which were cascading in cloud. Large fires were seen by many crews when they broke cloud at 6,000 feet after leaving the target area. Once again incendiaries were being jettisoned on the homeward route particularly in the Strasbourg area. Ground defences were slight but fighters were active over the target with several combats observed and aircraft seen going down in flames. Harry Ramsey brought PD253 'D-Dog' home on three engines after a fire just before Steve Nunns fetched up the rear landing NG125 at 03:56 hours.

Saturday 3rd February 1945 was a training day with a fighter affiliation exercise, three high level bombing exercises and an Air to Sea firing exercise. Sunday 4th February 1945, Lieutenant Ackerman SAAF was advised of an immediate award of the DFC which was announced in the London Gazette - Lieutenant Marthinus Theron Ackermann (32'8473V), S.A.A.F, 630 Sqn.

'One night in January, 1945, this officer was pilot and captain of an aircraft detailed to attack a target far into enemy territory. Whilst on the outward flight, the starboard inner engine became troublesome and later, Lieutenant Ackermann was forced to feather the propeller. Nevertheless, 'Lieutenant Ackermann, continued on 3 engines and eventually pressed home his attack at a height lower than that which was originally planned. He afterwards successfully completed the long flight home. This officer, who has completed numerous sorties displayed a very high standard of determination and devotion to duty'.

Poor weather for several days resulted in greatly reduced flying although a preliminary warning for night operations was received at 10:29 hours on Monday 5th February, the target was confirmed at 11:20 hours, preparations were completed, flight planning and aircrew briefings were held from 16:00 to 17:30 hours but the attack was called off at 19:30 hours.

Wednesday 7th February 1945.
Back to the Canals again, 177 Lancasters and 11 Mosquitoes of 5 Group attacked the stretch of the Dortmund-Ems Canal near Ladbergen. Briefing for the 630 Squadron crews was at 16:00 hours, 12 aircraft were detailed and armed with 12 x 1000lb HC (1 hour Delayed Action). At the same time 3 Lancasters of Six-thirty participated in a minelaying mission in the Kiel area each with 6 x Mk.VI mines.

7th/8th February 1945 : Night Bombing Attack on the Dortmund-Ems Canal
Take Off: at 20:38 hours Flight Commander, Squadron Leader Malcolm Eyre in LM260 took off at the head of the squadron.

ND554-E	F/O LA Barnes	
NN702-J	F/O EJ Monk	(F/O JL Bathgate RNZAF)
LM216-K	Lt DS Turner SAAF	
NN774-L	F/O GR Scott RAAF	
LM287-O	F/O A McGuffie	
NG259-N	Lt MT Ackerman SAAF	
LL966-P	F/O OJS Atkinson RAAF	
ME845-Q	F/O AV Cameron RAAF	
PB344-R	W/O GH Cowan	
LM260-S	S/L MA Eyre	
ME739-T*	F/O NG Roberts RAAF	
ND949-Z	W/O DI Plumb	

*Note – records are contradictory as to who flew 'T-Tare' on this attack, the 630 Squadron 'Operations Record Book' states that it was Lieutenant Lacey SAAF but the Ops Record details F/O Neil Roberts RAAF, this being supported by his Wireless Op's log book and also the list of completed ops in the recommendation for Robert's DFC. Confirmation from Ken Wallwork that the Flying Log Book of his Uncle, Albert Wallwork who was Bomb Aimer in the Lacey crew, shows that he did not fly on that night – further confirming that ME739 'T' was flown by the Roberts crew.

Weather was clear until well over the continent when two layers of cloud were encountered and 10/10ths cloud cover was found on arrival at Ladbergen. The target was punctually marked but the TIs were rather scattered in the prevailing weather conditions and crews found it difficult to determine which TI they were to attack. Attacking from 9,200 to 11,500 feet between 23:59 and 00:13 hours the majority of crews bombed the glow on the cloud from the Red TIs or the TI itself if it was momentarily visible but some crews did see sticks of bombs appearing to straddle the canal through gaps in the cloud. The ground defences were more active than on recent attacks and fighters were very active in the target area and on the track homeward as far as 0500E. The attack was not a success and little damage was caused. Malcolm Eyre had been the first to take off and was also the last to return to base at 03:31 hours, his crew and that of George Cowan had been unable to attack.

7th/8th February 1945 : Night Minelaying in 'Forget-Me-Nots' area
Take Off: Steve Nunns in PD253 was the first off at 19:18 hours.

PD253-D	F/L SA Nunns
NG413-M	F/O PS Weston RNZAF
NG123-U	F/O EC Harris RNZAF

Mines were planted in the allotted positions from 15,000 feet between 22:22 and 22:57 hours without any opposition, no fighters were seen and Eric Harris landed back at base last, at 02:09 hours.

Thursday 8th February 1945.
Lack of oil supply was crippling the Third Reich and the Synthetic Oil Plant at Pölitz was again the target for 475 Lancasters and 7 Mosquitoes of 1, 5 and 8 Groups. Briefing was at 13:00 hours for the crews of Six-thirty's 19 Lancasters detailed to operate, each was carrying 1 x 4000lb HC and 12 x 500lb AN-M64, except JB290, ND554, PB344 and ND949 which carried 1 x 4000lb HC and 9 x 500lb AN-M64 and ME739 which carried 1 x 4000lb HC and 11 x 500lb AN-M64.

8th/9th February 1945 : Night Bombing Attack on Pölitz
Take Off: South African Doug Turner in LM216 was the first airborne at 16:49 hours.

JB290-C	F/O JL Bathgate RNZAF
PD253-D	F/O HA Ramsey RNZAF
ND554-E	F/O RB Knight RNZAF
NG125-F	Capt DCB Reynolds SAAF
NN702-J	F/O PS Weston RNZAF
LM216-K	Lt DS Turner SAAF
NN774-L	F/O JW Wallace RNZAF
NG413-M	F/L GE Stemp
NG259-N	F/O RJ Sassoon
LM287-O	F/O A McGuffie
LL966-P	F/O OJS Atkinson RAAF
ME845-Q	F/O AV Cameron RAAF
PB344-R	W/O GH Cowan
LM260-S	Lt GR Lacey SAAF
ME739-T	F/O RA Stone RNZAF
PD254-W	F/O AM MacLean RCAF
NN703-X	F/O NG Roberts RAAF
PD327-Y	F/L TB Baker RAAF
ND949-Z	W/O DI Plumb

The attack was planned to take place in two waves, the first marked by 5 Group, the second by Pathfinders of 8 Group. Weather was clear with 3/10ths cloud at 4,000 – 6,000 feet and excellent visibility. Flying at about 13,000 feet in clear visibility at 20:51 hours Jimmy Wallace's NN774 'L-Love' was closing on the target when Sergeant John Albers (rear gunner) sighted a Lancaster about 800 yards astern suddenly catch fire and in the glow saw a single engined fighter on their port quarter level. He instructed a corkscrew to port and opened fire with a 200 round burst as the fighter passed astern and was lost to sight. It did not attack them and no definite result of his fire could be observed by him or by mid-upper gunner Sergeant Roger Willing.

At 21:09 hours while orbiting the target at 12,400 feet waiting to attack, Sergeant S.C 'Titch' Priest the mid upper gunner aboard PD254 'W-William' flown by Albert Maclean, saw two fighter flares about two miles astern of their Lancaster and in their light a JU88 flying on their port beam only 100 yards away on a parallel course. The German crew had apparently not seen their Lancaster and 'Titch' Priest opened fire scoring hits immediately on the JU88's starboard engine and fuselage. Sergeant Joe Cook in the rear turret was unable to bring his guns to bear as the JU88 flew ahead of the Lancaster into the fire of Pilot Officer Ron Norgrove (bomb aimer) who was manning the nose gun turret and at only 75 yards range saw his burst of machine gun bullets strike both engines and the fuselage, the JU88 banked and crossed the nose of the bomber to starboard as Norgrove continued to fire into it. Albert Maclean slowed their airspeed and turned to starboard into the fighter to enable both his mid-upper and nose gun turrets to maintain fire on the night fighter which inexplicably banked to port exposing its upper surfaces to both gunners who poured fire into it until it fell away diving towards the ground. While making their bombing run both bomb aimer and rear gunner reported an aircraft crashing beneath them. JU88 claimed as Destroyed.

Marking was punctual and accurate and the Controlling was excellent. Crews had no difficulty in making a bombing run on well concentrated markers, attacking between 21:15 and 21:29 hours from 12,000 to 13,000 feet. Many sticks of bombs were seen to fall across the target. A series of violent explosions particularly at 21:18 and 21:23 hours were reported. By the end of the attack smoke totally covered the target except for the tall chimneys. Early in the attack predicted heavy flak was accurate and a serious opposition, but as the attack developed it died away. Searchlights were few and ineffective and light flak was slight. Crews were briefed to descend on leaving the target to cross the Baltic at 1,000 to 3,000 feet climbing to cross Sweden at 4,000 to 6,000 feet where much light flak was seen before descending again to cross the North Sea under the weather fronts. Bombing by the entire force was rated as extremely accurate and German records show that the synthetic oil plant was put out of action for the remainder of the war, a total success. JB290 'C-Charlie' was the last to return at 03:17 hours. Fighters encountered in the target area, one of the squadron's Lancasters Failed To Return and without any clues as to its fate the seven crew were commemorated on the Runnymede Memorial.

Lancaster III, ND554 (Codes LE – E)

Pilot	– F/O Robert Baines Knight RNZAF. Age 25	Killed
Flight Eng	– Sgt Arthur Ronald Newby. Age 28	Killed
Navigator	– F/S James Montague. Age 27	Killed
Bomb Aimer	– F/S Norman Eric A Sharpe. Age 29	Killed
Wireless Op	– F/S John Lamont RNZAF. Age 28	Killed
Mid Upper	– Sgt Leon Young. Age 20	Killed
Rear Gunner	– Sgt Stanley Laidler Cameron. Age 19	Killed

Recent work on the victory claims by Luftwaffe night fighter crews shows that ND554 might have been the aircraft claimed as shot down at 22:03 hours over Stettin by Oberfeldwebel (Warrant Officer) Rudolf Mangelsdorf of 9/NGJ2 (9th Squadron of Night Fighter Group 2). The crew included John Lamont from Ballymoney, Northern Ireland who had emigrated to New Zealand at an early age where he found employment as a timber worker in Auckland. Arriving back in the UK after training in Canada he had crewed up at OTU with New Zealander Bob Knight and Norman Sharpe a married man with a young daughter who had been a successful builder and decorator in South London.

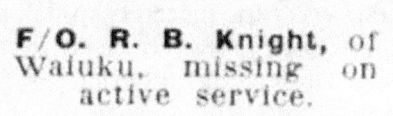

Bob Knight RNZAF (J Knight)   *Norman Sharpe (Sharpe family)*

Rainy drizzly days followed until Bomber Command and the USAAF commenced Operation Thunderclap, a series of attacks on Dresden, Chemnitz and Leipzig designed to dove-tail with Soviet military strategy, the targets situated just behind German lines on their Eastern Front.

Tuesday 13th February 1945.

796 Lancasters and 9 Mosquitoes were despatched in two distinct raids, the first by 5 Group using their own low-level markers. The 244 Lancasters on the first wave found some cloud cover over the target and their bombing was reportedly moderately successful. The second wave of 529 Lancasters of 1, 3, 6 and 8 Groups found the clear visibility and were able to bomb with great accuracy. Briefing for 630 Squadron was at 14:00 hours, 17 aircraft and crews were detailed for Ops and the bomb load was 1 x 4000lb HC and 12 x M.17 cluster incendiaries, except for NN774 and NN703 which carried 1 x 4000lb HC and 12 x Mk14 clusters and ND412 which carried 1 x 2000lb HC and 14 x M.17 clusters.

13th/14th February 1945 : Night Bombing Attack on Dresden

Take Off: at 17:40 hours Squadron Leader Marcel Cuelenaere RCAF was first away in NG413.

NG125-F	Capt DCB Reynolds SAAF
ND412-H	F/O LA Barnes
RF122-I	F/O DA Clifford
NN702-J	F/O HA Ramsey RNZAF
LM216-K	F/O GR Scott RAAF
NN774-L	F/O JW Hoare RAAF
NG413-M	S/L MR Cuelenaere RCAF
NG259-N	F/O RJ Sassoon
LM287-O	W/O DI Plumb

LL966-P	Lt GR Lacey SAAF	
ME845-Q	F/O AV Cameron RAAF	
LM260-S	Lt MT Ackerman SAAF	
ME739-T	F/O RA Stone RNZAF	
NG123-U	F/O EC Harris RNZAF	
NN703-X	F/O NG Roberts RAAF	
PD327-Y	F/L TB Baker RAAF	RD
JB290-C	F/O JL Bathgate RNZAF	

Crews took off in good visibility climbed to operational height forming up at 18:26 hours to set course. A gradual climb to 10,000 feet by the course change point was followed by a climb to bombing height between 14,000 to 15,000 feet flying towards the continent above the 10/10ths cloud. Flak was seen bursting either side of the bomber stream over the Ruhr Valley. Wanganui's with red and green stars were dropped ahead at Magdeburg before turning toward the target. A combat occurred in the Leipzig are on the route out but no results could be determined. Arriving over the target the squadron's crews reported 10/10ths cloud base at 15,000 feet. The marking was punctual and accurate, crews being ordered to attack the glow from the Red TIs at 22:12 hours as planned. Attacking from 12,500 to 14,900 feet the squadron was leaving the target area by 22:23 hours, diving rapidly to 2,000 feet as planned and flak was seen off track to starboard. Results were difficult to assess through the clouds but generally it was believed the attack went according to plan and the glow from the fires could be seen from 150 miles away on the return. Again reports of incendiaries jettisoned on the route home. No trouble was experienced from flak over the Ruhr Valley or the target area and very few fighters were seen. ME739 (Ron Stone) was the last to return, landing at 04:04 hours. 311 heavy bombers of the USAAF pounded Dresden again during the following day returning two or three times in the following days and weeks.

Wednesday 14th February 1945.
Next the Synthetic oil plant at Rösitz near Leipzig was again the target for 224 Lancasters and 5 Mosquitoes of 5 Group in an attempt to destroy any remaining oil reserves. Briefing for 630 Squadron crews was at 13:00 hours, 14 aircraft were despatched each carrying 1 x 4000lb HC and 12 x 500lb AN-M64, except JB290 and ND412 which carried 1 x 4000lb HC and 9 x 500lb AN-M64.

14th/15th February 1945 : Night Bombing Attack on Rösitz
Take Off: at 16:44 hours newly promoted Captain Doug Turner SAAF in LM216 was the first airborne.

JB290-C	F/O JL Bathgate RNZAF
NG125-F	F/O EJ Monk
ND412-H	F/O LA Barnes
RF122-I	F/O DA Clifford
LM216-K	Capt DS Turner SAAF
NN774-L	F/O JW Hoare RAAF
NG413-M	F/O GR Scott RAAF
NG259-N	F/O RJ Sassoon
LM287-O	F/O A McGuffie
LL966-P	Lt GR Lacey SAAF
ME845-Q	F/O AV Cameron RAAF
LM260-S	Lt MT Ackerman SAAF
ME739-T	F/O RA Stone RNZAF
PD254-W	F/O AM MacLean RCAF
NN703-X	W/O DI Plumb
PD327-Y	F/L TB Baker RAAF

Different parts of the force were to attack different sectors of the target. No. 55 Base (57, 207 and 630 Squadron) were to attack the most westerly sector of the plant from a height of 8,000 to 10,000 feet. Aircraft took off and immediately climbed to 7,000 feet, the weather was clear with a new moon until dusk at about 20:00 hours. At the target there was 6/10ths to 10/10ths cloud at 6,000 – 8,000 feet with a thin layer higher above. Marking at the oil plant was punctual and the attack went as planned. Attacking from 7,200 to 14,000 feet between 21:01 and 21:12 hours most crews saw the green and red TIs through gaps in the clouds or saw the glow below and every crew reported large explosions in the target area and a particularly large one at 21:06 hours at the north-western end of the works. Thick black smoke rose above the target. Ground defences were slight but fighters were seen in the target area. On the route home aircraft let down to 3,000 feet and flew home in clear visibility. Cliff Clifford's crew participated in this attack aboard RF122 'I-Item' although they are not listed in the 'Operations Record Book', the fact is confirmed by the log book of the pilot and the DFC recommendation for Flying Officer Gordon Mortiboys[i] (Deputy Bombing Leader) who flew with the crew on this occasion. NG413 (Aussie George Scott) was the last to return to East Kirkby at 02:49 hours. One crew Failed to Return.

Lancaster I, LL966 (Codes LE – P) 'Prune's Pride'

Pilot	– Lt Gordon Ramsey Lacey SAAF. Age	Killed
Flight Eng	– Sgt Duncan Kennedy Watson Mayes. Age 24	Killed
Navigator	– F/O Robert Edward Proudley. Age 21	Killed
Bomb Aimer	– F/O Albert Wallwork RAAF. Age 24	Killed
Wireless Op	– F/S Kevin Gregory Fogarty RAAF. Age 21	Killed
Mid Upper	– Sgt Alexander Carson. Age	Killed
Rear Gunner	– Sgt Herbert George Davies. Age	Killed

Gordon Lacey SAAF and crew. HG Davies is first left (Michael Davies)

In 1948 it was established that Lancaster LL966 was shot down by anti-aircraft fire 2 kilometres east of Rositz and crashed at Zschernitzsch, nearly 36 kilometres south of Leipzig. The rear gunner, Sgt. Bert Davies parachuted from the blazing aircraft and was captured but it is believed that he was murdered by German civilian police and his body was later located buried in Berlin. Gordon Lacey apparently stayed with his aircraft until it crashed, exploding on impact and scattering burning wreckage over a wide area. His body was recovered and buried but later located and exhumed by an American Graves Inspection Team and he now rests in the Heverlee War Cemetery, Leuven, Belgium. The remains of the other crew members were never found and they are all commemorated on the Runnymede Memorial for Missing Airmen at Surrey, United Kingdom.

Robert Proudley with his brother (photo: Linda Deakin)

Albert Wallwork RAAF (Ken Wallwork)

It was planned for 2 Lancasters of Six-thirty to participate in a mining operation on Thursday 15th February, both D and I were loaded with Mk.VI mines and their crews briefed but they did not take off as the weather closed in. Several hazy, misty overcast days followed with intermittent light rain – no flying was possible. Two new crews were posted to the squadron captained by 22 year old Aussie Leslie 'Jake' Jacobs[ii] and 23 year old Lincoln born Ken Gibson[iii].

Monday 19th February 1945.
To attack Böhlen 5 Group sent 254 Lancasters and 6 Mosquitoes led by the veteran 25 year old Master Bomber, Wing Commander Eric Benjamin DFC and Bar (627 Squadron). 15 aircraft of Six-thirty each carrying 1 x 4000lb HC and 12 x 500lb AN-M64, except JB290 and ND412 which carried 1 x 4000lb HC and 9 x 500lb AN-M64.

19th/20th February 1945 : Night Bombing Attack on Böhlen
Take Off: at 23:30 hours Squadron Leader Marcel Cuelenaere led the 630 squadron Lancasters from East Kirkby.

JB290-C	F/O JL Bathgate RNZAF
PD253-D	F/L SA Nunns
NG125-F	Capt DCB Reynolds SAAF
ND412-H	F/O LA Barnes

Leslie Jacobs RAAF and crew (Kay Rowland)

W/Cdr John Grindon and crew. Back row l to r: Ron Holding (WOp), Joe Brown (Nav), Grindon, Tom Cass (R/G), Front row l to r: Joe Pappin RCAF (MU/G), Perce Hollands (F/E), Gordon Mortiboys (A/B) (Tom Cass)

RF122-I	F/O GR Scott RAAF
LM216-K	Capt DS Turner SAAF
NN774-L	F/O HA Ramsey RNZAF
NG413-M	S/L MR Cuelenaere RCAF
NG259-N	F/O RJ Sassoon
LM287-O	F/L LF Ovens
ME845-Q	F/O EJ Monk
LM260-S	F/O AV Cameron RAAF
ME739-T	F/L RA Stone RNZAF
NG123-U	F/L EC Harris RNZAF
PD254-W	W/O DI Plumb
NN703-X	F/O NG Roberts RAAF

RF122 'I-Item' returned early after its front escape hatch came loose and was lost. Many aircraft flew below the cloud until crossing into enemy territory, after 530°East the force climbed to 7,000 feet to cross the battlefront. From 0800°East to 1100°East height was maintained at 5,000 to 7,000 feet thereafter climbing to bombing height. 10/10ths cloud in layers between 7,000 to 1,400 feet blanketed the target on arrival. The Master Bomber's Mosquito was quickly shot down by flak (Wing Commander EA Benjamin DFC and Bar with F/O JE Heath DFM as navigator, both killed). Instructions were to bomb the glow of Red TIs and crews did that even if it took 2 or 3 bombing runs. About H+4 a strange voice was heard on VHF directing crews to bomb the green TIs which had appeared about 10 miles distant. Nobody was misled by the German attempt to confuse bombing. Ground defences were not heavy and there was fighter activity in the TA and homeward to about 0700E. After attacking the target at 9,000 to 14,000 feet the force let down rapidly to 1,500 to 3,000 feet above the ground and headed for home. Richard Sassoon (NG259) was the last of the squadron to return and landed at 08:15 hours.

Tuesday 20th February 1945.

Not letting up the pressure on the German inland waterway system 5 Group despatched 154 Lancasters and 11 Mosquitoes to the section of the Mittelland Canal near Gravenhorst. 11 Lancasters of the squadron were detailed to participate each carrying 13 x 1000lb MC except ND412 which carried 12 x 1000lb MC.

20th/21st February 1945 : Night Bombing Attack on Mittelland Canal
Take Off: at 21:43 hours Lieutenant Ackerman SAAF lifted off ahead of the squadron.

PD253-D	F/O LA Barnes	
NG125-F	F/O JL Bathgate RNZAF	
RF122-I	F/L H Thompson	
NN774-L	F/O JW Hoare RAAF	
NG413-M	F/O GR Scott RAAF	
LM287-O	F/O NG Roberts RAAF	
ME739-T	F/O AV Cameron RAAF	
NG123-U	Lt MT Ackerman SAAF	
PD254-W	W/O DI Plumb	
PD327-Y	F/L TB Baker RAAF	
ND412-H	F/O RJ Sassoon	RD

All aircraft remained below 4,000 feet to 4° East crossing the front line above cloud at 5,000 feet. 10/10ths cloud covered the target as the bombers arrived. Red TIs were observed and an attack commenced on the starboard side followed by further flares but at 01:00 hours crews were told by the Controller to abandon mission and return to base. Fighters were active on both outward and homeward routes and 2 inconclusive combats took place. All crews returned safely with full bomb loads, the last to land being Neil Roberts and crew aboard 'O-Oboe' at 04:56 hours.

Wednesday 21st February 1945. 5 Group returned to the Mittelland Canal at Gravenhorst with a force of 165 Lancasters and 12 Mosquitoes. 630 Squadron crews were briefed at 13:30 hours, 13 aircraft were to attack, each carrying 13 x 1000lb MC Long Delay bombs.

21st/22nd February 1945 : Night Bombing Attack on Mittelland Canal
Take Off: at 17:05 hours PD253 (Steve Nunns) was first to get airborne.

PD253-D	F/L SA Nunns
RA520-E	F/L H Thompson
NG125-F	F/O EJ Monk
RF122-I	F/O GR Scott RAAF
NN774-L	F/O HA Ramsey RNZAF
NG413-M	F/L GE Stemp
NG259-N	F/L RG Waterfall
LM287-O	F/L LF Ovens
ME739-T	F/O RA Stone RNZAF
NG123-U	F/L EC Harris RNZAF
PD254-W	F/S R Grange
PD327-Y	F/L TB Baker RAAF
LM260-S	F/O OJS Atkinson RAAF

Weather was clear with slight ground haze. Take off was good in almost perfect weather but a nearly full moon made perfect conditions for fighters. Marking was punctual and accurate and crews were instructed to bomb the northern most of the three red TIs which were well placed by the canal. The attack took place between 20:36 to 20:43 hours from 8,600 to 11,000 feet. The results could not be assessed due to the nature of the bombs but two which exploded prematurely were well placed in between the Red TIs. Flak was only light in the TA but intense light flak was experienced on the homeward route and fighters were active over the target and as far as the Rhine afterwards when they infiltrated the bomber stream, three bombers were seen shot down in flames. RA520 (Henry Thompson) was the last of Six-thirty's aircraft to return safely at 23:46 hours. The stretch of canal was utterly destroyed in this attack draining many miles of connected inland waterway. The Court Martial of an airman was held at East Kirkby and attended by various officers from Skellingthorpe and Group HQ was the primary cause of interest around the station.

Friday 23rd February 1945. Just 2 Lancasters of 630 Squadron were required to participate in a minelaying operation, both were probably armed with 6 x MkVI mines.

23rd/24th February 1945 : Night Minelaying – 'Onions'
Take Off: at 17:22 hours in RF122 Reg Waterfall was first off the deck.

RF122-I	F/L RG Waterfall
NG123-U	F/L EC Harris RNZAF

Between 20:43 and 20:48 hours the mines were planted in the allotted positions from 13,500 feet without difficulty, several fighters were seen but no combats occurred. RF122 landed after NG123, at 00:08 hours.

Saturday 24th February 1945.

Unsurprisingly 5 Group were scheduled to attack the inland waterways again for their next operation and 166 Lancasters and 4 Mosquitoes set off to attack the Dortmund-Ems Canal at Ladbergen. Briefing was held at 10:30 hours for the crews of the 13 aircraft, each bombed up with 14 x 1000lb MC bombs.

24th February 1945 : Daylight Bombing Attack on Dortmund-Ems Canal
Take Off: at 13:44 hours Wing Commander Grindon (NG259) was first away.

JB290-C	F/O JW Wallace RNZAF
PD253-D	F/L SA Nunns
RA250-E	F/O RJ Sassoon
NG125-F	F/O EJ Monk
ND412-H	F/L H Thompson
LM216-K	F/O PS Weston RNZAF
NN774-L	F/O HA Ramsey RNZAF
NG413-M	F/L GE Stemp
NG259-N	W/C JE Grindon
LM287-O	F/L LF Ovens
LM260-S	F/S R Grange
ME739-T	F/O RA Stone RNZAF
PD327-Y	F/O OJS Atkinson RAAF

Forming up over the base the squadron set course at 14:57 hours, contact was made with 57 and 207 Squadrons over Hunstanton and Cromer and they joined the Group formation at 030° East. The weather was clear to the Dutch coast where cloud was encountered. The planned bombing height of 13,000 to 16,000 feet was attained but 10/10ths cloud covered the target area. There were no instructions from the Controller, no markers visible. No attack was made although the squadron over flew the target and some heavy flak was encountered in the TA. All aircraft returned with complete bomb loads except ND412 'H-How' and NG259 'N-Nan' which had to jettison their loads as both were on only three engines and Wing Commander Grindon had another engine running very rough. Ron Stone and crew board 'T-Tare' were the last to return to base landing at 19:15 hours.

The remainder of the month and early March was taken up with a series of fighter affiliation, high level bombing, cross country, air to sea firing, and minelaying exercises.

Some interesting figures are recorded for the East Kirkby Base staff as of 28th February 1945. These do not include 630 or 57 Squadron aircrew and total only Station staff and ground crews:

Officers

RAF	41	WAAF	4
RNZAF	1		
RCAF	2		
RAAF	1		

Airmen

W/O's	7	WAAF	0
SNCO's	112	SNCO's	8
Cpls and Ac's	886	Cpls and ACW's	217
RCAF	7		

March 1945

Saturday 3rd March 1945.
630 Squadron were detailed to participate in a raid on the Dortmund-Ems Canal at Ladbergen on 1st March but the attack was cancelled, however the Ladbergen Aqueduct on the canal was the target for 5 Group when 630 Squadron flew next. 212 Lancaster and 10 Mosquitoes were flying. 13 aircraft of the squadron were detailed and each armed with 13 x 1000lb MC bombs except ND412 which carried 12 x 1000lb MC bombs.

3rd/4th March 1945 : Night Bombing Attack on Ladbergen
Take Off: at 18:31 hours Wing Commander Grindon was first airborne in NG259.

PD253-D	F/O JW Wallace RNZAF
RA520-E	F/S R Grange
NG125-F	F/O EJ Monk
ND412-H	F/O JW Hoare RAAF
RF122-I	F/L H Thompson
NN774-L	F/L GE Stemp
NG259-N	W/C JE Grindon
LM287-O	F/O OJS Atkinson RAAF
ME845-Q	W/O GH Cowan
LM260-S	S/L MA Eyre
ME739-T	R/O RA Stone RNZAF
NG123-U	F/L EC Harris RNZAF
PD254-W	F/O AM MacLean RCAF

8/10ths cloud covered the target but the flares and TIs went down on time although the Red TIs were rather scattered and couldn't always be seen through clouds. The Controller ordered main force to bomb north-west of the red TI and later instructed to overshoot this TI by 3 seconds. Many crews reported that fighters were active during the run in and there was some light flak at target. Some fighter activity had been encountered approaching target and fighters were also active on the route homeward to about 0530E. No combats were reported by the squadron. PD254 reached the target too late and had to abort. The aqueduct was breached in 2 places and put completely out of action. At East Kirkby landings were almost complete after 10 of Six-thirty's Lancasters landed successfully by 00:12 hours when 'bandits' arrived in the circuit and all airfield lights were switched off, the remaining 2 were diverted without problem and after being engaged by a fighter PD253 (Jimmy Wallace) diverted and landed safely at Seighford.

A JU88 night fighter made a low diving attack on East Kirkby shooting up mainly the 57 Squadron side of the airfield with cannon and machine gun fire using incendiary and tracer rounds. Only superficial damage was caused to the MT Section and 57's briefing room but a debriefing team comprising 4 RAF officers and Squadron Officer Beth Hayward the WAAF CO were injured. Sadly 22 year old Flying Officer Arthur Heeley[i] (57 Squadron) the Signals Analysis Officer, died later that day of his injuries. Unternehmen (Operation) Gisela was in full swing, almost 200 Luftwaffe fighter crews had been briefed to cross the North Sea and patrol the East Coast from the Thames Estuary to the North Yorkshire Moors where they shot down both returning bombers and a number of Heavy Conversion Unit aircraft on night flying exercises.

> APPENDIX TO FORM 540 FOR MONTH OF MARCH 1945.
> R.A.F. STATION, EAST KIRKBY.
>
> On the night of 3/4th March, 1945, an air raid warning was received whilst the landing of aircraft was taking place on return from operations. Landing operations were suspended and airfield and camp lights doused, leaving only a few glim lamps on the perimeter track and hurricane lamps marking obstructions on the Technical Site roads.
>
> At 00.45 hours 4th March a low diving attack was made by a single J.U.88 with cannon and machine guns. There was 6/10ths cloud at 6/7000 feet and the moon was coming up with vis: at 4 miles. It would appear that the E/A sighted from the 5 glim lamps at the upward end of 02° Runway which was in use, and fired at M.T. Repair Bays and M.T. Dispersal area and the bullets carried on to 57 Squadron Briefing Block and Squadron Buildings and the following personnel who were waiting outside No. 57 Squadron Briefing Block for the return of the aircrews for de-briefing, were all injured in the attack and most injuries were caused by an explosive cannon shell.
>
> F/O. A. HEELEY (157528) GD(S) East Kirkby.
> F/O. G.E.PINE (170541) ASD/INT.East Kirkby.
> F/S. CLEGHORN. (572846) F/Arm. " "
> S/DIV/OFF.B.B.HAYWARD (166) Admin. H.Q.
> 55 Base.
> F/L D.R.G. FIFFIELD. 134029 57 Sqdn. A/G.
>
> They were admitted to S.S.Q. and subsequently transferred to Rauceby where F/O. Heeley died from his wounds on 4.3.45.
>
> Damage was caused to the buildings mentioned above and to 10 M.T. vehicles.
>
> Group Captain, Commanding,
> R.A.F. Station, East Kirkby.

Short report on the Operation Gisela attack against RAF East Kirkby (The National Archives)

3rd/4th March 1945 : Night Minelaying – 'Onions'

2 aircraft were detailed for minelaying each carrying 6 x Mk.1V mines. Reg Waterfall took off in LM216 just minutes before Leslie 'Jim' Ovens.

PD327-Y F/L LF Ovens
LM216-K F/L RG Waterfall

LM216's sortie was aborted and its crew landed at Bitteswell at 01:51 hours. At about 20:57 hours from 10,000 feet NG413 planted vegetables in the allotted garden utilising H2S, no enemy aircraft were seen but a little heavy flak was experienced in the garden area. The weather was reported to be clear and visibility excellent. Multiple sources suggest that 'Jim' Ovens flew 'Y-Yoke' and not NG413 'M-Mother' as shown in the 'Operations Record Book'.

Monday 5th March 1945.

Ensuring that what remained of Hitler's Germany was utterly starved of the oil which it desperately needed if it were to continue fighting, 5 Group despatched 248 Lancasters and 10 Mosquitoes to bomb a synthetic oil refinery. 17 aircraft of Six-thirty were detailed for Ops, each with 1 x 4000lb HC, 1 x 500lb MC and 11 x 500lb AN-M64, except ND412 and ND949 which carried 1 x 4000lb HC, 1 x 500lb MC and 8 x 500lb AN-M64 and NN774 and PD237 which carried 1 x 4000lb HC and 12 x 500lb AN-M64 bombs. Preliminary warning of the attack was received at 10:15 and flight planning and briefings commenced 13:30 hours.

5th/6th March 1945 : Night Bombing Attack on Böhlen

Take Off: at 16:56 hours in RA520 Wing Commander Grindon was first off the deck. 'Jerry' Monk and Neil Roberts' crews had Second Dickies aboard for the mission.

PD253-D	F/O JW Wallace RNZAF	
RA520-E	W/C JE Grindon	
NG125-F	F/O EJ Monk	(F/O LM Duggan RAAF)
ND412-H	F/O LW Jacobs RAAF	
RF122-I	F/O DA Clifford	
LM216-K	Capt DS Turner SAAF	RD
NN774-L	F/O JW Hoare RAAF	
NG413-M	F/O PS Weston RNZAF	RD
NG259-N	F/S R Grange	
LM287-O	F/O A McGuffie	
LM260-S	F/O KO Gibson	
ME739-T	F/O RA Stone RNZAF	
NG123-U	F/L EC Harris RNZAF	
PD254-W	F/O AM MacLean RCAF	
NN703-X	F/O NG Roberts RAAF	(F/O JC Clingin RAAF)
PD327-Y	W/O DI Plumb	
ND949-Z	F/L LF Ovens	

The squadron flew below the clouds from base, between 2,000 to 3,000 feet to Reading and then re-joined the bomber stream. 9/10ths to10/10ths cloud was encountered in the target area. 8 aircraft were seen going down in flames between 08°East and 1130°East. Near the target area the result of a collision was observed with parts of a wing falling to earth. Sky markers were all that could be seen for the most part and due to density of cloud they were sometimes obscure. Most crews bombed the sky markers although a few reported seeing TIs on the ground through slight breaks in the cloud. Three crews report that this TI was on the oil plant and that bombs were bursting amongst the buildings with a large oil tank on fire. Several heavy explosions were noted with a particularly large one at 21:53 hours. Moderate flak was encountered over the target and considerable fighter activity on the outward journey and over the target, but none on the homeward route. Combats began at 0800E. On the outward journey persistent contrails were seen above 14,000 feet. Homeward all crews reported moderate icing in cloud between 6,000 to 12,000 feet. The average airborne time was 10.20 hours. On three engines again PD327 flown by Warrant Officer Don Plumb this time was the last of the squadron's aircraft safely home at 03:43 hours. Despite the cloud cover damage was caused to the production capability of the refinery and to some storage sections. Jerry Monk and crew had flown their last op together, their tour was over and they were screened. Within just a week or so they had been posted away, their captain dashed down to Wimbledon in South London on leave and a week later married his sweetheart Olive.

Tuesday 6th March 1945.

5 Group were ordered to attack the small port of Sassnitz on the Baltic island of Rügen, 191 Lancasters and 7 Mosquitoes were despatched. Preliminary warning for both of the attacks came in at 10:40 hours and flight planning and briefings commenced at 14:30 hours. 630 Squadron crews were specifically briefed to attack shipping inside and outside the harbour. 11 Lancasters of 630 Squadron were detailed armed with a total of 96 x 1000lb AN-M65 TD .025 bombs. The squadron also provided one aircraft and crew for a night minelaying operation which was also conducted.

6th/7th March 1945 : Night Bombing Attack on Sassnitz
Take Off: at 18:02 hours Wing Commander Grindon was first away, in RA520,

PD253-D	F/O DA Clifford
ND412-H	F/L H Thompson
RA520-E	W/C JE Grindon
NG125-F	Capt DCB Reynolds SAAF
NN774-L	F/O JW Hoare RAAF
LM287-O	F/O A McGuffie
PA266-P	F/O OJS Atkinson RAAF
ME739-T	F/O RA Stone RNZAF
NG123-U	F/L EC Harris RNZAF
PD254-W	S/L MA Eyre
ND949-Z	F/L LF Ovens

Aside from a cold front the outward trip was in excellent weather conditions right up to the last sea crossing from Sweden to the target. Over the port 7/10ths to 9/10ths cloud obscured the visibility. Several crews attacked a large liner about 1 mile east of harbour breakwater but no results could be assessed due to cloud. Considerable light flak was fired from shipping but no fighters were seen. Aboard W/C Grinson's RA520 'E-Easy' the bomb aimer Gordon Mortiboys had a faulty bombsight so they attacked the town of Sassnitz dropping 10 x 1000lb from 9,500 feet. Kiwi Ron Stone was the last of the squadron to land back at base at 03:40 hours. Three ships were sunk in harbour and the massive 22,117 ton troop transport 'Hamburg' was sunk just off shore, obviously the liner attacked by Six-thirty.

The attack on Sassnitz was the last op flown with 630 Squadron by flight commander Squadron Leader Malcolm Eyre who was recommended for a DFC and posted shortly afterwards. His crew was dispersed, mostly posted over the following months, rear gunner George Arrowsmith and flight engineer John Nelson were recommended for DFCs which both later received.

6th/7th March 1945 : Night Minelaying in 'Willow' area
Take Off: at 18:09 hours Reg Waterfall's crew lifted off with a payload of 6 x Mk.VI mines.

NG259-N   F/L RG Waterfall

Having successfully laid 6 mines in the allotted position in excellent visibility and without opposition, NG259 touched down back at East Kirkby at 03:25 hours.

Wednesday 7th March 1945.

A warning was received from Group at 10:00 hours to prepare for an attack on Lutzkendorf but at 12:35 the target was changed to Harburg and at 14:15 hours flight planning and briefings commenced. The oil plant at Harburg was identified by intelligence reports as operating at a substantial capacity and passed to 5 Group for 'attention'. 234 Lancasters and 7 Mosquitoes were promptly despatched. 15 Lancasters of the squadron were detailed for Ops, each armed with 1 x 4000lb HC and 15 x 500lb MC bombs.

Left: Lancaster ME739 "T-Tare". Right: Frank Cummings (both photos Frank Cummings

7th/8th March 1945 : Night Bombing Attack on Harburg
Take Off: at 18:10 hours recently arrived Ken Gibson (ND412) was first away.

PD253-D	F/O GR Scott RAAF	
JB290-C	F/O JL Bathgate RNZAF	
RA520-E	F/L GE Stemp	
NG125-F	F/O PS Weston RNZAF	
ND412-H	F/O KO Gibson	
LM216-K	Capt DS Turner SAAF	RD
NN774-L	S/L MR Cuelenaere RCAF	
NG259-N	F/L RG Waterfall	
LM287-O	W/O DI Plumb	
ME739-T	F/S R Grange	RD
NG123-U	F/L H Thompson	
NG413-M	F/O NG Roberts RAAF	
PD327-Y	F/L TB Baker RAAF	
ND949-Z	F/O LW Jacobs RAAF	
PA266-P	F/O OJS Atkinson RAAF	

Several days of changeable weather followed during which more exercises were flown and an Op planned for Friday 9th March was cancelled whilst the aircrew were being briefed. Two replacement crews had been posted to 630 Squadron early in the month, both crews consisted mainly of British lads captained by Aussie Pilot Officers Jim Clingin[ii] a 32 year old from Camperdown, Victoria and Laurie Duggan[iii] respectively. Due to a last minute problem George Cowan's crew in 'W-William' were unable to take off from East Kirkby. Light ground haze or smoke hung over the target but the weather was clear below 14,000 feet although cloudy above. Most crews arrived early due to incorrectly forecast wind conditions and had to orbit whilst the Markers went to work. The marking was accurate and the attack started early as both the river and docks could clearly be seen by most crews, as the result the bombing was extremely accurate with sticks of bombs repeatedly seen to fall across the target. Large fires and explosions giving off volumes of black smoke were reported by most crews. Heavy flak was less than expected but light flak was intense and some searchlights were active but ineffective. Fighters were encountered over the target and on the homeward route as far as 0630E with several bombers seen to be shot down in flames. Over the target 'Jake' Jacobs bomb aimer aboard 'Z-Zebra' Sgt FA Lawton 'hit the tit' only to find that his bomb release switch was not working so the crew jettisoned their bomb load over the target. The crews of Gordon Stemp and Phil Weston were the last of the squadron to return safely when they landed almost simultaneously at 01:28 hours. German reports state that the oil refinery was damaged and an adjacent synthetic rubber factory was seriously damaged. Records are contradictory and some show the aircraft flown by the Thompson and Roberts crews transposed.

Sunday 11th March 1945.

In the last of many attacks on Essen Bomber Command sent a record number of bombers to raid industrial Essen, 1079 aircraft (750 Lancasters, 293 Halifaxes and 36 Mosquitoes). 15 Lancasters of 630 Squadron were detailed for Ops and bombed up with 1 x 4000lb HC, 4 x 500lb MC and 12 x 500 AN-M64 except JB290, ND412 and ND949 which carried 1 x 4000lb HC, 7 x 500lb MC and 9 x 500lb AN-M64 bombs

11th March 1945 : Daylight Bombing Attack on Essen
Take Off: at 11:49 hours Wing Commander Grindon was the first airborne.

JB290-C	F/O LW Jacobs RAAF
PD253-D	F/O PS Weston RNZAF
RA520-E	F/L GE Stemp
ND412-H	F/O JW Wallace RNZAF
RF122-I	F/L H Thompson
LM216-K	Capt DCB Reynolds SAAF
NN774-L	F/O JW Hoare RAAF
NG413-M	S/L MR Cuelenaere RCAF
NG259-N	W/C JE Grindon
LM287-O	F/O A McGuffie
PA266-P	F/L EC Harris RNZAF
LM260-S	F/O AM MacLean RCAF
ME739-T	F/O RA Stone RNZAF
PD327-Y	F/L TB Baker RAAF
ND949-Z	W/O DI Plumb

Tom Lockett (Carole Widdicombe).

Ron Stone RNZAF (Roy Calvert)

Aircraft formed up over base and joined the main force at Reading, on arrival over the target 10/10ths cloud blanketed the area with excellent visibility above. The PFF Master Bomber directed bombing onto various Oboe directed red and blue smoke sky markers. Flak was negligible and no fighters were seen. On leaving target black smoke was climbing through the clouds at 2000 feet and clouds were becoming discoloured. 4,661 tons of bombs fell on Essen in an accurate attack in a giant blow which virtually paralysed Essen and was followed up by the taking of the city by the

US Army shortly afterwards. Don Plumb brought ND949 'Z-Zebra' home at 17:30 hours. Two more of 630 Squadron's stalwart crews completed their tours in the attack on Essen, that of Cornish born New Zealander Eric Harris who was recommended for a DFC and his countryman Ron Stone and crew, both crews were dispersed as they received their next postings in early April.

Tom Lockett who had flown as mid upper gunner in the Harris crew throughout their tour joined the Manchester City Police post-war and during that service was awarded a George Medal for his bravery tackling an armed robber brandishing a pistol. (London Gazette 22 November 1957). That evening 2 aircraft and crews joined a minelaying force, each with a payload of 6 x Mk.VI mines.

11th/12th March 1945 : Night Minelaying 'Onions'
Take Off: at 17:42 hours 'Jim' Ovens and crew in PD344 were the first away.

PD254-W	F/L RG Waterfall
PB344-R	F/L LF Ovens

Both Lancasters planted their 'vegetables' as detailed utilising H2S. Both light and heavy flak was encountered in the garden area from the expected localities. An explosion was seen on the Northern most garden as mines were laid. Reg Waterfall returned 13 minutes after his squadron mate and landed at 00:37 hours. The 630 Squadron 'Operations Record Book' details F/O Alex McGuffie and crew flying PD254 'W-William' as Reg Waterfall's gardening partner although the McGuffie crew had only landed from the Essen attack 20 minutes before the 'gardeners' took off. 'W-Whisky' was apparently flown by the Waterfall crew (ref. pilots logbook) and 'R-Robert' was flown by Leslie 'Jim' Ovens' crew as confirmed by the list of ops in the recommendation for Ovens' DFC. Three recently arrived crews were preparing for ops, two were straight from training, the almost all entirely Aussie crews of F/O Keith Hallett RAAF[iv] with its token Englishman flight engineer Sgt W Cash, and from No. 75 Base (RAF Wigsley) after training at 27 OTU (Lichfield) 23 year old F/O Colin Richardson RAAF[v] with its English flight engineer Sgt Bernard Gibbons.

The other was captained by a 28 year old South African officer of the Southern Rhodesian Reserve, Squadron Leader Stan Flett[vi], a married man with two young sons who was returning to ops as B-Flight commander after a tour as an instructor.

Colin Richardson RAAF (LAHC Archive)

Monday 12th March 1945.
Setting an even greater record for the number of aircraft despatched, Bomber Command sent 1,108 bombers to Dortmund, also setting a tonnage record of bombs dropped (4,851 tons). Crews were briefed from 10:00/11:00 hours. 16 of the squadron's aircraft participated, each carrying 1 x 4000lb MC and 16 x 500lb MC bombs.

12th March 1945 : Daylight Bombing Attack on Dortmund
Take Off: at 13:29 hours Wing Commander Grindon and Captain Desmond Reynolds SAAF took off at the head of the squadron.

JB290-C	F/O LW Jacobs RAAF
PD253-D	F/O PS Weston RNZAF
RA520-E	F/O KO Gibson
ND412-H	F/O JW Wallace RNZAF
RF122-I	F/O DA Clifford
LM216-K	F/O GR Scott RAAF
NN774-L	F/O JW Hoare RAAF
NG413-M	Capt DCB Reynolds SAAF
NG259-N	W/C JE Grindon
LM287-O	F/O A McGuffie
PA266-P	F/O OJS Atkinson RAAF
PB344-R	W/O GH Cowan
LM260-S	W/O DI Plumb
ME739-T	F/O RJ Sassoon
PD254-W	F/O AM MacLean RCAF
ND949-Z	F/O JL Bathgate RNZAF

A large number of aircraft were by necessity concentrated into a small area during the second stage of the outward journey but flew in a very disciplined formation. Dortmund was blanketed by 10/10ths cloud at 6,000 feet with excellent visibility above. Just before bombing a Lancaster was seen hit in the port wing by flak, it went into a spin and was lost from view as it went down. The Master Bomber gave clear bombing instructions based on blue and green smoke sky markers which were constantly visible. A mass of dark smoke approximately 2 miles wide billowed through the cloud layer but no results could be seen. Flak was negligible and only one fighter was seen near the target. All of Six-thirty's aircraft returned safely, LM216 being the last to touch down at 19:38 hours. The post-war British bombing survey reported that this attack stopped war production so effectively that it would have been many months before any substantial recovery could have occurred. A planned attack on Lützkendorf was cancelled on Tuesday 13th March.

Wednesday 14th March 1945.
244 Lancasters and 11 Mosquitoes of 5 Group penetrated deep into Germany to attack Wintershall synthetic oil refinery at Lützkendorf. Preliminary warning was received at 10:00 and briefings commenced at 13:30 hours. 15 aircraft of Six-thirty were detailed for Ops and each bombed up with 1 x 4000lb HC and 12 x 500lb MC except ND412, PB344 and ND949 which carried 1 x 4000lb HC and 9 x 500lb MC.

14th/15th March 1945 : Night Bombing Attack on Lützkendorf
Take Off: at 16:46 hours Wing Commander Grindon led the squadron from East Kirkby.

PD253-D	F/O GR Scott RAAF	
RA250-E	F/O JL Bathgate RNZAF	RD
ND412-H	F/O JW Wallace RNZAF	
RF122-I	F/O DA Clifford	
LM216-K	F/O KO Gibson	
NN774-L	F/L H Thompson	
NG413-M	F/L GE Stemp	
NG259-N	W/C JE Grindon	
LM287-O	F/O A McGuffie	
PA266-P	F/O AV Cameron RAAF	
PB344-R	W/O GH Cowan	
ME739-T	F/O JC Clingin RAAF	
PD254-W	F/O AM MacLean RCAF	

ND949-Z	F/L LF Ovens
PD327-Y	Lt MT Ackerman SAAF
LM260-S	W/O DI Plumb

Phil Weston's crew were unable to take off in 'A-Able' as servicing had not been completed, 'C-Charlie' was unserviceable preventing 'Jake' Jacobs and crew from flying. Henry Thompson and crew had to 'boomerang' about 19:00 hours when the rear turret went unserviceable and jettisoned their Cookie and one 500 lb bomb over the North Sea at 19:09 hours. The force flew in clear conditions from base to the target area. Over the Lützkendorf the weather was clear but conditions for marking were difficult due to an attempted smoke screen coupled with a thick ground haze. Flak was moderate to heavy in the TA but directly over the target things were quieter and no searchlights were reported. The Germans deployed fake markers and all Reds had to be confirmed with a Yellow for the attacking force. F/O Jim Clingin's crew were unable to attack after their bomb release failed. All aircraft were diverted to Bruntingthorpe on the return but on arrival there the conditions were equally bad so they were re-diverted on to Bourne where all landed safely except for 'I-Item' and 'O-Oboe' which landed at Molesworth. ME739 (F/O Clingin) was the last to land at 03:15 hours. Photo reconnaissance showed that some sections of the refinery had been damaged.

Friday 16th March 1945.

630 Squadron next participated in a 5 Group attack by 225 Lancasters and 11 Mosquitoes against Würzburg. Preliminary warning for an attack on Wurzburg was received at 10:10, flight planning and briefings commenced at 13:00 hours. 18 of the squadron's aircraft were detailed, each armed with 1 x 4000lb HC and 1,800 x 4lb incendiaries except JB290, ND412, PB344 and ND949 which carried 1 x 4000lb HC and 1,350 x 4lb incendiaries.

16th/17th March 1945 : Night Bombing Attack on Würzburg

Take Off: at 17:37 hours the first airborne was ND949 (Richard Sassoon). Three crews were accompanied by Second Dickies, the crew of Steve Nunns had newly arrived Flight Commander S/L Stan Flett aboard.

RF192-A	F/O PS Weston RNZAF	
JB290-C	F/O LW Jacobs RAAF	
RA520-E	F/O JL Bathgate RNZAF	
NG125-F	F/L SA Nunns	(S/L SE Flett)
ND412-H	F/O JW Wallace RNZAF	
RF122-I	F/O DA Clifford	
LM216-K	F/O HA Ramsey RNZAF	
NN774-L	F/O KO Gibson	
NG413-M	F/O GR Scott RAAF	
NG259-N	F/L RG Waterfall	(F/O CRM Richardson RAAF)
PA266-P	F/O OJS Atkinson RAAF	
PB344-R	W/O GH Cowan	(F/O K Hallett RAAF)
LM260-S	W/O DI Plumb	
ME739-T	F/O AV Cameron RAAF	
NG123-U	F/O LM Duggan RAAF	
PD254-W	F/O AM MacLean RCAF	
PD327-Y	F/O JC Clingin RAAF	
ND949-Z	F/O RJ Sassoon	

PD327 'Y-Yoke' returned early due to a fire in Sgt Bob Loudon's rear turret, landing back at East Kirkby at 21:43 hours. Arriving over the target the bombers found the weather clear with some ground haze. The attack opened approximately 1 minute early with markers well placed and observed by all crews in good visibility. Incendiaries were well spread across the town. Some large explosions were seen and fires took a firm hold. Flak was light with only occasional bursts of heavy calibre being noted. Considerable fighter activity was encountered in the target area and on the homeward route. Several combats were observed and one bomber was seen to go down in flames. A collision was observed in the target area. Fighter flares were dropped on the homeward track as far as the front lines. 630 Squadron de-briefing reports stated that incendiaries were still being jettisoned on track at several points between the target and the Rhine. It was a tremendous blow by 5 Group with 1,127 tons of bombs dropped in 17 minutes with great accuracy. A post war survey records that 89% of the city was destroyed. On their first op, the crew of Lawrence Duggan RAAF were preparing to make their bombing run, the last by 630 Squadron in the attack, when the instruction was given not to attack and return to base. NG413 (Scott) was the last to return safely to base at 02:15 hours. One aircraft and crew Failed To Return.

Lancaster I, LM260 (Codes LE – S)

Pilot	– W/O Donald Ivor Plumb. Age 24	Killed
Flight Eng	– Sgt Peter Ackland. Age 21	Killed
Navigator	– F/S Arthur Michaels. Age 24	Killed
Bomb Aimer	– F/S John Harold Croucher. Age 21	Killed
Wireless Op	– Sgt Roy Jeffery. Age 23	Killed
Mid Upper	– Sgt Kenneth Howard Greenfield. Age 19	Killed
Rear Gunner	– Sgt John David Baker. Age 19	Killed

LM260 was shot down by a night fighter and crashed at Moos, 11km south of Würzburg. Researchers suggest the possibility is that it was shot down at 21:43 hours by either Hauptmann Wilhelm Johnen of Staff Flight, III Gruppe/NJG6 or approximately 21:44 hours by Oberleutnant Eric Jung of 5/NJG2, both claiming to have shot down Lancasters in the vicinity. The crew are buried together at Durnbach War Cemetery.

Several days of exercises followed, high level bombing, minelaying, fighter affiliation and similar. Replacement crews continued to arrive and prepare for ops, this late in the war the majority of new crews

Lancaster NG125 "F-Fox" (LAHC Archive)

reaching 630 Squadron comprised British NCO airmen and three of these were entirely British. The all NCO crew of 21 year old Flight Sergeant Don Tillett[vii] of Edmonton, North London who had joined the General Post Office as a boy Postman and been promoted to Sorter shortly before he joined the RAF, that captained by 21 year old Flight Sergeant Ron Mercer[viii] of Woolwich, South London his crew also being all NCO. Ron Mercer made a career with the RAF post-war, gaining a Permanent Commission and serving until June 1975. The third was captained by Pilot Officer Fred Robinson[ix] also British and heading a crew which was all NCO aside from himself. At about the same time 35 year old RAAF regular serviceman Flying Officer James Richardson[x] also arrived with his Aussie/British crew, Richardson had originally enlisted in December 1929 and served until 1948.

Don Plumb (Angela Plumb)   *John Baker (John Baker)*

Tuesday 20th March 1945.
Intelligence reports stated that Böhlen synthetic oil plant had been repaired and was able to achieve a level of meaningful production so 5 Group despatched 224 Lancasters and 11 Mosquitoes and also sent 12 Lancasters in a feint to Halle to confuse the night fighter defences. Warning to prepare for the attack was received at 10:40 hours, flight planning took place from 18:00 and briefings commenced at 22:00 hours. 16 Lancasters were detailed for Ops armed with 1 x 4000lb HC and 14 x 500lb MC or AN-M64 except for JB290, ND412, PB344 and ND949 which carried 1 x 4000lb and 12 x 500lb MC bombs.

20th/21st March 1945 : Night Bombing Attack on Böhlen
Take Off: at 23:16 hours PD237 (Colin Richardson) was the first to take off.

RF192-A	Capt DS Turner SAAF	
JB290-C	F/O LM Duggan RAAF	
PD253-D	F/L SA Nunns	(S/L SE Flett)
RA520-E	F/O NG Roberts RAAF	
NG125-F	Capt DCB Reynolds SAAF	
ND412-H	F/O JW Wallace RNZAF	
NN702-J	F/O JL Bathgate RNZAF	
LM216-K	F/S R Grange	
NN774-L	F/O HA Ramsey RNZAF	
NG259-N	F/O A McGuffie	
PA266-P	F/O RJ Sassoon	
PB344-R	F/O JC Clingin RAAF	
ME739-T	F/O K Hallett RAAF	
NG123-U	Lt MT Ackerman SAAF	
PD254-W	F/O AM MacLean RCAF	
PD327-Y	F/O CRM Richardson RAAF	

Jack Hoare RAAF in his office, Lancaster NN774-L (David Browne)

A thin layer of cloud hung at 6,000 to 7,000 feet over the target leaving visibility moderate. The Germans may have lit some decoy red TIs to the south of the target and others during the run up but crews attacked the correct red, green and yellow TIs and several large explosions were reported in the TA. Moderate to intense heavy flak was encountered as the attack commenced but it died down during the attack, numerous very active searchlights were present. Crews attributed the 9 casualties suffered by the attacking force to heavy flak from known defended localities on or near the route and round the target. There was little evidence of night fighters and few sightings at the target. Dawn was breaking as the aircraft crossed the Rhine on their route for home. PB344 (Jim Clingin RAAF) was the last aircraft to return at 08:35 hours.

The oil plant was completely put out of action and it remained inactive until it was captured by US forces some weeks later. It is believed that Steve Nunns crew with new flight commander Stan Flett in 'D-Dog' and Colin Richardson's in 'Y-Yankee' flying their first op both brought their bomb loads back to base after an ordnance problem, Steve Nunns reported that his bombs *'went safe of their own accord'*.

Nunns who had recently received a DFC and his crew were screened from ops on their return, tour expired. Nunns joined 617 Squadron the following month in the expectation of flying with 'Tiger Force' in the Far East and remained in the RAF post-war, receiving the AFC (London Gazette 13 June 1957) as a Squadron Leader, finally retiring as Squadron Leader in October 1963.

John Black who normally flew with Len Barnes made his last op that night as mid-upper gunner with Alex McGuffie's crew and completed his second tour being recommended for a DFC.

Three of Six-thirty's aircraft and crews participated in the diversionary attack each armed with 1 x 4000lb HC and 14 x 500lb MC or AN-M64 bombs.

20th/21st March 1945 : Night Diversionary Attack on Halle
Take-Off: at 23:17 hours 'Jim' Ovens in ND949 was the first to get off the deck.

RF122-I	F/L H Thompson	
ND949-Z	F/L LF Ovens	RD
NG413-M	F/L GE Stemp	

Halle was masked by a thin layer of cloud at 6,000-7,000 feet. The markers were seen as expected but some crews, including 'Jim' Ovens', lost sight of them and bombed on ETR results. Bombs were believed by the returning crews to have fallen on a built up area. Ground defences were active throughout the attack. 'S-Sugar' was the last of the three diversionary attackers to return at 08:00 hours.

Wednesday 21st March 1945.

5 Group's next target was the Deutsche Erdölwerke oil refinery at Hamburg. Originally the target advised at 10:40 hours was Hallendorf however at 11:30 it was changed to Hamburg, flight planning started at 17:30 hours and briefings commenced at 22:00 hours. 16 of the squadron's Lancasters were detailed and bombed up with 1 x 4000lb HC and 16 x 500lb MC except RF192, PA266 and NG123 which carried 1 x 4000lb HC and 16 x 500lb AN-M64.

21st/22nd March 1945 : Night Bombing Attack on Hamburg DPAG
Take Off: at 01:20 hours Alex McGuffie in NG259 was the first airborne.

RF192-A	F/O PS Weston RNZAF
PD253-D	F/O HA Ramsey RNZAF
RA520-E	F/O GR Scott RAAF
NG125-F	F/L H Thompson
ND412-H	F/O JW Wallace RNZAF
RF122-I	F/O DA Clifford
NN702-J	F/O JL Bathgate RNZAF
NN774-L	F/S R Grange

NG413-M	F/L GE Stemp
LM216-K	Capt DS Turner
NG259-N	F/O A McGuffie
PA266-P	F/O JC Clingin RAAF
PB344-R	W/O GH Cowan
NG123-U	Lt MT Ackerman SAAF
PD254-W	F/O K Hallett RAAF
PD327-Y	F/O RJ Sassoon

Crossing the North Sea at 3,000 feet the formation climbed to 12,000 to cross the enemy coast. Defences around Helgoland were very active and quite accurate with some aircraft sustaining flak damage. There was no cloud over the target but some ground haze possibly supplement by a smoke screen. The Markers were intent on accuracy and there was some delay before permission was given to attack. A well concentrated attack developed with a very large explosion at 04:11 hours causing a lot of black smoke. Flak was moderate in barrage form at the target and searchlights were active. Some fighters were seen in the target area and fighter flares followed the main force accurately on the route homeward until about 0530E. Several reports of red and green TIs 20-30 miles south of the target and one crew reported a red and yellow TI near Altone but these were likely decoys. It is possible that German countermeasures attempted VHF jamming in the target area. On leaving TA the force made a rapid descent to 3,000 feet until clear of the Kiel Canal where defences were as usual very active. 'U-Uncle' NG123 (Lieutenant Marthinus Ackerman SAAF) was the last to return at 07:30 hours. The attack was accurate, 20 huge storage tanks were destroyed and the refinery was put out of action for the remainder of the war. Another of 630 Squadron's veteran crews had completed their tour on this attack, 'Cliff' Clifford and crew had survived. Quite slowly the crew dispersed in later April and May 1945 to their next postings.

Friday 23rd March 1945.

The last raid against Wesel was carried out by 5 Group with 195 Lancasters and 23 Mosquitoes. The squadron were notified to begin preparations to attack Wesel at 10:54 hours, flight planning began at 14:30 and briefings t 16:30 hours. 17 Lancasters of Six-thirty participated, each armed with 13 x 1000lb MC and 1 x 500lb MC except JB290, ND412, PB344 and ND949 which carried 11 x 1000lb MC and 3 x 500lb MC bombs.

23rd/24th March 1945 : Night Bombing Attack on Wesel

Take Off: the South African Captains Des Reynolds and Doug Turner led the squadron from East Kirkby at 19:02 hours. This attack demonstrates very clearly the part played by Commonwealth airmen in Bomber Command at this stage of the war, 6 of the crews were headed by Australians, 4 were headed by New Zealanders, 3 by South Africans, 1 by a Canadian and 3 by British pilots.

RF192-A	F/O PS Weston RNZAF
JB290-C	F/O LM Duggan RAAF
PD253-D	F/O HA Ramsey RNZAF
RA520-E	F/O LA Barnes
NG125-F	Capt DCB Reynolds SAAF
ND412-H	F/O JW Wallace RNZAF
RF122-I	F/O GR Scott RAAF
NN702-J	F/O JL Bathgate RNZAF
LM216-K	Capt DS Turner SAAF
NN774-L	F/L HF Kirkwood
NG413-M	F/S R Grange
NG259-N	F/L NG Roberts RAAF
PA266-P	S/L SE Flett

PB344-R	F/O K Hallett RAAF
ME739-T	F/O JC Clingin RAAF
NG123-U	Lt MT Ackerman SAAF
PD254-W	F/O AM MacLean RCAF
PD327-Y	F/L TB Baker RAAF
ND949-Z	F/O CRM Richardson RAAF

RA520 'E-Easy' returned early due to an unserviceable bomb sight, this was a tactical target and accurate bombing a pre-requisite. Over the target the weather was clear with excellent visibility. Green TIs were accurately placed on aiming point by Mosquitoes and the target could also be visually identified. The attack commenced and a good concentration of bombing was seen on the north-western districts of Wesel with some bombs to the south of the main concentration. No enemy action reported apart from slight ineffective heavy flak at the target. Lieutenant Marthinus Ackerman SAAF in NG123 was the last to return at 01:35 hours. Wesel claims to be the most intensively bombed town of its size in Germany as 97% of the buildings in the main town were destroyed during the war. Neil Roberts' crew participated in this attack in NG259 'N-Nan', official records are contradictory however crew logbooks and other contemporary sources support this and the recommendation for his DFC specifically states, *'in an attack on Wesel on the night of the 23rd/24th March 1945 he orbited for over 15 minutes, being determined to make a perfect bombing run on a target which had to be attacked with extreme accurate'.*

On both Sunday 25th and Wednesday 28th March the squadron were warned for operations against a tactical target and an undisclosed target but both were scrubbed. A quiet week followed with occasional training, high level bombing and fighter affiliation in the main. A mining mission was expected to be mounted on the night of Friday 30th March but it was cancelled as was a possible daylight attack on Saturday 31st March.

April 1945

An American A-35 Vengeance tail number 41-31397 of 359 Fighter Group crash landed near Old Bolingbroke in the funnel of the main runway at East Kirkby on Sunday 1st April, its 4 USAAF crew members walked away unhurt. On Monday 2nd April at 11:50 the squadron was ordered to stand-by for a mining mission that night but the order was cancelled at 15:18 hours. The following day at 14:07 an order was received to prepare for a night attack on Nordhausen, flight planning commenced at 16:30 hours, aircrew were briefed from 18:00 to 19:00 hours and at 19:40 the attack order was cancelled. Air Commodore Louis Dickens DFC AFC[i] took over command of No. 55 Base.

Wednesday 4th April 1945. Crews were awoken to attend an 02:30 hours briefing to attack Nordhausen in daylight. 243 Lancasters and 1 Mosquito of 5 Group attacked troop concentrations and military barracks at the town of Nordhausen. 17 aircraft and crews of 630 Squadron were detailed for Ops, these were each armed with 1 x 4000lb HC and 14 x 500lb AN-M64 bombs, 9 aircraft attacked the barracks and the remaining 8 attacked the town of Nordhausen.

4th April 1945 : Daylight Bombing Attack on Nordhausen
Take Off: at 06:16 hours Tom Baker and crew (PD237) with a Second Dickie aboard, were first away.

RF192-A	F/O LW Jacobs RAAF	
JB290-C	F/O CRM Richardson RAAF	
PD253-D	F/O LM Duggan RAAF	
RA520-E	F/O LA Barnes	
NG125-F	Capt DCB Reynolds SAAF	
ND412-H	F/L HF Kirkwood	
NN702-J	F/O JL Bathgate RNZAF	
LM216-K	Capt DS Turner SAAF	
NN774-L	F/O GR Scott RAAF	
NG413-M	F/O HA Ramsey RNZAF	
NG259-N	F/L NG Roberts RAAF	
PA266-P	F/O K Hallett RAAF	
PB344-R	F/S DS Tillett	
RF122-S	F/O RJ Sassoon	
ME739-T	F/O AV Cameron RAAF	
NG123-U	Lt MT Ackerman SAAF	
PD254-W	F/O AM MacLean RCAF	
PD327-Y	F/L TB Baker RAAF	(P/O FA Robinson)
ND949-Z	F/L LF Ovens	

PA266 'P-Peter' returned early as its rear turret went unserviceable the Hallett crew jettisoned their Cookie and landed back at East Kirkby at 09:36 hours. Desmond Reynolds' NG125 'F-Fox' suffered an engine failure as it crossed the French coast at 10,000 feet on the way out, with at least six hours flying ahead and their port inner engine out of action he decided to press on and risk straggling. The outward leg of the sortie was accomplished without problem. On arrival crews had little difficulty in identifying the barracks but the target was soon covered in smoke and dust due to explosions on target and crews attacking after the first 2 minutes had to estimate the position using the road and railway lines. Several sticks of bombs were definitely seen to fall across the barracks. No opposition was encountered from the ground or in the air. Crews bombing the town did so on the Red TIs which were placed in the centre of the town. The Master Bomber reported he was quite satisfied with the attack, the SS barracks and town were severely damaged. Len Barnes and crew were the last to land back at base at 13:01 hours.

Desmond Reynolds and crew had completed their tour, they were promptly posted, their captain would receive a DFC for his leadership. Also completing their tour that night were Doug Turner and crew, two of the squadron's South African pilots would be returning home. At 16:40 hours that same afternoon aircraft were bombed-up in readiness for an army support attack if required but the operation was not ordered. On the morning of Thursday 5th April at 10:25 hours a preliminary warning for Ops was received but the projected operation was cancelled at 15:50 hours.

Desmond Reynolds SAAF (Di Thompson) *Marcel Cuelenaere RCAF (Cuelenaere family)*

Saturday 7th April 1945. At 09:45 hours a warning was received to prepare for a night attack on Molbis. At 10:39 a further instruction arrived to ready 3 aircraft for mining in Kiel Bay. The mining mission was confirmed at 11:12 but then cancelled at 12:55 hours but at 14:05 an instruction was received to bomb up the aircraft which had been detailed for mining, they were to join the attack on Molbis. Flight Planning commenced at 14:30 hours, briefings at 16:30 hours. At 17:05 the order to reduce the number of aircraft operating by one third came in. In the end 5 Group despatched 175 Lancasters and 11 Mosquitoes to the benzol refinery plant, electricity power station and tar refinery at Molbis near Leipzig. 11 aircraft of the squadron participated, these were all armed with 1 x 4000lb HC and 12 x 500lb AN-M64 bombs.

7th/8th April 1945 : Night Bombing Attack on Molbis
Take Off: at 18:11 hours Wing Commander Grindon was the first airborne.

RA520-E	F/O HA Ramsey RNZAF	
ND412-H	F/L H Thompson	(F/S RF Mercer)
NN702-J	F/O RJ Sassoon	
NN774-L	F/O JW Hoare RAAF	
NG259-N	W/C JE Grindon	
PA266-P	F/O K Hallett RAAF	
ME739-T	F/O AV Cameron RAAF	
ND949-Z	F/O JC Clingin RAAF	
NG123-U	F/L RG Waterfall	
NG413-M	F/L GE Stemp	
PD327-Y	F/L TB Baker RAAF	(F/O FA Robinson)

ND949 'Z-Zebra' returned early landing on 3 engines at 21:42 hours with the port inner unserviceable. Darkness fell as crews crossed the Rhine and with very much stronger head winds than predicted on the outward route resulting in a large number of crews arriving on target late and some not getting a chance to attack before the controller ordered stop bombing at 23:10 hours. Crews had been unwilling to force the pace upwards (using more fuel) due to fears of diversions as far north a Scotland for landing. Weather was clear in the target area with some ground haze being thickened by a smoke screen. Based on target photos bombing was very concentrated particularly in southern districts. A huge explosion at 23:10 hours was reported. Several large explosions were noted but some might have been decoys. Intense searchlight activity around target area and heavy flak was moderate but largely inaccurate. The only fighters seen were over the target.

Doug Turner SAAF standing left, Alf Hughes standing right, Jack Key RNZAF seated right (Paul and John Key)

NG123 'Oh U Beauty' had one engine fail, needing to be feathered just 15 minutes after take-off but her pilot Reg Waterfall and crew with station commander Group Captain Casey aboard pressed on and bombed on 3 engines, bringing 'U-Uncle' home safely, the last to land at 03:03 hours. Bombing was so effective that all production at the refinery ceased.

Aboard NN774 'L-Love' Jack Hoare's gunners JJ 'Sean' Drumm and Monty Blythe fought off an attacking Fw190 fighter.

Lancaster NG123 "Oh U Beauty" (LAHC Archive)

Jack Hoare RAAF and crew with NN774 "L-Love" (Kay Rowland)

Four of the squadron's veteran crews made their last op of the war that night, Geoff Stemp's crew had flown 32 ops, Henry Thompson's 34 ops, Aussie Tom Baker's 35 ops and that of Reg Waterfall 32 ops. All four pilots were recommended for DFCs and later received them.

Sunday 8th April 1945.

A preliminary warning for readiness was received at 10:15 hours, the target was confirmed as Lützkendorf, flight planning commenced at 14:00 and briefings at 15:00 hours. As the Lützkendorf oil refinery had not been destroyed on their previous attack 5 Group sent 231 Lancasters and 11 Mosquitoes to complete the job. 17 of the squadron's aircraft and crews were detailed to participate and the aircraft were bombed up with 1 x 4000lb HC and 14-16 x 500lb AN-M64 bombs.

8th/9th April 1945 : Night Bombing Attack on Lützkendorf
Take Off: at 18:00 hours Squadron Leader Marcel Cuelenaere in NG413 was the first away.

RF192-A	F/O LW Jacobs RAAF		
JB290-C	F/O JW Wallace RNZAF		
PD253-D	F/O LM Duggan RAAF		
RA520-E	F/O LA Barnes		
NG125-F	F/O KO Gibson		
ND412-H	F/S RF Mercer		
NN702-J	F/O JL Bathgate RNZAF		
LM216-K	F/L HF Kirkwood		
NG413-M	S/L MR Cuelenaere RCAF		
NG259-N	F/O NG Roberts RAAF		
PA266-P	F/L LF Ovens	(F/L JD Richardson)	RD
PB344-R	F/S DS Tillett		RD
RF122-S	F/O RJ Sassoon		
ME739-T	F/O AV Cameron RAAF		
PD254-W	F/O FA Robinson		
PD327-Y	F/O JC Clingin RAAF		RD
ND949-Z	F/O CRM Richardson RAAF		

Two Lancasters were unable to take off for this attack, 'L' (F/O GR Scott) and 'U' (W/O R Grange) due to last minute unserviceability. Darkness fell as the formation crossed the Rhine and there was no fighter or flak activity on the route to the target. With approximately 250 miles still to fly to reach the target and at only 5,000 feet the starboard outer engine of NG413 'M-Mother' failed but Squadron Leader Cuelenaere decided to press on aware that he would have to attack from lower than the expected bombing height of 8,000 feet. At the target where the weather conditions were hazy but with no cloud, markers were laid in good time for H-hour (22:45 hours) and the crews were called in to bomb at H -1 from 8,000 to 14,000 feet. Crews were able to attack the Red TIs with an 11 second overshoot. Major explosions followed and a particularly huge explosion was recorded by many crews at 22:52 hours. Consummated team work brought the Cuelenaere crew to the target on time and they are seen below attacking successfully from 7,500 feet. Staggered search light batteries were the main ground defences and flak was negligible.

Some combats were however reported. The oil refinery was comprehensively put out of action. Aircraft were diverted to Honeybourne on their return due to nasty weather conditions over base. The last of Six-thirty's aircraft to return safely was LM216 (Harold Kirkwood) at 03:37 hours.

At 03:10 hours ND949 'Z-Zebra' with its 'Almost – All Australian' crew had crashed at Foxton near Market Harborough before reaching the diversion airfield and sadly all of the crew were killed.

Lancaster III, ND949   (Codes LE – Z)

Pilot	– F/O Colin Robert Moore Richardson RAAF. Age 23	Killed
F/Eng-Pilot	– Sgt Bernard Gibbons. Age 21	Killed
Navigator	– F/S Herbert Eric Burton RAAF. Age 25	Killed
Bomb Aimer	– F/O Robert Martin RAAF. Age 23	Killed
Wireless Op	– F/O William Forrester RAAF. Age 20	Killed
Mid Upper	– F/S Anthony Ellis Bowman RAAF. Age 23	Killed
Rear Gunner	– F/S Fredrick James Howlett RAAF. Age 29	Killed

Colin Richardson RAAF (National Archives of Australia)   *Bob Martin RAAF (J Martin)*

Four of Colin Richardson's crew were buried at Oxford (Botley) Cemetery, Sgt Gibbons a qualified pilot was flying as F/Eng and is buried at Norton (St Nicholas) Churchyard, Letchworth, F/O Robert Martin RAAF who had served at Tobruk with the Australian Army before transferring for aircrew duty was buried by family members at Sunderland (Southwick) Cemetery and F/S Howlett RAAF is at Cambridge City Cemetery.

Tuesday 10th April 1945.
At 10:45 hours the crews at Honeybourne were ordered to prepare to return to East Kirkby about 13:00 hours. The Station had already been advised to provide 10 aircraft and crews from each squadron for a night attack. At 11:20 the decision was made to detail experienced crews only and at 12:00 the route was received. Flight planning commenced at 12:10 hours. In an operation in support of ground troops 76 Lancasters and 19 Mosquitoes of 5 and 8 Groups were sent to attack the Wahren railway marshalling yards near Leipzig. Briefing was held at 16:00 hours for the crews of the 11 aircraft of Six-thirty detailed to participate, their aircraft were each armed with 10 x 1000lb MC bombs.

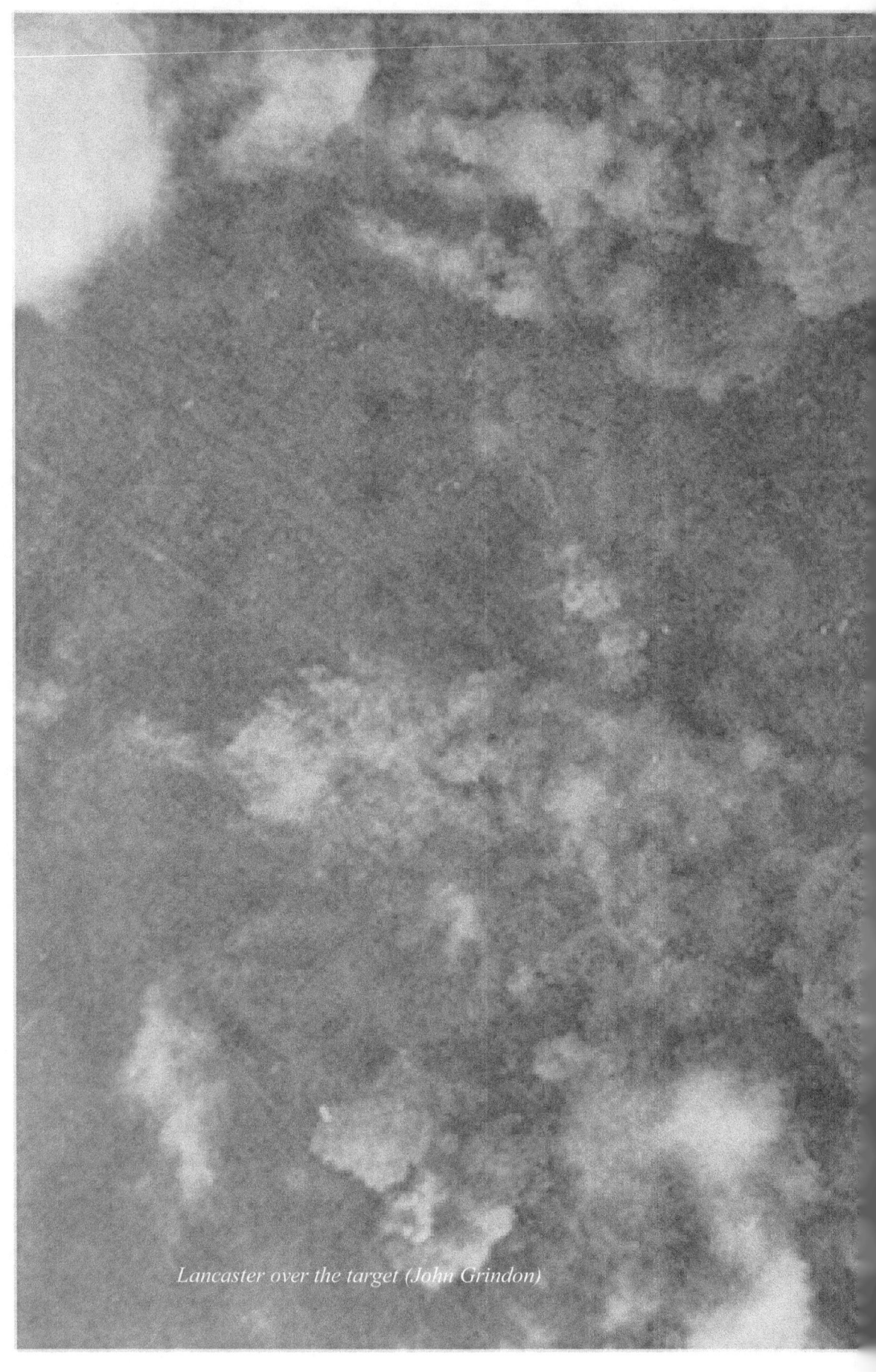

Lancaster over the target (John Grindon)

Lancaster ND949 "LE-Z" (S Hablethwaite/N Maconachie)

10th/11th April 1945 : Night Bombing Attack on Leipzig-Wahren

Take Off: at 18:20 hours Squadron Leader Marcel Cuelenaere in NG125 was the first off the deck.

RF192-A	F/O PS Weston RNZAF
JB290-C	F/O JW Hoare RAAF
PD253-D	F/O HA Ramsey RNZAF
NG125-F	S/L MR Cuelenaere RCAF
ND412-H	F/O LA Barnes
NG259-N	F/L NG Roberts RAAF 0317
PB344-R	Lt MT Ackerman SAAF
ME739-T	F/O AV Cameron RAAF
RF122-S	F/O RJ Sassoon
LM680-Z	F/L LF Ovens
PA266-P	F/L OJS Atkinson RAAF

The outward journey in excellent weather was uneventful but on arrival over the target area lack of flak suggested that fighter activity would be intense. Marking was completed punctually and accurately after which crews were ordered to attack the south western edge of the concentration of red and yellow TIs. Most crews visually identified the marshalling yards and bombing from 11,200 to 14,000 feet appeared well concentrated with a large explosion at 23:00 hours. The lower level attack was carried out by Neil Roberts and crew who attacked on 3 engines after their starboard inner engine failed. A large number of decoy TIs were lit by the Germans south of the target. Fighters were active over the target probably working with the searchlights but did not seem to follow the main force homeward. Once clear of the target the 5 Group 'rapid let down' to 3,000 feet was again deployed and fighter interference escaped on the route homeward. Jim Ovens crew aboard the replacement 'Z-Zebra' (LM680) were unable to attack as its bomb doors would not open after a hydraulics failure. Half of the railway yard was assessed as destroyed. Harry Ramsay's 'D-Dog' (PD253) had received the attentions of German night fighters, over the target a Fw190 attacked at high speed with machineguns and cannons but with warning given Ramsay was able to throw the Lancaster into a violent corkscrew as Sergeant Matt Barry in the mid-upper turret and Sergeant Hugh 'Mac' McDonald in the rear turret opened fire. The single engined fighter broke up in the air before their eyes. Leaving the target area another Fw190 was sighted, before it could manoeuvre to attack Matt Barry raked it with machinegun fire and it burst into flames spiralling into the ground where it exploded. Two Fw190's were destroyed within minutes. The last of the squadron's crews to return safely was unsurprisingly that of Neil Roberts crew in NG259 'N-Nan' which landed still on three engines at 03:17 hours. Two of the seven crews who Failed To Return from the attack were from Six-thirty.

Lancaster I, ME739 (Codes LE – T)

Pilot	– F/O Angus Vernon Cameron RAAF. Age 24	Prisoner
Flight Eng	– Sgt Reginald William Beardwell. Age 36	Prisoner
Navigator	– Sgt George Stanley W Hooper. Age 21	Prisoner
Bomb Aimer	– F/S Grenville (Nat) Gould. Age 22	Evaded
Wireless Op	– F/S John Edward (Ben) Hogan RAAF. Age 21	Prisoner
Mid Upper	– Sgt John Radford Dicken. Age 19	Killed
Rear Gunner	– Sgt Gerald George E Bourner. Age 23	Evaded

ME739 crashed at Zwochau just north west of Leipzig and is possibly the bomber claimed as shot down by Hauptmann Ernst-Georg Drünkler of 1/NJG 5 over Leipzig at about 23:05 hours, his 42nd victory. All of the crew baled out but the Sergeant Dicken's canopy caught fire and he fell to his death. Later an American Graves registration unit searching Zwochau for the crew of a missing B-17 located his grave and reburied him at Choloy in France as per the US policy of routinely moving casualties from within Germany for re-burial on friendly soil. Rear gunner Gerald Bourner, who had celebrated his 23rd birthday just two days previously, later recalled that on their bombing run there were sudden loud bangs in 'T-Tare' and the fuselage was immediately ablaze. He heard the order to bale out as the flames spread and promptly did so, landing with a thump in a ploughed field sometime after 23:00 hours. The Bournemouth former draftsman hid his chute in a ditch and headed westwards meeting his bomb aimer Grenville (Nat) Gould a former

Above : The fate of Lancaster ME739 and crew (B Moorcroft)
Right: Angus Cameron RAAF (RAAF official)

The Cameron crew. Back row l to r: Angus Cameron, Nat Gould, John Hooper
Front row l to r: Gerry Bourner, Ben Hogan, John Dicken (Philip Bourner)

engineer from Leamington Spa, as he went. As dawn broke they hid-up in a haystack where they were found by two Polish force labourers who gave them food. Moving on at midday they trudged towards Lansberg where they met two British prisoners of war from a nearby work camp who had been in a working party which had scattered when caught in an air attack and were resting up. Deciding to hide-up in plain sight the two airmen arrange to meet the soldiers that night at the perimeter of their camp, managing to sneak inside where they received military uniform, boots and could be fed. On 13th April the camp was evacuated by the Germans who were unwilling to march far for fear of marching towards the rapidly approaching Russians rather than falling into the hands of US forces. Eventually camping at a farm at Mutzchlena they were liberated by the US Army on 19th April. Grenville Gould recalled that he landed by parachute about 4-5 miles North of Leipzig before 23:30 hours, buried his parachute and harness and walked westwards for about an hour before joining Bourner. Just four days later Angus Cameron celebrated his 25th birthday.

Lancaster I, RF122   (Codes LE – S)

Pilot	– F/O Richard Joseph Sassoon. Age 21	Killed
Flight Eng	– Sgt Stanley Charles Walton. Age	Killed
Navigator	– P/O John Hopwood. Age 32	Killed
Bomb Aimer	– F/O Patrick Francis Fleming. Age 22	Prisoner
Wireless Op	– F/S Murray Swanson Munro. Age 24	Killed
Mid Upper	– Sgt William Howard Roger Jenkins. Age 22	Killed
Rear Gunner	– F/S Ivor Lancelot Lynn. Age 37	Prisoner

Sassoon crew. Back row l to r: Hopwood, Lynn and Sassoon. Front row l to r: Munro, Fleming, Jenkins (Thérèse Jeffery)

RF122 was shot down by a night fighter and crashed at Glebitzsch, 11km eastwards from Bitterfeld where the dead airmen were initially buried, they were later moved to Berlin War Cemetery. It is possible that Ernst-Georg Drünkler (see above) who may have shot down ME739 next attacked RF122 also shooting that down although the loss might also be attributed to pilots of NJG100 who were also operating in the area and did make claims.

Ivor Lynn was one of the oldest members of aircrew to serve with 630 Squadron; he was born in 1908 in Newport, Monmouthshire and had worked as a Brewers Drayman in Oxford prior to joining the RAF. Having previously served in the Tank Corps from 1927 to 1933 including a tour in India with 15/19 Hussars, he'd lied about his age to join the Army under age. Known as 'Pop' to his crew as the result of the age difference he recalled their Lancaster being hit hard in the mid-section from below, the explosion causing his chin to impact the breech of his .303 Browning machineguns. The force was so great it propelled him up head first through the Perspex which shattered. Fearing possibly being machine gunned in his parachute Lynn delayed deploying his chute on the way down, he saw their Lancaster spiralling down and a lone fighter circling down after it. He sprained his ankle on landing and paused to brush slivers of perspex out from around his neck. Hearing animals running around the field Lynn didn't move until daylight wary of the possibility of attack dogs and knowing that the live bomb load was still in the plane. Discounting the possibility of evasion due to his damaged ankle Lynn waited for dawn before hobbling into a nearby village on his damaged ankle and surrendered to the postman. He was very fortunate, in multiple incidents captured aircrew were very badly beaten or even lynched by crowds led by local Hitler Youth, Nazi Party district or block leaders while the authorities turned a blind eye.

Ivor Lynn (Thérèse Jeffery)

Len Barnes had flown the last op of the second half of his tour, which had been delayed for some months after he was shot down over occupied Europe and returned after evading capture. He remained with the squadron until it was disbanded. Post-war he became manager of the Printing Department of Williams and Glyns Bank being awarded an MBE in the Queen's Birthday Honours list of 1980 [London Gazette 14 June 1980]. At 10:10 on Wednesday 11th April orders were received for an attack on Leuna/Merseberg to commence at 22:30 hours, the route arrived at 11:10 and flight planning commenced at 14:00 hours. As the first aircraft took off at 17:45 hours a cancellation order was received from SHAEF. At 18:25 that evening a 158 Squadron Halifax code 'N' from Lissett which was on an attack against Nuremburg landed at East Kirkby due to a hydraulic leak. The Station's ground crews worked to repair the visitor's problem. Flying was restricted by several days of cloudy or foggy weather when even the best weather conditions always seemed to include a haze. Jeff Bignell RAAF and crew arrived at East Kirkby on 12 April.

Friday 13th April 1945.

A 'Raid Assessment Meeting' was held for both 57 and 630 Squadrons in the 630 Squadron Captain's briefing Room starting at 09:30 but during this at 10:05 a preliminary warning was received for a Gardening mission in Kiel Bay that night, expected H-hour 22:45 hours. Four of the squadron's Lancasters (and two of 57's) were detailed for mining and each armed with 6 x Mk.VI mines. Briefing for Navigators commenced at 14:00 hours, for Captain's at 14:30 and the main briefing at 15:00 or 16:30 hours by which time H-hour had been amended to 23:30 hours.

Back row l to r: Geoff Cohen (Rear Gunner), Cec Lawlan (Flight Eng). Front row l to r: Ken Clarke (Navigator), Len Barnes (Pilot), Cyril Holmes (Wireless Op) (photo: Sue Reid)

Jeff Bignell RAAF (John Bignell) *Geoff Cohen (Sue Reid)*

13th/14th April 1945 : Night Minelaying – Kiel Bay area
Take Off: at 20:30 hours George Cowan and crew in NN774 were the first away from East Kirkby.

RA520-E	F/O PS Weston RNZAF
NN774-L	F/O GH Cowan
NG123-U	W/O R Grange
PA266-P	F/L NG Roberts RAAF

The crew of 'L-Love' had to abort their task over the target area due to faulty H2S equipment however the others successfully planted mines in their allotted positions using H2S and without opposition. The last to return was Neil Roberts' PA266 at 02:12 hours. On Sunday 15th April warning was received at 10:20 hours for an attack on Pilsen, expected H-hour at 22:30, but the order was cancelled at 16:05 due to poor weather in the target area after completion of the aircrew briefings and five aircraft had to be de-bombed to participate in training flights. On Monday morning the College of Arms returned the crest and motto of 630 Squadron to 5 Group HQ complete with royal approval.

Monday 16th April 1945.

At 10:10 hours the squadron was ordered to prepare to attack Pilsen at 22:45 that night, aircraft were to be fuelled with 2,000 gallons of fuel, the route was received at 11:35 and flight planning commenced at 13:00 however an instruction was received to change H-hour to 04:00 so flight planning re-commenced at 16:30 with briefing times adjusted to 20:30 for navigators, and 21:00 for Captain's and main briefing. 5 Group despatched 222 Lancasters and 11 Mosquitoes to attack the railway marshalling yards at Pilsen. 14 aircraft and crews of Six-thirty were detailed to participate in the attack, each was armed with 1 x 4000lb HC and 14 x 500lb AM-N64 bombs.

16th/17th April 1945 : Night Bombing Attack on Pilsen

Take Off: at 23:36 hours the first away was RA520 flown by Ken Gibson. Four crews had Second Dickies aboard to gain operational experience.

RF192-A	F/O PS Weston RNZAF	(P/O JT Bignell RAAF)
JB290-C	F/L JD Richardson RAAF	
RA520-E	F/O KO Gibson	
NG125-F	F/O LM Duggan RAAF	
ND412-H	F/O JW Wallace RNZAF	
NN702-J	F/S RF Mercer	
LM216-K	F/L HF Kirkwood	
NN774-L	F/O LW Jacobs RAAF	
NG413-M	F/O HA Ramsey RNZAF	(F/O JB Dobbie)
NG259-N	W/C JE Grindon	(F/L J Barnes)
PA266-P	F/L OJS Atkinson RAAF	
PB344-R	F/S DS Tillett	
RF124-S	F/O FA Robinson	
NG123-U	Lt MT Ackerman SAAF	(F/OWM Taylor)
LM680-Z	F/L LF Ovens	

Harry Ramsey RNZAF(Peter and Gael Ramsey)

The outward journey was uneventful and until navigation lights were switched off at the English coast the stream appeared very well concentrated. Over the target marking was punctual and assessed as being within 50 yards of the aiming point, the attack opened at H-1. Crews were instructed to attack the north western tip of the red and yellow TIs from 03:58 and then at 04:03 hours to attack the north western tip of the Red TIs overshooting by 6 seconds. The attack, from 11,900 to 14,000 feet was quickly assessed as successful. Several large explosions were reported including a particularly big one at 04:00 hours. Search lights seemed to concentrate some 2,000 – 3,000 feet above the main force. Sergeants Art Ashby and John Brookes (mid-upper and rear) gunners aboard Lawrence Duggan flying NG125 'F-Freddy' fought off and damaged an attacking Fw190 fighter. Ground defences were slight and fighter activity on a small scale confined mainly to the TA and the first 50 miles of the route home. PB344 'R-Robert' was originally reported 'Overdue' from this operation but after landing at Juvincourt at 06:30 hours Don Tillett brought his crew back to base safely. At 08:18 hours 'H-How' touched down, the last to land.

Clear evidence that the air war was coming to a close is found in the number of the squadron's experienced crews who flew their last op against Pilsen, some had completed their tours but others had their routine pattern of leave due and on their return there were no more ops. 'Olly' Atkinson and 'Jim' Ovens crews were both tour expired and screened on their return, their captains recommended for DFCs which were later received, Harry Ramsey and Marthinus Ackerman were not to fly again on ops, both also later received DFCs, the CO Wing Commander John Grindon flew his last op with 630 Squadron, later in July he would be awarded a DSO in recognition of his courage and exceptional leadership of 630 Squadron and was posted to 617 Squadron, the Dam Busters, in command.

Don Tillett and crew (Kay Rowland)

LF "Jim" Ovens and crew (Stuart Hablethwaite)

At 17:40 hours on the evening of Tuesday 17th April 1945 as preparations were underway for an attack on a target near the German/Czech border, bombing-up was almost complete when fire broke out, it has been speculated from a petrol spillage, on the dispersal used by 57 Squadron's 'U-Uncle' close to Hagnaby Grange farm house and buildings. The ever efficient fire crew turned out with the tender arriving at the moment that two 1,000 lb bombs exploded. An RAF fire fighter and a soldier of the Pioneer Corps who had been employed on runway repairs but was keen to help were killed instantly. Fireman LAC William Thaxton was wounded but managed to carry his badly injured Corporal away from the worst of the fire and explosion as others began to fight the fires. Very quickly however the fires had spread to two more of 57 Squadron's Lancasters and quite quickly their bomb loads also began to explode. Fortunately the dispersal was on the far side of the station distant from the village. The Station Fire Officer, F/O Grebby arrived just after an ambulance attendant and one of the groundcrew had been killed.

The citations for gallantry awards later published in the London Gazette [27 November 1945] tell the story of what followed.

The KING has been graciously pleased to give orders for the following appointments to the Most Excellent Order of lie British Empire and to approve the following awards of the British Empire Medal: —
To be Additional Members of the Military Division of the Most Excellent Order of the British Empire:—

Flying Officer John Aidan Hastings Gott, G.M. (154963), Royal Air Force Volunteer Reserve.
Flying Officer Courtenay Cecil GREBBY (133289), Royal Air Force Volunteer Reserve.

<u>*Awarded the British Empire Medal (Military Division).*</u>

916695 Corporal Raymond Graham FORSTER, Royal Air Force.
1184210 Corporal Leslie John Daniel FRISWELL, Royal Air Force Volunteer Reserve.
1863590 Leading Aircraftman Frederick Phillip BROWN, Royal Air Force Volunteer Reserve.
1037853 Leading Aircraftman William Edward THAXTON, Royal Air Force Volunteer Reserve.

Citation-

'On the evening of 17th April, 1945, an explosion occurred in an aircraft which was being prepared for operations on the airfield at East Kirkby. A number of airmen and soldiers working in the vicinity were injured, two of them fatally. Two, and eventually three, aircraft already fully bombed up on adjacent dispersal positions caught fire, and shortly afterwards the bombs on these aircraft started to explode. Flying Officers Gott and Grebby went to the scene immediately after the first explosion. They found a soldier lying near the blazing wreckage with his clothing on fire, put out the flames and rendered first aid to his wounds. These officers then proceeded to extinguish fires which had taken hold of the tyres of some loaded bomb trolleys. Next, in spite of further explosions of bombs, they helped to remove wounded men to places of safety. Explosions were now occurring at frequent intervals, causing further casualties, some fatal. Orders were given to evacuate the area but Flying Officer Grebby continued to help with the wounded and asked permission to remove a body lying by the burning wreckage of an aircraft. At that moment a further bomb exploded and Flying Officer Grebby sustained a deep wound in the thigh. When in great .pain, and lying on a stretcher, he asked to be assured that no injured persons were being left in danger while he was being given a place in the ambulance. Flying Officer Gott was the last to leave the scene, taking with him in his car the last of the injured men. Corporal Forster, who was in charge of the airmen engaged in servicing the aircraft in which the initial explosion occurred, was in a hut some 50 yards away. Although injured and severely shaken, he immediately went to the scene and assisted Flying Officers Gott and Grebby in their rescue work. After having removed one injured man to safety, Corporal Forster returned to the aircraft and continued to render assistance until he was instructed to leave the area. Corporal Friswell was in charge of a party of airmen engaged in servicing an aircraft a short distance away. When the explosion occurred he was thrown to the ground and sustained slight injuries. Before he could reach safety a further explosion occurred and several men sustained injuries. Corporal Friswell went to the scene of the accident, removed

one man to safety and arranged for his conveyance to sick quarters. Corporal Friswell then returned to the aircraft and continued the rescue work until he was ordered to retire. Leading Aircraftman Brown was in a flight hut some 50 yards away when the first explosion occurred and was knocked down by the blast. Leading Aircraftman Brown quickly extricated himself from the wreckage of the hut, and then proceeded to the scene of the accident. Soon 4 aircraft were ablaze and, although further explosions and fires were occurring, Leading Aircraftman Brown made every endeavour to help the injured personnel and also assisted in extinguishing isolated fires. Leading Aircraftman Thaxton, a member of the Station fire party, was injured by the explosion of a bomb as he arrived on the scene; his corporal was thrown to the ground and severely injured. Leading Aircraftman Thaxton carried the corporal to safety and then returned to the scene of the explosion. Despite the intermittent explosions which were still occurring this airman assisted in the rescue work and was instrumental in evacuating many of the injured personnel. Throughout the incident these officers and airmen displayed outstanding courage and initiative which resulted in the saving of many lives. Losing blood at a terrific rate from his leg wound F/O Grebby's life was saved by a tourniquet made from braces worn by Group Captain Bernard Casey OBE (Station Commander). The station commander and F/L Jim MacBean, Station Armament Officer had arrived on the scene just as Lancaster LM673 blew up killing Corporal Dixon (Ambulance) and a fireman. Group Captain Casey ordered the evacuation of the vicinity and as explosions and fires continued, the evacuation of the station. The casualties were moved clear as the fourth Lancaster caught fire just as the fire tenders arrived from neighbouring Coningsby and Spilsby. At 09:30 hours the following morning another bomb exploded as the Bomb Disposal Squad waited to commence work and they had to remain clear until later that afternoon after the remaining aircraft had been de-bombed. They carried out controlled explosions on a number of bombs in dangerous condition wherever they had been thrown across the airfield by the explosions and rendered the area safe so that the airfield could resume duties. The fire had completely burned out.

Four of 57 Squadron's Lancasters had been destroyed, 10 seriously damaged and six more lightly damaged. The Incendiary Hangar/Store beside the dispersal was extensively damaged and the dispersal hard standings were cratered as was a section of the track. Flight dispersal huts were blown flat and damage was done to two of the unoccupied houses of Hagnaby Grange on the aerodrome. Inn that aftermath it was discovered that 9 x 1,000 lb and 34 x 500 lb Medium Capacity bombs had exploded.

Those killed were –

1009063 Corporal Thomas Stanley Dixon RAFVR, age 30 of Dukinfield.
1048598 LAC Arnold Price RAFVR, age 24 of Chorlton-cum-Hardy.
1018928 Corporal George William Johnson RAFVR, age 33 of Wombwell.
13062628 Corporal Matthew Bulmer, 829 Company Pioneer Corps, age 29 (a Sunderland man).

Corporal Dixon was buried at Marple (All Saints) Churchyard, LAC Dixon at Manchester Southern Cemetery, Corporal Johnson at Wombwell Cemetery in Yorkshire and Corporal Bulmer at Lincoln (Newport) Cemetery.

The names of those recorded as injured were –

LAC A Daley RAFVR	RAF East Kirkby
F/O CC Grebby RAFVR	RAF East Kirkby
Cpl RJ Piper RAFVR	RAF East Kirkby
Pte E Turner (Army)	829 Company Pioneer Corps
Cpl Dougherty RAFVR	RAF East Kirkby
LAC F Challis RAFVR	RAF East Kirkby
Cpl J Martin RAFVR	RAF East Kirkby
LAC R Stubbs RAFVR	RAF East Kirkby

Bombing up (J Grindon)

Three views of the scene of devastation, the remains of a Lanc in the right foreground of the middle photo (TL Redding)

Station Fire Officer Courtenay Grebby MBE (Jerry Monks)

On Thursday 19th April Flight Sergeant Maxwell Hartcher RAAF, bomb aimer in Keith Hallett's recently arrived Aussie crew was receiving treatment for sickness at the RAF Hospital Rauceby he was later repatriated to Australia. Exercises were the routine for several days although at 18:20 hours on Friday 20th April the squadron received preliminary warning for an Op on the 21st, but it did not take place and on Sunday 22nd at 19:00 hours another warning was received for a daylight attack on the following day. Four new crews were on the Battle Order for the next op, they were captained by Flight Lieutenant Jack Barnes[ii] from 1660 CU heading a crew including some pre-war RAF regular service airmen commencing their second tours, Aussie F/O Jeff Bignell RAAF[iii] with his mainly British crew on their first tour, 25 year old Flying Officer John Dobbie[iv] a recently married Glaswegian pre-war Regular airman with his crew of British NCO's and finally the crew of British NCO's headed by 31 year old Flying Officer Mick Taylor[v] a veterinary surgeon from Codsall in Staffordshire.

Monday 23rd April 1945.
At 04:00 hours the planned attack was postponed due to poor weather in the Target Area but at 10:00 hours the operation was back 'On' now planned for 17:30 hours. Briefings commenced at 11:00 and at 12:10 H-Hour was put back until 18:30 but the Op was confirmed 'On'. 5 Group despatched 148 Lancasters to attack the railway yards at Flensburg on the North German coast with shipping in harbour as alternative. The 12 Lancasters of 630 Squadron were each bombed up with 14 x 1000lb AN-M65 bombs.

23rd April 1945 : Daylight Bombing Attack on Flensburg

Take Off: at 15:06 hours Squadron Leader Marcel Cuelenaere and 'Jake' Jacobs led the squadron away.

RF192-A	F/O JB Dobbie
NG125-F	F/O LW Jacobs RAAF
NN702-J	F/S RF Mercer
NN774-L	F/O JW Hoare RAAF
NG413-M	S/L MR Cuelenaere RCAF
NG259-N	F/L NG Roberts RAAF
PA266-P	F/O JT Bignell RAAF
RF124-S	F/O WM Taylor
NG123-U	F/L J Barnes
ND412-H	F/O KO Gibson
PB784-Q	F/L JD Richardson RAAF
PA322-V	F/O FA Robinson
LM680-Z	F/O A McGuffie

Climbing through a thin sheet layer of cloud the squadron joined the 'gaggle' on time and in position. Cloud began to break on leaving the English coast and near the enemy coast it had cleared completely. Over the target however the Controller ordered the force to *'abandon attack'* as a solid layer of cloud covered the target at 6,000 to 8,000 feet. No ground opposition was encountered and there were only one or two sightings of enemy aircraft but none attacked. All aircraft returned safely, Neil Roberts in NG259 'N-Nan' being the last to land at East Kirkby at 21:06 hours.

George Dobbie's crew. Back row l to r: Gaze, Courtnay, Telling, Constable. Front row l to r: Cruickshank, Dobbie, Turne. (Neale McCarthy)

24th April 1945.

After an initial signal that the Squadron would not be required for Ops that night – a mining operation in Oslofjord was ordered. Briefings commenced at 18:00 hours and the 4 Lancasters detailed for the mining mission were each armed with 6 x Mk.VI mines.

24th/25th April 1945 : Night Minelaying – 'Onions'

Take Off: at 20:09 hours aboard NN774 'Jake' Jacobs and crew were the first of the 'All Commonwealth' force to leave East Kirkby.

RF124-S	F/O AM MacLean RCAF
NN774-L	F/O LW Jacobs RAAF
RF192-A	F/O PS Weston RNZAF
NG123-U	F/O JL Bathgate RNZAF

All mines were laid in the allotted positions using H2S equipment. Minimal light flak was encountered from Horten area but no other opposition. Four searchlights were active in the garden area. Determination to be as accurate as possible shows clearly as Albert MacLean's crew aborted their first run and made a second to ensure that their 'Vegetable' was correctly 'planted' and Phil Weston's crew did not release until their 4th run. 'Jake' Jacobs' crew were the last to return landing at 02:53 hours. Note – one record states that the crew of F/O Jim Bathgate flew this op aboard a 57 Squadron Lancaster 'X-X ray'. About to fly his first op with 630 Squadron was recently arrived replacement B-flight commander, 23 year old Squadron Leader Lawrence Pilgrim DFC[vi] until recently a long serving flight commander at 1660 HCU, heading a veteran crew comprising Australians, British and a New Zealander. Pilgrim had flown a successful first tour with 44 Squadron.

Wednesday 25th April 1945.

In the early hours crews prepared for briefings which commenced at 01:00 hours. The Op was declared definitely 'On' at 03:05 hours. 359 Lancasters and 16 Mosquitoes of 1, 5 and 8 Groups were despatched to bomb Hitler's personal 'Eagles Nest' chalet complex and the adjoining SS Barracks at Berchtesgaden. 5 aircraft of 630 Squadron participated each armed with 12 x 1000lb AN-M59 bombs.

25th April 1945 : Daylight Bombing Attack on Berchtesgaden

Take Off: at 04:15 hours aboard NG125 Ken Gibson's crew were the first airborne.

RA520-E	F/O JW Hoare RAAF
NG125-F	F/O KO Gibson
NN702-J	F/O GR Scott RAAF
PA322-V	S/L LW Pilgrim
PB784-Q	F/O GH Cowan

The bombers took off and made their ways individually to the rendezvous point at St Quentin where the group formed up in the early morning light. Other sections of the formation joined up later. Weather at the target was clear with excellent visibility although low cloud hung in many of the deep valleys. The expected Red TIs were not seen. The attack took place from 16,000 to 16,500 feet between 09:00 to 09:03 hours. Several crews reported seeing the barracks rectangle which was quickly obscured by bomb bursts. It is noted that overshoots were observed and that some aircraft attacked the railway bridge north of the target whilst others bombed the village itself. High mountains on the run in prevented several crews from seeing the target until the last minute with mist in the valleys making map reading difficult. F/O GR Scott's crew had an unsuccessful op receiving no bombing instructions. No enemy fighters were seen but moderate heavy flak was met at the target and from Salzburg. Amongst the force were 16 Lancasters of 617 Squadron dropping their last 'Tallboy' bombs. The mission was assessed as accurate and effective. George Cowan

Jack Hoare RAAF (standing left) and crew (D Browne)

was the last of the squadron to return to base at 12:54 hours. Jack Hoare's crew had flown their 30th and last Op, and they had survived.

On 26th April 1945 Wing Commander Frederick 'Jimmy' Wild[vii] took command of 630 Squadron. He was an adventurous 33 year old Bradford man, who had been a Cadet in the Merchant Navy at the age of 16 and worked in the USA and Canada in the late 1920's before returning to the UK to take up a regular commission in the RAF in 1931. Having served in the Middle East pre-war and then flying from North Africa to bomb Italian targets with 38 Squadron (Wellington bombers) in late 1940/early 1941, he was a highly respected officer. Postwar Wild returned to Canada where he settled and became a citizen.

The out-going CO Wing Commander John Grindon was recommended for a DSO for his outstanding leadership and bravery whilst in command of 630 Squadron, he was posted to command 617 Squadron. The month closed with several days of cloudy weather. The remaining days of April and those of May were mainly fair but with occasional showers and Six-thirty were kept busy with high level bombing exercises, fighter affiliation missions and occasional Air to Sea firing.

May 1945

W/Cdr Wild (3rd from left) flanked by his flight commanders (LAHC Archive)

On 2nd May 1945 nine aircraft of No. 630 Squadron were detailed to participate in 'Operation Exodus' the repatriation by air of liberated British Prisoners of War. Wing Commander Wild joined the pilots participating as did another recent arrival with the squadron F/L Mike Karop[i] a 23 year old married man from Norwich who worked in the Southern Cameroons post-war and sadly died there in 1959.

RA520-E	F/O JL Bathgate RNZAF
LM216-K	F/L HF Kirkwood
LM680-Z	F/O A McGuffie
NG413-M	S/L MR Cuelenaere RCAF
NN774-L	F/L MC Karop
PB344-R	F/O GH Cowan
PA322-V	W/C FWL Wild
ND412-H	F/O GR Scott RAAF

Due to transportation problems Military authorities had been unable to muster the numbers of former prisoners expected and only two aircraft (S/L Cuelenaere and F/O Cowan) ferried men home, the others returning empty. On 4th May both 630 Squadron and 57 Squadron again participated in Operation Exodus each providing 12 aircraft. 57 Squadron repatriated 281 service personnel to Westcott and Six-thirty brought back 287 service personnel and 1 civilian. 630's 'C' (Flying Officer Dobbie) remained at Westcott after the flight as their Gee had become unserviceable.

NG125-F	F/O GR Scott RAAF
PB784-Q	F/O K Hallett RAAF
LM216-P	F/O A McGuffie
LM216-K	F/L HF Kirkwood
NG259-N	S/L LW Pilgrim
ND412-H	F/O JW Wallace RNZAF
RA520-E	F/O LA Barnes
PB344-R	F/O GH Cowan
RF124-S	F/O AM MacLean

NG413-M	F/L MC Karop
JB290-C	F/O JB Dobbie
NG123-U	Lt MT Ackerman SAAF

On 8th May both squadrons from East Kirkby again flew round trips repatriating former POW's home from the continent. Returning from Juvincourt, 57 Squadron's 8 aircraft brought 192 servicemen and 630 Squadron's 7 brought back 163 servicemen. This time two more recently arrived pilots and their crews participated, 21 year old Warrant Officer Pete Frampton[ii] from Steyning who would become a planter in Malaya after wartime service and Australian F/O Robert 'Hammy' Hamilton[iii].

PD253-D	F/O JW Wallace RNZAF
NN702-J	F/O RE Hamilton RAAF
LM216-K	W/O PGS Frampton
NG413-M	F/O WM Taylor
NG259-N	F/S DS Tillett
PB784-Q	S/L LW Pilgrim
ME739-T	F/O JC Clingin RAAF

Back at base the Station Commander called a parade for 14:30 hours so that at 15:00 hours on 8th May the broadcast by the Prime Minister Winston Churchill was heard, war with Germany was over. This was followed by a short service held by the Chaplain Squadron Leader the Rev. George Dunbar[iv]. An 'Exodus' operation to Brussels was aborted on 12th May due to lousy weather and re-mounted successfully on 14th when 16 aircraft of 57 Squadron and 13 of 630 Squadron ferried 717 service personnel home safely from Lille-Vendeville.

LM216-K	F/L HF Kirkwood
PA266-P	F/O GH Cowan
NG125-F	F/O GR Scott RAAF
PA322-V	F/O AM MacLean RCAF
PD253-D	F/O LM Duggan RAAF
ME739-T	F/O K Hallett RAAF
RA520-E	F/O LA Barnes
LM680-Z	F/S DS Tillett
ND412-H	F/O JW Wallace RNZAF
RF124-S	W/O R Grange
NG123-U	F/O LW Jacobs RAAF
PB784-Q	S/L LW Pilgrim
NG413-M	F/O JL Bathgate RNZAF

On 15th May the squadron mounted a cross country flight by 4 aircraft, across the Ruhr Valley, 24 year old Section Officer Kay Seward WAAF[v] was one of the Base Staff who flew and decades later vividly recalled the excitement of sitting in a gun turret and sitting beside the pilot of her aircraft. She was a war widow, her husband Flight Lieutenant Fred Seward had been killed on 29th June 1943 flying with 97 Squadron.

Note: on 16th May 1945, Lt William Adams USAAF formerly of 630 Squadron but now flying with 617 Squadron crashed Lancaster Mark I PD139 while flying fast and very low near Oberg/Braunschweig clipping the roof of a house while on a training exercise. The entire crew walked away unhurt. One month earlier he'd written off another Lancaster near Lossiemouth, soon afterwards he returned to service with the USAAF.

On 17th May 1945 the recently arrived crew of 24 year old Bernard Hall[vi] crashed while carrying out a routine cross country training flight in RF124. At 17:15 hours a message was received at East Kirkby to the effect that the aircraft had been seen near Wolverhampton coming out of the clouds apparently out of control and crashing into a roadway near Moat House Farm at Short Heath, Wednesfield. The aircraft was completely destroyed and the whole crew killed. The cause of this accident is not known.

Lancaster I, RF124   (Codes LE – S)

Pilot	– F/O Bernard Hall. Age 24	Killed
Flight Eng	– F/O Ronald James O'Donnell. Age 21	Killed
Navigator	– Sgt Reginald Henry (Reggie) Smith. Age 21	Killed
Bomb Aimer	– F/O Victor Francis Dobell Meade. Age 23	Killed
Wireless Op	– Sgt Gordon Leonard Rabbetts. Age 21	Killed
Mid Upper	– Sgt Vincent Reginald W Southworth. Age 19	Killed
Rear Gunner	– Sgt John Alfred Sills. Age 21	Killed

The Hall crew (LAHC Archive)

Vincent Southworth was only 19 years old. The sad loss of this aircraft and crew was the first fatal accident involving a Bomber Command aircraft since the official cease fire at the end of the Second World War on 8th May 1945. Hall was buried at Boulton (St Mary) Churchyard, O'Donnell at Plymouth (Ford Park) Cemetery, Smith at Henley (Reading Road) Cemetery, Meade at Wiveliscombe (St Andrew) Churchyard, Rabbetts at Mangotsfield (Downend) Cemetery, Southworth at Watford North Cemetery and Sills at Cleethorpes Cemetery.

On 18th May 1945 Steve Nunns and crew were posted to 617 Squadron. On 21st May and 28th May in between a continually building program of training exercises 14 aircraft of 630 Squadron were detailed to jettison incendiaries into the North Sea on the first occasion and 12 on the second. The latter half of month was more inclined to thundery showers but training missions continued as rumours abounded concerning 'Tiger Force' the expected transfer of heavy bomber squadrons to participate in the war in the Far East.

630 Squadron completed 595.30 non-operational flying hours during the month.

Kay Rowland about to fly with the recently arrived crew of Bob Hamilton (Kay Rowland)

June 1945

June 1945 commenced with showery weather and during the first week crews of Six-thirty flew various Air Tests and on 4th June five of the squadrons aircraft and crews participated in incendiary dropping off the East Coast to dispose of more of the remaining stocks of volatile incendiary bombs. The 5th and 8th June brought a cross country flight over the Ruhr. On 7th June the squadron despatched seven aircraft to drop incendiaries into the North Sea and on the 9th carried out 48 similar flights and on 14th June two aircraft of 57 Squadron and 2 of 630 Squadron carried out 'Ruhr tours' Even more wet and windy days followed with occasional training missions until 15th June 1945 when four aircraft were detailed for another round of incendiary dropping.

On 8 June 1945 the award of the French Croix de Guerre was announced to Flight Lieut 'Pancho' O'Dwyer who had completed his tour and been posted away from the squadron in January 1945. Sadly one crew failed to return. The last news from the crew was at 11:47 hours when they reported having dropped their incendiaries and that they were turning for home. A search mission followed by 6 aircraft of 630 Squadron supported by 2 Warwicks, 1 Walrus and a Hight Speed Launch of 16 Group, but no trace could be found and no wreckage was seen floating. That evening a search mission was planned for early the following morning with 13 aircraft of 57 Squadron flying. At 22:05 hours a dinghy search was flown by 280 Squadron.

Lancaster III, PB344 (Codes LE – R)

Pilot	– F/O George Hamilton Cowan. Age 22	Killed
Flight Eng	– F/S David Porter Currie. Age 24	Killed
Navigator	– F/S Wilfred Ernest Smith. Age	Killed
Bomb Aimer	– F/S Jonah Rhodes. Age 25	Killed
Wireless Op	– F/S Frederick Reynolds. Age	Killed
Rear Gunner	– F/S James Porter. Age 20	Killed

The entire crew are commemorated on Runnymede Memorial. George Cowan's operational crew included David Currie, Wilf Smith, Fred Reynolds and Jim Porter, together they had completed 28 operations over enemy territory only to sadly be lost on a bomb disposal flight. Confusingly Jonah Rhodes is shown as a member of 51 Squadron on the Memorial.

In fine weather on the following day a dinghy search was flown by ten aircraft commencing at 04:50 hours but it was without result. At 09:10 hours ten aircraft from Spilsby commenced a search to the south of the area previously searched but sighted nothing. Nothing was heard from George Cowan's crew again but some wreckage was sighted between 12:37 and 15:54 hours in an Air Sea Rescue search 105 nautical miles off Flamborough Head by 44 and 207 Squadron aircraft. On 18th June a signal was received from HQ No.5 Group that the squadron was to prepare to move to RAF Skellingthorpe, the Advance Party to move on the 24th June, the Main Party on 25th and the Rear Part on 26th, work

David Currie (Matt Currie)

immediately commenced. The rolling program of training missions continued and on 19th June one aircraft toured the Ruhr Valley, several completed training missions whilst one took aerial photos of East Kirkby airfield. Incendiary dropping into the North Sea re-commenced on 20th and 21st June. After several days of frantic activity it was announced on 22nd June that with packing virtually complete, the move to Skellingthorpe was cancelled. Both squadrons at East Kirkby commenced some elements of training for 'Tiger Force', the RAF Heavy Bomber force expected to be despatched to the Far East.

In thunder storms and generally poor weather the squadron was stood down until 25th June when two further aircraft toured the Ruhr and high level bombing exercises resumed. The remainder of June was rainy, foggy and hazy although training flights continued until the end of the month. New British personnel continued to arrive to replace the Commonwealth aircrew who were quickly being posted in large numbers to Holding Units pending repatriation to their homes. In early June both flight commanders, Squadron Leaders Marcel Cuelenaere DFC RCAF and Lawrence Pilgrim DFC were posted away, Pilgrim back to 44 Squadron to train for 'Tiger Force'. Their replacements being Squadron Leader Ian George Fadden DFC BEM previously of 61 Squadron who had earned a BEM for gallantry crash landing a Wellington in the Western Desert while serving with 148 Squadron in October 1941 and Squadron Leader Terry Forshaw a pre-war regular pilot. 630 Squadron completed 308.15 non-operational flying hours during the month.

July 1945

With little change to the weather July commenced with occasional fine days in between showers, localised thunder and wider spread thunderstorms. Reconnaissance missions, training exercises and incendiary dropping into the North Sea were the order of the day but were interrupted by Ruhr tours by two Lancasters on 9th July.

Later in the month foggy and cloudy weather set in and most training flights were cancelled although on 12th July twelve cross country flights relieved the boredom and two more Ruhr tours were flown with two more following on 16th.

On 18th July the Appendix to the Operations Record Book abruptly reports the names of the aircrew still serving with 630 Squadron when it disbanded, the list is headed:

Commanding Officer	:	Wing Commander FWL Wild
Squadron Adjutant	:	Flight Lieutenant AHL Britton
'A' Flight Commander	:	Squadron Leader T Forshaw[i]
'B' Flight Commander	:	Squadron Leader IG Fadden DFC BEM[ii]
Training Officer	:	Flight Lieutenant GA Mitchell[iii]
Gunnery Leader	:	Flight Lieutenant TL Cass DFM[iv]
Navigation Leader	:	Flight Lieutenant HTA Evans DFC[v]
Bombing Leader	:	Flight Lieutenant A Barnard[vi]
Engineer Leader	:	Flying Officer SA Mitton[vii]
Signals Leader	:	Flying Officer DW Hobrough[viii]

630 Squadron Leadership

Commanding Officers
Squadron Leader M Crocker DFC and Bar	15/11/43 to 12/12/43
Wing Commander JD Rollinson DFC	12/12/43 to 29/01/44
Wing Commander WI Deas DSO DFC and Bar	01/02/44 to 08/07/44
Wing Commander LM Blome-Jones DFC	12/07/44 to 14/10/44
Wing Commander JE Grindon DSO	14/10/44 to 26/04/45
Wing Commander FWL Wild	26/04/45 to 19/07/45

A-Flight
Squadron Leader ER Butler DFC and 2 Bars	December 1943 – June 1944
Squadron Leader AE Foster DFC	June 1944 – June 1944
Squadron Leader RE Millichap DFC	June 1944 – November 1944
Squadron Leader MR Cuelenaere DFC and Bar	November 1944 – May 1945
Squadron Leader THT Forshaw	June 1945 – July 1945

B-Flight
Flight Lieut. WH Kellaway DSO and Bar	December 1943 to January 1944
Squadron Leader RO Calvert DFC and 2 Bars	January 1944 – August 1944
Squadron Leader MA Eyre DFC	August 1944 – March 1945
Squadron Leader SE Flett	March 1945 – April 1945
Squadron Leader LW Pilgrim DFC	April 1945 – May 1945
Squadron Leader IG Fadden DFC BEM	June 1945 – July 1945

Bombing Leader
Flight Lieutenant GGH Farara DFC DFM   November 1943 – July 1944
Flight Lieutenant RK Foulkes DFC   July 1944 – Jan 1945
Flight Lieutenant GKW Arkieson DFC   Jan 1945 – April 1945
Flight Lieutenant A Bernard   May 1945 – July 1945

Engineer Leader
Flight Lieutenant FD Spencer DFC   November 1943 – October 1944
Flight Lieutenant JJ Nelson DFC   October 1944 – April 1945
Flying Officer SA Mitton   May 1945 – July 1945

Gunnery Leader
Flight Lieutenant E Stead   November 1943 – February 1944
Flying Officer WLC Kirkpatrick   February 1944 – March 1944
Flight Lieutenant T Neison DFC   April 1944 – June 1944
Flight Lieutenant T Cass DFM   July 1944 – July 1945

Navigator Leader
Flight Lieutenant L Ehrman DFC   November 1943 – January 1944
Flight Lieutenant R Adams DFC   March 1944 – June 1944
Flight Lieutenant JW Martin DFC   July 1944 – October 1944
Flight Lieutenant HTA Evans DFC   February 1945 – July 1945

Signals Leader
Flying Officer WT Upton DFM   February 1944 – March 1944
Flight Lieutenant HG Cawdron DFM   March 1944 – December 1944
Flight Lieutenant DW Hobrough   February 1945 – July 1945

RAF East Kirkby
    Group Captain RT Taaffe OBE   20/08/43 to 30/11/44
    Group Captain BA Casey OBE   01/12/44 to 30/11/45

No.55 Base
    Group Captain RT Taaffe OBE   15/04/44 to 15/05/44
    Air Commodore HN Thornton MBE   15/05/44 to late March 45
    Air Commodore LW Dickens DFC AFC   April 45 to October 45
    Group Captain BA Casey OBE   October 45 to November 45

Awards

Bar to Distinguished Service Order

09/05/1944　　A/F/L Winston Herbert Kellaway DSO RAF (Pilot)

Distinguished Service Order

26/09/1944　　A/W/C William Inglis Deas DFC and Bar RAFVR (Pilot)
17/07/1945　　A/W/C John Evelyn Grindon RAF (Pilot)

2nd Bar to Distinguished Flying Cross

15/09/1944　　A/S/L Edward Robert Butler RAFVR (Navigator)
15/09/1944　　A/S/L Roy Oldfield Calvert RNZAF (Pilot)

Bar to Distinguished Flying Cross

18/01/1944　　A/S/L Malcolm Crocker DFC RAFVR (Pilot)
30/06/1944　　A/F/L Kenneth Robert Ames RAFVR (Pilot)
04/12/1945　　A/S/L Marcel Redmond Cuelenaere RCAF (Pilot)

Distinguished Flying Cross

07/01/1944　　A/F/L Douglas Allister MacDonald RCAF (Pilot)
11/02/1944　　F/L Donald Savigny Paterson RCAF (Pilot)
15/02/1944　　P/O Alexander Herbert Gibson RAFVR (Nav)
15/02/1944　　P/O Albert Edward A Matthews RAFVR (F/E)
15/02/1944　　P/O James Robert Worthington RAFVR (WOp/AG)
11/04/1944　　A/F/L James Charles W Weller RAFVR (Pilot)
21/04/1944　　F/O Carl Helmer Johnson RCAF (Nav)
21/04/1944　　F/O Harold Martin MacDonald RCAF (Pilot)
23/05/1944　　P/O Robert Cecil Hooper RAFVR (Pilot)
23/05/1944　　A/F/L Thomas Neison RAFVR (A/G)
23/05/1944　　F/O John Henry Pratt RCAF (Pilot)
02/06/1944　　F/O Anthony Gervase Blois RAFVR (A/B)
02/06/1944　　P/O Thomas Smart RAFVR (Nav)
06/06/1944　　F/O Gordon William Brake RAFVR (Nav)
06/06/1944　　P/O Robert Thomas Hughes RAFVR (Pilot)
06/06/1944　　W/O Lorne Hudson Todd RCAF (A/G)
30/06/1944　　P/O Harvey Glasby RAAF (WOp/AG)
30/06/1944　　P/O Frederick Richard G A Higgins RAFVR (A/G)
30/06/1944　　A/F/L David Roberts RAFVR (Pilot)
30/06/1944　　F/O Albert James Wright RAFVR (Nav)
11/07/1944　　A/F/L Geoffrey Harry Probert RAFVR (Pilot)
15/08/1944　　A/F/L Harold Walter Hill RAFVR (Pilot)
15/08/1944　　F/O Herbert Clifford Rogers RAF (Pilot
15/08/1944　　A/F/L Frederick David Spencer RAFVR (F/E)
19/09/1944　　F/O Andrew Kuzma RCAF (A/B)

19/09/1944	P/O Andrew John Lucas RAFVR (Nav)
19/09/1944	P/O Alan John Payne RAFVR (Nav)
13/10/1944	F/O Kenneth George Chamberlain RAFVR (Nav)
13/10/1944	F/O Alan William G Connor DFM RAAF (WOp/AG)
13/10/1944	F/O William Mooney DFM RAFVR (F/E)
17/10/1944	P/O William Charles R Jones RAFVR
17/10/1944	P/O Lionel Norman Rackley RAAF (Pilot)
08/12/1944	F/O Geoffrey John L Bate RAFVR (A/G)
08/12/1944	F/L Joseph Alcide M Beaudoin RCAF (Nav)
08/12/1944	F/L James William Martin RAFVR (Nav)
08/12/1944	A/S/L Roy Edgar Millichap RAFVR (Pilot)
08/12/1944	F/L Leonard Herbert V Wood RAFVR (WOp/AG)
12/12/1944	F/O Douglas Elwood Hawker RNZAF (Pilot)
12/12/1944	F/O Joseph William Lennon RNZAF (Pilot)
16/01/1945	A/W/C Leslie Milburne Blome-Jones RAFO (Pilot)
16/01/1945	F/O Hazen Herbert Long RCAF (Pilot)
16/01/1945	F/O Richard Lawrier McCann RCAF (Nav)
19/01/1945	P/O Winston Kimberley Goodhew RCAF (Nav)
19/01/1945	F/O Alan Ripley Kerr RAFVR (Pilot)
19/01/1945	F/O Donald Rhodes Mallinson RAFVR (Pilot)
19/01/1945	A/F/O Eugene Patrick Mitchell RAFVR (Pilot)
19/01/1945	A/F/O Matthew Alec Swain RAFVR (Pilot)
16/02/1945	A/F/L Terence Gillespie O'Dwyer RAFVR (Pilot)
09/03/1945	Lt Marthinus Theron Ackermann SAAF (Pilot)
22/05/1945	F/L Robert Kenrick Foulkes RAFVR (A/B)
22/05/1945	F/L Charles Wade Rodgers RAAF (Pilot)
22/05/1945	W/O George Alfred Whitby RAFVR (A/B)
29/06/1945	A/F/L George Grafton H Farara DFM RAFVR (A/B)
17/07/1945	F/L Henry David Archer RAFVR (Pilot)
20/07/1945	F/O Francis Ewen H Millar RNZAF (Pilot)
18/09/1945	A/F/L George Russell Joblin RNZAF (Pilot)
18/09/1945	A/F/L Geoffrey Eustace Stemp RAFVR (Pilot)
21/09/1945	A/F/L Thomas Bruce Baker RAAF (Pilot)
21/09/1945	F/L Malcolm Albert Eyre RAFVR (Pilot)
21/09/1945	A/F/L Eric Clifton Harris RNZAF (Pilot)
21/09/1945	A/F/L Stephen Arnold Nunns RAFVR (Pilot)
21/09/1945	A/F/L Harry Thompson RAF (Pilot)
23/10/1945	F/O George Alan Arrowsmith RAFVR (A/G)
26/10/1945	F/O John Black RAFVR (A/G)
04/12/1945	F/L George Kay Walker Arkieson RAFVR (A/B)
04/12/1945	A/F/L Oliver John Scott Atkinson RAAF (Pilot)
04/12/1945	F/L Gordon Louis Mortiboys RAFVR (A/B)
04/12/1945	Capt Desmond Charles B Reynolds SAAF (Pilot)
04/12/1945	A/F/L Neil Geoffrey Roberts RAAF (Pilot)
07/12/1945	F/O Jack William Hoare RAAF (Pilot)
07/12/1945	A/F/L John James Nelson RAFVR (F/E)
07/12/1945	F/O Leslie Frank Ovens RAFVR (Pilot)
07/12/1945	F/O Harry Alexander Ramsey RNZAF (Pilot)
07/12/1945	Capt Douglas Stacey Turner SAAF (Pilot)
07/12/1945	A/F/L Reginald George Waterfall RAFVR (Pilot)
21/12/1945	P/O Wilson Birwell Yates RAFVR (Pilot)

Distinguished Flying Medal

31/12/1943	F/S James White RAFVR (Pilot)
11/02/1944	F/S James George L Martin RAFVR (A/G)
07/04/1944	Sgt Richard Stafford Parle RAFVR (A/G)
21/04/1944	Sgt Peter William Vaggs RAF (A/G)
19/05/1944	Sgt Donald James Taylor RAFVR (F/E)
30/06/1944	F/S Thomas Hiett Savage RAFVR (A/B)
15/08/1944	F/S George Arthur Davies RAFVR (A/B)
15/08/1944	F/S Allan Wilkie Jeffrey RAFVR (Nav)
15/09/1944	F/S Douglas William Allen RCAF (A/B)
13/10/1944	F/S William Edwin J Cox RAFVR (F/E)
16/01/1945	F/S Edward Joseph Browne RCAF (A/G)
04/12/1945	F/S Mathew Barry RAFVR (A/G)

British Empire Medal (awarded for gallantry)

03/11/1944   F/S Douglas Stewart Morgan RAAF (A/B)

Croix de Guerre (France)

08/06/1945   A/F/L Terence Gillespie O'Dwyer RAFVR (Pilot)

Croix de Guerre 1940 avec Palme (Belgium)

27/06/1947   Engineer II John Gittings RAF (F/E)

Aircraft of 630 Squadron

Serial	Code	From	To	Fate	Ops	inc E/Rs
ED308	D	15/11/1943	22/11/1943	Later FTR -50 Sqn	0	0
ED413	M	15/11/1943	20/01/1944	Later SOC	9	2
ED655	J	15/11/1943	16/02/1944	crashed on return	16	2
ED698	R	15/11/1943	11/01/1944	Later crashed-207 Sqn	9	2
ED758	H	15/11/1943	13/01/1944	Later FTR - 207 Sqn	5	1
ED777	Q	15/11/1943	02/12/1943	FTR	2	0
ED920	P/D	15/11/1943	04/12/1943	FTR	6	1
ED944	Z	15/11/1943	19/04/1944	to 5455M in 7/45	19	4
JA872	N	15/11/1943	05/06/1944	SOC 10/01/1947	25	1
JB135	L	15/11/1943	24/11/1943	FTR	3	0
JB236	O-Bar	15/11/1943	24/11/1943	FTR	3	0
JB288	H	04/01/1944	31/03/1944	FTR	17	3
JB290	D/C	04/01/1944	18/09/1944	SOC 29/07/1946	62	2
JB294	R	04/01/1944	22/01/1944	FTR	3	0
JB532	X	20/11/1943	02/01/1944	FTR	7	1
JB546	A	17/11/1943	23/05/1944	FTR	34	1
JB556	Y	23/11/1943	24/04/1944	crashed on take off	30	2
JB561	W	20/11/1943	04/12/1943	Later FTR - 300 Sqn	3	1
JB597	S	17/11/1943	27/11/1943	crashed on return	2	1
JB654	C	17/11/1943	29/01/1944	FTR	14	1
JB665	B	17/11/1943	16/02/1944	FTR	16	0
JB666	O	17/11/1943	29/01/1944	FTR	14	2
JB672	F	17/11/1943	22/05/1944	FTR	40	0
JB710	W	27/12/1943	20/02/1944	FTR	10	1
LL886	I	19/03/1944	25/03/1944	FTR	1	0
LL949	E	28/04/1944	23/11/1944	FTR	56	1
LL950	Y	28/04/1944	22/05/1944	FTR	5	0
LL966	P	06/05/1944	15/02/1945	FTR	65	1
LL972	T	11/05/1944	17/08/1944	FTR	28	0
LM117	J	24/05/1944	19/07/1944	FTR	14	0
LM118	V	24/05/1944	22/06/1944	FTR	10	0
LM215		24/06/1944	29/06/1944	SOC 21/06/47	0	0
LM216	K	24/06/1944	25/07/1944	SOC 05/03/46	84	1
LM259	F	20/07/1944	09/10/1944	Later FTR - 227 Sqn	34	0
LM260	S	21/07/1944	17/03/1945	FTR	48	0
LM262	G	21/07/1944	08/08/1944	FTR	4	0
LM269	I	24/07/1944	18/08/1944	FTR	11	0
LM287	O	28/07/1944	21/05/1945	to 5759M in 12/45	70	0
LM537	X	25/04/1944	19/07/1944	FTR	26	0

Serial	Code	From	To	Fate	Ops	inc E/Rs
LM637	V	21/06/1944	09/12/1944	FTR	42	0
LM649		15/07/1944	09/09/1944	SOC 27/01/47	0	0
LM649		13/07/1945	20/07/1945			
LM673	B	17/09/1944	08/10/1944	SOC 27/04/45	7	0
LM680	Z	27/03/1945	06/11/1945		3	0
ME312	A	28/10/1944	28/12/1944	SOC 14/08/46	10	2
ME532		03/03/1945	12/03/1945	SOC 15/05/47	0	0
ME650	B	24/02/1944	27/08/1944	FTR	42	1
ME664	T	24/02/1944	31/03/1944	FTR	8	1
ME717	E	31/03/1944	27/04/1944	crashed on return	6	0
ME729	T/I	30/03/1944	19/07/1944	crashed on exercise	9	0
ME737	S	31/03/1944	12/05/1944	FTR	12	0
ME739	D/T	10/04/1944	11/04/1945	FTR	91	0
ME782	N	01/05/1944	22/06/1944	FTR	15	0
ME795	G	14/05/1944	22/06/1944	crashed on return	15	0
ME796	S	14/05/1944	19/07/1944	FTR	23	1
ME843	U	11/06/1944	22/06/1944	FTR	3	0
ME845	Q	04/06/1944	16/05/1945	SOC 27/05/47	68	0
ME845		18/06/1945	06/07/1945			
ME867	N	24/06/1944	05/07/1944	FTR	1	0
ND335	L	12/12/1943	28/08/1944	to 5793M in 5/46	63	3
ND337	S	12/12/1943	31/03/1944	FTR	23	1
ND338	Q	12/12/1943	21/02/1944	FTR	13	0
ND412	H	07/08/1944	01/09/1945		52	1
ND527	O	27/01/1944	27/07/1944	FTR	50	0
ND530	P	25/01/1944	16/03/1944	FTR	7	3
ND531	K	27/01/1944	22/06/1944	FTR	36	2
ND532	N	25/01/1944	20/02/1944	FTR	2	0
ND554	C/A/E	27/01/1944	09/02/1945	FTR	49	3
ND561	R	30/01/1944	02/03/1944	FTR	6	0
ND563	T	30/01/1944	20/02/1944	crashed on take off	3	0
ND580	G	05/02/1944	12/05/1944	FTR	15	0
ND583	V	05/02/1944	16/03/1944	FTR	6	0
ND655	J	28/02/1944	23/05/1944	FTR	19	2
ND657	W	29/02/1944	25/03/1944	FTR	5	0
ND685	Q	29/02/1944	07/06/1944	FTR	29	1
ND686	M	29/02/1944	19/03/1944	FTR	2	0
ND688	R	04/03/1944	08/07/1944	FTR	17	0
ND788	U	18/03/1944	25/03/1944	FTR	1	0
ND789	I	26/03/1944	27/04/1944	FTR	10	0
ND793	V	26/03/1944	26/08/1944	SOC	14	1
ND797	W	26/03/1944	29/07/1944	FTR	31	0

Serial	Code	From	To	Fate	Ops	inc E/Rs
ND949	Z	22/04/1944	09/04/1945	crashed on return	75	2
ND982	Y	07/08/1944	30/08/1944	FTR	10	0
NF961	L	24/08/1944	18/10/1944	crashed	10	1
NG123	U	08/09/1944	03/10/1945	SOC 07/08/1947	55	0
NG125	N/F	09/09/1944	17/09/1945	SOC 22/05/1947	55	1
NG145	I	17/09/1944	03/12/1944	Later FTR - 57 Sqn	14	0
NG258	B	06/11/1944	22/12/1944	crashed	10	0
NG259	N	15/10/1944	06/07/1945	SOC 15/01/1947	45	1
NG413	V/M	28/12/1944	31/07/1945	SOC 02/06/1945	29	0
NN702	J	20/07/1944	06/07/1945	SOC 15/01/1947	77	0
NN703	X	21/07/1944	25/07/1945	SOC 03/06/1947	68	2
NN774	L	05/01/1945	25/07/1945	SOC 21/02/1946	27	1
PA266	P	27/02/1945	19/07/1945	SOC 12/03/1948	16	1
PA322	V	06/04/1945	19/07/1945	SOC 22/05/1947	2	0
PA992	Y	29/05/1944	25/07/1944	FTR	18	1
PB121	F	05/06/1944	10/06/1944	FTR	1	0
PB211	H	08/07/1944	24/07/1944	FTR	7	0
PB236	F	27/06/1944	19/07/1944	FTR	7	0
PB244	N	08/07/1944	18/08/1944	FTR	21	0
PB344	R	14/07/1944	15/06/1945	crashed at sea	75	0
PB742		26/10/1944	05/11/1944	Later FTR - 189 Sqn	0	0
PB865		17/12/1944	03/01/1945	SOC 30/10/46	0	0
PB880	B	17/12/1944	14/01/1945	FTR	5	0
PB894	A	27/12/1944	01/01/1945	FTR	1	0
PD253	D	04/08/1944	09/08/1945	SOC 19/10/45	62	1
PD254	W	11/08/1944	25/07/1945	SOC 15/05/47	63	0
PD283	G	24/08/1944	12/09/1944	FTR	5	0
PD317	G	18/09/1944	08/01/1945	crashed on landing	31	3
PD327	Y/E	17/09/1944	23/07/1945	SOC 19/10/45	52	2
RA520	E	20/02/1945	06/07/1945	SOC 03/09/47	19	1
RA603		23/04/1945	06/07/1945	SOC 09/01/47	0	0
RF122	I/S	06/02/1945	11/04/1945	FTR	18	0
RF124	S	11/04/1945	17/05/1945	crashed on exercise	3	0
RF192	A	14/03/1945	06/07/1945	SOC 31/10/47	10	0
RF202		31/05/1945	25/09/1945	SS 07/05/47	0	0
RF266		17/04/1945	22/04/1945	SS 29/08/47	0	0

East Kirkby

RAF East Kirkby control with G/Capt Taaffe (Imperial War Museum)

RAF East Kirkby – 'Call Sign – Silksheen'

The RAF Form 540 'Operations Record Book' of RAF East Kirkby[i] opens in mid-July 1943 showing frantic activity as an operational heavy bomber airfield was under construction. Civilian contractors, primarily John Laing and Son Ltd were at work to provide an Air Ministry Class A standard specification airfield, ie: two 1,400 yard long runways in a 'V' pattern, 08-26 and 13-31, in this instance converging at the Stickney road. Crossing the two was the main 2,000 yard runway 02-20 running slightly east of North towards the old windmill at Old Bolingbroke run by Mr and Mrs Ely which served as a perfect landmark for crews struggling to get a damaged aircraft home or seeking the safety of home in poor weather.

During August 1943 as the base took shape the senior officers of various branches began to arrive:

S/L AHL Marwood[ii]   Station Admin Officer (from RAF Syerston)
F/L WL Collis[iii]   Accountant Officer (from RAF Linton)
F/O BJ Roberts[iv]   Equipment Officer (from RAF Grange over Sands)
A/F/L CJ Morley[v]   Catering Officer (from HQ Bomber Command)
F/L LF Woolcott[vi]   Signals Officer (from RAF Waddington)

By mid-month the records reported that two accommodation sites were fully equipped and the means were available to provide 2 more.

Site 2 – for 23 officers, 60 NCO's and 270 Airmen.
Site 3 – for 37 officers, 64 NCO's and 240 Airmen.

The WAAF site was ready for occupation and would be furnished as WAAF's arrived. Services were laid on, electric lighting was available throughout the camp, suppliers of coal and laundry services had been arranged with tenders invited for boot repairs and funerals.

A/F/L CW Martin[vii]	Engineer Officer (from RAF Wigsley)
F/O EW Buckler[viii]	Flying Control (from RAF Scampton)

On 20th August Group Captain RT Taaffe OBE[ix] (Station Commander) reported from 5 Group on attachment pending his formal posting as Station Commander which was to be effective 1st September 1943 and had the RAF standard flying above the station.

A/P/O SI Hollingsworth[x]	Electrical Engineer (from RAF Swinderby)
F/L GN Sellers DFC[xi]	Station Adjutant (from RAF Driffield)
F/O WD Evans[xii]	Flying Control (from RAF Syerston)

On the 24th and 26th Group Captain Taaffe and Squadron Leader Marwood visited RAF Coningsby and RAF Scampton to discuss the move of 57 Squadron to East Kirkby and to attend the Farewell Party held at Scampton for the departing squadron. Advanced parties from 57 Squadron commenced their move the very next morning.

Station staff officers continued to arrive:

S/L RN Benjamin MC[xiii]	OC, 2785 AA Squadron, RAF Regt.
A/S/L EA Dearman[xiv]	Intelligence Officer (from RAF Scampton)
A/F/L H Watson MBE[xv]	Armament Officer (from RAF Scampton)
S/O AN Grant WAAF[xvi]	Code and Cypher Officer (from RAF Hethel)
F/O CAS Lowndes[xvii]	Meteorological Officer (from RAF Scampton)
F/O AA StClair-Miller[xviii]	Navigation Officer (from 1660 Conversion Unit)
F/O AR Morris[xix]	Signals (RDF) Officer (from RAF Fiskerton)
P/O J Pye	Signals (attached from 5 Group)
S/O MJ Barclay WAAF[xx]	Intelligence (attached from RAF Waddington)
S/O IG Bruce WAAF[xxi]	Attached temporarily from RAF Annan.

Marion Barclay from Dorking had been a W.V.S. ambulance driver prior to joining the W.A.A.F.

On 29th August 57 Squadron arrived at RAF East Kirkby, their aircraft were flown in fully crewed and the following night they participated in an attack on Monchen-Gladbach.

Station staff officers continued to arrive:

F/L JR O'Dowd[xxii]	Medical Officer (from RAF Uxbridge)
F/O H Mellor[xxiii]	Intelligence Officer (from RAF Uxbridge)
A/F/L M Carty[xxiv]	Intelligence Officer (from RAF Scampton)
S/O J Pellow WAAF[xxv]	Intelligence Officer (from RAF Scampton)

The closing days of August had seen RAF East Kirkby (Group Captain Rudolph Taaffe OBE, Station Commander) declared operational and receive the prompt transfer of No. 57 Squadron (Wing Commander HWH Fisher DFC) from Scampton.

Further Station staff officers arrived during September:

S/O DJ Burnett WAAF[xxvi]	Catering Officer (from RAF Walton)
A/F/L WC Hawken[xxvii]	Tech Armament (from RAF Bottesford)
F/L CU Lloyd[xxviii]	Motor Transport (from RAF Bottesford)
P/O RR Bennett[xxix]	FCO (from RAF Scampton)
S/L B Peter Jones[xxx]	Admin and Special Duties (from RAF Syerston)
P/O PS Griffiths[xxxi]	Meteorological Officer (from RAF Syerston)
F/O F Oldfield[xxxii]	Accounts Officer (from RAF Topcliff)
S/L AW Heward DFC AFC[xxxiii]	Pilot, from 1654 Conversion Unit.
S/L P Alderson[xxxiv]	Station Equipment Officer (from the Air Ministry)
S/O JA Mouat WAAF[xxxv]	Admin Officer (from RAF Stannington)
S/O DJ Babington WAAF[xxxvi]	Intelligence Officer (from RAF Scampton)
F/O RG Dunnett[xxxvii]	FCO (from RAF Langar)
A/Flt/O OF Webber WAAF[xxxviii]	'G' (from 11 Base)

During September Group Captain Taaffe lent advice and support as RAF Spilsby took shape just as East Kirkby had been and 57 Squadron continued to fly operational missions as works on the station continued. On 21st September the AOC 5 Group AVM the Hon. Sir Ralph Cochrane CB CBE AFC[xxxix] visited the station. As a reminder, as if any were needed in the face of the squadrons' losses over Germany, that the air war was not a distant one, a Luftwaffe night fighter intruder shot up a returning 57 Squadron Lancaster in circuit above the base at about 00:40 hours on the morning of 23rd September 1943. The crew of Pilot Officer GA Duff in W4948 (DX – S) were caught unawares and five were killed, two baling out unhurt, as it crashed in flames near Spilsby. Five Me410 long-range night fighter intruders of V/KG 2 (5th Wing of Bomber Group 2) had joined the returning bomber stream carrying out seven attacks over the bomber bases. Their commanding officer Major Wolf-Dietrich Meister was responsible for shooting down W4948.

Another enemy night fighter intruder opened fire with cannons and machine guns across the centre of East Kirkby airfield at about midnight on the 27th and on the following day whilst in transit from a stop-over at RAF Waterbeach following an attack on Hannover the 57 Squadron crew of P/O GM Hargrave aboard ED941 (DX – V) had both port engines cut out as they came in to land at East Kirkby causing their Lancaster to crash on the north side of the airfield. The pilot, flight engineer and navigator were sadly killed, survivors were treated for injuries at RAF Hospital Rauceby.

Minor changes to the staff positions took place during the month and new staff officers arrived into October as 57 Squadron continued to fly operations as required.

F/L WG Giles[xl]	PT Officer (from RAF High Wycombe)
S/L A Haskell[xli]	Station Engineer Officer (from RAF Bottesford)
Lt-Colonel S Astle[xlii]	Local Defence Adviser (from 5 Group HQ)
A/P/O Kirby	Flying Control Officer (from 5 Group HQ)
F/O CC Grebby[xliii]	Gas/Fire Officer (from RAF Bottesford)
S/O DM deSausmarez[xliv]	'G' (from RAF Bottesford)
S/O MP Vickers[xlv]	Catering Officer (from RAF Kidbrooke)

Lt-Colonel S. Astle MC TD was to work with 2756 Squadron RAF Regiment who guarded the station and provided Anti-Aircraft defence.

On 15th April 1944 Headquarters No. 55 Base RAF formed at East Kirkby as per Bomber Command BC/S.29757/5/Org. of 22nd April 1944. The Base comprised RAF Station East Kirkby and sub-stations RAF Strubby and RAF Spilsby.
W/C RN Stidolph (GB Branch) was posted from 61 Squadron for Operations.
W/C RW Holloway (A&SD) was posted from RAF Foulsham as Senior Admin Officer
W/C JS Eley (Equipment) was posted from HQ Bomber Command as Eqpt Officer
S/O Hopcroft (Intelligence) was posted from No. 5 Group
S/O Crabbe (Signals) was posted from No. 5 Group

Bob Baldwin (media producer and playwright) wrote the highly rated play 'Wireless Operator' based on the service of his father Joe Baldwin who flew in Jerry Monk's crew, 630 Squadron.

Joe Baldwin, Wireless Operator(Bob Baldwin)

Footnotes

Formation

[i] Hurtle William Hamilton Fisher DFC (41915). GD Branch. DFC LG. 21/11/41, 49 Sqdn.
[ii] Malcolm Crocker (125256), GD Branch. DFC and Bar, KIA (see text). born 02/02/1917 at Fitchburg, Worcester, Massachusetts, USA.
[iii] John Dudley Rollinson (90391). GD Branch. DFC, KIA (see text)
[iv] John Douglas Henderson (NZ411403), RNZAF. DFC LG. 12/11/43, 619 Sqdn.
[v] Cyril Raymond Savage (J13415), RCAF. DFC LG. 18/01/44, 44 Sqdn.
[vi] The Rev. Gordon Robert Cooper (120458), RAFVR. Chaplains Branch.
[vii] The Rev. Charles Edward Heap, B.A. (127019). Chaplains Branch.
[viii] Frederick Harry Jones (123171), A&SD Branch. Previously 771265, LAC.
[ix] Herbert Francis George Dawson (53130), A&SD Branch. Previously 517794, W/O.

November 1943

[i] Frank Cheetham (60633). A&SD Branch.
[ii] National Archives, London (Air27/538)
[iii] Donald Savigny Paterson (J.3523) RCAF. DFC LG.11/02/44, 630 Squadron. (born 22/04/1918 Fort Worth/Canada – died 24/05/2006 Winnipeg/NB).
[iv] Frederick Leonard Perrers (NZ414672) RNZAF. KIA (see text).
[v] John Henry Pratt (J.16836) RCAF. DFC LG. 23/05/44, 630 Sqdn.
[vi] Joseph Howe (149545),RAFVR. KIA (see text)
[vii] Peter John Piggin (147781), RAFVR. KIA (see text) (born 28/04/1922 Tanganyika/Zambia – KIA 02/03/1944 on Ops) Educated at Cranbrook School, Kent.
[viii] Donald William Story (A.4048) RAAF. KIA (see text)
[ix] Sidney Albert Edwards (1382668, 170938). RAFVR.Later KIA 10/05/44.
[x] John Walter Homewood, 1392321, RAFVR. KIA (see text)
[xi] James White, 657977, RAFVR. DFM LG. 31/12/43. Later KIA (see text)
[xii] Wilson Birwell Yates (1303926, 161407), RAFVR. DFC LG. 21/12/45. KIA (see text).
[xiii] National Archives, London (Air27/2152)
[xiv] William English (117836), RAFVR. KIA (see text)
[xv] John Syme (A.416725) RAAF. KIA (see text)
[xvi] Gordon William Burness, RNZAF. NZ416191.DFM LG 14/12/43, 44 Sqdn. AFC LG. 07/09/45. (born 26/09/1921 Waimate/New Zealand – died 14/01/1968 Timaru/New Zealand).
[xvii] Kenneth Robert Ames (133400), RAFVR. DFC LG. 23/11/43, 61 Sqn, Bar to DFC LG.30/06/44, 630 Squadron. (born April 1922 Wandsworth/London – died 22/09/1975 at his home in Vienna)
[xviii] Donald Harry Cheney (J.18295) RCAF. DFC LG. 16/01/45, 617 Sqn.
[xix] Reginald Cartwright (157429), RAFVR. DFC LG. 10/10/43, 207 Sqn.
[xx] Douglas Allister MacDonald (J.14691) RCAF. DFC LG. 07/01/44, 630 Sqdn, KIA (see text)
[xxi] Robert Thomas Hughes (658169, 169008), RAFVR. DFC LG. 06/06/44, 630 Sqdn.
[xxii] Geoffrey Harry Probert (135407), RAFVR. DFC LG. 11/07/44, 630 Sqdn.
[xxiii] David Robets (150196), RAFVR. DFC LG. 30/06/44, 630 Sqdn. Later awarded AFC.
[xxiv] William Alfred Clark (156304), RAFVR. KIA (see text)
[xxv] Austin Drinkall (1388354, 161594), RAFVR. Later KIA 06/08/44. DFC LG 12/09/44, 582 Sqdn.
[xxvi] Allan George Garth Johnson (1384953, 161590), RAFVR. KIA (see text)
[xxvii] Clifford Harold Armour (142201), RAFVR. KIA (see text)
[xxviii] Winston Herbert Kellaway (49688), RAF. DSO LG. 30/03/43, 149 Sqdn. Citation published.
[xxix] Leopold Ehrman (1388632, 126033), RAFVR. DFC LG. 11/06/43, 44 Sqdn. KIA (see text)

[xxx] Frederick David Spencer (968957, 143793) RAFVR. DFC LG. 15/08/44, 630 Sqdn.
[xxxi] George Grafton Haig Farara (920368, 143472), RAFVR. DFM LG. 15/06/43, 97 Sqdn. DFC LG. 29/06/45, 630 Sqdn. KIA (see text).
[xxxii] Ernest Stead (1050900, 124125), RAFVR. MinD LG. 01/01/43. KIA (see text)
[xxxiii] Douglas Edward James (1267376), RAFVR. KIA (see text)
[xxxiv] James Wilson Harrower (133129), A&SD Branch, RAFVR. Previously AC2, 1558919
[xxxv] RAF Museum, Hendon (AC91/8/39)
[xxxvi] Anthony Gervase Blois (156046), RAFVR. DFC LG. 02/06/44, 630 Sqdn.
[xxxvii] National Archives, London (Air 2/9149)
[xxxviii] Francis Eric Whalley (136322), Suffolk Regt. Retired as Hon Lt-Col, 07/12/47.
[xxxix] Herbert Clifford Rogers (574463, 54091), RAF. DFC LG.15/08/44, 630 Sqdn. OBE LG. 08/06/1968 as Chief Test Pilot, Rolls Royce.

December 1943

[i] Harold Charles Leeton Mackintosh (A 414052), RAAF. KIA (see text)
[ii] Wilfrid Lewis Dunn (90074), Accounts Branch, RAF.
[iii] Joseph Wagstaff (50814), Technical Branch, RAF. Previously W/O (508844).
[iv] Howard Derbyshire Elloitt, M.B., Ch.B. (88625). Medical Branch.
[v] Robert Hugh Clover (60968). RAF Regt. Previously 1351936 Sergeant.
[vi] James Charles William Weller (55014), RAF. DFC LG. 11/04/44, 630 Sqdn.
[vii] Dermott John Hegarty (A.420561) RAAF. Later KIA 16/07/44. DFC LG.13/10/44, 83 Sqdn.
[viii] Edward Robert Butler (107923), GD Branch, RAFVR. DFC LG. 03/11/42, 97 Sqdn. Bar to DFC LG. 20/11/42, 97 Sqdn. 2nd Bar to DFC LG. 15/09/44, 630 Sqdn.
[ix] Peter Greenhalgh (73899), Royal Artillery. DFC LG. 8/11/44.
[x] William Neil McKechnie GC DFC (26144), RAF, Later KIA 30/08/44, 106 Sqdn.
[xi] Anthony Caron Evans-Evans DFC (19018), RAF. Later KIA 21/02/45, 83 Sqdn, age 43.
[xii] Kenneth Rodbourn (1577414, 169004), RAFVR. KIA (see text).
[xiii] Harold Walter Hill (161806), RAFVR. DFC LG.11/08/44, 630 Sqdn.
[xiv] Kenneth Frederick Vare (40273). RAF. AFC LG. 01/01/44

January 1944

[i] Vaughan Charles Simson Bach (72776), RAFVR. A&SD Branch. (born 02/10/1899 Overstone Rectory, Northampton – died 20/07/1946 Northampton, serving as Flight Lieut). Prob. Commission Flight Officer RNAS on 02/09/1917; transfer to RAF commission 15/05/1918 as pilot, flew DH6, Avro, BE2c and Handley Page. Commissioned Pilot Officer RAF on 14/03/1939 A&SD Branch.
[ii] Roy Oldfield Calvert (NZ404890) RNZAF. DFC LG. 20/10/42, 50 Sqdn. Bar to DFC LG. 18/12/42, 50 Sqdn. 2nd Bar to DFC LG. 15/09/44, 630 Sqdn.
[iii] Frederick Henry Arthur Watts (170742), RAFVR. DFC LG. 23/03/45, 617 Sqdn.
[iv] Leonard Alfred Barnes (168998), RAFVR. Shot down and Evaded. (see text). MBE LG. 10/06/80.
[v] Thomas Smart (1346545, 155578), RAFVR. DFC LG. 02/06/44, 630 Sqdn. MinD LG. 06/06/45. MinD LG. 01/01/46.
[vi] Anthony Gervase Blois (156046), RAFVR. DFC LG. 02/06/44.
[vii] The Rev. Thomas Freyne (126135), RAFVR. Chaplains Branch.

February 1944

[i] William Inglis Deas (87060), RAFVR. DSO LG. 26/09/44, 630 Sqdn. DFC LG. 21/11/41, 61 Sqdn. Bar to DFC LG. 20/04/43, 61 Sqdn.
[ii] John Benner Nall (125936), RAFVR. Transferred to 83 Sqdn.
[iii] Joseph Seddon Kilgour (170959), RAFVR. KIA (see text)
[iv] Arthur John Perry (A.17335), RAAF. POW (see text)
[v] Clifford Leslie Eldridge Allen (170941), RAFVR. KIA (see text)
[vi] Edgar John Murray (170229), RAFVR. KIA (see text)
[vii] Reginald Neville Stidolph (37513). DFC LG.25/01/44, 61 Sqdn. Station Ops Officer.
[viii] Robert Lawrence Bowes (70072), RAF. GD Branch. DFC LG 19/10/43, Bar to DFC LG. 03/03/44, both awards with 44 Sqdn.
[ix] Kenneth Watson Orchiston (NZ.422310) RNZAF. KIA (see text)
[x] William Leopold Carver Kirkpatrick (2202818, 144459), RAFVR. KIA (see text).
[xi] Alan Geoffrey Hardy, B.M., B.Ch., M.R.C.S., L.R.C.P. (137263). MBE LG. 14/06/45.
[xii] John Mason Cockshott, L.D.S. (109394). Dental Branch.
[xiii] Peter Albert Nash (1321180, 172182), RAFVR. Died following accidental injuries (see text)
[xiv] Alan William Wilson (A.410510) RAAF. KIA (see text)
[xv] Ronald Walter Bailey (170965). KIA (see text)
[xvi] John Ogilvie Langlands (132799). POW (see text)
[xvii] Lionel Norman (Blue) Rackley (A.414828) RAAF. DFC LG. 17/10/44, 630 Sqdn.. Later awarded Air Efficiency Award and made a member of the Order of Australia in 1982, promoted 1998.

March 1944

[i] Ronald Leslie Clark (A.408328) RAAF. KIA (see text)
[ii] Robert Adams (120247). DFC LG. 11/06/43, 61 Sqdn.KIA (see text)
[iii] Thomas Neison (1365541, 138890), RAFVR. DFC LG. 23/05/44, 630 Sqdn.KIA (see text)
[iv] George Russell Joblin (NZ424982), RNZAF. DFC LG. 18/09/45, 630 Sqdn. KIA (see text)
[v] Donald Rhodes Mallinson (1425572, 174315), RAFVR. DFC LG. 19/01/45, 630 Sqdn.
[vi] Robert Cecil Hooper (1410555, 172176), RAFVR. DFC LG. 23/05/44, 630 Sqdn.KIA (see text)
[vii] Alfred Thomas Jackson (904877, 172175), RAFVR. KIA (see text)
[viii] Charles Wade Rodgers (A.409948), RAAF. DFC LG. 22/05/45, 630 Sqdn.
[ix] Hurtle William Hamilton Fisher DFC (41915). GD Branch. DFC LG. 21/11/41, 49 Sqdn.
[x] Herbert York Humphreys (33003), RAFVR. GD Branch. DFC LG. 03/10/44, 57 Sqdn.
[xi] Maurice John Stancer (1452104, 179431), RAFVR. DFM LG. 13/10/44, 44 Sqdn.

April 1944

[i] Marcus George Radcliffe (67172). A&SD Branch. M in D LG. 14/06/45.
[ii] Rev. Hugh Deerin (172818). Chaplains Branch.
[iii] Douglas Elwood Hawker (NZ 42401), RNZAF. DFC LG. 12/12/44, 630 Sqdn.
[iv] Wilfred Arthur Watt (NZ421800) RNZAF. KIA (see text)
[v] Joseph William Lennon (NZ.421732) RNZAF. DFC LG. 12/12/44, 630 Sqdn.
[vi] Vivian William Brown (A.414903), RAAF. KIA (see text)
[vii] Edward Frank Champness (A.421858), RAAF. KIA (see text)
[viii] Charles Theodore Martin MM (76921). A&SD Branch.
[ix] Eugene Patrick Mitchell (1508002, 178308), RAFVR. DFC LG. 19/01/45, 630 Sqdn.
[x] John Banks McGinn (46263), RAF. Tech Branch. Previously W/O, 331779. MBE LG. 01/01/42. Mentioned in Despatches twice in 1941 as Wt.Offr, again in 1943. Later W/Cdr. (1902-1959)
[xi] Alan Flowerdew (34220), A&SD Branch, RAF. (formerly General Duties Branch).

May 1944

[i] Brian Benjamin Lindsay (A. 420216), RAAF. DFC LG. 06/10/44, 97 Sqdn.
[ii] Howard Wallace Smith (J.24995) RCAF. KIA (see text)
[iii] Gordon Edward Maxwell (A.425331) RAAF. KIA (see text)
[iv] East Kirkby 'Raids Book' (RAF Museum, AC91/8/25)
[v] Alfred George Henriquez (1800848, 171932), RAFVR. KIA (see text)
[vi] Douglas George Gamble (172478), RAFVR. DFC LG. 20/07/45, 83 Sqdn.
[vii] Terence Gillespie O'Dwyer (1397484, 142353), RAFVR. DFC LG. 16/02/45, 630 Sqdn.
[viii] Henry Norman Thornton MBE, RAF. MBE LG. 03/06/35. promoted Acting AVM 04/05/45.
[ix] Robert George Percy Jaggard MBE (21252), RAF. MBE LG. 01/01/41.
[x] Bethea Barbara Hayward (166), WAAF. M in D LG 01/01/45. Wounded in action 04/03/45. Died 3/7/1973 at Balsham Cambs aged 62.
[xi] Kenyon Cameron Brigden (111140). RAFVR. Technical Branch.
[xii] Henry Allan Astbury (76107). Accountant Branch.
[xiii] William Barrett Rawling (88294). A&SD Branch.
[xiv] Lawrence Harold Button (88760), RAFVR. GD Branch. M in D LG 14/01/44.
[xv] Delia Emily Holey (5284), WAAF.
[xvi] Bernard Victor Smith (47246), RAF. Tech Branch. Previously W/O, 509877. M in D LG. 01/01/43 and 08/06/44.
[xvii] Hazen Herbert Long (J.25982), RCAF. DFC LG. 16/01/45, 630 Sqdn. (born 23/05/1914 New Brunswick/Canada – died 24/03/1977 Moncton/New Brunswick)
[xviii] Ronald Thomas Hayes (1324704, 175961), RAFVR. KIA (see text)
[xix] Bruce William Brittain (A.414756), RAAF. Shot down and Evaded (see text)
[xx] Claud Morley Houghton AFM (1165631, 176435) RAFVR. AFM LG. 08/06/44. KIA (see text). (born 22/04/1915, a journalist pre-war, resident at Barford Road, Sheringham).
[xxi] Douglas Haig Simpson (J.24995) RCAF. DFC LG. 17/07/45, 97 Sqdn.
[xxii] Harold Earl Wilson (R.166063, J.86677), RCAF. KIA (see text)
[xxiii] Alan Ripley Kerr (1601498, 172185), RAFVR. DFC LG. 19/01/45, 630 Sqdn.
[xxiv] Arthur Edgar Foster DFC (1169809,113416), RAFVR. DFC LG. 12/03/43, 61 Sqdn. KIA (see text)

June 1944

[i] John Francis Grey DSO DFC (37767), RAF. DSO LG. 28/11/44. DFC LG. 30/05/44, both awards 207 Sqdn.
[ii] Matthew Alec Swain (1335451, 176282), RAFVR. DFC LG. 19/01/45, 630 Sqdn.
[iii] Edward Docherty (1550988, 170951), RAFVR.
[iv] Thomas George Hart (R.160011, J.86480). KIA (see text).
[v] John Henry George Smith (1602443, 175502), RAFVR. KIA (see text).
[vi] Thomas Selskar Fenning (548080, 54967), RAF. Later DFC LG. 25/09/45, 189 Sqdn.
[vii] John Herbert Bolton (1443886, 175108), RAFVR. Shot down and Evaded (see text)
[viii] Ralph Norman Taft (1394743, 176763), RAFVR. KIA (see text)
[ix] Arthur Frederick Kemp (J.25975) RCAF. Shot down and Evaded (see text)
[x] William Alexander McNeil (1342663, 176956), RAFVR.
[xi] Roy Edgar Millichap (1187343, 111781), RAFVR. DFC LG. 08/12/44, 630 Sqdn. (born 22/07/1916 Plymouth – died 15/11/1995) post-war pilot with British Airways and BOAC. Flew the Comet which carried HM Queen Elizabeth 2 to Newfoundland 06/1959.

July 1944

[i] Evelyn George William Bowers (1575110, 178512), RAFVR. KIA (see text).
[ii] Peter Buck Dennett (A.418927), RAAF. KIA (see text)
[iii] Alexander James Sargent (1333723, 173311), RAFVR. KIA (see text)
[iv] Joseph Thomas Taylor (1136019, 143798), RAFVR. DFC LG. 14/09/43, 49 Sqdn. KIA (see text).
[v] Walter Thomas Upton (1254726, 157278), RAFVR. DFM LG. 29/12/42, 61 Sqdn. POW (see text).
[vi] Thomas Leonard Cass (745238, 137343), RAFVR. DFM LG. 29/12/42, 61 Sqdn.
[vii] George Kay Walker Arkieson (131133), RAFVR. DFC LG. 04/12/45, 630 Sqdn.
[viii] Leslie Milburn Blome-Jones (37760), RAF. DFC LG. 16/01/45, 630 Sqdn. (born 17/01/1912 Sheppey/Kent – died 02/05/2011 Cape Town/South Africa) Farmer in Southern Rhodesia.
[ix] James William Martin (921384, 128020), RAFVR. DFC LG. 08/12/44, 630 Sqdn.
[x] Andrew John Kuzma (J.24633), RCAF. DFC LG. 19/09/44, 630 Sqdn.
[xi] Ian David James MacDougall (103374), RAFVR.
[xii] Edmund Keith Creswell (902162, 107461), RAFVR. DFC LG. 06/11/42. DSO LG. 27/07/43, 35 Sqdn. Bar to DSO LG. 29/09/44, 35 Sqdn.
[xiii] Stanley Arthur Hawken (A.418663), RAAF. Evaded capture (see text). OBE LG. 15/06/74 as Councillor and JP for public service.
[xiv] William Angus Sparks (657867, 130251), RAFVR. Later killed 11/11/44.
[xv] George Vernon Bentley Patterson (NZ 421525), RNZAF. KIA (see text)
[xvi] Joseph Alcide Marcel Beaudoin (J,21913), RCAF. DFC LG. 08/12/44, 630 Sqdn.
[xvii] William Mooney (1501390,171182), RAFVR. DFM LG. 14/09/43, 50 Sqdn. DFC LG. 13/10/44, 630 Sqdn. Murdered in India by bandits 11/12/1945, buried at Calcutta.
[xviii] Alan William Gooderham Connor (A.400898), RAAF. DFM LG. 15/06/43, 50 Sqdn. DFC LG. 13/10/44, 630 Sqdn.
[xix] William Howard Gordon (1333881, 128951), RAFVR. DFC LG. 22/05/45, 189 Sqdn.
[xx] Charles Robson Faulkner (656908, 178519), RAFVR. KIA (see text)
[xxi] Stephen Arnold Nunns (1020024, 179592). DFC LG. 30/06/44, 630 Sqdn. Later awarded AFC.

August 1944

[i] Standish Ian Douglas Herbert (NZ 428818), RNZAF. Later POW 04/12/44.
[ii] Francis Ewan Hewison Millar (NZ 42171), RNZAF. DFC LG. 20/07/45, 630 Sqdn.
[iii] Henry David Archer (1302597, 128870), RAFVR. DFC LG. 17/07/45, 630 Sqdn.
[iv] Matthew Miller (1563659, 179571), RAFVR.
[v] Eric John Monk (1332562, 179063), RAFVR.
[vi] Douglas George Twidle (NZ 42819), RNZAF
[vii] John Outram Davies (1029607, 133640), RAFVR. Later KIA 02/02/45.
[viii] Cyril Edwin Thomas Peters (1394562, 179597), RAFVR, Later KIA 10/11/44.
[ix] Walter George Frederick Filby (553457, 55086), RAF. KIA (see text)
[xi] Deryck Anthony Clifford (138706, 179701), RAFVR.
[x] George Ross Flood (NZ 421502), RNZAF. KIA (see text)
[xii] Ronald Athol Stone (NZ 425601), RNZAF.
[xiii] Eric Clifton Harris (NZ 425788), RNZAF. DFC LG. 21/09/45, 630 Sqdn.
[xiv] Eric Ivor Britton (657650, 144279), RAFVR. Later KIA 04/12/44.
[xv] Arthur Bates (1431043, 172782), RAFVR.
[xvi] Malcolm Albert Eyre (111548), RAFVR. DFC LG. 21/09/45, 630 Squadron. (born 12/01/1922 Willesden/London – died 09/08/1966 Paget/Bermuda). A clerk for the local Council pre-war, post-war employed by BOAC as a pilot.
[xvii] James Irvin Campnett (1545933, 145592), RAFVR. M in D LG. 01/01/45.
[xviii] George Ernest Billing (1385810, 182601), RAFVR.

September 1944

[i] Desmond Charles Bursey Reynolds (88566), SAAF. DFC LG. 04/12/45, 630 Sqdn.
[ii] Douglas Stacey Turner (144736V), SAAF. DFC LG. 07/12/45, 630 Sqdn
[iii] Oliver John Scott Atknison (A.426019), RAAF. DFC LG. 04/12/45, 630 Sqdn.
[iv] Anthony John Rees Wilson (NZ424540). Later POW 18/12/44.
[v] Geoffrey William Daggett (1335734, 161271), RAFVR. Later DFC LG. 21/09/45, 44 Sqdn.
[vi] Geoffrey Eustace Stemp (1332937, 176731), RAFVR. DFC LG. 21/09/45, 630 Sqdn.
[vii] Henry Thompson (628426, 55918), RAF. DFC LG. 21/09/45, 630 Sqdn.
[viii] Richard Lawrier McCann (J.27578), RCAF. DFC LG. 16/01/45, 630 Sqdn.
[ix] Edward Joseph Browne (R.218062), RCAF. DFM LG. 16/01/45, 630 Sqdn.
[x] James William Martin (128020), RAFVR. DFC LG. 08/12/44, 630 Sqdn.
[xi] Robert Kenrick Foulkes (131129), RAFVR. DFC LG. 22/05/45, 630 Sqdn.
[xii] Rendel Forrest Lewis (655297, 129118), RAFVR. KIA (see text)
[xiii] Henry Terence Ryan (A.415025), RAAF. Posted to 189 Sqdn.
[xiv] Leslie Frank (Jim) Ovens (1339200, 183444), RAFVR. DFC LG. 07/12/45, 630 Sqdn
[xv] Donald Alexander McGillivray (NZ.426176), RNZAF. Posted to 189 Sqdn.
[xvi] George Hamilton Cowan (1097956, 195174), RAFVR. KIFA (see text)
[xvii] Edward Ainsley Thomas (1337751,132619), RAFVR. KIA (see text)
[xviii] Reginald George Waterfall (150506), RAFVR. DFC LG. 07/12/45, 630 Sqdn.
[xix] Thomas Bruce Baker (A.427282), RAAF. DFC LG. 21/09/45, 630 Sqdn.
[xx] Harry Grayson (1483345, 133413), RAFVR. DFC LG. 16/11/45, 189 Sqdn.

October 1944

[i] John Evelyn Grindon (33206), RAF. DSO LG. 17/07/45, 630 Sqdn.
[ii] John Black (1319289), RAFVR. DFC LG. 26/10/45, 630 Squadron. MinD LG. 08/06/44.
[iii] Dennis Archibald Brammer (1037153, 151568), RAFVR. KIFA (see text)
[iv] Jack William Hoare (A.427473), RAAF. DFC LG. 07/12/45, 630 Sqdn.
[v] John William Langley (1330135, 184936), RAFVR. Interned Sweden 14/01/45 (see text).
[vi] Alexander McGuffie (658409, 179533), RAFVR.

November 1944

[i] Albert MacLean (J.28539), RCAF.
[ii] Richard Joseph Sassoon (1802851, 150614), RAFVR.
[iii] George Richard Scott (051658, A.427555), RAAF.
[iv] Harry Alexander Ramsey (NZ 415017), RNZAF. Later 59606, RAF. DFC LG. 07/12/45, 630 Sqdn.
[v] Philip Samuel Weston (NZ 425628), RNZAF.
[vi] Neil Geoffrey Roberts (A.409877), RAAF. DFC LG. 04/12/45, 630 Sqdn.
[vii] Arnold Stockill (1044116, 142550), RAFVR. KIFA (see text).
[viii] William Henry Horsman (1578151, 142450), RAFVR.
[ix] Gordon Ramsey Lacey (1105V), SAAF. KIA (see text)
[x] Marthinus Theron Ackerman (328473V), SAAF. DFC LG. 09/03/45, 630 Sqdn.
[xi] Marcel Redmond Cuelenaere (J.16384), RCAF. DFC LG. 15/06/43, 97 Sqdn. Bar to DFC LG. 04/12/45, 630 Sqdn. (born Leask, Saskatchewan 1918 – died 1995). Postwar he was a successful lawyer.
[xii] Bernard Adolf Casey (29185), GD Branch, RAF. OBE LG. 01/01/1942.
[xiii] Alfred Henry Lionel Britton (107865) A&SD Branch RAFVR. (born 02/12/1905 – died 1970 Wiltshire).

January 1945

[i] The Rev. William Joseph Mulholland, B.A. (148781), Chaplains Branch, RAFVR.
[ii] Robert Baines Knight (NZ.422292), RNZAF. KIA (see text)
[iii] James Lewis Bathgate (NZ.416195), RNZAF.
[iv] Angus Vernon Cameron (A.429171), RAAF. POW (see text)
[v] Harold Francis Kirkwood (104544), RAFVR.
[vi] Donald Ivan Plumb (1334292, 196398), RAFVR. KIA (see text)
[vii] James William Wallace (NZ.428771), RNZAF.
[viii] Richard Grange (1425529), RAFVR
[ix] David Loudon Timmins (755329, 134659), RAFVR.

February 1945

[i] Gordon Louis Mortiboys (851377, 147124), RAuxAF. DFC LG. 04/12/45, 630 Sqdn.
[ii] Leslie Warren Jacobs (A.417750), RAAF.
[iii] Kenneth Osborn Gibson (1436400, 185972), RAFVR.

March 1945

[i] Arthur Heeley (157528) RAFVR, Killed at East Kirkby 04/03/45.
[ii] James Carlisle Clingin (A.410306), RAAF. Discharged from RAAF on 29/11/1945. (born 24/10/1912 Camperdown, Victoria – died 22/09/1972 Eildon, Victoria)
[iii] Lawrence Michael Duggan (A.429868), RAAF.
[iv] Keith Hallett (A.414228) RAAF.
[v] Colin Robert Moore Richardson (A.412697), RAAF. KIA (see text)
[vi] Stanley Edward Flett (80042), RAF. Posted to command 44 Sqdn.
[vii] Donald Stanley Tillett (1802895), RAFVR
[viii] Ronald Frank Mercer (1800, 196951), RAFVR
[ix] Frederick Albert Robinson (186955), RAFVR.
[x] James Douglas Richardson (A.403377), RAAF.

April 1945

[i] Louis Walter Dickens DFC AFC (16108), RAFVR. AFC LG. 06/06/39. DFC LG. 31/05/40, 139 Sqdn. Sir Louis, KB DFC AFC DL. MinD LGs. 14/01/44, 01/01/45, 01/01/46.
[ii] Jack Barnes (144021), RAFVR.
[iii] Jeffrey Thompson Bignell (1385810, 182601), RAFVR.
[iv] John Basil Dobbie (550970, 56478), RAF.
[v] Walter Michael Taylor (156945), RAFVR.
[vi] Lawrence William Pilgrim (122092), RAFVR. DFC LG. 12/10/43, 44 Sqdn.
[vii] Frederick William Lyder Wild (32115), RAF.

May 1945

[i] Michael Churchill Karop (150084), RAFVR. Commissioned 1943, formerly 902476. (born 01/07/1921 Bromley/South London – died 01/07/1959, Bota/Southern Cameroon)
[ii] Peter Geoffrey Selwyn Frampton. (1217271,198535). RAFVR
[iii] Robert Edward Hamilton (A424035), RAAF.
[iv] Rev. George Alban Charles Dunbar (184661), RAFVR.
[v] Edith Kathleen Mary Seward, nee Curtis (5574), WAAF, Later a nurse, re-married (Rowland).
[vi] Bernard Hall (168650), RAFVR. KIFA (see text)

July 1945

[i] Terence Henry Trimble Forshaw (39165), RAF. (born 1916 Kent)
[ii] Ian George Fadden DFC BEM (758062, 113490), RAFVR. BEM awarded for bravery crash landing Wellington Z8733 of 148 Squadron in the desert 05/10/41 and then rescuing an injured crew member despite the flames, LG.08/06/42. DFC LG.11/08/44, 61 Sqdn. (born 27/01/1916, resided Harrow, RAF Regular serviceman, 758062 Sgt No. 2 Squadron in 1939, died 17/09/1999 buried Whatlington/Sussex)
[iii] Gerald Arthur Mitchell (1061588, 174328), RAFVR. G.D. Branch (Aircrew).
[iv] Thomas Leonard Cass DFM (745238, 137343),RAFVR. DFM LG.29/12/42, 61 Sqdn. (born 18/11/1918 Lincoln – died 18/05/2001 Lincoln) Pre-war RAFVR No. 745238.
[v] Henry Thomas Alfred Evans DFC (1800700,138089), RAFVR. DFC LG.11/08/44, 550 Sqdn.
[vi] Alfred Barnard (936803, 146025), RAFVR.
[vii] Stanley Allenby Mitton (54000), RAF. Previously 537513, Sergeant.
[viii] David Walter Hobrough (1336831, 184544), RAFVR. Previously 617 Sqdn. (born 1923 Hammersmith – died 2011 Winchester/Hants)

East Kirkby

[i] National Archives, London (Air 28/244)
[ii] Arthur Henry Lysaght Marwood (75822). Administrative and Special Duties Branch. (born 1885 – died 1955) Previously Major, Yorks and Lancs Regiment 1914-18.
[iii] William Leslie Collis (44119) A&SD Branch, previously 618717 Corporal.
[iv] Bernard James Roberts (145999). Equipment Branch, previously 965041 Corporal.
[v] Cecil John Morley (67163), A&SD Branch.
[vi] Leslie Frank Woolcott (47048), Technical Branch, RAF. Previously W/O (362729). born 6 Sep 1905 – died 11 Jul 1969 Epsom.
[vii] Cecil William Martin (44917). A&SD Branch, previously 362529 Sergeant.
[viii] Eric Wilfred Buckler (106780). A&SD Branch, previously 845075 Corporal. (1900 – 1962 Chichester)
[x] Stephen Ian Hollingsworth (134457). Technical Branch, previously 1126162 Corporal. M in D LG 14/06/1945.
[ix] Rudolph Trevor Taaffe (17211), General Duties Branch. OBE LG. 11/07/1940. M in D LG. 08/06/1944. Rudolph Trevor Aloysius Patrick Taaffe, (born 21 Jun 1901 Ardee, County Louth, died 15 Feb 1985 Dublin). Commissioned RAF 14 May 1923. 41 Squadron Fighter pilot until posted to HQ Iraq in 1934. Promoted W/Cdr 12 Mar 1940. Retired 21 Sep 1951 as Group Capt.
[xi] Godfrey Norman Sellers, DFC. (77663). A&SD Branch. Served Great War in France from April 1915, Corporal until commissioned in West Yorks Regt 25 Apr 1917, transferred to Royal Air Force). Awarded the DFC for a night aerial recce operation in terrible weather (LG 7 Aug 1918). Recommissioned for wartime service and retired due to ill health in July 1944. (born March 1896 Yorkshire – died 10 May 1955 Bradford).
[xii] William Dennis Evans (117527). A&SD Branch.
[xiii] Roy Neville Benjamin, MC (79822). MC LG. 11/01/1919 Royal Fusiliers – gallantry citation.
[xiv] Edward Alfred Dearman (81808). A&SD Branch. He was M in D LG. 02/06/44.
[xv] Henry Watson MBE (50873), Tech (Armament) Branch, RAF. Previously 564490 W/O. MBE LG. 11/06/42. MinD LG 14/01/44.
[xvi] Alathea Noel Grant, nee Stevenson (657), WAAF. Previously ACW1, 885060.
[xvii] Charles Arthur Standing Lowndes (140149), RAFVR. Meteorological Branch. (26 Jan 1918 – July 1978 Berkshire)
[xviii] Alexander Augustus St.Clair-Miller DFC (123011), RAFVR. General Duties Branch. (born 31/01/1912 – died Feb 1989 Richmond/Surrey)

[xix] Arthur Percy Morris (142430), Tech (Signals), RAFVR. Previously 1248140, Sergeant. MinD LG. 14/06/45.
[xx] Marion Jean Barclay (2639). WAAF. (31 Oct 1919 – 3 Dec 1980 Chelsea)
[xxi] Isabel Grassie Bruce (3226). WAAF. (2 April 1907 – 29 Jul 1984) formerly an A.R.P. Warden and Clitheroe Girls Grammar School Mistress.
[xxii] Joseph Robert O'Dowd, MRCS., LRCP (84837). Medical Branch. M in D LG. 01/01/43.
[xxiii] Harold Mellor (69630). A&SD Branch. Previously 1426212 Aircraftman 2nd class.
[xxiv] Matthew Carty (109609). A&SD Branch . M in D – 08/06/44
[xxv] Rose Marion Jean Pellow (4867). WAAF known as Jean (14 June 1919 – 25 Oct 2010 Buckfastleigh, Devon)
[xxvi] Doreen Joan Burnett (4321). WAAF
[xxvii] William Clement Hawken (48576). Tech Branch. Previously W/O 513264. MBE LG 02/06/44.
[xxviii] Clifford Underwood Lloyd (90990). A&SD Branch. Previously Balloon Branch, Aux AF.
[xxix] Ronald Reginald Bennett (145205). A&SD Branch. Previously 844186 Sergeant.
[xxx] Bernard Peter Jones (37739). A&SD Branch. M in D 08/06/44
[xxxi] Philip Sidney Griffiths (140817), RAFVR. Met Branch.
[xxxii] Frank Oldfield (141237). Accoutant Branch. Previously 1232504 Corporal.
[xxxiii] Anthony Wilkinson Heward (39044), Reserve of Air Force Officers. AFC LG. 31/03/42. DFC LG. 18/04/44 50 Sqdn. Bar to DFC 30/03/45 97 Sqdn.
[xxxiv] Percival Alderson (21022), RAF. Equipment Branch.
[xxxv] Jeannette Ainslie Mouat (4849). WAAF. (born 3 Jul 1924 Sheffield/Yorks – died 2 May 2017 USA)
[xxxvi] Damaris Jean Babington (3877). WAAF. daughter of Air Marshal Sir John Tremayne Babington. (1918 – 7 July 2010 Cornwall). She returned to England from the Straits Settlements in 1941 to join the W.A.A.F.
[xxxvii] Richard George Dunnett (110353). A&SD Branch. Previously 1147737 Aircraftman 2nd class.
[xxxviii] Olive Florence Webber (1652), WAAF. Previously 894976 Aircraftwoman 1st Class
[xxxix] the Hon. Sir Ralph Alexander Cochrane, CB CBE AFC, GD Branch, RAF. CBE LG. 02/01/38. AFC LG. 01/01/1919. CB LG. 01/01/43. KCB in 1948 and GBE in 1950.
[xl] William George Giles (77659), RAFVR. A&SD Branch.
[xli] Arthur James Haskell (35296), RAF. Engineer Branch. M in D LG 11/06/42
[xlii] Sydney Astle, MC TD, Cheshire Regt, TA. MC LG 13/05/18 (trench raid). Of Bramhall, Cheshire. Formerly Lieut., Cheshire Regt later Major RA, TA. (born 1897 – died 9 Jan 1966 Wilmslow/Cheshire).
[xliii] Courtenay Cecil Grebby (133289). A&SD Branch. Previously 1618174 Aircraftman 2nd class. (18 Oct 1904 – 14 Sep 1985 Fulham, London) Awarded M.B.E. for gallantry at the explosion at East Kirkby on 17 April 1945 (LG 27/11/45). M in D LG 08/06/44.
[xliv] Damaris Mary De Sausmarez (1417), WAAF. Previously 888316 Aircraftwoman 1st Class
[xlv] Margaret Pauline Vickers (6092) WAAF

The Faces of Aircrew Representing 630 Squadron

In honoured memory of them all

Dennis Bradd Dennis Brammer Cyril Cook,

Bill Brentnall Reg Burrows Jim DiBondi

Les Duck JR 'Reg' Fletcher H 'Tex' Glasby

Vern Goodwin

Bob Guthrie

Bob Hay

WPR Hewitt

Mike Howley

Jack Key

Johnny Kiesow

Vic Lawrence

Bruce Lawton

Ernie Leese Harry LeMarchant Gordon 'Flash' Love

Norm Machonachie Matt Miller Joe Morgan

Harry Parkins Don Plumb 'Rocky' Roche

John Quinlivan   *FP Peter Settle*   *Norman Sharpe*

Wilf Shillito   *Ken Sinclair*   *Trev Tanner*

RA 'George' Toogood   *AE 'Bertie' Truesdale*   *CW Walter Walker*

Idris Smith-Warren — *Ted Watson* — *Geoff Watts*

Ev Wildey — *Aneurin Williams* — *Doug Williamson*

Melvyn White — *Charles Wright* — *Jim Wright*

Dennis George Bradd, born Orsett, Essex 1924, joined the RAF to train as an air gunner, flew primarily as mid-upper gunner in the Probert crew but also as a 'spare bod'. Killed in action 22 June 1944 aged 20 as he completed his tour.

Dennis Archibald Brammer, born Stoke-on-Trent 1920, worked pre-war as a bank clerk in Worcester, trained as a pilot and was completing training ready for going operational when his aircraft crashed on 18 Oct 1944 and he was killed.

Cyril Cook, born West Pinchbeck, Lincs 1924, joined the RAF aged 18 and flew as wireless operator in the Lewis crew. Killed in action 8 Dec 1944 aged 19, half way through his tour of ops.

William Beresford Brentnall, born Oldham 1914, completed a tour as bomb aimer in the Reynolds crew, returned to work in London post-war, died in Waltham, Lincolnshire 1984.

Reginald Bertie Burrows, born Iwerne Minster, Dorset 1923, pre-war student at Shaftesbury, completed a tour as navigator in the Ramsey crew, died in Poole, Dorset 1990.

James DeBondi, born Stannary Hills, Queensland, Australia 1922, worked as a cost clerk in Queensland, joined RAAF, completed a tour as wireless operator in the Atkinson crew, died Perth, West Australia 2000.

Leslie Sidney Duck, born New Malden, Surrey 1925, joined the RAF age 17, completed a tour as flight engineer in the Ramsey crew, lived and worked in Battersea, South London all of his life, retired to Poole and died Poole, Dorset 2016.

James Reginald Fletcher, born Lancashire 1922, survived serious crash Nov 1944 as wireless operator in a 619 Squadron crew, transferred to 630 Squadron as a 'spare bod' and flew with seven different crews, died 2007 Preston, Lancs.

Harvey Glasby DFC, born Toowoomba, Queensland, Australia 1920, worked there as a driver and shop assistant, joined RAAF, trained as wireless op/air gunner, flew a complete tour in the Ames crew in 61 and 630 Squadrons then continued with 617 Squadron but was killed in action 30 Jul 1944.

Vernon Alfred Goodwin, born Edmonton, Alberta, Canada 1925, working as a truck driver when he joined the RCAF aged 17 to train as air gunner, flew as mid-upper gunner in Howard Smith's crew, on his 3rd op killed in action 22 May 1944.

Robert Martin Guthrie, born Reading 1923, a clerk, joined the RAF, flew as navigator with the Langlands crew until shot down over Germany 31 March 1944, prisoner of war in Stalag Luft I until liberation, died Stamford, Lincolnshire 2008.

Spottiswoode Robert Hay, born Portobello, Midlothian 1922, joined the RAF and trained as an air gunner, completed a tour with the Hegarty crew as mid-upper gunner on 630 and later 83 Squadrons, died Windlesham, Surrey, 1991.

William Phillip Revenhall Hewitt, born North Sydney, New South Wales 1923, worked on a dairy farm, joined RAAF to train as air gunner, flew on 9 and 630 Squadrons as rear gunner in the English crew, on 25th op killed in action 15 February 1944.

Michael James Howley, born Northwood, Middlesex 1923, joined the RAF from school, completed his tour as navigator in the Ovens crew, worked in the media, died in Luton 2007.

Jack Cleland Key, born Waimate, Canterbury, New Zealand 1923, joined the RNZAF, completed his tour as navigator in the Turner crew, died Okato, Taranaki, New Zealand 1989.

John Birney Kiesow, born Phillips/Montana, USA 1924, worked at Peswegin/Saskatchewan, Canada. Enlisted in the RCAF, transferred to USAAF, attached to RAF, flew as mid-upper gunner in the crew of Bill Adams USAAF. Killed in action 25 July 1944 aged 20 half way through his tour.

Victor Dennis Lawrence, born London 1923, worked as a clerk in London, joined the RAF, completed his tour as wireless operator in the Probert crew, emigrated to Canada 1947, died Montreal, Canada 2008.

Bruce Robert Lawton, born Killara, New South Wales 1923, worked as a clerk, joined RAAF, completed a tour as wireless operator in the Ramsey crew, died Sydney, NSW 2000.

Ernest Albert Leese, born Hemel Hempstead 1920, pre-war aircraft engineer, enlisted in the RAF and flew a complete tour as Flight Engineer in the Mitchell crew, settled in Surrey, retired in Perth/WA, died 1998.

Harry Frederick LeMarchant, born Hadley Wood 1922, completed his tour as bomb aimer in the Crocker crew in 57 and 630 Squadrons, lived at Amersham, retired RAF Reserve of Officers 1959, died Stoke Mandeville, Buckinghamshire 2014.

Henry Ernest Gordon Love, born Chelmsford, Essex 1924, furniture trade apprentice, joined the RAF, completed his tour as mid-upper gunner in the Miller crew, died Chelmsford, Essex 1993.

Norman Maconachie, born Newcastle, New South Wales 1924, joined the RAAF, completed his tour as wireless operator with the Ovens crew, a mercer by trade, died Australia 2020.

Joseph Anthony Morgan, born Crook, Durham 1925, joined the RAF from school, flew as rear gunner in the Lewis crew until shot down, sole survivor, deprived of medical treatment as prisoner of war, post-war school teacher, died Carlisle 2002.

Henry William Parkins, born Bethnal Green, London 1924, joined the RAF from school, completed his tour as flight engineer in the Lennon crew, married and settled in Lincoln post-war, died in Lincoln 2020.

Donald Ivan Plumb, born Norwich 1922, joined the RAF, trained as a pilot at Napier Field, Alabama/USA, almost half way through his tour he and his crew were killed in action 17 March 1945.

John Henry Quinlivan, born Clerkenwell, London 1924, joined the RAF from school, flew as mid-upper gunner in the Stockill crew, killed in action 22 December 1944.

William Joseph Roche, born Myrtleford/Wangaratta, New South Wales 1914, worked as a farm labourer before joining RAAF, flew as rear gunner in the Yates crew on 57 and 630 Squadrons before being killed in action with MacDonald crew 2 January 1944.

Frederick Peter Settle, born Camberwell, London 1923, worked as a junior clerk for a solicitor in Islington, flew as wireless operator/air gunner in the White crew on 49, 57 and 630 Squadrons, shot down and prisoner of war 25 March 1944, held at Stalag Luft 1. Died at Sheringham, Norfolk 1985.

Norman Eric Sharpe, born Lambeth, London 1915, worked as a builder, painter/decorator, married with a daughter, joined the RAF, flew as bomb aimer in the Knight crew until killed in action 9 February 1945.

Wilfred Shillito, born Doncaster 1923, joined the RAF, flew as wireless operator/air gunner in the Sparks crew, survived their 18 Jul 1944 flying accident, rejoined 207 Squadron to complete his tour, died Doncaster 2017.

Kenneth Arthur Sinclair, born Cottesloe, Western Australia 1921, working as a clerk when he joined RAAF, flew as navigator in the Brown crew until killed in action 23 May 1944.

Trevor William Tanner, born Cardiff, Wales 1924, pre-war boy seaman Merchant Navy, flew as flight engineer in the Adams crew, shot down half way through his tour 25 July 1944, evaded capture in France, post-war joined RCAF, died Victoria, British Columbia, Canada 1998.

Arthur Reginald Toogood, born Bath, Somerset 1922, flew as navigator in the Adams crew, shot down half way through his tour 25 July 1944, evaded capture in France, post-war employed as an Education Officer, died Radstock, Somerset 2006.

Albert Edward Truesdale, born Newry, Down, Northern Ireland 1922, flew as wireless operator/air gunner in the Bailey crew, almost half way through his tour when killed in action 22 May 1944.

Charles Walter Walker, born Blaydon, Durham 1924, pre-war apprentice motor mechanic, trained as air gunner brief service with 57 Squadron then flew a complete tour as rear gunner in the Roberts crew, died Chester-le-Street, Durham 2005.

Idris Smith Warren, born Chesterfield, Derbyshire 1920, flew a complete tour as wireless operator/air gunner in the Burness crew on 44 and 630 Squadrons, Mentioned in Despatches 8 June 1944, died Bradford, Yorkshire 1967.

Edwin Watson, born Cockfield, Durham 1925. Awarded Kings Scout pre-war, ATC member, flew a complete tour as flight engineer in the Monks crew plus several extra ops with other crews, post-war aviation industry and engineering.

Geoffrey Ernest Watts AFM, born Warwickshire 1921, RAF regular, Halton apprentice, flew as flight engineer in the Johnson crew until shot down and taken prisoner 31 March 1944, remained in the RAF, awarded Air Force Medal 2 Jan 1950, retired as Squadron Leader 1973, died Stevenage 1998.

Wilfred Everleigh Wildey, born Christchurch, New Zealand 1919, flew a complete tour as navigator in the Millar crew, post-war lived at Lyttleton, New Zealand working as a crane driver, died Canterbury, New Zealand 2001.

Aneurin Garfield Williams, born Tonypandy, Wales 1925, apprentice coach builder, flew a complete tour as rear gunner in the Grayson crew with 630 and 189 Squadrons, died Downham Market, Norfolk 2014.

Douglas Ernest Williamson, born Holbeach, Lincolnshire 1922, pre-war junior clerk in March, Cambridgeshire, flew a complete tour as navigator in the Weller crew, died Peterborough 1975.

Melvyn White, born Bedwelty, Wales 1915, foreman with a concrete company, flew as mid upper gunner in the Kilgour crew, killed in action 27 April 1944 half way through their tour.

Charles Norman Wright, born Buckley, Wales 1915, joiner and pattern maker, flew as navigator in the Nash crew and later W/C Deas crew until killed in action 8 July 1944 half way through his tour.

Albert James Wright DFC, born 1922, flew a complete tour with 61, 630 and 97 Squadrons as navigator in the Ames crew. Wounded in action. Distinguished Flying Cross 27 June 1944. Retired as Wing Commander in 1976, died Abingdon, Oxfordshire 2022.

These four unidentified commissioned pilots of 630 Squadron (c.late April 1944) probably included John Nall, Pete Nash and David Roberts. (Patti Kellaway)

www.ingramcontent.com/pod-product-compliance
Lightning Source LLC
Chambersburg PA
CBHW080419230426
43662CB00015B/2152